Exam 70-461: Querying Microsoft SQL Server 2012

OBJECTIVE	CHAPTER	LESSON
1. CREATE DATABASE OBJECTS		
1.1 Create and alter tables using T-SQL syntax (simple statements).	8	1
1.2 Create and alter views (simple statements).	9 15	1 1
1.3 Design views.	9	1
1.4 Create and modify constraints (simple statements).	8	2
1.5 Create and alter DML triggers.	13	2
2. WORK WITH DATA		
2.1 Query data by using SELECT statements.	1 2 3 4 5 6 8 9 12	1 2 All lessons All lessons 3 Lessons 2 and 3 2 2 3
2.2 Implement sub-queries.	4 5 17	2 2 1
2.3 Implement data types.	2 3	2 1
2.4 Implement aggregate queries.	5	Lessons 1 and 3
2.5 Query and manage XML data.	7	All lessons
3. MODIFY DATA		
3.1 Create and alter stored procedures (simple statements).	13	All lessons
3.2 Modify data by using INSERT, UPDATE, and DELETE statements.	10 11	All lessons 3
3.3 Combine datasets.	2 4 11	2 3 2
3.4 Work with functions.	2 3 6 13	2 1 3 3
4. TROUBLESHOOT & OPTIMIZE		
4.1 Optimize queries.	12 14 15 17	Both lessons All lessons All lessons All lessons
4.2 Manage transactions.	12	1
4.3 Evaluate the use of row-based operations vs. set-based operations.	16	1
4.4 Implement error handling.	12 16	2 1

Exam Objectives The exam objectives listed here are current as of this book's publication date. Exam objectives are subject to change at any time without prior notice and at Microsoft's sole discretion. Please visit the Microsoft Learning website for the most current listing of exam objectives: *http://www.microsoft.com/learning/en/us/exam.aspx?ID=70-461&locale=en-us*.

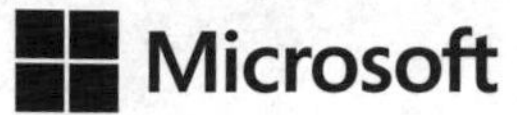

Querying Microsoft® SQL Server® 2012

Exam 70-461 Training Kit

Itzik Ben-Gan
Dejan Sarka
Ron Talmage

Published with the authorization of Microsoft Corporation by:

O'Reilly Media, Inc.
1005 Gravenstein Highway North
Sebastopol, California 95472

ISBN: 978-0-7356-6605-4

5 6 7 8 9 10 11 12 13 QG 8 7 6 5 4 3

Printed and bound in the United States of America.

Microsoft Press books are available through booksellers and distributors worldwide. If you need support related to this book, email Microsoft Press Book Support at *mspinput@microsoft.com*. Please tell us what you think of this book at *http://www.microsoft.com/learning/booksurvey*.

Acquisitions & Developmental Editor: Ken Jones

Production Editor: Melanie Yarbrough

Editorial Production: Online Training Solutions, Inc.

Technical Reviewer: Herbert Albert

Indexer: WordCo Indexing Services

Cover Design: Twist Creative • Seattle

Cover Composition: Zyg Group, LLC

[2013-12-13]

Contents at a Glance

Contents

Chapter 3 Filtering and Sorting Data 61

Chapter 6 Querying Full-Text Data 191

Chapter 9 Designing and Creating Views, Inline Functions, and Synonyms 299

What do you think of this book? We want to hear from you!

Microsoft is interested in hearing your feedback so we can continually improve our books and learning resources for you. To participate in a brief online survey, please visit:

www.microsoft.com/learning/booksurvey/

Introduction

This Training Kit is designed for information technology (IT) professionals who need to query data in Microsoft SQL Server 2012 and who also plan to take Exam 70-461, "Querying Microsoft SQL Server 2012." It is assumed that before you begin using this Training Kit, you have a foundation-level understanding of using Transact-SQL (T-SQL) to query data in SQL Server 2012 and have some experience using the product. Although this book helps prepare you for the 70-461 exam, you should consider it as one part of your exam preparation plan. Meaningful, real-world experience with SQL Server 2012 is required to pass this exam.

The material covered in this Training Kit and on Exam 70-461 relates to the technologies in SQL Server 2012. The topics in this Training Kit cover what you need to know for the exam as described on the Skills Measured tab for the exam, which is available at *http://www.microsoft.com/learning/en/us/exam.aspx?ID=70-461&locale=en-us#tab2.*

By using this Training Kit, you will learn how to do the following:

- Create database objects
- Work with data
- Modify data
- Troubleshoot and optimize T-SQL code

Refer to the objective mapping page in the front of this book to see where in the book each exam objective is covered.

System Requirements

The following are the minimum system requirements your computer needs to meet to complete the practice exercises in this book and to run the companion CD.

SQL Server Software and Data Requirements

You can find the minimum SQL Server software and data requirements here:

- **SQL Server 2012** You need access to a SQL Server 2012 instance with a logon that has permissions to create new databases—preferably one that is a member of the sysadmin role. For the purposes of this Training Kit, you can use almost any edition of on-premises SQL Server (Standard, Enterprise, Business Intelligence, or Developer), both 32-bit and 64-bit editions. If you don't have access to an existing SQL Server instance, you can install a trial copy that you can use for 180 days. You can download a trial copy from *http://www.microsoft.com/sqlserver/en/us/get-sql-server/try-it.aspx.*

- **SQL Server 2012 Setup Feature Selection** In the Feature Selection dialog box of the SQL Server 2012 setup program, choose at minimum the following components:
  - Database Engine Services
    - Full-Text And Semantic Extractions For Search
    - Documentation Components
    - Management Tools—Basic (required)
    - Management Tools—Complete (recommended)
- **TSQL2012 sample database and source code** Most exercises in this Training Kit use a sample database called TSQL2012. The companion content for the Training Kit includes a compressed file called TK70461-YYYYMMDD.zip (where YYYYMMDD reflects the date of the last revision) that contains the book's source code, exercises, and a script file called TSQL2012.sql that you use to create the sample database. You can download the compressed file from O'Reilly's website at *http://go.microsoft.com/FWLink/?Linkid=263548* and from the authors' website at *http://tsql.solidq.com/books/tk70461/*.

Hardware and Operating System Requirements

You can find the minimum hardware and operating system requirements for installing and running SQL Server 2012 at *http://msdn.microsoft.com/en-us/library/ms143506(v=sql.110).aspx*.

Using the Companion CD

A companion CD is included with this Training Kit. The companion CD contains the following:

- **Practice tests** You can reinforce your understanding of the topics covered in this Training Kit by using electronic practice tests that you customize to meet your needs. You can practice for the 70-461 certification exam by using tests created from a pool of 200 practice exam questions, which give you many practice exams to help you prepare for the certification exam. These questions are not from the exam; they are for practice and preparation.
- **An eBook** An electronic version (eBook) of this book is included for when you do not want to carry the printed book with you.

How to Install the Practice Tests

To install the practice test software from the companion CD to your hard disk, perform the following steps:

1. Insert the companion CD into your CD drive and accept the license agreement. A CD menu appears.

> ***NOTE*** **IF THE CD MENU DOES NOT APPEAR**
>
> **If the CD menu or the license agreement does not appear, AutoRun might be disabled on your computer. Refer to the Readme.txt file on the CD for alternate installation instructions.**

2. Click Practice Tests and follow the instructions on the screen.

How to Use the Practice Tests

To start the practice test software, follow these steps:

1. Click Start, All Programs, and then select Microsoft Press Training Kit Exam Prep.

   A window appears that shows all the Microsoft Press Training Kit exam prep suites installed on your computer.

2. Double-click the practice test you want to use.

When you start a practice test, you choose whether to take the test in Certification Mode, Study Mode, or Custom Mode:

- **Certification Mode** Closely resembles the experience of taking a certification exam. The test has a set number of questions. It is timed, and you cannot pause and restart the timer.
- **Study Mode** Creates an untimed test during which you can review the correct answers and the explanations after you answer each question.
- **Custom Mode** Gives you full control over the test options so that you can customize them as you like.

In all modes, the user interface when you are taking the test is basically the same but with different options enabled or disabled, depending on the mode.

When you review your answer to an individual practice test question, a "References" section is provided that lists where in the Training Kit you can find the information that relates to that question and provides links to other sources of information. After you click Test Results to score your entire practice test, you can click the Learning Plan tab to see a list of references for every objective.

How to Uninstall the Practice Tests

To uninstall the practice test software for a Training Kit, use the Program And Features option in Windows Control Panel.

Acknowledgments

A book is put together by many more people than the authors whose names are listed on the cover page. We'd like to express our gratitude to the following people for all the work they have done in getting this book into your hands: Herbert Albert (technical editor), Lilach Ben-Gan (project manager), Ken Jones (acquisitions and developmental editor), Melanie Yarbrough (production editor), Jaime Odell (copyeditor), Marlene Lambert (PTQ project manager), Jeanne Craver (graphics), Jean Trenary (desktop publisher), Kathy Krause (proofreader), and Kerin Forsyth (PTQ copyeditor).

Errata & Book Support

We've made every effort to ensure the accuracy of this book and its companion content. Any errors that have been reported since this book was published are listed on our Microsoft Press site at oreilly.com:

http://go.microsoft.com/FWLink/?Linkid=263549

If you find an error that is not already listed, you can report it to us through the same page.

If you need additional support, email Microsoft Press Book Support at *mspinput@microsoft.com.*

Please note that product support for Microsoft software is not offered through the addresses above.

We Want to Hear from You

At Microsoft Press, your satisfaction is our top priority, and your feedback our most valuable asset. Please tell us what you think of this book at:

http://www.microsoft.com/learning/booksurvey

The survey is short, and we read every one of your comments and ideas. Thanks in advance for your input!

Stay in Touch

Let's keep the conversation going! We're on Twitter: *http://twitter.com/MicrosoftPress*.

Preparing for the Exam

Microsoft certification exams are a great way to build your resume and let the world know about your level of expertise. Certification exams validate your on-the-job experience and product knowledge. While there is no substitution for on-the-job experience, preparation through study and hands-on practice can help you prepare for the exam. We recommend that you round out your exam preparation plan by using a combination of available study materials and courses. For example, you might use the Training Kit and another study guide for your "at home" preparation, and take a Microsoft Official Curriculum course for the classroom experience. Choose the combination that you think works best for you.

NOTE **PASSING THE EXAM**

Take a minute (well, one minute and two seconds) to look at the "Passing a Microsoft Exam" video at *http://www.youtube.com/watch?v=Jp5qg2NhgZ0&feature=youtu.be*. It's true. Really!

CHAPTER 1

Foundations of Querying

Exam objectives in this chapter:

- Work with Data
  - Query data by using SELECT statements.

Transact-SQL (T-SQL) is the main language used to manage and manipulate data in Microsoft SQL Server. This chapter lays the foundations for querying data by using T-SQL. The chapter describes the roots of this language, terminology, and the mindset you need to adopt when writing T-SQL code. It then moves on to describe one of the most important concepts you need to know about the language—logical query processing.

> IMPORTANT
> ***Have you read page xxx?***
> **It contains valuable information regarding the skills you need to pass the exam.**

Although this chapter doesn't directly target specific exam objectives other than discussing the design of the SELECT statement, which is the main T-SQL statement used to query data, the rest of the chapters in this Training Kit do. However, the information in this chapter is critical in order to correctly understand the rest of the book.

Lessons in this chapter:

- Lesson 1: Understanding the Foundations of T-SQL
- Lesson 2: Understanding Logical Query Processing

Before You Begin

To complete the lessons in this chapter, you must have:

- An understanding of basic database concepts.
- Experience working with SQL Server Management Studio (SSMS).
- Some experience writing T-SQL code.
- Access to a SQL Server 2012 instance with the sample database TSQL2012 installed. (Please see the book's introduction for details on how to create the sample database.)

Lesson 1: Understanding the Foundations of T-SQL

Many aspects of computing, like programming languages, evolve based on intuition and the current trend. Without strong foundations, their lifespan can be very short, and if they do survive, often the changes are very rapid due to changes in trends. T-SQL is different, mainly because it has strong foundations—mathematics. You don't need to be a mathematician to write good SQL (though it certainly doesn't hurt), but as long as you understand what those foundations are, and some of their key principles, you will better understand the language you are dealing with. Without those foundations, you can still write T-SQL code—even code that runs successfully—but it will be like eating soup with a fork!

After this lesson, you will be able to:

- Describe the foundations that T-SQL is based on.
- Describe the importance of using T-SQL in a relational way.
- Use correct terminology when describing T-SQL–related elements.

Estimated lesson time: 40 minutes

Evolution of T-SQL

As mentioned, unlike many other aspects of computing, T-SQL is based on strong mathematical foundations. Understanding some of the key principals from those foundations can help you better understand the language you are dealing with. Then you will think in T-SQL terms when coding in T-SQL, as opposed to coding with T-SQL while thinking in procedural terms.

Figure 1-1 illustrates the evolution of T-SQL from its core mathematical foundations.

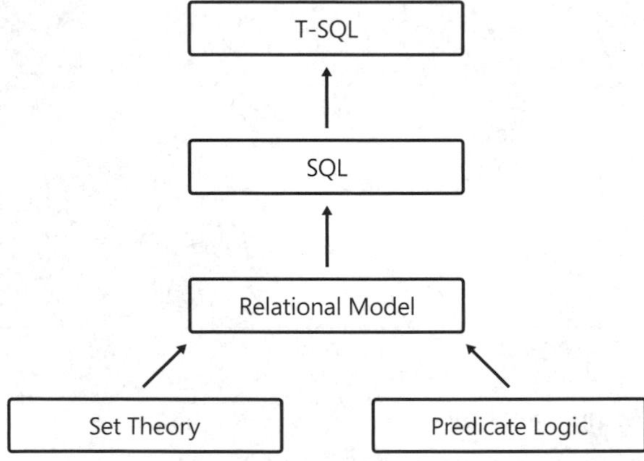

FIGURE 1-1 Evolution of T-SQL.

T-SQL is the main language used to manage and manipulate data in Microsoft's main relational database management system (RDBMS), SQL Server—whether on premises or in the cloud (Microsoft Windows Azure SQL Database). SQL Server also supports other languages, like Microsoft Visual C# and Microsoft Visual Basic, but T-SQL is usually the preferred language for data management and manipulation.

T-SQL is a dialect of standard SQL. SQL is a standard of both the International Organization for Standards (ISO) and the American National Standards Institute (ANSI). The two standards for SQL are basically the same. The SQL standard keeps evolving with time. Following is a list of the major revisions of the standard so far:

- SQL-86
- SQL-89
- SQL-92
- SQL:1999
- SQL:2003
- SQL:2006
- SQL:2008
- SQL:2011

All leading database vendors, including Microsoft, implement a dialect of SQL as the main language to manage and manipulate data in their database platforms. Therefore, the core language elements look the same. However, each vendor decides which features to implement and which not to. Also, the standard sometimes leaves some aspects as an implementation choice. Each vendor also usually implements extensions to the standard in cases where the vendor feels that an important feature isn't covered by the standard.

Writing in a standard way is considered a best practice. When you do so, your code is more portable. Your knowledge is more portable, too, because it is easy for you to start working with new platforms. When the dialect you're working with supports both a standard and a nonstandard way to do something, you should always prefer the standard form as your default choice. You should consider a nonstandard option only when it has some important benefit to you that is not covered by the standard alternative.

As an example of when to choose the standard form, T-SQL supports two "not equal to" operators: <> and !=. The former is standard and the latter is not. This case should be a no-brainer: go for the standard one!

As an example of when the choice of standard or nonstandard depends on the circumstances, consider the following: T-SQL supports multiple functions that convert a source value to a target type. Among them are the CAST and CONVERT functions. The former is standard and the latter isn't. The nonstandard CONVERT function has a style argument that CAST doesn't support. Because CAST is standard, you should consider it your default choice for conversions. You should consider using CONVERT only when you need to rely on the style argument.

Yet another example of choosing the standard form is in the termination of T-SQL statements. According to standard SQL, you should terminate your statements with a semicolon. T-SQL currently doesn't make this a requirement for all statements, only in cases where there would otherwise be ambiguity of code elements, such as in the WITH clause of a common table expression (CTE). You should still follow the standard and terminate all of your statements even where it is currently not required.

Standard SQL is based on the *relational model*, which is a mathematical model for data management and manipulation. The relational model was initially created and proposed by Edgar F. Codd in 1969. Since then, it has been explained and developed by Chris Date, Hugh Darwen, and others.

A common misconception is that the name "relational" has to do with relationships between tables (that is, foreign keys). Actually, the true source for the model's name is the mathematical concept *relation*.

A relation in the relational model is what SQL calls a *table*. The two are not synonymous. You could say that a table is an attempt by SQL to represent a relation (in addition to a relation variable, but that's not necessary to get into here). Some might say that it is not a very successful attempt. Even though SQL is based on the relational model, it deviates from it in a number of ways. But it's important to note that as you understand the model's principles, you can use SQL—or more precisely, the dialect you are using—in a relational way. More on this, including a further reading recommendation, is in the next section, "Using T-SQL in a Relational Way."

Getting back to a relation, which is what SQL attempts to represent with a table: a relation has a heading and a body. The heading is a set of attributes (what SQL attempts to represent with columns), each of a given type. An attribute is identified by name and type name. The body is a set of tuples (what SQL attempts to represent with rows). Each tuple's heading is the heading of the relation. Each value of each tuple's attribute is of its respective type.

Some of the most important principals to understand about T-SQL stem from the relational model's core foundations—set theory and predicate logic.

Remember that the heading of a relation is a set of attributes, and the body a set of tuples. So what is a set? According to the creator of mathematical set theory, Georg Cantor, a *set* is described as follows:

> *By a "set" we mean any collection M into a whole of definite, distinct objects m (which are called the "elements" of M) of our perception or of our thought.*
>
> —George Cantor, in "Georg Cantor" by Joseph W. Dauben (Princeton University Press, 1990)

There are a number of very important principles in this definition that, if understood, should have direct implications on your T-SQL coding practices. For one, notice the term *whole*. A set should be considered as a whole. This means that you do not interact with the individual elements of the set, rather with the set as a whole.

Notice the term *distinct*—a set has no duplicates. Codd once remarked on the no duplicates aspect: "If something is true, then saying it twice won't make it any truer." For example, the set {a, b, c} is considered equal to the set {a, a, b, c, c, c}.

Another critical aspect of a set doesn't explicitly appear in the aforementioned definition by Cantor, but rather is implied—there's no relevance to the order of elements in a set. In contrast, a sequence (which is an *ordered* set), for example, does have an order to its elements. Combining the no duplicates and no relevance to order aspects means that the set {a, b, c} is equal to the set {b, a, c, c, a, c}.

The other branch of mathematics that the relational model is based on is called predicate logic. A *predicate* is an expression that when attributed to some object, makes a proposition either true or false. For example, "salary greater than $50,000" is a predicate. You can evaluate this predicate for a specific employee, in which case you have a proposition. For example, suppose that for a particular employee, the salary is $60,000. When you evaluate the proposition for that employee, you get a true proposition. In other words, a predicate is a parameterized proposition.

The relational model uses predicates as one of its core elements. You can enforce data integrity by using predicates. You can filter data by using predicates. You can even use predicates to define the data model itself. You first identify propositions that need to be stored in the database. Here's an example proposition: an order with order ID 10248 was placed on February 12, 2012 by the customer with ID 7, and handled by the employee with ID 3. You then create predicates from the propositions by removing the data and keeping the heading. Remember, the heading is a set of attributes, each identified by name and type name. In this example, you have orderid INT, orderdate DATE, custid INT, and empid INT.

Quick Check

1. **What are the mathematical branches that the relational model is based on?**
2. **What is the difference between T-SQL and SQL?**

Quick Check Answer

1. **Set theory and predicate logic.**
2. **SQL is standard; T-SQL is the dialect of and extension to SQL that Microsoft implements in its RDBMS—SQL Server.**

Using T-SQL in a Relational Way

As mentioned in the previous section, T-SQL is based on SQL, which in turn is based on the relational model. However, there are a number of ways in which SQL—and therefore, T-SQL—deviates from the relational model. But the language gives you enough tools so that if you understand the relational model, you can use the language in a relational manner, and thus write more-correct code.

MORE INFO SQL AND RELATIONAL THEORY

For detailed information about the differences between SQL and the relational model and how to use SQL in a relational way, see *SQL and Relational Theory,* Second Edition by C. J. Date (O'Reilly Media, 2011). It's an excellent book that all database practitioners should read.

Remember that a relation has a heading and a body. The heading is a set of attributes and the body is a set of tuples. Remember from the definition of a set that a set is supposed to be considered as a whole. What this translates to in T-SQL is that you're supposed to write queries that interact with the tables as a whole. You should try to avoid using iterative constructs like cursors and loops that iterate through the rows one at a time. You should also try to avoid thinking in iterative terms because this kind of thinking is what leads to iterative solutions.

For people with a procedural programming background, the natural way to interact with data (in a file, record set, or data reader) is with iterations. So using cursors and other iterative constructs in T-SQL is, in a way, an extension to what they already know. However, the correct way from the relational model's perspective is not to interact with the rows one at a time; rather, use relational operations and return a relational result. This, in T-SQL, translates to writing queries.

Remember also that a set has no duplicates. T-SQL doesn't always enforce this rule. For example, you can create a table without a key. In such a case, you are allowed to have duplicate rows in the table. To follow relational theory, you need to enforce uniqueness in your tables—for example, by using a primary key or a unique constraint.

Even when the table doesn't allow duplicate rows, a query against the table can still return duplicate rows in its result. You'll find further discussion about duplicates in subsequent chapters, but here is an example for illustration purposes. Consider the following query.

```
USE TSQL2012;

SELECT country
FROM HR.Employees;
```

The query is issued against the TSQL2012 sample database. It returns the country attribute of the employees stored in the HR.Employees table. According to the relational model, a relational operation against a relation is supposed to return a relation. In this case, this should translate to returning the set of countries where there are employees, with an emphasis on set, as in no duplicates. However, T-SQL doesn't attempt to remove duplicates by default.

Here's the output of this query.

```
Country
---------------
USA
USA
USA
USA
UK
UK
UK
USA
UK
```

In fact, T-SQL is based more on multiset theory than on set theory. A *multiset* (also known as a bag or a superset) in many respects is similar to a set, but can have duplicates. As mentioned, the T-SQL language does give you enough tools so that if you want to follow relational theory, you can do so. For example, the language provides you with a DISTINCT clause to remove duplicates. Here's the revised query.

```
SELECT DISTINCT country
FROM HR.Employees;
```

Here's the revised query's output.

```
Country
---------------
UK
USA
```

Another fundamental aspect of a set is that there's no relevance to the order of the elements. For this reason, rows in a table have no particular order, conceptually. So when you issue a query against a table and don't indicate explicitly that you want to return the rows in particular presentation order, the result is supposed to be relational. Therefore, you shouldn't assume any specific order to the rows in the result, never mind what you know about the physical representation of the data, for example, when the data is indexed.

As an example, consider the following query.

```
SELECT empid, lastname
FROM HR.Employees;
```

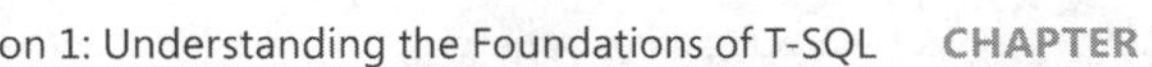

When this query was run on one system, it returned the following output, which looks like it is sorted by the column lastname.

```
empid  lastname
------ -------------
5      Buck
8      Cameron
1      Davis
9      Dolgopyatova
2      Funk
7      King
3      Lew
4      Peled
6      Suurs
```

Even if the rows were returned in a different order, the result would have still been considered correct. SQL Server can choose between different physical access methods to process the query, knowing that it doesn't need to guarantee the order in the result. For example, SQL Server could decide to parallelize the query or scan the data in file order (as opposed to index order).

If you do need to guarantee a specific presentation order to the rows in the result, you need to add an ORDER BY clause to the query, as follows.

```
SELECT empid, lastname
FROM HR.Employees
ORDER BY empid;
```

This time, the result isn't relational—it's what standard SQL calls a *cursor*. The order of the rows in the output is guaranteed based on the empid attribute. Here's the output of this query.

```
empid  lastname
------ -------------
1      Davis
2      Funk
3      Lew
4      Peled
5      Buck
6      Suurs
7      King
8      Cameron
9      Dolgopyatova
```

The heading of a relation is a set of attributes that are supposed to be identified by name and type name. There's no order to the attributes. Conversely, T-SQL does keep track of ordinal positions of columns based on their order of appearance in the table definition. When you issue a query with SELECT *, you are guaranteed to get the columns in the result based on definition order. Also, T-SQL allows referring to ordinal positions of columns from the result in the ORDER BY clause, as follows.

```
SELECT empid, lastname
FROM HR.Employees
ORDER BY 1;
```

Beyond the fact that this practice is not relational, think about the potential for error if at some point you change the SELECT list and forget to change the ORDER BY list accordingly. Therefore, the recommendation is to always indicate the names of the attributes that you need to order by.

T-SQL has another deviation from the relational model in that it allows defining result columns based on an expression without assigning a name to the target column. For example, the following query is valid in T-SQL.

```
SELECT empid, firstname + ' ' + lastname
FROM HR.Employees;
```

This query generates the following output.

```
empid
------ ------------------
1      Sara Davis
2      Don Funk
3      Judy Lew
4      Yael Peled
5      Sven Buck
6      Paul Suurs
7      Russell King
8      Maria Cameron
9      Zoya Dolgopyatova
```

But according to the relational model, all attributes must have names. In order for the query to be relational, you need to assign an alias to the target attribute. You can do so by using the AS clause, as follows.

```
SELECT empid, firstname + ' ' + lastname AS fullname
FROM HR.Employees;
```

Also, T-SQL allows a query to return multiple result columns with the same name. For example, consider a join between two tables, T1 and T2, both with a column called keycol. T-SQL allows a SELECT list that looks like the following.

```
SELECT T1.keycol, T2.keycol ...
```

For the result to be relational, all attributes must have unique names, so you would need to use different aliases for the result attributes, as in the following.

```
SELECT T1.keycol AS key1, T2.keycol AS key2 ...
```

As for predicates, following the *law of excluded middle* in mathematical logic, a predicate can evaluate to true or false. In other words, predicates are supposed to use two-valued logic. However, Codd wanted to reflect the possibility for values to be missing in his model. He referred to two kinds of missing values: missing but applicable and missing but inapplicable. Take a mobilephone attribute of an employee as an example. A missing but applicable value would be if an employee has a mobile phone but did not want to provide this information, for example, for privacy reasons. A missing but inapplicable value would be when the employee simply doesn't have a mobile phone. According to Codd, a language based on his model should provide two different marks for the two cases. T-SQL—again, based on standard SQL—implements only one general purpose mark called NULL for any kind of missing value. This leads to three-valued predicate logic. Namely, when a predicate compares two values, for example, mobilephone = '(425) 555-0136', if both are present, the result evaluates to either true or false. But if one of them is NULL, the result evaluates to a third logical value—unknown.

Note that some believe that a valid relational model should follow two-valued logic, and strongly object to the concept of NULLs in SQL. But as mentioned, the creator of the relational model believed in the idea of supporting missing values, and predicates that extend beyond two-valued logic. What's important from a perspective of coding with T-SQL is to realize that if the database you are querying supports NULLs, their treatment is far from being trivial. That is, you need to carefully understand what happens when NULLs are involved in the data you're manipulating with various query constructs, like filtering, sorting, grouping, joining, or intersecting. Hence, with every piece of code you write with T-SQL, you want to ask yourself whether NULLs are possible in the data you're interacting with. If the answer is yes, you want to make sure that you understand the treatment of NULLs in your query, and ensure that your tests address treatment of NULLs specifically.

Quick Check

1. **Name two aspects in which T-SQL deviates from the relational model.**
2. **Explain how you can address the two items in question 1 and use T-SQL in a relational way.**

Quick Check Answer

1. **A relation has a body with a distinct set of tuples. A table doesn't have to have a key. T-SQL allows referring to ordinal positions of columns in the ORDER BY clause.**
2. **Define a key in every table. Refer to attribute names—not their ordinal positions—in the ORDER BY clause.**

Using Correct Terminology

Your use of terminology reflects on your knowledge. Therefore, you should make an effort to understand and use correct terminology. When discussing T-SQL–related topics, people often use incorrect terms. And if that's not enough, even when you do realize what the correct terms are, you also need to understand the differences between the terms in T-SQL and those in the relational model.

As an example of incorrect terms in T-SQL, people often use the terms "field" and "record" to refer to what T-SQL calls "column" and "row," respectively. Fields and records are physical. Fields are what you have in user interfaces in client applications, and records are what you have in files and cursors. Tables are logical, and they have logical rows and columns.

Another example of an incorrect term is referring to "NULL values." A NULL is a mark for a missing value—not a value itself. Hence, the correct usage of the term is either "NULL mark" or just "NULL."

Besides using correct T-SQL terminology, it's also important to understand the differences between T-SQL terms and their relational counterparts. Remember from the previous section that T-SQL attempts to represent a relation with a table, a tuple with a row, and an attribute with a column; but the T-SQL concepts and their relational counterparts differ in a number of ways. As long as you are conscious of those differences, you can, and should, strive to use T-SQL in a relational way.

Quick Check

1. **Why are the terms "field" and "record" incorrect when referring to column and row?**
2. **Why is the term "NULL value" incorrect?**

Quick Check Answer

1. **Because "field" and "record" describe physical things, whereas columns and rows are logical elements of a table.**
2. **Because NULL isn't a value; rather, it's a mark for a missing value.**

PRACTICE Using T-SQL in a Relational Way

In this practice, you exercise your knowledge of using T-SQL in a relational way.

If you encounter a problem completing an exercise, you can install the completed projects from the companion content for this chapter and lesson.

EXERCISE 1 Identify Nonrelational Elements in a Query

In this exercise, you are given a query. Your task is to identify the nonrelational elements in the query.

1. Open SQL Server management Studio (SSMS) and connect to the sample database TSQL2012. (See the book's introduction for instructions on how to create the sample database and how to work with SSMS.)
2. Type the following query in the query window and execute it.

```
SELECT custid, YEAR(orderdate)
FROM Sales.Orders
ORDER BY 1, 2;
```

You get the following output shown here in abbreviated form.

```
custid
----------- -----------
1           2007
1           2007
1           2007
1           2008
1           2008
1           2008
2           2006
2           2007
2           2007
2           2008
...
```

3. Review the code and its output. The query is supposed to return for each customer and order year the customer ID (custid) and order year (YEAR(orderdate)). Note that there's no presentation ordering requirement from the query. Can you identify what the nonrelational aspects of the query are?

   Answer: The query doesn't alias the expression YEAR(orderdate), so there's no name for the result attribute. The query can return duplicates. The query forces certain presentation ordering to the result and uses ordinal positions in the ORDER BY clause.

EXERCISE 2 Make the Nonrelational Query Relational

In this exercise, you work with the query provided in Exercise 1 as your starting point. After you identify the nonrelational elements in the query, you need to apply the appropriate revisions to make it relational.

- In step 3 of Exercise 1, you identified the nonrelational elements in the last query. Apply revisions to the query to make it relational.

  A number of revisions are required to make the query relational.

  - Define an attribute name by assigning an alias to the expression YEAR(orderdate).
  - Add a DISTINCT clause to remove duplicates.
  - Also, remove the ORDER BY clause to return a relational result.
  - Even if there was a presentation ordering requirement (not in this case), you should not use ordinal positions; instead, use attribute names. Your code should look like the following.

    ```
    SELECT DISTINCT custid, YEAR(orderdate) AS orderyear
    FROM Sales.Orders;
    ```

Lesson Summary

- T-SQL is based on strong mathematical foundations. It is based on standard SQL, which in turn is based on the relational model, which in turn is based on set theory and predicate logic.
- It is important to understand the relational model and apply its principals when writing T-SQL code.
- When describing concepts in T-SQL, you should use correct terminology because it reflects on your knowledge.

Lesson Review

Answer the following questions to test your knowledge of the information in this lesson. You can find the answers to these questions and explanations of why each answer choice is correct or incorrect in the "Answers" section at the end of this chapter.

1. Why is it important to use standard SQL code when possible and know what is standard and what isn't? (Choose all that apply.)
   - **A.** It is not important to code using standard SQL.
   - **B.** Standard SQL code is more portable between platforms.
   - **C.** Standard SQL code is more efficient.
   - **D.** Knowing what standard SQL code is makes your knowledge more portable.
2. Which of the following is not a violation of the relational model?
   - **A.** Using ordinal positions for columns
   - **B.** Returning duplicate rows
   - **C.** Not defining a key in a table
   - **D.** Ensuring that all attributes in the result of a query have names
3. What is the relationship between SQL and T-SQL?
   - **A.** T-SQL is the standard language and SQL is the dialect in Microsoft SQL Server.
   - **B.** SQL is the standard language and T-SQL is the dialect in Microsoft SQL Server.
   - **C.** Both SQL and T-SQL are standard languages.
   - **D.** Both SQL and T-SQL are dialects in Microsoft SQL Server.

Lesson 2: Understanding Logical Query Processing

T-SQL has both logical and physical sides to it. The logical side is the conceptual interpretation of the query that explains what the correct result of the query is. The physical side is the processing of the query by the database engine. Physical processing must produce the result defined by logical query processing. To achieve this goal, the database engine can apply optimization. Optimization can rearrange steps from logical query processing or remove steps altogether—but only as long as the result remains the one defined by logical query processing. The focus of this lesson is *logical query processing*—the conceptual interpretation of the query that defines the correct result.

After this lesson, you will be able to:

- Understand the reasoning for the design of T-SQL.
- Describe the main logical query processing phases.
- Explain the reasons for some of the restrictions in T-SQL.

Estimated lesson time: 40 minutes

T-SQL As a Declarative English-Like Language

T-SQL, being based on standard SQL, is a declarative English-like language. In this language, declarative means you define *what* you want, as opposed to *imperative* languages that define also *how* to achieve what you want. Standard SQL describes the logical interpretation of the declarative request (the "what" part), but it's the database engine's responsibility to figure out how to physically process the request (the "how" part).

For this reason, it is important not to draw any performance-related conclusions from what you learn about logical query processing. That's because logical query processing only defines the correctness of the query. When addressing performance aspects of the query, you need to understand how optimization works. As mentioned, optimization can be quite different from logical query processing because it's allowed to change things as long as the result achieved is the one defined by logical query processing.

It's interesting to note that the standard language SQL wasn't originally called so; rather, it was called SEQUEL; an acronym for "structured English query language." But then due to a trademark dispute with an airline company, the language was renamed to SQL, for "structured query language." Still, the point is that you provide your instructions in an English-like manner. For example, consider the instruction, "Bring me a soda from the refrigerator." Observe that in the instruction in English, the object comes before the location. Consider the following request in T-SQL.

```
SELECT shipperid, phone, companyname
FROM Sales.Shippers;
```

Observe the similarity of the query's keyed-in order to English. The query first indicates the SELECT list with the attributes you want to return and then the FROM clause with the table you want to query.

Now try to think of the order in which the request needs to be logically interpreted. For example, how would you define the instructions to a robot instead of a human? The original English instruction to get a soda from the refrigerator would probably need to be revised to something like, "Go to the refrigerator; open the door; get a soda; bring it to me."

Similarly, the logical processing of a query must first know which table is being queried before it can know which attributes can be returned from that table. Therefore, contrary to the keyed-in order of the previous query, the logical query processing has to be as follows.

```
FROM Sales.Shippers
SELECT shipperid, phone, companyname
```

This is a basic example with just two query clauses. Of course, things can get more complex. If you understand the concept of logical query processing well, you will be able to explain many things about the way the language behaves—things that are very hard to explain otherwise.

Logical Query Processing Phases

This section covers logical query processing and the phases involved. Don't worry if some of the concepts discussed here aren't clear yet. Subsequent chapters in this Training Kit provide more detail, and after you go over those, this topic should make more sense. To make sure you really understand these concepts, make a first pass over the topic now and then revisit it later after going over Chapters 2 through 5.

The main statement used to retrieve data in T-SQL is the SELECT statement. Following are the main query clauses specified in the order that you are supposed to type them (known as "keyed-in order"):

1. SELECT
2. FROM
3. WHERE
4. GROUP BY
5. HAVING
6. ORDER BY

But as mentioned, the logical query processing order, which is the conceptual interpretation order, is different. It starts with the FROM clause. Here is the logical query processing order of the six main query clauses:

1. FROM
2. WHERE

3. GROUP BY
4. HAVING
5. SELECT
6. ORDER BY

Each phase operates on one or more tables as inputs and returns a virtual table as output. The output table of one phase is considered the input to the next phase. This is in accord with operations on relations that yield a relation. Note that if an ORDER BY is specified, the result isn't relational. This fact has implications that are discussed later in this Training Kit, in Chapter 3, "Filtering and Sorting Data," and Chapter 4, "Combining Sets."

Consider the following query as an example.

```
SELECT country, YEAR(hiredate) AS yearhired, COUNT(*) AS numemployees
FROM HR.Employees
WHERE hiredate >= '20030101'
GROUP BY country, YEAR(hiredate)
HAVING COUNT(*) > 1
ORDER BY country , yearhired DESC;
```

This query is issued against the HR.Employees table. It filters only employees that were hired in or after the year 2003. It groups the remaining employees by country and the hire year. It keeps only groups with more than one employee. For each qualifying group, the query returns the hire year and count of employees, sorted by country and hire year, in descending order.

The following sections provide a brief description of what happens in each phase according to logical query processing.

1. Evaluate the FROM Clause

In the first phase, the FROM clause is evaluated. That's where you indicate the tables you want to query and table operators like joins if applicable. If you need to query just one table, you indicate the table name as the input table in this clause. Then, the output of this phase is a table result with all rows from the input table. That's the case in the following query: the input is the HR.Employees table (nine rows), and the output is a table result with all nine rows (only a subset of the attributes are shown).

```
empid  hiredate    country
------ ----------- --------
1      2002-05-01  USA
2      2002-08-14  USA
3      2002-04-01  USA
4      2003-05-03  USA
5      2003-10-17  UK
6      2003-10-17  UK
7      2004-01-02  UK
8      2004-03-05  USA
9      2004-11-15  UK
```

2. Filter Rows Based on the WHERE Clause

The second phase filters rows based on the predicate in the WHERE clause. Only rows for which the predicate evaluates to true are returned.

EXAM TIP

Rows for which the predicate evaluates to false, or evaluates to an unknown state, are not returned.

In this query, the WHERE filtering phase filters only rows for employees hired on or after January 1, 2003. Six rows are returned from this phase and are provided as input to the next one. Here's the result of this phase.

```
empid  hiredate    country
------ ----------- --------
4      2003-05-03  USA
5      2003-10-17  UK
6      2003-10-17  UK
7      2004-01-02  UK
8      2004-03-05  USA
9      2004-11-15  UK
```

A typical mistake made by people who don't understand logical query processing is attempting to refer in the WHERE clause to a column alias defined in the SELECT clause. This isn't allowed because the WHERE clause is evaluated before the SELECT clause. As an example, consider the following query.

```
SELECT country, YEAR(hiredate) AS yearhired
FROM HR.Employees
WHERE yearhired >= 2003;
```

This query fails with the following error.

```
Msg 207, Level 16, State 1, Line 3
Invalid column name 'yearhired'.
```

If you understand that the WHERE clause is evaluated before the SELECT clause, you realize that this attempt is wrong because at this phase, the attribute yearhired doesn't yet exist. You can indicate the expression YEAR(hiredate) >= 2003 in the WHERE clause. Better yet, for optimization reasons that are discussed in Chapter 3 and Chapter 15, "Implementing Indexes and Statistics," use the form hiredate >= '20030101' as done in the original query.

3. Group Rows Based on the GROUP BY Clause

This phase defines a group for each distinct combination of values in the grouped elements from the input table. It then associates each input row to its respective group. The query you've been working with groups the rows by country and YEAR(hiredate). Within the six rows in the input table, this step identifies four groups. Here are the groups and the detail rows that are associated with them (redundant information removed for purposes of illustration).

```
group    group          detail detail  detail
country  YEAR(hiredate) empid  country hiredate
-------- -------------- ------ ------- ----------
UK       2003           5      UK      2003-10-17
                        6      UK      2003-10-17
UK       2004           7      UK      2004-01-02
                        9      UK      2004-11-15
USA      2003           4      USA     2003-05-03
USA      2004           8      USA     2004-03-05
```

As you can see, the group UK, 2003 has two associated detail rows with employees 5 and 6; the group for UK, 2004 also has two associated detail rows with employees 7 and 9; the group for USA, 2003 has one associated detail row with employee 4; the group for USA, 2004 also has one associated detail row with employee 8.

The final result of this query has one row representing each group (unless filtered out). Therefore, expressions in all phases that take place after the current grouping phase are somewhat limited. All expressions processed in subsequent phases must guarantee a single value per group. If you refer to an element from the GROUP BY list (for example, country), you already have such a guarantee, so such a reference is allowed. However, if you want to refer to an element that is not part of your GROUP BY list (for example, empid), it must be contained within an aggregate function like MAX or SUM. That's because multiple values are possible in the element within a single group, and the only way to guarantee that just one will be returned is to aggregate the values. For more details on grouped queries, see Chapter 5, "Grouping and Windowing."

4. Filter Rows Based on the HAVING Clause

This phase is also responsible for filtering data based on a predicate, but it is evaluated after the data has been grouped; hence, it is evaluated per group and filters groups as a whole. As is usual in T-SQL, the filtering predicate can evaluate to true, false, or unknown. Only groups for which the predicate evaluates to true are returned from this phase. In this case, the HAVING clause uses the predicate COUNT(*) > 1, meaning filter only country and hire year groups that have more than one employee. If you look at the number of rows that were associated with each group in the previous step, you will notice that only the groups UK, 2003 and UK, 2004 qualify. Hence, the result of this phase has the following remaining groups, shown here with their associated detail rows.

```
group    group          detail detail  detail
country  YEAR(hiredate) empid  country hiredate
-------- -------------- ------ ------- ----------
UK       2003           5      UK      2003-10-17
                        6      UK      2003-10-17
UK       2004           7      UK      2004-01-02
                        9      UK      2004-11-15
```

Quick Check

- What is the difference between the WHERE and HAVING clauses?

Quick Check Answer

- The WHERE clause is evaluated before rows are grouped, and therefore is evaluated per row. The HAVING clause is evaluated after rows are grouped, and therefore is evaluated per group.

5. Process the SELECT Clause

The fifth phase is the one responsible for processing the SELECT clause. What's interesting about it is the point in logical query processing where it gets evaluated—almost last. That's interesting considering the fact that the SELECT clause appears first in the query.

This phase includes two main steps. The first step is evaluating the expressions in the SELECT list and producing the result attributes. This includes assigning attributes with names if they are derived from expressions. Remember that if a query is a grouped query, each group is represented by a single row in the result. In the query, two groups remain after the processing of the HAVING filter. Therefore, this step generates two rows. In this case, the SELECT list returns for each country and order year group a row with the following attributes: country, YEAR(hiredate) aliased as yearhired, and COUNT(*) aliased as numemployees.

The second step in this phase is applicable if you indicate the DISTINCT clause, in which case this step removes duplicates. Remember that T-SQL is based on multiset theory more than it is on set theory, and therefore, if duplicates are possible in the result, it's your responsibility to remove those with the DISTINCT clause. In this query's case, this step is inapplicable. Here's the result of this phase in the query.

```
country  yearhired  numemployees
-------- ---------- ------------
UK       2003       2
UK       2004       2
```

If you need a reminder of what the query looks like, here it is again.

```
SELECT country, YEAR(hiredate) AS yearhired, COUNT(*) AS numemployees
FROM HR.Employees
WHERE hiredate >= '20030101'
GROUP BY country, YEAR(hiredate)
HAVING COUNT(*) > 1
ORDER BY country , yearhired DESC;
```

The fifth phase returns a relational result. Therefore, the order of the rows isn't guaranteed. In this query's case, there is an ORDER BY clause that guarantees the order in the result, but this will be discussed when the next phase is described. What's important to note is that the outcome of the phase that processes the SELECT clause is still relational.

Also, remember that this phase assigns column aliases, like yearhired and numemployees. This means that newly created column aliases are not visible to clauses processed in previous phases, like FROM, WHERE, GROUP BY, and HAVING.

Note that an alias created by the SELECT phase isn't even visible to other expressions that appear in the same SELECT list. For example, the following query isn't valid.

```
SELECT empid, country, YEAR(hiredate) AS yearhired, yearhired - 1 AS prevyear
FROM HR.Employees;
```

This query generates the following error.

```
Msg 207, Level 16, State 1, Line 1
Invalid column name 'yearhired'.
```

The reason that this isn't allowed is that, conceptually, T-SQL evaluates all expressions that appear in the same logical query processing phase in an all-at-once manner. Note the use of the word *conceptually*. SQL Server won't necessarily physically process all expressions at the same point in time, but it has to produce a result as if it did. This behavior is different than many other programming languages where expressions usually get evaluated in a left-to-right order, making a result produced in one expression visible to the one that appears to its right. But T-SQL is different.

Quick Check

1. **Why are you not allowed to refer to a column alias defined by the SELECT clause in the WHERE clause?**
2. **Why are you not allowed to refer to a column alias defined by the SELECT clause in the same SELECT clause?**

Quick Check Answer

1. **Because the WHERE clause is logically evaluated in a phase earlier to the one that evaluates the SELECT clause.**
2. **Because all expressions that appear in the same logical query processing phase are evaluated conceptually at the same point in time.**

6. Handle Presentation Ordering

The sixth phase is applicable if the query has an ORDER BY clause. This phase is responsible for returning the result in a specific presentation order according to the expressions that appear in the ORDER BY list. The query indicates that the result rows should be ordered first by country (in ascending order by default), and then by yearhired, descending, yielding the following output.

```
country  yearhired  numemployees
-------- ---------- ------------
UK       2004       2
UK       2003       2
```

Notice that the ORDER BY clause is the first and only clause that is allowed to refer to column aliases defined in the SELECT clause. That's because the ORDER BY clause is the only one to be evaluated after the SELECT clause.

Unlike in previous phases where the result was relational, the output of this phase isn't relational because it has a guaranteed order. The result of this phase is what standard SQL calls a cursor. Note that the use of the term cursor here is conceptual. T-SQL also supports an object called a cursor that is defined based on a result of a query, and that allows fetching rows one at a time in a specified order.

You might care about returning the result of a query in a specific order for presentation purposes or if the caller needs to consume the result in that manner through some cursor mechanism that fetches the rows one at a time. But remember that such processing isn't relational. If you need to process the query result in a relational manner—for example, define a table expression like a view based on the query (details later in Chapter 4)—the result will need to be relational. Also, sorting data can add cost to the query processing. If you don't care about the order in which the result rows are returned, you can avoid this unnecessary cost by not adding an ORDER BY clause.

A query may specify the TOP or OFFSET-FETCH filtering options. If it does, the same ORDER BY clause that is normally used to define presentation ordering also defines which rows to filter for these options. It's important to note that such a filter is processed after the SELECT phase evaluates all expressions and removes duplicates (in case a DISTINCT clause was specified). You might even consider the TOP and OFFSET-FETCH filters as being processed in their own phase number 7. The query doesn't indicate such a filter, and therefore, this phase is inapplicable in this case.

PRACTICE Logical Query Processing

In this practice, you exercise your knowledge of logical query processing.

If you encounter a problem completing an exercise, you can install the completed projects from the companion content for this chapter and lesson.

EXERCISE 1 Fix a Problem with Grouping

In this exercise, you are presented with a grouped query that fails when you try to execute it. You are provided with instructions on how to fix the query.

1. Open SSMS and connect to the sample database TSQL2012.

2. Type the following query in the query window and execute it.

```
SELECT custid, orderid
FROM Sales.Orders
GROUP BY custid;
```

The query was supposed to return for each customer the customer ID and the maximum order ID for that customer, but instead it fails. Try to figure out why the query failed and what needs to be revised so that it would return the desired result.

3. The query failed because orderid neither appears in the GROUP BY list nor within an aggregate function. There are multiple possible orderid values per customer. To fix the query, you need to apply an aggregate function to the orderid attribute. The task is to return the maximum orderid value per customer. Therefore, the aggregate function should be MAX. Your query should look like the following.

```
SELECT custid, MAX(orderid) AS maxorderid
FROM Sales.Orders
GROUP BY custid;
```

EXERCISE 2 Fix a Problem with Aliasing

In this exercise, you are presented with another grouped query that fails, this time because of an aliasing problem. As in the first exercise, you are provided with instructions on how to fix the query.

1. Clear the query window, type the following query, and execute it.

```
SELECT shipperid, SUM(freight) AS totalfreight
FROM Sales.Orders
WHERE freight > 20000.00
GROUP BY shipperid;
```

   The query was supposed to return only shippers for whom the total freight value is greater than 20,000, but instead it returns an empty set. Try to identify the problem in the query.

2. Remember that the WHERE filtering clause is evaluated per row—not per group. The query filters individual orders with a freight value greater than 20,000, and there are none. To correct the query, you need to apply the filter per each shipper group—not per each order. You need to filter the total of all freight values per shipper. This can be achieved by using the HAVING filter. You try to fix the problem by using the following query.

```
SELECT shipperid, SUM(freight) AS totalfreight
FROM Sales.Orders
GROUP BY shipperid
HAVING totalfreight > 20000.00;
```

   But this query also fails. Try to identify why it fails and what needs to be revised to achieve the desired result.

3. The problem now is that the query attempts to refer in the HAVING clause to the alias totalfreight, which is defined in the SELECT clause. The HAVING clause is evaluated before the SELECT clause, and therefore, the column alias isn't visible to it. To fix the problem, you need to refer to the expression SUM(freight) in the HAVING clause, as follows.

```
SELECT shipperid, SUM(freight) AS totalfreight
FROM Sales.Orders
GROUP BY shipperid
HAVING SUM(freight) > 20000.00;
```

Lesson Summary

- T-SQL was designed as a declarative language where the instructions are provided in an English-like manner. Therefore, the keyed-in order of the query clauses starts with the SELECT clause.
- Logical query processing is the conceptual interpretation of the query that defines the correct result, and unlike the keyed-in order of the query clauses, it starts by evaluating the FROM clause.
- Understanding logical query processing is crucial for correct understanding of T-SQL.

Lesson Review

Answer the following questions to test your knowledge of the information in this lesson. You can find the answers to these questions and explanations of why each answer choice is correct or incorrect in the "Answers" section at the end of this chapter.

1. Which of the following correctly represents the logical query processing order of the various query clauses?
   - **A.** SELECT > FROM > WHERE > GROUP BY > HAVING > ORDER BY
   - **B.** FROM > WHERE > GROUP BY > HAVING > SELECT > ORDER BY
   - **C.** FROM > WHERE > GROUP BY > HAVING > ORDER BY > SELECT
   - **D.** SELECT > ORDER BY > FROM > WHERE > GROUP BY > HAVING
2. Which of the following is invalid? (Choose all that apply.)
   - **A.** Referring to an attribute that you group by in the WHERE clause
   - **B.** Referring to an expression in the GROUP BY clause; for example, GROUP BY YEAR(orderdate)
   - **C.** In a grouped query, referring in the SELECT list to an attribute that is not part of the GROUP BY list and not within an aggregate function
   - **D.** Referring to an alias defined in the SELECT clause in the HAVING clause

3. What is true about the result of a query without an ORDER BY clause?
   - **A.** It is relational as long as other relational requirements are met.
   - **B.** It cannot have duplicates.
   - **C.** The order of the rows in the output is guaranteed to be the same as the insertion order.
   - **D.** The order of the rows in the output is guaranteed to be the same as that of the clustered index.

Case Scenarios

In the following case scenarios, you apply what you've learned about T-SQL querying. You can find the answers to these questions in the "Answers" section at the end of this chapter.

Case Scenario 1: Importance of Theory

You and a colleague on your team get into a discussion about the importance of understanding the theoretical foundations of T-SQL. Your colleague argues that there's no point in understanding the foundations, and that it's enough to just learn the technical aspects of T-SQL to be a good developer and to write correct code. Answer the following questions posed to you by your colleague:

1. Can you give an example for an element from set theory that can improve your understanding of T-SQL?
2. Can you explain why understanding the relational model is important for people who write T-SQL code?

Case Scenario 2: Interviewing for a Code Reviewer Position

You are interviewed for a position as a code reviewer to help improve code quality. The organization's application has queries written by untrained people. The queries have numerous problems, including logical bugs. Your interviewer poses a number of questions and asks for a concise answer of a few sentences to each question. Answer the following questions addressed to you by your interviewer:

1. Is it important to use standard code when possible, and why?
2. We have many queries that use ordinal positions in the ORDER BY clause. Is that a bad practice, and if so why?
3. If a query doesn't have an ORDER BY clause, what is the order in which the records are returned?
4. Would you recommend putting a DISTINCT clause in every query?

Suggested Practices

To help you successfully master the exam objectives presented in this chapter, complete the following tasks.

Visit T-SQL Public Newsgroups and Review Code

To practice your knowledge of using T-SQL in a relational way, you should review code samples written by others.

- **Practice 1** List as many examples as you can for aspects of T-SQL coding that are not relational.
- **Practice 2** After creating the list in Practice 1, visit the Microsoft public forum for T-SQL at *http://social.msdn.microsoft.com/Forums/en/transactsql/threads*. Review code samples in the T-SQL threads. Try to identify cases where nonrelational elements are used; if you find such cases, identify what needs to be revised to make them relational.

Describe Logical Query Processing

To better understand logical query processing, we recommend that you complete the following tasks:

- **Practice 1** Create a document with a numbered list of the phases involved with logical query processing in the correct order. Provide a brief paragraph summarizing what happens in each step.
- **Practice 2** Create a graphical flow diagram representing the flow of the logical query processing phases by using a tool such as Microsoft Visio, Microsoft PowerPoint, or Microsoft Word.

Answers

This section contains the answers to the lesson review questions and solutions to the case scenarios in this chapter.

Lesson 1

1. **Correct Answers: B and D**
   - **A. Incorrect:** It is important to use standard code.
   - **B. Correct:** Use of standard code makes it easier to port code between platforms because fewer revisions are required.
   - **C. Incorrect:** There's no assurance that standard code will be more efficient.
   - **D. Correct:** When using standard code, you can adapt to a new environment more easily because standard code elements look similar in the different platforms.
2. **Correct Answer: D**
   - **A. Incorrect:** A relation has a header with a set of attributes, and tuples of the relation have the same heading. A set has no order, so ordinal positions do not have meaning and constitute a violation of the relational model. You should refer to attributes by their name.
   - **B. Incorrect:** A query is supposed to return a relation. A relation has a body with a set of tuples. A set has no duplicates. Returning duplicate rows is a violation of the relational model.
   - **C. Incorrect:** Not defining a key in the table allows duplicate rows in the table, and like the answer to B, that's a violation of the relational model.
   - **D. Correct:** Because attributes are supposed to be identified by name, ensuring that all attributes have names is relational, and hence not a violation of the relational model.
3. **Correct Answer: B**
   - **A. Incorrect:** T-SQL isn't standard and SQL isn't a dialect in Microsoft SQL Server.
   - **B. Correct:** SQL is standard and T-SQL is a dialect in Microsoft SQL Server.
   - **C. Incorrect:** T-SQL isn't standard.
   - **D. Incorrect:** SQL isn't a dialect in Microsoft SQL Server.

Lesson 2

1. **Correct Answer: B**
   - **A. Incorrect:** Logical query processing doesn't start with the SELECT clause.
   - **B. Correct:** Logical query processing starts with the FROM clause, and then moves on to WHERE, GROUP BY, HAVING, SELECT, and ORDER BY.
   - **C. Incorrect:** The ORDER BY clause isn't evaluated before the SELECT clause.
   - **D. Incorrect:** Logical query processing doesn't start with the SELECT clause.
2. **Correct Answer: C and D**
   - **A. Incorrect:** T-SQL allows you to refer to an attribute that you group by in the WHERE clause.
   - **B. Incorrect:** T-SQL allows grouping by an expression.
   - **C. Correct:** If the query is a grouped query, in phases processed after the GROUP BY phase, each attribute that you refer to must appear either in the GROUP BY list or within an aggregate function.
   - **D. Correct:** Because the HAVING clause is evaluated before the SELECT clause, referring to an alias defined in the SELECT clause within the HAVING clause is invalid.
3. **Correct Answer: A**
   - **A. Correct:** A query with an ORDER BY clause doesn't return a relational result. For the result to be relational, the query must satisfy a number of requirements, including the following: the query must not have an ORDER BY clause, all attributes must have names, all attribute names must be unique, and duplicates must not appear in the result.
   - **B. Incorrect:** A query without a DISTINCT clause in the SELECT clause can return duplicates.
   - **C. Incorrect:** A query without an ORDER BY clause does not guarantee the order of rows in the output.
   - **D. Incorrect:** A query without an ORDER BY clause does not guarantee the order of rows in the output.

Case Scenario 1

1. One of the most typical mistakes that T-SQL developers make is to assume that a query without an ORDER BY clause always returns the data in a certain order—for example, clustered index order. But if you understand that in set theory, a set has no particular order to its elements, you know that you shouldn't make such assumptions. The only way in SQL to guarantee that the rows will be returned in a certain order is to add an ORDER BY clause. That's just one of many examples for aspects of T-SQL that can be better understood if you understand the foundations of the language.

2. Even though T-SQL is based on the relational model, it deviates from it in a number of ways. But it gives you enough tools that if you understand the relational model, you can write in a relational way. Following the relational model helps you write code more correctly. Here are some examples:
   - You shouldn't rely on order of columns or rows.
   - You should always name result columns.
   - You should eliminate duplicates if they are possible in the result of your query.

Case Scenario 2

1. It is important to use standard SQL code. This way, both the code and people's knowledge is more portable. Especially in cases where there are both standard and nonstandard forms for a language element, it's recommended to use the standard form.

2. Using ordinal positions in the ORDER BY clause is a bad practice. From a relational perspective, you are supposed to refer to attributes by name, and not by ordinal position. Also, what if the SELECT list is revised in the future and the developer forgets to revise the ORDER BY list accordingly?

3. When the query doesn't have an ORDER BY clause, there are no assurances for any particular order in the result. The order should be considered arbitrary. You also notice that the interviewer used the incorrect term *record* instead of *row*. You might want to mention something about this, because the interviewer may have done so on purpose to test you.

4. From a pure relational perspective, this actually could be valid, and perhaps even recommended. But from a practical perspective, there is the chance that SQL Server will try to remove duplicates even when there are none, and this will incur extra cost. Therefore, it is recommended that you add the DISTINCT clause only when duplicates are possible in the result and you're not supposed to return the duplicates.

CHAPTER 2

Getting Started with the SELECT Statement

Exam objectives in this chapter:

- Work with Data
  - Query data by using SELECT statements.
  - Implement data types.
- Modify Data
  - Work with functions.

The previous chapter provided you with the foundations to T-SQL. This chapter starts by covering two of the principal query clauses—FROM and SELECT. It then continues by covering the data types supported by Microsoft SQL Server and the considerations in choosing the appropriate data types for your columns. This chapter also covers the use of built-in scalar functions, the CASE expression, and variations like ISNULL and COALESCE.

Lessons in this chapter:

- Lesson 1: Using the FROM and SELECT Clauses
- Lesson 2: Working with Data Types and Built-in Functions

Before You Begin

To complete the lessons in this chapter, you must have:

- Experience working with SQL Server Management Studio (SSMS).
- Some experience writing T-SQL code.
- Access to a SQL Server 2012 instance with the sample database TSQL2012 installed.

Lesson 1: Using the FROM and SELECT Clauses

The FROM and SELECT clauses are two principal clauses that appear in almost every query that retrieves data. This lesson explains the purpose of these clauses, how to use them, and best practices associated with them.

After this lesson, you will be able to:

- Write queries that use the FROM and SELECT clauses.
- Define table and column aliases.
- Describe best practices associated with the FROM and SELECT clauses.

Estimated lesson time: 30 minutes

The FROM Clause

According to logical query processing (see details in Chapter 1, "Foundations of Querying," explaining the concept), the FROM clause is the first clause to be evaluated logically in a SELECT query. The FROM clause has two main roles:

- It's the clause where you indicate the tables that you want to query.
- It's the clause where you can apply table operators like joins to input tables.

This chapter focuses on the first role. Chapter 4, "Combining Sets," and Chapter 5, "Grouping and Windowing," cover the use of table operators.

As a basic example, assuming you are connected to the sample database TSQL2012, the following query uses the FROM clause to specify that HR.Employees is the table being queried.

```
SELECT empid, firstname, lastname
FROM HR.Employees;
```

Observe the use of the two-part name to refer to the table. The first part (HR) is the schema name and the second part (Employees) is the table name. In some cases, T-SQL supports omitting the schema name, as in FROM Employees, in which case it uses an implicit schema name resolution process. It is considered a best practice to always explicitly indicate the schema name. This practice can prevent you from ending up with a schema name that you did not intend to be used, and can also remove the cost involved in the implicit resolution process, although this cost is minor.

In the FROM clause, you can alias the queried tables with your chosen names. You can use the form <*table*> <*alias*>, as in HR.Employees E, or <*table*> AS <*alias*>, as in HR.Employees AS E. The latter form is more readable. When using aliases, the convention is to use short names, typically one letter that is somehow indicative of the queried table, like E for Employees. The reasons why you might want to alias tables become apparent in Chapter 4. For now, it's sufficient for you to know that the language supports such table aliases and the syntax to assign them.

Note that if you assign an alias to a table, you basically rename the table for the duration of the query. The original table name isn't visible anymore; only the alias is. Normally, you can prefix a column name you refer to in a query with the table name, as in Employees.empid. However, if you aliased the Employees table as E, the reference Employees.empid is invalid; you have to use E.empid, as the following example demonstrates.

```
SELECT E.empid, firstname, lastname
FROM HR.Employees AS E;
```

If you try running this code by using the full table name as the column prefix, the code will fail.

As mentioned, Chapter 4 gets into the details of why table aliasing is needed.

The SELECT Clause

The SELECT clause of a query has two main roles:

- It evaluates expressions that define the attributes in the query's result, assigning them with aliases if needed.
- Using a DISTINCT clause, you can eliminate duplicate rows in the result if needed.

I'll start with the first role. Take the following query as an example.

```
SELECT empid, firstname, lastname
FROM HR.Employees;
```

The FROM clause indicates that the HR.Employees table is the input table of the query. The SELECT clause then projects only three of the attributes from the input as the returned attributes in the result of the query.

T-SQL supports using an asterisk (*) as an alternative to listing all attributes from the input tables, but this is considered a bad practice for a number of reasons. Often, you need to return only a subset of the input attributes, and using an * is just a matter of laziness. By returning more attributes than you really need, you can prevent SQL Server from using what would normally be considered covering indexes in respect to the interesting set of attributes. You also send more data than is needed over the network, and this can have a negative impact on the system's performance. In addition, the underlying table definition could change over time; even if, when the query was initially authored, * really represented all attributes you needed; it might not be the case anymore at a later point in time. For these reasons and others, it is considered a best practice to always explicitly list the attributes that you need.

In the SELECT clause, you can assign your own aliases to the expressions that define the result attributes. There are a number of supported forms of aliasing: *<expression>* AS *<alias>* as in empid AS employeeid, *<expression>* *<alias>* as in empid employeeid, and *<alias>* = *<expression>* as in employeeid = empid.

REAL WORLD **A PREFERRED METHOD**

We prefer to use the first form with the AS clause because it's both standard and we find it to be the most readable. The second form is both unreadable and makes it hard to spot a certain bug in the code.

Consider the following query.

```
SELECT empid, firstname lastname
FROM HR.Employees;
```

The developer who authored the query intended to return the attributes empid, firstname, and lastname but missed indicating the comma between firstname and lastname. The query doesn't fail; instead, it returns the following result.

```
empid       lastname
----------- ----------
1           Sara
2           Don
3           Judy
...
```

Although not the author's intention, SQL Server interprets the request as assigning the alias lastname to the attribute firstname instead of returning both. If you're used to aliasing expressions with the space form as a common practice, it will be harder for you to spot such bugs.

Back to intentional attribute aliasing, there are two main uses for those. One is renaming—when you need the result attribute to be named differently than the source attribute—for example, if you need to name the result attribute employeeid instead of empid, as follows.

```
SELECT empid AS employeeid, firstname, lastname
FROM HR.Employees;
```

Another use is to assign a name to an attribute that results from an expression that would otherwise be unnamed. For example, suppose you need to generate a result attribute from an expression that concatenates the firstname attribute, a space, and the lastname attribute. You use the following query.

```
SELECT empid, firstname + N' ' + lastname
FROM HR.Employees;
```

You get a nonrelational result because the result attribute has no name.

```
empid
----------- -------------------------------
1           Sara Davis
2           Don Funk
3           Judy Lew
...
```

By aliasing the expression, you assign a name to the result attribute, making the result of the query relational, as follows.

```
SELECT empid, firstname + N' ' + lastname AS fullname
FROM HR.Employees;
```

Here's an abbreviated form of the result of this query.

```
empid       fullname
----------- -------------------------------
1           Sara Davis
2           Don Funk
3           Judy Lew
...
```

Remember from the discussions in Chapter 1 that if duplicates are possible in the result, T-SQL won't try to eliminate those unless instructed. A result with duplicates is considered nonrelational because relations—being sets—are not supposed to have duplicates. Therefore, if duplicates are possible in the result, and you want to eliminate them in order to return a relational result, you can do so by adding a DISTINCT clause, as in the following.

```
SELECT DISTINCT country, region, city
FROM HR.Employees;
```

The HR.Employees table has nine rows but five distinct locations; hence, the output of this query has five rows.

```
country         region          city
--------------- --------------- ---------------
UK              NULL            London
USA             WA              Kirkland
USA             WA              Redmond
USA             WA              Seattle
USA             WA              Tacoma
```

There's an interesting difference between standard SQL and T-SQL in terms of minimal SELECT query requirements. According to standard SQL, a SELECT query must have at minimum FROM and SELECT clauses. Conversely, T-SQL supports a SELECT query with only a SELECT clause and without a FROM clause. Such a query is as if issued against an imaginary table that has only one row. For example, the following query is invalid according to standard SQL but is valid according to T-SQL.

```
SELECT 10 AS col1, 'ABC' AS col2;
```

The output of this query is a single row with attributes resulting from the expressions with names assigned using the aliases.

```
col1        col2
----------- ----
10          ABC
```

Delimiting Identifiers

When referring to identifiers of attributes, schemas, tables, and other objects, there are cases in which you are required to use delimiters vs. cases in which the use of delimiters is optional. T-SQL supports both a standard form to delimit identifiers using double quotation marks, as in "Sales"."Orders", as well as a proprietary form using square brackets, as in [Sales].[Orders].

When the identifier is "regular," delimiting it is optional. In a regular identifier, the identifier complies with the rules for formatting identifiers. The rules say that the first character must be a letter defined by the Unicode Standard 3.2 (a-z, A-Z, and letters from other Unicode languages), underscore (_), at sign (@), or number sign (#). Subsequent characters can include letters, decimal numbers, at sign, dollar sign ($), number sign, or underscore. The identifier cannot be a reserved keyword in T-SQL, cannot have embedded spaces, and must not include supplementary characters.

An identifier that doesn't comply with these rules must be delimited. For example, an attribute called 2006 is considered an irregular identifier because it starts with a digit, and therefore must be delimited as "2006" or [2006]. A regular identifier such as y2006 can be referenced without delimiters simply as y2006, or it can be optional with delimiters. You might prefer not to delimit regular identifiers because the delimiters tend to clutter the code.

Quick Check

1. **What are the forms of aliasing an attribute in T-SQL?**
2. **What is an irregular identifier?**

Quick Check Answer

1. **The forms are <*expression*> AS <*alias*>, <*expression*> <*alias*>, and <*alias*> = <*expression*>.**
2. **An identifier that does not follow the rules for formatting identifiers; for example, it starts with a digit, has an embedded space, or is a reserved T-SQL keyword.**

PRACTICE Using the FROM and SELECT Clauses

In this practice, you exercise your knowledge of using the FROM and SELECT clauses.

If you encounter a problem completing an exercise, you can install the completed projects from the companion content for this chapter and lesson.

EXERCISE 1 Write a Simple Query and Use Table Aliases

In this exercise, you practice the use of the FROM and SELECT clauses, including the use of table aliases.

1. Open SSMS and connect to the sample database TSQL2012.
2. To practice writing a simple query that uses the FROM and SELECT clauses, type the following query and execute it.

```
USE TSQL2012;

SELECT shipperid, companyname, phone
FROM Sales.Shippers;
```

   The USE statement ensures that you are connected to the target database TSQL2012. The FROM clause indicates that the Sales.Shippers table is the queried table, and the SELECT clause projects the attributes shipperid, companyname, and phone from this table. Here's the result of the query.

```
shipperid  companyname    phone
---------- -------------- ---------------
1          Shipper GVSUA  (503) 555-0137
2          Shipper ETYNR  (425) 555-0136
3          Shipper ZHISN  (415) 555-0138
```

3. If there was more than one table involved in the query and another table had an attribute called shipperid, you would need to prefix the shipperid attribute with the table name, as in Shippers.shipperid. For brevity, you can alias the table with a shorter name, like S, and then refer to the attribute as S.shipperid. Here's an example for aliasing the table and prefixing the attribute with the new table name.

```
SELECT S.shipperid, companyname, phone
FROM Sales.Shippers AS S;
```

EXERCISE 2 Use Column Aliases and Delimited Identifiers

In this exercise, you practice the use of column aliases, including the use of delimited identifiers. As your starting point, you use the query from step 3 in the previous exercise.

1. Suppose you want to rename the result attribute phone to **phone number**. Here's an attempt to alias the attribute with the identifier phone number without delimiters.

```
SELECT S.shipperid, companyname, phone AS phone number
FROM Sales.Shippers AS S;
```

2. This code fails because phone number is not a regular identifier, and therefore has to be delimited, as follows.

```
SELECT S.shipperid, companyname, phone AS [phone number]
FROM Sales.Shippers AS S;
```

3. Remember that T-SQL supports both a proprietary way to delimit identifiers by using square brackets, and the standard form using double quotation marks, as in "phone number".

Lesson Summary

- The FROM clause is the first clause to be logically processed in a SELECT query. In this clause, you indicate the tables you want to query and table operators. You can alias tables in the FROM clause with your chosen names and then use the table alias as a prefix to attribute names.
- With the SELECT clause, you can indicate expressions that define the result attributes. You can assign your own aliases to the result attributes, and in this way, create a relational result. If duplicates are possible in the result, you can eliminate those by specifying the DISTINCT clause.
- If you use regular identifiers as object and attribute names, using delimiters is optional. If you use irregular identifiers, delimiters are required.

Lesson Review

Answer the following questions to test your knowledge of the information in this lesson. You can find the answers to these questions and explanations of why each answer choice is correct or incorrect in the "Answers" section at the end of this chapter.

1. What is the importance of the ability to assign attribute aliases in T-SQL? (Choose all that apply.)
   - **A.** The ability to assign attribute aliases is just an aesthetic feature.
   - **B.** An expression that is based on a computation results in no attribute name unless you assign one with an alias, and this is not relational.
   - **C.** T-SQL requires all result attributes of a query to have names.
   - **D.** Using attribute aliases, you can assign your own name to a result attribute if you need it to be different than the source attribute name.
2. What are the mandatory clauses in a SELECT query, according to T-SQL?
   - **A.** The FROM and SELECT clauses
   - **B.** The SELECT and WHERE clauses
   - **C.** The SELECT clause
   - **D.** The FROM and WHERE clauses
3. Which of the following practices are considered bad practices? (Choose all that apply.)
   - **A.** Aliasing columns by using the AS clause
   - **B.** Aliasing tables by using the AS clause
   - **C.** Not assigning column aliases when the column is a result of a computation
   - **D.** Using * in the SELECT list

Lesson 2: Working with Data Types and Built-in Functions

When defining columns in tables, parameters in procedures and functions, and variables in T-SQL batches, you need to choose a data type for those. The data type constrains the data that is supported, in addition to encapsulating behavior that operates on the data, exposing it through operators and other means. Because data types are such a fundamental component of your data—everything is built on top—your choices of data types will have dramatic implications for your application at many different layers. Therefore, this is an area that should not be taken lightly, but instead treated with a lot of care and attention. That's also the reason why this topic is covered so early in this Training Kit, even though the first few chapters of the kit focus on querying, and only later chapters deal with data definition, like creating and altering tables. Your knowledge of types is critical for both data definition and data manipulation.

T-SQL supports many built-in functions that you can use to manipulate data. Because functions operate on input values and return output values, an understanding of built-in functions goes hand in hand with an understanding of data types.

Note that this chapter is not meant to be an exhaustive coverage of all types and all functions that T-SQL supports—this would require a whole book in its own right. Instead, this chapter explains the factors you need to consider when choosing a data type, and key aspects of working with functions, usually in the context of certain types of data, like date and time data or character data. For details and technicalities about data types, see Books Online for SQL Server 2012, under the topic "Data Types (Transact-SQL)" at *http://msdn.microsoft.com/en-us/library/ms187752(v=SQL.110).aspx*. For details about built-in functions, see the topic "Built-in Functions (Transact-SQL)" at *http://msdn.microsoft.com/en-us/library/ms174318(v=SQL.110).aspx*.

After this lesson, you will be able to:

- Choose the appropriate data type.
- Choose a type for your keys.
- Work with date and time, in addition to character data.
- Work with the CASE expression and related functions.

Estimated lesson time: 50 minutes

Choosing the Appropriate Data Type

Choosing the appropriate data types for your attributes is probably one of the most important decisions that you will make regarding your data. SQL Server supports many data types from different categories: exact numeric (INT, NUMERIC), character strings (CHAR, VARCHAR), Unicode character strings (NCHAR, NVARCHAR), approximate numeric (FLOAT, REAL), binary strings (BINARY, VARBINARY), date and time (DATE, TIME, DATETIME2, SMALLDATETIME, DATETIME, DATETIMEOFFSET), and others. There are many options, so it might seem like a difficult task, but as long as you follow certain principles, you can be smart about your choices, which results in a robust, consistent, and efficient database.

One of the great strengths of the relational model is the importance it gives to enforcement of data integrity as part of the model itself, at multiple levels. One important aspect in choosing the appropriate type for your data is to remember that a type is a constraint. This means that it has a certain domain of supported values and will not allow values outside that domain. For example, the DATE type allows only valid dates. An attempt to enter something that isn't a date, like 'abc' or '20120230', is rejected. If you have an attribute that is supposed to represent a date, such as birthdate, and you use a type such as INT or CHAR, you don't benefit from built-in validating of dates. An INT type won't prevent a value such as 99999999 and a CHAR type won't prevent a value such as '20120230'.

Much like a type is a constraint, NOT NULL is a constraint as well. If an attribute isn't supposed to allow NULLs, it's important to enforce a NOT NULL constraint as part of its definition. Otherwise, NULLs will find their way into your attribute.

Also, you want to make sure that you do not confuse the formatting of a value with its type. Sometimes, people use character strings to store dates because they think of storing a date in a certain format. The formatting of a value is supposed to be the responsibility of the application when data is presented. The type is a property of the value stored in the database, and the internal storage format shouldn't be your concern. This aspect has to do with an important principle in the relational model called *physical data independence*.

A data type encapsulates behavior. By using an inappropriate type, you miss all the behavior that is encapsulated in the type in the form of operators and functions that support it. As a simple example, for types representing numbers, the plus (+) operator represents addition, but for character strings, the same operator represents concatenation. If you chose an inappropriate type for your value, you sometimes have to convert the type (explicitly or implicitly), and sometimes juggle the value quite a bit, in order to treat it as what it is supposed to be.

Another important principle in choosing the appropriate type for your data is size. Often one of the major aspects affecting query performance is the amount of I/O involved. A query that reads less simply tends to run faster. The bigger the type that you use, the more storage it uses. Tables with many millions of rows, if not billions, are commonplace nowadays. When you start multiplying the size of a type by the number of rows in the table, the numbers can quickly become significant. As an example, suppose you have an attribute representing test scores, which are integers in the range 0 to 100. Using an INT data type for this purpose is overkill. It would use 4 bytes per value, whereas a TINYINT would use only 1 byte, and is therefore the more appropriate type in this case. Similarly, for data that is supposed to represent dates, people have a tendency to use DATETIME, which uses 8 bytes of storage. If the value is supposed to represent a date without a time, you should use DATE, which uses only 3 bytes of storage. If the value is supposed to represent both date and time, you should consider DATETIME2 or SMALLDATETIME. The former requires storage between 6 to 8 bytes (depending on precision), and as an added value, provides a wider range of dates and improved, controllable precision. The latter uses only 4 bytes of storage, so as long as its supported range of dates and precision cover your needs, you should use it. In short, you should use the smallest type that serves your needs. Though of course, this applies not in the short run, but in the long run. For example, using an INT type for a key in a table that at one point or another will grow to a degree of billions of rows is a bad idea. You should be using BIGINT. But using INT for an attribute representing test scores or DATETIME for date and time values that require a minute precision are both bad choices even when thinking about the long run.

Be very careful with the imprecise types FLOAT and REAL. The first two sentences in the documentation describing these types should give you a good sense of their nature: "Approximate-number data types for use with floating point numeric data. Floating point data is approximate; therefore, not all values in the data type range can be represented exactly." (You can find this documentation in the Books Online for SQL Server 2012 article "float and real [Transact-SQL]" at *http://msdn.microsoft.com/en-us/library/ms173773.aspx*.) The benefit in these types is that they can represent very large and very small numbers beyond what any other numeric type that SQL Server supports can represent. So, for example, if you need to represent very large or very small numbers for scientific purposes and don't need complete accuracy, you may find these types useful. They're also quite economic (4 bytes for REAL and 8 bytes for FLOAT). But do not use them for things that are supposed to be precise.

REAL WORLD **FLOAT TROUBLE**

We remember a case where a customer used FLOAT to represent barcode numbers of products, and was then surprised by not getting the right product when scanning the products' barcodes. Also, recently, we got a query about conversion of a FLOAT value to NUMERIC, resulting in a different value than what was entered. Here's the case.

```
DECLARE @f AS FLOAT = '29545428.022495';
SELECT CAST(@f AS NUMERIC(28, 14)) AS value;
```

Can you guess what the output of this code is? Here it is.

```
Value
---------------------------------------
29545428.02249500200000
```

As mentioned, some values cannot be represented precisely.

In short, make sure you use exact numeric types when you need to represent values precisely, and reserve the use of the approximate numeric types only to cases where you're certain that it's acceptable for the application.

Another important aspect in choosing a type has to do with choosing fixed types (CHAR, NCHAR, BINARY) vs. dynamic ones (VARCHAR, NVARCHAR, VARBINARY). Fixed types use the storage for the indicated size; for example, CHAR(30) uses storage for 30 characters, whether you actually specify 30 characters or less. This means that updates will not require the row to physically expand, and therefore no data shifting is required. So for attributes that get updated frequently, where the update performance is a priority, you should consider fixed types. Note that when compression is used—specifically row compression—SQL Server stores fixed types like variable ones, but with less overhead.

Variable types use the storage for what you enter, plus a couple of bytes for offset information (or 4 bits with row compression). So for widely varying sizes of strings, if you use variable types you can save a lot of storage. As already mentioned, the less storage used, the less there is for a query to read, and the faster the query can perform. So variable length types are usually preferable in such cases when read performance is a priority.

With character strings, there's also the question of using regular character types (CHAR, VARCHAR) vs. Unicode types (NCHAR, NVARCHAR). The former use 1 byte of storage per character and support only one language (based on collation properties) besides English. The latter use 2 bytes of storage per character (unless compressed) and support multiple languages. If a surrogate pair is needed, a character will require 4 bytes of storage. So if data is in multiple languages and you need to represent only one language besides English in your data, you can benefit from using regular character types, with lower storage requirements. When data is international, or your application natively works with Unicode data, you should use Unicode data types so you don't lose information. The greater storage requirements of Unicode data are mitigated starting with SQL Server 2008 R2 with Unicode compression.

When using types that can have a length associated with them, such as CHAR and VARCHAR, T-SQL supports omitting the length and then uses a default length. However, in different contexts, the defaults can be different. It is considered a best practice to always be explicit about the length, as in CHAR(1) or VARCHAR(30).

When defining attributes that represent the same thing across different tables—especially ones that will later be used as join columns (like the primary key in one table and the foreign key in another)—it's very important to be consistent with the types. Otherwise, when comparing one attribute with another, SQL Server has to apply implicit conversion of one attribute's type to the other, and this could have negative performance implications, like preventing efficient use of indexes.

You also want to make sure that when indicating a literal of a type, you use the correct form. For example, literals of regular character strings are delimited with single quotation marks, as in 'abc', whereas literals of Unicode character strings are delimited with a capital N and then single quotation marks, as in N'abc'. When an expression involves elements with different types, SQL Server needs to apply implicit conversion when possible, and this may result in performance penalties. Note that in some cases the interpretation of a literal may not be what you think intuitively. In order to force a literal to be of a certain type, you may need to apply explicit conversion with functions like CAST, CONVERT, PARSE, or TRY_CAST, TRY_CONVERT, and TRY_PARSE. As an example, the literal 1 is considered an INT by SQL Server in any context. If you need the literal 1 to be considered, for example, a BIT, you need to convert the literal's type explicitly, as in CAST(1 AS BIT). Similarly, the literal 4000000000 is considered NUMERIC and not BIGINT. If you need the literal to be the latter, use CAST(4000000000 AS BIGINT). The difference between the functions without the TRY and their counterparts with the TRY is that those without the TRY fail if the value isn't convertible, whereas those with the TRY return a NULL in such a case. For example, the following code fails.

```
SELECT CAST('abc' AS INT);
```

Conversely, the following code returns a NULL.

```
SELECT TRY_CAST('abc' AS INT);
```

As for the difference between CAST, CONVERT, and PARSE, with CAST, you indicate the expression and the target type; with CONVERT, there's a third argument representing the style for the conversion, which is supported for some conversions, like between character strings and date and time values. For example, CONVERT(DATE, '1/2/2012', 101) converts the literal character string to DATE using style 101 representing the United States standard. With PARSE, you can indicate the culture by using any culture supported by the Microsoft .NET Framework. For example, PARSE('1/2/2012' AS DATE USING 'en-US') parses the input literal as a DATE by using a United States English culture.

When using expressions that involve operands of different types, SQL Server usually converts the one that has the lower data type precedence to the one with the higher. Consider the expression 1 + '1' as an example. One operand is INT and the other is VARCHAR. If you look in Books Online for SQL Server 2012, under "Data Type Precedence (Transact-SQL)," at *http://msdn.microsoft.com/en-us/library/ms190309.aspx*, you will find that INT precedes VARCHAR; hence, SQL Server implicitly converts the VARCHAR value '1' to the INT value 1, and the result of the expression is therefore 2 and not the string '11'. Of course, you can always take control by using explicit conversion.

If all operands of the expression are of the same type, that's also going to be the type of the result, and you might not want it to be the case. For example, the result of the expression 5 / 2 in T-SQL is the INT value 2 and not the NUMERIC value 2.5, because both operands are integers, and therefore the result is an integer. If you were dealing with two integer columns, like col1 / col2, and wanted the division to be NUMERIC, you would need to convert the columns explicitly, as in CAST(col1 AS NUMERIC(12, 2)) / CAST(col2 AS NUMERIC(12, 2)).

Choosing a Data Type for Keys

When defining intelligent keys in your tables—namely keys based on already existing attributes derived from the application—there's no question about types because you already chose those for your attributes. But when you need to create surrogate keys—ones that are added solely for the purpose of being used as keys—you need to determine an appropriate type for the attribute in addition to a mechanism to generate the key values. The reality is that you will hear many different opinions as to what is the best solution—some based on theory, and some backed by empirical evidence. But different systems and different workloads could end up with different optimal solutions. What's more, in some systems, write performance might be the priority, whereas in others, the read performance is. One solution can make the inserts faster but the reads slower, and another solution might work the other way around. At the end of the day, to make smart choices, it's important to learn the theory, learn about others' experiences, but eventually make sure that you run benchmarks in the target system. In this respect, a sentence in a book called *Bubishi* by Patrick McCarthy (Tuttle Publishing, 2008) is very fitting. It says, "Wisdom is putting knowledge into action."

Note that this section refers to elements like sequence objects, the identity column property, and indexes, which are covered in more detail later in the book. Chapter 11, "Other Data Modification Aspects," covers sequence objects and the identity property, and Chapter 15, "Implementing Indexes and Statistics," covers indexes. You may want to revisit this section after finishing those chapters.

The typical options people use to generate surrogate keys are:

- **The identity column property** A property that automatically generates keys in an attribute of a numeric type with a scale of 0; namely, any integer type (TINYINT, SMALLINT, INT, BIGINT) or NUMERIC/DECIMAL with a scale of 0.
- **The sequence object** An independent object in the database from which you can obtain new sequence values. Like identity, it supports any numeric type with a scale of 0. Unlike identity, it's not tied to a particular column; instead, as mentioned, it is an independent object in the database. You can also request a new value from a sequence object before using it. There are a number of other advantages over identity that will be covered in Chapter 11.
- **Nonsequential GUIDs** You can generate nonsequential global unique identifiers to be stored in an attribute of a UNIQUEIDENTIFIER type. You can use the T-SQL function NEWID to generate a new GUID, possibly invoking it with a default expression attached to the column. You can also generate one from anywhere—for example, the client—by using an application programming interface (API) that generates a new GUID. The GUIDs are guaranteed to be unique across space and time.
- **Sequential GUIDs** You can generate sequential GUIDs within the machine by using the T-SQL function NEWSEQUENTIALID.
- **Custom solutions** If you do not want to use the built-in tools that SQL Server provides to generate keys, you need to develop your own custom solution. The data type for the key then depends on your solution.

EXAM TIP

Understanding the built-in tools T-SQL provides for generating surrogate keys like the sequence object, identity column property, and the NEWID and NEWSEQUENTIALID functions, and their impact on performance, is an important skill for the exam.

One thing to consider regarding your choice of surrogate key generator and the data type involved is the size of the data type. The bigger the type, the more storage is required, and hence the slower the reads are. A solution using an INT data type requires 4 bytes per value, BIGINT requires 8 bytes, UNIQUEIDENTIFIER requires 16 bytes, and so on. The storage requirements for your surrogate key can have a cascading effect if your clustered index is defined on the same key columns (the default for a primary key constraint). The clustered index key columns are used by all nonclustered indexes internally as the means to locate rows in the table. So if you define a clustered index on a column x, and nonclustered indexes—one on column a, one on b, and one on c—your nonclustered indexes are internally created on column (a, x), (b, x), and (c, x), respectively. In other words, the effect is multiplied.

Regarding the use of sequential keys (as with identity, sequence, and NEWSEQUENTIALID) vs. nonsequential ones (as with NEWID or a custom randomized key generator), there are several aspects to consider.

Starting with sequential keys, all rows go into the right end of the index. When a page is full, SQL Server allocates a new page and fills it. This results in less fragmentation in the index, which is beneficial for read performance. Also, insertions can be faster when a single session is loading the data, and the data resides on a single drive or a small number of drives. However, with high-end storage subsystems that have many spindles, the situation can be different. When loading data from multiple sessions, you will end up with page latch contention (*latches* are objects used to synchronize access to database pages) against the rightmost pages of the index leaf level's linked list. This bottleneck prevents use of the full throughput of the storage subsystem.

Note that if you decide to use sequential keys and you're using numeric ones, you can always start with the lowest value in the type to use the entire range. For example, instead of starting with 1 in an INT type, you could start with -2,147,483,648.

Consider nonsequential keys, such as random ones generated with NEWID or with a custom solution. When trying to force a row into an already full page, SQL Server performs a classic page split—it allocates a new page and moves half the rows from the original page to the new one. A page split has a cost, plus it results in index fragmentation. Index fragmentation can have a negative impact on the performance of reads. However, in terms of insert performance, if the storage subsystem contains many spindles and you're loading data from multiple sessions, the random order can actually be better than sequential despite the splits. That's because there's no hot spot at the right end of the index, and you use the storage subsystem's available throughput better. A good example for a benchmark demonstrating this strategy can be found in a blog by Thomas Kejser at *http://blog.kejser.org/2011/10/05/boosting-insert-speed-by-generating-scalable-keys/*.

Note that splits and index fragmentation can be mitigated by periodic index rebuilds as part of the usual maintenance activities—assuming you have a window available for this.

If for aforementioned reasons you decide to rely on keys generated in random order, you will still need to decide between GUIDs and a custom random key generator solution. As already mentioned, GUIDs are stored in a UNIQUEIDENTIFIER type that is 16 bytes in size; that's large. But one of the main benefits of GUIDs is the fact that they can be generated anywhere and not conflict across time and space. You can generate GUIDs not just in SQL Server using the NEWID function, but anywhere, using APIs. Otherwise, you could come up with a custom solution that generates smaller random keys. The solution can even be a mix of a built-in tool and some tweaking on top. For example, you can find a creative solution by Wolfgang 'Rick'

Kutschera at *http://dangerousdba.blogspot.com/2011/10/day-sequences-saved-world.html*. Rick uses the SQL Server sequence object, but flips the bits of the values so that the insertion is distributed across the index leaf.

To conclude this section about keys and types for keys, remember that there are multiple options. Smaller is generally better, but then there's the question of the hardware that you use, and where your performance priorities are. Also remember that although it is very important to make educated guesses, it is also important to benchmark solutions in the target environment.

Date and Time Functions

T-SQL supports a number of date and time functions that allow you to manipulate your date and time data. Support for date and time functions keeps improving, with the last two versions of SQL Server adding a number of new functions.

This section covers some of the important functions supported by T-SQL and provides some examples. For the full list, as well as the technical details and syntax elements, see Books Online for SQL Server 2012, under the topic "Date and Time Data Types and Functions (Transact-SQL)" at *http://msdn.microsoft.com/en-us/library/ms186724(v=SQL.110).aspx*.

Current Date and Time

One important category of functions is the category that returns the current date and time. The functions in this category are GETDATE, CURRENT_TIMESTAMP, GETUTCDATE, SYSDATETIME, SYSUTCDATETIME, and SYSDATETIMEOFFSET.

GETDATE is T-SQL–specific, returning the current date and time in the SQL Server instance you're connected to as a DATETIME data type. CURRENT_TIMESTAMP is the same, only it's standard, and hence the recommended one to use. SYSDATETIME and SYSDATETIMEOFFSET are similar, only returning the values as the more precise DATETIME2 and DATETIMEOFFSET types (including offset), respectively. Note that there are no built-in functions to return the current date or the current time; to get such information, simply cast the SYSDATETIME function to DATE or TIME, respectively. For example, to get the current date, use CAST(SYSDATETIME() AS DATE). The GETUTCDATE function returns the current date and time in UTC terms as a DATETIME type, and SYSUTCDATETIME does the same, only returning the result as the more precise DATETIME2 type.

Date and Time Parts

This section covers date and time functions that either extract a part from a date and time value (like DATEPART) or construct a date and time value from parts (like DATEFROMPARTS).

Using the DATEPART function, you can extract from an input date and time value a desired part, such as a year, minute, or nanosecond, and return the extracted part as an integer. For example, the expression DATEPART(month, '20120212') returns 2. T-SQL provides the functions YEAR, MONTH, and DAY as abbreviations to DATEPART, not requiring you to specify the part. The DATENAME function is similar to DATEPART, only it returns the name of the part as a character string, as opposed to the integer value. Note that the function is language-dependent. That is, if the effective language in your session is us_english, the expression DATENAME(month, '20120212') returns 'February', but for Italian, it returns 'febbraio'.

T-SQL provides a set of functions that construct a desired date and time value from its numeric parts. You have such a function for each of the six available date and time types: DATEFROMPARTS, DATETIME2FROMPARTS, DATETIMEFROMPARTS, DATETIMEOFFSETFROMPARTS, SMALLDATETIMEFROMPARTS, and TIMEFROMPARTS. For example, to build a DATE value from its parts, you would use an expression such as DATEFROMPARTS(2012, 02, 12).

Finally, the EOMONTH function computes the respective end of month date for the input date and time value. For example, suppose that today was February 12, 2012. The expression EOMONTH(SYSDATETIME()) would then return the date '2012-02-29'. This function supports a second optional input indicating how many months to add to the result.

Add and Diff

T-SQL supports addition and difference date and time functions called DATEADD and DATEDIFF.

DATEADD is a very commonly used function. With it, you can add a requested number of units of a specified part to a specified date and time value. For example, the expression DATEADD(year, 1, '20120212') adds one year to the input date February 12, 2012.

DATEDIFF is another commonly used function; it returns the difference in terms of a requested part between two date and time values. For example, the expression DATEDIFF(day, '20110212', '20120212') computes the difference in days between February 12, 2011 and February 12, 2012, returning the value 365. Note that this function looks only at the parts from the requested one and above in the date and time hierarchy—not below. For example, the expression DATEDIFF(year, '20111231', '20120101') looks only at the year part, and hence returns 1. It doesn't look at the month and day parts of the values.

Offset

T-SQL supports two functions related to date and time values with an offset: SWITCHOFFSET and TODATETIMEOFFSET.

With the SWITCHOFFSET function, you can return an input DATETIMEOFFSET value in a requested offset term. For example, consider the expression SWITCHOFFSET(SYSDATETIMEOFFSET(), '-08:00'). Regardless of the offset of the instance you are connected to, you request to present the current date and time value in terms of offset '-08:00'. If the system's offset is, say, '-05:00', the function will compensate for this by subtracting three hours from the input value.

The TODATETIMEOFFSET function is used for a different purpose. You use it to construct a DATETIMEOFFSET value from two inputs: the first is a date and time value that is not offset-aware, and the second is the offset. You can use this function when migrating from data that is not offset-aware, where you keep the local date and time value in one attribute, and the offset in another, to offset-aware data. Say you have the local date and time in an attribute called dt, and the offset in an attribute called theoffset. You add an attribute called dto of a DATETIMEOFFSET type to the table. You then update the new attribute to the expression TODATETIMEOFFSET(dt, theoffset), and then drop the original attributes dt and theoffset from the table.

The following code demonstrates using both functions.

```
SELECT
  SWITCHOFFSET('20130212 14:00:00.0000000 -08:00', '-05:00') AS [SWITCHOFFSET],
  TODATETIMEOFFSET('20130212 14:00:00.0000000', '-08:00') AS [TODATETIMEOFFSET];
```

Here's the output of this code.

```
SWITCHOFFSET                       TODATETIMEOFFSET
---------------------------------- ----------------------------------
2013-02-12 17:00:00.0000000 -05:00 2013-02-12 14:00:00.0000000 -08:00
```

Character Functions

T-SQL was not really designed to support very sophisticated character string manipulation functions, so you won't find a very large set of such functions. This section describes the character string functions that T-SQL does support, arranged in categories.

Concatenation

Character string concatenation is a very common need. T-SQL supports two ways to concatenate strings—one with the plus (+) operator, and another with the CONCAT function.

Here's an example for concatenating strings in a query by using the + operator.

```
SELECT empid, country, region, city,
  country + N',' + region + N',' + city AS location
FROM HR.Employees;
```

Here's the result of this query.

```
empid  country  region  city      location
------ -------- ------- --------- ----------------
1      USA      WA      Seattle   USA,WA,Seattle
2      USA      WA      Tacoma    USA,WA,Tacoma
3      USA      WA      Kirkland  USA,WA,Kirkland
4      USA      WA      Redmond   USA,WA,Redmond
5      UK       NULL    London    NULL
6      UK       NULL    London    NULL
7      UK       NULL    London    NULL
8      USA      WA      Seattle   USA,WA,Seattle
9      UK       NULL    London    NULL
```

Observe that when any of the inputs is NULL, the + operator returns a NULL. That's standard behavior that can be changed by turning off a session option called CONCAT_NULL_YIELDS_NULL, though it's not recommended to rely on nonstandard behavior. If you want to substitute a NULL with an empty string, there are a number of ways for you to do this programmatically. One option is to use COALESCE(<*expression*>, ''). For example, in this data, only region can be NULL, so you can use the following query to replace a comma plus region with an empty string when region is NULL.

```
SELECT empid, country, region, city,
  country + COALESCE( N',' + region, N'') + N',' + city AS location
FROM HR.Employees;
```

Another option is to use the CONCAT function which, unlike the + operator, substitutes a NULL input with an empty string. Here's how the query looks.

```
SELECT empid, country, region, city,
  CONCAT(country, N',' + region, N',' + city) AS location
FROM HR.Employees;
```

Here's the output of this query.

```
empid  country  region  city      location
------ -------- ------- --------- ----------------
1      USA      WA      Seattle   USA,WA,Seattle
2      USA      WA      Tacoma    USA,WA,Tacoma
3      USA      WA      Kirkland  USA,WA,Kirkland
4      USA      WA      Redmond   USA,WA,Redmond
5      UK       NULL    London    UK,London
6      UK       NULL    London    UK,London
7      UK       NULL    London    UK,London
8      USA      WA      Seattle   USA,WA,Seattle
9      UK       NULL    London    UK,London
```

Observe that this time, when region was NULL, it was replaced with an empty string.

Substring Extraction and Position

This section covers functions that you can use to extract a substring from a string, and identify the position of a substring within a string.

With the SUBSTRING function, you can extract a substring from a string given as the first argument, starting with the position given as the second argument, and a length given as the third argument. For example, the expression SUBSTRING('abcde', 1, 3) returns 'abc'. If the third argument is greater than what would get you to the end of the string, the function doesn't fail; instead, it just extracts the substring until the end of the string.

The LEFT and RIGHT functions extract a requested number of characters from the left and right ends of the input string, respectively. For example, LEFT('abcde', 3) returns 'abc' and RIGHT('abcde', 3) returns 'cde'.

The CHARINDEX function returns the position of the first occurrence of the string provided as the first argument within the string provided as the second argument. For example, the expression CHARINDEX(' ','Itzik Ben-Gan') looks for the first occurrence of a space in the second input, returning 6 in this example. Note that you can provide a third argument indicating to the function where to start looking.

You can combine, or nest, functions in the same expression. For example, suppose you query a table with an attribute called fullname formatted as '<*first*> <*last*>', and you need to write an expression that extracts the first name part. You can use the following expression.

```
LEFT(fullname, CHARINDEX(' ', fullname) - 1)
```

T-SQL also supports a function called PATINDEX that, like CHARINDEX, you can use to locate the first position of a string within another string. But whereas with CHARINDEX you're looking for a constant string, with PATINDEX you're looking for a pattern. The pattern is formed very similar to the LIKE patterns that you're probably familiar with, where you use wildcards like % for any string, _ for a single character, and square brackets ([]) representing a single character from a certain list or range. If you're not familiar with such pattern construction, see the topics "PATINDEX (Transact-SQL)" and "LIKE (Transact-SQL)" in Books Online for SQL Server 2012 at *http://msdn.microsoft.com/en-us/library/ms188395(v=SQL.110).aspx* and *http://msdn.microsoft.com/en-us/library/ms179859(v=SQL.110).aspx*. As an example, the expression PATINDEX('%[0-9]%', 'abcd123efgh') looks for the first occurrence of a digit (a character in the range 0–9) in the second input, returning the position 5 in this case.

String Length

T-SQL provides two functions that you can use to measure the length of an input value—LEN and DATALENGTH.

The LEN function returns the length of an input string in terms of the number of characters. Note that it returns the number of characters, not bytes, whether the input is a regular character or Unicode character string. For example, the expression LEN(N'xyz') returns 3. If there are any trailing spaces, LEN removes them.

The DATALENGTH function returns the length of the input in terms of number of bytes. This means, for example, that if the input is a Unicode character string, it will count 2 bytes per character. For example, the expression DATALENGTH(N'xyz') returns 6. Note also that, unlike LEN, the DATALENGTH function doesn't remove trailing spaces.

String Alteration

T-SQL supports a number of functions that you can use to apply alterations to an input string. Those are REPLACE, REPLICATE, and STUFF.

With the REPLACE function, you can replace in an input string provided as the first argument all occurrences of the string provided as the second argument, with the string provided as the third argument. For example, the expression REPLACE('.1.2.3.', '.', '/') substitutes all occurrences of a dot (.) with a slash (/), returning the string '/1/2/3/'.

The REPLICATE function allows you to replicate an input string a requested number of times. For example, the expression REPLICATE('0', 10) replicates the string '0' ten times, returning '0000000000'.

The STUFF function operates on an input string provided as the first argument; then, from the character position indicated as the second argument, deletes the number of characters indicated by the third argument. Then it inserts in that position the string specified as the fourth argument. For example, the expression STUFF(',x,y,z', 1, 1, '') removes the first character from the input string, returning 'x,y,z'.

String Formatting

This section covers functions that you can use to apply formatting options to an input string. Those are the UPPER, LOWER, LTRIM, RTRIM, and FORMAT functions.

The first four functions are self-explanatory (uppercase form of the input, lowercase form of the input, input after removal of leading spaces, and input after removal of trailing spaces). Note that there's no TRIM function that removes both leading and trailing spaces; to achieve this, you need to nest one function call within another, as in RTRIM(LTRIM(<input>)).

With the FORMAT function, you can format an input value based on a format string, and optionally specify the culture as a third input where relevant. You can use any format string supported by the .NET Framework. (For details, see the topics "FORMAT (Transact-SQL)" and "Formating Types" at *http://msdn.microsoft.com/en-us/library/hh213505(v=sql.110).aspx* and *http://msdn.microsoft.com/en-us/library/26etazsy.aspx*.) As an example, the expression FORMAT(1759, '0000000000') formats the input number as a character string with a fixed size of 10 characters with leading zeros, returning '0000001759'.

CASE Expression and Related Functions

T-SQL supports an expression called CASE and a number of related functions that you can use to apply conditional logic to determine the returned value. Many people incorrectly refer to CASE as a statement. A statement performs some kind of an action or controls the flow of the code, and that's not what CASE does; CASE returns a value, and hence is an expression.

The CASE expression has two forms—the *simple* form and the *searched* form. Here's an example of the simple CASE form issued against the sample database TSQL2012.

```
SELECT productid, productname, unitprice, discontinued,
  CASE discontinued
    WHEN 0 THEN 'No'
    WHEN 1 THEN 'Yes'
    ELSE 'Unknown'
  END AS discontinued_desc
FROM Production.Products;
```

The simple form compares an *input expression* (in this case the attribute discontinued) to multiple possible scalar *when expressions* (in this case, 0 and 1), and returns the *result expression* (in this case, 'No' and 'Yes', respectively) associated with the first match. If there's no match and an ELSE clause is specified, the *else expression* (in this case, 'Unknown') is returned. If there's no ELSE clause, the default is ELSE NULL. Here's an abbreviated form of the output of this query.

```
productid  productname    unitprice  discontinued discontinued_desc
---------- -------------- ---------- ------------ -----------------
1          Product HHYDP  18.00      0            No
2          Product RECZE  19.00      0            No
3          Product IMEHJ  10.00      0            No
4          Product KSBRM  22.00      0            No
5          Product EPEIM  21.35      1            Yes
...
```

The searched form of the CASE expression is more flexible. Instead of comparing an input expression to multiple possible expressions, it uses predicates in the WHEN clauses, and the first predicate that evaluates to true determines which when expression is returned. If none is true, the CASE expression returns the else expression. Here's an example.

```
SELECT productid, productname, unitprice,
  CASE
    WHEN unitprice < 20.00 THEN 'Low'
    WHEN unitprice < 40.00 THEN 'Medium'
    WHEN unitprice >= 40.00 THEN 'High'
    ELSE 'Unknown'
  END AS pricerange
FROM Production.Products;
```

In this example, the CASE expression returns a description of the product's unit price range. When the unit price is below $20.00, it returns 'Low', when it's $20.00 or more and below $40.00, it returns 'Medium', and when it's $40.00 or more, it returns 'High'. There's an ELSE clause for safety; if the input is NULL, the else expression returned is 'Unknown'. Notice that the second when predicate didn't need to check whether the value is $20.00 or more explicitly. That's because the when predicates are evaluated in order and the first when predicate did not evaluate to true. Here's an abbreviated form of the output of this query.

```
productid  productname    unitprice  pricerange
---------- -------------- ---------- ----------
1          Product HHYDP  18.00      Low
2          Product RECZE  19.00      Low
3          Product IMEHJ  10.00      Low
4          Product KSBRM  22.00      Medium
5          Product EPEIM  21.35      Medium
...
```

T-SQL supports a number of functions that can be considered as abbreviates of the CASE expression. Those are the standard COALESCE and NULLIF functions, and the nonstandard ISNULL, IIF, and CHOOSE.

The COALESCE function accepts a list of expressions as input and returns the first that is not NULL, or NULL if all are NULLs. If all inputs are the untyped NULL constant, SQL Server generates an error. For example, the expression COALESCE(NULL, 'x', 'y') returns 'x'. More generally, the expression:

```
COALESCE(<exp1>, <exp2>, …, <expn>)
```

is similar to the following.

```
CASE
  WHEN <exp1> IS NOT NULL THEN <exp1>
  WHEN <exp2> IS NOT NULL THEN <exp2>
  …
  WHEN <expn> IS NOT NULL THEN <expn>
  ELSE NULL
END
```

A typical use of COALESCE is to substitute a NULL with something else. For example, the expression COALESCE(region, '') returns region if it's not NULL and returns an empty string if it is NULL.

T-SQL supports a nonstandard function called ISNULL that is similar to the standard COALESCE, but it's a bit more limited in the sense that it supports only two inputs. Like COALESCE, it returns the first input that is not NULL. So, instead of COALESCE(region, ''), you could use ISNULL(region, ''). Generally, it is recommended to stick to standard features unless there's some flexibility or performance advantage in the nonstandard feature that is a higher priority. ISNULL is actually more limited than COALESCE, so generally, it is recommended to stick to COALESCE.

There are a couple of subtle differences between COALESCE and ISNULL that you might be interested in. One difference is in which input determines the type of the output. Consider the following code.

```
DECLARE
  @x AS VARCHAR(3) = NULL,
  @y AS VARCHAR(10) = '1234567890';

SELECT COALESCE(@x, @y) AS [COALESCE], ISNULL(@x, @y) AS [ISNULL];
```

Here's the output of this code.

```
COALESCE   ISNULL
---------- ------
1234567890 123
```

Observe that the type of the COALESCE expression is determined by the returned element, whereas the type of the ISNULL expression is determined by the first input.

The other difference between COALESCE and ISNULL is when you are using SELECT INTO, which is discussed in more detail in Chapter 11. Suppose the SELECT list of a SELECT INTO statement contains the expressions COALESCE(col1, 0) AS newcol1 vs. ISNULL(col1, 0) AS newcol1. If the source attribute col1 is defined as NOT NULL, both expressions will produce an attribute in the result table defined as NOT NULL. However, if the source attribute col1 is defined as allowing NULLs, COALESCE will create a result attribute allowing NULLs, whereas ISNULL will create one that disallows NULLs.

EXAM TIP

COALESCE and ISNULL can impact performance when you are combining sets; for example, with joins or when you are filtering data. Consider an example where you have two tables T1 and T2 and you need to join them based on a match between T1.col1 and T2.col1. The attributes do allow NULLs. Normally, a comparison between two NULLs yields unknown, and this causes the row to be discarded. You want to treat two NULLs as equal. What some do in such a case is use COALESCE or ISNULL to substitute a NULL with a value that they know cannot appear in the data. For example, if the attributes are integers, and you know that you have only positive integers in your data (you can even have constraints that ensure this), you might try to use the predicate COALESCE(T1.col1, -1) = COALESCE(T2.col1, -1), or ISNULL(T1.col1, -1) = ISNULL(T2.col1, -1). The problem with this form is that, because you apply manipulation to the attributes you're comparing, SQL Server will not rely on index ordering. This can result in not using available indexes efficiently. Instead, it is recommended to use the longer form: T1.col1 = T2.col1 OR (T1.col1 IS NULL AND T2.col1 IS NULL), which SQL Server understands as just a comparison that considers NULLs as equal. With this form, SQL Server can efficiently use indexing.

T-SQL also supports the standard NULLIF function. This function accepts two input expressions, returns NULL if they are equal, and returns the first input if they are not. For example, consider the expression NULLIF(col1, col2). If col1 is equal to col2, the function returns a NULL; otherwise, it returns the col1 value.

As for IIF and CHOOSE, these are nonstandard T-SQL functions that were added to simplify migrations from Microsoft Access platforms. Because these functions aren't standard and there are simple standard alternatives with CASE expressions, it is not usually recommended that you use them. However, when you are migrating from Access to SQL Server, these functions can help with smoother migration, and then gradually you can refactor your code to use the available standard functions. With the IIF function, you can return one value if an input predicate is true and another value otherwise. The function has the following form.

```
IIF(<predicate>, <true_result>, <false_or_unknown_result>)
```

This expression is equivalent to the following.

```
CASE WHEN <predicate> THEN <true_result> ELSE <false_or_unknown_result> END
```

For example, the expression IIF(orderyear = 2012, qty, 0) returns the value in the qty attribute when the orderyear attribute is equal to 2012, and zero otherwise.

The CHOOSE function allows you to provide a position and a list of expressions, and returns the expression in the indicated position. The function takes the following form.

```
CHOOSE(<pos>, <exp1>, <exp2>, …, <expn>)
```

For example, the expression CHOOSE(2, 'x', 'y', 'z') returns 'y'. Again, it's straightforward to replace a CHOOSE expression with a logically equivalent CASE expression; but the point in supporting CHOOSE, as well as IIF, is to simplify migrations from Access to SQL Server as a temporary solution.

Quick Check

1. **Would you use the type FLOAT to represent a product unit price?**
2. **What is the difference between NEWID and NEWSEQUENTIALID?**
3. **Which function returns the current date and time value as a DATETIME2 type?**
4. **When concatenating character strings, what is the difference between the plus (+) operator and the CONCAT function?**

Quick Check Answer

1. **No, because FLOAT is an approximate data type and cannot represent all values precisely.**
2. **The NEWID function generates GUID values in random order, whereas the NEWSEQUENTIALID function generates GUIDs that increase in a sequential order.**
3. **The SYSDATETIME function.**
4. **The + operator by default yields a NULL result on NULL input, whereas the CONCAT function treats NULLs as empty strings.**

PRACTICE Working with Data Types and Built-in Functions

In this practice, you exercise your knowledge of data types and functions. You query data from existing tables and manipulate existing attributes by using functions. You are provided with exercises that contain requests to write queries that address certain tasks. It is recommended that you first try to write the query yourself and then compare your answer with the given solution.

If you encounter a problem completing an exercise, you can install the completed projects from the companion content for this chapter and lesson.

EXERCISE 1 Apply String Concatenation and Use a Date and Time Function

In this exercise, you practice string concatenation and the use of a date and time function.

1. Open SSMS and connect to the sample database TSQL2012.
2. Write a query against the HR.Employees table that returns the employee ID, the full name of the employee (concatenate the attributes firstname, space, and lastname), and the birth year (apply a function to the birthdate attribute). Here's one possible query that achieves this task.

```
SELECT empid,
  firstname + N' ' + lastname AS fullname,
  YEAR(birthdate) AS birthyear
FROM HR.Employees;
```

EXERCISE 2 Use Additional Date and Time Functions

In this exercise, you practice the use of additional date and time functions.

Write an expression that computes the date of the last day of the current month. Also write an expression that computes the last day of the current year. Of course, there are a number of ways to achieve such tasks. Here's one way to compute the end of the current month.

```
SELECT EOMONTH(SYSDATETIME()) AS end_of_current_month;
```

And here's one way to compute the end of the current year.

```
SELECT DATEFROMPARTS(YEAR(SYSDATETIME()), 12, 31) AS end_of_current_year;
```

Using the YEAR function, you extract the current year. Then provide the current year along with the month 12 and the day 31 to the DATEFROMPARTS function to construct the last day of the current year.

EXERCISE 3 Use String and Conversion Functions

In this exercise, you practice the use of string and conversion functions.

1. Write a query against the Production.Products table that returns the existing numeric product ID, in addition to the product ID formatted as a fixed-sized string with 10 digits with leading zeros. For example, for product ID 42, you need to return the string '0000000042'. One way to address this need is by using the following code.

```
SELECT productid,
  RIGHT(REPLICATE('0', 10) + CAST(productid AS VARCHAR(10)), 10) AS str_productid
FROM Production.Products;
```

2. Using the REPLICATE function, you generate a string made of 10 zeros. Next you concatenate the character form of the product ID. Then you extract the 10 rightmost characters from the result string.

Can you think of a simpler way to achieve the same task using new functions that were introduced in SQL Server 2012? A much simpler way to achieve the same thing is by using the FORMAT function, as in the following query.

```
SELECT productid,
  FORMAT(productid, 'd10') AS str_productid
FROM Production.Products;
```

Lesson Summary

- Your choices of data types for your attributes will have a dramatic effect on the functionality and performance of the T-SQL code that interacts with the data—even more so for attributes used as keys. Therefore, much care and consideration should be taken when choosing types.
- T-SQL supports a number of functions that you can use to apply manipulation of date and time data, character string data, and other types of data. Remember that T-SQL was mainly designed to handle data manipulation, and not formatting and similar needs. Therefore, in those areas, you will typically find only fairly basic support. Such tasks are usually best handled in the client.
- T-SQL provides the CASE expression that allows you to return a value based on conditional logic, in addition to a number of functions that can be considered abbreviations of CASE.

Lesson Review

Answer the following questions to test your knowledge of the information in this lesson. You can find the answers to these questions and explanations of why each answer choice is correct or incorrect in the "Answers" section at the end of this chapter.

1. Why is it important to use the appropriate type for attributes?
   - **A.** Because the type of your attribute enables you to control the formatting of the values
   - **B.** Because the type constrains the values to a certain domain of supported values
   - **C.** Because the type prevents duplicates
   - **D.** Because the type prevents NULLs
2. Which of the following functions would you consider using to generate surrogate keys? (Choose all that apply.)
   - **A.** NEWID
   - **B.** NEWSEQUENTIALID
   - **C.** GETDATE
   - **D.** CURRENT_TIMESTAMP

3. What is the difference between the simple CASE expression and the searched CASE expression?
   - **A.** The simple CASE expression is used when the database recovery model is simple, and the searched CASE expression is used when it's full or bulk logged.
   - **B.** The simple CASE expression compares an input expression to multiple possible expressions in the WHEN clauses, and the searched CASE expression uses independent predicates in the WHEN clauses.
   - **C.** The simple CASE expression can be used anywhere in a query, and the searched CASE expression can be used only in the WHERE clause.
   - **D.** The simple CASE expression can be used anywhere in a query, and the searched CASE expression can be used only in query filters (ON, WHERE, HAVING).

Case Scenarios

In the following case scenarios, you apply what you've learned about the SELECT statement. You can find the answers to these questions in the "Answers" section at the end of this chapter.

Case Scenario 1: Reviewing the Use of Types

You are hired as a consultant to help address performance issues in an existing system. The system was developed originally by using SQL Server 2005 and has recently been upgraded to SQL Server 2012. Write rates in the system are fairly low, and their performance is more than adequate. Also, write performance is not a priority. However, read performance is a priority, and currently it is not satisfactory. One of the main goals of the consulting engagement is to provide recommendations that will help improve read performance. You have a meeting with representatives of the customer, and they ask for your recommendations in different potential areas for improvement. One of the areas they inquire about is the use of data types. Your task is to respond to the following customer queries:

1. We have many attributes that represent a date, like order date, invoice date, and so on, and currently we use the DATETIME data type for those. Do you recommend sticking to the existing type or replacing it with another? Any other recommendations along similar lines?
2. We have our own custom table partitioning solution because we're using the Standard edition of SQL Server. We use a surrogate key of a UNIQUEIDENTIFIER type with the NEWID function invoked by a default constraint expression as the primary key for the tables. We chose this approach because we do not want keys to conflict across the different tables. This primary key is also our clustered index key. Do you have any recommendations concerning our choice of a key?

Case Scenario 2: Reviewing the Use of Functions

The same company who hired you to review their use of data types would like you to also review their use of functions. They pose the following question to you:

- Our application has worked with SQL Server so far, but due to a recent merger with another company, we need to support other database platforms as well. What can you recommend in terms of use of functions?

Suggested Practices

To help you successfully master the exam objectives presented in this chapter, complete the following tasks.

Analyze the Data Types in the Sample Database

To practice your knowledge of data types, analyze the data types in the sample database TSQL2012.

- **Practice 1** Using the Object Explorer in SSMS, navigate to the sample database TSQL2012. Analyze the choices of the data types for the different attributes and try to reason about the choices. Also, evaluate whether the choices made are optimal and think about whether there's any room for improvement in some cases.
- **Practice 2** Visit Books Online under "Data Type Precedence (Transact-SQL)," at *http://msdn.microsoft.com/en-us/library/ms190309.aspx*. Identify the precedence order among the types INT, DATETIME, and VARCHAR. Try to reason about Microsoft's choice of this precedence order.

Analyze Code Samples in Books Online for SQL Server 2012

To better understand the use of built-in functions, analyze and execute the code samples provided in Books Online for SQL Server 2012.

- **Practice 1** Visit the Books Online article "Date and Time Data Types and Functions (Transact-SQL)" at *http://msdn.microsoft.com/en-us/library/ms186724(v=SQL.110).aspx*. From there, follow the links that lead to articles about individual functions that seem useful to you. In those articles, go to the Examples section. Analyze those examples, execute them, and make sure that you understand them.
- **Practice 2** Similar to Practice 1, go to the Books Online article "String Functions (Transact-SQL)" at *http://msdn.microsoft.com/en-us/library/ms181984(v=SQL.110).aspx*. Follow the links for functions that seem useful to you. In those articles, go to the Examples section. Analyze and execute the examples, and make sure you understand them.

Answers

This section contains the answers to the lesson review questions and solutions to the case scenarios in this chapter.

Lesson 1

1. **Correct Answers: B and D**
   - **A. Incorrect:** Attribute aliasing allows you to meet relational requirements, so it's certainly more than an aesthetic feature.
   - **B. Correct:** The relational model requires that all attributes have names.
   - **C. Incorrect:** T-SQL allows a result attribute to be without a name when the expression is based on a computation without an alias.
   - **D. Correct:** You can assign your own name to a result attribute by using an alias.
2. **Correct Answer: C**
   - **A. Incorrect:** The FROM and SELECT clauses are mandatory in a SELECT query according to standard SQL but not T-SQL.
   - **B. Incorrect:** The WHERE clause is optional in T-SQL.
   - **C. Correct:** According to T-SQL, the only mandatory clause is the SELECT clause.
   - **D. Incorrect:** The FROM and WHERE clauses are both optional in T-SQL.
3. **Correct Answers: C and D**
   - **A. Incorrect:** Aliasing columns with the AS clause is standard and considered a best practice.
   - **B. Incorrect:** Aliasing tables with the AS clause is standard and considered a best practice.
   - **C. Correct:** Not aliasing a column that is a result of a computation is nonrelational and is considered a bad practice.
   - **D. Correct:** Using * in the SELECT list is considered a bad practice.

Lesson 2

1. **Correct Answer: B**
   - **A. Incorrect:** Formatting isn't a responsibility of the type or the data layer in general; rather, it is the responsibility of the presentation layer.
   - **B. Correct:** The type should be considered a constraint because it limits the values allowed.

C. **Incorrect:** The type itself doesn't prevent duplicates. If you need to prevent duplicates, you use a primary key or unique constraint.

D. **Incorrect:** A type doesn't prevent NULLs. For this, you use a NOT NULL constraint.

2. **Correct Answers: A and B**

A. **Correct:** The NEWID function creates GUIDs in random order. You would consider it when the size overhead is not a major issue and the ability to generate a unique value across time and space, from anywhere, in random order is a higher priority.

B. **Correct:** The NEWSEQUENTIALID function generates GUIDs in increasing order within the machine. It helps reduce fragmentation and works well when a single session loads the data, and the number of drives is small. However, you should carefully consider an alternative using another key generator, like a sequence object, with a smaller type when possible.

C. **Incorrect:** There's no assurance that GETDATE will generate unique values; therefore, it's not a good choice to generate keys.

D. **Incorrect:** The CURRENT_TIMESTAMP function is simply the standard version of GETDATE, so it also doesn't guarantee uniqueness.

3. **Correct Answer: B**

A. **Incorrect:** CASE expressions have nothing to do with the database recovery model.

B. **Correct:** The difference between the two is that the simple form compares expressions and the searched form uses predicates.

C. **Incorrect:** Both CASE expressions are allowed wherever a scalar expression is allowed—anywhere in the query.

D. **Incorrect:** Both CASE expressions are allowed wherever a scalar expression is allowed—anywhere in the query.

Case Scenario 1

1. The DATETIME data type uses 8 bytes of storage. SQL Server 2012 supports the DATE data type, which uses 3 bytes of storage. In all those attributes that represent a date only, it is recommended to switch to using DATE. The lower the storage requirement, the better the reads can perform.

   As for other recommendations, the general rule "smaller is better, provided that you cover the needs of the attribute in the long run" is suitable for read performance. For example, if you have descriptions of varying lengths stored in a CHAR or NCHAR type, consider switching to VARCHAR or NVARCHAR, respectively. Also, if you're currently using Unicode types but need to store strings of only one language—say, US English—consider using regular characters instead.

2. For one, the UNIQUEIDENTIFIER type is large—16 bytes. And because it's also the clustered index key, it is copied to all nonclustered indexes. Also, due to the random order in which the NEWID function generates values, there's probably a high level of fragmentation in the index. A different approach to consider (and test!) is switching to an integer type and using the sequence object to generate keys that do not conflict across tables. Due to the reduced size of the type, with the multiplied effect on nonclustered indexes, performance of reads will likely improve. The values will be increasing, and as a result, there will be less fragmentation, which will also likely have a positive effect on reads.

Case Scenario 2

- To improve the portability of the code, it's important to use standard code when possible, and this of course applies more specifically to the use of built-in functions. For example, use COALESCE and not ISNULL, use CURRENT_TIMESTAMP and not GETDATE, and use CASE and not IIF.

CHAPTER 3

Filtering and Sorting Data

Exam objectives in this chapter:

- Work with Data
  - Query data by using SELECT statements.
  - Implement data types.
- Modify Data
  - Work with functions.

Filtering and sorting data are the most foundational, as well as most common, aspects of querying data. Almost every query that you write needs to filter data, and many queries involve sorting. The traditional way to filter data in T-SQL is based on predicates. However, T-SQL also supports filtering data based on another concept—a specified number of rows and ordering. The options T-SQL supports based on this concept are TOP and OFFSET-FETCH. As for sorting, even though it might seem like a trivial aspect of querying, it's actually a source for quite a lot of confusion and misunderstanding, which this chapter tries to clarify.

Lessons in this chapter:

- Lesson 1: Filtering Data with Predicates
- Lesson 2: Sorting Data
- Lesson 3: Filtering Data with TOP and OFFSET-FETCH

Before You Begin

To complete the lessons in this this chapter, you must have:

- Experience working with Microsoft SQL Server Management Studio (SSMS).
- Some experience writing T-SQL code.
- Access to a SQL Server 2012 instance with the sample database TSQL2012 installed.

Lesson 1: Filtering Data with Predicates

T-SQL supports three query clauses that enable you to filter data based on predicates. Those are the ON, WHERE, and HAVING clauses. The ON and HAVING clauses are covered later in the book. ON is covered as part of the discussions about joins in Chapter 4, "Combining Sets," and HAVING is covered as part of the discussions about grouping data in Chapter 5, "Grouping and Windowing." Lesson 1 in this chapter focuses on filtering data with the WHERE clause.

After this lesson, you will be able to:

- Use the WHERE clause to filter data based on predicates.
- Filter data involving NULLs correctly.
- Use search arguments to filter data efficiently.
- Combine predicates with logical operators.
- Understand the implications of three-valued logic on filtering data.
- Filter character data.
- Filter date and time data.

Estimated lesson time: 60 minutes

Predicates, Three-Valued Logic, and Search Arguments

In the very first SQL queries that you ever wrote, you very likely already started using the WHERE clause to filter data based on predicates. Initially, it seems like a very simple and straightforward concept. But with time, as you gain deeper understanding of T-SQL, you probably realize that there are filtering aspects that are not that obvious. For example, you need to understand how predicates interact with NULLs, and how filters based on such predicates behave. You also need to understand how to form your predicates to maximize the efficiency of your queries, and for this you need to be familiar with the concept of a *search argument*.

Some of the examples in this chapter use the HR.Employees table from the TSQL2012 sample database. Here's the content of the table (only relevant columns shown).

```
empid  firstname  lastname      country  region  city
------ ---------- ------------- -------- ------- ---------
1      Sara       Davis         USA      WA      Seattle
2      Don        Funk          USA      WA      Tacoma
3      Judy       Lew           USA      WA      Kirkland
4      Yael       Peled         USA      WA      Redmond
5      Sven       Buck          UK       NULL    London
6      Paul       Suurs         UK       NULL    London
7      Russell    King          UK       NULL    London
8      Maria      Cameron       USA      WA      Seattle
9      Zoya       Dolgopyatova  UK       NULL    London
```

To start with a simple example, consider the following query, which filters only employees from the United States.

```
SELECT empid, firstname, lastname, country, region, city
FROM HR.Employees
WHERE country = N'USA';
```

Recall from Chapter 1, "Foundations of Querying," that a predicate is a logical expression. When NULLs are not possible in the data (in this case, the country column is defined as not allowing NULLs), the predicate can evaluate to true or false. The type of logic used in such a case is known as *two-valued logic*. The WHERE filter returns only the rows for which the predicate evaluates to true. Here's the result of this query.

```
empid  firstname  lastname  country  region  city
------ ---------- --------- -------- ------- ---------
1      Sara       Davis     USA      WA      Seattle
2      Don        Funk      USA      WA      Tacoma
3      Judy       Lew       USA      WA      Kirkland
4      Yael       Peled     USA      WA      Redmond
8      Maria      Cameron   USA      WA      Seattle
```

However, when NULLs are possible in the data, things get trickier. Consider the customer location columns country, region, and city in the Sales.Customers table. Suppose that these columns reflect the location hierarchy based on the sales organization. For some places in the world, such as in the United States, all three location columns are applicable; for example:

Country: USA

Region: WA

City: Seattle

But other places, like the United Kingdom, have only two applicable parts—the country and the city. In such cases, the region column is set to NULL; for example:

Country: UK

Region: NULL

City: London

Consider then a query filtering only employees from Washington State.

```
SELECT empid, firstname, lastname, country, region, city
FROM HR.Employees
WHERE region = N'WA';
```

Recall from Chapter 1 that when NULLs are possible in the data, a predicate can evaluate to true, false, and unknown. This type of logic is known as *three-valued logic*. When using an equality operator in the predicate like in the previous query, you get true when both operands are not NULL and equal; for example, WA and WA. You get false when both are not NULL and different; for example, OR and WA. So far, it's straightforward. The tricky part is when NULL marks are involved. You get an unknown when at least one operand is NULL; for example, NULL and WA, or even NULL and NULL.

As mentioned, the WHERE filter returns rows for which the predicate evaluates to true, meaning that it discards both false and unknown cases. Therefore, the query returns only employees where the region is not NULL and equal to WA, as shown in the following.

```
empid  firstname  lastname  country  region  city
------ ---------- --------- -------- ------- ---------
1      Sara       Davis     USA      WA      Seattle
2      Don        Funk      USA      WA      Tacoma
3      Judy       Lew       USA      WA      Kirkland
4      Yael       Peled     USA      WA      Redmond
8      Maria      Cameron   USA      WA      Seattle
```

You might consider this behavior as intuitive, but consider a request to return only employees that are not from Washington State. You issue the following query.

```
SELECT empid, firstname, lastname, country, region, city
FROM HR.Employees
WHERE region <> N'WA';
```

Run the query and you get an empty set back:

```
empid  firstname  lastname  country  region  city
------ ---------- --------- -------- ------- ---------
```

Can you make sense of the result?

As it turns out, all of the employees that aren't from Washington State are from the UK; recall that the region for places in the UK is set to NULL to indicate that it's inapplicable. Even though it may be clear to you that someone from the UK isn't from Washington State, it's not clear to T-SQL. To T-SQL, a NULL represents a missing value that could be applicable, and could be WA just like it could be anything else. So it cannot conclude with certainty that the region is different from WA. In other words, when region is NULL, the predicate region <> 'WA' evaluates to unknown, and the row is discarded. So such a predicate would return only cases that are not NULL and are known to be different from WA. For example, if you had an employee in the table with a region NY, such an employee would have been returned.

Knowing that in the Employees table a NULL region represents a missing and inapplicable region, how do you make T-SQL return such employees when looking for places where the region is different from WA?

If you're considering a predicate such as region <> N'WA' OR region = NULL, you need to remember that two NULLs are not considered equal to each other. The result of the expression NULL = NULL is, in fact, unknown—not true. T-SQL provides the predicate IS NULL to return a true when the tested operand is NULL. Similarly, the predicate IS NOT NULL returns true when the tested operand is not NULL. So the solution to this problem is to use the following form.

```
SELECT empid, firstname, lastname, country, region, city
FROM HR.Employees
WHERE region <> N'WA'
   OR region IS NULL;
```

Here's the result of this query.

```
empid  firstname  lastname      country  region  city
------ ---------- ------------- -------- ------- -------
5      Sven       Buck          UK       NULL    London
6      Paul       Suurs         UK       NULL    London
7      Russell    King          UK       NULL    London
9      Zoya       Dolgopyatova  UK       NULL    London
```

Query filters have an important performance side to them. For one thing, by filtering rows in the query (as opposed to in the client), you reduce network traffic. Also, based on the query filters that appear in the query, SQL Server can evaluate the option to use indexes to get to the data efficiently without requiring a full scan of the table. It's important to note, though, that the predicate needs to be of a form known as a *search argument* (SARG) to allow efficient use of the index. Chapter 15, "Implementing Indexes and Statistics," goes into details about indexing and the use of search arguments; here, I'll just briefly describe the concept and provide simple examples.

A predicate in the form *column operator value* or *value operator column* can be a search argument. For example, predicates like col1 = 10, and col1 > 10 are search arguments. Applying manipulation to the filtered column in most cases prevents the predicate from being a search argument. An example for manipulation of the filtered column is applying a function to it, as in F(col1) = 10, where F is some function. There are some exceptions to this rule, but they are very uncommon.

For example, suppose you have a stored procedure that accepts an input parameter @dt representing an input shipped date. The procedure is supposed to return orders that were shipped on the input date. If the shippeddate column did not allow NULLs, you could use the following query to address this task.

```
SELECT orderid, orderdate, empid
FROM Sales.Orders
WHERE shippeddate = @dt;
```

However, the shippeddate column does allow NULLs; those represent orders that weren't shipped yet. When users will need all orders that were not shipped yet, the users will provide a NULL as the input shipped date, and your query would need to be able to cope with such a case. Remember that when comparing two NULLs, you get unknown and the row is filtered out. So the current form of the predicate doesn't address NULL inputs correctly. Some address this need by using COALESCE or ISNULL to substitute NULLs with a value that doesn't exist in the data normally, as in the following.

```
SELECT orderid, orderdate, empid
FROM Sales.Orders
WHERE COALESCE(shippeddate, '19000101') = COALESCE(@dt, '19000101');
```

The problem is that even though the solution now returns the correct result—even when the input is NULL—the predicate isn't a search argument. This means that SQL Server cannot efficiently use an index on the shippeddate column. To make the predicate a search argument, you need to avoid manipulating the filtered column and rewrite the predicate like the following.

```
SELECT orderid, orderdate, empid
FROM Sales.Orders
WHERE shippeddate = @dt
   OR (shippeddate IS NULL AND @dt IS NULL);
```

EXAM TIP

Understanding the impact of using COALESCE and ISNULL on performance is an important skill for the exam.

Interestingly, standard SQL has a predicate called IS NOT DISTINCT FROM that has the same meaning as the predicate used in the last query (return true when both sides are equal or when both are NULLs, otherwise false). Unfortunately, T-SQL doesn't support this predicate.

Another example for manipulation involves the filtered column in an expression; for example, col1 - 1 <= @n. Sometimes, you can rewrite the predicate to a form that is a search argument, and then allow efficient use of indexing. The last predicate, for example, can be rewritten using simple math as col1 <= @n + 1.

In short, when a predicate involves manipulation of the filtered column, and there are alternative ways to phrase it without the manipulation, you can increase the likelihood for efficient use of indexing. There are a couple of additional examples in the sections "Filtering Character Data" and "Filtering Date and Time Data" later in this chapter. And as mentioned, more extensive coverage of the topic is in Chapter 15.

Combining Predicates

You can combine predicates in the WHERE clause by using the logical operators AND and OR. You can also negate predicates by using the NOT logical operator. This section starts by describing important aspects of negation and then discusses combining predicates.

Negation of true and false is straightforward—NOT true is false, and NOT false is true. What can be surprising to some is what happens when you negate unknown—NOT unknown is still unknown.

Recall from earlier in this chapter the query that returned all employees from Washington State; the query used the predicate region = N'WA' in the WHERE clause. Suppose that you want to return the employees that are not from WA, and for this you use the predicate NOT region = N'WA'. It's clear that cases that return false from the positive predicate (say the region is NY) return true from the negated predicate. It's also clear that cases that return true from the positive predicate (say the region is WA) return false from the negated predicate. However, when the region is NULL, both the positive predicate and the negated one return unknown and the row is discarded. So the right way for you to include NULL cases in the result—if that's what you know that you need to do—is to use the IS NULL operator, as in NOT region = N'WA' OR region IS NULL.

As for combining predicates, there are several interesting things to note. Some precedence rules determine the logical evaluation order of the different predicates. The NOT operator precedes AND and OR, and AND precedes OR. For example, suppose that the WHERE filter in your query had the following combination of predicates.

```
WHERE col1 = 'w' AND col2 = 'x' OR col3 = 'y' AND col4 = 'z'
```

Because AND precedes OR, you get the equivalent of the following.

```
WHERE (col1 = 'w' AND col2 = 'x') OR (col3 = 'y' AND col4 = 'z')
```

Trying to express the operators as pseudo functions, this combination of operators is equivalent to OR(AND(col1 = 'w', col2 = 'x'), AND(col3 = 'y', col4 = 'z')).

Because parentheses have the highest precedence among all operators, you can always use those to fully control the logical evaluation order that you need, as the following example shows.

```
WHERE col1 = 'w' AND (col2 = 'x' OR col3 = 'y') AND col4 = 'z'
```

Again, using pseudo functions, this combination of operators and use of parentheses is equivalent to AND(col1 = 'w', OR(col2 = 'x', col3 = 'y'), col4 = 'z').

Recall from Chapter 1 that all expressions that appear in the same logical query processing phase—for example, the WHERE phase—are conceptually evaluated at the same point in time. For example, consider the following filter predicate.

```
WHERE propertytype = 'INT' AND CAST(propertyval AS INT) > 10
```

Suppose that the table being queried holds different property values. The propertytype column represents the type of the property (an INT, a DATE, and so on), and the propertyval column holds the value in a character string. When propertytype is 'INT', the value in propertyval is convertible to INT; otherwise, not necessarily.

Some assume that unless precedence rules dictate otherwise, predicates will be evaluated from left to right, and that short circuiting will take place when possible. In other words, if the first predicate propertytype = 'INT' evaluates to false, SQL Server won't evaluate the second predicate CAST(propertyval AS INT) > 10 because the result is already known. Based on this assumption, the expectation is that the query should never fail trying to convert something that isn't convertible.

The reality, though, is different. SQL Server does internally support a short-circuit concept; however, due to the all-at-once concept in the language, it is not necessarily going to evaluate the expressions in left-to-right order. It could decide, based on cost-related reasons, to start with the second expression, and then if the second expression evaluates to true, to evaluate the first expression as well. This means that if there are rows in the table where propertytype is different than 'INT', and in those rows propertyval isn't convertible to INT, the query can fail due to a conversion error.

You can deal with this problem in a number of ways. A simple option is to use the TRY_CAST function instead of CAST. When the input expression isn't convertible to the target type, TRY_CAST returns a NULL instead of failing. And comparing a NULL to anything yields unknown. Eventually, you will get the correct result, without allowing the query to fail. So your WHERE clause should be revised like the following.

```
WHERE propertytype = 'INT' AND TRY_CAST(propertyval AS INT) > 10
```

Filtering Character Data

In many respects, filtering character data is the same as filtering other types of data. This section covers a couple of items that are specific to character data: proper form of literals and the LIKE predicate.

As discussed in Chapter 2, "Getting Started with the SELECT Statement," a literal has a type. If you write an expression that involves operands of different types, SQL Server will have to apply implicit conversion to align the types. Depending on the circumstances, implicit conversions can sometimes hurt performance. It is important to know the proper form of literals of different types and make sure you use the right ones. A classic example for using incorrect literal types is with Unicode character strings (NVARCHAR and NCHAR types). The right form for a Unicode character string literal is to prefix the literal with a capital N and delimit the literal with single quotation marks; for example, N'literal'. For a regular character string literal, you just delimit the literal with single quotation marks; for example, 'literal'. It's a very typical bad habit to specify a regular character string literal when the filtered column is of a Unicode type, as in the following example.

```
SELECT empid, firstname, lastname
FROM HR.Employees
WHERE lastname = 'Davis';
```

Because the column and the literal have different types, SQL Server implicitly converts one operand's type to the other. In this example, fortunately, SQL Server converts the literal's type to the column's type, so it can still efficiently rely on indexing. However, there may be cases where implicit conversion hurts performance. It is a best practice to use the proper form, like in the following.

```
SELECT empid, firstname, lastname
FROM HR.Employees
WHERE lastname = N'Davis';
```

T-SQL provides the LIKE predicate, which you can use to filter character string data (regular and Unicode) based on pattern matching. The form of a predicate using LIKE is as follows.

```
<column> LIKE <pattern>
```

The LIKE predicate supports wildcards that you can use in your patterns. Table 3-1 describes the available wildcards, their meaning, and an example demonstrating their use.

TABLE 3-1 Wildcards used in LIKE patterns

Wildcard	Meaning	Example
% (percent sign)	Any string including an empty one	'D%': string starting with D
_ (underscore)	A single character	'_D%': string where second character is D
[<*character list*>]	A single character from a list	'[AC]%': string where first character is A or C
[<*character range*>]	A single character from a range	'[0-9]%': string where first character is a digit
[^<*character list or range*>]	A single character that is not in the list or range	'[^0-9]%': string where first character is not a digit

As an example, suppose you want to return all employees whose last name starts with the letter D. You would use the following query.

```
SELECT empid, firstname, lastname
FROM HR.Employees
WHERE lastname LIKE N'D%';
```

This query returns the following output.

```
empid  firstname  lastname
------ ---------- -------------
1      Sara       Davis
9      Zoya       Dolgopyatova
```

If you want to look for a character that is considered a wildcard, you can indicate it after a character that you designate as an escape character by using the ESCAPE keyword. For example, the expression col1 LIKE '!_%' ESCAPE '!' looks for strings that start with an underscore (_) by using an exclamation point (!) as the escape character.

IMPORTANT **PERFORMANCE OF THE LIKE PREDICATE**

When the LIKE pattern starts with a known prefix—for example, col LIKE 'ABC%'—SQL Server can potentially efficiently use an index on the filtered column; in other words, SQL Server can rely on index ordering. When the pattern starts with a wildcard—for example, col LIKE '%ABC%'—SQL Server cannot rely on index ordering anymore. Also, when looking for a string that starts with a known prefix (say, ABC) make sure you use the LIKE predicate, as in col LIKE 'ABC%', because this form is considered a search argument. Recall that applying manipulation to the filtered column prevents the predicate from being a search argument. For example, the form LEFT(col, 3) = 'ABC' isn't a search argument and will prevent SQL Server from being able to use an index efficiently.

Filtering Date and Time Data

There are several important considerations when filtering date and time data that are related to both the correctness of your code and to its performance. You want to think of things like how to express literals, filter ranges, and use search arguments.

I'll start with literals. Suppose that you need to query the Sales.Orders table and return only orders placed on February 12, 2007. You use the following query.

```
SELECT orderid, orderdate, empid, custid
FROM Sales.Orders
WHERE orderdate = '02/12/07';
```

If you're an American, this form probably means February 12, 2007, to you. However, if you're British, this form probably means December 2, 2007. If you're Japanese, it probably means December 7, 2002. The question is, when SQL Server converts this character string to a date and time type to align it with the filtered column's type, how does it interpret the value? As it turns out, it depends on the language of the logon that runs the code. Each logon has a default language associated with it, and the default language sets various session options on the logon's behalf, including one called DATEFORMAT. A logon with us_english will have the DATEFORMAT setting set to mdy, British to dmy, and Japanese to ymd. The problem is, how do you as a developer express a date if you want it to be interpreted the way you intended, regardless of who runs your code?

There are two main approaches. One is to use a form that is considered language-neutral. For example, the form '20070212' is always interpreted as ymd, regardless of your language. Note that the form '2007-02-12' is considered language-neutral only for the data types DATE, DATETIME2, and DATETIMEOFFSET. Unfortunately, due to historic reasons, this form is considered language-dependent for the types DATETIME and SMALLDATETIME. The advantage of the form without the separators is that it is language-neutral for all date and time types. So the recommendation is to write the query like the following.

```
SELECT orderid, orderdate, empid, custid
FROM Sales.Orders
WHERE orderdate = '20070212';
```

> ***NOTE*** **STORING DATES IN A DATETIME COLUMN**
>
> **The filtered column orderdate is of a DATETIME data type representing both date and time. Yet the literal specified in the filter contains only a date part. When SQL Server converts the literal to the filtered column's type, it assumes midnight when a time part isn't indicated. If you want such a filter to return all rows from the specified date, you need to ensure that you store all values with midnight as the time.**

Another approach is to use the CONVERT or PARSE functions, which you can use to indicate how you want SQL Server to interpret the literal that you specify. The CONVERT function supports a style number representing the conversion style, and the PARSE function supports indicating a culture name. You can find details about both functions in Chapter 2.

Another important aspect of filtering date and time data is trying whenever possible to use search arguments. For example, suppose that you need to filter only orders placed in February 2007. You can use the YEAR and MONTH functions, as in the following.

```
SELECT orderid, orderdate, empid, custid
FROM Sales.Orders
WHERE YEAR(orderdate) = 2007 AND MONTH(orderdate) = 2;
```

However, because here you apply manipulation to the filtered column, the predicate is not considered a search argument, and therefore, SQL Server won't be able to rely on index ordering. You could revise your predicate as a range, like the following.

```
SELECT orderid, orderdate, empid, custid
FROM Sales.Orders
WHERE orderdate >= '20070201' AND orderdate < '20070301';
```

Now that you don't apply manipulation to the filtered column, the predicate is considered a search argument, and there's the potential for SQL Server to rely on index ordering.

If you're wondering why this code expresses the date range by using greater than or equal to (>=) and less than (<) operators as opposed to using BETWEEN, there's a reason for this. When you are using BETWEEN and the column holds both date and time elements, what do you use as the end value? As you might realize, for different types, there are different precisions. What's more, suppose that the type is DATETIME, and you use the following predicate.

```
WHERE orderdate BETWEEN '20070201' AND '20070228 23:59:59.999'
```

This type's precision is three and a third milliseconds. The milliseconds part of the end point 999 is not a multiplication of the precision unit, so SQL Server ends up rounding the value to midnight of March 1, 2007. As a result, you may end up getting some orders that you're not supposed to see. In short, instead of BETWEEN, use >= and <, and this form will work correctly in all cases, with all date and time types, whether the time portion is applicable or not.

Quick Check

1. **What are the performance benefits in using the WHERE filter?**
2. **What is the form of a filter predicate that can rely on index ordering called?**

Quick Check Answer

1. **You reduce network traffic by filtering in the database server instead of in the client, and you can potentially use indexes to avoid full scans of the tables involved.**
2. **A search argument, or SARG, for short.**

PRACTICE Filtering Data with Predicates

In this practice, you exercise your knowledge of filtering data with predicates.

If you encounter a problem completing an exercise, you can install the completed projects from the companion content for this chapter and lesson.

EXERCISE 1 Use the WHERE Clause to Filter Rows with NULLs

In this exercise, you practice the use of the WHERE clause to filter unshipped orders from the Sales.Orders table.

1. Open SSMS and connect to the sample database TSQL2012.
2. You are asked to write a query that returns orders that were not shipped yet. Such orders have a NULL in the shippeddate column. For your first attempt, use the following query.

   ```
   SELECT orderid, orderdate, custid, empid
   FROM Sales.Orders
   WHERE shippeddate = NULL;
   ```

   However, when you run this code, you get an empty result set.

   ```
   orderid     orderdate               custid      empid
   ----------- ----------------------- ----------- -----------
   ```

   The reason for this is that when the expression compares two NULLs, the result is unknown, and the row is filtered out.
3. Revise the filter predicate to use the IS NULL operator instead of equality (=), as in the following.

   ```
   SELECT orderid, orderdate, custid, empid
   FROM Sales.Orders
   WHERE shippeddate IS NULL;
   ```

   This time, you do get the correct result, shown here in abbreviated form.

   ```
   orderid     orderdate               custid      empid
   ----------- ----------------------- ----------- -----------
   11008       2008-04-08 00:00:00.000 20          7
   11019       2008-04-13 00:00:00.000 64          6
   11039       2008-04-21 00:00:00.000 47          1
   ...
   ```

EXERCISE 2 Use the WHERE Clause to Filter a Range of Dates

In this exercise, you practice the use of the WHERE clause to filter orders within a certain range of dates from the Sales.Orders table.

1. You are requested to return all orders that were placed between February 11, 2008, and February 12, 2008. The orderdate column you're supposed to filter by is of a DATETIME type. With the current data in the table, all orderdate values have the time set to midnight, but suppose this wasn't the case—namely, that the time portion could be a value other than midnight. For your first attempt, use the BETWEEN predicate, as follows.

   ```
   SELECT orderid, orderdate, custid, empid
   FROM Sales.Orders
   WHERE orderdate BETWEEN '20080211' AND '20080212 23:59:59.999';
   ```

   Because 999 is not a multiplication of the DATETIME type's precision unit (three and a third milliseconds), the end value in the range gets rounded to the next midnight, and the result includes rows from February 13 that you didn't ask for.

   ```
   orderid     orderdate               custid      empid
   ----------- ----------------------- ----------- -----------
   10881       2008-02-11 00:00:00.000 12          4
   10887       2008-02-13 00:00:00.000 29          8
   10886       2008-02-13 00:00:00.000 34          1
   10884       2008-02-12 00:00:00.000 45          4
   10883       2008-02-12 00:00:00.000 48          8
   10882       2008-02-11 00:00:00.000 71          4
   10885       2008-02-12 00:00:00.000 76          6
   ```

2. To fix the problem, revise the range filter to use the >= and < operators, as follows.

   ```
   SELECT orderid, orderdate, custid, empid
   FROM Sales.Orders
   WHERE orderdate >= '20080211' AND orderdate < '20080213';
   ```

   This time, you get the correct result.

Lesson Summary

- With the WHERE clause, you can filter data by using predicates. Predicates in T-SQL use three-valued logic. The WHERE clause returns cases where the predicate evaluates to true and discards the rest.
- Filtering data by using the WHERE clause helps reduce network traffic and can potentially enable using indexes to minimize I/O. It is important to try and phrase your predicates as search arguments to enable efficient use of indexes.
- When filtering different types of data, like character and date and time data, it is important to be familiar with best practices that will ensure that you write both correct and efficient code.

Lesson Review

Answer the following questions to test your knowledge of the information in this lesson. You can find the answers to these questions and explanations of why each answer choice is correct or incorrect in the "Answers" section at the end of this chapter.

1. What does the term three-valued logic refer to in T-SQL?
   - **A.** The three possible logical result values of a predicate: true, false, and NULL
   - **B.** The three possible logical result values of a predicate: true, false, and unknown
   - **C.** The three possible logical result values of a predicate: 1, 0, and NULL
   - **D.** The three possible logical result values of a predicate: -1, 0, and 1
2. Which of the following literals are language-dependent for the DATETIME data type? (Choose all that apply.)
   - **A.** '2012-02-12'
   - **B.** '02/12/2012'
   - **C.** '12/02/2012'
   - **D.** '20120212'
3. Which of the following predicates are search arguments? (Choose all that apply.)
   - **A.** DAY(orderdate) = 1
   - **B.** companyname LIKE 'A%'
   - **C.** companyname LIKE '%A%'
   - **D.** companyname LIKE '%A'
   - **E.** orderdate > = '20120212' AND orderdate < '20120213'

Lesson 2: Sorting Data

Sorting data is supposed to be a trivial thing, but as it turns out, it's a source of a lot of confusion in T-SQL. This lesson describes the critical difference in T-SQL between unsorted and sorted data. It then describes the tools T-SQL provides you to sort data.

After this lesson, you will be able to:

- Use the ORDER BY clause to determine the order of rows in the result of a query.
- Describe the difference between a query with and without an ORDER BY clause.
- Control ascending and descending direction of ordering.
- Follow ordering best practices.
- Identify ordering restrictions when DISTINCT is used.
- Order by aliases that were assigned in the SELECT clause.

Estimated lesson time: 30 minutes

Understanding When Order Is Guaranteed

Probably one of the most confusing aspects of working with T-SQL is understanding when a query result is guaranteed to be returned in particular order versus when it isn't. Correct understanding of this aspect of the language ties directly to the foundations of T-SQL—particularly mathematical set theory. If you understand this from the very early stages of writing T-SQL code, you will have a much easier time than many who simply have incorrect assumptions and expectations from the language.

Consider the following query as an example.

```
SELECT empid, firstname, lastname, city, MONTH(birthdate) AS birthmonth
FROM HR.Employees
WHERE country = N'USA' AND region = N'WA';
```

Is there a guarantee that the rows will be returned in particular order, and if so, what is that order?

Some make an intuitive assumption that the rows will be returned in insertion order; some assume primary key order; some assume clustered index order; others know that there's no guarantee for any kind of order.

If you recall from Chapter 1, a table in T-SQL is supposed to represent a relation; a relation is a set, and a set has no order to its elements. With this in mind, unless you explicitly instruct the query otherwise, the result of a query has no guaranteed order. For example, this query gave the following output when run on one system.

```
empid  firstname  lastname  city      birthmonth
------ ---------- --------- --------- -----------
1      Sara       Davis     Seattle   12
2      Don        Funk      Tacoma    2
3      Judy       Lew       Kirkland  8
4      Yael       Peled     Redmond   9
8      Maria      Cameron   Seattle   1
```

It might seem like the output is sorted by empid, but that's not guaranteed. What could be more confusing is that if you run the query repeatedly, it seems like the result keeps being returned in the same order; but again, that's not guaranteed. When the database engine (SQL Server in this case) processes this query, it knows that it can return the data in any order because there is no explicit instruction to return the data in a specific order. It could be that, due to optimization and other reasons, the SQL Server database engine chose to process the data in a particular way *this time*. There's even some likelihood that such choices will be repeated if the physical circumstances remain the same. But there's a big difference between what's likely to happen due to optimization and other reasons and what's actually guaranteed.

The database engine may—and sometimes does—change choices that can affect the order in which rows are returned, knowing that it is free to do so. Examples for such changes in choices include changes in data distribution, availability of physical structures such as indexes, and availability of resources like CPUs and memory. Also, with changes in the engine after an upgrade to a newer version of the product, or even after application of a service pack, optimization aspects may change. In turn, such changes could affect, among other things, the order of the rows in the result.

In short, this cannot be stressed enough: A query that doesn't have an explicit instruction to return the rows in a particular order doesn't guarantee the order of rows in the result. When you do need such a guarantee, the only way to provide it is by adding an ORDER BY clause to the query, and that's the focus of the next section.

Using the ORDER BY Clause to Sort Data

The only way to truly guarantee that the rows are returned from a query in a certain order is by adding an ORDER BY clause.

For example, if you want to return information about employees from Washington State in the United States, sorted by city, you specify the city column in the ORDER BY clause as follows.

```
SELECT empid, firstname, lastname, city, MONTH(birthdate) AS birthmonth
FROM HR.Employees
WHERE country = N'USA' AND region = N'WA'
ORDER BY city;
```

Here's the output of this query.

```
empid  firstname  lastname  city      birthmonth
------ ---------- --------- --------- -----------
3      Judy       Lew       Kirkland  8
4      Yael       Peled     Redmond   9
8      Maria      Cameron   Seattle   1
1      Sara       Davis     Seattle   12
2      Don        Funk      Tacoma    2
```

If you don't indicate a direction for sorting, ascending order is assumed by default. You can be explicit and specify city ASC, but it means the same thing as not indicating the direction. For descending ordering, you need to explicitly specify DESC, as follows.

```
SELECT empid, firstname, lastname, city, MONTH(birthdate) AS birthmonth
FROM HR.Employees
WHERE country = N'USA' AND region = N'WA'
ORDER BY city DESC;
```

This time, the output shows the rows in city order, descending direction.

```
empid  firstname  lastname  city      birthmonth
------ ---------- --------- --------- -----------
2      Don        Funk      Tacoma    2
1      Sara       Davis     Seattle   12
8      Maria      Cameron   Seattle   1
4      Yael       Peled     Redmond   9
3      Judy       Lew       Kirkland  8
```

The city column isn't unique within the filtered country and region, and therefore, the ordering of rows with the same city (see Seattle, for example) isn't guaranteed. In such a case, it is said that the ordering isn't deterministic. Just like a query without an ORDER BY clause doesn't guarantee order among result rows in general, a query with ORDER BY city, when city isn't unique, doesn't guarantee order among rows with the same city. Fortunately, you can specify multiple expressions in the ORDER BY list, separated by commas. One use case of this capability is to apply a tiebreaker for ordering. For example, you could define empid as the secondary sort column, as follows.

```
SELECT empid, firstname, lastname, city, MONTH(birthdate) AS birthmonth
FROM HR.Employees
WHERE country = N'USA' AND region = N'WA'
ORDER BY city, empid;
```

Here's the output of this query.

```
empid  firstname  lastname  city      birthmonth
------ ---------- --------- --------- -----------
3      Judy       Lew       Kirkland  8
4      Yael       Peled     Redmond   9
1      Sara       Davis     Seattle   12
8      Maria      Cameron   Seattle   1
2      Don        Funk      Tacoma    2
```

The ORDER BY list is now unique; hence, the ordering is deterministic. As long as the underlying data doesn't change, the results are guaranteed to be repeatable, in addition to their presentation ordering. You can indicate the ordering direction on an expression-by-expression basis, as in ORDER BY col1 DESC, col2, col3 DESC (col1 descending, then col2 ascending, then col3 descending).

With T-SQL, you can sort by ordinal positions of columns in the SELECT list, but it is considered a bad practice. Consider the following query as an example.

```
SELECT empid, firstname, lastname, city, MONTH(birthdate) AS birthmonth
FROM HR.Employees
WHERE country = N'USA' AND region = N'WA'
ORDER BY 4, 1;
```

In this query, you're asking to order the rows by the fourth expression in the SELECT list (city), and then by the first (empid). In this particular query, it is equivalent to using ORDER BY city, empid. However, this practice is considered a bad one for a number of reasons. For one, T-SQL does keep track of ordinal positions of columns in a table, in addition to in a query result, but this is nonrelational. Recall that the header of a relation is a set of attributes, and a set has no order. Also, when you are using ordinal positions, it is very easy after making changes to the SELECT list to miss changing the ordinals accordingly. For example, suppose that you decide to apply changes to your previous query, returning city right after empid in the SELECT list. You apply the change to the SELECT list but forget to change the ORDER BY list accordingly, and end up with the following query.

```
SELECT empid, city, firstname, lastname, MONTH(birthdate) AS birthmonth
FROM HR.Employees
WHERE country = N'USA' AND region = N'WA'
ORDER BY 4, 1;
```

Now the query is ordering the data by lastname and empid instead of by city and empid. In short, it's a best practice to refer to column names, or expressions based on those, and not to ordinal positions.

Note that you can order the result rows by elements that you're not returning. For example, the following query returns, for each qualifying employee, the employee ID and city, ordering the result rows by the employee birth date.

```
SELECT empid, city
FROM HR.Employees
WHERE country = N'USA' AND region = N'WA'
ORDER BY birthdate;
```

Here's the output of this query.

```
empid       city
----------- ---------------
4           Redmond
1           Seattle
2           Tacoma
8           Seattle
3           Kirkland
```

Of course, the result would appear much more meaningful if you included the birthdate attribute, but if it makes sense for you not to, it's perfectly valid. The rule is, you can order the result rows by elements that are not part of the SELECT list, as long as the result rows would have normally been allowed there. This rule changes when the DISTINCT clause is also specified—and for a good reason. When DISTINCT is used, duplicates are removed; then the result rows don't necessarily map to source rows in a one-to-one manner, rather than one-to-many. For example, try to reason why the following query isn't valid.

```
SELECT DISTINCT city
FROM HR.Employees
WHERE country = N'USA' AND region = N'WA'
ORDER BY birthdate;
```

You can have multiple employees—each with a different birth date—from the same city. But you're returning only one row for each distinct city in the result. So given one city (say, Seattle) with multiple employees, which of the employee birth dates should apply as the ordering value? The query won't just pick one; rather, it simply fails.

So, in case the DISTINCT clause is used, you are limited in the ORDER BY list to only elements that appear in the SELECT list, as in the following query.

```
SELECT DISTINCT city
FROM HR.Employees
WHERE country = N'USA' AND region = N'WA'
ORDER BY city;
```

Now the query is perfectly sensible, returning the following output.

```
city
---------
Kirkland
Redmond
Seattle
Tacoma
```

What's also interesting to note about the ORDER BY clause is that it gets evaluated conceptually after the SELECT clause—unlike most other query clauses. This means that column aliases assigned in the SELECT clause are actually visible to the ORDER BY clause. As an example, the following query uses the MONTH function to return the birth month, assigning the expression with the column alias birthmonth. The query then refers to the column alias birthmonth directly in the ORDER BY clause.

```
SELECT empid, firstname, lastname, city, MONTH(birthdate) AS birthmonth
FROM HR.Employees
WHERE country = N'USA' AND region = N'WA'
ORDER BY birthmonth;
```

This query returns the following output.

```
empid  firstname  lastname  city      birthmonth
------ ---------- --------- --------- -----------
8      Maria      Cameron   Seattle   1
2      Don        Funk      Tacoma    2
3      Judy       Lew       Kirkland  8
4      Yael       Peled     Redmond   9
1      Sara       Davis     Seattle   12
```

Another tricky aspect of ordering is treatment of NULLs. Recall that a NULL represents a missing value, so when comparing a NULL to anything, you get the logical result unknown. That's the case even when comparing two NULLs. So it's not that trivial to ask how NULLs should behave in terms of sorting. Should they all sort together? If so, should they sort before or after non-NULL values? Standard SQL says that NULLs should sort together, but leaves it to the implementation to decide whether to sort them before or after non-NULL values. In SQL Server the decision was to sort them before non-NULLs (when using an ascending direction). As an example, the following query returns for each order the order ID and shipped date, ordered by the latter.

```
SELECT orderid, shippeddate
FROM Sales.Orders
WHERE custid = 20
ORDER BY shippeddate;
```

Remember that unshipped orders have a NULL in the shippeddate column; hence, they sort before shipped orders, as the query output shows.

```
orderid     shippeddate
----------- -----------------------
11008       NULL
11072       NULL
10258       2006-07-23 00:00:00.000
10263       2006-07-31 00:00:00.000
10351       2006-11-20 00:00:00.000
...
```

Standard SQL supports the options NULLS FIRST and NULLS LAST to control how NULLs sort, but T-SQL doesn't support this option. As an interesting challenge, see if you can figure out how to sort the orders by shipped date ascending, but have NULLs sort last. (Hint: You can specify expressions in the ORDER BY clause; think of how to use the CASE expression to achieve this task.)

So remember, a query without an ORDER BY clause returns a relational result (at least from an ordering perspective), and hence doesn't guarantee any order. The only way to guarantee order is with an ORDER BY clause. According to standard SQL, a query with an ORDER BY clause conceptually returns a *cursor* and not a relation.

Indexing is discussed later in the Training Kit, but for now, suffice it to say that creating the right indexes can help SQL Server avoid the need to actually sort the data to address an ORDER BY request. Without good indexes, SQL Server needs to sort the data, and sorting can be expensive, especially when a large set is involved. If you don't need to return the data sorted, make sure you do not specify an ORDER BY clause, to avoid unnecessary costs.

Quick Check

1. **How do you guarantee the order of the rows in the result of a query?**
2. **What is the difference between the result of a query with and one without an ORDER BY clause?**

Quick Check Answer

1. **The only way to do so is by adding an ORDER BY clause.**
2. **Without an ORDER BY clause, the result is relational (from an ordering perspective); with an ORDER BY clause, the result is conceptually what the standard calls a cursor.**

PRACTICE Sorting Data

In this practice, you exercise your knowledge of sorting data with the ORDER BY clause.

If you encounter a problem completing an exercise, you can install the completed projects from the companion content for this chapter and lesson.

EXERCISE 1 Use the ORDER BY Clause with Nondeterministic Ordering

In this exercise, you practice using the ORDER BY clause to sort data, practicing nondeterministic ordering.

1. Open SSMS and connect to the sample database TSQL2012.
2. You are asked to write a query that returns the orders for customer 77. Use the following query.

   ```
   SELECT orderid, empid, shipperid, shippeddate
   FROM Sales.Orders
   WHERE custid = 77;
   ```

   You get the following result set.

   ```
   orderid  empid  shipperid  shippeddate
   -------- ------ ---------- -----------------------
   10992    1      3          2008-04-03 00:00:00.000
   10805    2      3          2008-01-09 00:00:00.000
   10708    6      2          2007-11-05 00:00:00.000
   10310    8      2          2006-09-27 00:00:00.000
   ```

   Note that because you didn't specify an ORDER BY clause, there's no assurance that the rows will be returned in the order shown in the previous code. The only assurance that you have is that you will get this particular set of rows.

3. You are asked to revise your query such that the rows will be sorted by shipperid. Add an ORDER BY clause, as follows.

```
SELECT orderid, empid, shipperid, shippeddate
FROM Sales.Orders
WHERE custid = 77
ORDER BY shipperid;
```

The query now returns the following result.

```
orderid  empid  shipperid  shippeddate
-------- ------ ---------- -----------------------
10708    6      2          2007-11-05 00:00:00.000
10310    8      2          2006-09-27 00:00:00.000
10992    1      3          2008-04-03 00:00:00.000
10805    2      3          2008-01-09 00:00:00.000
```

Now you guarantee that the rows will be returned by shipperid ordering, but is the ordering deterministic? For example, can you tell with certainty what will be the order among rows with the same shipper ID? The answer is no.

EXERCISE 2 Use the ORDER BY Clause with Deterministic Ordering

In this exercise, you practice using the ORDER BY clause to sort data, practicing deterministic ordering.

1. You start this step with the query you wrote in step 3 of Exercise 1. You are given a requirement to add secondary ordering by shipped date, descending. Add shippeddate DESC to the ORDER BY clause, as follows.

```
SELECT orderid, empid, shipperid, shippeddate
FROM Sales.Orders
WHERE custid = 77
ORDER BY shipperid, shippeddate DESC;
```

The query now returns the following result.

```
orderid  empid  shipperid  shippeddate
-------- ------ ---------- -----------------------
10708    6      2          2007-11-05 00:00:00.000
10310    8      2          2006-09-27 00:00:00.000
10992    1      3          2008-04-03 00:00:00.000
10805    2      3          2008-01-09 00:00:00.000
```

Unlike in step 3, now it's guaranteed that the rows with the same shipper ID will be sorted by shipped date, descending. Is ordering now deterministic? Can you tell with certainty what will be the order among rows with the same shipper ID and shipped date? The answer is still no, because the combination of columns shipperid and shippeddate isn't unique, never mind what the current values that you see in the table might lead you to think. Technically, there could be multiple rows in the result of this query with the same shipperid and shippeddate values.

2. You are asked to revise the query from step 1 by guaranteeing deterministic ordering. You need to define a tiebreaker. For example, define orderid DESC as a tiebreaker, as follows.

```
SELECT orderid, empid, shipperid, shippeddate
FROM Sales.Orders
WHERE custid = 77
ORDER BY shipperid, shippeddate DESC, orderid DESC;
```

Now, in case of ties in the shipperid and shippeddate values, the row with the greater orderid value will be sorted first.

Lesson Summary

- Queries normally return a relational result where ordering isn't guaranteed. If you need to guarantee presentation ordering, you need to add an ORDER BY clause to your query.
- With the ORDER BY clause, you can specify a list of expressions for primary ordering, secondary ordering, and so on. With each expression, you can indicate ASC or DESC for ascending or descending ordering, with ascending being the default.
- Even when an ORDER BY clause is specified, the result could still have nondeterministic ordering. For deterministic ordering, the ORDER BY list must be unique.
- You can use ordinal positions of expressions from the SELECT list in the ORDER BY clause, but this is considered a bad practice.
- You can sort by elements that do not appear in the SELECT list unless the DISTINCT clause is also specified.
- Because the ORDER BY clause is conceptually evaluated after the SELECT clause, you can refer to aliases assigned in the SELECT clause within the ORDER BY clause.
- For sorting purposes, SQL Server considers NULLs as being lower than non-NULL marks and equal to each other. This means that when ascending ordering is used, they sort together before non-NULL marks.

Lesson Review

Answer the following questions to test your knowledge of the information in this lesson. You can find the answers to these questions and explanations of why each answer choice is correct or incorrect in the "Answers" section at the end of this chapter.

1. When a query doesn't have an ORDER BY clause, what is the order in which the rows are returned?

   A. Arbitrary order

   B. Primary key order

   C. Clustered index order

   D. Insertion order

2. You want result rows to be sorted by orderdate descending, and then by orderid, descending. Which of the following clauses gives you what you want?

   A. ORDER BY orderdate, orderid DESC

   B. ORDER BY DESC orderdate, DESC orderid

   C. ORDER BY orderdate DESC, orderid DESC

   D. DESC ORDER BY orderdate, orderid

3. You want result rows to be sorted by orderdate ascending, and then by orderid, ascending. Which of the following clauses gives you what you want? (Choose all that apply.)

   A. ORDER BY ASC(orderdate, orderid)

   B. ORDER BY orderdate, orderid ASC

   C. ORDER BY orderdate ASC, orderid ASC

   D. ORDER BY orderdate, orderid

Lesson 3: Filtering Data with TOP and OFFSET-FETCH

The first lesson covered filtering data by using predicates, and the second covered sorting data. This third lesson in a sense mixes filtering and sorting concepts. Often, you need to filter data based on given ordering and a specified number of rows. Think about requests such as "return the three most recent orders" and "return the five most expensive products." The filter involves some ordering specification and a requested number of rows. T-SQL provides two options to handle such filtering needs: one is the proprietary TOP option and the other is the standard OFFSET-FETCH option that was introduced in SQL Server 2012.

After this lesson, you will be able to:

- Filter data by using the TOP option.
- Filter data by using the OFFSET-FETCH option.

Estimated lesson time: 45 minutes

Filtering Data with TOP

With the TOP option, you can filter a requested number or percent of rows from the query result based on indicated ordering. You specify the TOP option in the SELECT clause followed by the requested number of rows in parentheses (BIGINT data type). The ordering specification of the TOP filter is based on the same ORDER BY clause that is normally used for presentation ordering.

As an example, the following query returns the three most recent orders.

```
SELECT TOP (3) orderid, orderdate, custid, empid
FROM Sales.Orders
ORDER BY orderdate DESC;
```

You specify 3 as the number of rows you want to filter, and orderdate DESC as the ordering specification. So you get the three rows with the most recent order dates. Here's the output of this query.

```
orderid     orderdate               custid      empid
----------- ----------------------- ----------- -----------
11077       2008-05-06 00:00:00.000 65          1
11076       2008-05-06 00:00:00.000 9           4
11075       2008-05-06 00:00:00.000 68          8
```

> ***NOTE*** **TOP AND PARENTHESES**
>
> **T-SQL supports specifying the number of rows to filter using the TOP option in SELECT queries without parentheses, but that's only for backward-compatibility reasons. The correct syntax is with parentheses.**

You can also specify a percent of rows to filter instead of a number. To do so, specify a FLOAT value in the range 0 through 100 in the parentheses, and the keyword PERCENT after the parentheses, as follows.

```
SELECT TOP (1) PERCENT orderid, orderdate, custid, empid
FROM Sales.Orders
ORDER BY orderdate DESC;
```

The PERCENT option puts a ceiling on the resulting number of rows if it's not whole. In this example, without the TOP option, the number of rows in the result is 830. Filtering 1 percent gives you 8.3, and then the ceiling of this value gives you 9; hence, the query returns 9 rows.

```
orderid     orderdate               custid      empid
----------- ----------------------- ----------- -----------
11076       2008-05-06 00:00:00.000 9           4
11077       2008-05-06 00:00:00.000 65          1
11075       2008-05-06 00:00:00.000 68          8
11074       2008-05-06 00:00:00.000 73          7
11070       2008-05-05 00:00:00.000 44          2
11071       2008-05-05 00:00:00.000 46          1
11073       2008-05-05 00:00:00.000 58          2
11072       2008-05-05 00:00:00.000 20          4
11067       2008-05-04 00:00:00.000 17          1
```

The TOP option isn't limited to a constant input; instead, it allows you to specify a self-contained expression. From a practical perspective, this capability is especially important when you need to pass a parameter or a variable as input, as the following code demonstrates.

```
DECLARE @n AS BIGINT = 5;

SELECT TOP (@n) orderid, orderdate, custid, empid
FROM Sales.Orders
ORDER BY orderdate DESC;
```

This query generates the following output.

```
orderid     orderdate               custid      empid
----------- ----------------------- ----------- -----------
11076       2008-05-06 00:00:00.000 9           4
11077       2008-05-06 00:00:00.000 65          1
11075       2008-05-06 00:00:00.000 68          8
11074       2008-05-06 00:00:00.000 73          7
11070       2008-05-05 00:00:00.000 44          2
```

In most cases, you need your TOP option to rely on some ordering specification, but as it turns out, an ORDER BY clause isn't mandatory. For example, the following query is technically valid.

```
SELECT TOP (3) orderid, orderdate, custid, empid
FROM Sales.Orders;
```

However, the query isn't deterministic. The query filters three rows, but you have no guarantee which three rows will be returned. You end up getting whichever three rows SQL Server happened to access first, and that's dependent on optimization. For example, this query gave the following output on one system.

```
orderid     orderdate               custid      empid
----------- ----------------------- ----------- -----------
11011       2008-04-09 00:00:00.000 1           3
10952       2008-03-16 00:00:00.000 1           1
10835       2008-01-15 00:00:00.000 1           1
```

But there's no guarantee that the same rows will be returned if you run the query again. If you are really after three arbitrary rows, it might be a good idea to add an ORDER BY clause with the expression (SELECT NULL) to let people know that your choice is intentional and not an oversight. Here's how your query would look.

```
SELECT TOP (3) orderid, orderdate, custid, empid
FROM Sales.Orders
ORDER BY (SELECT NULL);
```

Note that even when you do have an ORDER BY clause, in order for the query to be completely deterministic, the ordering must be unique. For example, consider again the first query from this section.

```
SELECT TOP (3) orderid, orderdate, custid, empid
FROM Sales.Orders
ORDER BY orderdate DESC;
```

The orderdate column isn't unique, so the ordering in case of ties is arbitrary. When this query was run, the system returned the following output.

```
orderid     orderdate               custid      empid
----------- ----------------------- ----------- -----------
11077       2008-05-06 00:00:00.000 65          1
11076       2008-05-06 00:00:00.000 9           4
11075       2008-05-06 00:00:00.000 68          8
```

But what if there are other rows in the result without TOP that have the same order date as in the last row here? You don't always care about guaranteeing deterministic or repeatable results; but if you do, two options are available to you. One option is to ask to include all ties with the last row by adding the WITH TIES option, as follows.

```
SELECT TOP (3) WITH TIES orderid, orderdate, custid, empid
FROM Sales.Orders
ORDER BY orderdate DESC;
```

Of course, this could result in returning more rows than you asked for, as the output of this query shows.

```
orderid     orderdate               custid      empid
----------- ----------------------- ----------- -----------
11077       2008-05-06 00:00:00.000 65          1
11076       2008-05-06 00:00:00.000 9           4
11075       2008-05-06 00:00:00.000 68          8
11074       2008-05-06 00:00:00.000 73          7
```

The other option to guarantee determinism is to break the ties by adding a tiebreaker that makes the ordering unique. For example, in case of ties in the order date, suppose you wanted the row with the greater order ID to "win." To do so, add orderid DESC to your ORDER BY clause, as follows.

```
SELECT TOP (3) orderid, orderdate, custid, empid
FROM Sales.Orders
ORDER BY orderdate DESC, orderid DESC;
```

Here's the output of this query.

```
orderid     orderdate               custid      empid
----------- ----------------------- ----------- -----------
11077       2008-05-06 00:00:00.000 65          1
11076       2008-05-06 00:00:00.000 9           4
11075       2008-05-06 00:00:00.000 68          8
```

The query is now deterministic, and the results are guaranteed to be repeatable, as long as the underlying data doesn't change.

To conclude this section, we'd just like to note that the TOP option can also be used in modification statements to limit how many rows get modified, but modifications are covered later in this Training Kit.

Filtering Data with OFFSET-FETCH

The OFFSET-FETCH option is a filtering option that, like TOP, you can use to filter data based on a specified number of rows and ordering. But unlike TOP, it is standard, and also has a skipping capability, making it useful for ad-hoc paging purposes.

The OFFSET and FETCH clauses appear right after the ORDER BY clause, and in fact, in T-SQL, they require an ORDER BY clause to be present. You first specify the OFFSET clause indicating how many rows you want to skip (0 if you don't want to skip any); you then optionally specify the FETCH clause indicating how many rows you want to filter. For example, the following query defines ordering based on order date descending, followed by order ID descending; it then skips 50 rows and fetches the next 25 rows.

```
SELECT orderid, orderdate, custid, empid
FROM Sales.Orders
ORDER BY orderdate DESC, orderid DESC
OFFSET 50 ROWS FETCH NEXT 25 ROWS ONLY;
```

Here's an abbreviated form of the output.

```
orderid     orderdate               custid      empid
----------- ----------------------- ----------- -----------
11027       2008-04-16 00:00:00.000 10          1
11026       2008-04-15 00:00:00.000 27          4
...
11004       2008-04-07 00:00:00.000 50          3
11003       2008-04-06 00:00:00.000 78          3
```

The ORDER BY clause now plays two roles: One role is telling the OFFSET-FETCH option which rows it needs to filter. Another role is determining presentation ordering in the query.

As mentioned, in T-SQL, the OFFSET-FETCH option requires an ORDER BY clause to be present. Also, in T-SQL—contrary to standard SQL—a FETCH clause requires an OFFSET clause to be present. So if you do want to filter some rows but skip none, you still need to specify the OFFSET clause with 0 ROWS.

In order to make the syntax intuitive, you can use the keywords NEXT or FIRST interchangeably. When skipping some rows, it might be more intuitive to you to use the keywords FETCH NEXT to indicate how many rows to filter; but when not skipping any rows, it might be more intuitive to you to use the keywords FETCH FIRST, as follows.

```
SELECT orderid, orderdate, custid, empid
FROM Sales.Orders
ORDER BY orderdate DESC, orderid DESC
OFFSET 0 ROWS FETCH FIRST 25 ROWS ONLY;
```

For similar reasons, you can use the singular form ROW or the plural form ROWS interchangeably, both for the number of rows to skip and for the number of rows to filter. But it's not like you will get an error if you say FETCH NEXT 1 ROWS or FETCH NEXT 25 ROW. It's up to you to use a proper form, just like with English.

While in T-SQL, a FETCH clause requires an OFFSET clause, and the OFFSET clause doesn't require a FETCH clause. In other words, by indicating an OFFSET clause, you're requesting to skip some rows; then by not indicating a FETCH clause, you're requesting to return all remaining rows. For example, the following query requests to skip 50 rows, returning all the rest.

```
SELECT orderid, orderdate, custid, empid
FROM Sales.Orders
ORDER BY orderdate DESC, orderid DESC
OFFSET 50 ROWS;
```

Here's an abbreviated form of the output.

```
orderid     orderdate               custid      empid
----------- ----------------------- ----------- -----------
11027       2008-04-16 00:00:00.000 10          1
11026       2008-04-15 00:00:00.000 27          4
...
10249       2006-07-05 00:00:00.000 79          6
10248       2006-07-04 00:00:00.000 85          5

(780 row(s) affected)
```

As mentioned earlier, the OFFSET-FETCH option requires an ORDER BY clause. But what if you need to filter a certain number of rows based on arbitrary order? To do so, you can specify the expression (SELECT NULL) in the ORDER BY clause, as follows.

```
SELECT orderid, orderdate, custid, empid
FROM Sales.Orders
ORDER BY (SELECT NULL)
OFFSET 0 ROWS FETCH FIRST 3 ROWS ONLY;
```

This code simply filters three arbitrary rows. Here's the output one system returned after running the code.

```
orderid     orderdate               custid      empid
----------- ----------------------- ----------- -----------
11011       2008-04-09 00:00:00.000 1           3
10952       2008-03-16 00:00:00.000 1           1
10835       2008-01-15 00:00:00.000 1           1
```

With both the OFFSET and the FETCH clauses, you can use expressions as inputs. This is very handy when you need to compute the input values dynamically. For example, suppose that you're implementing a paging concept where you return to the user one page of rows at a time. The user passes as input parameters to your procedure or a function the page number they are after (@pagenum parameter) and page size (@pagesize parameter). This means that you need to skip as many rows as @pagenum minus one times @pagesize, and fetch the next @pagesize rows. This can be implemented using the following code (using local variables for simplicity).

```
DECLARE @pagesize AS BIGINT = 25, @pagenum AS BIGINT = 3;

SELECT orderid, orderdate, custid, empid
FROM Sales.Orders
ORDER BY orderdate DESC, orderid DESC
OFFSET (@pagenum - 1) * @pagesize ROWS FETCH NEXT @pagesize ROWS ONLY;
```

With these inputs, the code returns the following output.

```
orderid     orderdate               custid      empid
----------- ----------------------- ----------- -----------
10477       2007-03-17 00:00:00.000 60          5
10476       2007-03-17 00:00:00.000 35          8
...
10454       2007-02-21 00:00:00.000 41          4
10453       2007-02-21 00:00:00.000 4           1

(25 row(s) affected)
```

You can feel free to change the input values and see how the result changes accordingly.

Because the OFFSET-FETCH option is standard and TOP isn't, in cases where they are logically equivalent, it's recommended to stick to the former. Remember that OFFSET-FETCH also has an advantage over TOP in the sense that it supports a skipping capability. However, for now, OFFSET-FETCH does not support options similar to TOP's PERCENT and WITH TIES.

From a performance standpoint, you should evaluate indexing the ORDER BY columns to support the TOP and OFFSET-FETCH options. Such indexing serves a very similar purpose to indexing filtered columns and can help avoid scanning unnecessary data as well as sorting.

Quick Check

1. **How do you guarantee deterministic results with TOP?**
2. **What are the benefits of using OFFSET-FETCH over TOP?**

Quick Check Answer

1. **By either returning all ties by using the WITH TIES option or by defining unique ordering to break ties.**
2. **OFFSET-FETCH is standard and TOP isn't; also, OFFSET-FETCH supports a skipping capability that TOP doesn't.**

PRACTICE Filtering Data with TOP and OFFSET-FETCH

In this practice, you exercise your knowledge of filtering data with TOP and OFFSET-FETCH.

If you encounter a problem completing an exercise, you can install the completed projects from the companion content for this chapter and lesson.

EXERCISE 1 Use the TOP Option

In this exercise, you practice using the TOP option to filter data.

1. Open SSMS and connect to the sample database TSQL2012.
2. You are tasked with writing a query against the Production.Products table, returning the five most expensive products from category 1. Write the following query.

   ```
   SELECT TOP (5) productid, unitprice
   FROM Production.Products
   WHERE categoryid = 1
   ORDER BY unitprice DESC;
   ```

   You get the following result set.

   ```
   productid   unitprice
   ----------- ---------------------
   38          263.50
   43          46.00
   2           19.00
   1           18.00
   35          18.00
   ```

   This query returns the desired result, except it doesn't have any handling of ties. In other words, the ordering among products with the same unit price is nondeterministic.
3. You are requested to provide solutions to turn the previous query into a deterministic one—one solution that includes ties and another that breaks the ties. First, address the version that includes all ties by using the WITH TIES option. Add this option to the query, as follows.

   ```
   SELECT TOP (5) WITH TIES productid, unitprice
   FROM Production.Products
   WHERE categoryid = 1
   ORDER BY unitprice DESC;
   ```

   You get the following output, which includes ties.

   ```
   productid   unitprice
   ----------- ---------------------
   38          263.50
   43          46.00
   2           19.00
   1           18.00
   39          18.00
   35          18.00
   76          18.00
   ```

4. Address the second version that breaks the ties by using productid, descending, as follows.

   ```
   SELECT TOP (5) productid, unitprice
   FROM Production.Products
   WHERE categoryid = 1
   ORDER BY unitprice DESC, productid DESC;
   ```

   This query generates the following output.

   ```
   productid   unitprice
   ----------- ---------------------
   38          263.50
   43          46.00
   2           19.00
   76          18.00
   39          18.00
   ```

EXERCISE 2 Use the OFFSET-FETCH Option

In this exercise, you practice using the OFFSET-FETCH option to filter data.

1. Open SSMS and connect to the sample database TSQL2012.
2. You are requested to write a set of queries that page through products, five at a time, in unit price ordering, using the product ID as the tie breaker. Start by writing a query that returns the first five products.

   ```
   SELECT productid, categoryid, unitprice
   FROM Production.Products
   ORDER BY unitprice, productid
   OFFSET 0 ROWS FETCH FIRST 5 ROWS ONLY;
   ```

   You could have used either the FIRST or the NEXT keyword, but say you decided to use FIRST because it was the more natural option when not skipping any rows. This query generates the following output.

   ```
   productid   categoryid  unitprice
   ----------- ----------- ---------------------
   33          4           2.50
   24          1           4.50
   13          8           6.00
   52          5           7.00
   54          6           7.45
   ```

3. Next, write a query that returns the next five rows (rows 6 through 10) using the following query.

   ```
   SELECT productid, categoryid, unitprice
   FROM Production.Products
   ORDER BY unitprice, productid
   OFFSET 5 ROWS FETCH NEXT 5 ROWS ONLY;
   ```

This time, use the NEXT keyword because you are skipping some rows. This query generates the following output.

```
productid   categoryid  unitprice
----------- ----------- ---------------------
75          1           7.75
23          5           9.00
19          3           9.20
45          8           9.50
47          3           9.50
```

4. Similarly, write the following query to return rows 11 through 15:

```
SELECT productid, categoryid, unitprice
FROM Production.Products
ORDER BY unitprice, productid
OFFSET 10 ROWS FETCH NEXT 5 ROWS ONLY;
```

This query generates the following output.

```
productid   categoryid  unitprice
----------- ----------- ---------------------
41          8           9.65
3           2           10.00
21          3           10.00
74          7           10.00
46          8           12.00
```

You would follow a similar process for subsequent pages.

Lesson Summary

- With the TOP and OFFSET-FETCH options, you can filter data based on a specified number of rows and ordering.
- The ORDER BY clause that is normally used in the query for presentation ordering is also used by TOP and OFFSET FETCH to indicate which rows to filter.
- The TOP option is a proprietary T-SQL feature that you can use to indicate a number or a percent of rows to filter.
- You can make a TOP query deterministic in two ways: one is by using the WITH TIES option to return all ties, and the other is by using unique ordering to break ties.
- The OFFSET-FETCH option is a standard option similar to TOP, supported by SQL Server 2012. Unlike TOP, it allows you to specify how many rows to skip before indicating how many rows to filter. As such, it can be used for ad-hoc paging purposes.
- Both TOP and OFFSET-FETCH support expressions as inputs and not just constants.

Lesson Review

Answer the following questions to test your knowledge of the information in this lesson. You can find the answers to these questions and explanations of why each answer choice is correct or incorrect in the "Answers" section at the end of this chapter.

1. You execute a query with a TOP (3) option. Which of the following options most accurately describes how many rows will be returned?
   - **A.** Fewer than three rows
   - **B.** Three rows or fewer
   - **C.** Three rows
   - **D.** Three rows or more
   - **E.** More than three rows
   - **F.** Fewer than three, three, or more than three rows
2. You execute a query with TOP (3) WITH TIES and nonunique ordering. Which of the following options most accurately describes how many rows will be returned?
   - **A.** Fewer than three rows
   - **B.** Three rows or fewer
   - **C.** Three rows
   - **D.** Three rows or more
   - **E.** More than three rows
   - **F.** Fewer than three, three, or more than three rows
3. Which of the following OFFSET-FETCH options are valid in T-SQL? (Choose all that apply.)
   - **A.** SELECT ... ORDER BY orderid OFFSET 25 ROWS
   - **B.** SELECT ... ORDER BY orderid FETCH NEXT 25 ROWS ONLY
   - **C.** SELECT ... ORDER BY orderid OFFSET 25 ROWS FETCH NEXT 25 ROWS ONLY
   - **D.** SELECT ... <no ORDER BY> OFFSET 0 ROWS FETCH FIRST 25 ROWS ONLY

Case Scenarios

In the following case scenarios, you apply what you've learned about filtering and sorting data. You can find the answers to these questions in the "Answers" section at the end of this chapter.

Case Scenario 1: Filtering and Sorting Performance Recommendations

You are hired as a consultant to help address query performance problems in a beer factory running SQL Server 2012. You trace a typical workload submitted to the system and observe very slow query run times. You see a lot of network traffic. You see that many queries return all rows to the client and then the client handles the filtering. Queries that do filter data often manipulate the filtered columns. All queries have ORDER BY clauses, and when you inquire about this, you are told that it's not really needed, but the developers got accustomed to doing so—just in case. You identify a lot of expensive sort operations. The customer is looking for recommendations to improve performance and asks you the following questions:

1. Can anything be done to improve the way filtering is handled?
2. Is there any harm in specifying ORDER BY even when the data doesn't need to be returned ordered?
3. Any recommendations related to queries with TOP and OFFSET-FETCH?

Case Scenario 2: Tutoring a Junior Developer

You are tutoring a junior developer regarding filtering and sorting data with T-SQL. The developer seems to be confused about certain topics and poses some questions to you. Answer the following to the best of your knowledge:

1. When I try to refer to a column alias that I defined in the SELECT list in the WHERE clause, I get an error. Can you explain why this isn't allowed and what the workarounds are?
2. Referring to a column alias in the ORDER BY clause seems to be supported. Why is that?
3. Why is it that Microsoft made it mandatory to specify an ORDER BY clause when using OFFSET-FETCH but not when using TOP? Does this mean that only TOP queries can have nondeterministic ordering?

Suggested Practices

To help you successfully master the exam objectives presented in this chapter, complete the following tasks.

Identify Logical Query Processing Phases and Compare Filters

To practice your knowledge of logical query processing, list the elements you've learned about so far in their right order.

- **Practice 1** In this chapter, you learned about using the WHERE clause to filter data based on predicates, the ORDER BY clause to sort data, and the TOP and OFFSET-FETCH options as another way to filter data. Combined with your knowledge from Chapter 1, list the query elements SELECT, FROM, WHERE, GROUP BY, HAVING, ORDER BY, TOP, and OFFSET-FETCH in correct logical query processing order. Note that because TOP and OFFSET-FETCH cannot be combined in the same query, you need to create two such lists.
- **Practice 2** List the capabilities that the OFFSET-FETCH filter has that aren't available to TOP in SQL Server 2012, and also the other way around.

Understand Determinism

Recall that a deterministic query is one that has only one correct result. To demonstrate your knowledge of query determinism, provide examples for deterministic and nondeterministic queries.

- **Practice 1** Provide examples for queries with deterministic and nondeterministic ordering. Describe in your own words what is required to get deterministic ordering.
- **Practice 2** Provide examples for deterministic and nondeterministic queries by using TOP and OFFSET-FETCH. Explain how you can enforce determinism in both cases.

Answers

This section contains the answers to the lesson review questions and solutions to the case scenarios in this chapter.

Lesson 1

1. **Correct Answer: B**

   A. Incorrect: NULL is not part of the three possible logical results of a predicate in T-SQL.

   B. Correct: Three-valued logic refers to true, false, and unknown.

   C. Incorrect: 1, 0, and NULL are not part of the three possible logical results of a predicate.

   D. Incorrect: -1, 0, and 1 are not part of the three possible logical results of a predicate.

2. **Correct Answers: A, B, and C**

   A. Correct: The form '2012-02-12' is language-neutral for the data types DATE, DATETIME2, and DATETIMEOFFSET, but language-dependent for DATETIME and SMALLDATETIME.

   B. Correct: The form '02/12/2012' is language-dependent.

   C. Correct: The form '12/02/2012' is language-dependent.

   D. Incorrect: The form '20120212' is language-neutral.

3. **Correct Answers: B and E**

   A. Incorrect: This predicate applies manipulation to the filtered column, and hence isn't a search argument.

   B. Correct: The LIKE predicate is a search argument when the pattern starts with a known prefix.

   C. Incorrect: The LIKE predicate isn't a search argument when the pattern starts with a wild card.

   D. Incorrect: The LIKE predicate isn't a search argument when the pattern starts with a wild card.

   E. Correct: Because no manipulation is applied to the filtered column, the predicate is a search argument.

Lesson 2

1. **Correct Answer: A**
   - **A. Correct:** Without an ORDER BY clause, ordering isn't guaranteed and is said to be arbitrary—it's optimization-dependent.
   - **B. Incorrect:** Without an ORDER BY clause, there's no guarantee for ordering.
   - **C. Incorrect:** Without an ORDER BY clause, there's no guarantee for ordering.
   - **D. Incorrect:** Without an ORDER BY clause, there's no guarantee for ordering.
2. **Correct Answer: C**
   - **A. Incorrect:** This uses ascending ordering for orderdate and descending just for orderid.
   - **B. Incorrect:** This is invalid syntax.
   - **C. Correct:** The correct syntax is to specify DESC after each expression whose ordering direction needs to be descending.
   - **D. Incorrect:** This is invalid syntax.
3. **Correct Answer: B, C, and D**
   - **A. Incorrect:** This is invalid syntax.
   - **B. Correct:** The default direction is ascending, so this clause uses ascending order for both orderdate and orderid.
   - **C. Correct:** This clause explicitly uses ascending order for both orderdate and orderid.
   - **D. Correct:** The default direction is ascending, so this clause uses ascending order for both orderdate and orderid.

Lesson 3

1. **Correct Answer: B**
   - **A. Incorrect:** If there are at least three rows in the query result without TOP, the query will return three rows.
   - **B. Correct:** If there are fewer rows than three in the query result without TOP, the query will return only those rows. If there are three rows or more without TOP, the query will return three rows.
   - **C. Incorrect:** If there are fewer rows than three in the query result without TOP, the query will return only those rows.
   - **D. Incorrect:** Unless the WITH TIES option is used, the query won't return more than the requested number of rows.
   - **E. Incorrect:** Unless the WITH TIES option is used, the query won't return more than the requested number of rows.
   - **F. Incorrect:** Unless the WITH TIES option is used, the query won't return more than the requested number of rows.

2. **Correct Answer: F**

   A. **Incorrect:** If there are at least three rows in the query result without TOP, the query will return at least three rows.

   B. **Incorrect:** If there are more than three rows in the result, as well as ties with the third row, the query will return more than three rows.

   C. **Incorrect:** If there are fewer rows than three in the query result without TOP, the query will return only those rows. If there are more than three rows in the result, as well as ties with the third row, the query will return more than three rows.

   D. **Incorrect:** If there are fewer rows than three in the query result without TOP, the query will return only those rows.

   E. **Incorrect:** If there are three rows or less in the query result without TOP, the query won't return more than three rows.

   F. **Correct:** If there are fewer rows than three in the query result without TOP, the query will return only those rows. If there are at least three rows in the result and no ties with the third, the query will return three rows. If there are more than three rows in the result, as well as ties with the third row, the query will return more than three rows.

3. **Correct Answer: A and C**

   A. **Correct:** T-SQL supports indicating an OFFSET clause without a FETCH clause.

   B. **Incorrect:** Contrary to standard SQL, T-SQL does not support a FETCH clause without an OFFSET clause.

   C. **Correct:** T-SQL supports indicating both OFFSET and FETCH clauses.

   D. **Incorrect:** T-SQL does not support OFFSET-FETCH without an ORDER BY clause.

Case Scenario 1

1. For one thing, as much filtering as possible should be done in the database. Doing most of the filtering in the client means that you're scanning more data, which increases the stress on the storage subsystem, and also that you cause unnecessary network traffic. When you do filter in the databases, for example by using the WHERE clause, you should use search arguments that increase the likelihood for efficient use of indexes. You should try as much as possible to avoid manipulating the filtered columns.

2. Adding an ORDER BY clause means that SQL Server needs to guarantee returning the rows in the requested order. If there are no existing indexes to support the ordering requirements, SQL Server will have no choice but to sort the data. Sorting is expensive with large sets. So the general recommendation is to avoid adding ORDER BY clauses to queries when there are no ordering requirements. And when you do need to return the rows in a particular order, consider arranging supporting indexes that can prevent SQL Server from needing to perform expensive sort operations.

3. The main way to help queries with TOP and OFFSET-FETCH perform well is by arranging indexes to support the ordering elements. This can prevent scanning all data, in addition to sorting.

Case Scenario 2

1. To be able to understand why you can't refer to an alias that was defined in the SELECT list in the WHERE clause, you need to understand logical query processing. Even though the keyed-in order of the clauses is SELECT-FROM-WHERE-GROUP BY-HAVING-ORDER BY, the logical query processing order is FROM-WHERE-GROUP BY-HAVING-SELECT-ORDER BY. As you can see, the WHERE clause is evaluated prior to the SELECT clause, and therefore aliases defined in the SELECT clause aren't visible to the WHERE clause.
2. Logical query processing order explains why the ORDER BY clause can refer to aliases defined in the SELECT clause. That's because the ORDER BY clause is logically evaluated after the SELECT clause.
3. The ORDER BY clause is mandatory when using OFFSET-FETCH because this clause is standard, and standard SQL decided to make it mandatory. Microsoft simply followed the standard. As for TOP, this feature is proprietary, and when Microsoft designed it, they chose to allow using TOP in a completely nondeterministic manner—without an ORDER BY clause. Note that the fact that OFFSET-FETCH requires an ORDER BY clause doesn't mean that you must use deterministic ordering. For example, if your ORDER BY list isn't unique, the ordering isn't deterministic. And if you want the ordering to be completely nondeterministic, you can specify ORDER BY (SELECT NULL) and then it's equivalent to not specifying an ORDER BY clause at all.

CHAPTER 4

Combining Sets

Exam objectives in this chapter:

- Work with Data
  - Query data by using SELECT statements.
  - Implement sub-queries.
- Modify Data
  - Combine datasets.

T-SQL provides a number of different ways to combine data from multiple tables; this chapter describes the different options. The chapter covers joins, subqueries, table expressions, the APPLY operator, and set operators.

Lessons in this chapter:

- Lesson 1: Using Joins
- Lesson 2: Using Subqueries, Table Expressions, and the APPLY Operator
- Lesson 3: Using Set Operators

Before You Begin

To complete the lessons in this chapter, you must have:

- Experience working with Microsoft SQL Server Management Studio (SSMS).
- Some experience writing T-SQL code.
- Access to a SQL Server 2012 instance with the sample database TSQL2012 installed.
- An understanding of filtering and sorting data.

Also, before you run the queries in this chapter, add a new supplier to the Production.Suppliers table by running the following code.

```
USE TSQL2012;

INSERT INTO Production.Suppliers
  (companyname, contactname, contacttitle, address, city, postalcode, country, phone)
  VALUES(N'Supplier XYZ', N'Jiru', N'Head of Security', N'42 Sekimai Musashino-shi',
         N'Tokyo', N'01759', N'Japan', N'(02) 4311-2609');
```

This supplier does not have any related products in the Production.Products table and is used in examples demonstrating nonmatches.

Lesson 1: Using Joins

Often, data that you need to query is spread across multiple tables. The more normalized the environment is, the more tables you usually have. The tables are usually related through keys, such as a foreign key in one side and a primary key in the other. Then you can use joins to query the data from the different tables and match the rows that need to be related. This lesson covers the different types of joins that T-SQL supports: cross, inner, and outer.

After this lesson, you will be able to:

- Write queries that use cross joins, inner joins, and outer joins.
- Describe the difference between the ON and WHERE clauses.
- Write queries that combine multiple joins.

Estimated lesson time: 60 minutes

Cross Joins

A *cross join* is the simplest type of join, though not the most commonly used one. This join performs what's known as a *Cartesian product* of the two input tables. In other words, it performs a multiplication between the tables, yielding a row for each combination of rows from both sides. If you have *m* rows in table T1 and *n* rows in table T2, the result of a cross join between T1 and T2 is a virtual table with $m \times n$ rows. Figure 4-1 provides an illustration of a cross join.

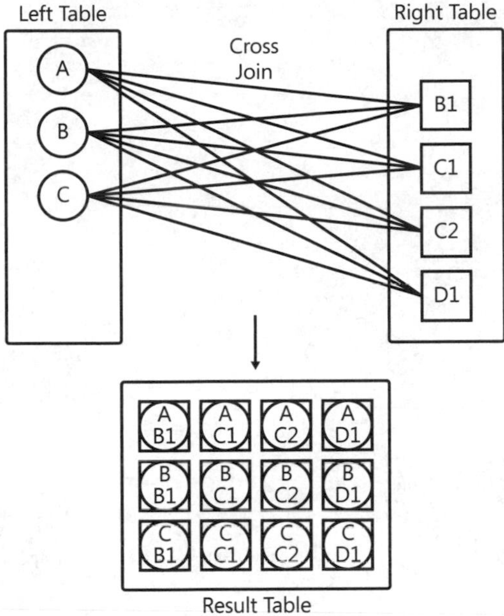

FIGURE 4-1 Cross join.

The left table has three rows with the key values A, B, and C. The right table has four rows with the key values B1, C1, C2, and D1. The result is a table with 12 rows containing all possible combinations of rows from the two input tables.

Consider an example from the TSQL2012 sample database. This database contains a table called dbo.Nums that has a column called n with a sequence of integers from 1 on. Your task is to use the Nums table to generate a result with a row for each weekday (1 through 7) and shift number (1 through 3), assuming there are three shifts a day. The result can later be used as the basis for building information about activities in the different shifts in the different days. With seven days in the week and three shifts every day, the result should have 21 rows.

Here's a query that achieves the task by performing a cross join between two instances of the Nums table—one representing the days (aliased as D), and the other representing the shifts (aliased as S).

```
SELECT D.n AS theday, S.n AS shiftno
FROM dbo.Nums AS D
  CROSS JOIN dbo.Nums AS S
WHERE D.n <= 7
  AND S.N <= 3
ORDER BY theday, shiftno;
```

Here's the output of this query.

```
theday      shiftno
----------- -----------
1           1
1           2
1           3
2           1
2           2
2           3
3           1
3           2
3           3
4           1
4           2
4           3
5           1
5           2
5           3
6           1
6           2
6           3
7           1
7           2
7           3
```

The Nums table has 100,000 rows. According to logical query processing, the first step in the processing of the query is evaluating the FROM clause. The cross join operates in the FROM clause, performing a Cartesian product between the two instances of Nums, yielding a table with 10,000,000,000 rows (not to worry, that's only conceptually). Then the WHERE clause filters only the rows where the column D.n is less than or equal to 7, and the column S.n is less than or equal to 3. After applying the filter, the result has 21 qualifying rows. The SELECT clause then returns D.n naming it theday, and S.n naming it shiftno.

Fortunately, SQL Server doesn't have to follow logical query processing literally as long as it can return the correct result. That's what optimization is all about—returning the result as fast as possible. SQL Server knows that with a cross join followed by a filter it can evaluate the filters first (which is especially efficient when there are indexes to support the filters), and then match the remaining rows.

Note the importance of aliasing the tables in the join. For one, it's convenient to refer to a table by using a shorter name. But in a self-join like ours, table aliasing is mandatory. If you don't assign different aliases to the two instances of the table, you end up with an invalid result because there are duplicate column names even when including the table name as a prefix. By aliasing the tables differently, you can refer to columns in an unambiguous way using the form table_alias.column_name, as in D.n vs. S.n.

Also note that in addition to supporting the syntax for cross joins with the CROSS JOIN keywords, both standard SQL and T-SQL support an older syntax where you specify a comma between the table names, as in FROM T1, T2. However, for a number of reasons, it is recommended to stick to the newer syntax; it is less prone to errors and allows for more consistent code.

Inner Joins

With an *inner join*, you can match rows from two tables based on a predicate—usually one that compares a primary key value in one side to a foreign key value in another side. Figure 4-2 illustrates an inner join.

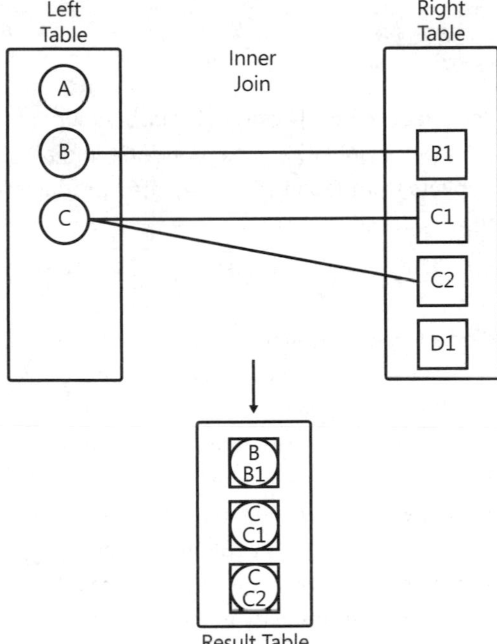

FIGURE 4-2 Inner join.

The letters represent primary key values in the left table and foreign key values in the right table. Assuming the join is an equijoin (using a predicate with an equality operator such as lefttable.keycol = righttable.keycol), the inner join returns only matching rows for which the predicate evaluates to true. Rows for which the predicate evaluates to false or unknown are discarded.

As an example, the following query returns suppliers from Japan and the products they supply.

```
SELECT
  S.companyname AS supplier, S.country,
  P.productid, P.productname, P.unitprice
FROM Production.Suppliers AS S
  INNER JOIN Production.Products AS P
    ON S.supplierid = P.supplierid
WHERE S.country = N'Japan';
```

Here's the output of this query.

```
supplier        country  productid   productname    unitprice
--------------- -------- ----------- -------------- ----------
Supplier QOVFD  Japan    9           Product AOZBW  97.00
Supplier QOVFD  Japan    10          Product YHXGE  31.00
Supplier QOVFD  Japan    74          Product BKAZJ  10.00
Supplier QWUSF  Japan    13          Product POXFU  6.00
Supplier QWUSF  Japan    14          Product PWCJB  23.25
Supplier QWUSF  Japan    15          Product KSZOI  15.50
```

Observe that the join's matching predicate is specified in the ON clause. It matches suppliers and products that share the same supplier ID. Rows from either side that don't find a match in the other are discarded. For example, suppliers from Japan with no related products aren't returned.

EXAM TIP

Often, when joining tables, you join them based on a foreign key–unique key relationship. For example, there's a foreign key defined on the supplierid column in the Production .Products table (the referencing table), referencing the primary key column supplierid in the Production.Suppliers table (the referenced table). It's also important to note that when you define a primary key or unique constraint, SQL Server creates a unique index on the constraint columns to enforce the constraint's uniqueness property. But when you define a foreign key, SQL Server doesn't create any indexes on the foreign key columns. Such indexes could improve the performance of joins based on those relationships. Because SQL Server doesn't create such indexes automatically, it's your responsibility to identify the cases where they can be useful and create them. So when working on index tuning, one interesting area to examine is foreign key columns, and evaluating the benefits of creating indexes on those.

Regarding the last query, again, notice the convenience of using short table aliases when needing to refer to ambiguous column names like supplierid. Observe that the query uses table aliases to prefix even nonambiguous column names such as s.country. This practice isn't mandatory as long as the column name is not ambiguous, but it is still considered a best practice for clarity.

A very common question is, "What's the difference between the ON and the WHERE clauses, and does it matter if you specify your predicate in one or the other?" The answer is that for inner joins it doesn't matter. Both clauses perform the same filtering purpose. Both filter only rows for which the predicate evaluates to true and discard rows for which the predicate evaluates to false or unknown. In terms of logical query processing, the WHERE is evaluated right after the FROM, so conceptually it is equivalent to concatenating the predicates with an AND operator. SQL Server knows this, and therefore can internally rearrange the order in which it evaluates the predicates in practice, and it does so based on cost estimates.

For these reasons, if you wanted, you could rearrange the placement of the predicates from the previous query, specifying both in the ON clause, and still retain the original meaning, as follows.

```
SELECT
  S.companyname AS supplier, S.country,
  P.productid, P.productname, P.unitprice
FROM Production.Suppliers AS S
  INNER JOIN Production.Products AS P
    ON S.supplierid = P.supplierid
    AND S.country = N'Japan';
```

For many people, though, it's intuitive to specify the predicate that matches columns from both sides in the ON clause, and predicates that filter columns from only one side in the WHERE clause. But again, with inner joins it doesn't matter. In the discussion of outer joins in the next section, you will see that, with those, ON and WHERE play different roles; you need to figure out, according to your needs, which is the appropriate clause for each of your predicates.

As another example for an inner join, the following query joins two instances of the HR.Employees table to match employees with their managers. (A manager is also an employee, hence the self-join.)

```
SELECT E.empid,
  E.firstname + N' ' + E.lastname AS emp,
  M.firstname + N' ' + M.lastname AS mgr
FROM HR.Employees AS E
  INNER JOIN HR.Employees AS M
    ON E.mgrid = M.empid;
```

Here's the output of this query.

```
empid  emp                 mgr
------ ------------------- -----------
2      Don Funk            Sara Davis
3      Judy Lew            Don Funk
4      Yael Peled          Judy Lew
5      Sven Buck           Don Funk
6      Paul Suurs          Sven Buck
7      Russell King        Sven Buck
8      Maria Cameron       Judy Lew
9      Zoya Dolgopyatova   Sven Buck
```

Observe the join predicate: ON E.mgrid = M.empid. The employee instance is aliased as E and the manager instance as M. To find the right matches, the employee's manager ID needs to be equal to the manager's employee ID.

Note that only eight rows were returned even though there are nine rows in the table. The reason is that the CEO (Sara Davis, employee ID 1) has no manager, and therefore, her mgrid column is NULL. Remember that an inner join does not return rows that don't find matches.

As with cross joins, both standard SQL and T-SQL support an older syntax for inner joins where you specify a comma between the table names, and then all predicates in the WHERE clause. But as mentioned, it is considered a best practice to stick to the newer syntax with the JOIN keyword. When using the older syntax, if you forget to indicate the join predicate, you end up with an unintentional cross join. When using the newer syntax, an inner join isn't valid syntactically without an ON clause, so if you forget to indicate the join predicate, the parser will generate an error.

Because an inner join is the most commonly used type of join, the standard decided to make it the default in case you specify just the JOIN keyword. So T1 JOIN T2 is equivalent to T1 INNER JOIN T2.

Outer Joins

With *outer joins*, you can request to preserve all rows from one or both sides of the join, never mind if there are matching rows in the other side based on the ON predicate.

By using the keywords LEFT OUTER JOIN (or LEFT JOIN for short), you ask to preserve the left table. The join returns what an inner join normally would—that is, matches (call those inner rows). In addition, the join also returns rows from the left that had no matches in the right table (call those outer rows), with NULLs used as placeholders in the right side. Figure 4-3 shows an illustration of a left outer join.

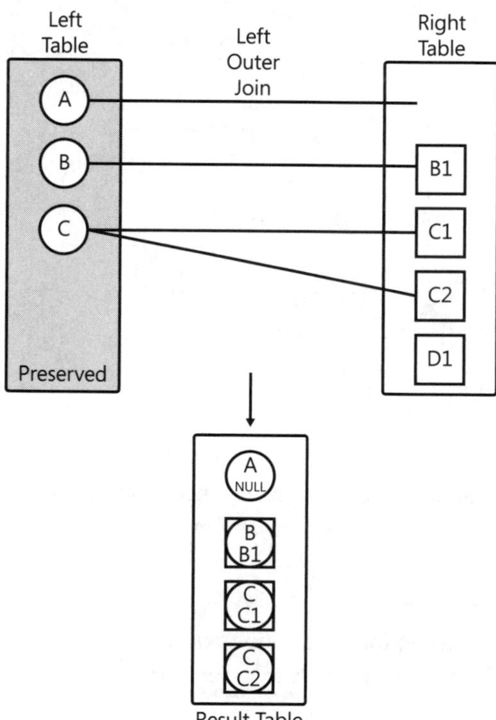

FIGURE 4-3 Left outer join.

Unlike in the inner join, the left row with the key A is returned even though it had no match in the right side. It's returned with NULLs as placeholders in the right side.

As an example, the following query returns suppliers from Japan and the products they supply, including suppliers from Japan that don't have related products.

```
SELECT
  S.companyname AS supplier, S.country,
  P.productid, P.productname, P.unitprice
FROM Production.Suppliers AS S
  LEFT OUTER JOIN Production.Products AS P
    ON S.supplierid = P.supplierid
WHERE S.country = N'Japan';
```

Here's the output of this query.

```
supplier        country  productid  productname    unitprice
--------------- -------- ---------- -------------- ----------
Supplier QOVFD  Japan    9          Product AOZBW  97.00
Supplier QOVFD  Japan    10         Product YHXGE  31.00
Supplier QOVFD  Japan    74         Product BKAZJ  10.00
Supplier QWUSF  Japan    13         Product POXFU  6.00
Supplier QWUSF  Japan    14         Product PWCJB  23.25
Supplier QWUSF  Japan    15         Product KSZOI  15.50
Supplier XYZ    Japan    NULL       NULL           NULL
```

Because the Production.Suppliers table is the preserved side of the join, Supplier XYZ is returned even though it has no matching products. As you recall, an inner join did not return this supplier.

It is very important to understand that, with outer joins, the ON and WHERE clauses play very different roles, and therefore, they aren't interchangeable. The WHERE clause still plays a simple filtering role—namely, it keeps true cases and discards false and unknown cases. In our query, the WHERE clause filters only suppliers from Japan, so suppliers that aren't from Japan simply don't show up in the output.

However, the ON clause doesn't play a simple filtering role; rather, it's more a *matching* role. In other words, a row in the preserved side will be returned whether the ON predicate finds a match for it or not. So the ON predicate only determines which rows from the non-preserved side get matched to rows from the preserved side—not whether to return the rows from the preserved side. In our query, the ON clause matches rows from both sides by comparing their supplier ID values. Because it's a matching predicate (as opposed to a filter), the join won't discard suppliers; instead, it only determines which products get matched to each supplier. But even if a supplier has no matches based on the ON predicate, the supplier is still returned. In other words, ON is not final with respect to the preserved side of the join. WHERE is final. So when in doubt whether to specify the predicate in the ON or WHERE clauses, ask yourself: Is the predicate used to filter or match? Is it supposed to be final or nonfinal?

Can you guess what happens if you specify both the predicate that compares the supplier IDs from both sides and the one comparing the supplier country to Japan in the ON clause? Try it.

```
SELECT
  S.companyname AS supplier, S.country,
  P.productid, P.productname, P.unitprice
FROM Production.Suppliers AS S
  LEFT OUTER JOIN Production.Products AS P
    ON S.supplierid = P.supplierid
   AND S.country = N'Japan';
```

Observe what's different in the result (shown here in abbreviated form) and see if you can explain in your own words what the query returns now.

```
supplier        country  productid  productname    unitprice
--------------- -------- ---------- -------------- ----------
Supplier SWRXU  UK       NULL       NULL           NULL
Supplier VHQZD  USA      NULL       NULL           NULL
Supplier STUAZ  USA      NULL       NULL           NULL
Supplier QOVFD  Japan    9          Product AOZBW  97.00
Supplier QOVFD  Japan    10         Product YHXGE  31.00
Supplier QOVFD  Japan    74         Product BKAZJ  10.00
Supplier EQPNC  Spain    NULL       NULL           NULL
...
```

Now that both predicates appear in the ON clause, both serve a matching purpose. What this means is that all suppliers are returned—even those that aren't from Japan. But in order to match a product to a supplier, the supplier IDs in both sides need to match, and the supplier country needs to be Japan.

Back to the query that matched employees and their managers: Remember that the inner join eliminated the CEO's row because it found no matching manager. If you want to include the CEO's row, you need to use an outer join preserving the side representing the employees (E), as follows.

```
SELECT E.empid,
  E.firstname + N' ' + E.lastname AS emp,
  M.firstname + N' ' + M.lastname AS mgr
FROM HR.Employees AS E
  LEFT OUTER JOIN HR.Employees AS M
    ON E.mgrid = M.empid;
```

Here's the output of this query, this time including the CEO's row.

```
empid  emp                mgr
------ ------------------ -----------
1      Sara Davis         NULL
2      Don Funk           Sara Davis
3      Judy Lew           Don Funk
4      Yael Peled         Judy Lew
5      Sven Buck          Don Funk
6      Paul Suurs         Sven Buck
7      Russell King       Sven Buck
8      Maria Cameron      Judy Lew
9      Zoya Dolgopyatova  Sven Buck
```

Just like you can use a left outer join to preserve the left side, you can use a right outer join to preserve the right side. Use the keywords RIGHT OUTER JOIN (or RIGHT JOIN in short). Figure 4-4 shows an illustration of a right outer join.

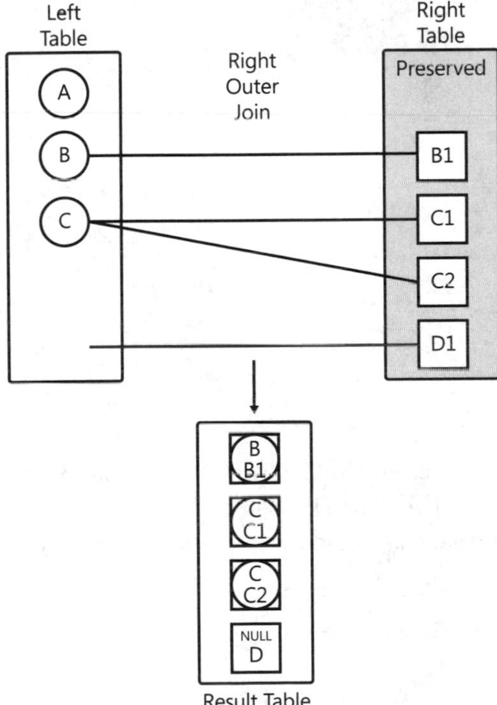

FIGURE 4-4 Right outer join.

T-SQL also supports a full outer join (FULL OUTER JOIN, or FULL JOIN in short), that preserves both sides. Figure 4-5 shows an illustration of this type of join.

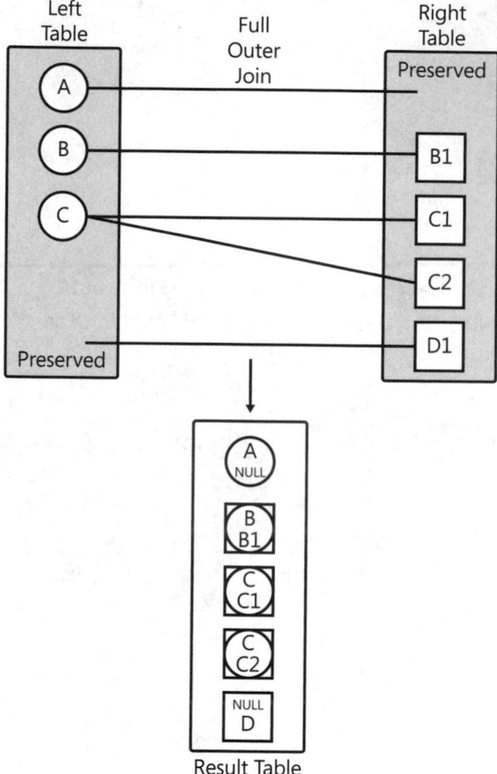

FIGURE 4-5 Full outer join.

A full outer join returns the inner rows that are normally returned from an inner join; plus rows from the left that don't have matches in the right, with NULLs used as placeholders in the right side; plus rows from the right that don't have matches in the left, with NULLs used as placeholders in the left side.

Multi-Join Queries

It's important to remember that a join in T-SQL takes place conceptually between two tables at a time. A multi-join query evaluates the joins conceptually from left to right. So the result of one join is used as the left input to the next join. If you don't understand this, you can end up with logical bugs, especially when outer joins are involved. (With inner and cross joins, the order cannot affect the meaning.)

As an example, suppose that you wanted to return all suppliers from Japan, and matching products where relevant. For this, you need an outer join between Production.Suppliers and Production.Products, preserving Suppliers. But you also want to include product category information, so you add an inner join to Production.Categories, as follows.

```
SELECT
  S.companyname AS supplier, S.country,
  P.productid, P.productname, P.unitprice,
  C.categoryname
FROM Production.Suppliers AS S
  LEFT OUTER JOIN Production.Products AS P
    ON S.supplierid = P.supplierid
  INNER JOIN Production.Categories AS C
    ON C.categoryid = P.categoryid
WHERE S.country = N'Japan';
```

Look at the output of this query.

```
supplier        country  productid  productname    unitprice  categoryname
--------------- -------- ---------- -------------- ---------- --------------
Supplier QOVFD  Japan    9          Product AOZBW  97.00      Meat/Poultry
Supplier QOVFD  Japan    10         Product YHXGE  31.00      Seafood
Supplier QOVFD  Japan    74         Product BKAZJ  10.00      Produce
Supplier QWUSF  Japan    13         Product POXFU  6.00       Seafood
Supplier QWUSF  Japan    14         Product PWCJB  23.25      Produce
Supplier QWUSF  Japan    15         Product KSZOI  15.50      Condiments
```

Supplier XYZ from Japan was discarded. Can you explain why?

Conceptually, the first join included outer rows (suppliers with no products) but produced NULLs in the product attributes in those rows. Then the join to Production.Categories compared the NULL categoryid values in the outer rows to categoryid values in Production. Categories, and discarded those rows. In short, the inner join that followed the outer join nullified the outer part of the join.

There are a number of ways to address this problem, but probably the most natural is to use an interesting capability in the language—separate some of the joins to their own independent logical phase. What you're after is a left outer join between Production.Suppliers and the result of the inner join between Production.Products and Production.Categories. You can phrase your query exactly like this.

```
SELECT
  S.companyname AS supplier, S.country,
  P.productid, P.productname, P.unitprice,
  C.categoryname
FROM Production.Suppliers AS S
  LEFT OUTER JOIN
    (Production.Products AS P
       INNER JOIN Production.Categories AS C
         ON C.categoryid = P.categoryid)
    ON S.supplierid = P.supplierid
WHERE S.country = N'Japan';
```

Now the result retains suppliers from Japan without products.

```
supplier        country  productid  productname    unitprice  categoryname
--------------- -------- ---------- -------------- ---------- -------------
Supplier QOVFD  Japan    9          Product AOZBW  97.00      Meat/Poultry
Supplier QOVFD  Japan    10         Product YHXGE  31.00      Seafood
Supplier QOVFD  Japan    74         Product BKAZJ  10.00      Produce
Supplier QWUSF  Japan    13         Product POXFU  6.00       Seafood
Supplier QWUSF  Japan    14         Product PWCJB  23.25      Produce
Supplier QWUSF  Japan    15         Product KSZOI  15.50      Condiments
Supplier XYZ    Japan    NULL       NULL           NULL       NULL
```

This aspect of the language can indeed be confusing, but fortunately there is a fix.

Interestingly, outer joins have only one standard syntax—based on the JOIN keyword and the ON clause. In fact, the introduction of outer joins to the standard is what led to changing the syntax, where the standard realized the need for separation between the clauses where you specify the matching predicate (ON) and the filter predicate (WHERE). Then, probably for consistency's sake, the standard added support for similar syntax based on the JOIN keyword for cross and inner joins.

Quick Check

1. **What is the difference between the old and new syntax for cross joins?**
2. **What are the different types of outer joins?**

Quick Check Answer

1. **The new syntax has the CROSS JOIN keywords between the table names and the old syntax has a comma.**
2. **Left, right, and full.**

PRACTICE Using Joins

In this practice, you exercise your knowledge of joins.

EXERCISE 1 Match Customers and Orders with Inner Joins

In this exercise, you practice matching customers and orders by using inner joins.

1. Open SSMS and connect to the sample database TSQL2012.
2. Write a query that matches customers with their respective orders, returning only matches. You are not required to return customers with no related orders.

Issue the following query by using an inner join.

```
USE TSQL2012;

SELECT C.custid, C.companyname, O.orderid, O.orderdate
FROM Sales.Customers AS C
  INNER JOIN Sales.Orders AS O
    ON C.custid = O.custid;
```

This query generates the following output:

```
custid  companyname     orderid  orderdate
------- --------------- -------- -----------------------
85      Customer ENQZT  10248    2006-07-04 00:00:00.000
79      Customer FAPSM  10249    2006-07-05 00:00:00.000
34      Customer IBVRG  10250    2006-07-08 00:00:00.000
...

(830 rows affected)
```

EXERCISE 2 Match Customers and Orders with Outer Joins

In this exercise, you practice matching customers and orders by using outer joins.

1. You start with the query you wrote in step 2 of Exercise 1. Revise your query to also include customers without orders. Alter the join type to a left outer join, as follows.

```
SELECT C.custid, C.companyname, O.orderid, O.orderdate
FROM Sales.Customers AS C
  LEFT OUTER JOIN Sales.Orders AS O
    ON C.custid = O.custid;
```

The output now also includes customers without orders, with NULLs in the order attributes.

```
custid  companyname     orderid  orderdate
------- --------------- -------- -----------------------
85      Customer ENQZT  10248    2006-07-04 00:00:00.000
79      Customer FAPSM  10249    2006-07-05 00:00:00.000
34      Customer IBVRG  10250    2006-07-08 00:00:00.000
...
22      Customer DTDMN  NULL     NULL
57      Customer WVAXS  NULL     NULL

(832 rows affected)
```

2. Return only customers without orders. To achieve this, add to the previous query a WHERE clause that filters only rows with a NULL in the key from the nonpreserved side (O.orderid), as follows.

```
SELECT C.custid, C.companyname, O.orderid, O.orderdate
FROM Sales.Customers AS C
  LEFT OUTER JOIN Sales.Orders AS O
    ON C.custid = O.custid
WHERE O.orderid IS NULL;
```

The output shows that there are two customers without orders.

```
custid  companyname      orderid  orderdate
------- ---------------- -------- -------------------------
22      Customer DTDMN   NULL     NULL
57      Customer WVAXS   NULL     NULL
```

3. Write a query that returns all customers, but match orders only if they were placed in February 2008. Because both the comparison between the customer's customer ID and the order's customer ID, and the date range are considered part of the matching logic, both should appear in the ON clause, as follows.

```
SELECT C.custid, C.companyname, O.orderid, O.orderdate
FROM Sales.Customers AS C
  LEFT OUTER JOIN Sales.Orders AS O
    ON C.custid = O.custid
   AND O.orderdate >= '20080201'
   AND O.orderdate < '20080301';
```

This query returns 110 rows; here's a portion of the output.

```
custid  companyname      orderid  orderdate
------- ---------------- -------- -------------------------
1       Customer NRZBB   NULL     NULL
2       Customer MLTDN   NULL     NULL
3       Customer KBUDE   NULL     NULL
4       Customer HFBZG   10864    2008-02-02 00:00:00.000
5       Customer HGVLZ   10866    2008-02-03 00:00:00.000
5       Customer HGVLZ   10875    2008-02-06 00:00:00.000
...
```

If you specify the date range predicate in the WHERE clause, customers who did not place orders in that month will be filtered out, and that's not what you want.

Lesson Summary

- Cross joins return a Cartesian product of the rows from both sides.
- Inner joins match rows based on a predicate and return only matches.
- Outer joins match rows based on a predicate and return both matches and non-matches from the tables marked as preserved.
- Multi-join queries involve multiple joins. They can have a mix of different join types. You can control the logical join ordering by using parentheses and by repositioning the ON clauses.

Lesson Review

Answer the following questions to test your knowledge of the information in this lesson. You can find the answers to these questions and explanations of why each answer choice is correct or incorrect in the "Answers" section at the end of this chapter.

1. What is the difference between the ON clause and the WHERE clause?
   - **A.** The ON clause uses two-valued logic and the WHERE clause uses three-valued logic.
   - **B.** The ON clause uses three-valued logic and the WHERE clause uses two-valued logic.
   - **C.** In outer joins, the ON clause determines filtering and the WHERE clause determines matching.
   - **D.** In outer joins, the ON clause determines matching and the WHERE clause determines filtering.
2. Which keywords can be omitted in the new standard join syntax without changing the meaning of the join? (Choose all that apply.)
   - **A.** JOIN
   - **B.** CROSS
   - **C.** INNER
   - **D.** OUTER
3. Which syntax is recommended to use for cross joins and inner joins, and why?
   - **A.** The syntax with the JOIN keyword because it's consistent with outer join syntax and is less prone to errors.
   - **B.** The syntax with the comma between the table names because it's consistent with outer join syntax and is less prone to errors.
   - **C.** It is recommended to avoid using cross and inner joins.
   - **D.** It is recommended to use only lowercase characters and omit default keywords, as in join instead of INNER JOIN because it increases energy consumption.

Lesson 2: Using Subqueries, Table Expressions, and the APPLY Operator

T-SQL supports nesting of queries. This is a convenient part of the language that you can use to refer to one query's result from another. You do not need to store the result of one query in a variable in order to be able to refer to that result from another query. This lesson covers the different types of subqueries. This lesson also covers the use of table expressions, which are named queries. Finally, this lesson also covers the APPLY table operator.

After this lesson, you will be able to:

- Use self-contained subqueries and correlated subqueries.
- Use subqueries that return scalar, multi-valued, and table-valued results.
- Use derived tables and common table expressions (CTEs) in your queries.
- Create and use views and inline table-valued functions.
- Use the APPLY operator.

Estimated lesson time: 60 minutes

Subqueries

Subqueries can be self-contained—namely, independent of the outer query; or they can be correlated—namely, having a reference to a column from the table in the outer query. In terms of the result of the subquery, it can be scalar, multi-valued, or table-valued.

This section starts by covering the simpler self-contained subqueries and then continues to correlated subqueries.

Self-Contained Subqueries

Self-contained subqueries are subqueries that have no dependency on the outer query. If you want, you can highlight the inner query and run it independently. This makes the troubleshooting of problems with self-contained subqueries easier compared to correlated subqueries.

As mentioned, a subquery can return different forms of results. It can return a single value, multiple values, or even an entire table result. Table-valued subqueries, or table expressions, are discussed in the section "Views and Inline Table-Valued Functions" later in this chapter.

Subqueries that return a single value, or scalar subqueries, can be used where a single-valued expression is expected, like in one side of a comparison. For example, the following query uses a self-contained subquery to return the products with the minimum unit price.

```
SELECT productid, productname, unitprice
FROM Production.Products
WHERE unitprice =
  (SELECT MIN(unitprice)
   FROM Production.Products);
```

Here's the output of this query.

```
productid  productname     unitprice
---------- -------------- ----------
33         Product ASTMN  2.50
```

As you can see, the subquery returns the minimum unit price from the Production.Products table. The outer query then returns information about products with the minimum unit price. Try highlighting only the inner query and executing it, and you will find that this is possible.

Note that if what's supposed to be a scalar subquery returns in practice more than one value, the code fails at run time. If the scalar subquery returns an empty set, it is converted to a NULL.

A subquery can also return multiple values in the form of a single column. Such a subquery can be used where a multi-valued result is expected—for example, when using the IN predicate. As an example, the following query uses a multi-valued subquery to return products supplied by suppliers from Japan.

```
SELECT productid, productname, unitprice
FROM Production.Products
WHERE supplierid IN
  (SELECT supplierid
   FROM Production.Suppliers
   WHERE country = N'Japan');
```

This query generates the following output.

```
productid  productname    unitprice
---------- -------------- ----------
9          Product AOZBW  97.00
10         Product YHXGE  31.00
74         Product BKAZJ  10.00
13         Product POXFU  6.00
14         Product PWCJB  23.25
15         Product KSZOI  15.50
```

The inner query returns supplier IDs of suppliers from Japan. The outer query then returns information about products whose supplier ID is in the set returned by the subquery. As with predicates in general, you can negate an IN predicate, so if you wanted to return products supplied by suppliers that are not from Japan, simply change IN to NOT IN.

Correlated Subqueries

Correlated subqueries are subqueries where the inner query has a reference to a column from the table in the outer query. They are trickier to work with compared to self-contained subqueries because you can't just highlight the inner portion and run it independently.

As an example, suppose that you need to return products with the minimum unit price per category. You can use a correlated subquery to return the minimum unit price out of the products where the category ID is equal to the one in the outer row (the correlation), as follows.

```
SELECT categoryid, productid, productname, unitprice
FROM Production.Products AS P1
WHERE unitprice =
  (SELECT MIN(unitprice)
   FROM Production.Products AS P2
   WHERE P2.categoryid = P1.categoryid);
```

This query generates the following output.

```
categoryid  productid  productname    unitprice
----------- ---------- -------------- ----------
1           24         Product QOGNU  4.50
2           3          Product IMEHJ  10.00
3           19         Product XKXDO  9.20
4           33         Product ASTMN  2.50
5           52         Product QSRXF  7.00
6           54         Product QAQRL  7.45
7           74         Product BKAZJ  10.00
8           13         Product POXFU  6.00
```

Notice that the outer query and the inner query refer to different instances of the same table, Production.Products. In order for the subquery to be able to distinguish between the two, you must assign different aliases to the different instances. The query assigns the alias P1 to the outer instance and P2 to the inner instance, and by using the table alias as a prefix, you can refer to columns in an unambiguous way. The subquery uses a correlation in the predicate P2.categoryid = P1.categoryid, meaning that it filters only the products where the category ID is equal to the one in the outer row. So when the outer row has category ID 1, the inner query returns the minimum unit price out of all products where the category ID is 1; when the outer row has category ID 2, the inner query returns the minimum unit price out of all products where the category ID is 2; and so on.

As another example of a correlated subquery, the following query returns customers who placed orders on February 12, 2007.

```
SELECT custid, companyname
FROM Sales.Customers AS C
WHERE EXISTS
  (SELECT *
   FROM Sales.Orders AS O
   WHERE O.custid = C.custid
     AND O.orderdate = '20070212');
```

This query generates the following output.

```
custid  companyname
------- ---------------
5       Customer HGVLZ
66      Customer LHANT
```

The EXISTS predicate accepts a subquery as input and returns true when the subquery returns at least one row and false otherwise. In this case, the subquery returns orders placed by the customer whose ID is equal to the customer ID in the outer row (the correlation) and where the order date is February 12, 2007. So the outer query returns a customer only if there's at least one order placed by that customer on the date in question.

As a predicate, EXISTS doesn't need to return the result set of the subquery; rather, it returns only true or false, depending on whether the subquery returns any rows. For this reason, the SQL Server Query Optimizer ignores the SELECT list of the subquery, and therefore, whatever you specify there will not affect optimization choices like index selection.

As with other predicates, you can negate the EXISTS predicate as well. The following query negates the previous query's predicate, returning customers who did not place orders on February 12, 2007.

```
SELECT custid, companyname
FROM Sales.Customers AS C
WHERE NOT EXISTS
  (SELECT *
   FROM Sales.Orders AS O
   WHERE O.custid = C.custid
     AND O.orderdate = '20070212');
```

This query generates the following output, shown here in abbreviated form.

```
custid  companyname
------- ---------------
72      Customer AHPOP
58      Customer AHXHT
25      Customer AZJED
18      Customer BSVAR
91      Customer CCFIZ
...
```

Table Expressions

Table expressions are named queries. You write an inner query that returns a relational result set, name it, and query it from an outer query. T-SQL supports four forms of table expressions:

- Derived tables
- Common table expressions (CTEs)
- Views
- Inline table-valued functions

The first two are visible only to the statement that defines them. As for the last two, you preserve the definition of the table expression in the database as an object; therefore, it's reusable, and you can also control access to the object with permissions.

Note that because a table expression is supposed to represent a relation, the inner query defining it needs to be relational. This means that all columns returned by the inner query must have names (use aliases if the column is a result of an expression), and all column names must be unique. Also, the inner query is not allowed to have an ORDER BY clause. (Remember, a set has no order.) There's an exception to the last rule: If you use the TOP or OFFSET-FETCH option in the inner query, the ORDER BY serves a meaning that is not related to presentation ordering; rather, it's part of the filter's specification. So if the inner query uses the TOP or OFFSET-FETCH option, it's allowed to have an ORDER BY clause as well. But then the outer query has no presentation ordering guarantees if it doesn't have its own ORDER BY clause.

IMPORTANT **OPTIMIZATION OF TABLE EXPRESSIONS**

It's important to note that, from a performance standpoint, when SQL Server optimizes queries involving table expressions, it first unnests the table expression's logic, and therefore interacts with the underlying tables directly. It does not somehow persist the table expression's result in an internal work table and then interact with that work table. This means that table expressions don't have a performance side to them—neither good nor bad—just no side.

Now that you understand the requirements of the inner query, you are ready to learn about the different forms of table expressions that T-SQL supports.

Derived Tables

A derived table is probably the form of table expression that most closely resembles a subquery—only a subquery that returns an entire table result. You define the derived table's inner query in parentheses in the FROM clause of the outer query, and specify the name of the derived table after the parentheses.

Before demonstrating the use of derived tables, this section describes a query that returns a certain desired result. Then it explains a need that cannot be addressed directly in the query, and shows how you can address that need by using a derived table (or any other table expression type for that matter).

Consider the following query, which computes row numbers for products, partitioned by categoryid, and ordered by unitprice and productid.

```
SELECT
  ROW_NUMBER() OVER(PARTITION BY categoryid
                    ORDER BY unitprice, productid) AS rownum,
  categoryid, productid, productname, unitprice
FROM Production.Products;
```

This query generates the following output, shown here in abbreviated form.

```
rownum  categoryid  productid  productname    unitprice
------- ----------- ---------- -------------- ----------
1       1           24         Product QOGNU  4.50
2       1           75         Product BWRLG  7.75
3       1           34         Product SWNJY  14.00
4       1           67         Product XLXQF  14.00
5       1           70         Product TOONT  15.00
...
1       2           3          Product IMEHJ  10.00
2       2           77         Product LUNZZ  13.00
3       2           15         Product KSZOI  15.50
4       2           66         Product LQMGN  17.00
5       2           44         Product VJIEO  19.45
...
```

You learn about the ROW_NUMBER function, as well as other window functions, in Chapter 5, "Grouping and Windowing." But for now, suffice it to say that the ROW_NUMBER function computes unique incrementing integers from 1 and on based on indicated ordering, possibly within partitions of rows. As you can see in the query's result, the ROW_NUMBER function generates unique incrementing integers from 1 and on based on unitprice and productid ordering, within each partition defined by categoryid.

The thing with the ROW_NUMBER function—and window functions in general—is that they are only allowed in the SELECT and ORDER BY clauses of a query. So, what if you want to filter rows based on such a function's result? For example, suppose you want to return only the rows where the row number is less than or equal to 2; namely, in each category, you want to return the two products with the lowest unit prices, with the product ID used as a tiebreaker. You are not allowed to refer to the ROW_NUMBER function in the query's WHERE clause. Remember also that according to logical query processing, you're not allowed to refer to a column alias that was assigned in the SELECT list in the WHERE clause, because the WHERE clause is conceptually evaluated before the SELECT clause.

You can circumvent the restriction by using a table expression. You write a query such as the previous query that computes the window function in the SELECT clause, and assign a column alias to the result column. You then define a table expression based on that query, and refer to the column alias in the outer query's WHERE clause, as follows.

```
SELECT categoryid, productid, productname, unitprice
FROM (SELECT
        ROW_NUMBER() OVER(PARTITION BY categoryid
                          ORDER BY unitprice, productid) AS rownum,
        categoryid, productid, productname, unitprice
      FROM Production.Products) AS D
WHERE rownum <= 2;
```

This query generates the following output, shown here in abbreviated form.

```
categoryid  productid  productname    unitprice
----------- ---------- -------------- ----------
1           24         Product QOGNU  4.50
1           75         Product BWRLG  7.75
2           3          Product IMEHJ  10.00
2           77         Product LUNZZ  13.00
3           19         Product XKXDO  9.20
3           47         Product EZZPR  9.50
...
```

As you can see, the derived table is defined in the FROM clause of the outer query in parentheses, followed by the derived table name. Then the outer query is allowed to refer to column aliases that were assigned by the inner query. That's a classic use of table expressions.

Two column aliasing options are available to you when working with derived tables: *inline* and *external*. With the inline form, you specify the column alias as part of the expression, as in <*expression*> AS *alias*. The last query used the inline form to assign the alias rownum to the expression with the ROW_NUMBER function. With the external aliasing form, you don't specify result column aliases as part of the column expressions; instead, you name all target columns right after the derived table's name, as in FROM (...) AS D(rownum, categoryid, productid, productname, unitprice). With the external form, you must specify all target column names and not just those that are results of computations.

There are a couple of problematic aspects to working with derived tables that stem from the fact that a derived table is defined in the FROM clause of the outer query. One problem has to do with cases where you want to refer to one derived table from another. In such a case, you end up nesting derived tables, and nesting often complicates the logic, making it hard to follow and increasing the likelihood for errors. Consider the following general form of nesting of derived tables.

```
SELECT ...
FROM (SELECT
      FROM (SELECT ...
            FROM T1
            WHERE ...) AS D1
      WHERE ...) AS D2
WHERE ...;
```

The other problem with derived tables has to do with the "all-at-once" property of the language. Remember that all expressions that appear in the same logical query processing phase are conceptually evaluated at the same point in time. This is true even for table expressions. As a result, the name assigned to a derived table is not visible to other elements that appear in the same logical query processing phase where the derived table name was defined. This means that if you want to join multiple instances of the same derived table, you can't. You have no choice but to duplicate the code, defining multiple derived tables based on the same query. The general form of such a query looks like the following.

```
SELECT ...
FROM (SELECT ...
      FROM T1) AS D1
  INNER JOIN
     (SELECT ...
      FROM T1) AS D2
    ON ...;
```

The derived tables D1 and D2 are based on the same query. This repetition of code increases the likelihood for errors when you need to make revisions to the inner queries.

CTEs

A *common table expression (CTE)* is a similar concept to a derived table in the sense that it's a named table expression that is visible only to the statement that defines it. Like a query against a derived table, a query against a CTE involves three main parts:

- The inner query
- The name you assign to the query and its columns
- The outer query

However, with CTEs, the arrangement of the three parts is different. Recall that with derived tables the inner query appears in the FROM clause of the outer query—kind of in the middle of things. With CTEs, you first name the CTE, then specify the inner query, and then the outer query—a much more modular approach.

```
WITH <CTE_name>
AS
(
  <inner_query>
)
<outer_query>;
```

Recall the example from the section about derived tables where you returned for each product category the two products with the lowest unit prices. Here's how you can implement the same task with a CTE.

```
WITH C AS
(
  SELECT
    ROW_NUMBER() OVER(PARTITION BY categoryid
                      ORDER BY unitprice, productid) AS rownum,
    categoryid, productid, productname, unitprice
  FROM Production.Products
)
SELECT categoryid, productid, productname, unitprice
FROM C
WHERE rownum <= 2;
```

As you can see, it's a similar concept to derived tables, except the inner query is not defined in the middle of the outer query; instead, first you define the inner query—from start to end—then the outer query—from start to end. This design leads to much clearer code that is easier to understand.

You don't nest CTEs like you do derived tables. If you need to define multiple CTEs, you simply separate them by commas. Each can refer to the previously defined CTEs, and the outer query can refer to all of them. After the outer query terminates, all CTEs defined in that WITH statement are gone. The fact that you don't nest CTEs makes it easier to follow the logic and therefore reduces the chances for errors. For example, if you want to refer to one CTE from another, you can use the following general form.

```
WITH C1 AS
(
  SELECT ...
  FROM T1
  WHERE ...
),
C2 AS
```

```
(
  SELECT
  FROM  C1
  WHERE ...
)
SELECT ...
FROM C2
WHERE ...;
```

Because the CTE name is assigned before the start of the outer query, you can refer to multiple instances of the same CTE name, unlike with derived tables. The general form looks like the following.

```
WITH C AS
(
  SELECT ...
  FROM T1
)
SELECT ...
FROM C AS C1
  INNER JOIN C AS C2
    ON ...;
```

CTEs also have a recursive form. The body of the recursive query has two or more queries, usually separated by a UNION ALL operator. At least one of the queries in the CTE body, known as the anchor member, is a query that returns a valid relational result. The anchor query is invoked only once. In addition, at least one of the queries in the CTE body, known as the recursive member, has a reference to the CTE name. This query is invoked repeatedly until it returns an empty result set. In each iteration, the reference to the CTE name from the recursive member represents the previous result set. Then the reference to the CTE name from the outer query represents the unified results of the invocation of the anchor member and all invocations of the recursive member.

As an example, the following code uses a recursive CTE to return the management chain leading all the way up to the CEO for a specified employee.

```
WITH EmpsCTE AS
(
  SELECT empid, mgrid, firstname, lastname, 0 AS distance
  FROM HR.Employees
  WHERE empid = 9

  UNION ALL

  SELECT M.empid, M.mgrid, M.firstname, M.lastname, S.distance + 1 AS distance
  FROM EmpsCTE AS S
    JOIN HR.Employees AS M
      ON S.mgrid = M.empid
)
SELECT empid, mgrid, firstname, lastname, distance
FROM EmpsCTE;
```

This code returns the following output.

```
empid       mgrid       firstname  lastname             distance
----------- ----------- ---------- -------------------- -----------
9           5           Zoya       Dolgopyatova         0
5           2           Sven       Buck                 1
2           1           Don        Funk                 2
1           NULL        Sara       Davis                3
```

As you can see, the anchor member returns the row for employee 9. Then the recursive member is invoked repeatedly, and in each round joins the previous result set with the HR.Employees table to return the direct manager of the employee from the previous round. The recursive query stops as soon as it returns an empty set—in this case, after not finding a manager of the CEO. Then the outer query returns the unified results of the invocation of the anchor member (the row for employee 9) and all invocations of the recursive member (all managers above employee 9).

Views and Inline Table-Valued Functions

As you learned in the previous sections, derived tables and CTEs are table expressions that are visible only in the scope of the statement that defines them. After that statement terminates, the table expression is gone. Hence, derived tables and CTEs are not reusable. For reusability, you need to store the definition of the table expression as an object in the database, and for this you can use either views or inline table-valued functions. Because these are objects in the database, you can control access by using permissions.

The main difference between views and inline table-valued functions is that the former doesn't accept input parameters and the latter does. As an example, suppose you need to persist the definition of the query with the row number computation from the examples in the previous sections. To achieve this, you create the following view.

```
IF OBJECT_ID('Sales.RankedProducts', 'V') IS NOT NULL DROP VIEW Sales.RankedProducts;
GO
CREATE VIEW Sales.RankedProducts
AS

SELECT
  ROW_NUMBER() OVER(PARTITION BY categoryid
                    ORDER BY unitprice, productid) AS rownum,
  categoryid, productid, productname, unitprice
FROM Production.Products;
GO
```

Note that it's not the result set of the view that is stored in the database; rather, only its definition is stored. Now that the definition is stored, the object is reusable. Whenever you need to query the view, it's available to you, assuming you have the permissions to query it.

```
SELECT categoryid, productid, productname, unitprice
FROM Sales.RankedProducts
WHERE rownum <= 2;
```

As for inline table-valued functions, they are very similar to views in concept; however, as mentioned, they do support input parameters. So if you want to define something like a view with parameters, the closest you have is an inline table-valued function. As an example, consider the recursive CTE from the section about CTEs that retuned the management chain leading all the way up to the CEO for a specified employee. Suppose that you wanted to encapsulate the logic in a table expression for reusability, but also wanted to parameterize the input employee instead of using the constant 9. You can achieve this by using an inline table-valued function with the following definition.

```
IF OBJECT_ID('HR.GetManagers', 'IF') IS NOT NULL DROP FUNCTION HR.GetManagers;
GO
CREATE FUNCTION HR.GetManagers(@empid AS INT) RETURNS TABLE
AS

RETURN
  WITH EmpsCTE AS
  (
    SELECT empid, mgrid, firstname, lastname, 0 AS distance
    FROM HR.Employees
    WHERE empid = @empid

    UNION ALL

    SELECT M.empid, M.mgrid, M.firstname, M.lastname, S.distance + 1 AS distance
    FROM EmpsCTE AS S
      JOIN HR.Employees AS M
        ON S.mgrid = M.empid
  )
  SELECT empid, mgrid, firstname, lastname, distance
  FROM EmpsCTE;
GO
```

Observe that the header assigns the function with a name (HR.GetManagers), defines the input parameter (@empid AS INT), and indicates that the function returns a table result (defined by the returned query). Then the function has a RETURN clause returning the result of the recursive query, and the anchor member of the recursive CTE filters the employee whose ID is equal to the input employee ID. When querying the function, you pass a specific input employee ID as the following example shows.

```
SELECT *
FROM HR.GetManagers(9) AS M;
```

APPLY

The APPLY operator is a powerful operator that you can use to apply a table expression given to it as the right input to each row from a table expression given to it as the left input. What's interesting about the APPLY operator as compared to a join is that the right table expression can be correlated to the left table; in other words, the inner query in the right table expression can have a reference to an element from the left table. So conceptually, the right table expression is evaluated separately for each left row. This means that you can replace the use of cursors in some cases with the APPLY operator.

For example, suppose that you have a query that performs some logic for a particular customer. Suppose that you need to apply this query logic to each customer from the Sales .Customers table. You could use a cursor to iterate through the customers, and in each iteration invoke the query for the current customer. Instead, you can use the APPLY operator, providing the Sales.Customers table as the left input, and a table expression based on your query as the right input. You can correlate the customer ID in the inner query of the right table expression to the customer ID from the left table.

The two forms of the APPLY operator—CROSS and OUTER—are described in the next sections.

CROSS APPLY

The CROSS APPLY operator operates on left and right table expressions as inputs. The right table expression can have a correlation to elements from the left table. The right table expression is applied to each row from the left input. What's special about the CROSS APPLY operator as compared to OUTER APPLY is that if the right table expression returns an empty set for a left row, the left row isn't returned. Figure 4-6 shows an illustration of the CROSS APPLY operator.

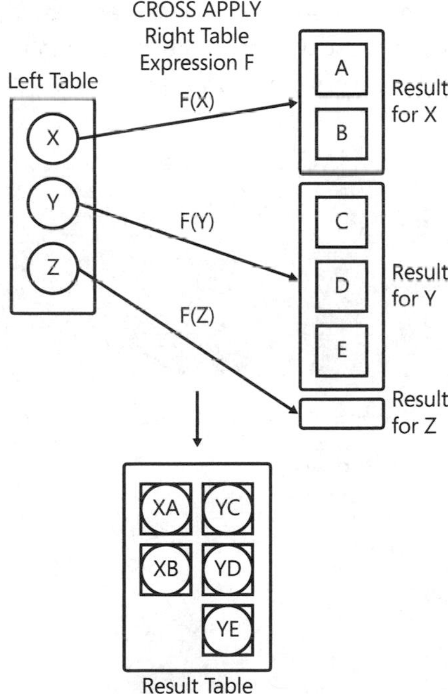

FIGURE 4-6 The CROSS APPLY operator.

The letters X, Y, and Z represent key values from the left table. F represents the table expression provided as the right input, and in parentheses, you can see the key value from the left row passed as the correlated element. On the right side of the illustration, you can see the result returned from the right table expression for each left row. Then at the bottom, you can see the result of the CROSS APPLY table operator, where left rows are matched with the respective right rows that were returned for them. Notice that a left row that gets an empty set back from the right table expression isn't returned. Such is the case with the row with the key value Z.

As a more practical example, suppose that you write a query that returns the two products with the lowest unit prices for a specified supplier—say, supplier 1.

```
SELECT productid, productname, unitprice
FROM Production.Products
WHERE supplierid = 1
ORDER BY unitprice, productid
OFFSET 0 ROWS FETCH FIRST 2 ROWS ONLY;
```

This query generates the following output.

```
productid  productname    unitprice
---------- -------------- ----------
3          Product IMEHJ  10.00
1          Product HHYDP  18.00
```

Next, suppose that you need to apply this logic to each of the suppliers from Japan that you have in the Production.Suppliers table. You don't want to use a cursor to iterate through the suppliers one at a time and invoke a separate query for each. Instead, you can use the CROSS APPLY operator like in the following.

```
SELECT S.supplierid, S.companyname AS supplier, A.*
FROM Production.Suppliers AS S
  CROSS APPLY (SELECT productid, productname, unitprice
               FROM Production.Products AS P
               WHERE P.supplierid = S.supplierid
               ORDER BY unitprice, productid
               OFFSET 0 ROWS FETCH FIRST 2 ROWS ONLY) AS A
WHERE S.country = N'Japan';
```

This query generates the following output.

```
supplierid  supplier        productid  productname    unitprice
----------- --------------- ---------- -------------- ----------
4           Supplier QOVFD  74         Product BKAZJ  10.00
4           Supplier QOVFD  10         Product YHXGE  31.00
6           Supplier QWUSF  13         Product POXFU  6.00
6           Supplier QWUSF  15         Product KSZOI  15.50
```

As you can see in the query, the left input to the APPLY operator is the Production .Suppliers table, with only suppliers from Japan filtered. The right table expression is a correlated derived table returning the two products with the lowest prices for the left supplier. Because the APPLY operator applies the right table expression to each supplier from the left, you get the two products with the lowest prices per each supplier from Japan. Because the CROSS APPLY operator doesn't return left rows for which the right table expression returns an empty set, suppliers from Japan who don't have any related products aren't returned.

OUTER APPLY

The OUTER APPLY operator does what the CROSS APPLY operator does, but also includes in the result rows from the left side that get an empty set back from the right side. NULLs are used as placeholders for the result columns from the right side. In other words, the OUTER APPLY operator preserves the left side. In a sense, the difference between OUTER APPLY and CROSS APPLY is similar to the difference between a LEFT OUTER JOIN and an INNER JOIN. Figure 4-7 shows an illustration of the OUTER APPLY operator:

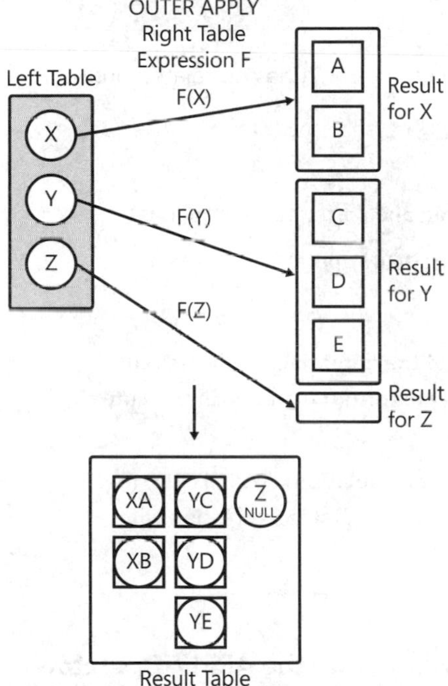

FIGURE 4-7 The OUTER APPLY operator.

Observe that this time the left row with the key value Z is preserved.

Back to the example returning the two products with the lowest prices per each supplier from Japan: If you use the OUTER APPLY operator instead of CROSS APPLY, you will preserve the left side. Here's the revised query.

```
SELECT S.supplierid, S.companyname AS supplier, A.*
FROM Production.Suppliers AS S
  OUTER APPLY (SELECT productid, productname, unitprice
               FROM Production.Products AS P
               WHERE P.supplierid = S.supplierid
               ORDER BY unitprice, productid
               OFFSET 0 ROWS FETCH FIRST 2 ROWS ONLY) AS A
WHERE S.country = N'Japan';
```

Here's the output of this query.

```
supplierid  supplier        productid  productname    unitprice
----------- --------------- ---------- -------------- ----------
4           Supplier QOVFD  74         Product BKAZJ  10.00
4           Supplier QOVFD  10         Product YHXGE  31.00
6           Supplier QWUSF  13         Product POXFU  6.00
6           Supplier QWUSF  15         Product KSZOI  15.50
30          Supplier XYZ    NULL       NULL           NULL
```

Observe that supplier 30 was preserved this time even though it has no related products.

Quick Check

1. **What is the difference between self-contained and correlated subqueries?**
2. **What is the difference between the APPLY and JOIN operators?**

Quick Check Answer

1. **Self-contained subqueries are independent of the outer query, whereas correlated subqueries have a reference to an element from the table in the outer query.**
2. **With a JOIN operator, both inputs represent static relations. With APPLY, the left side is a static relation, but the right side can be a table expression with correlations to elements from the left table.**

PRACTICE Using Subqueries, Table Expressions, and the APPLY Operator

In this practice, you exercise your knowledge of subqueries, table expressions, and the APPLY operator.

EXERCISE 1 Return Products with Minimum Unit Price per Category

In this exercise, you write a solution that uses a CTE to return the products with the lowest unit price per category.

1. Open SSMS and connect to the sample database TSQL2012.

2. As a first step in your solution, write a query against the Production.Products table that groups the products by categoryid, and returns for each category the minimum unit price. Here's a query that achieves this step.

```
SELECT categoryid, MIN(unitprice) AS mn
FROM Production.Products
GROUP BY categoryid;
```

This query generates the following output.

```
categoryid  mn
----------- ---------------------
1           4.50
2           10.00
3           9.20
4           2.50
5           7.00
6           7.45
7           10.00
8           6.00
```

3. The next step in the solution is to define a CTE based on the previous query, and then join the CTE to the Production.Products table to return per each category the products with the minimum unit price. This step can be achieved with the following code.

```
WITH CatMin AS
(
  SELECT categoryid, MIN(unitprice) AS mn
  FROM Production.Products
  GROUP BY categoryid
)
SELECT P.categoryid, P.productid, P.productname, P.unitprice
FROM Production.Products AS P
  INNER JOIN CatMin AS M
    ON P.categoryid = M.categoryid
    AND P.unitprice = M.mn;
```

This code represents the complete solution returning the desired result.

```
categoryid  productid  productname    unitprice
----------- ---------- -------------- ----------
1           24         Product QOGNU  4.50
2           3          Product IMEHJ  10.00
3           19         Product XKXDO  9.20
4           33         Product ASTMN  2.50
5           52         Product QSRXF  7.00
6           54         Product QAQRL  7.45
7           74         Product BKAZJ  10.00
8           13         Product POXFU  6.00
```

EXERCISE 2 Return *N* Products with Lowest Unit Price per Supplier

In this exercise, you practice using the CROSS APPLY and OUTER APPLY operators.

1. Define an inline table-valued function that accepts a supplier ID as input (@supplierid), in addition to a number (@n), and returns the @n products with the lowest prices for the input supplier. In case of ties in the unit price, use the product ID as the tiebreaker. Use the following code to define the function.

```
IF OBJECT_ID('Production.GetTopProducts', 'IF') IS NOT NULL DROP FUNCTION
Production.GetTopProducts;
GO
CREATE FUNCTION Production.GetTopProducts(@supplierid AS INT, @n AS BIGINT)
RETURNS TABLE
AS

RETURN
  SELECT productid, productname, unitprice
  FROM Production.Products
  WHERE supplierid = @supplierid
  ORDER BY unitprice, productid
  OFFSET 0 ROWS FETCH FIRST @n ROWS ONLY;
GO
```

2. Query the function to test it, providing the supplier ID 1 and the number 2 to return the two products with the lowest prices for the input supplier.

```
SELECT * FROM Production.GetTopProducts(1, 2) AS P;
```

This code generates the following output:

```
productid  productname    unitprice
---------- -------------- ----------
3          Product IMEHJ  10.00
1          Product HHYDP  18.00
```

3. Next, return per each supplier from Japan the two products with the lowest prices. To achieve this, use the CROSS APPLY operator, with Production.Suppliers as the left side and the Production.GetTopProducts function as the right side, as follows.

```
SELECT S.supplierid, S.companyname AS supplier, A.*
FROM Production.Suppliers AS S
  CROSS APPLY Production.GetTopProducts(S.supplierid, 2) AS A
WHERE S.country = N'Japan';
```

This code generates the following output.

```
supplierid  supplier        productid  productname    unitprice
----------- --------------- ---------- -------------- ----------
4           Supplier QOVFD  74         Product BKAZJ  10.00
4           Supplier QOVFD  10         Product YHXGE  31.00
6           Supplier QWUSF  13         Product POXFU  6.00
6           Supplier QWUSF  15         Product KSZOI  15.50
```

4. In the previous step, you used the CROSS APPLY operator, and therefore, suppliers from Japan with no related products were discarded. Suppose that you need to return those as well. You need to preserve the left side, and to achieve this, use the OUTER APPLY operator, as follows.

```
SELECT S.supplierid, S.companyname AS supplier, A.*
FROM Production.Suppliers AS S
  OUTER APPLY Production.GetTopProducts(S.supplierid, 2) AS A
WHERE S.country = N'Japan';
```

This time the output includes suppliers without products.

```
supplierid  supplier        productid  productname     unitprice
----------- --------------- ---------- -------------- ----------
4           Supplier QOVFD  74         Product BKAZJ  10.00
4           Supplier QOVFD  10         Product YHXGE  31.00
6           Supplier QWUSF  13         Product POXFU  6.00
6           Supplier QWUSF  15         Product KSZOI  15.50
30          Supplier XYZ    NULL       NULL           NULL
```

5. When you're done, run the following code for cleanup.

```
IF OBJECT_ID('Production.GetTopProducts', 'IF') IS NOT NULL DROP FUNCTION
Production.GetTopProducts;
```

Lesson Summary

- With subqueries, you can nest queries within queries. You can use self-contained subqueries as well as correlated ones. You can use subqueries that return single-valued results, multi-valued results, and table-valued results.
- T-SQL supports four kinds of table expressions, which are named query expressions. Derived tables and CTEs are types of table expressions that are visible only in the scope of the statement that defined them. Views and inline table-valued functions are reusable table expressions whose definitions are stored as objects in the database. Views do not support input parameters, whereas inline table-valued functions do.
- The APPLY operator operates on two table expressions as input. It applies the right table expression to each row from the left side. The inner query in the right table expression can be correlated to elements from the left table. The APPLY operator has two versions; the CROSS APPLY version doesn't return left rows that get an empty set back from the right side. The OUTER APPLY operator preserves the left side, and therefore, does return left rows when the right side returns an empty set. NULLs are used as placeholders in the attributes from the right side in the outer rows.

Lesson Review

Answer the following questions to test your knowledge of the information in this lesson. You can find the answers to these questions and explanations of why each answer choice is correct or incorrect in the "Answers" section at the end of this chapter.

1. What happens when a scalar subquery returns more than one value?
   - **A.** The query fails at run time.
   - **B.** The first value is returned.
   - **C.** The last value is returned.
   - **D.** The result is converted to a NULL.
2. What are the benefits of using a CTE over derived tables? (Choose all that apply.)
   - **A.** CTEs are better performing than derived tables.
   - **B.** CTEs don't nest; the code is more modular, making it easier to follow the logic.
   - **C.** Unlike with derived tables, you can refer to multiple instances of the same CTE name, avoiding repetition of code.
   - **D.** Unlike derived tables, CTEs can be used by all statements in the session, and not just the statement defining them.
3. What is the difference between the result of T1 CROSS APPLY T2 and T1 CROSS JOIN T2 (the right table expression isn't correlated to the left)?
   - **A.** CROSS APPLY filters only rows where the values of columns with the same name are equal; CROSS JOIN just returns all combinations.
   - **B.** If T1 has rows and T2 doesn't, CROSS APPLY returns an empty set and CROSS JOIN still returns the rows from T1.
   - **C.** If T1 has rows and T2 doesn't, CROSS APPLY still returns the rows from T1 and CROSS join returns an empty set.
   - **D.** There is no difference.

Lesson 3: Using Set Operators

Set operators operate on two result sets of queries, comparing complete rows between the results. Depending on the result of the comparison and the set operator used, the operator determines whether to return the row or not. T-SQL supports three set operators: UNION, INTERSECT, and EXCEPT; it also supports one multiset operator: UNION ALL.

The general form of code using a set operator is as follows.

```
<query 1>
<set operator>
<query 2>
[ORDER BY <order_by_list>]
```

Working with set operators follows a number of guidelines:

- Because complete rows are matched between the result sets, the number of columns in the queries has to be the same and the column types of corresponding columns need to be compatible (implicitly convertible).
- Set operators consider two NULLs as equal for the purpose of comparison. This is quite unusual when compared to filtering clauses like WHERE and ON.
- Because the operators are set operators and not cursor operators, the individual queries are not allowed to have ORDER BY clauses.
- You can optionally add an ORDER BY clause that determines presentation ordering of the result of the set operator.
- The column names of result columns are determined by the first query.

After this lesson, you will be able to:

- Unify query results by using the UNION and UNION ALL operators.
- Produce an intersection of query results by using the INTERSECT operator.
- Perform a difference between query results by using the EXCEPT operator.

Estimated lesson time: 30 minutes

UNION and UNION ALL

The UNION set operator unifies the results of the two input queries. As a *set* operator, UNION has an implied DISTINCT property, meaning that it does not return duplicate rows. Figure 4-8 shows an illustration of the UNION operator, using a *Venn diagram*.

FIGURE 4-8 The UNION operator.

As an example for using the UNION operator, the following query returns locations that are employee locations or customer locations or both.

```
SELECT country, region, city
FROM HR.Employees

UNION

SELECT country, region, city
FROM Sales.Customers;
```

This query generates the following output, shown here in abbreviated form.

```
country         region          city
--------------- --------------- ---------------
UK              NULL            London
USA             WA              Kirkland
USA             WA              Seattle
...

(71 row(s) affected)
```

The HR.Employees table has 9 rows and the Sales.Customers table has 91 rows, but there are 71 distinct locations in the unified results; hence, the UNION operator returns 71 rows.

If you want to keep the duplicates—for example, to later group the rows and count occurrences—you need to use the UNION ALL multiset operator instead of UNION. The UNION ALL operator unifies the results of the two input queries, but doesn't try to eliminate duplicates. Figure 4-9 has an illustration of the UNION ALL operator using a Venn diagram.

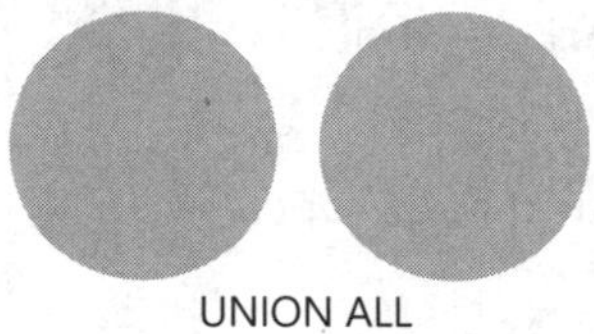

FIGURE 4-9 The UNION ALL operator.

As an example, the following query unifies employee locations and customer locations using the UNION ALL operator.

```
SELECT country, region, city
FROM HR.Employees

UNION ALL

SELECT country, region, city
FROM Sales.Customers;
```

Because UNION ALL doesn't attempt to remove duplicates, the result has 100 rows (9 employees + 91 customers).

```
country         region          city
--------------- --------------- ---------------
USA             WA              Seattle
USA             WA              Tacoma
USA             WA              Kirkland
USA             WA              Redmond
UK              NULL            London
UK              NULL            London
UK              NULL            London
...

(100 row(s) affected)
```

IMPORTANT **UNION VS. UNION ALL**

If the sets you're unifying are disjoint and there's no potential for duplicates, UNION and UNION ALL will return the same result. However, it's important to use UNION ALL in such a case from a performance standpoint because with UNION, SQL Server may try to eliminate duplicates, incurring unnecessary cost.

INTERSECT

The INTERSECT operator returns only distinct rows that are common to both sets. In other words, if a row appears at least once in the first set and at least once in the second set, it will appear once in the result of the INTERSECT operator. Figure 4-10 illustrates the INTERSECT operator using a Venn diagram.

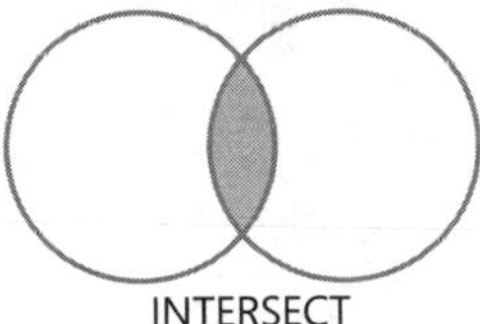

FIGURE 4-10 The INTERSECT operator.

As an example, the following code uses the INTERSECT operator to return distinct locations that are both employee and customer locations (locations where there's at least one employee and at least one customer).

```
SELECT country, region, city
FROM HR.Employees

INTERSECT

SELECT country, region, city
FROM Sales.Customers;
```

This query generates the following output.

```
country         region          city
--------------- --------------- ---------------
UK              NULL            London
USA             WA              Kirkland
USA             WA              Seattle
```

Observe that the location (UK, NULL, London) was returned because it appears in both sides. When comparing the NULLs in the region column in the rows from the two sides, the INTERSECT operator considered them as equal. Also note that never mind how many times the same location appears in each side, as long as it appears at least once in both sides, it's returned only once in the output.

EXCEPT

The EXCEPT operator performs set difference. It returns distinct rows that appear in the first query but not the second. In other words, if a row appears at least once in the first query and zero times in the second, it's returned once in the output. Figure 4-11 illustrates the EXCEPT operator with a Venn diagram.

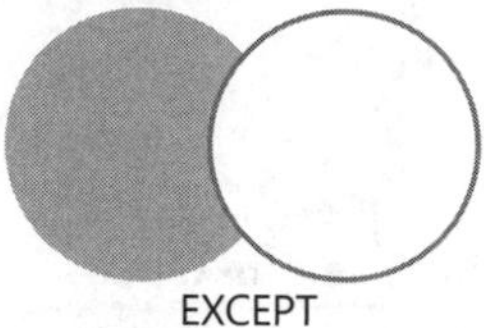

FIGURE 4-11 The EXCEPT operator.

As an example for using EXCEPT, the following query returns locations that are employee locations but not customer locations.

```
SELECT country, region, city
FROM HR.Employees

EXCEPT

SELECT country, region, city
FROM Sales.Customers;
```

This query generates the following output.

```
country         region          city
--------------- --------------- ---------------
USA             WA              Redmond
USA             WA              Tacoma
```

With UNION and INTERSECT, the order of the input queries doesn't matter. However, with EXCEPT, there's different meaning to <query 1> EXCEPT <query 2> vs. <query 2> EXCEPT <query 1>.

Finally, set operators have precedence: INTERSECT precedes UNION and EXCEPT, and UNION and EXCEPT are evaluated from left to right based on their position in the expression. Consider the following set operators.

```
<query 1> UNION <query 2> INTERSECT <query 3>;
```

First, the intersection between query 2 and query 3 takes place, and then a union between the result of the intersection and query 1. You can always force precedence by using parentheses. So, if you want the union to take place first, you use the following form.

```
(<query 1> UNION <query 2>) INTERSECT <query 3>;
```

When you're done, run the following code for cleanup.

```
DELETE FROM Production.Suppliers WHERE supplierid > 29;
IF OBJECT_ID('Sales.RankedProducts', 'V') IS NOT NULL DROP VIEW Sales.RankedProducts;
IF OBJECT_ID('HR.GetManagers', 'IF') IS NOT NULL DROP FUNCTION HR.GetManagers;
```

 **Quick Check**

1. Which set operators does T-SQL support?
2. Name two requirements for the queries involved in a set operator.

Quick Check Answer

1. The UNION, INTERSECT, and EXCEPT set operators, as well as the UNION ALL multiset operator.
2. The number of columns in the two queries needs to be the same, and corresponding columns need to have compatible types.

PRACTICE Using Set Operators

In this practice, you exercise your knowledge of set operators.

EXERCISE 1 Use the EXCEPT Set Operator

In this exercise, you practice identifying relationships between customers and employees through orders by using the EXCEPT set operator.

1. Open SSMS and connect to the sample database TSQL2012.
2. Write a query that returns employees who handled orders for customer 1 but not customer 2. To achieve this, use the EXCEPT set operator, as follows.

```
SELECT empid
FROM Sales.Orders
WHERE custid = 1

EXCEPT

SELECT empid
FROM Sales.Orders
WHERE custid = 2;
```

The first query returns employees who handled orders for customer 1, and the second query returns employees who handled orders for customer 2. Because the EXCEPT operator is used between the first and second query, you get employees who handled orders for customer 1 but not 2, as requested. Remember that EXCEPT doesn't return duplicate rows, so you don't need to worry about an employee appearing more than once in the output. Your solution code returns the following employees.

```
empid
-----------
1
6
```

EXERCISE 2 Use the INTERSECT Set Operator

In this exercise, you practice identifying relationships between customers and employees through orders by using the INTERSECT set operator.

Using the same Sales.Orders table you used in Exercise 1, return employees who handled orders for both customer 1 and customer 2. To achieve this, use the same two input queries, but this time intersect the results by using the INTERSECT operator, as follows.

```
SELECT empid
FROM Sales.Orders
WHERE custid = 1

INTERSECT

SELECT empid
FROM Sales.Orders
WHERE custid = 2;
```

This code returns the following output.

```
empid
-----------
3
4
```

Lesson Summary

- Set operators compare complete rows between the result sets of two queries.
- The UNION operator unifies the input sets, returning distinct rows.
- The UNION ALL operator unifies the inputs without eliminating duplicates.
- The INTERSECT operator returns only rows that appear in both input sets, returning distinct rows.
- The EXCEPT operator returns the rows that appear in the first set but not the second, returning distinct rows.

Lesson Review

Answer the following questions to test your knowledge of the information in this lesson. You can find the answers to these questions and explanations of why each answer choice is correct or incorrect in the "Answers" section at the end of this chapter.

1. Which of the following operators removes duplicates from the result? (Choose all that apply.)

   A. UNION

   B. UNION ALL

   C. INTERSECT

   D. EXCEPT

2. In which operator does the order of the input queries matter?
   - **A.** UNION
   - **B.** UNION ALL
   - **C.** INTERSECT
   - **D.** EXCEPT
3. Which of the following is the equivalent of <query 1> UNION <query 2> INTERSECT <query 3> EXCEPT <query 4>?
   - **A.** (<query 1> UNION <query 2>) INTERSECT (<query 3> EXCEPT <query 4>)
   - **B.** <query 1> UNION (<query 2> INTERSECT <query 3>) EXCEPT <query 4>
   - **C.** <query 1> UNION <query 2> INTERSECT (<query 3> EXCEPT <query 4>)
   - **D.** <query 1> UNION (<query 2> INTERSECT <query 3> EXCEPT <query 4>)

Case Scenarios

In the following case scenarios, you apply what you've learned about combining sets. You can find the answers to these questions in the "Answers" section at the end of this chapter.

Case Scenario 1: Code Review

You are asked to review the code in a system that suffers from both code maintainability problems and performance problems. You come up with the following findings and need to determine what to recommend to the customer:

1. You find many queries that use a number of nesting levels of derived tables, making it very hard to follow the logic. You also find a lot of queries that join multiple derived tables that are based on the same query, and you find that some queries are repeated in a number of places in the code. What can you recommend to the customer to reduce the complexity and improve maintainability?
2. During your review, you identify a number of cases where cursors are used to access the instances of a certain entity (like customer, employee, shipper) one at a time; next the code invokes a query per each of those instances, storing the result in a temporary table; then the code just returns all the rows from the temporary tables. The customer has both code maintainability and performance problems with the existing code. What can you recommend?
3. You identify performance issues with joins. You realize that there are no indexes created explicitly in the system; there are only the ones created by default through primary key and unique constraints. What can you recommend?

Case Scenario 2: Explaining Set Operators

You are presenting a session about set operators in a conference. At the end of the session, you give the audience an opportunity to ask questions. Answer the following questions presented to you by attendees:

1. In our system, we have a number of views that use a UNION operator to combine disjoint sets from different tables. We see performance problems when querying the views. Do you have any suggestions to try and improve the performance?
2. Can you point out the advantages of using set operators like INTERSECT and EXCEPT compared to the use of inner and outer joins?

Suggested Practices

To help you successfully master the exam objectives presented in this chapter, complete the following tasks.

Combine Sets

To practice your knowledge of combining sets, use joins, subqueries, and set operators in the TSQL2012 sample database.

- **Practice 1** In this practice, you join tables in the TSQL2012 sample database. You identify how different tables are related based on foreign key–unique key relationships and write joins to match rows from the related tables. Use the Object Explorer in SSMS to navigate to the TSQL2012 database. Expand the folder for the Sales.Orders table, and then the folder Keys. Double-click the different foreign keys, and then expand Tables and Columns Specifications to identify the referencing and referenced tables and columns. Construct join queries to match rows between Sales.Orders and all related tables based on the identified relationships, and make sure that, in your query, you return columns from all joined tables. You can perform a similar practice with other tables in order to get comfortable with joins.
- **Practice 2** In this practice, you identify rows that appear in one table but have no matches in another. You are given a task to return the IDs of employees from the HR.Employees table who did not handle orders (in the Sales.Orders table) on February 12, 2008. Write three different solutions using the following: joins, subqueries, and set operators. To verify the validity of your solution, you are supposed to return employee IDs: 1, 2, 3, 5, 7, and 9.

Answers

This section contains the answers to the lesson review questions and solutions to the case scenarios in this chapter.

Lesson 1

1. **Correct Answer: D**
   - **A. Incorrect:** Both clauses use three-valued logic.
   - **B. Incorrect:** Both clauses use three-valued logic.
   - **C. Incorrect:** ON determines matching and WHERE determines filtering.
   - **D. Correct:** ON determines matching and WHERE determines filtering.
2. **Correct Answers: C and D**
   - **A. Incorrect:** The JOIN keyword cannot be omitted in the new syntax for joins.
   - **B. Incorrect:** If the CROSS keyword is omitted from CROSS JOIN, the keyword JOIN alone means inner join and not cross join anymore.
   - **C. Correct:** If the INNER keyword is omitted from INNER JOIN, the meaning is retained.
   - **D. Correct:** If the OUTER keyword is omitted from LEFT OUTER JOIN, RIGHT OUTER JOIN, and FULL OUTER JOIN, the meaning is retained.
3. **Correct Answer: A**
   - **A. Correct:** The syntax with the JOIN keyword is consistent with the only standard syntax available for outer joins and is less prone to errors.
   - **B. Incorrect:** Outer joins don't have a standard syntax based on commas.
   - **C. Incorrect:** There's no such recommendation. Cross and inner joins have a reason to exist.
   - **D. Incorrect:** There's no such evidence.

Lesson 2

1. **Correct Answer: A**
   - **A. Correct:** The query fails at run time, indicating that more than one value is returned.
   - **B. Incorrect:** The query fails.
   - **C. Incorrect:** The query fails.
   - **D. Incorrect:** The scalar subquery is converted to NULL when it returns an empty set—not multiple values.

2. **Correct Answers: B and C**
   - **A. Incorrect:** All types of table expressions are treated the same in terms of optimization—they get unnested.
   - **B. Correct:** If you want to refer to one derived table from another, you need to nest them. With CTEs, you separate those by commas, so the code is more modular and easier to follow.
   - **C. Correct:** Because the CTE name is defined before the outer query that uses it, the outer query is allowed to refer to multiple instances of the same CTE name.
   - **D. Incorrect:** CTEs are visible only in the scope of the statement that defined them.
3. **Correct Answer: D**
   - **A. Incorrect:** Both return all combinations.
   - **B. Incorrect:** Both return an empty set.
   - **C. Incorrect:** Both return an empty set.
   - **D. Correct:** Both return the same result when there's no correlation because CROSS APPLY applies all rows from T2 to each row from T1.

Lesson 3

1. **Correct Answers: A, C, and D**
   - **A. Correct:** UNION removes duplicates.
   - **B. Incorrect:** UNION ALL doesn't remove duplicates.
   - **C. Correct:** INTERSECT removes duplicates.
   - **D. Correct:** EXCEPT removes duplicates.
2. **Correct Answer: D**
   - **A. Incorrect:** With UNION, the order of the inputs doesn't matter.
   - **B. Incorrect:** With UNION ALL, the order of the inputs doesn't matter.
   - **C. Incorrect:** With INTERSECT, the order of the inputs doesn't matter.
   - **D. Correct:** With EXCEPT, the order of the inputs matters.
3. **Correct Answer: B**
   - **A. Incorrect:** Without the parentheses, the INTERSECT precedes the other operators, and with the specified parentheses, it gets evaluated last.
   - **B. Correct:** Without the parentheses, the INTERSECT precedes the other operators, and with the specified parentheses, it's the same.
   - **C. Incorrect:** Without the parentheses, the INTERSECT precedes the other operators, and with the specified parentheses, EXCEPT is evaluated first.
   - **D. Incorrect:** Without the parentheses, the UNION operator is evaluated second (after the INTERSECT), and with the specified parentheses, UNION is evaluated last

Case Scenario 1

1. To address the nesting complexity of derived tables, in addition to the duplication of derived table code, you can use CTEs. CTEs don't nest; instead, they are more modular. Also, you can define a CTE once and refer to it multiple times in the outer query. As for queries that are repeated in different places in your code for reusability you can use views and inline table-valued functions. Use the former if you don't need to pass parameters and the latter if you do.

2. The customer should evaluate the use of the APPLY operator instead of the cursor plus the query per row. The APPLY operator involves less code and therefore improves the maintainability, and it does not incur the performance hit that cursors usually do.

3. The customer should examine foreign key relationships and evaluate creating indexes on the foreign key columns.

Case Scenario 2

1. The UNION operator returns distinct rows. When the unified sets are disjoint, there are no duplicates to remove, but the SQL Server Query Optimizer may not realize it. Trying to remove duplicates even when there are none involves extra cost. So when the sets are disjoint, it's important to use the UNION ALL operator and not UNION. Also, adding CHECK constraints that define the ranges supported by each table can help the optimizer realize that the sets are disjoint. Then, even when using UNION, the optimizer can realize it doesn't need to remove duplicates.

2. Set operators have a number of benefits. They allow simpler code because you don't explicitly compare the columns from the two inputs like you do with joins. Also, when set operators compare two NULLs, they consider them the same, which is not the case with joins. When this is the desired behavior, it is easier to use set operators. With join, you have to add predicates to get such behavior.

CHAPTER 5

Grouping and Windowing

Exam objectives in this chapter:

- Work with Data
  - Query data by using SELECT statements.
  - Implement sub-queries.
  - Implement aggregate queries.

This chapter focuses on data analysis operations. A data analysis function is a function applied to a set of rows, and it returns a single value. An example of such a function is the SUM aggregate function. A data analysis function can be either a group function or a window function. The two types differ in how you define the set of rows for the function to operate on. You can use grouped queries to define grouped tables, and then a group function is applied to each group. Or, you can use windowed queries that define windowed tables, and then a window function is applied to each window.

The lessons in this chapter cover grouped queries and pivoting and unpivoting of data. Pivoting can be considered a specialized form of grouping, and unpivoting can be considered the inverse of pivoting. This chapter also covers windowed queries.

Lessons in this chapter:

- Lesson 1: Writing Grouped Queries
- Lesson 2: Pivoting and Unpivoting Data
- Lesson 3: Using Window Functions

Before You Begin

To complete the lessons in this chapter, you must have:

- Experience working with Microsoft SQL Server Management Studio (SSMS).
- Some experience writing T-SQL code.
- An understanding of how to combine sets.
- Access to a SQL Server 2012 instance with the sample database TSQL2012 installed.

Lesson 1: Writing Grouped Queries

You can use grouped queries to define groups in your data, and then you can perform data analysis computations per group. You group the data by a set of attributes known as a *grouping set*. Traditional T-SQL queries define a single grouping set; namely, they group the data in only one way. More recently, T-SQL introduced support for features that enable you to define multiple grouping sets in one query. This lesson starts by covering queries that define a single grouping set, and then it covers queries that define multiple ones.

After this lesson, you will be able to:

- Group data by using a single grouping set.
- Use group functions.
- Group data by using multiple grouping sets.

Estimated lesson time: 60 minutes

Working with a Single Grouping Set

With grouped queries, you can arrange the rows you're querying in groups and apply data analysis computations like aggregate functions against those groups. A query becomes a grouped query when you use a group function, a GROUP BY clause, or both.

A query that invokes a group function but doesn't have an explicit GROUP BY clause arranges all rows in one group. Consider the following query as an example.

```
USE TSQL2012;

SELECT COUNT(*) AS numorders
FROM Sales.Orders;
```

This query generates the following output.

```
numorders
-----------
830
```

Because there's no explicit GROUP BY clause, all rows queried from the Sales.Orders table are arranged in one group, and then the COUNT(*) function counts the number of rows in that group. Grouped queries return one result row per group, and because the query defines only one group, it returns only one row in the result set.

Using an explicit GROUP BY clause, you can group the rows based on a specified grouping set of expressions. For example, the following query groups the rows by shipper ID and counts the number of rows (orders, in this case) per each distinct group.

```
SELECT shipperid, COUNT(*) AS numorders
FROM Sales.Orders
GROUP BY shipperid;
```

This query generates the following output.

```
shipperid   numorders
----------- -----------
1           249
2           326
3           255
```

The query identifies three groups because there are three distinct shipper IDs.

The grouping set can be made of multiple elements. For example, the following query groups the rows by shipper ID and shipped year.

```
SELECT shipperid, YEAR(shippeddate) AS shippedyear,
   COUNT(*) AS numorders
FROM Sales.Orders
GROUP BY shipperid, YEAR(shippeddate);
```

This query generates the following output.

```
shipperid   shippedyear numorders
----------- ----------- -----------
1           2008        79
3           2008        73
1           NULL        4
3           NULL        6
1           2006        36
2           2007        143
2           NULL        11
3           2006        51
1           2007        130
2           2008        116
2           2006        56
3           2007        125
```

Notice that you get a group for each distinct shipper ID and shipped year combination that exists in the data, even when the shipped year is NULL. Remember that a NULL in the shippeddate column represents unshipped orders, so a NULL in the shippedyear column represents the group of unshipped orders for the respective shipper.

If you need to filter entire groups, you need a filtering option that is evaluated at the group level—unlike the WHERE clause, which is evaluated at the row level. For this, T-SQL provides the HAVING clause. Like the WHERE clause, the HAVING clause uses a predicate but evaluates the predicate per group as opposed to per row. This means that you can refer to aggregate computations because the data has already been grouped.

For example, suppose that you need to group only shipped orders by shipper ID and shipping year, and filter only groups having fewer than 100 orders. You can use the following query to achieve this task.

```
SELECT shipperid, YEAR(shippeddate) AS shippedyear,
   COUNT(*) AS numorders
FROM Sales.Orders
WHERE shippeddate IS NOT NULL
GROUP BY shipperid, YEAR(shippeddate)
HAVING COUNT(*) < 100;
```

This query generates the following output.

```
shipperid   shippedyear numorders
----------- ----------- -----------
1           2008        79
3           2008        73
1           2006        36
3           2006        51
2           2006        56
```

Notice that the query filters only shipped orders in the WHERE clause. This filter is applied at the row level conceptually before the data is grouped. Next the query groups the data by shipper ID and shipped year. Then the HAVING clause filters only groups that have a count of rows (orders) that is less than 100. Finally, the SELECT clause returns the shipper ID, shipped year, and count of orders per each remaining group.

T-SQL supports a number of aggregate functions. Those include COUNT(*) and a few general set functions (as they are categorized by standard SQL) like COUNT, SUM, AVG, MIN, and MAX. General set functions are applied to an expression and ignore NULLs.

The following query invokes the COUNT(*) function, in addition to a number of general set functions, including COUNT.

```
SELECT shipperid,
  COUNT(*) AS numorders,
  COUNT(shippeddate) AS shippedorders,
  MIN(shippeddate) AS firstshipdate,
  MAX(shippeddate) AS lastshipdate,
  SUM(val) AS totalvalue
FROM Sales.OrderValues
GROUP BY shipperid;
```

This query generates the following output (dates formatted for readability).

```
shipperid   numorders  shippedorders firstshipdate lastshipdate  totalvalue
----------- ---------- ------------- ------------- ------------- -----------
3           255        249           2006-07-15    2008-05-01    383405.53
1           249        245           2006-07-10    2008-05-04    348840.00
2           326        315           2006-07-11    2008-05-06    533547.69
```

Notice the difference between the results of COUNT(shippeddate) and COUNT(*). The former ignores NULLs in the shippeddate column, and therefore the counts are less than or equal to those produced by the latter.

With general set functions, you can work with distinct occurrences by specifying a DISTINCT clause before the expression, as follows.

```
SELECT shipperid, COUNT(DISTINCT shippeddate) AS numshippingdates
FROM Sales.Orders
GROUP BY shipperid;
```

This query generates the following output.

```
shipperid   numshippingdates
----------- -----------------
1           188
2           215
3           198
```

Note that the DISTINCT option is available not only to the COUNT function, but also to other general set functions. However, it's more common to use it with COUNT.

From a logical query processing perspective, the GROUP BY clause is evaluated after the FROM and WHERE clauses, and before the HAVING, SELECT, and ORDER BY clauses. So the last three clauses already work with a grouped table, and therefore the expressions that they support are limited. Each group is represented by only one result row; therefore, all expressions that appear in those clauses must guarantee a single result value per group. There's no problem referring directly to elements that appear in the GROUP BY clause because each of those returns only one distinct value per group. But if you want to refer to elements from the underlying tables that don't appear in the GROUP BY list, you must apply an aggregate function to them. That's how you can be sure that the expression returns only one value per group. As an example, the following query isn't valid.

```
SELECT S.shipperid, S.companyname, COUNT(*) AS numorders
FROM Sales.Shippers AS S
  JOIN Sales.Orders AS O
    ON S.shipperid = O.shipperid
GROUP BY S.shipperid;
```

This query generates the following error.

```
Msg 8120, Level 16, State 1, Line 1
Column 'Sales.Shippers.companyname' is invalid in the select list because it is not
contained in either an aggregate function or the GROUP BY clause.
```

Even though you know that there can't be more than one distinct company name per each distinct shipper ID, T-SQL doesn't know this. Because the S.companyname column neither appears in the GROUP BY list nor is it contained in an aggregate function, it's not allowed in the HAVING, SELECT, and ORDER BY clauses.

You can use a number of workarounds. One solution is to add the S.companyname column to the GROUP BY list, as follows.

```
SELECT S.shipperid, S.companyname,
  COUNT(*) AS numorders
FROM Sales.Shippers AS S
  INNER JOIN Sales.Orders AS O
    ON S.shipperid = O.shipperid
GROUP BY S.shipperid, S.companyname;
```

This query generates the following output.

```
shipperid   companyname    numorders
----------- -------------- -----------
1           Shipper GVSUA  249
2           Shipper ETYNR  326
3           Shipper ZHISN  255
```

Another workaround is to apply an aggregate function like MAX to the column, as follows.

```
SELECT S.shipperid,
  MAX(S.companyname) AS companyname,
  COUNT(*) AS numorders
FROM Sales.Shippers AS S
  INNER JOIN Sales.Orders AS O
    ON S.shipperid = O.shipperid
GROUP BY S.shipperid;
```

In this case, the aggregate function is an artificial one because there can't be more than one distinct company name per each distinct shipper ID. The first workaround, though, tends to produce more optimal plans, and also seems to be the more natural solution.

The third workaround is to group and aggregate the rows from the Orders table first, define a table expression based on the grouped query, and then join the table expression with the Shippers table to get the shipper company names. Here's the solution's code.

```
WITH C AS
(
  SELECT shipperid, COUNT(*) AS numorders
  FROM Sales.Orders
  GROUP BY shipperid
)
SELECT S.shipperid, S.companyname, numorders
FROM Sales.Shippers AS S
  INNER JOIN C
    ON S.shipperid = C.shipperid;
```

SQL Server usually optimizes the third solution like it does the first. The first solution might be preferable because it involves much less code.

Note that SQL Server 2012 allows you to create user defined aggregates (UDA) using .NET code based on the Common Language Runtime (CLR). SQL Server 2012 provides some built-in CLR UDAs for the spatial data types GEOMETRY and GEOGRAPHY and also allows you to create new UDAs operating on spatial types as inputs. For more details please refer to books online.

Working with Multiple Grouping Sets

With T-SQL, you can define multiple grouping sets in the same query. In other words, you can use one query to group the data in more than one way. T-SQL supports three clauses that allow defined multiple grouping sets: GROUPING SETS, CUBE, and ROLLUP. You use these in the GROUP BY clause.

You can use the GROUPING SETS clause to list all grouping sets that you want to define in the query. As an example, the following query defines four grouping sets.

```
SELECT shipperid, YEAR(shippeddate) AS shipyear, COUNT(*) AS numorders
FROM Sales.Orders
WHERE shippeddate IS NOT NULL -- exclude unshipped orders
GROUP BY GROUPING SETS
(
  ( shipperid, YEAR(shippeddate) ),
  ( shipperid                    ),
  ( YEAR(shippeddate)            ),
  (                              )
);
```

You list the grouping sets separated by commas within the outer pair of parentheses belonging to the GROUPING SETS clause. You use an inner pair of parentheses to enclose each grouping set. If you don't indicate an inner pair of parentheses, each individual element is considered a separate grouping set.

This query defines four grouping sets. One of them is the empty grouping set, which defines one group with all rows for computation of grand aggregates. The query generates the following output.

```
shipperid   shipyear    numorders
----------- ----------- -----------
1           2006        36
2           2006        56
3           2006        51
NULL        2006        143
1           2007        130
2           2007        143
3           2007        125
NULL        2007        398
1           2008        79
2           2008        116
3           2008        73
NULL        2008        268
NULL        NULL        809
3           NULL        249
1           NULL        245
2           NULL        315
```

The output combines the results of grouping and aggregating the data of four different grouping sets. As you can see in the output, NULLs are used as placeholders in rows where an element isn't part of the grouping set. For example, in result rows that are associated with the grouping set (shipperid), the shipyear result column is set to NULL. Similarly, in rows that are associated with the grouping set (YEAR(shippeddate)), the shipperid column is set to NULL.

You could achieve the same result by writing four separate grouped queries—each defining only a single grouping set—and unifying their results with a UNION ALL operator. However, such a solution would involve much more code and won't get optimized as efficiently as the query with the GROUPING SETS clause.

T-SQL supports two additional clauses called CUBE and ROLLUP, which you can consider as abbreviations of the GROUPING SETS clause. The CUBE clause accepts a list of expressions as inputs and defines all possible grouping sets that can be generated from the inputs—including the empty grouping set. For example, the following query is a logical equivalent of the previous query that used the GROUPING SETS clause.

```
SELECT shipperid, YEAR(shippeddate) AS shipyear, COUNT(*) AS numorders
FROM Sales.Orders
GROUP BY CUBE( shipperid, YEAR(shippeddate) );
```

The CUBE clause defines all four possible grouping sets from the two inputs:

1. (shipperid, YEAR(shippeddate))
2. (shipperid)
3. (YEAR(shippeddate))
4. ()

The ROLLUP clause is also an abbreviation of the GROUPING SETS clause, but you use it when there's a hierarchy formed by the input elements. In such a case, only a subset of the possible grouping sets is really interesting. Consider, for example, a location hierarchy made of the elements shipcountry, shipregion, and shipcity, in this order. It's only interesting to roll up the data in one direction, computing aggregates for the following grouping sets:

1. (shipcountry, shipregion, shipcity)
2. (shipcountry, shipregion)
3. (shipcountry)
4. ()

The other grouping sets are simply not interesting. For example, even though the same city name can appear in different places in the world, it's not interesting to aggregate all of the occurrences—irrespective of region and country.

So, when the elements form a hierarchy, you use the ROLLUP clause and this way avoid computing unnecessary aggregates. Here's an example of a query using the ROLLUP clause based on the aforementioned hierarchy.

```
SELECT shipcountry, shipregion, shipcity, COUNT(*) AS numorders
FROM Sales.Orders
GROUP BY ROLLUP( shipcountry, shipregion, shipcity );
```

This query generates the following output (shown here in abbreviated form).

```
shipcountry     shipregion      shipcity        numorders
--------------- --------------- --------------- -----------
Argentina       NULL            Buenos Aires    16
Argentina       NULL            NULL            16
Argentina       NULL            NULL            16
...
USA             AK              Anchorage       10
USA             AK              NULL            10
USA             CA              San Francisco   4
USA             CA              NULL            4
USA             ID              Boise           31
USA             ID              NULL            31
...
USA             NULL            NULL            122
...
NULL            NULL            NULL            830
```

As mentioned, NULLs are used as placeholders when an element isn't part of the grouping set. If all grouped columns disallow NULLs in the underlying table, you can identify the rows that are associated with a single grouping set based on a unique combination of NULLs and non-NULLs in those columns. A problem arises in identifying the rows that are associated with a single grouping set when a grouped column allows NULLs—as is the case with the shipregion column. How do you tell whether a NULL in the result represents a placeholder (meaning "all regions") or an original NULL from the table (meaning "inapplicable region")? T-SQL provides two functions to help address this problem: GROUPING and GROUPING_ID.

The GROUPING function accepts a single element as input and returns 0 when the element is part of the grouping set and 1 when it isn't. The following query demonstrates using the GROUPING function.

```
SELECT
  shipcountry, GROUPING(shipcountry) AS grpcountry,
  shipregion , GROUPING(shipregion)  AS grpregion,
  shipcity   , GROUPING(shipcity)    AS grpcity,
  COUNT(*) AS numorders
FROM Sales.Orders
GROUP BY ROLLUP( shipcountry, shipregion, shipcity );
```

This query generates the following output (shown here in abbreviated form).

```
shipcountry   grpcountry  shipregion   grpregion  shipcity      grpcitry   numorders
------------  ----------  -----------  ---------- ------------- ---------- ----------
Argentina     0           NULL         0          Buenos Aires  0          16
Argentina     0           NULL         0          NULL          1          16
Argentina     0           NULL         1          NULL          1          16
...
USA           0           AK           0          Anchorage     0          10
USA           0           AK           0          NULL          1          10
USA           0           CA           0          San Francisco 0          4
USA           0           CA           0          NULL          1          4
USA           0           ID           0          Boise         0          31
USA           0           ID           0          NULL          1          31
...
USA           0           NULL         1          NULL          1          122
...
NULL          1           NULL         1          NULL          1          830
```

Now you can identify a grouping set by looking for 0s in the elements that are part of the grouping set and 1s in the rest.

Another function that you can use to identify the grouping sets is GROUPING_ID. This function accepts the list of grouped columns as inputs and returns an integer representing a bitmap. The rightmost bit represents the rightmost input. The bit is 0 when the respective element is part of the grouping set and 1 when it isn't. Each bit represents 2 raised to the power of the bit position minus 1; so the rightmost bit represents 1, the one to the left of it 2, then 4, then 8, and so on. The result integer is the sum of the values representing elements that are not part of the grouping set because their bits are turned on. Here's a query demonstrating the use of this function.

```
SELECT GROUPING_ID( shipcountry, shipregion, shipcity ) AS grp_id,
  shipcountry, shipregion, shipcity,
  COUNT(*) AS numorders
FROM Sales.Orders
GROUP BY ROLLUP( shipcountry, shipregion, shipcity );
```

This query generates the following output (shown here in abbreviated form).

```
grp_id      shipcountry     shipregion      shipcity        numorders
----------- --------------- --------------- --------------- -----------
0           Argentina       NULL            Buenos Aires    16
1           Argentina       NULL            NULL            16
3           Argentina       NULL            NULL            16
...
0           USA             AK              Anchorage       10
1           USA             AK              NULL            10
0           USA             CA              San Francisco   4
1           USA             CA              NULL            4
0           USA             ID              Boise           31
1           USA             ID              NULL            31
...
```

```
3           USA           NULL          NULL          122
...
7           NULL          NULL          NULL          830
```

The last row in this output represents the empty grouping set—none of the three elements is part of the grouping set. Therefore, the respective bits (values 1, 2, and 4) are turned on. The sum of the values that those bits represent is 7.

> ***TIP*** **GROUPING SETS ALGEBRA**
>
> **You can specify multiple GROUPING SETS, CUBE, and ROLLUP clauses in the GROUP BY clause separated by commas. By doing so, you achieve a multiplication effect. For example the clause CUBE(a, b, c) defines eight grouping sets and the clause ROLLUP(x, y, z) defines four grouping sets. By specifying a comma between the two, as in CUBE(a, b, c), ROLLUP(x, y, z), you multiply them and get 32 grouping sets.**

Quick Check

1. **What makes a query a grouped query?**
2. **What are the clauses that you can use to define multiple grouping sets in the same query?**

Quick Check Answer

1. **When you use an aggregate function, a GROUP BY clause, or both.**
2. **GROUPING SETS, CUBE, and ROLLUP.**

PRACTICE Writing Grouped Queries

In this practice, you exercise your knowledge of grouped queries. You write grouped queries that define a single grouping set, in addition to multiple ones.

If you encounter a problem completing an exercise, you can install the completed projects from the companion content for this chapter and lesson.

EXERCISE 1 Aggregate Information About Customer Orders

In this exercise, you group and aggregate data involving customers and orders. When given a task, try first to come up with your own query solution before you look at the provided query.

1. Open SSMS and connect to the sample database TSQL2012.
2. Write a query that computes the number of orders per each customer for customers from Spain.

To achieve this task, you first need to join the Sales.Customers and Sales.Orders tables based on a match between the customer's customer ID and the order's customer ID. You then filter only the rows where the customer's country is Spain. Then you group the remaining rows by customer ID. Because there's a custid column in both input tables, you need to prefix the column with the table source. For example, if you prefer to use the one from the Sales.Customers table, and you alias that table C, you need to specify C.custid in the GROUP BY clause. Finally, you return the customer ID and the count of rows in the SELECT list. Here's the complete query.

```
USE TSQL2012;

SELECT C.custid, COUNT(*) AS numorders
FROM Sales.Customers AS C
  INNER JOIN Sales.Orders AS O
    ON C.custid = O.custid
WHERE C.country = N'Spain'
GROUP BY C.custid;
```

This query generates the following output.

```
custid      numorders
----------- -----------
8           3
29          5
30          10
69          5
```

3. Add the city information in the output of the query. First, attempt to just add C.city to the SELECT list, as follows.

```
SELECT C.custid, C.city, COUNT(*) AS numorders
FROM Sales.Customers AS C
  INNER JOIN Sales.Orders AS O
    ON C.custid = O.custid
WHERE C.country = N'Spain'
GROUP BY C.custid;
```

You get the following error.

```
Msg 8120, Level 16, State 1, Line 1

Column 'Sales.Customers.city' is invalid in the select list because it is not
contained in either an aggregate function or the GROUP BY clause.
```

4. Find a solution that would allow returning the city as well.

One possible solution is to add city to the GROUP BY clause, as follows.

```
SELECT C.custid, C.city, COUNT(*) AS numorders
FROM Sales.Customers AS C
  INNER JOIN Sales.Orders AS O
    ON C.custid = O.custid
WHERE C.country = N'Spain'
GROUP BY C.custid, C.city;
```

This query generates the following output.

```
custid      city            numorders
----------- --------------- -----------
8           Madrid          3
29          Barcelona       5
30          Sevilla         10
69          Madrid          5
```

EXERCISE 2 Define Multiple Grouping Sets

In this exercise, you define multiple grouping sets.

- Your starting point is the query you wrote in step 4 of Exercise 1. In addition to the counts by customer returned by that query, also include in the same output the grand count. You need the output to show first the counts by customer and then the grand count.

  You can use the GROUPING SETS clause to define two grouping sets: one for (C.custid, C.city), and another for the empty grouping set (). To sort the customer counts before the grand counts, order the data by GROUPING(C.custid). Here's the complete query.

```
SELECT C.custid, C.city, COUNT(*) AS numorders
FROM Sales.Customers AS C
  INNER JOIN Sales.Orders AS O
    ON C.custid = O.custid
WHERE C.country = N'Spain'
GROUP BY GROUPING SETS ( (C.custid, C.city), () )
ORDER BY GROUPING(C.custid);
```

  This query generates the following output.

```
custid      city            numorders
----------- --------------- -----------
8           Madrid          3
29          Barcelona       5
30          Sevilla         10
69          Madrid          5
NULL        NULL            23
```

Lesson Summary

- With T-SQL, you can group your data and perform data analysis operations against the groups.
- You can apply aggregate functions to the groups, such as COUNT, SUM, AVG, MIN, and MAX.
- Traditional grouped queries define only one grouping set.
- You can use newer features in the language to define multiple grouping sets in one query by using the GROUPING SETS, CUBE, and ROLLUP clauses.

Lesson Review

Answer the following questions to test your knowledge of the information in this lesson. You can find the answers to these questions and explanations of why each answer choice is correct or incorrect in the "Answers" section at the end of this chapter.

1. What is the restriction that grouped queries impose on your expressions?
   - **A.** If the query is a grouped query, you must invoke an aggregate function.
   - **B.** If the query has an aggregate function, it must have a GROUP BY clause.
   - **C.** The elements in the GROUP BY clause must also be specified in the SELECT clause.
   - **D.** If you refer to an element from the queried tables in the HAVING, SELECT, or ORDER BY clauses, it must either appear in the GROUP BY list or be contained by an aggregate function.
2. What is the purpose of the GROUPING and GROUPING_ID functions? (Choose all that apply.)
   - **A.** You can use these functions in the GROUP BY clause to group data.
   - **B.** You can use these functions to tell whether a NULL in the result represents a placeholder for an element that is not part of the grouping set or an original NULL from the table.
   - **C.** You can use these functions to uniquely identify the grouping set that the result row is associated with.
   - **D.** These functions can be used to sort data based on grouping set association—that is, first detail, and then aggregates.
3. What is the difference between the COUNT(*) aggregate function and the COUNT(<*expression*>) general set function?
   - **A.** COUNT(*) counts rows; COUNT(<*expression*>) counts rows where <*expression*> is not NULL.
   - **B.** COUNT(*) counts columns; COUNT(<*expression*>) counts rows.
   - **C.** COUNT(*) returns a BIGINT; COUNT(<*expression*>) returns an INT.
   - **D.** There's no difference between the functions.

Lesson 2: Pivoting and Unpivoting Data

Pivoting is a specialized case of grouping and aggregating of data. Unpivoting is, in a sense, the inverse of pivoting. T-SQL supports native operators for both. The first part of this lesson describes pivoting and the second part describes unpivoting.

> **After this lesson, you will be able to:**
>
> - Use the PIVOT operator to pivot data.
> - Use the UNPIVOT operator to unpivot data.
>
> **Estimated lesson time: 40 minutes**

Pivoting Data

Pivoting is a technique that groups and aggregates data, transitioning it from a state of rows to a state of columns. In all pivot queries, you need to identify three elements:

- What do you want to see on rows? This element is known as the *on rows*, or *grouping element*.
- What do you want to see on columns? This element is known as the *on cols*, or *spreading element*.
- What do you want to see in the intersection of each distinct row and column value? This element is known as the *data*, or *aggregation element*.

As an example of a pivot request, suppose that you want to query the Sales.Orders table. You want to return a row for each distinct customer ID (the grouping element), a column for each distinct shipper ID (the spreading element), and in the intersection of each customer and shipper you want to see the sum of freight values (the aggregation element). With T-SQL, you can achieve such a pivoting task by using the PIVOT table operator. The recommended form for a pivot query is generally like the following.

```
WITH PivotData AS
(
  SELECT
    < grouping column >,
    < spreading column >,
    < aggregation column >
  FROM < source table >
)
SELECT < select list >
FROM PivotData
  PIVOT( < aggregate function >(< aggregation column >)
    FOR < spreading column > IN (< distinct spreading values >) ) AS P;
```

This recommended general form is made of the following elements:

- You define a table expression (like the one named PivotData) that returns the three elements that are involved in pivoting. It is not recommended to query the underlying source table directly; the reason for this is explained shortly.
- You issue the outer query against the table expression and apply the PIVOT operator to that table expression. The PIVOT operator returns a table result. You need to assign an alias to that table, for example, P.
- The specification for the PIVOT operator starts by indicating an aggregate function applied to the aggregation element—in this example, SUM(freight).
- Then you specify the FOR clause followed by the spreading column, which in this example is shipperid.
- Then you specify the IN clause followed by the list of distinct values that appear in the spreading element, separated by commas. What used to be values in the spreading column (in this, case shipper IDs) become column names in the result table. Therefore, the items in the list should be expressed as column identifiers. Remember that if a column identifier is irregular, it has to be delimited. Because shipper IDs are integers, they have to be delimited: [1],[2],[3].

Following this recommended syntax for pivot queries, the following query addresses the example task (return customer IDs on rows, shipper IDs on columns, and the total freight in the intersections).

```
WITH PivotData AS
(
  SELECT
    custid   , -- grouping column
    shipperid, -- spreading column
    freight    -- aggregation column
  FROM Sales.Orders
)
SELECT custid, [1], [2], [3]
FROM PivotData
  PIVOT(SUM(freight) FOR shipperid IN ([1],[2],[3]) ) AS P;
```

This query generates the following output (shown here in abbreviated form).

```
custid  1        2        3
------- -------- -------- --------
1       95.03    61.02    69.53
2       43.90    NULL     53.52
3       63.09    116.56   88.87
4       41.95    358.54   71.46
5       189.44   1074.51  295.57
6       0.15     126.19   41.92
7       217.96   215.70   190.00
8       16.16    175.01   NULL
9       341.16   419.57   597.14
10      129.42   162.17   502.36
...

(89 row(s) affected)
```

If you look carefully at the specification of the PIVOT operator, you will notice that you indicate the aggregation and spreading elements, but not the grouping element. The grouping element is identified by elimination—it's what's left from the queried table besides the aggregation and spreading elements. This is why it is recommended to prepare a table expression for the pivot operator returning only the three elements that should be involved in the pivoting task. If you query the underlying table directly (Sales.Orders in this case), all columns from the table besides the aggregation (freight) and spreading (shipperid) columns will implicitly become your grouping elements. This includes even the primary key column orderid. So instead of getting a row per customer, you end up getting a row per order. You can see it for yourself by running the following code.

```
SELECT custid, [1], [2], [3]
FROM Sales.Orders
  PIVOT(SUM(freight) FOR shipperid IN ([1],[2],[3]) ) AS P;
```

This query generates the following output (shown here in abbreviated form).

```
custid  1       2       3
------- ------- ------- -------
85      NULL    NULL    32.38
79      11.61   NULL    NULL
34      NULL    65.83   NULL
84      41.34   NULL    NULL
76      NULL    51.30   NULL
34      NULL    58.17   NULL
14      NULL    22.98   NULL
68      NULL    NULL    148.33
88      NULL    13.97   NULL
35      NULL    NULL    81.91
...

(830 row(s) affected)
```

You get 830 rows back because there are 830 rows in the Sales.Orders table. By defining a table expression as was shown in the recommended solution, you control which columns will be used as the grouping columns. If you return custid, shipperid, and freight in the table expression, and use the last two as the spreading and aggregation elements, respectively, the PIVOT operator implicitly assumes that custid is the grouping element. Therefore, it groups the data by custid, and as a result, returns a single row per customer.

You should be aware of a few limitations of the PIVOT operator:

- The aggregation and spreading elements cannot directly be results of expressions; instead, they must be column names from the queried table. You can, however, apply expressions in the query defining the table expression, assign aliases to those expressions, and then use the aliases in the PIVOT operator.
- The COUNT(*) function isn't allowed as the aggregate function used by the PIVOT operator. If you need a count, you have to use the general COUNT(<*col name*>) aggregate function. A simple workaround is to define a dummy column in the table expression made of a constant, as in 1 AS agg_col, and then in the PIVOT operator apply the aggregate function to that column: COUNT(agg_col).

- A PIVOT operator is limited to using only one aggregate function.
- The IN clause of the PIVOT operator accepts a static list of spreading values. It doesn't support a subquery as input. You need to know ahead what the distinct values are in the spreading column and specify those in the IN clause. When the list isn't known ahead, you can use dynamic SQL to construct and execute the query string after querying the distinct values from the data. For details about dynamic SQL, see Chapter 12, "Implementing Transactions, Error Handling, and Dynamic SQL."

Unpivoting Data

Unpivoting data can be considered the inverse of pivoting. The starting point is some pivoted data. When unpivoting data, you rotate the input data from a state of columns to a state of rows. Just like T-SQL supports the native PIVOT table operator to perform pivoting, it supports a native UNPIVOT operator to perform unpivoting. Like PIVOT, UNPIVOT is implemented as a table operator that you use in the FROM clause. The operator operates on the input table that is provided to its left, which could be the result of other table operators, like joins. The outcome of the UNPIVOT operator is a table result that can be used as the input to other table operators that appear to its right.

To demonstrate unpivoting, use as an example a sample table called Sales.FreightTotals. The following code creates the sample data and queries it to show its contents.

```
USE TSQL2012;
IF OBJECT_ID(N'Sales.FreightTotals', N'U') IS NOT NULL DROP TABLE Sales.FreightTotals;
GO

WITH PivotData AS
(
  SELECT
    custid    , -- grouping column
    shipperid, -- spreading column
    freight    -- aggregation column
  FROM Sales.Orders
)
SELECT *
INTO Sales.FreightTotals
FROM PivotData
  PIVOT( SUM(freight) FOR shipperid IN ([1],[2],[3]) ) AS P;

SELECT * FROM Sales.FreightTotals;
```

This code generates the following output, shown here in abbreviated form.

```
custid  1        2        3
------- -------- -------- --------
1       95.03    61.02    69.53
2       43.90    NULL     53.52
3       63.09    116.56   88.87
4       41.95    358.54   71.46
5       189.44   1074.51  295.57
6       0.15     126.19   41.92
7       217.96   215.70   190.00
```

```
8        16.16    175.01    NULL
9        341.16   419.57    597.14
10       129.42   162.17    502.36
...
```

As you can see, the source table has a row for each customer and a column for each shipper (shippers 1, 2, and 3). The intersection of each customer and shipper has the total freight values. The unpivoting task at hand is to return a row for each customer and shipper holding the customer ID in one column, the shipper ID in a second column, and the freight value in a third column.

Unpivoting always takes a set of source columns and rotates those to multiple rows, generating two target columns: one to hold the source column values and another to hold the source column names. The source columns already exist, so their names should be known to you. But the two target columns are created by the unpivoting solution, so you need to choose names for those. In our example, the source columns are [1], [2], and [3]. As for names for the target columns, you need to decide on those. In this case, it might be suitable to call the values column freight and the names column shipperid. So remember, in every unpivoting task, you need to identify the three elements involved:

- The set of source columns that you're unpivoting (in this case, [1],[2],[3])
- The name you want to assign to the target values column (in this case, freight)
- The name you want to assign to the target names column (in this case, shipperid)

After you identify these three elements, you use the following query form to handle the unpivoting task.

```
SELECT < column list >, < names column >, < values column >
FROM < source table >
  UNPIVOT( < values column > FOR < names column > IN( <source columns> ) ) AS U;
```

Based on this syntax, the following query addresses the current task.

```
SELECT custid, shipperid, freight
FROM Sales.FreightTotals
  UNPIVOT( freight FOR shipperid IN([1],[2],[3]) ) AS U;
```

This query generates the following output (shown here in abbreviated form).

```
custid  shipperid  freight
------- ---------- --------
1       1          95.03
1       2          61.02
1       3          69.53
2       1          43.90
2       3          53.52
3       1          63.09
3       2          116.56
3       3          88.87
4       1          41.95
4       2          358.54
4       3          71.46
...
```

Besides unpivoting the data, the UNPIVOT operator filters out rows with NULLs in the value column (freight in this case). The assumption is that those represent inapplicable cases. There was no escape from keeping NULLs in the source if the column was applicable to at least one other customer. But after unpivoting the data, there's no reason to keep a row for a certain customer-shipper pair if it's inapplicable—if that shipper did not ship orders to that customer.

In terms of data types, the names column is defined as a Unicode character string (NVARCHAR(128)). The values column is defined with the same type as the type of the source columns that were unpivoted. For this reason, the types of all columns that you're unpivoting must be the same.

When you're done, run the following code for cleanup.

```
IF OBJECT_ID(N'Sales.FreightTotals', N'U') IS NOT NULL DROP TABLE Sales.FreightTotals;
```

Quick Check

1. **What is the difference between PIVOT and UNPIVOT?**
2. **What type of language constructs are PIVOT and UNPIVOT implemented as?**

Quick Check Answer

1. **PIVOT rotates data from a state of rows to a state of columns; UNPIVOT rotates the data from columns to rows.**
2. **PIVOT and UNPIVOT are implemented as table operators.**

PRACTICE Pivoting Data

In this practice, you exercise your knowledge of pivoting data.

If you encounter a problem completing an exercise, you can install the completed projects from the companion content for this chapter and lesson.

EXERCISE 1 Pivot Data by Using a Table Expression

In this exercise, you pivot data by using a table expression.

1. Open SSMS and connect to the sample database TSQL2012.
2. Write a PIVOT query against the Sales.Orders table that returns the maximum shipping date for each order year and shipper ID. Return order years on rows, shipper IDs (1, 2, and 3) on columns, and the maximum shipping dates in the data part.

   You first attempt to address the task by using the following query.

```
SELECT YEAR(orderdate) AS orderyear, [1], [2], [3]
FROM Sales.Orders
  PIVOT( MAX(shippeddate) FOR shipperid IN ([1],[2],[3]) ) AS P;
```

You expect to get three rows in the result for the years 2006, 2007, and 2008, but instead you get 830 rows in the result, like the number of orders in the table.

3. Try to explain why you got the undesired result and figure out a solution.

   The reason you got the undesired result is that you queried the Sales.Orders table directly. The way SQL Server determined which columns to group by is by using elimination; the grouping columns are all columns that you didn't specify as spreading (shipperid, in this case) and aggregation (shippeddate, in this case). All remaining columns—including orderID—became implicitly part of the group by list. Therefore, you got a row per order instead of a row per year. To fix the problem, you define a table expression that contains only the grouping, spreading, and aggregation columns, and provide the table expression as input to the PIVOT query. Your solution should look like the following.

```
WITH PivotData AS
(
  SELECT YEAR(orderdate) AS orderyear, shipperid, shippeddate
  FROM Sales.Orders
)
SELECT orderyear, [1], [2], [3]
FROM PivotData
  PIVOT( MAX(shippeddate) FOR shipperid IN ([1],[2],[3]) ) AS P;
```

   Here's the output with dates formatted for brevity.

```
orderyear   1           2           3
----------- ----------- ----------- -----------
2007        2008-01-30  2008-01-21  2008-01-09
2008        2008-05-04  2008-05-06  2008-05-01
2006        2007-01-03  2006-12-30  2007-01-16
```

EXERCISE 2 Pivot Data and Compute Counts

In this exercise, you apply the COUNT aggregate when pivoting data. As in Exercise 1, you work with the Sales.Orders table in the TSQL2012 sample database.

1. Write a PIVOT query that returns a row for each distinct customer ID, a column for each distinct shipper ID, and the count of orders in the customer-shipper intersections. Prepare a table expression that returns only the custid and shipperid columns from the Sales.Orders table, and provide this table expression as input to the PIVOT operator.

   As your first attempt, try to use the COUNT(*) aggregate function, as follows.

```
WITH PivotData AS
(
  SELECT
    custid    ,  -- grouping column
    shipperid    -- spreading column
  FROM Sales.Orders
)
SELECT custid, [1], [2], [3]
FROM PivotData
  PIVOT( COUNT(*) FOR shipperid IN ([1],[2],[3]) ) AS P;
```

Because the PIVOT operator doesn't support the COUNT(*) aggregate function, you get the following error.

```
Msg 102, Level 15, State 1, Line 10
Incorrect syntax near '*'.
```

2. Try to think of a workaround to this problem.

   To solve the problem, you need to use the COUNT(<*col_name*>) general set function, but remember that the input to the aggregate function cannot be a result of an expression; instead, it must be a column name that exists in the queried table. So one option you have is to use the spreading column as the aggregation column, as in COUNT(shipperid). The other option is to create a dummy column from a constant expression in the table expression, and then use that column as input to the COUNT function, as follows.

```
WITH PivotData AS
(
  SELECT
    custid    ,  -- grouping column
    shipperid,   -- spreading column
    1 AS aggcol  -- aggregation column
  FROM Sales.Orders
)
SELECT custid, [1], [2], [3]
FROM PivotData
  PIVOT( COUNT(aggcol) FOR shipperid IN ([1],[2],[3]) ) AS P;
```

   This query generates the desired output.

```
custid  1   2   3
------- --- --- ---
1       4   1   1
2       1   0   3
3       2   3   2
4       1   8   4
5       5   9   4
6       1   3   3
7       5   3   3
8       1   2   0
9       6   7   4
10      3   3   8
...
```

Lesson Summary

- Pivoting is a special form of grouping and aggregating data where you rotate data from a state of rows to a state of columns.
- When you pivot data, you need to identify three things: the grouping element, spreading element, and aggregation element.
- T-SQL supports a native table operator called PIVOT that you can use to pivot the data from the input table.
- Unpivoting rotates data from a state of columns to a state of rows.
- To unpivot data, you need to identify three things: the source columns that you need to unpivot, the target names column, and the target values column.
- T-SQL supports a native operator called UNPIVOT that you can use to unpivot data from the input table.

Lesson Review

Answer the following questions to test your knowledge of the information in this lesson. You can find the answers to these questions and explanations of why each answer choice is correct or incorrect in the "Answers" section at the end of this chapter.

1. How does the PIVOT operator determine what the grouping element is?
   - **A.** It's the element specified as input to the GROUPING function.
   - **B.** It's determined by elimination—the element(s) from the queried table that were not specified as the spreading or aggregation elements.
   - **C.** It's the element specified in the GROUP BY clause.
   - **D.** It's the primary key.
2. Which of the following are not allowed in the PIVOT operator's specification? (Choose all that apply.)
   - **A.** Specifying a computation as input to the aggregate function
   - **B.** Specifying a computation as the spreading element
   - **C.** Specifying a subquery in the IN clause
   - **D.** Specifying multiple aggregate functions
3. What is the data type of the target values column in the result of an UNPIVOT operator?
   - **A.** INT
   - **B.** NVARCHAR(128)
   - **C.** SQL_VARIANT
   - **D.** The data type of the source columns that you unpivot

Lesson 3: Using Window Functions

Like group functions, window functions also enable you to perform data analysis computations. The difference between the two is in how you define the set of rows for the function to work with. With group functions, you use grouped queries to arrange the queried rows in groups, and then the group functions are applied to each group. You get one result row per group—not per underlying row. With window functions, you define the set of rows per function—and then return one result value per each underlying row and function. You define the set of rows for the function to work with using a clause called OVER.

This lesson covers three types of window functions: aggregate, ranking, and offset.

> **After this lesson, you will be able to:**
>
> - Use window aggregate functions, window ranking functions, and window offset functions.
> - Define window partitioning, ordering, and framing in your window functions.
>
> **Estimated lesson time: 60 minutes**

Window Aggregate Functions

Window aggregate functions are the same as the group aggregate functions (for example, SUM, COUNT, AVG, MIN, and MAX), except window aggregate functions are applied to a window of rows defined by the OVER clause.

One of the benefits of using window functions is that unlike grouped queries, windowed queries do not hide the detail—they return a row for every underlying query's row. This means that you can mix detail and aggregated elements in the same query, and even in the same expression. Using the OVER clause, you define a set of rows for the function to work with per each underlying row. In other words, a windowed query defines a window of rows per each function and row in the underlying query.

As mentioned, you use an OVER clause to define a window of rows for the function. The window is defined in respect to the current row. When using empty parentheses, the OVER clause represents the entire underlying query's result set. For example, the expression SUM(val) OVER() represents the grand total of all rows in the underlying query. You can use a window partition clause to restrict the window. For example, the expression SUM(val) OVER(PARTITION BY custid) represents the current customer's total. As an example, if the current row has customer ID 1, the OVER clause filters only those rows from the underlying query's result set where the customer ID is 1; hence, the expression returns the total for customer 1.

Here's an example of a query against the Sales.OrderValues view returning for each order the customer ID, order ID, and order value; using window functions, the query also returns the grand total of all values and the customer total.

```
SELECT custid, orderid,
  val,
  SUM(val) OVER(PARTITION BY custid) AS custtotal,
  SUM(val) OVER() AS grandtotal
FROM Sales.OrderValues;
```

This query generates the following output (shown here in abbreviated form).

```
custid  orderid  val     custtotal  grandtotal
------- -------- ------- ---------- -----------
1       10643    814.50  4273.00    1265793.22
1       10692    878.00  4273.00    1265793.22
1       10702    330.00  4273.00    1265793.22
1       10835    845.80  4273.00    1265793.22
1       10952    471.20  4273.00    1265793.22
1       11011    933.50  4273.00    1265793.22
2       10926    514.40  1402.95    1265793.22
2       10759    320.00  1402.95    1265793.22
2       10625    479.75  1402.95    1265793.22
2       10308    88.80   1402.95    1265793.22
...
```

The grand total is of course the same for all rows. The customer total is the same for all rows with the same customer ID.

You can mix detail elements and windowed aggregates in the same expression. For example, the following query computes for each order the percent of the current order value out of the customer total, and also the percent of the grand total.

```
SELECT custid, orderid,
  val,
  CAST(100.0 * val / SUM(val) OVER(PARTITION BY custid) AS NUMERIC(5, 2)) AS pctcust,
  CAST(100.0 * val / SUM(val) OVER()                    AS NUMERIC(5, 2)) AS pcttotal
FROM Sales.OrderValues;
```

This query generates the following output (shown here in abbreviated form).

```
custid  orderid  val     pctcust  pcttotal
------- -------- ------- -------- ---------
1       10643    814.50  19.06    0.06
1       10692    878.00  20.55    0.07
1       10702    330.00  7.72     0.03
1       10835    845.80  19.79    0.07
1       10952    471.20  11.03    0.04
1       11011    933.50  21.85    0.07
2       10926    514.40  36.67    0.04
2       10759    320.00  22.81    0.03
2       10625    479.75  34.20    0.04
2       10308    88.80   6.33     0.01
...
```

The sum of all percentages out of the grand total is 100. The sum of all percentages out of the customer total is 100 for each partition of rows with the same customer.

Window aggregate functions support another filtering option called framing. The idea is that you define ordering within the partition by using a window order clause, and then based on that order, you can confine a frame of rows between two delimiters. You define the delimiters by using a window frame clause. The window frame clause requires a window order clause to be present because a set has no order, and without order, limiting rows between two delimiters would have no meaning.

In the window frame clause, you indicate the window frame units (ROWS or RANGE) and the window frame extent (the delimiters). With the ROWS window frame unit, you can indicate the delimiters as one of three options:

- UNBOUNDED PRECEDING or FOLLOWING, meaning the beginning or end of the partition, respectively
- CURRENT ROW, obviously representing the current row
- *<n>* ROWS PRECEDING or FOLLOWING, meaning *n* rows before or after the current, respectively

As an example, suppose that you wanted to query the Sales.OrderValues view and compute the running total values from the beginning of the current customer's activity until the current order. You need to use the SUM aggregate. You partition the window by custid. You order the window by orderdate, orderid. You then frame the rows from the beginning of the partition (UNBOUNDED PRECEDING) until the current row. Your query should look like the following.

```
SELECT custid, orderid, orderdate, val,
  SUM(val) OVER(PARTITION BY custid
                ORDER BY orderdate, orderid
                ROWS BETWEEN UNBOUNDED PRECEDING
                         AND CURRENT ROW) AS runningtotal
FROM Sales.OrderValues;
```

This query generates the following output (shown here in abbreviated form).

```
custid  orderid  orderdate   val     runningtotal
------- -------- ----------- ------- -------------
1       10643    2007-08-25  814.50  814.50
1       10692    2007-10-03  878.00  1692.50
1       10702    2007-10-13  330.00  2022.50
1       10835    2008-01-15  845.80  2868.30
1       10952    2008-03-16  471.20  3339.50
1       11011    2008-04-09  933.50  4273.00
2       10308    2006-09-18  88.80   88.80
2       10625    2007-08-08  479.75  568.55
2       10759    2007-11-28  320.00  888.55
2       10926    2008-03-04  514.40  1402.95
...
```

Observe how the values keep accumulating from the beginning of the customer partition until the current row. By the way, instead of the verbose form of the frame extent ROWS BETWEEN UNBOUNDED PRECEDING AND CURRENT ROW, you can use the shorter form ROWS UNBOUNDED PRECEDING, and retain the same meaning.

Using window aggregate functions to perform computations such as running totals, you typically get much better performance compared to using joins or subqueries and group aggregate functions. Window functions lend themselves to good optimization—especially when using UNBOUNDED PRECEDING as the first delimiter.

In terms of logical query processing, a query's result is achieved when you get to the SELECT phase—after the FROM, WHERE, GROUP BY, and HAVING phases have been processed. Because window functions are supposed to operate on the underlying query's result set, they are allowed only in the SELECT and ORDER BY clauses. If you need to refer to the result of a window function in any clause that is evaluated before the SELECT clause, you need to use a table expression. You invoke the window function in the SELECT clause of the inner query, assigning the expression with a column alias. Then you can refer to that column alias in the outer query in all clauses.

For example, suppose that you need to filter the result of the last query, returning only those rows where the running total is less than 1,000.00. The following code achieves this by defining a common table expression (CTE) based on the previous query and then doing the filtering in the outer query.

```
WITH RunningTotals AS
(
  SELECT custid, orderid, orderdate, val,
    SUM(val) OVER(PARTITION BY custid
                  ORDER BY orderdate, orderid
                  ROWS BETWEEN UNBOUNDED PRECEDING
                           AND CURRENT ROW) AS runningtotal
  FROM Sales.OrderValues
)
SELECT *
FROM RunningTotals
WHERE runningtotal < 1000.00;
```

This query generates the following output (shown here in abbreviated form).

```
custid  orderid  orderdate   val     runningtotal
------- -------- ----------- ------- -------------
1       10643    2007-08-25  814.50  814.50
2       10308    2006-09-18  88.80   88.80
2       10625    2007-08-08  479.75  568.55
2       10759    2007-11-28  320.00  888.55
3       10365    2006-11-27  403.20  403.20
...
```

As another example for a window frame extent, if you wanted the frame to include only the last three rows, you would use the form ROWS BETWEEN 2 PRECEDING AND CURRENT ROW.

As for the RANGE window frame extent, according to standard SQL, it allows you to define delimiters based on logical offsets from the current row's sort key. Remember that ROWS defines the delimiters based on physical offsets in terms of number of rows from the current row. However, SQL Server 2012 has a very limited implementation of the RANGE option, supporting only UNBOUNDED PRECEDING or FOLLOWING and CURRENT ROW as delimiters. One subtle difference between ROWS and RANGE when using the same delimiters is that the former doesn't include peers (tied rows in terms of the sort key) and the latter does.

IMPORTANT **ROWS VS. RANGE**

In SQL Server 2012, the ROWS option usually gets optimized much better than RANGE when using the same delimiters. If you define a window with a window order clause but without a window frame clause, the default is RANGE BETWEEN UNBOUNDED PRECEDING AND CURRENT ROW. Therefore, unless you are after the special behavior you get from RANGE that includes peers, make sure you explicitly use the ROWS option.

Window Ranking Functions

With window ranking functions, you can rank rows within a partition based on specified ordering. As with the other window functions, if you don't indicate a window partition clause, the entire underlying query result is considered one partition. The window order clause is mandatory. Window ranking functions do not support a window frame clause. T-SQL supports four window ranking functions: ROW_NUMBER, RANK, DENSE_RANK, and NTILE.

The following query demonstrates the use of these functions.

```
SELECT custid, orderid, val,
  ROW_NUMBER() OVER(ORDER BY val) AS rownum,
  RANK()       OVER(ORDER BY val) AS rnk,
  DENSE_RANK() OVER(ORDER BY val) AS densernk,
  NTILE(100)   OVER(ORDER BY val) AS ntile100
FROM Sales.OrderValues;
```

This query generates the following output (shown here in abbreviated form).

```
custid  orderid  val    rownum  rnk  densernk  ntile100
------- -------- ------ ------- ---- --------- ---------
12      10782    12.50  1       1    1         1
27      10807    18.40  2       2    2         1
66      10586    23.80  3       3    3         1
76      10767    28.00  4       4    4         1
54      10898    30.00  5       5    5         1
88      10900    33.75  6       6    6         1
48      10883    36.00  7       7    7         1
41      11051    36.00  8       7    7         1
71      10815    40.00  9       9    8         1
38      10674    45.00  10      10   9         2
53      11057    45.00  11      10   9         2
75      10271    48.00  12      12   10        2
...
```

IMPORTANT **PRESENTATION ORDERING VS. WINDOW ORDERING**

The sample query doesn't have a presentation ORDER BY clause, and therefore, there's no assurance that the rows will be presented in any particular order. The window order clause only determines ordering for the window function's computation. If you invoke a window function in your query but don't specify a presentation ORDER BY clause, there's no guarantee that the rows will be presented in the same order as the window function's ordering. If you need such a guarantee, you need to add a presentation ORDER BY clause.

The ROW_NUMBER function computes a unique sequential integer starting with 1 within the window partition based on the window ordering. Because the example query doesn't have a window partition clause, the function considers the entire query's result set as one partition; hence, the function assigns unique row numbers across the entire query's result set.

Note that if the ordering isn't unique, the ROW_NUMBER function is not deterministic. For example, notice in the result that two rows have the same ordering value of 36.00, but the two rows got different row numbers. That's because the function must generate unique integers in the partition. Currently, there's no explicit tiebreaker, and therefore the choice of which row gets the higher row number is arbitrary (optimization dependent). If you need a deterministic computation (guaranteed repeatable results), you need to add a tiebreaker. For example, you could add the primary key to make the ordering unique, as in ORDER BY val, orderid.

RANK and DENSE_RANK differ from ROW_NUMBER in the sense that they assign the same ranking value to all rows that share the same ordering value. The RANK function returns the number of rows in the partition that have a lower ordering value than the current, plus 1. For example, consider the rows in the sample query's result that have an ordering value of 45.00. Nine rows have ordering values that are lower than 45.00; hence, these rows got the rank 10 (9 + 1).

The DENSE_RANK function returns the number of distinct ordering values that are lower than the current, plus 1. For example, the same rows that got the rank 10 got the dense rank 9. That's because these rows have an ordering value 45.00, and there are eight distinct ordering values that are lower than 45.00. Because RANK considers rows and DENSE_RANK considers distinct values, the former can have gaps between result ranking values, and the latter cannot have gaps. Because the RANK and DENSE_RANK functions compute the same ranking value to rows with the same ordering value, both functions are deterministic even when the ordering isn't unique. In fact, if you use unique ordering, both functions return the same result as the ROW_NUMBER function. So usually these functions are interesting to use when the ordering isn't unique.

With the NTILE function, you can arrange the rows within the partition in a requested number of equally sized tiles, based on the specified ordering. You specify the desired number of tiles as input to the function. In the sample query, you requested 100 tiles. There are 830 rows in the result set, and hence the base tile size is 830 / 100 = 8 with a remainder of 30. Because there is a remainder of 30, the first 30 tiles are assigned with an additional row.

Namely, tiles 1 through 30 will have nine rows each, and all remaining tiles (31 through 100) will have eight rows each. Observe in the result of this sample query that the first nine rows (according to val ordering) are assigned with tile number 1, then the next nine rows are assigned with tile number 2, and so on. Like ROW_NUMBER, the NTILE function isn't deterministic when the ordering isn't unique. If you need to guarantee determinism, you need to define unique ordering.

EXAM TIP

As explained in the discussion of window aggregate functions, window functions are allowed only in the SELECT and ORDER BY clauses of the query. If you need to refer to those in other clauses—for example, in the WHERE clause—you need to use a table expression such as a CTE. You invoke the window function in the inner query's SELECT clause, assigning the expression with a column alias. Then you refer to that column alias in the outer query's WHERE clause. You have a chance to practice this technique in this lesson's exercises.

Window Offset Functions

Window offset functions return an element from a single row that is in a given offset from the current row in the window partition, or from the first or last row in the window frame. T-SQL supports the following window offset functions: LAG, LEAD, FIRST_VALUE, and LAST_VALUE. The LAG and LEAD functions rely on an offset with respect to the current row, and the FIRST_VALUE and LAST_VALUE functions operate on the first or last row in the frame, respectively.

The LAG and LEAD functions support window partition and ordering clauses. They don't support a window frame clause. The LAG function returns an element from the row in the current partition that is a requested number of rows before the current row (based on the window ordering), with 1 assumed as the default offset. The LEAD function returns an element from the row that is in the requested offset after the current row.

As an example, the following query uses the LAG and LEAD functions to return along with each order the value of the previous customer's order, in addition to the value from the next customer's order.

```
SELECT custid, orderid, orderdate, val,
  LAG(val)  OVER(PARTITION BY custid
                 ORDER BY orderdate, orderid) AS prev_val,
  LEAD(val) OVER(PARTITION BY custid
                 ORDER BY orderdate, orderid) AS next_val
FROM Sales.OrderValues;
```

This query generates the following output (shown here in abbreviated form).

```
custid  orderid  orderdate   val     prev_val  next_val
------- -------- ----------- ------- --------- ---------
1       10643    2007-08-25  814.50  NULL      878.00
1       10692    2007-10-03  878.00  814.50    330.00
1       10702    2007-10-13  330.00  878.00    845.80
1       10835    2008-01-15  845.80  330.00    471.20
1       10952    2008-03-16  471.20  845.80    933.50
1       11011    2008-04-09  933.50  471.20    NULL
2       10308    2006-09-18  88.80   NULL      479.75
2       10625    2007-08-08  479.75  88.80     320.00
2       10759    2007-11-28  320.00  479.75    514.40
2       10926    2008-03-04  514.40  320.00    NULL
...
```

Because an explicit offset wasn't specified, both functions relied on the default offset of 1. If you want a different offset than 1, you specify it as the second argument, as in LAG(val, 3). Notice that if a row does not exist in the requested offset, the function returns a NULL by default. If you want to return a different value in such a case, specify it as the third argument, as in LAG(val, 3, 0).

The FIRST_VALUE and LAST_VALUE functions return a value expression from the first or last rows in the window frame, respectively. Naturally, the functions support window partition, order, and frame clauses. As an example, the following query returns along with each order the values of the customer's first and last orders.

```
SELECT custid, orderid, orderdate, val,
  FIRST_VALUE(val)  OVER(PARTITION BY custid
                         ORDER BY orderdate, orderid
                         ROWS BETWEEN UNBOUNDED PRECEDING
                                  AND CURRENT ROW) AS first_val,
  LAST_VALUE(val) OVER(PARTITION BY custid
                       ORDER BY orderdate, orderid
                       ROWS BETWEEN CURRENT ROW
                                AND UNBOUNDED FOLLOWING) AS last_val
FROM Sales.OrderValues;
```

This query generates the following output (shown here in abbreviated form).

```
custid  orderid  orderdate   val     first_val  last_val
------- -------- ----------- ------- ---------- ----------
1       11011    2008-04-09  933.50  814.50     933.50
1       10952    2008-03-16  471.20  814.50     933.50
1       10835    2008-01-15  845.80  814.50     933.50
1       10702    2007-10-13  330.00  814.50     933.50
1       10692    2007-10-03  878.00  814.50     933.50
1       10643    2007-08-25  814.50  814.50     933.50
2       10926    2008-03-04  514.40  88.80      514.40
2       10759    2007-11-28  320.00  88.80      514.40
2       10625    2007-08-08  479.75  88.80      514.40
2       10308    2006-09-18  88.80   88.80      514.40
...
```

IMPORTANT **DEFAULT FRAME AND PERFORMANCE OF RANGE**

As a reminder, when a window frame is applicable to a function but you do not specify an explicit window frame clause, the default is RANGE BETWEEN UNBOUNDED PRECEDING AND CURRENT ROW. For performance reasons, it is generally recommended to avoid the RANGE option; to do so, you need to be explicit with the ROWS clause. Also, if you're after the first row in the partition, using the FIRST_VALUE function with the default frame at least gives you the correct result. However, if you're after the last row in the partition, using the LAST_VALUE function with the default frame won't give you what you want because the last row in the default frame is the current row. So with the LAST_VALUE, you need to be explicit about the window frame in order to get what you are after. And if you need an element from the last row in the partition, the second delimiter in the frame should be UNBOUNDED FOLLOWING.

Quick Check

1. What are the clauses that the different types of window functions support?
2. What do the delimiters UNBOUNDED PRECEDING and UNBOUNDED FOLLOWING represent?

Quick Check Answer

1. Partitioning, ordering, and framing clauses.
2. The beginning and end of the partition, respectively.

PRACTICE Using Window Functions

In this practice, you exercise your knowledge of window functions.

If you encounter a problem completing an exercise, you can install the completed projects from the companion content for this chapter and lesson.

EXERCISE 1 Use Window Aggregate Functions

In this exercise, you are given a task that requires you to write queries by using window aggregate functions. Try to first come up with your own solution before looking at the provided one.

1. Open SSMS and connect to the sample database TSQL2012.
2. Write a query against the Sales.OrderValues view that returns per each customer and order the moving average value of the customer's last three orders.

Your solution query should be similar to the following query.

```
SELECT custid, orderid, orderdate, val,
  AVG(val) OVER(PARTITION BY custid
                ORDER BY orderdate, orderid
                ROWS BETWEEN 2 PRECEDING
                         AND CURRENT ROW) AS movingavg
FROM Sales.OrderValues;
```

This query generates the following output, shown here in abbreviated form.

```
custid orderid  orderdate   val     movingavg
------ -------- ----------- ------- -----------
1      10643    2007-08-25  814.50  814.500000
1      10692    2007-10-03  878.00  846.250000
1      10702    2007-10-13  330.00  674.166666
1      10835    2008-01-15  845.80  684.600000
1      10952    2008-03-16  471.20  549.000000
1      11011    2008-04-09  933.50  750.166666
2      10308    2006-09-18  88.80   88.800000
2      10625    2007-08-08  479.75  284.275000
2      10759    2007-11-28  320.00  296.183333
2      10926    2008-03-04  514.40  438.050000
...
```

EXERCISE 2 Use Window Ranking and Offset Functions

In this exercise, you are given tasks that require you to write queries by using window ranking and offset functions. You are requested to filter rows based on the result of a window function, and write expressions that mix detail elements and window functions.

1. As the next task, write a query against the Sales.Orders table, and filter the three orders with the highest freight values per each shipper using orderid as the tiebreaker.

   You need to use the ROW_NUMBER function to filter the desired rows. But remember that you are not allowed to refer to window functions directly in the WHERE clause. The workaround is to define a table expression based on a query that invokes the ROW_NUMBER function and assigns the expression with a column alias. Then you can handle the filtering in the outer query using that column alias. Here's the complete solution query.

```
WITH C AS
(
  SELECT shipperid, orderid, freight,
    ROW_NUMBER() OVER(PARTITION BY shipperid
                      ORDER BY freight DESC, orderid) AS rownum
  FROM Sales.Orders
)
SELECT shipperid, orderid, freight
FROM C
WHERE rownum <= 3
ORDER BY shipperid, rownum;
```

This query generates the following output.

```
shipperid  orderid  freight
---------- -------- ---------
1          10430    458.78
1          10836    411.88
1          10658    364.15
2          10372    890.78
2          11030    830.75
2          10691    810.05
3          10540    1007.64
3          10479    708.95
3          11032    606.19
```

2. As your last task, query the Sales.OrderValues view. You need to compute the difference between the current order value and the value of the customer's previous order, in addition to the difference between the current order value and the value of the customer's next order.

   To get the values of the customer's previous and next orders, you can use the LAG and LEAD functions, respectively. Then you can subtract the results of those functions from the val column to get the desired differences. Here's the complete solution query.

```
SELECT custid, orderid, orderdate, val,
  val - LAG(val)  OVER(PARTITION BY custid
                       ORDER BY orderdate, orderid) AS diffprev,
  val - LEAD(val) OVER(PARTITION BY custid
                       ORDER BY orderdate, orderid) AS diffnext
FROM Sales.OrderValues;
```

   This query generates the following output, shown here in abbreviated form.

```
custid  orderid  orderdate   val     diffprev  diffnext
------- -------- ----------- ------- --------- ---------
1       10643    2007-08-25  814.50  NULL      -63.50
1       10692    2007-10-03  878.00  63.50     548.00
1       10702    2007-10-13  330.00  -548.00   -515.80
1       10835    2008-01-15  845.80  515.80    374.60
1       10952    2008-03-16  471.20  -374.60   -462.30
1       11011    2008-04-09  933.50  462.30    NULL
2       10308    2006-09-18  88.80   NULL      -390.95
2       10625    2007-08-08  479.75  390.95    159.75
2       10759    2007-11-28  320.00  -159.75   -194.40
2       10926    2008-03-04  514.40  194.40    NULL
...
```

Lesson Summary

- Window functions perform data analysis computations. They operate on a set of rows defined for each underlying row by using a clause called OVER.
- Unlike grouped queries, which hide the detail rows and return only one row per group, windowed queries do not hide the detail. They return a row per each row in the underlying query, and allow mixing detail elements and window functions in the same expressions.
- T-SQL supports window aggregate, ranking, and offset functions. All window functions support window partition and window order clauses. Aggregate window functions, in addition to FIRST_VALUE and LAST_VALUE, also support a window frame clause.

> ***MORE INFO* WINDOW FUNCTIONS**
>
> **For more detailed information about window functions, their optimization, and practical uses, refer to the book *Microsoft SQL Server 2012 High-Performance T-SQL Using Window Functions*, by Itzik Ben-Gan (Microsoft Press, 2012).**

Lesson Review

Answer the following questions to test your knowledge of the information in this lesson. You can find the answers to these questions and explanations of why each answer choice is correct or incorrect in the "Answers" section at the end of this chapter.

1. What is the default frame window functions use when a window order clause is specified but an explicit window frame clause isn't? (Choose all that apply.)
   - **A.** ROWS BETWEEN UNBOUNDED PRECEDING AND CURRENT ROW
   - **B.** ROWS UNBOUNDED PRECEDING
   - **C.** RANGE BETWEEN UNBOUNDED PRECEDING AND CURRENT ROW
   - **D.** RANGE UNBOUNDED PRECEDING
2. What do the RANK and DENSE_RANK functions compute?
   - **A.** The RANK function returns the number of rows that have a lower ordering value (assuming ascending ordering) than the current; the DENSE_RANK function returns the number of distinct ordering values that are lower than the current.
   - **B.** The RANK function returns one more than the number of rows that have a lower ordering value than the current; the DENSE_RANK function returns one more than the number of distinct ordering values that are lower than the current.
   - **C.** The RANK function returns one less than the number of rows that have a lower ordering value than the current; the DENSE_RANK function returns one less than the number of distinct ordering values that are lower than the current.
   - **D.** The two functions return the same result unless the ordering is unique.

3. Why are window functions allowed only in the SELECT and ORDER BY clauses of a query?
   A. Because they are supposed to operate on the underlying query's result, which is achieved when logical query processing gets to the SELECT phase.
   B. Because Microsoft didn't have time to implement them in other clauses.
   C. Because you never need to filter or group data based on the result of window functions.
   D. Because in the other clauses, the functions are considered door functions (also known as backdoor functions).

Case Scenarios

In the following case scenarios, you apply what you've learned about grouping and windowing. You can find the answers to these questions in the "Answers" section at the end of this chapter.

Case Scenario 1: Improving Data Analysis Operations

You are a data analyst in a financial company that uses SQL Server 2012 for its database. The company has just recently upgraded the system from SQL Server 2000. You often use T-SQL queries against the company's database to analyze the data. So far, you were limited to code that was compatible with SQL Server 2000, relying mainly on joins, subqueries, and grouped queries. Your queries were often complex and slow. You are now evaluating the use of features available in SQL Server 2012.

1. You often need to compute things like running totals, year-to-date calculations, and moving averages. What will you consider now to handle those? What are the things you should watch out for in order to get good performance?
2. Occasionally, you need to create crosstab reports where you rotate the data from rows to columns or the other way around. So far, you imported data to Microsoft Excel and handled such needs there, but you prefer to do it in T-SQL. What will you consider using for this purpose? What should you be careful about when using the features you're considering?
3. In many of your queries, you need to perform recency computations—that is, identify the time passed between a previous event and the current, or between the current event and the next. So far, you used subqueries for this. What will you consider now instead?

Case Scenario 2: Interviewing for a Developer Position

You are interviewed for a position as a T-SQL developer. Respond to the following questions presented to you by your interviewer.

1. Describe the difference between ROW_NUMBER and RANK.
2. Describe the difference between the ROWS and RANGE window frame units.
3. Why can you not refer to a window function in the WHERE clause of a query and what is the workaround for that?

Suggested Practices

To help you successfully master the exam objectives presented in this chapter, complete the following tasks.

Logical Query Processing

To practice your knowledge of logical query processing, identify the order in which the various query clauses are evaluated. Also identify the clauses in which the computations learned in this chapter are allowed.

- **Practice 1** At this point in this Training Kit you should be familiar with all major SELECT query clauses: SELECT, FROM, WHERE, GROUP BY, HAVING, ORDER BY, TOP, and OFFSET-FETCH. Identify the order in which these clauses are conceptually evaluated according to logical query processing. Also, identify the clauses in which the PIVOT and UNPIVOT operators operate. Finally, identify the clauses in which group functions are allowed and the clauses in which window functions are allowed.
- **Practice 2** Think of and identify the logical advantages that window aggregate functions have over grouped aggregates and over aggregates computed in subqueries.

Answers

This section contains the answers to the lesson review questions and solutions to the case scenarios in this chapter.

Lesson 1

1. **Correct Answer: D**
   - **A. Incorrect:** You can group rows without invoking an aggregate function.
   - **B. Incorrect:** A query can have an aggregate function without a GROUP BY clause. The grouping is implied—all rows make one group.
   - **C. Incorrect:** There's no requirement for grouped elements to appear in the SELECT list, though it's common to return the elements that you group by.
   - **D. Correct:** A grouped query returns only one row per group. For this reason, all expressions that appear in phases that are evaluated after the GROUP BY clause (HAVING, SELECT, and ORDER BY) must guarantee returning a single value per group. That's where the restriction comes from.
2. **Correct Answers: B, C, and D**
   - **A. Incorrect:** These functions cannot be used in the GROUP BY clause.
   - **B. Correct:** When the functions return a 1 bit, a NULL is a placeholder; when they return a 0 bit, the NULL originates from the table.
   - **C. Correct:** Each grouping set can be identified with a unique combination of 1s and 0s returned by these functions.
   - **D. Correct:** These functions can be used for sorting because they return a 0 bit for a detail element and a 1 bit for an aggregated element. So if you want to see detail first, sort by the result of the function in ascending order.
3. **Correct Answer: A**
   - **A. Correct:** The COUNT(*) function doesn't operate on an input expression; instead, it counts the number of rows in the group. The COUNT(<*expression*>) function operates on an expression and ignores NULLs. Interestingly, COUNT(<*expression*>) returns 0 when all inputs are NULLs, whereas other general set functions like MIN, MAX, SUM, and AVG return a NULL in such a case.
   - **B. Incorrect:** COUNT(*) counts rows.
   - **C. Incorrect:** COUNT(*) returns an INT.
   - **D. Incorrect:** Clearly, there is a difference between the functions in the treatment of NULLs.

Lesson 2

1. **Correct Answer: B**
   - **A. Incorrect:** The GROUPING function is related to grouping sets—not to pivoting.
   - **B. Correct:** The PIVOT operator determines the grouping element by elimination—it's what's left besides the spreading and aggregation elements.
   - **C. Incorrect:** When using the PIVOT operator, the grouping for pivoting happens as part of the PIVOT operator—before the GROUP BY clause gets evaluated.
   - **D. Incorrect:** The PIVOT operator doesn't look at constraint definitions to determine the grouping element.
2. **Correct Answers: A, B, C, and D**
   - **A. Correct:** You cannot specify a computation as input to the aggregate function, rather just a name of a column from the input table.
   - **B. Correct:** You cannot specify a computation as the spreading element, rather just a name of a column from the input table.
   - **C. Correct:** You cannot specify a subquery in the IN clause, rather just a static list.
   - **D. Correct:** You cannot specify multiple aggregate functions, rather just one.
3. **Correct Answer: D**
   - **A. Incorrect:** The type of the values column is not necessarily always an INT.
   - **B. Incorrect:** The type of the values column is not necessarily always an NVARCHAR(128)—that's the case with the names column.
   - **C. Incorrect:** The type of the values column is not SQL_VARIANT.
   - **D. Correct:** The type of the values column is the same as the type of the columns that you unpivot, and therefore they must all have a common type.

Lesson 3

1. **Correct Answers: C and D**
   - **A. Incorrect:** The default frame is based on the RANGE unit.
   - **B. Incorrect:** The default frame is based on the RANGE unit.
   - **C. Correct:** This is the default frame.
   - **D. Correct:** This is an abbreviated form of the default frame, having the same meaning.
2. **Correct Answer: B**
   - **A. Incorrect:** These definitions are one less than the correct ones.
   - **B. Correct:** These are the correct definitions.
   - **C. Incorrect:** These definitions are two less than the correct ones.
   - **D. Incorrect:** The opposite is true—the two functions return the same result when the ordering is unique.

3. **Correct Answer: A**

   A. **Correct:** Window functions are supposed to operate on the underlying query's result set. In terms of logical query processing, this result set is reached in the SELECT phase.

   B. **Incorrect:** Standard SQL defines this restriction, so it has nothing to do with Microsoft's time constraints.

   C. **Incorrect:** There are practical reasons to want to filter or group data based on the results of window functions.

   D. **Incorrect:** There are neither door functions nor backdoor functions in SQL.

Case Scenario 1

1. Window aggregate functions are excellent for such computations. As for things to watch out for, with the current implementation in SQL Server 2012, you should generally try to avoid using the RANGE window frame unit. And remember that without an explicit window frame clause, you get RANGE by default, so you want to be explicit and use the ROWS option.

2. The PIVOT and UNPIVOT operators are handy for crosstab queries. One thing to be careful about when using PIVOT is related to the fact that the grouping element is determined by elimination—what's left from the input table that wasn't specified as either spreading or aggregation elements. Therefore, it is recommended to always define a table expression returning the grouping, spreading, and aggregation elements, and use that table as the input to the PIVOT operator.

3. The LAG and LEAD functions are natural for this purpose.

Case Scenario 2

1. The ROW_NUMBER function isn't sensitive to ties in the window ordering values. Therefore, the computation is deterministic only when the window ordering is unique. When the window ordering isn't unique, the function isn't deterministic. The RANK function is sensitive to ties and produces the same rank value to all rows with the same ordering value. Therefore, it is deterministic even when the window ordering isn't unique.

2. The difference between ROWS and RANGE is actually similar to the difference between ROW_NUMBER and RANK, respectively. When the window ordering isn't unique, ROWS doesn't include peers, and therefore it isn't deterministic, whereas RANGE includes peers, and therefore it is deterministic. Also, the ROWS option can be optimized with an efficient in-memory spool; RANGE is optimized with an on-disk spool and therefore is usually slower.

3. Window functions are allowed only in the SELECT and ORDER BY clauses because the initial window they are supposed to work with is the underlying query's result set. If you need to filter rows based on a window function, you need to use a table expression like a CTE or derived table. You specify the window function in the inner query's SELECT clause and assign the target column an alias. You can then filter the rows by referring to that column alias in the outer query's WHERE clause.

CHAPTER 6

Querying Full-Text Data

Exam objectives in this chapter:

- Work with Data
  - Query data by using SELECT statements.
- Modify Data
  - Work with functions.

It is hard to imagine searching for something on the web without modern search engines like Bing or Google. However, most contemporary applications still limit users to exact searches only. For end users, even the standard SQL LIKE operator is not powerful enough for approximate searches. In addition, many documents are stored in modern databases; end users would probably like to have powerful search capabilities inside document contents as well.

Microsoft SQL Server 2012 enhances the full-text search support that was substantially available in previous editions. This chapter explains how to use full-text search and even semantic search inside a SQL Server database.

Lessons in this chapter:

- Lesson 1: Creating Full-Text Catalogs and Indexes
- Lesson 2: Using the CONTAINS and FREETEXT Predicates
- Lesson 3: Using the Full-Text and Semantic Search Table-Valued Functions

Before You Begin

To complete the lessons in this chapter, you must have:

- An understanding of relational database concepts.
- Experience working with SQL Server Management Studio (SSMS).
- Some experience writing T-SQL code.
- Access to a SQL Server 2012 instance with the sample database TSQL2012 installed.
- Full-Text Search installed on your SQL Server instance.

Lesson 1: Creating Full-Text Catalogs and Indexes

Full-text search allows approximate searches in SQL Server 2012 databases. Before you start using full-text predicates and functions, you must create *full-text indexes* inside *full-text catalogs*. After you create full-text indexes over character columns in your database, you are able to search for:

- *Simple* terms—that is, one or more specific words or phrases.
- *Prefix* terms, which are terms the words or phrases begin with.
- *Generation* terms, meaning inflectional forms of words.
- *Proximity* terms, or words or phrases close to another word or phrase.
- *Thesaurus* terms, or synonyms of a word.
- *Weighted* terms, which are words or phrases that use values with your custom weight.
- *Statistical semantic* search, or key phrases in a document.
- *Similar* documents, where similarity is defined by semantic key phrases.

After this lesson, you will be able to:

- Create full-text catalogs and full-text indexes.
- Enable statistical semantic indexing.

Estimated lesson time: 60 minutes

Full-Text Search Components

In order to start using full-text search, you have to understand full-text components. For a start, you can check whether Full-Text Search is installed by using the following query.

```
SELECT SERVERPROPERTY('IsFullTextInstalled');
```

If Full-Text Search is not installed, you must re-run the setup.

You can create full-text indexes on columns of type CHAR, VARCHAR, NCHAR, NVARCHAR, TEXT, NTEXT, IMAGE, XML, and VARBINARY(MAX). Besides using full-text indexes on SQL Server character data, you can store whole documents in binary or XML columns, and use full-text queries on those documents. Columns of data type VARBINARY(MAX), IMAGE, or XML require an additional type column in which you store the file extension (such as .docx, .pdf, or .xlsx) of the document in each row.

You need appropriate filters for documents. Filters, called *ifilters* in full-text terminology, extract the textual information and remove formatting from the documents. You can check which filters are installed in your instance by using the following query.

```
EXEC sys.sp_help_fulltext_system_components 'filter';
```

In addition to using the system stored procedure, you can also check which filters are installed in your instance by querying the sys.fulltext_document_types catalog view, as follows.

```
SELECT document_type, path
FROM sys.fulltext_document_types;
```

Many popular formats are supported by default. You can install additional filters, such as filters for Microsoft Office 2010 document formats. You can download Microsoft Office 2010 filter packs at *http://www.microsoft.com/en-us/download/details.aspx?id=17062*.

After you download the filter packs, you install them on your computer with your SQL Server instance by using the instructions provided with the filter packs. For an Office 2010 filter pack, for example, all you need to do is run the self-extracting downloaded file.

After you install the filter pack on your computer, you need to register the filters in SQL Server by using the following command.

```
EXEC sys.sp_fulltext_service 'load_os_resources', 1;
```

You might need to restart SQL Server. After you restart it, check whether the filters were successfully installed by using the sys.sp_help_fulltext_system_components system procedure again.

Word breakers and stemmers perform linguistic analysis on all full-text data. Because rules differ from language to language, word breakers and stemmers are language specific. A *word breaker* identifies individual words (or *tokens*). Tokens are inserted in a full-text index in compressed format. The *stemmer* generates inflectional forms of a word based on the rules of a language. You can use the following query to check which languages are supported in SQL Server.

```
SELECT lcid, name
FROM sys.fulltext_languages
ORDER BY name;
```

Stemmers are language specific. If you use a localized version of SQL Server, SQL Server Setup sets the default full-text language to the language of your instance, if the language is supported on your instance. If the language is not supported, or if you use a nonlocalized version of SQL Server, the default full-text language is English. You can specify a different language for each full-text indexed column. You can change the default language by using the sys.sp_configure system procedure.

Word breakers are language specific as well. If a word breaker does not exist for the language of your instance, a neutral word breaker is used. The neutral word breaker uses only neutral characters as spaces for breaking text into individual words.

Imagine that you have documents about SQL Server. The phrase "SQL Server" probably appears in every document. Such a phrase does not help you with searches; however, it bloats a full-text index. You can prevent indexing such noise words by creating *stoplists* of *stopwords*. You can check current stopwords and stoplists in your database by using the following queries.

```
SELECT stoplist_id, name
FROM sys.fulltext_stoplists;
SELECT stoplist_id, stopword, language
FROM sys.fulltext_stopwords;
```

Full-text queries can search not only for words you provide in a query; they can search for synonyms as well. SQL Server finds synonyms in *thesaurus* files. Each language has an associated XML thesaurus file. The location of the thesaurus files for a default instance is SQL_Server_install_path\Microsoft SQL Server\MSSQL11.MSSQLSERVER\MSSQL\FTDATA\. You can manually edit each thesaurus file and configure the following elements:

- **diacritics_sensitive** Set the value of this element to 0 if the language is accent insensitive, or to 1 if it is accent sensitive.
- **expansion** Use this element to add expansion words for a word. For example, you can add the expansion word "author" to the word "writer" in order to search for "author" as well when an end user searches for the word "writer."
- **replacement** Use this element to define replacement words or terms for a specific word or term. For example, "Windows 2008" could be a replacement for "Win 2k8." In such an example, SQL Server would search for "Windows 2008," even though "Win 2k8" was used in a search term.

After you edit the thesaurus file for a specific language, you must load it with the following system procedure call.

```
EXEC sys.sp_fulltext_load_thesaurus_file 1033;
```

The parameter of the procedure denotes language ID; in this case, (1033), which is the US English language.

Full-text queries can search on document properties as well. Which properties can be searched for depends on the document filter. You can create a *search property list* to define searchable properties for your documents. You can include properties that a specific filter can extract from a document.

EXAM TIP

Although full-text search is not on the list of the exam objectives, an indirect question about it could appear. Remember that full text predicates can also be a part of the WHERE clause of a query.

Creating and Managing Full-Text Catalogs and Indexes

After you have all of the full-text infrastructure in place, you can start using it. Full-text indexes are stored in full-text catalogs. A full-text catalog is a virtual object, a container for full-text indexes. As a virtual object, it does not belong to any filegroup.

Following is the syntax for creating full-text catalogs.

```
CREATE FULLTEXT CATALOG catalog_name
     [ON FILEGROUP filegroup ]
     [IN PATH 'rootpath']
     [WITH <catalog_option>]
     [AS DEFAULT]
     [AUTHORIZATION owner_name ]
<catalog_option>::=
     ACCENT_SENSITIVITY = {ON|OFF}
```

The ON FILEGROUP and IN PATH options are for backward-compatibility for SQL Server 2008 and earlier and have no effect in SQL Server 2012; you should avoid using them. The ACCENT_SENSITIVITY option determines whether full-text indexes in this catalog are accent sensitive or not. If you change this option later, you have to rebuild all full-text indexes in the catalog.

You alter a full-text catalog by using the ALTER FULLTEXT CATALOG statement, and drop it with the DROP FULLTEXT CATALOG statement.

After you have a full-text catalog, you can create appropriate full-text indexes. The syntax for creating a full-text index is as follows.

```
CREATE FULLTEXT INDEX ON table_name
   [ ( { column_name
             [ TYPE COLUMN type_column_name ]
             [ LANGUAGE language_term ]
             [ STATISTICAL_SEMANTICS ]
        } [ ,...n]
      ) ]
    KEY INDEX index_name
    [ ON <catalog_filegroup_option> ]
    [ WITH [ ( ] <with_option> [ ,...n] [ ) ] ]
[;]
<catalog_filegroup_option>::=
 {
    fulltext_catalog_name
 | ( fulltext_catalog_name, FILEGROUP filegroup_name )
 | ( FILEGROUP filegroup_name, fulltext_catalog_name )
 | ( FILEGROUP filegroup_name )
 }
<with_option>::=
 {
   CHANGE_TRACKING [ = ] { MANUAL | AUTO | OFF [, NO POPULATION ] }
 | STOPLIST [ = ] { OFF | SYSTEM | stoplist_name }
 | SEARCH PROPERTY LIST [ = ] property_list_name
 }
```

Most of the options are self-describing. You learn about them in the practice for this lesson. The following describes some advanced options:

- **KEY INDEX index_name** This is the name of the unique key index on a table. You have to use a unique, single-key, non-nullable column. Integers are recommended.
- **CHANGE_TRACKING [=] { MANUAL | AUTO | OFF [, NO POPULATION] }** This option specifies whether SQL Server updates a full-text index automatically. SQL Server uses a change tracking mechanism to track changes.
- **STATISTICAL_SEMANTICS** This option creates additional key phrase and document similarity indexes that are part of statistical semantic indexing.

The last option mentioned, the STATISTICAL_SEMANTICS option, deserves deeper explanation. *Statistical semantic search* gives you deeper insight into documents by extracting and indexing statistically relevant key phrases. Full-text search uses these key phrases to identify and index documents that are similar or related. You query these semantic indexes by using three T-SQL rowset functions to retrieve the results as structured data. You use these functions in the practices in this chapter. Semantic search extends full-text search functionality. It enables you to query the meaning of the documents. For example, you can query the index of key phrases to build the taxonomy of documents. You can query the document similarity index to identify résumés that match a job description. Semantic search gives you the possibility to create your own text-mining solution. Semantic search could be especially interesting in conjunction with text-mining components of SQL Server Integration Services (SSIS).

In order to use the Semantic Search feature, you have to have Full-Text Search installed. In addition, you need to install the Semantic Language Statistics Database. You install it in the practice for this lesson.

Quick Check

- **Can you store indexes from the same full-text catalog to different filegroups?**

Quick Check Answer

- **Yes. A full-text catalog is a virtual object only; full-text indexes are physical objects. You can store each full-text index from the same catalog to a different file group.**

PRACTICE Creating a Full-Text Index

In this practice, you create a table, populate it with some documents and text data, and create a full-text catalog and index on this table. This practice assumes that the default language of your instance is US English.

If you encounter a problem completing an exercise, you can install the completed projects from the companion content for this chapter and lesson.

EXERCISE 1 Create a Table and Full-Text Components

In this exercise, you create a demo table, populate it with some demo text, and then create stopwords and a stoplist and search document properties.

1. Start SSMS and connect to your SQL Server instance.
2. Open a new query window by clicking the New Query button.
3. Change the context to the TSQL2012 database.
4. Check whether Full-Text Search is installed by using the following query.

   ```
   SELECT SERVERPROPERTY('IsFullTextInstalled');
   ```

5. If Full-Text Search is not installed, run SQL Server Setup and install it. Also install the Microsoft Office 2010 filter packs.
6. Create a table that you will use for full-text search. Create it in the dbo schema and name it **Documents**. Use the information from Table 6-1 for the columns of your dbo. Documents table.

   TABLE 6-1 Column information for the dbo.Documents table

Column name	Data type	Nullability	Remarks
id	INT	NOT NULL	IDENTITY, PRIMARY KEY
title	NVARCHAR(100)	NOT NULL	Name of the documents you are going to import
doctype	NCHAR(4)	NOT NULL	Type of the documents you are going to import
docexcerpt	NVARCHAR(1000)	NOT NULL	Excerpt of the documents you are going to import
doccontent	VARBINARY(MAX)	NOT NULL	Documents you are going to import

   Use the following code for creating the table.

   ```
   CREATE TABLE dbo.Documents
   (
     id INT IDENTITY(1,1) NOT NULL,
     title NVARCHAR(100) NOT NULL,
     doctype NCHAR(4) NOT NULL,
     docexcerpt NVARCHAR(1000) NOT NULL,
     doccontent VARBINARY(MAX) NOT NULL,
     CONSTRAINT PK_Documents
      PRIMARY KEY CLUSTERED(id)
   );
   ```

7. Import the four documents included in the folder for this book. If the folder is C:\TK70461, then you can use the following code directly; otherwise, change the folder in the OPENROWSET functions appropriately.

```
INSERT INTO dbo.Documents
(title, doctype, docexcerpt, doccontent)
SELECT N'Columnstore Indices and Batch Processing',
 N'docx',
 N'You should use a columnstore index on your fact tables,
   putting all columns of a fact table in a columnstore index.
   In addition to fact tables, very large dimensions could benefit
   from columnstore indices as well.
   Do not use columnstore indices for small dimensions. ',
 bulkcolumn
FROM OPENROWSET(BULK 'C:\TK70461\ColumnstoreIndicesAndBatchProcessing.docx',
                SINGLE_BLOB) AS doc;
INSERT INTO dbo.Documents
(title, doctype, docexcerpt, doccontent)
SELECT N'Introduction to Data Mining',
 N'docx',
 N'Using Data Mining is becoming more a necessity for every company
   and not an advantage of some rare companies anymore. ',
 bulkcolumn
FROM OPENROWSET(BULK 'C:\TK70461\IntroductionToDataMining.docx',
                SINGLE_BLOB) AS doc;
INSERT INTO dbo.Documents
(title, doctype, docexcerpt, doccontent)
SELECT N'Why Is Bleeding Edge a Different Conference',
 N'docx',
 N'During high level presentations attendees encounter many questions.
   For the third year, we are continuing with the breakfast Q&A session.
   It is very popular, and for two years now,
   we could not accommodate enough time for all questions and discussions! ',
 bulkcolumn
FROM OPENROWSET(BULK 'C:\TK70461\WhyIsBleedingEdgeADifferentConference.docx',
                SINGLE_BLOB) AS doc;
INSERT INTO dbo.Documents
(title, doctype, docexcerpt, doccontent)
SELECT N'Additivity of Measures',
 N'docx',
 N'Additivity of measures is not exactly a data warehouse design problem.
   However, you have to realize which aggregate functions you will use
   in reports for which measure, and which aggregate functions
   you will use when aggregating over which dimension.',
 bulkcolumn
FROM OPENROWSET(BULK 'C:\TK70461\AdditivityOfMeasures.docx',
                SINGLE_BLOB) AS doc;
```

8. Create a search property list called **WordSearchPropertyList**. Add the property Authors to the list. Document properties have predefined GUIDs and integer IDs. See the Books OnLine for SQL Server 2012 article "Find Property Set GUIDs and

Property Integer IDs for Search Properties" at *http://msdn.microsoft.com/en-us/library/ee677618.aspx* for the list of some well-known ones. For the Authors property of Office documents, the GUID is F29F85E0-4FF9-1068-AB91-08002B27B3D9, and the integer ID is 4. Use the following code.

```
CREATE SEARCH PROPERTY LIST WordSearchPropertyList;
GO
ALTER SEARCH PROPERTY LIST WordSearchPropertyList
 ADD 'Authors'
 WITH (PROPERTY_SET_GUID = 'F29F85E0-4FF9-1068-AB91-08002B27B3D9',
       PROPERTY_INT_ID = 4,
       PROPERTY_DESCRIPTION = 'System.Authors - authors of a given item.');
```

9. Create a stopwords list called **SQLStopList**. Add the word **SQL** to it, using English as the language. Use the following code.

```
CREATE FULLTEXT STOPLIST SQLStopList;
GO
ALTER FULLTEXT STOPLIST SQLStopList
 ADD 'SQL' LANGUAGE 'English';
```

10. Check the stopwords list and remember the stoplist ID. Use the following query.

```
SELECT w.stoplist_id,
 l.name,
 w.stopword,
 w.language
FROM sys.fulltext_stopwords AS w
 INNER JOIN sys.fulltext_stoplists AS l
  ON w.stoplist_id = l.stoplist_id;
```

11. Use the sys.dm_fts_parser dynamic management view to check how full-text search is parsing strings according to your stoplist, thesaurus info, word breaking in the selected language, and stemming in the selected language. For example, the next two queries check how a string is broken into words and what inflectional forms of a word full-text search can use. Note the parameters of the dynamic management view: The first one is the character string to analyze, the second one is the language ID (1033 for US English), the third one is the stoplist ID you got from the previous query, and the fourth one is a flag showing whether the parsing should be accent sensitive or not.

```
SELECT *
FROM sys.dm_fts_parser
(N'"Additivity of measures is not exactly a data warehouse design problem.
   However, you have to realize which aggregate functions you will use
   in reports for which measure, and which aggregate functions
   you will use when aggregating over which dimension."', 1033, 5, 0);
SELECT *
FROM sys.dm_fts_parser
('FORMSOF(INFLECTIONAL,'+ 'function' + ')', 1033, 5, 0);
```

EXERCISE 2 Install a Semantic Database and Create a Full-Text Index

In this exercise, you install a semantic database and then create a full-text index.

1. Check whether the Semantic Language Statistics Database is installed. If the following query does not return a row, you must install it.

   ```
   SELECT *
   FROM sys.fulltext_semantic_language_statistics_database;
   ```

   To install the Semantic Language Statistics Database, run the SemanticLanguageDatabase.msi package from the x64\Setup (if you are using a 64-bit instance) or x86\Setup (if your instance is 32-bit) folder from the SQL Server Setup drive.

2. Check whether the SQL Server service account has Read and Write permissions on the folder where you installed the Semantic Language Statistics Database files. The default folder is C:\Program Files\Microsoft Semantic Language Database. If you installed the database in the default folder, then you can attach it by using the following command.

   ```
   CREATE DATABASE semanticsdb ON
    (FILENAME = 'C:\Program Files\Microsoft Semantic Language Database\semanticsdb.
   mdf'),
    (FILENAME = 'C:\Program Files\Microsoft Semantic Language Database\semanticsdb_
   log.ldf')
    FOR ATTACH;
   ```

3. After you attach the database, register it by using the following code.

   ```
   EXEC sp_fulltext_semantic_register_language_statistics_db
    @dbname = N'semanticsdb';
   ```

4. Check whether the Semantic Language Statistics Database was successfully installed by repeating the query from step 1. This time, the query should return one row.

5. Finally, it is time to create a catalog. Name it **DocumentsFtCatalog**. Use the following code.

   ```
   CREATE FULLTEXT CATALOG DocumentsFtCatalog;
   ```

6. Now create a full-text index. You should index the docexcerpt and doccontent columns. Set change tracking for populating the index to AUTO. Use the following code.

   ```
   CREATE FULLTEXT INDEX ON dbo.Documents
   (
     docexcerpt Language 1033,
     doccontent TYPE COLUMN doctype
     Language 1033
     STATISTICAL_SEMANTICS
   )
   KEY INDEX PK_Documents
   ON DocumentsFtCatalog
   WITH STOPLIST = SQLStopList,
        SEARCH PROPERTY LIST = WordSearchPropertyList,
        CHANGE_TRACKING AUTO;
   ```

Lesson Summary

- You can create full-text catalogs and indexes by using SQL Server Full-Text Search and Semantic Search.
- You can improve full-text searches by adding stopwords to stoplists, enhancing a thesaurus, and enabling a search over document properties.
- You can use the sys.dm_fts_parser dynamic management object to check how Full-Text Search breaks your documents into words, creates inflectional forms of words, and more.

Lesson Review

Answer the following questions to test your knowledge of the information in this lesson. You can find the answers to these questions and explanations of why each answer choice is correct or incorrect in the "Answers" section at the end of this chapter.

1. Which full-text search elements can you use to prevent indexing noisy words? (Choose all that apply.)

   A. Stopwords

   B. Thesaurus

   C. Stemmer

   D. Stoplists

2. Which database do you have to install in order to enable the Semantic Search feature?

   A. msdb

   B. distribution

   C. semanticsdb

   D. tempdb

3. How can you create synonyms for the words searched?

   A. You can edit the thesaurus file.

   B. You can create a thesaurus table.

   C. You can use the stopwords for synonyms as well.

   D. Full-text search does not support synonyms.

Lesson 2: Using the CONTAINS and FREETEXT Predicates

SQL Server supports two very powerful predicates for limiting the result set of a query by using full-text indexes. These two predicates are the CONTAINS and FREETEXT predicates. Both of them support various term searching. Besides these two predicates, SQL Server supports two table-valued functions for full-text searches, and three table-valued functions for semantic searches. You learn about the two predicates in this lesson and about the five functions in the next lesson.

After this lesson, you will be able to:

- Use the CONTAINS predicate in your queries.
- Use the FREETEXT predicate.

Estimated lesson time: 40 minutes

The CONTAINS Predicate

With the CONTAINS predicate, you can search for the following:

- Words and phrases in text
- Exact or fuzzy matches
- Inflectional forms of a word
- Text in which a search word is close to another search word
- Synonyms of a searched word
- A prefix of a word or a phrase only

You can also add your custom weight to words you are searching for. You use the CONTAINS predicate in the WHERE clause of your T-SQL statements.

For all details about this predicate, see the Books Online for SQL Server 2012 article "CONTAINS (Transact-SQL)" at *http://msdn.microsoft.com/en-us/library/ms187787.aspx*. Here are the most important forms of queries with the CONTAINS predicate in pseudocode, where FTcolumn stands for a full-text indexed column and 'SearchWord?' stands for the word or phrase searched:

- **SELECT...FROM...WHERE CONTAINS(FTcolumn, 'SearchWord1')** This is the simplest form. You are searching for rows where the FTcolumn contains an exact match for 'SearchWord1'. This is a *simple* term.
- **SELECT...FROM...WHERE CONTAINS(FTcolumn, 'SearchWord1 OR SearchWord2')** You are searching for rows where the FTcolumn contains an exact match for 'SearchWord1' or for the word 'SearchWord2'. You can also use AND and AND NOT logical operators and change the order of evaluation of the operators in an expression with parentheses.

- **SELECT…FROM…WHERE CONTAINS(FTcolumn, '"SearchWord1 SearchWord2"')** You are searching for rows where the FTcolumn contains an exact match for the phrase "SearchWord1 SearchWord2."
- **SELECT…FROM…WHERE CONTAINS(FTcolumn, '"SearchWord1*"')** You are searching for rows where the FTcolumn contains at least one word that starts with the letters 'SearchWord1'. This is a *prefix* term.
- **SELECT…FROM…WHERE CONTAINS(FTcolumn, 'NEAR(SearchWord1, SearchWord2)')** You are searching for rows where the FTcolumn contains SearchWord1 and SearchWord2. This is the simplest custom *proximity term*. In this simplest version, it searches only for occurrences of both words, no matter what the distance and order of terms. The result is similar to a simple term where two words or phrases are connected with the logical AND operator.
- **SELECT…FROM…WHERE CONTAINS(FTcolumn, 'NEAR((SearchWord1, SearchWord2), distance)')** You are searching for rows where the FTcolumn contains SearchWord1 and SearchWord2. The order of the search words is not important; however, the distance is an integer that tells how many nonsearch terms can be maximally between the searched terms in order to qualify a row for the result set.
- **SELECT…FROM…WHERE CONTAINS(FTcolumn, 'NEAR((SearchWord1, SearchWord2), distance, flag)')** You are searching for rows where the FTcolumn contains SearchWord1 and SearchWord2. The two searched terms must be closer together than the distance. The flag can take values TRUE or FALSE; the default is FALSE. If the flag is set to TRUE, then the order of the searched terms is important; SearchWord1 must be in text before SearchWord2.
- **SELECT…FROM…WHERE CONTAINS(FTcolumn, 'FORMSOF(INFLECTIONAL, SearchWord1)')** This is the *generation term* format of the predicate. You are searching for the rows where the FTcolumn includes any of the inflectional form of the word SearchWord1.
- **SELECT…FROM…WHERE CONTAINS(FTcolumn, 'FORMSOF(THESAURUS, SearchWord1)')** This is again the generation term format of the predicate. You are searching for the rows where the FTcolumn includes either the word SearchWord1 or any of the synonyms for this word defined in the thesaurus file.
- **SELECT…FROM…WHERE CONTAINS(FTcolumn, 'ISABOUT(SearchWord1 weight(w1), SearchWord2 weight(w2))')** This is a *weighted term*. Weights have influence on the rank of the documents returned. However, because the CONTAINS predicate does not rank the results, this form has no influence on it. The weighted form is useful for the CONTAINSTABLE function.
- **SELECT…FROM…WHERE CONTAINS(PROPERTY(FTcolumn, 'PropertyName'), 'SearchWord1')** This is a property search. You need to have documents with some known properties. In such a query, you are searching for rows with documents that have the property PropertyName that contain the value SearchWord1.

The FREETEXT Predicate

The FREETEXT predicate is less specific and thus returns more rows than the CONTAINS predicate. It searches for the values that match the meaning of a phrase and not just exact words. When you use the FREETEXT predicate, the engine performs word breaking of the search phrase, generates inflectional forms (does the stemming), and identifies a list of expansions or replacements for the words in the searched term with words from the thesaurus. The form is much simpler than the form of the CONTAINS predicate: SELECT...FROM...WHERE FREETEXT(FTcolumn, 'SearchWord1 SearchWord2'). With this, you are searching for rows where the FTcolumn includes any of the inflectional forms and any of the defined synonyms of the words SearchWord1 and SearchWord2.

EXAM TIP

The FREETEXT predicate is less selective than the CONTAINS predicate, and thus it usually returns more rows than the CONTAINS predicate.

Quick Check

1. **How do you search for synonyms of a word with the CONTAINS predicate?**
2. **Which is a more specific predicate, CONTAINS or FREETEXT?**

Quick Check Answers

1. **You have to use the CONTAINS(FTcolumn, 'FORMSOF(THESAURUS, SearchWord1)') syntax.**
2. **You use the CONTAINS predicate for more specific searches.**

PRACTICE Using the CONTAINS and FREETEXT Predicates

After you create all components needed for a full-text search solution, it is time to start using the full-text search.

If you encounter a problem completing an exercise, you can install the completed projects from he companion content for this chapter and lesson.

EXERCISE 1 Use the CONTAINS Predicate

In this exercise, you use the CONTAINS predicate. In addition, you edit and use a thesaurus file.

1. If you closed SSMS, start it and connect to your SQL Server instance. Open a new query window by clicking the New Query button.

2. Connect to your TSQL2012 database.

3. Find all rows where the docexcerpt column of the dbo.Documents table includes the word "data". Use the following query.

```
SELECT id, title, docexcerpt
FROM dbo.Documents
WHERE CONTAINS(docexcerpt, N'data');
```

4. Find all rows where the docexcerpt column of the dbo.Documents table includes the word "data" or the word "index". Use the following query.

```
SELECT id, title, docexcerpt
FROM dbo.Documents
WHERE CONTAINS(docexcerpt, N'data OR index');
```

5. Find all rows where the docexcerpt column of the dbo.Documents table includes the word "data" and not the word "mining". Use the following query.

```
SELECT id, title, docexcerpt
FROM dbo.Documents
WHERE CONTAINS(docexcerpt, N'data AND NOT mining');
```

6. Find all rows where the docexcerpt column of the dbo.Documents table includes the word "data" or the words "fact" and "warehouse". Use the following query.

```
SELECT id, title, docexcerpt
FROM dbo.Documents
WHERE CONTAINS(docexcerpt, N'data OR (fact AND warehouse)');
```

7. Find all rows where the docexcerpt column of the dbo.Documents table includes the phrase "data warehouse". Use the following query.

```
SELECT id, title, docexcerpt
FROM dbo.Documents
WHERE CONTAINS(docexcerpt, N'"data warehouse"');
```

8. Find all rows where the docexcerpt column of the dbo.Documents table includes words that start with the prefix "add". Use the following query.

```
SELECT id, title, docexcerpt
FROM dbo.Documents
WHERE CONTAINS(docexcerpt, N'"add*"');
```

9. Find all rows where the docexcerpt column of the dbo.Documents table includes the word "problem" anywhere near the word "data". Use the following query.

```
SELECT id, title, docexcerpt
FROM dbo.Documents
WHERE CONTAINS(docexcerpt, N'NEAR(problem, data)');
```

10. Find all rows where the docexcerpt column of the dbo.Documents table includes the word "problem" anywhere near the word "data". Try it with a query that searches for excerpts where the words are fewer than five and then with a query where the words are fewer than one nonsearch terms away. From the following two queries, the first one should return one row and the second one no rows.

```
SELECT id, title, docexcerpt
FROM dbo.Documents
WHERE CONTAINS(docexcerpt, N'NEAR((problem, data),5)');

SELECT id, title, docexcerpt
FROM dbo.Documents
WHERE CONTAINS(docexcerpt, N'NEAR((problem, data),1)');
```

11. Find all rows where the docexcerpt column of the dbo.Documents table includes the word "problem" anywhere near the word "data". Try it with a query that searches for excerpts where the words are fewer than five nonsearch terms away. However, specify that the word "problem" must be before the word "data". Use the following query.

```
SELECT id, title, docexcerpt
FROM dbo.Documents
WHERE CONTAINS(docexcerpt, N'NEAR((problem, data),5, TRUE)');
```

12. Find all rows where the docexcerpt column of the dbo.Documents table includes the word "presentation". Try with a query that searches for exact match and with a query that searches for any inflectional form of the word. From the following two queries, the first query should return no rows and the second query one row.

```
SELECT id, title, docexcerpt
FROM dbo.Documents
WHERE CONTAINS(docexcerpt, N'presentation');

SELECT id, title, docexcerpt
FROM dbo.Documents
WHERE CONTAINS(docexcerpt, N'FORMSOF(INFLECTIONAL, presentation)');
```

EXERCISE 2 Use Synonyms and FREETEXT

In this exercise, you edit and use a thesaurus file to add a synonym.

1. Use Notepad to edit the thesaurus file for the US English language. Add a synonym "necessity" for the word "need". The file to edit is the tsenu.xml file, located in a default installation in the C:\Program Files\Microsoft SQL Server\MSSQL11.MSSQLSERVER\MSSQL\FTData folder. If you didn't use the default path for the installation or use a nondefault instance, then the path in a general form is SQL_Server_install_path\Microsoft SQL Server\MSSQL11.Instance_id\MSSQL\FTData. Clear the XML comments from the file.

After editing, the content of the file should be as follows.

```
<XML ID="Microsoft Search Thesaurus">
    <thesaurus xmlns="x-schema:tsSchema.xml">
    <diacritics_sensitive>0</diacritics_sensitive>
        <expansion>
            <sub>Internet Explorer</sub>
            <sub>IE</sub>
            <sub>IE5</sub>
        </expansion>
        <replacement>
            <pat>NT5</pat>
            <pat>W2K</pat>
            <sub>Windows 2000</sub>
        </replacement>
        <expansion>
            <sub>run</sub>
            <sub>jog</sub>
        </expansion>
        <expansion>
            <sub>need</sub>
            <sub>necessity</sub>
        </expansion>
    </thesaurus>
</XML>
```

2. Load the thesaurus file for US English.

```
EXEC sys.sp_fulltext_load_thesaurus_file 1033;
```

3. Find all rows where the docexcerpt column of the dbo.Documents table includes the word "need" or its synonym. Try with a query that searches for exact match and with a query that searches for synonyms of the word. From the following two queries, the first query should return no rows and the second query one row.

```
SELECT id, title, docexcerpt
FROM dbo.Documents
WHERE CONTAINS(docexcerpt, N'need');

SELECT id, title, docexcerpt
FROM dbo.Documents
WHERE CONTAINS(docexcerpt, N'FORMSOF(THESAURUS, need)');
```

4. Search for all rows from the dbo.Documents table where the document in the doccontent column contains a property called "Authors" with a value that includes the word "Dejan". Use the following query.

```
SELECT id, title, docexcerpt
FROM dbo.Documents
WHERE CONTAINS(PROPERTY(doccontent,'Authors'), 'Dejan');
```

5. Finally, find all rows where the docexcerpt column contains any of the words "data", "presentation", or "need". The words can be in any inflectional form. Search for synonyms as well. Use the following query.

```
SELECT id, title, doctype, docexcerpt
FROM dbo.Documents
WHERE FREETEXT(docexcerpt, N'data presentation need');
```

Lesson Summary

- You can use the CONTAINS predicate for selective searches.
- The FREETEXT predicate can be used for more general searches.

Lesson Review

Answer the following questions to test your knowledge of the information in this lesson. You can find the answers to these questions and explanations of why each answer choice is correct or incorrect in the "Answers" section at the end of this chapter.

1. Which of the following is not a part of the CONTAINS predicate?
   - **A.** FORMSOF
   - **B.** THESAURUS
   - **C.** NEAR
   - **D.** PROPERTY
   - **E.** TEMPORARY
2. Which form of the proximity term defines the distance and the order?
   - **A.** NEAR((SearchWord1, SearchWord2), 5, TRUE)
   - **B.** NEAR((SearchWord1, SearchWord2), CLOSE, ORDER)
   - **C.** NEAR((SearchWord1, SearchWord2), 5)
   - **D.** NEAR(SearchWord1, SearchWord2)
3. What can you search for with the CONTAINS predicate? (Choose all that apply.)
   - **A.** Inflectional forms of a word
   - **B.** Synonyms of a searched word
   - **C.** Translations of a word
   - **D.** Text in which a search word is close to another search word
   - **E.** A prefix of a word or a phrase only

Lesson 3: Using the Full-Text and Semantic Search Table-Valued Functions

In the previous lesson, you learned that terms in a full-text search can be weighted to change the rank of documents. However, you cannot see the rank by using the CONTAINS predicate. You need to get a table of documents (or document IDs) and their rank. This table is returned by the CONTAINSTABLE and FREETEXTTABLE functions. In addition, you installed the Semantic Language Statistics Database in the practice for Lesson 1. You are now going to exploit semantic search through three table-valued functions: SEMANTICKEYPHRASETABLE, SEMANTICSIMILARITYDETAILSTABLE, and SEMANTICSIMILARITYTABLE.

After this lesson, you will be able to:

- Use full-text table-valued functions.
- Use semantic search table-valued functions.

Estimated lesson time: 30 minutes

Using the Full-Text Search Functions

The CONTAINSTABLE and FREETEXTTABLE functions return two columns: KEY and RANK. The KEY column is the unique key from the index used in the KEY INDEX clause of the CREATE FULLTEXT INDEX statement. RANK returns an ordinal value between 0 and 1000. This is the rank value. It tells you how well a row matches your search criteria. The number is always relative to a query; it tells you only relative order of relevance for a particular rowset. A lower value means lower relevance. The actual values are not important; they might even change when you run the same query next time.

The calculation of the rank is quite complex. SQL Server takes into account term frequency—that is, frequency of a searched word in a document, number of words in a document, proximity terms (the NEAR clause), weight (the ISABOUT clause), number of indexed rows, and more. There is a different calculation for the CONTAINSTABLE function and for the FREETEXTTABLE function, because the latter does not support the majority of the parameters that the first one does, like proximity and weight terms.

The shortened syntax for the CONTAINSTABLE is as follows.

```
CONTAINSTABLE ( table , { column_name | ( column_list ) | * } ,
 ' <contains_search_condition> ' [ , LANGUAGE language_term]  [ , top_n_by_rank ] )
```

Search conditions are the same as in the CONTAINS predicate. You can use a simple term, a prefix term, a generation term, a proximity term, or a weighted term. The top_n_by_rank is an integer that specifies that only the *n* rows with highest rank should be returned in the rowset. This parameter could be important for performance, because your query might return huge rowsets.

The syntax for the FREETEXTTABLE is as follows.

```
FREETEXTTABLE (table , { column_name | (column_list) | * }
          , 'freetext_string'  [ , LANGUAGE language_term ]  [ , top_n_by_rank ] )
```

Because this syntax is so simple, the complete syntax is shown.

> ***NOTE*** **WORD BREAKING, STEMMING, THESAURUS, AND STOPWORDS LANGUAGE**
>
> **It is worth mentioning what *language_term* stands for. This is the language SQL Server uses for word breaking, stemming, and thesaurus and stopword removal as part of the query. If no value is specified, the column full-text language is used. This parameter could be useful when you store documents of different languages in a single column. The locale identifier (LCID) of a document determines what language SQL Server uses to index its content. When you query such a column, the language_term can increase the quality of matches. You can use the language_term in the CONTAINS and FREETEXT predicates and CONTAINSTABLE function as well. You can specify it as an integer, representing the LCID, or as a string, representing the language alias. In addition, you can even specify LCID as a hexadecimal string.**

Using the Semantic Search Functions

There are three table-valued functions that enable the semantic search. The syntax for the first one, the SEMANTICKEYPHRASETABLE, is as follows.

```
SEMANTICKEYPHRASETABLE
    ( table, { column | (column_list) | * }  [ , source_key ] )
```

This function returns a table with key phrases associated with the full-text indexed column from the column_list. The source_key parameter specifies the unique key from the index used in the KEY INDEX clause of the CREATE FULLTEXT INDEX statement. If you omit it, SQL Server returns key phrases for all rows.

EXAM TIP

Semantic search is available through the table-valued functions only; it does not support any specific predicates for the WHERE clause of a query.

The syntax for the second semantic search function, SEMANTICSIMILARITYDETAILSTABLE, is as follows.

```
SEMANTICSIMILARITYDETAILSTABLE
    ( table, source_column, source_key, matched_column, matched_key )
```

This function returns a table with key phrases that are common across two documents. You define the source document with the source_key, which is again the unique key from the index used in the KEY INDEX clause of the CREATE FULLTEXT INDEX statement, and with source_column, which is the name of the full-text indexed column.

The last semantic search function is the SEMANTICSIMILARITYTABLE function, as shown here.

```
SEMANTICSIMILARITYTABLE
    ( table, { column | (column_list) | * }, source_key )
```

This function returns a table with documents scored by semantic similarity to the searched document specified with the source_key parameter. The source_key parameter specifies the unique key from the index used in the KEY INDEX clause of the CREATE FULLTEXT INDEX statement. You can use this function to find which documents are the most similar to a specified document.

Quick Check

- **How many full-text search and how many semantic search functions are supported by SQL Server?**

Quick Check Answer

- **SQL Server supports two full-text search and three semantic search functions.**

PRACTICE Using the Full-Text and Semantic Search Functions

In this practice, you use the full-text and semantic search table-valued functions.

If you encounter a problem completing an exercise, you can install the completed projects from the companion content for this chapter and lesson.

EXERCISE 1 Use the Full-Text Search Functions

In this exercise, you query data with the CONTAINSTABLE and FREETEXTTABLE functions.

1. If you closed SSMS, start it and connect to your SQL Server instance. Open a new query window by clicking the New Query button.
2. Connect to your TSQL2012 database.

3. Write a query that uses the CONTAINSTABLE function to rank the documents based on containment of the words "data" or "level" in the docexcerpt column. Use the following query.

```
SELECT D.id, D.title, CT.[RANK], D.docexcerpt
FROM CONTAINSTABLE(dbo.Documents, docexcerpt,
      N'data OR level') AS CT
 INNER JOIN dbo.Documents AS D
  ON CT.[KEY] = D.id
ORDER BY CT.[RANK] DESC;
```

4. Write a query that uses the FREETEXTTABLE function to rank the documents based on containment of the words "data" or "level" in the docexcerpt column. Compare the result with the result from the previous query. Use the following query.

```
SELECT D.id, D.title, FT.[RANK], D.docexcerpt
FROM FREETEXTTABLE (dbo.Documents, docexcerpt,
      N'data level') AS FT
 INNER JOIN dbo.Documents AS D
  ON FT.[KEY] = D.id
ORDER BY FT.[RANK] DESC;
```

5. Write a query that retrieves the rank of the documents based on containment of the words "data" or "level" in the docexcerpt column. Give the word "data" a weight of 0.8, and the word "level" a weight of 0.2. Compare the results with the results from the first CONTAINSTABLE query in this exercise. Use the following query.

```
SELECT D.id, D.title, CT.[RANK], D.docexcerpt
FROM CONTAINSTABLE
      (dbo.Documents, docexcerpt,
       N'ISABOUT(data weight(0.8), level weight(0.2))') AS CT
 INNER JOIN dbo.Documents AS D
  ON CT.[KEY] = D.id
ORDER BY CT.[RANK] DESC;
```

6. Write a query that retrieves the rank of the documents based on containment of the words "data" and "row" in the doccontent column. The words must be fewer than 30 search terms away. Use the following query.

```
SELECT D.id, D.title, CT.[RANK]
FROM CONTAINSTABLE (dbo.Documents, doccontent,
      N'NEAR((data, row), 30)') AS CT
 INNER JOIN dbo.Documents AS D
  ON CT.[KEY] = D.id
ORDER BY CT.[RANK] DESC;
```

7. Test the previous query with a different distance between search terms.

EXERCISE 2 Use the Semantic Search Functions

In this exercise, you query data by using the SEMANTICKEYPHRASETABLE, SEMANTICSIMILARITYDETAILSTABLE, and SEMANTICSIMILARITYTABLE functions.

1. Write a query that retrieves the 20 most important semantic search phrases in the documents in the doccontent column. Use the following query.

```
SELECT TOP (20)
 D.id, D.title, SKT.keyphrase, SKT.score
FROM SEMANTICKEYPHRASETABLE
      (dbo.Documents, doccontent) AS SKT
 INNER JOIN dbo.Documents AS D
  ON SKT.document_key = D.id
ORDER BY SKT.score DESC;
```

2. Return all documents but the document with ID equal to 1, ordered by semantic similarity to the document in the doccontent column with ID equal to 1. Use the following query.

```
SELECT SST.matched_document_key,
 D.title, SST.score
FROM SEMANTICSIMILARITYTABLE
     (dbo.Documents, doccontent, 1) AS SST
 INNER JOIN dbo.Documents AS D
  ON SST.matched_document_key = D.id
ORDER BY SST.score DESC;
```

3. Return semantic search key phrases that are common across the document with ID equal to 1 and the document with ID equal to 4. Order the phrases by similarity score. Use the following query.

```
SELECT SSDT.keyphrase, SSDT.score
FROM SEMANTICSIMILARITYDETAILSTABLE
      (dbo.Documents, doccontent, 1,
       doccontent, 4) AS SSDT
ORDER BY SSDT.score DESC;
```

4. Clean up the database.

```
DROP TABLE dbo.Documents;
DROP FULLTEXT CATALOG DocumentsFtCatalog;
DROP SEARCH PROPERTY LIST WordSearchPropertyList;
DROP FULLTEXT STOPLIST SQLStopList;
```

5. Exit SSMS.

Lesson Summary

- Full-text functions are useful for ranking results.
- Semantic similarity functions give you a lot of insight into the documents. You can find key phrases and compare documents.

Lesson Review

Answer the following questions to test your knowledge of the information in this lesson. You can find the answers to these questions and explanations of why each answer choice is correct or incorrect in the "Answers" section at the end of this chapter.

1. Which function can be used to rank documents based on proximity of words?
   - **A.** CONTAINSTABLE()
   - **B.** FREETEXTTABLE()
   - **C.** SEMANTICKEYPHRASETABLE()
   - **D.** SEMANTICSIMILARITYTABLE()
   - **E.** SEMANTICSIMILARITYDETAILSTABLE()
2. Which function can be used to find the document that is most semantically similar to a specified document?
   - **A.** CONTAINSTABLE()
   - **B.** FREETEXTTABLE()
   - **C.** SEMANTICKEYPHRASETABLE()
   - **D.** SEMANTICSIMILARITYTABLE()
   - **E.** SEMANTICSIMILARITYDETAILSTABLE()
3. Which function returns a table with key phrases associated with the full-text indexed column?
   - **A.** CONTAINSTABLE()
   - **B.** FREETEXTTABLE()
   - **C.** SEMANTICKEYPHRASETABLE()
   - **D.** SEMANTICSIMILARITYTABLE()
   - **E.** SEMANTICSIMILARITYDETAILSTABLE()

Case Scenarios

In the following case scenarios, you apply what you've learned about querying full-text data and using a semantic search. You can find the answers to these questions in the "Answers" section at the end of this chapter.

Case Scenario 1: Enhancing the Searches

After you deploy a line-of-business (LOB) application to your customer, you realize it is not user friendly enough. End users have to perform many searches; however, they always have to know the exact phrase they are searching for.

1. How could you enhance the end users' experience?
2. How should you change your queries to support the enhanced user interface?

Case Scenario 2: Using the Semantic Search

You need to analyze some Microsoft Word documents to find the documents that are semantically similar to a document that you get from your manager. You need to provide a quick and simple solution for this problem.

1. Would you create a Microsoft .NET application or use T-SQL queries for this problem?
2. If you decide to use a T-SQL solution, which T-SQL function would you use?

Suggested Practices

To help you successfully master the exam objectives presented in this chapter, complete the following tasks.

Check the FTS Dynamic Management Views and Backup and Restore of a Full-Text Catalog and Indexes

There is also some administrative work involved with full-text indexes. For a brief introduction to this administrative work, you should review the information provided by the dynamic management views that deal with full-text search and semantic search, and learn how to back up full-text catalogs and full-text indexes.

- **Practice 1** In order to understand full-text search thoroughly, check the information provided in the following dynamic management views:
  - sys.dm_fts_active_catalogs
  - sys.dm_fts_fdhosts
  - sys.dm_fts_index_keywords_by_document
  - sys.dm_fts_index_keywords_by_property
  - sys.dm_fts_index_keywords
  - sys.dm_fts_index_population
  - sys.dm_fts_memory_buffers
  - sys.dm_fts_memory_pools
  - sys.dm_fts_outstanding_batches
  - sys.dm_fts_parser
  - sys.dm_fts_population_ranges
  - sys.dm_fts_semantic_similarity_population
- **Practice 2** Backup and restore is a very typical DBA job. You should have basic knowledge of how to include full-text catalogs and indexes in a backup. See the Books Online for SQL Server 2012 article "Back Up and Restore Full-Text Catalogs and Indexes" at *http://msdn.microsoft.com/en-us/library/ms142511.aspx* to study how to perform the following tasks:
  - Finding the full-text indexes of a full-text catalog
  - Finding the file group or file that contains a full-text index
  - Backing up the file groups that contain full-text indexes

Answers

This section contains answers to the lesson review questions and solutions to the case scenarios in this chapter.

Lesson 1

1. **Correct Answers: A and D**
   - **A. Correct:** Stopwords include noisy words.
   - **B. Incorrect:** Thesaurus is used for synonyms.
   - **C. Incorrect:** Stemmer is used for generating inflectional forms of words.
   - **D. Correct:** You group stopwords in stoplists.
2. **Correct Answer: C**
   - **A. Incorrect:** The msdb database is installed by default and is used for SQL Server Agent.
   - **B. Incorrect:** The distribution database is installed and used by replication.
   - **C. Correct:** You need the semanticsdb database in order to enable semantic search.
   - **D. Incorrect:** The tempdb database is installed by default and is used for all temporary objects.
3. **Correct Answer: A**
   - **A. Correct:** You can add synonyms by editing the thesaurus file.
   - **B. Incorrect:** Full-text search uses thesaurus files and not tables for synonyms.
   - **C. Incorrect:** You cannot use stopwords for synonyms.
   - **D. Incorrect:** Full-text search supports synonyms.

Lesson 2

1. **Correct Answer: E**
   - **A. Incorrect:** FORMSOF is a valid keyword of the CONTAINS predicate.
   - **B. Incorrect:** THESAURUS is a valid keyword.
   - **C. Incorrect:** NEAR is a valid keyword.
   - **D. Incorrect:** PROPERTY is a valid keyword.
   - **E. Correct:** TEMPORARY is not a valid keyword of the CONTAINS predicate.

2. **Correct Answer: A**
   - **A. Correct:** This proximity term defines both distance and order of searched terms.
   - **B. Incorrect:** This is not a valid syntax.
   - **C. Incorrect:** This proximity term defines distance of searched terms only.
   - **D. Incorrect:** This proximity term does not define either distance or order of searched terms.
3. **Correct Answers: A, B, D, and E**
   - **A. Correct:** You can search for inflectional forms of a word.
   - **B. Correct:** You can search for synonyms of a searched word.
   - **C. Incorrect:** Full-text search does not support translations.
   - **D. Correct:** You can search for text in which a search word is close to another search word.
   - **E. Correct:** You can search for a prefix of a word or a phrase only.

Lesson 3

1. **Correct Answer: A**
   - **A. Correct:** You use the CONTAINSTABLE function to rank documents based on proximity of words.
   - **B. Incorrect:** You use the FREETEXTTABLE function to rank documents based on containment of words.
   - **C. Incorrect:** You use the SEMANTICKEYPHRASETABLE function to return key phrases associated with the full-text indexed column.
   - **D. Incorrect:** You use the SEMANTICSIMILARITYTABLE function to retrieve documents scored by similarity to a specified document.
   - **E. Incorrect:** You use the SEMANTICSIMILARITYDETAILSTABLE function to return key phrases that are common across two documents.
2. **Correct Answer: D**
   - **A. Incorrect:** You use the CONTAINSTABLE function to rank documents based on proximity of words.
   - **B. Incorrect:** You use the FREETEXTTABLE function to rank documents based on containment of words.
   - **C. Incorrect:** You use the SEMANTICKEYPHRASETABLE function to return key phrases associated with the full-text indexed column.

- **D.** **Correct:** You use the SEMANTICSIMILARITYTABLE function to retrieve documents scored by similarity to a specified document.
- **E.** **Incorrect:** You use the SEMANTICSIMILARITYDETAILSTABLE function to return key phrases that are common across two documents.

3. **Correct Answer: C**
   - **A.** **Incorrect:** You use the CONTAINSTABLE function to rank documents based on proximity of words.
   - **B.** **Incorrect:** You use the FREETEXTTABLE function to rank documents based on containment of words.
   - **C.** **Correct:** You use the SEMANTICKEYPHRASETABLE function to return key phrases associated with the full-text indexed column.
   - **D.** **Incorrect:** You use the SEMANTICSIMILARITYTABLE function to retrieve documents scored by similarity to a specified document.
   - **E.** **Incorrect:** You use the SEMANTICSIMILARITYDETAILSTABLE function to return key phrases that are common across two documents.

Case Scenario 1

1. You should use the Full-Text Search feature of SQL Server.
2. You should revise your queries to include the full-text predicates, or use the full-text and semantic search table-valued functions.

Case Scenario 2

1. A T-SQL solution is simpler in this scenario because the SQL Server Full-Text Search and Semantic Search features support the functionality you need out of the box.
2. You should use the SEMANTICSIMILARITYTABLE function.

CHAPTER 7

Querying and Managing XML Data

Exam objectives in this chapter:

- Work with Data
  - Query and manage XML data.

Microsoft SQL Server 2012 includes extensive support for XML. This support includes creating XML from relational data with a query and shredding XML into relational tabular format. Additionally, SQL Server has a native XML data type. You can store XML data, constrain it with XML schemas, index it with specialized XML indexes, and manipulate it using XML data type methods. All of the T-SQL XML data type methods accept an XQuery string as a parameter. XQuery (short for XML Query Language) is the standard language used to query and manipulate XML data.

In this chapter, you learn how to use all of the XML features mentioned. In addition, you get a couple of ideas about why you would use XML in a relational database.

> ***IMPORTANT*** **USE OF THE TERM XML IN THIS CHAPTER**
>
> **XML is used in this chapter to refer to both the open standard and T-SQL data type.**

Lessons in this chapter:

- Lesson 1: Returning Results As XML with FOR XML
- Lesson 2: Querying XML Data with XQuery
- Lesson 3: Using the XML Data Type

Before You Begin

To complete the lessons in this chapter, you must have:

- An understanding of relational database concepts.
- Experience working with SQL Server Management Studio (SSMS).
- Some experience writing T-SQL code.
- Access to a SQL Server 2012 instance with the sample database TSQL2012 installed.

Lesson 1: Returning Results As XML with FOR XML

XML is a widely used standard for data exchange, calling web services methods, configuration files, and more. This lesson starts with a short introduction to XML. After that, you learn how you can create XML as the result of a query by using different flavors of the FOR XML clause. The lesson finishes with information on shredding XML to relational tables by using the OPENXML rowset function.

After this lesson, you will be able to:

- Describe XML documents.
- Convert relational data to XML.
- Shred XML to tables.

Estimated lesson time: 40 minutes

Introduction to XML

This lesson introduces XML through samples. The following is an example of an XML document, created with a FOR XML clause of the SELECT statement.

```
<CustomersOrders>
  <Customer custid="1" companyname="Customer NRZBB">
    <Order orderid="10692" orderdate="2007-10-03T00:00:00" />
    <Order orderid="10702" orderdate="2007-10-13T00:00:00" />
    <Order orderid="10952" orderdate="2008-03-16T00:00:00" />
  </Customer>
  <Customer custid="2" companyname="Customer MLTDN">
    <Order orderid="10308" orderdate="2006-09-18T00:00:00" />
    <Order orderid="10926" orderdate="2008-03-04T00:00:00" />
  </Customer>
</CustomersOrders>
```

NOTE **COMPANION CODE**

The query that produces the XML output from the previous example and other queries for other examples are provided in the companion code files.

As you can see, XML uses tags to name parts of an *XML document*. These parts are called *elements*. Every begin *tag*, such as <Customer>, must have a corresponding end tag, in this case </Customer>. If an element has no nested elements, the notation can be abbreviated to a single tag that denotes the beginning and end of an element, such as <Order ... />. Elements can be nested. Tags cannot be interleaved; the end tag of a parent element must be after the end tag of the last nested element. If every begin tag has a corresponding end tag, and if tags are nested properly, the XML document is *well-formed*.

XML documents are *ordered*. This does not mean they are ordered by any specific element value; it means that the position of elements matters. For example, the element with orderid equal to 10702 in the preceding example is the second Order element under the first Customer element.

XML is *case-sensitive Unicode text*. You should never forget that XML is case sensitive. In addition, some characters in XML, such as <, which introduces a tag, are processed as *markup* and have special meanings. If you want to include these characters in the values of your XML document, they must be escaped by using an ampersand (&), followed by a special code, followed by a semicolon (;), as shown in Table 7-1.

TABLE 7-1 Characters with special values in XML documents

Character	Replacement text
& (ampersand)	&
" (quotation mark)	"
< (less than)	<
> (greater than)	>
' (apostrophe)	'

Alternatively, you can use the special XML CDATA section, written as <![CDATA[...]]>. You can replace the three dots with any character string that does not include the string literal "]]>"; this will prevent special characters in the string from being parsed as XML markup.

Processing instructions, which are information for applications that process XML, are written similarly to elements, between less than (<) and greater than (>) characters, and they start and end with a question mark (?), like <?PItarget data?>. The engine that processes XML—for example, the SQL Server Database Engine — receives those instructions.

In addition to elements and processing instructions, XML can include comments in the format <!-- This is a comment -->.

Finally, XML can have a prolog at the beginning of the document, denoting the XML version and encoding of the document, such as <?xml version="1.0" encoding="ISO-8859-15"?>.

In addition to XML documents, you can also have *XML fragments*. The only difference between a document and a fragment is that a document has a single *root node*, like <CustomersOrders> in the preceding example. If you delete this node, you get the following XML fragment.

```
<Customer custid="1" companyname="Customer NRZBB">
  <Order orderid="10692" orderdate="2007-10-03T00:00:00" />
  <Order orderid="10702" orderdate="2007-10-13T00:00:00" />
  <Order orderid="10952" orderdate="2008-03-16T00:00:00" />
</Customer>
```

```
  <Customer custid="2" companyname="Customer MLTDN">
    <Order orderid="10308" orderdate="2006-09-18T00:00:00" />
    <Order orderid="10926" orderdate="2008-03-04T00:00:00" />
  </Customer>
```

If you delete the second customer, you get an XML document because it will have a single root node again.

As you can see from the examples so far, elements can have *attributes*. Attributes have their own names, and their values are enclosed in quotation marks. This is *attribute-centric* presentation. However, you can write XML differently; every attribute can be a nested element of the original element. This is *element-centric* presentation.

Finally, element names do not have to be unique, because they can be referred to by their position; however, to distinguish between elements from different business areas, different departments, or different companies, you can add *namespaces*. You declare namespaces used in the root element of an XML document. You can also use an *alias* for every single namespace. Then you prefix element names with a namespace alias. The following code is an example of element-centric XML that uses a namespace; the data is the same as in the first example of this lesson.

```
<CustomersOrders xmlns:co="TK461-CustomersOrders">
  <co:Customer>
    <co:custid>1</co:custid>
    <co:companyname>Customer NRZBB</co:companyname>
    <co:Order>
      <co:orderid>10692</co:orderid>
      <co:orderdate>2007-10-03T00:00:00</co:orderdate>
    </co:Order>
    <co:Order>
      <co:orderid>10702</co:orderid>
      <co:orderdate>2007-10-13T00:00:00</co:orderdate>
    </co:Order>
    <co:Order>
      <co:orderid>10952</co:orderid>
      <co:orderdate>2008-03-16T00:00:00</co:orderdate>
    </co:Order>
  </co:Customer>
  <co:Customer>
    <co:custid>2</co:custid>
    <co:companyname>Customer MLTDN</co:companyname>
    <co:Order>
      <co:orderid>10308</co:orderid>
      <co:orderdate>2006-09-18T00:00:00</co:orderdate>
    </co:Order>
    <co:Order>
      <co:orderid>10926</co:orderid>
      <co:orderdate>2008-03-04T00:00:00</co:orderdate>
    </co:Order>
  </co:Customer>
</CustomersOrders>
```

XML is very flexible. As you've seen so far, there are very few rules for creating a well-formed XML document. In an XML document, the actual data is mixed with *metadata*, such as element and attribute names. Because XML is text, it is very convenient for exchanging data between different systems and even between different platforms. However, when exchanging data, it becomes important to have metadata fixed. If you had to import a document with customers' orders, as in the preceding examples, every couple of minutes, you'd definitely want to automate the import process. Imagine how hard you'd have to work if the metadata changed with every new import. For example, imagine that the Customer element gets renamed to Client, and the Order element gets renamed to Purchase. Or imagine that the orderdate attribute (or element) suddenly changes its data type from timestamp to integer. You'd quickly conclude that you should have more fixed *schema* for the XML documents you are importing.

Many different standards have evolved to describe the metadata of XML documents. Currently, the most widely used metadata description is with *XML Schema Description* (XSD) documents. XSD documents are XML documents that describe the metadata of other XML documents. The schema of an XSD document is predefined. With the XSD standard, you can specify element names, data types, and number of occurrences of an element, constraints, and more. The following example shows an XSD schema describing the element-centric version of customers and their orders.

```
<xsd:schema targetNamespace="TK461-CustomersOrders" xmlns:schema="TK461-CustomersOrders"
  xmlns:xsd=http://www.w3.org/2001/XMLSchema
  xmlns:sqltypes=http://schemas.microsoft.com/sqlserver/2004/sqltypes
  elementFormDefault="qualified">
  <xsd:import namespace=http://schemas.microsoft.com/sqlserver/2004/sqltypes
    schemaLocation="http://schemas.microsoft.com/sqlserver/2004/sqltypes/sqltypes.xsd"
/>
  <xsd:element name="Customer">
    <xsd:complexType>
      <xsd:sequence>
        <xsd:element name="custid" type="sqltypes:int" />
        <xsd:element name="companyname">
          <xsd:simpleType>
            <xsd:restriction base="sqltypes:nvarchar" sqltypes:localeId="1033"
               sqltypes:sqlCompareOptions="IgnoreCase IgnoreKanaType IgnoreWidth"
               sqltypes:sqlSortId="52">
              <xsd:maxLength value="40" />
            </xsd:restriction>
          </xsd:simpleType>
        </xsd:element>
        <xsd:element ref="schema:Order" minOccurs="0" maxOccurs="unbounded" />
      </xsd:sequence>
    </xsd:complexType>
  </xsd:element>
  <xsd:element name="Order">
    <xsd:complexType>
      <xsd:sequence>
        <xsd:element name="orderid" type="sqltypes:int" />
        <xsd:element name="orderdate" type="sqltypes:datetime" />
      </xsd:sequence>
    </xsd:complexType>
  </xsd:element>
</xsd:schema>
```

When you check whether an XML document complies with a schema, you *validate* the document. A document with a predefined schema is said to be a *typed* XML document.

Producing XML from Relational Data

With the T-SQL SELECT statement, you can create all XML shown in this lesson. This section explains how you can convert a query result set to XML by using the FOR XML clause of the SELECT T-SQL statement. You learn about the most useful options and directives of this clause; for a detailed description of the complete syntax, see the Books Online for SQL Server 2012 article "FOR XML (SQL Server)" at *http://msdn.microsoft.com/en-us/library/ms178107.aspx.*

FOR XML RAW

The first option for creating XML from a query result is the RAW option. The XML created is quite close to the relational (tabular) presentation of the data. In RAW mode, every row from returned rowsets converts to a single element named row, and columns translate to the attributes of this element. Here is an example of an XML document created with the FOR XML RAW option.

```
<row custid="1" companyname="Customer NRZBB" orderid="10692"
 orderdate="2007-10-03T00:00:00" />
<row custid="1" companyname="Customer NRZBB" orderid="10702"
 orderdate="2007-10-13T00:00:00" />
<row custid="1" companyname="Customer NRZBB" orderid="10952"
 orderdate="2008-03-16T00:00:00" />
<row custid="2" companyname="Customer MLTDN" orderid="10308"
 orderdate="2006-09-18T00:00:00" />
<row custid="2" companyname="Customer MLTDN" orderid="10926"
 orderdate="2008-03-04T00:00:00" />
```

You can enhance the RAW mode by renaming the row element, adding a root element, including namespaces, and making the XML returned element-centric. The following is an example of enhanced XML created with the FOR XML RAW option.

```
<CustomersOrders>
  <Order custid="1" companyname="Customer NRZBB" orderid="10692"
   orderdate="2007-10-03T00:00:00" />
  <Order custid="1" companyname="Customer NRZBB" orderid="10702"
   orderdate="2007-10-13T00:00:00" />
  <Order custid="1" companyname="Customer NRZBB" orderid="10952"
   orderdate="2008-03-16T00:00:00" />
  <Order custid="2" companyname="Customer MLTDN" orderid="10308"
   orderdate="2006-09-18T00:00:00" />
  <Order custid="2" companyname="Customer MLTDN" orderid="10926"
   orderdate="2008-03-04T00:00:00" />
</CustomersOrders>
```

As you can see, this is a document instead of a fragment. It looks more like "real" XML; however, it does not include any additional level of nesting. The customer with custid equal to 1 is repeated three times, once for each order; it would be nicer if it appeared once only and included orders as nested elements. You can produce XML that is easier to read with the FOR XML AUTO option, described in the following section.

FOR XML AUTO

The FOR XML AUTO option gives you nice XML documents with nested elements, and it is not complicated to use. In AUTO and RAW modes, you can use the keyword ELEMENTS to produce element-centric XML. The WITH NAMESPACES clause, preceding the SELECT part of the query, defines namespaces and aliases in the returned XML. So far, you have seen XML results only. In the practice for this lesson, you create queries that produce similar results. However, in order to give you a better presentation of how SELECT with the FOR XML clause looks, here is an example.

```
WITH XMLNAMESPACES('TK461-CustomersOrders' AS co)
SELECT [co:Customer].custid AS [co:custid],
 [co:Customer].companyname AS [co:companyname],
 [co:Order].orderid AS [co:orderid],
 [co:Order].orderdate AS [co:orderdate]
FROM Sales.Customers AS [co:Customer]
 INNER JOIN Sales.Orders AS [co:Order]
  ON [co:Customer].custid = [co:Order].custid
WHERE [co:Customer].custid <= 2
  AND [co:Order].orderid %2 = 0
ORDER BY [co:Customer].custid, [co:Order].orderid
FOR XML AUTO, ELEMENTS, ROOT('CustomersOrders');
```

The T-SQL table and column aliases in the query are used to produce element names, prefixed with a namespace. A colon is used in XML to separate the namespace from the element name. The WHERE clause of the query limits the output to two customers, with only every second order for each customer retrieved. The output is a quite nice element-centric XML document.

```
<CustomersOrders xmlns:co="TK461-CustomersOrders">
  <co:Customer>
    <co:custid>1</co:custid>
    <co:companyname>Customer NRZBB</co:companyname>
    <co:Order>
      <co:orderid>10692</co:orderid>
      <co:orderdate>2007-10-03T00:00:00</co:orderdate>
    </co:Order>
    <co:Order>
      <co:orderid>10702</co:orderid>
      <co:orderdate>2007-10-13T00:00:00</co:orderdate>
    </co:Order>
    <co:Order>
      <co:orderid>10952</co:orderid>
      <co:orderdate>2008-03-16T00:00:00</co:orderdate>
    </co:Order>
  </co:Customer>
```

```
    <co:Customer>
      <co:custid>2</co:custid>
      <co:companyname>Customer MLTDN</co:companyname>
      <co:Order>
        <co:orderid>10308</co:orderid>
        <co:orderdate>2006-09-18T00:00:00</co:orderdate>
      </co:Order>
      <co:Order>
        <co:orderid>10926</co:orderid>
        <co:orderdate>2008-03-04T00:00:00</co:orderdate>
      </co:Order>
    </co:Customer>
  </CustomersOrders>
```

Note that a proper ORDER BY clause is very important. With T-SQL SELECT, you are actually formatting the returned XML. Without the ORDER BY clause, the order of rows returned is unpredictable, and you can get a weird XML document with an element repeated multiple times with just part of nested elements every time.

EXAM TIP

The FOR XML clause comes after the ORDER BY clause in a query.

It is not only the ORDER BY clause that is important; the order of columns in the SELECT clause also influences the XML returned. SQL Server uses column order to determine the nesting of elements. The order of the columns should follow one-to-many relationships. A customer can have many orders; therefore, you should have customer columns before order columns in your query.

You might be vexed by the fact that you have to take care of column order; in a relation, the order of columns and rows is not important. Nevertheless, you have to realize that the result of your query is not a relation; it is text in XML format, and parts of your query are used for formatting the text.

In RAW and AUTO mode, you can also return the *XSD schema* of the document you are creating. This schema is included inside the XML that is returned, before the actual XML data; therefore, it is called *inline* schema. You return XSD with the XMLSCHEMA directive. This directive accepts a parameter that defines a target namespace. If you need schema only, without data, simply include a WHERE condition in your query with a predicate that no row can satisfy. The following query returns the schema of the XML generated in the previous query.

```
SELECT [Customer].custid AS [custid],
 [Customer].companyname AS [companyname],
 [Order].orderid AS [orderid],
 [Order].orderdate AS [orderdate]
FROM Sales.Customers AS [Customer]
 INNER JOIN Sales.Orders AS [Order]
  ON [Customer].custid = [Order].custid
WHERE 1 = 2
FOR XML AUTO, ELEMENTS,
    XMLSCHEMA('TK461-CustomersOrders');
```

Here is the output, the XSD document.

```
<xsd:schema targetNamespace="TK461-CustomersOrders" xmlns:schema="TK461-CustomersOrders"
  xmlns:xsd=http://www.w3.org/2001/XMLSchema
  xmlns:sqltypes=http://schemas.microsoft.com/sqlserver/2004/sqltypes
  elementFormDefault="qualified">
  <xsd:import namespace=http://schemas.microsoft.com/sqlserver/2004/sqltypes
   schemaLocation=http://schemas.microsoft.com/sqlserver/2004/sqltypes/sqltypes.xsd
  />
  <xsd:element name="Customer">
    <xsd:complexType>
      <xsd:sequence>
        <xsd:element name="custid" type="sqltypes:int" />
        <xsd:element name="companyname">
          <xsd:simpleType>
            <xsd:restriction base="sqltypes:nvarchar" sqltypes:localeId="1033"
              sqltypes:sqlCompareOptions="IgnoreCase IgnoreKanaType IgnoreWidth"
              sqltypes:sqlSortId="52">
              <xsd:maxLength value="40" />
            </xsd:restriction>
          </xsd:simpleType>
        </xsd:element>
        <xsd:element ref="schema:Order" minOccurs="0" maxOccurs="unbounded" />
      </xsd:sequence>
    </xsd:complexType>
  </xsd:element>
  <xsd:element name="Order">
    <xsd:complexType>
      <xsd:sequence>
        <xsd:element name="orderid" type="sqltypes:int" />
        <xsd:element name="orderdate" type="sqltypes:datetime" />
      </xsd:sequence>
    </xsd:complexType>
  </xsd:element>
</xsd:schema>
```

FOR XML PATH

With the last two flavors of the FOR XML clause —the EXPLICIT and PATH options—you can manually define the XML returned. With these two options, you have total control of the XML document returned. The EXPLICIT mode is included for backward compatibility only; it uses proprietary T-SQL syntax for formatting XML. The PATH mode uses standard XML XPath expressions to define the elements and attributes of the XML you are creating. This section focuses on the PATH mode; if you want to learn more about the EXPLICIT mode, see the Books Online for SQL Server 2012 article "Use EXPLICIT Mode with FOR XML" at *http://msdn.microsoft.com/en-us/library/ms189068.aspx*.

In PATH mode, column names and aliases serve as XPath expressions. XPath expressions define the path to the element in the XML generated. Path is expressed in a hierarchical way; levels are delimited with the slash (/) character. By default, every column becomes an element; if you want to generate attribute-centric XML, prefix the alias name with the "at" (@) character.

Here is an example of a simple XPATH query.

```
SELECT Customer.custid AS [@custid],
 Customer.companyname AS [companyname]
FROM Sales.Customers AS Customer
WHERE Customer.custid <= 2
ORDER BY Customer.custid
FOR XML PATH ('Customer'), ROOT('Customers');
```

The query returns the following output.

```
<Customers>
  <Customer custid="1">
    <companyname>Customer NRZBB</companyname>
  </Customer>
  <Customer custid="2">
    <companyname>Customer MLTDN</companyname>
  </Customer>
</Customers>
```

If you want to create XML with nested elements for child tables, you have to use subqueries in the SELECT part of the query in the PATH mode. Subqueries have to return a scalar value in a SELECT clause. However, you know that a parent row can have multiple child rows; a customer can have multiple orders. You return a scalar value by returning XML from the subquery. Then the result is returned as a single scalar XML value. You format nested XML from the subquery with the FOR XML clause, like you format XML in an outer query. Additionally, you have to use the TYPE directive of the FOR XML clause to produce a value of the XML data type, and not XML as text, which cannot be consumed by the outer query.

You create XML with nested elements by using the FOR XML PATH clause in the practice for this lesson.

Quick Check

- **How can you get an XSD schema together with an XML document from your SELECT statement?**

Quick Check Answer

- **You should use the XMLSCHEMA directive in the FOR XML clause.**

Shredding XML to Tables

You just learned how to create XML from relational data. Of course, you can also do the opposite process: convert XML to tables. Converting XML to relational tables is known as *shredding* XML. You can do this by using the nodes method of the XML data type; you learn about this method in Lesson 3, "Using the XML Data Type." Starting with SQL Server 2000, you can do the shredding also with the OPENXML rowset function.

The OPENXML function provides a rowset over in-memory XML documents by using *Document Object Model* (DOM) presentation. Before parsing the DOM, you need to prepare it. To prepare the DOM presentation of XML, you need to call the system stored procedure sys.sp_xml_preparedocument. After you shred the document, you must remove the DOM presentation by using the system procedure sys.sp_xml_removedocument.

The OPENXML function uses the following parameters:

- An XML DOM document handle, returned by sp_xml_preparedocument
- An XPath expression to find the nodes you want to map to rows of a rowset returned
- A description of the rowset returned
- Mapping between XML nodes and rowset columns

The document handle is an integer. This is the simplest parameter. The XPath expression is specified as rowpattern, which defines how XML nodes translate to rows. The path to a node is used as a pattern; nodes below the selected node define rows of the returned rowset.

You can map XML elements or attributes to rows and columns by using the WITH clause of the OPENXML function. In this clause, you can specify an existing table, which is used as a template for the rowset returned, or you can define a table with syntax similar to that in the CREATE TABLE T-SQL statement.

The OPENXML function accepts an optional third parameter, called flags, which allows you to specify the mapping used between the XML data and the relational rowset. A value of 1 means attribute-centric mapping, 2 means element-centric, and 3 means both. However, flag value 3 is undocumented, and it is a best practice not to use it. Flag value 8 can be combined with values 1 and 2 with a bitwise logical OR operator to get both attribute and element-centric mapping. The XML used for the following OPENXML examples uses attributes and elements; for example, custid is the attribute and companyname is the element. The intention of this slightly overcomplicated XML is to show you the difference between attribute-centric and element-centric mappings. The following code shreds the same XML three times to show you the difference between different mappings by using the following values for the flags parameter: 1, 2, and 11 (8+1+2); all three queries use the same rowset description in the WITH clause.

```
DECLARE @DocHandle AS INT;
DECLARE @XmlDocument AS NVARCHAR(1000);
SET @XmlDocument = N'
<CustomersOrders>
  <Customer custid="1">
    <companyname>Customer NRZBB</companyname>
    <Order orderid="10692">
      <orderdate>2007-10-03T00:00:00</orderdate>
    </Order>
    <Order orderid="10702">
      <orderdate>2007-10-13T00:00:00</orderdate>
    </Order>
    <Order orderid="10952">
      <orderdate>2008-03-16T00:00:00</orderdate>
    </Order>
  </Customer>
```

```
  <Customer custid="2">
    <companyname>Customer MLTDN</companyname>
    <Order orderid="10308">
      <orderdate>2006-09-18T00:00:00</orderdate>
    </Order>
    <Order orderid="10926">
      <orderdate>2008-03-04T00:00:00</orderdate>
    </Order>
  </Customer>
</CustomersOrders>';
-- Create an internal representation
EXEC sys.sp_xml_preparedocument @DocHandle OUTPUT, @XmlDocument;
-- Attribute-centric mapping
SELECT *
FROM OPENXML (@DocHandle, '/CustomersOrders/Customer',1)
     WITH (custid INT,
           companyname NVARCHAR(40));
-- Element-centric mapping
SELECT *
FROM OPENXML (@DocHandle, '/CustomersOrders/Customer',2)
     WITH (custid INT,
           companyname NVARCHAR(40));
-- Attribute- and element-centric mapping
-- Combining flag 8 with flags 1 and 2
SELECT *
FROM OPENXML (@DocHandle, '/CustomersOrders/Customer',11)
     WITH (custid INT,
           companyname NVARCHAR(40));
-- Remove the DOM
EXEC sys.sp_xml_removedocument @DocHandle;
GO
```

Results of the preceding three queries are as follows.

```
custid      companyname
----------- ----------------------------------------
1           NULL
2           NULL
custid      companyname
----------- ----------------------------------------
NULL        Customer NRZBB
NULL        Customer MLTDN
custid      companyname
----------- ----------------------------------------
1           Customer NRZBB
2           Customer MLTDN
```

As you can see, you get attributes with attribute-centric mapping, elements with element-centric mapping, and both if you combine the two mappings. The nodes method of the XML data type is more efficient for shredding an XML document only once and is therefore the preferred way of shredding XML documents in such a case. However, if you need to shred the same document multiple times, like shown in the three-query example for the OPENXML function, then preparing the DOM presentation once, using OPENXML multiple times, and removing the DOM presentation might be faster.

PRACTICE Using the FOR XML Clause

In this practice, you create XML from relational data. You return XML data as a document and as a fragment.

If you encounter a problem completing an exercise, you can install the completed projects from the companion content for this chapter and lesson.

EXERCISE 1 Return an XML Document

In this exercise, you return XML formatted as a document from relational data.

1. Start SSMS and connect to your SQL Server instance.
2. Open a new query window by clicking the New Query button.
3. Change the current database context to the TSQL2012 database.
4. Return customers with their orders as XML in RAW mode. Return the custid and companyname columns from the Sales.Customers table, and orderid and orderdate columns from the Sales.Orders table. You can use the following query.

```
SELECT Customer.custid, Customer.companyname,
 [Order].orderid, [Order].orderdate
FROM Sales.Customers AS Customer
 INNER JOIN Sales.Orders AS [Order]
  ON Customer.custid = [Order].custid
ORDER BY Customer.custid, [Order].orderid
FOR XML RAW;
```

5. Observe the results.
6. Improve the XML created with the previous query by changing from RAW to AUTO mode. Make the result element-centric by using TK461-CustomersOrders as the namespace and CustomersOrders as the root element. You can use the following code.

```
WITH XMLNAMESPACES('TK461-CustomersOrders' AS co)
SELECT [co:Customer].custid AS [co:custid],
 [co:Customer].companyname AS [co:companyname],
 [co:Order].orderid AS [co:orderid],
 [co:Order].orderdate AS [co:orderdate]
FROM Sales.Customers AS [co:Customer]
 INNER JOIN Sales.Orders AS [co:Order]
  ON [co:Customer].custid = [co:Order].custid
ORDER BY [co:Customer].custid, [co:Order].orderid
FOR XML AUTO, ELEMENTS, ROOT('CustomersOrders');
```

7. Observe the results.

EXERCISE 2 **Return an XML Fragment**

In this exercise, you return XML formatted as a fragment from relational data.

1. Return the third XML as a fragment, not as a document. Return the top element Customer with custid and companyname attributes. Return the Order nested element with orderid and orderdate attributes. Use the FOR XML PATH clause for explicit formatting of XML. You can use the following code.

```
SELECT Customer.custid AS [@custid],
 Customer.companyname AS [@companyname],
 (SELECT [Order].orderid AS [@orderid],
   [Order].orderdate AS [@orderdate]
  FROM Sales.Orders AS [Order]
  WHERE Customer.custid = [Order].custid
    AND [Order].orderid %2 = 0
  ORDER BY [Order].orderid
  FOR XML PATH('Order'), TYPE)
FROM Sales.Customers AS Customer
WHERE Customer.custid <= 2
ORDER BY Customer.custid
FOR XML PATH('Customer');
```

2. Observe the results.

Lesson Summary

- You can use the FOR XML clause of the SELECT T-SQL statement to produce XML.
- Use the OPENXML function to shred XML to tables.

Lesson Review

Answer the following questions to test your knowledge of the information in this lesson. You can find the answers to these questions and explanations of why each answer choice is correct or incorrect in the "Answers" section at the end of this chapter.

1. Which FOR XML options are valid? (Choose all that apply.)
   - **A.** FOR XML AUTO
   - **B.** FOR XML MANUAL
   - **C.** FOR XML DOCUMENT
   - **D.** FOR XML PATH
2. Which directive of the FOR XML clause should you use to produce element-centric XML?
   - **A.** ATTRIBUTES
   - **B.** ROOT
   - **C.** ELEMENTS
   - **D.** XMLSCHEMA

3. Which FOR XML options can you use to manually format the XML returned? (Choose all that apply.)
   - A. FOR XML AUTO
   - B. FOR XML EXPLICIT
   - C. FOR XML RAW
   - D. FOR XML PATH

Lesson 2: Querying XML Data with XQuery

XQuery is a standard language for browsing XML instances and returning XML. It is much richer than *XPath* expressions, an older standard, which you can use for simple navigation only. With XQuery, you can navigate as with XPath; however, you can also loop over nodes, shape the returned XML instance, and much more.

For a query language, you need a query-processing engine. The SQL Server database engine processes XQuery inside T-SQL statements through XML data type methods. Not all XQuery features are supported in SQL Server. For example, XQuery user-defined functions are not supported in SQL Server because you already have T-SQL and CLR functions available. Additionally, T-SQL supports nonstandard extensions to XQuery, called *XML DML*, that you can use to modify elements and attributes in XML data. Because an XML data type is a large object, it could be a huge performance bottleneck if the only way to modify an XML value were to replace the entire value.

This lesson introduces XQuery for data retrieval purposes only; you learn more about the XML data type in Lesson 3. In this lesson, you use variables of the XML data type and the query method of the XML data type only. The query method accepts an XQuery string as its parameter, and it returns the XML you shape in XQuery.

The implementation of XQuery in SQL Server follows the World Wide Web Consortium (W3C) standard, and it is supplemented with extensions to support data modifications. You can find more about W3C on the web at *http://www.w3.org/*, and news and additional resources about XQuery at *http://www.w3.org/XML/Query/*.

After this lesson, you will be able to:

- Use XPath expressions to navigate through nodes of an XML instance.
- Use XQuery predicates.
- Use XQuery FLWOR expressions.

Estimated lesson time: 60 minutes

XQuery Basics

XQuery is, like XML, case sensitive. Therefore, if you want to check the examples manually, you have to write the queries exactly as they are written in this chapter. For example, if you write Data() instead of data(), you will get an error stating that there is no Data() function.

XQuery returns sequences. Sequences can include *atomic* values or *complex* values (XML nodes). Any node, such as an element, attribute, text, processing instruction, comment, or document, can be included in the sequence. Of course, you can format the sequences to get well-formed XML. The following code shows different sequences returned from a simple XML instance by three XML queries.

```
DECLARE @x AS XML;
SET @x=N'
<root>
 <a>1<c>3</c><d>4</d></a>
 <b>2</b>
</root>';
SELECT
 @x.query('*') AS Complete_Sequence,
 @x.query('data(*)') AS Complete_Data,
 @x.query('data(root/a/c)') AS Element_c_Data;
```

Here are the sequences returned.

```
Complete_Sequence                               Complete_Data Element_c_Data
----------------------------------------------- ------------- --------------
<root><a>1<c>3</c><d>4</d></a><b>2</b></root>            1342              3
```

The first XQuery expression uses the simplest possible path expression, which selects everything from the XML instance; the second uses the data() function to extract all atomic data values from the complete document; the third uses the data() function to extract atomic data from the element c only.

Every identifier in XQuery is a qualified name, or a *QName*. A QName consists of a local name and, optionally, a namespace prefix. In the preceding example, root, a, b, c, and d are QNames; however, they are without namespace prefixes. The following standard namespaces are predefined in SQL Server:

- **xs** The namespace for an XML schema (the uniform resource identifier, or URI, is *http://www.w3.org/2001/XMLSchema*)
- **xsi** The XML schema instance namespace, used to associate XML schemas with instance documents (*http://www.w3.org/2001/XMLSchema-instance*)
- **xdt** The namespace for XPath and XQuery data types (*http://www.w3.org/2004/07/xpath-datatypes*)
- **fn** The functions namespace (*http://www.w3.org/2004/07/xpath-functions*)
- **sqltypes** The namespace that provides mapping for SQL Server data types (*http://schemas.microsoft.com/sqlserver/2004/sqltypes*)
- **xml** The default XML namespace (*http://www.w3.org/XML/1998/namespace*)

You can use these namespaces in your queries without defining them again. You define your own data types in the *prolog*, which belongs at the beginning of your XQuery. You separate the prolog from the query body with a semicolon. In addition, in T-SQL, you can declare namespaces used in XQuery expressions in advance in the WITH clause of the T-SQL SELECT command. If your XML uses a single namespace, you can also declare it as the default namespace for all elements in the XQuery prolog.

You can also include comments in your XQuery expressions. The syntax for a comment is text between parentheses and colons: (: this is a comment :). Do not mix this with comment nodes in your XML document; this is the comment of your XQuery and has no influence on the XML returned. The following code shows all three methods of namespace declaration and uses XQuery comments. It extracts orders for the first customer from an XML instance.

```
DECLARE @x AS XML;
SET @x='
<CustomersOrders xmlns:co="TK461-CustomersOrders">
  <co:Customer co:custid="1" co:companyname="Customer NRZBB">
    <co:Order co:orderid="10692" co:orderdate="2007-10-03T00:00:00" />
    <co:Order co:orderid="10702" co:orderdate="2007-10-13T00:00:00" />
    <co:Order co:orderid="10952" co:orderdate="2008-03-16T00:00:00" />
  </co:Customer>
  <co:Customer co:custid="2" co:companyname="Customer MLTDN">
    <co:Order co:orderid="10308" co:orderdate="2006-09-18T00:00:00" />
    <co:Order co:orderid="10926" co:orderdate="2008-03-04T00:00:00" />
  </co:Customer>
</CustomersOrders>';
-- Namespace in prolog of XQuery
SELECT @x.query('
(: explicit namespace :)
declare namespace co="TK461-CustomersOrders";
//co:Customer[1]/*') AS [Explicit namespace];
-- Default namespace for all elements in prolog of XQuery
SELECT @x.query('
(: default namespace :)
declare default element namespace "TK461-CustomersOrders";
//Customer[1]/*') AS [Default element namespace];
-- Namespace defined in WITH clause of T-SQL SELECT
WITH XMLNAMESPACES('TK461-CustomersOrders' AS co)
SELECT @x.query('
(: namespace declared in T-SQL :)
//co:Customer[1]/*') AS [Namespace in WITH clause];
```

Here is the abbreviated output.

```
Explicit namespace
--------------------------------------------------------------------------------
<co:Order xmlns:co="TK461-CustomersOrders" co:orderid="10692" co:orderd

Default element namespace
--------------------------------------------------------------------------------
<Order xmlns="TK461-CustomersOrders" xmlns:p1="TK461-Customers

Namespace in WITH clause
--------------------------------------------------------------------------------
<co:Order xmlns:co="TK461-CustomersOrders" co:orderid="10692" co:orderd
```

NOTE THE DEFAULT NAMESPACE

If you use a default element namespace, the namespace is not included for the elements in the resulting XML; it is included for the attributes. Therefore, only the first and third queries are completely equivalent. In addition, when you use the default element namespace, you can't define your own namespace abbreviation. You should prefer an explicit namespace definition to using the default element namespace.

The queries used a relative path to find the Customer element. Before looking at all the different ways of navigation in XQuery, you should first read through the most important XQuery data types and functions, described in the following two sections.

XQuery Data Types

XQuery uses about 50 predefined data types. Additionally, in the SQL Server implementation you also have the sqltypes namespace, which defines SQL Server types. You already know about SQL Server types. Do not worry too much about XQuery types; you'll never use most of them. This section lists only the most important ones, without going into details about them.

XQuery data types are divided into node types and atomic types. The node types include attribute, comment, element, namespace, text, processing-instruction, and document-node. The most important atomic types you might use in queries are xs:boolean, xs:string, xs:QName, xs:date, xs:time, xs:datetime, xs:float, xs:double, xs:decimal, and xs:integer.

You should just do a quick review of this much-shortened list. The important thing to understand is that XQuery has its own type system, that it has all of the commonly used types you would expect, and that you can use specific functions on specific types only. Therefore, it is time to introduce a couple of important XQuery functions.

XQuery Functions

Just as there are many data types, there are dozens of functions in XQuery as well. They are organized into multiple categories. The *data()* function, used earlier in the chapter, is a data accessor function. Some of the most useful XQuery functions supported by SQL Server are:

- **Numeric functions** ceiling(), floor(), and round()
- **String functions** concat(), contains(), substring(), string-length(), lower-case(), and upper-case()
- **Boolean and Boolean constructor functions** not(), true(), and false()
- **Nodes functions** local-name() and namespace-uri()
- **Aggregate functions** count(), min(), max(), avg(), and sum()
- **Data accessor functions** data() and string()
- **SQL Server extension functions** sql:column() and sql:variable()

You can easily conclude what a function does and what data types it supports from the function and category names. For a complete list of functions with detailed descriptions, see the Books Online for SQL Server 2012 article "XQuery Functions against the xml Data Type" at *http://msdn.microsoft.com/en-us/library/ms189254.aspx*.

The following query uses the aggregate functions count() and max() to retrieve information about orders for each customer in an XML document.

```
DECLARE @x AS XML;
SET @x='
<CustomersOrders>
  <Customer custid="1" companyname="Customer NRZBB">
    <Order orderid="10692" orderdate="2007-10-03T00:00:00" />
    <Order orderid="10702" orderdate="2007-10-13T00:00:00" />
    <Order orderid="10952" orderdate="2008-03-16T00:00:00" />
  </Customer>
  <Customer custid="2" companyname="Customer MLTDN">
    <Order orderid="10308" orderdate="2006-09-18T00:00:00" />
    <Order orderid="10926" orderdate="2008-03-04T00:00:00" />
  </Customer>
</CustomersOrders>';
SELECT @x.query('
for $i in //Customer
return
   <OrdersInfo>
      { $i/@companyname }
      <NumberOfOrders>
        { count($i/Order) }
      </NumberOfOrders>
      <LastOrder>
        { max($i/Order/@orderid) }
      </LastOrder>
   </OrdersInfo>
');
```

As you can see, this XQuery is more complicated than previous examples. The query uses iterations, known as XQuery FLWOR expressions, and formats the XML returned in the return part of the query. The FLWOR expressions are discussed later in this lesson. For now, treat this query as an example of how you can use aggregate functions in XQuery. The result of this query is as follows.

```
<OrdersInfo companyname="Customer NRZBB">
  <NumberOfOrders>3</NumberOfOrders>
  <LastOrder>10952</LastOrder>
</OrdersInfo>
<OrdersInfo companyname="Customer MLTDN">
  <NumberOfOrders>2</NumberOfOrders>
  <LastOrder>10926</LastOrder>
</OrdersInfo>
```

Navigation

You have plenty of ways to navigate through an XML document with XQuery. Actually, there is not enough space in this book to fully describe all possibilities of XQuery navigation; you have to realize this is far from a complete treatment of the topic. The basic approach is to use XPath expressions. With XQuery, you can specify a path absolutely or relatively from the current node. XQuery takes care of the current position in the document; this means that you can refer to a path relatively, starting from the current node, to which you navigated through a previous path expression. Every path consists of a sequence of steps, listed from left to right. A complete path might take the following form.

```
Node-name/child::element-name[@attribute-name=value]
```

Steps are separated with slashes; therefore, the path example described here has two steps. In the second step you can see in detail from which parts a step can be constructed. A step may consist of three parts:

- **Axis** Specifies the direction of travel. In the example, the axis is child::, which specifies child nodes of the node from the previous step.
- **Node test** Specifies the criterion for selecting nodes. In the example, element-name is the node test; it selects only nodes named element-name.
- **Predicate** Further narrows down the search. In the example, there is one predicate: [@attribute-name=value], which selects only nodes that have an attribute named attribute-name with value value, such as [@orderid=10952].

Note that in the predicate example, there is a reference to the attribute:: axis; the at sign (@) is an abbreviation for the axis attribute::. This looks a bit confusing; it might help if you think of navigation in an XML document in four directions: up (in the hierarchy), down (in the hierarchy), here (in current node), and right (in the current context level, to find attributes). Table 7-2 describes the axes supported in SQL Server.

TABLE 7-2 Axes supported in SQL Server

Axis	Abbrevation	Description
child::		Returns children of the current context node. This is the default axis; you can omit it. Direction is down.
descendant::		Retrieves all descendants of the context node. Direction is down.
self::		Retrieves the context node. Direction is here.
descendant-or-self::	//	Retrieves the context node and all its descendants. Direction is here and then down.
attribute::	@	Retrieves the specified attribute of the context node. Direction is right.
parent::	..	Retrieves the parent of the context node. Direction is up.

A *node test* follows the axis you specify. A node test can be as simple as a name test. Specifying a name means that you want nodes with that name. You can also use wildcards. An asterisk (*) means that you want any *principal node*, with any name. A principal node is the default node kind for an axis. The principal node is an attribute if the axis is attribute::, and it is an element for all other axes. You can also narrow down wildcard searches. If you want all principal nodes in the namespace prefix, use prefix:*. If you want all principal nodes named local-name, no matter which namespace they belong to, use *:local-name.

You can also perform node kind tests, which help you query nodes that are not principal nodes. You can use the following node type tests:

- **comment()** Allows you to select comment nodes.
- **node()** True for any kind of node. Do not mix this with the asterisk (*) wildcard; * means any principal node, whereas node() means any node at all.
- **processing-instruction()** Allows you to retrieve a processing instruction node.
- **text()** Allows you to retrieve text nodes, or nodes without tags.

EXAM TIP

Navigation through XML can be quite tricky; make sure you understand the complete path.

Predicates

Basic predicates include *numeric* and *Boolean* predicates. Numeric predicates simply select nodes by position. You include them in brackets. For example, /x/y[1] means the first y child element of each x element. You can also use parentheses to apply a numeric predicate to the entire result of a path. For example, (/x/y)[1] means the first element out of all nodes selected by x/y.

Boolean predicates select all nodes for which the predicate evaluates to true. XQuery supports logical and and or operators. However, you might be surprised by how comparison operators work. They work on both atomic values and sequences. For sequences, if one atomic value in a sequence leads to a true exit of the expression, the whole expression is evaluated to true. Look at the following example.

```
DECLARE @x AS XML = N'';
SELECT @x.query('(1, 2, 3) = (2, 4)');      -- true
SELECT @x.query('(5, 6) < (2, 4)');         -- false
SELECT @x.query('(1, 2, 3) = 1');           -- true
SELECT @x.query('(1, 2, 3) != 1');          -- true
```

The first expression evaluates to true because the number 2 is in both sequences. The second evaluates to false because none of the atomic values from the first sequence is less than any of the values from the second sequence. The third expression is true because there is an atomic value in the sequence on the left that is equal to the atomic value on the right. The fourth expression is true because there is an atomic value in the sequence on the left that is not equal to the atomic value on the right. Interesting result, right? Sequence (1, 2, 3) is both equal and not equal to atomic value 1. If this confuses you, use the *value comparison operators.* (The familiar symbolic operators in the preceding example are called *general comparison operators* in XQuery.) Value comparison operators do not work on sequences, they work on singletons. The following example shows usage of value comparison operators.

```
DECLARE @x AS XML = N'';
SELECT @x.query('(5) lt (2)');              -- false
SELECT @x.query('(1) eq 1');                -- true
SELECT @x.query('(1) ne 1');                -- false
GO
DECLARE @x AS XML = N'';
SELECT @x.query('(2, 2) eq (2, 2)');      -- error
GO
```

Note that the last query, which is in a separate batch, produces an error because it is trying to use a value comparison operator on sequences. Table 7-3 lists the general comparison operators and their value comparison operator counterparts.

TABLE 7-3 General and value comparison operators

General	Value	Description
=	eq	equal
!=	ne	not equal
<	lt	less than
<=	le	less than or equal to
>	gt	greater than
>=	ge	greater than or equal to

XQuery also supports conditional if..then..else expressions with the following syntax.

```
if (<expression1>)
then
  <expression2>
else
  <expression3>
```

Note that the if..then..else expression is not used to change the program flow of the XQuery query. It is more like a function that evaluates a logical expression parameter and returns one expression or another depending on the value of the logical expression. It is more like the T-SQL CASE expression than the T-SQL IF statement.

The following code shows usage of a conditional expression.

```
DECLARE @x AS XML = N'
<Employee empid="2">
  <FirstName>fname</FirstName>
  <LastName>lname</LastName>
</Employee>
';
DECLARE @v AS NVARCHAR(20) = N'FirstName';
SELECT @x.query('
 if (sql:variable("@v")="FirstName") then
  /Employee/FirstName
 else
   /Employee/LastName
') AS FirstOrLastName;
GO
```

In this case, the result would be the first name of the employee with ID equal to 2. If you change the value of the variable *@v,* the result of the query would be the employee's last name.

FLWOR Expressions

The real power of XQuery lies in its so-called *FLWOR* expressions. FLWOR is the acronym for for, let, where, order by, and return. A FLWOR expression is actually a for each loop. You can use it to iterate through a sequence returned by an XPath expression. Although you typically iterate through a sequence of nodes, you can use FLWOR expressions to iterate through any sequence. You can limit the nodes to be processed with a predicate, sort the nodes, and format the returned XML. The parts of a FLWOR statement are:

- **For** With a for clause, you bind iterator variables to input sequences. Input sequences are either sequences of nodes or sequences of atomic values. You create atomic value sequences by using literals or functions.
- **Let** With the optional let clause, you assign a value to a variable for a specific iteration. The expression used for an assignment can return a sequence of nodes or a sequence of atomic values.
- **Where** With the optional where clause, you filter the iteration.
- **Order by** Using the order by clause, you can control the order in which the elements of the input sequence are processed. You control the order based on atomic values.
- **Return** The return clause is evaluated once per iteration, and the results are returned to the client in the iteration order. With this clause, you format the resulting XML.

Here is an example of usage of all FLWOR clauses.

```
DECLARE @x AS XML;
SET @x = N'
<CustomersOrders>
  <Customer custid="1">
    <!-- Comment 111 -->
    <companyname>Customer NRZBB</companyname>
    <Order orderid="10692">
      <orderdate>2007-10-03T00:00:00</orderdate>
    </Order>
    <Order orderid="10702">
      <orderdate>2007-10-13T00:00:00</orderdate>
    </Order>
    <Order orderid="10952">
      <orderdate>2008-03-16T00:00:00</orderdate>
    </Order>
  </Customer>
  <Customer custid="2">
    <!-- Comment 222 -->
    <companyname>Customer MLTDN</companyname>
    <Order orderid="10308">
      <orderdate>2006-09-18T00:00:00</orderdate>
    </Order>
    <Order orderid="10952">
      <orderdate>2008-03-04T00:00:00</orderdate>
    </Order>
  </Customer>
</CustomersOrders>';
SELECT @x.query('for $i in CustomersOrders/Customer/Order
                 let $j := $i/orderdate
                 where $i/@orderid < 10900
                 order by ($j)[1]
                 return
                 <Order-orderid-element>
                  <orderid>{data($i/@orderid)}</orderid>
                  {$j}
                 </Order-orderid-element>')
       AS [Filtered, sorted and reformatted orders with let clause];
```

The query iterates, as you can see from the for clause, through all Order nodes using an iterator variable and returns those nodes. The name of the iterator variable must start with a dollar sign ($) in XQuery. The where clause limits the Order nodes processed to those with an orderid attribute smaller than 10900.

The expression passed to the order by clause must return values of a type compatible with the gt XQuery operator. As you'll recall, the gt operator expects atomic values. The query orders the XML returned by the orderdate element. Although there is a single orderdate element per order, XQuery does not know this, and it considers orderdate to be a sequence, not an atomic value. The numeric predicate specifies the first orderdate element of an order as the value to order by. Without this numeric predicate, you would get an error.

The return clause shapes the XML returned. It converts the orderid attribute to an element by creating the element manually and extracting only the value of the attribute with the data() function. It returns the orderdate element as well, and wraps both in the Order-orderid-element element. Note the braces around the expressions that extract the value of the orderid element and the orderdate element. XQuery evaluates expressions in braces; without braces, everything would be treated as a string literal and returned as such.

The let clause assigns a name to the $i/orderdate expression. This expression repeats twice in the query, in the order by and the return clauses. To name the expression, you have to use a variable different from $i. XQuery inserts the expression every time the new variable is referenced. Here is the result of the query.

```
<Order-orderid-element>
  <orderid>10308</orderid>
  <orderdate>2006-09-18T00:00:00</orderdate>
</Order-orderid-element>
<Order-orderid-element>
  <orderid>10692</orderid>
  <orderdate>2007-10-03T00:00:00</orderdate>
</Order-orderid-element>
<Order-orderid-element>
  <orderid>10702</orderid>
  <orderdate>2007-10-13T00:00:00</orderdate>
</Order-orderid-element>
```

Quick Check

1. What do you do in the return clause of the FLWOR expressions?
2. What would be the result of the expression (12, 4, 7) != 7?

Quick Check Answers

1. In the return clause, you format the resulting XML of a query.
2. The result would be true.

PRACTICE Using XQuery/XPath Navigation

In this practice, you use XPath expressions for navigation inside XQuery. You start with simple path expressions, and then use more complex path expressions with predicates.

If you encounter a problem completing an exercise, you can install the completed projects from the companion content for this chapter and lesson.

EXERCISE 1 Use Simple XPath Expressions

In this exercise, you use simple XPath expressions to return subsets of XML data.

1. If you closed SSMS, start it and connect to your SQL Server instance. Open a new query window by clicking the New Query button.
2. Connect to your TSQL2012 database.
3. Use the following XML instance for testing the navigation.

```
DECLARE @x AS XML;
SET @x = N'
<CustomersOrders>
  <Customer custid="1">
    <!-- Comment 111 -->
    <companyname>Customer NRZBB</companyname>
    <Order orderid="10692">
      <orderdate>2007-10-03T00:00:00</orderdate>
    </Order>
    <Order orderid="10702">
      <orderdate>2007-10-13T00:00:00</orderdate>
    </Order>
    <Order orderid="10952">
      <orderdate>2008-03-16T00:00:00</orderdate>
    </Order>
  </Customer>
  <Customer custid="2">
    <!-- Comment 222 -->
    <companyname>Customer MLTDN</companyname>
    <Order orderid="10308">
      <orderdate>2006-09-18T00:00:00</orderdate>
    </Order>
    <Order orderid="10952">
      <orderdate>2008-03-04T00:00:00</orderdate>
    </Order>
  </Customer>
</CustomersOrders>';
```

4. Write a query that selects Customer nodes with child nodes. Select principal nodes (elements in this context) only. The result should be similar to the abbreviated result here.

```
1. Principal nodes
--------------------------------------------------------------------------------
<companyname>Customer NRZBB</companyname><Order orderid="10692"><orderdate>2007-
```

Use the following query to get the desired result.

```
SELECT @x.query('CustomersOrders/Customer/*')
       AS [1. Principal nodes];
```

5. Now return all nodes, not just the principal ones. The result should be similar to the abbreviated result here.

```
2. All nodes
--------------------------------------------------------------------------------
<!-- Comment 111 --><companyname>Customer NRZBB</companyname><Order orderid="106
```

Use the following query to get the desired result.

```
SELECT @x.query('CustomersOrders/Customer/node()')
       AS [2. All nodes];
```

6. Return comment nodes only. The result should be similar to the result here.

```
3. Comment nodes
--------------------------------------------------------------------------------
<!-- Comment 111 --><!-- Comment 222 -->
```

Use the following query to get the desired result.

```
SELECT @x.query('CustomersOrders/Customer/comment()')
       AS [3. Comment nodes];
```

EXERCISE 2 Use XPath Expressions with Predicates

In this exercise, you use XPath expressions with predicates to return filtered subsets of XML data.

1. Use the following XML instance (the same as in the previous exercise) for testing the navigation.

```
DECLARE @x AS XML;
SET @x = N'
<CustomersOrders>
  <Customer custid="1">
    <!-- Comment 111 -->
    <companyname>Customer NRZBB</companyname>
    <Order orderid="10692">
      <orderdate>2007-10-03T00:00:00</orderdate>
    </Order>
    <Order orderid="10702">
      <orderdate>2007-10-13T00:00:00</orderdate>
    </Order>
    <Order orderid="10952">
      <orderdate>2008-03-16T00:00:00</orderdate>
    </Order>
  </Customer>
  <Customer custid="2">
    <!-- Comment 222 -->
    <companyname>Customer MLTDN</companyname>
    <Order orderid="10308">
      <orderdate>2006-09-18T00:00:00</orderdate>
    </Order>
    <Order orderid="10952">
      <orderdate>2008-03-04T00:00:00</orderdate>
    </Order>
  </Customer>
</CustomersOrders>';
```

2. Return all orders for customer 2. The result should be similar to the abbreviated result here.

```
4. Customer 2 orders
--------------------------------------------------------------------------------
<Order orderid="10308"><orderdate>2006-09-18T00:00:00</orderdate></Order><Order
```

Use the following query to get the desired result.

```
SELECT @x.query('//Customer[@custid=2]/Order')
       AS [4. Customer 2 orders];
```

3. Return all orders with order number 10952, no matter who the customer is. The result should be similar to the abbreviated result here.

```
5. Orders with orderid=10952
--------------------------------------------------------------------------------
<Order orderid="10952"><orderdate>2008-03-16T00:00:00</orderdate></Order><Order
```

Use the following query to get the desired result.

```
SELECT @x.query('//Order[@orderid=10952]')
       AS [5. Orders with orderid=10952];
```

4. Return the second customer who has at least one order. The result should be similar to the abbreviated result here.

```
6. 2nd Customer with at least one Order
--------------------------------------------------------------------------------
<Customer custid="2"><!-- Comment 222 --><companyname>Customer MLTDN</companyname
```

Use the following query to get the desired result.

```
SELECT @x.query('(/CustomersOrders/Customer/
                 Order/parent::Customer)[2]')
       AS [6. 2nd Customer with at least one Order];
```

Lesson Summary

- You can use the XQuery language inside T-SQL queries to query XML data.
- XQuery supports its own data types and functions.
- You use XPath expressions to navigate through an XML instance.
- The real power of XQuery is in the FLWOR expressions.

Lesson Review

Answer the following questions to test your knowledge of the information in this lesson. You can find the answers to these questions and explanations of why each answer choice is correct or incorrect in the "Answers" section at the end of this chapter.

1. Which of the following is not a FLWOR clause?

   A. for

   B. let

   C. where

   D. over

   E. return

2. Which node type test can be used to retrieve all nodes of an XML instance?

   A. Asterisk (*)

   B. comment()

   C. node()

   D. text()

3. Which conditional expression is supported in XQuery?

   A. IIF

   B. if..then..else

   C. CASE

   D. switch

Lesson 3: Using the XML Data Type

XML is the standard format for exchanging data among different applications and platforms. It is widely used, and almost all modern technologies support it. Databases simply have to deal with XML. Although XML could be stored as simple text, plain text representation means having no knowledge of the structure built into an XML document. You could decompose the text, store it in multiple relational tables, and use relational technologies to manipulate the data. Relational structures are quite static and not so easy to change. Think of dynamic or volatile XML structures. Storing XML data in a native XML data type solves these problems, enabling functionality attached to the type that can accommodate support for a wide variety of XML technologies.

After this lesson, you will be able to:

- Use the XML data type and its methods.
- Index XML data.

Estimated lesson time: 45 minutes

When to Use the XML Data Type

A database schema is sometimes volatile. Think about situations in which you have to support many different schemas for the same kind of event. SQL Server has many such cases within it. Data definition language (DDL) triggers and extended events are good examples. There are dozens of different DDL events. Each event returns different event information; each event returns data with a different schema. A conscious design choice was that DDL triggers return event information in XML format via the eventdata() function. Event information in XML format is quite easy to manipulate. Furthermore, with this architecture, SQL Server will be able to extend support for new DDL events in future versions more easily.

Another interesting example of internal XML support is XML showplan. You can generate execution plan information in XML format by using the SET SHOWPLAN_XML and SET STATISTICS XML statements. Think of the value for applications and tools that need execution plan information—it's easy to request and parse now. You can even force the optimizer to use a specified execution plan by providing the XML plan in a USE PLAN query hint.

Another place to use XML is to represent data that is sparse. Your data is sparse and you have a lot of NULLs if some columns are not applicable to all rows. Standard solutions for such a problem introduce subtypes or implement an open schema model in a relational environment. However, a solution based on XML could be the easiest to implement. A solution that introduces subtypes can lead to many new tables. SQL Server 2008 introduced sparse columns and filtered indexes. Sparse columns could be another solution for having attributes that are not applicable for all rows in a table. Sparse columns have optimized storage for NULLs. If you have to index them, you can efficiently use filtered indexes to index known values only; this way, you optimize table and index storage. In addition, you can have access to all sparse columns at once through a column set. A column set is an XML representation of all the sparse columns that is even updateable. However, with sparse columns and a column set, the schema is more complicated than a schema with an explicit XML column.

You could have other reasons to use an XML model. XML inherently supports hierarchical and sorted data. If ordering is inherent in your data, you might decide to store it as XML. You could receive XML documents from your business partner, and you might not need to shred the document to tables. It might be more practical to just store the complete XML documents in your database, without shredding.

XML Data Type Methods

In the XQuery introduction in this chapter, you already saw the XML data type. XQuery was a parameter for the query() method of this type. An XML data type includes five methods that accept XQuery as a parameter. The methods support querying (the query() method), retrieving atomic values (the value() method), checking existence (the exist() method), modifying sections within the XML data (the modify() method) as opposed to overwriting the whole thing, and shredding XML data into multiple rows in a result set (the nodes() method). You use the XML data type methods in the practice for this lesson.

The value() method of the XML data type returns a scalar value, so it can be specified anywhere where scalar values are allowed; for example, in the SELECT list of a query. Note that the value() method accepts an XQuery expression as the first input parameter. The second parameter is the SQL Server data type returned. The value() method must return a scalar value; therefore, you have to specify the position of the element in the sequence you are browsing, even if you know that there is only one.

You can use the exist() method to test if a specific node exists in an XML instance. Typical usage of this clause is in the WHERE clause of T-SQL queries. The exist() method returns a bit, a flag that represents true or false. It can return the following:

- 1, representing true, if the XQuery expression in a query returns a nonempty result. That means that the node searched for exists in the XML instance.
- 0, representing false, if the XQuery expression returns an empty result.
- NULL, if the XML instance is NULL.

The query() method, as the name implies, is used to query XML data. You already know this method from the previous lesson of this chapter. It returns an instance of an untyped XML value.

The XML data type is a large object type. The amount of data stored in a column of this type can be very large. It would not be very practical to replace the complete value when all you need is just to change a small portion of it; for example, a scalar value of some subelement. The SQL Server XML data type provides you with the modify() method, similar in concept to the WRITE method that can be used in a T-SQL UPDATE statement for VARCHAR(MAX) and the other MAX types. You invoke the modify() method in an UPDATE T-SQL statement.

The W3C standard doesn't support data modification with XQuery. However, SQL Server provides its own language extensions to support data modification with XQuery. SQL Server XQuery supports three data manipulation language (DML) keywords for data modification: insert, delete, and replace value of.

The nodes() method is useful when you want to shred an XML value into relational data. Its purpose is therefore the same as the purpose of the OPENXML rowset function introduced in Lesson 1 of this chapter. However, using the nodes() method is usually much faster than preparing the DOM with a call to sp_xml_preparedocument, executing a SELECT..FROM OPENXML statement, and calling sp_xml_removedocument. The nodes() method prepares DOM internally, during the execution of the T-SQL SELECT. The OPENXML approach could be faster if you prepared the DOM once and then shredded it multiple times in the same batch.

The result of the nodes() method is a result set that contains logical copies of the original XML instances. In those logical copies, the context node of every row instance is set to one of the nodes identified by the XQuery expression, meaning that you get a row for every single node from the starting point defined by the XQuery expression. The nodes() method returns copies of the XML values, so you have to use additional methods to extract the scalar values out of them. The nodes() method has to be invoked for every row in the table. With the T-SQL APPLY operator, you can invoke a right table expression for every row of a left table expression in the FROM part.

Using the XML Data Type for Dynamic Schema

In this lesson, you learn how to use an XML data type inside your database through an example. This example shows how you can make a relational database schema dynamic. The example extends the Products table from the TSQL2012 database.

Suppose that you need to store some specific attributes only for beverages and other attributes only for condiments. For example, you need to store the percentage of recommended daily allowance (RDA) of vitamins only for beverages, and a short description only for condiments to indicate the condiment's general character (such as sweet, spicy, or salty). You could add an XML data type column to the Production.Products table of the TSQL2012 database; for this example, call it additionalattributes. Because the other product categories have no additional attributes, this column has to be nullable. The following code alters the Production.Products table to add this column.

```
ALTER TABLE Production.Products
 ADD additionalattributes XML NULL;
```

Before inserting data in the new column, you might want to constrain the values of this column. You should use a typed XML, an XML validated against a schema. With an XML schema, you constrain the possible nodes, the data type of those nodes, and more. In SQL Server, you can validate XML data against an XML schema collection. This is exactly what you need for a dynamic schema; if you could validate XML data against a single schema only, you could not use an XML data type for a dynamic schema solution, because XML instances would be limited to a single schema. Validation against a collection of schemas enables support of different schemas for beverages and condiments. If you wanted to validate XML values only against a single schema, you would define only a single schema in the collection.

You create the schema collection by using the CREATE XML SCHEMA COLLECTION T-SQL statement. You have to supply the XML schema, an XSD document, as input. Creating the schema is a task that should not be taken lightly. If you make an error in the schema, some invalid data might be accepted and some valid data might be rejected.

The easiest way to create XML schemas is to create relational tables first, and then use the XMLSCHEMA option of the FOR XML clause. Store the resulting XML value (the schema) in a variable, and provide the variable as input to the CREATE XML SCHEMA COLLECTION statement. The following code creates two auxiliary empty tables for beverages and condiments, and then uses SELECT with the FOR XML clause to create an XML schema from those tables. Then it stores the schemas in a variable, and creates a schema collection from that variable. Finally, after the schema collection is created, the code drops the auxiliary tables.

```
-- Auxiliary tables
CREATE TABLE dbo.Beverages
(
  percentvitaminsRDA INT
);
CREATE TABLE dbo.Condiments
(
  shortdescription NVARCHAR(50)
);
GO
-- Store the Schemas in a Variable and Create the Collection
DECLARE @mySchema NVARCHAR(MAX);
SET @mySchema = N'';
SET @mySchema = @mySchema +
  (SELECT *
   FROM Beverages
   FOR XML AUTO, ELEMENTS, XMLSCHEMA('Beverages'));
SET @mySchema = @mySchema +
  (SELECT *
   FROM Condiments
   FOR XML AUTO, ELEMENTS, XMLSCHEMA('Condiments'));
SELECT CAST(@mySchema AS XML);
CREATE XML SCHEMA COLLECTION dbo.ProductsAdditionalAttributes AS @mySchema;
GO
-- Drop Auxiliary Tables
DROP TABLE dbo.Beverages, dbo.Condiments;
GO
```

The next step is to alter the XML column from a well-formed state to a schema-validated one.

```
ALTER TABLE Production.Products
  ALTER COLUMN additionalattributes
   XML(dbo.ProductsAdditionalAttributes);
```

You can get information about schema collections by querying the catalog views sys.xml_schema_collections, sys.xml_schema_namespaces, sys.xml_schema_components, and some others views in the sys schema with names that start with xml_schema_. However, a schema collection is stored in SQL Server in tabular format, not in XML format. It would make sense to perform the same schema validation on the client side as well. Why would you send data to the server side if the relational database management system (RDBMS) will reject it? You can perform schema collection validation in Microsoft .NET code as well, as long as you have the schemas. Therefore, it makes sense to save the schemas you create with T-SQL in files in a file system as well. If you forgot to save the schemas in files, you can still retrieve them from SQL Server schema collections with the xml_schema_namespace system function. Note that the schema returned by this function might not be lexically the same as the original schema used when you created your schema collection. Comments, annotations, and white spaces are lost. However, the aspects of the schema used for validation are preserved.

Before using the new data type, you have to take care of one more issue. How do you avoid binding the wrong schema to a product of a specific category? For example, how do you prevent binding a condiments schema to a beverage? You could solve this issue with a trigger; however, having a declarative constraint, a check constraint, is preferable. This is why the code added namespaces to the schemas. You need to check whether the namespace is the same as the product category name. You cannot use XML data type methods inside constraints. You have to create two additional functions: one retrieves the XML namespace of the additionalattributes XML column, and the other retrieves the category name of a product. In the check constraint, you can check whether the return values of both functions are equal. Here is the code that creates both functions and adds a check constraint to the Production.Products table.

```
-- Function to Retrieve the Namespace
CREATE FUNCTION dbo.GetNamespace(@chkcol XML)
 RETURNS NVARCHAR(15)
AS
BEGIN
 RETURN @chkcol.value('namespace-uri((/*)[1])','NVARCHAR(15)')
END;
GO
-- Function to Retrieve the Category Name
CREATE FUNCTION dbo.GetCategoryName(@catid INT)
 RETURNS NVARCHAR(15)
AS
BEGIN
 RETURN
  (SELECT categoryname
   FROM Production.Categories
   WHERE categoryid = @catid)
END;
GO
-- Add the Constraint
ALTER TABLE Production.Products ADD CONSTRAINT ck_Namespace
 CHECK (dbo.GetNamespace(additionalattributes) =
        dbo.GetCategoryName(categoryid));
GO
```

The infrastructure is prepared. You can try to insert some valid XML data in your new column.

```
-- Beverage
UPDATE Production.Products
   SET additionalattributes = N'
<Beverages xmlns="Beverages">
  <percentvitaminsRDA>27</percentvitaminsRDA>
</Beverages>'
WHERE productid = 1;
-- Condiment
UPDATE Production.Products
   SET additionalattributes = N'
<Condiments xmlns="Condiments">
  <shortdescription>very sweet</shortdescription>
</Condiments>'
WHERE productid = 3;
```

To test whether the schema validation and check constraint work, you should try to insert some invalid data as well.

```
-- String instead of int
UPDATE Production.Products
   SET additionalattributes = N'
<Beverages xmlns="Beverages">
   <percentvitaminsRDA>twenty seven</percentvitaminsRDA>
</Beverages>'
WHERE productid = 1;
-- Wrong namespace
UPDATE Production.Products
   SET additionalattributes = N'
<Condiments xmlns="Condiments">
  <shortdescription>very sweet</shortdescription>
</Condiments>'
WHERE productid = 2;
-- Wrong element
UPDATE Production.Products
   SET additionalattributes = N'
<Condiments xmlns="Condiments">
  <unknownelement>very sweet</unknownelement>
</Condiments>'
WHERE productid = 3;
```

You should get errors for all three UPDATE statements. You can check the data with the SELECT statement. When you are done, you could clean up the TSQL2012 database with the following code.

```
ALTER TABLE Production.Products
 DROP CONSTRAINT ck_Namespace;
ALTER TABLE Production.Products
 DROP COLUMN additionalattributes;
DROP XML SCHEMA COLLECTION dbo.ProductsAdditionalAttributes;
DROP FUNCTION dbo.GetNamespace;
DROP FUNCTION dbo.GetCategoryName;
GO
```

Quick Check

- **Which XML data type method would you use to retrieve scalar values from an XML instance?**

Quick Check Answer

- **The value() XML data type method retrieves scalar values from an XML instance.**

XML Indexes

The XML data type is actually a large object type. There can be up to 2 gigabytes (GB) of data in every single column value. Scanning through the XML data sequentially is not a very efficient way of retrieving a simple scalar value. With relational data, you can create an index on a filtered column, allowing an index seek operation instead of a table scan. Similarly, you can index XML columns with specialized *XML indexes*. The first index you create on an XML column is the *primary XML index*. This index contains a shredded persisted representation of the XML values. For each XML value in the column, the index creates several rows of data. The number of rows in the index is approximately the number of nodes in the XML value. Such an index alone can speed up searches for a specific element by using the exist() method. After creating the primary XML index, you can create up to three other types of *secondary XML indexes*:

- **PATH** This secondary XML index is especially useful if your queries specify path expressions. It speeds up the exist() method better than the Primary XML index. Such an index also speeds up queries that use value() for a fully specified path.
- **VALUE** This secondary XML index is useful if queries are value-based and the path is not fully specified or it includes a wildcard.
- **PROPERTY** This secondary XML index is very useful for queries that retrieve one or more values from individual XML instances by using the value() method.

The primary XML index has to be created first. It can be created only on tables with a clustered primary key.

PRACTICE Using XML Data Type Methods

In this practice, you use XML data type methods.

If you encounter a problem completing an exercise, you can install the completed projects from the companion content for this chapter and lesson.

EXERCISE 1 Use the value() and exist() Methods

In this exercise, you use the value() and exist() XML data type methods.

1. If you closed SSMS, start it and connect to your SQL Server instance. Open a new query window by clicking the New Query button.
2. Connect to your TSQL2012 database.

3. Use the following XML instance for testing the XML data type methods.

```
DECLARE @x AS XML;
SET @x = N'
<CustomersOrders>
  <Customer custid="1">
    <!-- Comment 111 -->
    <companyname>Customer NRZBB</companyname>
    <Order orderid="10692">
      <orderdate>2007-10-03T00:00:00</orderdate>
    </Order>
    <Order orderid="10702">
      <orderdate>2007-10-13T00:00:00</orderdate>
    </Order>
    <Order orderid="10952">
      <orderdate>2008-03-16T00:00:00</orderdate>
    </Order>
  </Customer>
  <Customer custid="2">
    <!-- Comment 222 -->
    <companyname>Customer MLTDN</companyname>
    <Order orderid="10308">
      <orderdate>2006-09-18T00:00:00</orderdate>
    </Order>
    <Order orderid="10952">
      <orderdate>2008-03-04T00:00:00</orderdate>
    </Order>
  </Customer>
</CustomersOrders>';
```

4. Write a query that retrieves the first customer name as a scalar value. The result should be similar to the result here.

```
First Customer Name
--------------------
Customer NRZBB
```

Use the following query to get the desired result.

```
SELECT @x.value('(/CustomersOrders/Customer/companyname)[1]',
       'NVARCHAR(20)')
        AS [First Customer Name];
```

5. Now check whether companyname and address nodes exist under the Customer node. The result should be similar to the result here.

```
Company Name Exists Address Exists
------------------- --------------
1                   0
```

Use the following query to get the desired result.

```
SELECT @x.exist('(/CustomersOrders/Customer/companyname)')
        AS [Company Name Exists],
       @x.exist('(/CustomersOrders/Customer/address)')
        AS [Address Exists];
```

EXERCISE 2 Use the query(), nodes(), and modify() Methods

In this exercise, you use the query(), nodes(), and modify() XML data type methods.

1. Use the following XML instance (the same instance as in the previous exercise) for testing the XML data type methods.

```
DECLARE @x AS XML;
SET @x = N'
<CustomersOrders>
  <Customer custid="1">
    <!-- Comment 111 -->
    <companyname>Customer NRZBB</companyname>
    <Order orderid="10692">
      <orderdate>2007-10-03T00:00:00</orderdate>
    </Order>
    <Order orderid="10702">
      <orderdate>2007-10-13T00:00:00</orderdate>
    </Order>
    <Order orderid="10952">
      <orderdate>2008-03-16T00:00:00</orderdate>
    </Order>
  </Customer>
  <Customer custid="2">
    <!-- Comment 222 -->
    <companyname>Customer MLTDN</companyname>
    <Order orderid="10308">
      <orderdate>2006-09-18T00:00:00</orderdate>
    </Order>
    <Order orderid="10952">
      <orderdate>2008-03-04T00:00:00</orderdate>
    </Order>
  </Customer>
</CustomersOrders>';
```

2. Return all orders for the customer with @custid equal to 1 (the first customer in the XML document) as XML. The result should be similar to the result here.

```
<Order orderid="10692">
  <orderdate>2007-10-03T00:00:00</orderdate>
</Order>
<Order orderid="10702">
  <orderdate>2007-10-13T00:00:00</orderdate>
</Order>
<Order orderid="10952">
  <orderdate>2008-03-16T00:00:00</orderdate>
</Order>
```

Use the following query to get the desired result.

```
SELECT @x.query('//Customer[@custid=1]/Order')
       AS [Customer 1 orders];
```

3. Shred all orders information for the customer with @custid equal to 1 (the first customer in the XML document). The result should be similar to the result here.

```
Order Id    Order Date
----------- -----------------------
10692       2007-10-03 00:00:00.000
10702       2007-10-13 00:00:00.000
10952       2008-03-16 00:00:00.000
```

Use the following query to get the desired result.

```
SELECT  T.c.value('./@orderid[1]', 'INT') AS [Order Id],
 T.c.value('./orderdate[1]', 'DATETIME') AS [Order Date]
FROM @x.nodes('//Customer[@custid=1]/Order')
      AS T(c);
```

4. Update the name of the first customer and then retrieve the new name. The result should be similar to the result here.

```
First Customer New Name
------------------------
New Company Name
```

Use the following query to get the desired result.

```
SET @x.modify('replace value of
    /CustomersOrders[1]/Customer[1]/companyname[1]/text()[1]
  with "New Company Name"');
SELECT @x.value('(/CustomersOrders/Customer/companyname)[1]',
       'NVARCHAR(20)')
       AS [First Customer New Name];
```

5. Now Exit SSMS.

Lesson Summary

- The XML data type is useful for many scenarios inside a relational database.
- You can validate XML instances against a schema collection.
- You can work with XML data through XML data type methods.

Lesson Review

Answer the following questions to test your knowledge of the information in this lesson. You can find the answers to these questions and explanations of why each answer choice is correct or incorrect in the "Answers" section at the end of this chapter.

1. Which of the following is not an XML data type method?
   - **A.** merge()
   - **B.** nodes()
   - **C.** exist()
   - **D.** value()
2. What kind of XML indexes can you create? (Choose all that apply.)
   - **A.** PRIMARY
   - **B.** PATH
   - **C.** ATTRIBUTE
   - **D.** PRINCIPALNODES
3. Which XML data type method do you use to shred XML data to tabular format?
   - **A.** modify()
   - **B.** nodes()
   - **C.** exist()
   - **D.** value()

Case Scenarios

In the following case scenarios, you apply what you've learned about querying and managing XML data. You can find the answers to these questions in the "Answers" section at the end of this chapter.

Case Scenario 1: Reports from XML Data

A company that hired you as a consultant uses a website to get reviews of their products from their customers. They store those reviews in an XML column called reviewsXML of a table called ProductReviews. The XML column is validated against a schema and contains, among others, firstname, lastname, and datereviewed elements. The company wants to generate a report with names of the reviewers and dates of reviews. Additionally, because there are already many very long reviews, the company worries about the performance of this report.

1. How could you get the data needed for the report?
2. What would you do to maximize the performance of the report?

Case Scenario 2: Dynamic Schema

You need to provide a solution for a dynamic schema for the Products table in your company. All products have the same basic attributes, like product ID, product name, and list price. However, different groups of products have different additional attributes. Besides dynamic schema for the variable part of the attributes, you need to ensure at least basic constraints, like data types, for these variable attributes.

1. How would you make the schema of the Products table dynamic?
2. How would you ensure that at least basic constraints would be enforced?

Suggested Practices

To help you successfully master the exam objectives presented in this chapter, complete the following tasks.

Query XML Data

In the AdventureWorks2012 demo database, there is the HumanResources.JobCandidate table. It contains a Resume XML data type column.

- **Practice 1** Find all first and last names in this column.
- **Practice 2** Find all candidates from Chicago.
- **Practice 3** Return distinct states found in all resumes.

Answers

This section contains the answers to the lesson review questions and solutions to the case scenarios in this chapter.

Lesson 1

1. **Correct Answers: A and D**
   - **A. Correct:** FOR XML AUTO is a valid option to produce automatically formatted XML.
   - **B. Incorrect:** There is no FOR XML MANUAL option.
   - **C. Incorrect:** There is no FOR XML DOCUMENT option.
   - **D. Correct:** With the FOR XML PATH option, you can format XML explicitly.
2. **Correct Answer: C**
   - **A. Incorrect:** There is no specific ATTRIBUTES directive. Attribute-centric formatting is the default.
   - **B. Incorrect:** With the ROOT option, you can specify a name for the root element.
   - **C. Correct:** Use the ELEMENTS option to produce element-centric XML.
   - **D. Incorrect:** With the XMLSCHEMA option, you produce inline XSD.
3. **Correct Answers: B and D**
   - **A. Incorrect:** FOR XML AUTO automatically formats the XML retuned.
   - **B. Correct:** FOR XML EXPLICIT allows you to manually format the XML returned.
   - **C. Incorrect:** FOR XML RAW automatically formats the XML retuned.
   - **D. Correct:** FOR XML PATH allows you to manually format the XML returned.

Lesson 2

1. **Correct Answer: D**
   - **A. Incorrect:** for is a FLWOR clause.
   - **B. Incorrect:** let is a FLWOR clause.
   - **C. Incorrect:** where is a FLWOR clause.
   - **D. Correct:** over is not a FLWOR clause; O stands for the order by clause.
   - **E. Incorrect:** return is a FLWOR clause.

2. **Correct Answer: C**
   - **A. Incorrect:** With the asterisk (*), you retrieve all principal nodes.
   - **B. Incorrect:** With comment(), you retrieve comment nodes.
   - **C. Correct:** You use the node() node-type test to retrieve all nodes.
   - **D. Incorrect:** With text(), you retrieve text nodes.
3. **Correct Answer: B**
   - **A. Incorrect:** IIF is not an XQuery expression.
   - **B. Correct:** XQuery supports the if..then..else conditional expression.
   - **C. Incorrect:** CASE is not an XQuery expression.
   - **D. Incorrect:** switch is not an XQuery expression.

Lesson 3

1. **Correct Answer: A**
   - **A. Correct:** merge() is not an XML data type method.
   - **B. Incorrect:** nodes() is an XML data type method.
   - **C. Incorrect:** exist() is an XML data type method.
   - **D. Incorrect:** value() is an XML data type method.
2. **Correct Answers: A and B**
   - **A. Correct:** You create a PRIMARY XML index before any other XML indexes.
   - **B. Correct:** A PATH XML index is especially useful if your queries specify path expressions.
   - **C. Incorrect:** There is no general ATTRIBUTE XML index.
   - **D. Incorrect:** There is no general PRINCIPALNODES XML index.
3. **Correct Answer: B**
   - **A. Incorrect:** You use the modify() method to update XML data.
   - **B. Correct:** You use the nodes() method to shred XML data.
   - **C. Incorrect:** You use the exist() method to test whether a node exists.
   - **D. Incorrect:** You use the value() method to retrieve a scalar value from XML data.

Case Scenario 1

1. You could use the value() XML data type method to retrieve the scalar values needed for the report.
2. You should consider using XML indexes in order to maximize the performance of the report.

Case Scenario 2

1. You could use the XML data type column to store the variable attributes in XML format.
2. You could validate the XML against an XML schema collection.

CHAPTER 8

Creating Tables and Enforcing Data Integrity

Exam objectives in this chapter:

- Create Database Objects
  - Create and alter tables using T-SQL syntax (simple statements).
  - Create and modify constraints (simple statements).

Tables are the primary method of data storage in Microsoft SQL Server. To use tables, you need to master how to create them, in addition to adding constraints to protect the integrity of the stored data. In this chapter, you learn how to create and alter tables, in addition to enforcing data integrity between tables by using table constraints.

Lessons in this chapter:

- Lesson 1: Creating and Altering Tables
- Lesson 2: Enforcing Data Integrity

Before You Begin

To complete the lessons in this chapter, you must have:

- An understanding of basic database concepts.
- Experience working with SQL Server Management Studio (SSMS).
- Some experience writing T-SQL code.
- Access to a SQL Server 2012 instance with the sample database TSQL2012 installed.

Lesson 1: Creating and Altering Tables

Because database tables are how SQL Server stores data, it is vital to understand the T-SQL commands for creating and altering tables. In this lesson, you learn about these commands and their related options.

After this lesson, you will be able to:

- Use the CREATE TABLE statement to create a table.
- Understand how to specify data types for columns.
- Use the ALTER TABLE statement to change some properties of columns.
- Create a table with table compression.

Estimated lesson time: 45 minutes

Introduction

In SQL Server, the table is the main method used for storing data. Every table belongs to exactly one database, so when data is stored in the table, SQL Server protects it through backup/restore processes, in addition to transactional behavior, described as follows:

- When you back up a database, all its tables are backed up, and when you restore the database, all those tables are restored with the same data they had when the backup occurred.
- When you query a database for data, ultimately that data is located in tables either in that database or another database referenced by the query.
- Even system data in SQL Server is stored in specially reserved tables called system tables.

In SQL Server, tables containing data are often called base tables to distinguish them from other objects or expressions that might be derived from tables, such as views or queries. A base table is permanent in the sense that the table's definition and contents remain in the database even if SQL Server is shut down and restarted.

Other variations on tables that are covered elsewhere in this Training Kit are as follows:

- *Temporary tables* are base tables that exist in tempdb and last only as long as a session or scope referencing them endures (covered in Chapter 16, "Understanding Cursors, Sets, and Temporary Tables").
- *Table variables* are variables that can store data but only for the duration of a T-SQL batch (also covered in Chapter 16).
- *Views*, which are not base tables but are derived from queries against base tables, appear just like tables but do not store data (covered in Chapter 9, "Designing and Creating Views, Inline Functions, and Synonyms").
- *Indexed views* store data but are defined as views and are updated whenever the base tables are updated (covered in Chapter 15, "Implementing Indexes and Statistics").
- *Derived tables* and *table expressions* are subqueries that are referenced like tables in queries (covered in Chapter 4, "Combining Sets").

When working with tables, you need to know how to create, drop, and alter a table.

Creating a Table

You can create a table in T-SQL in two ways:

- By using the CREATE TABLE statement, where you explicitly define the components of the table
- By using the SELECT INTO statement, which creates a table automatically by using the output of a query for the basic table definition

This lesson covers just the CREATE TABLE statement.

The basic syntax of the CREATE TABLE statement is shown in the Books Online for SQL Server 2012 article "CREATE TABLE (Transact-SQL)" at *http://msdn.microsoft.com/en-us/library/ms174979.aspx*. Although the full details are too complex to go into here, they can be simplified by looking at the first section of the syntax diagram.

```
CREATE TABLE
    [ database_name . [ schema_name ] . | schema_name . ] table_name
    [ AS FileTable ]
    ( { <column_definition> | <computed_column_definition>
        | <column_set_definition> | [ <table_constraint> ] [ ,...n ] } )
    [ ON { partition_scheme_name ( partition_column_name ) | filegroup
        | "default" } ]
    [ { TEXTIMAGE_ON { filegroup | "default" } ]
    [ FILESTREAM_ON { partition_scheme_name | filegroup
        | "default" } ]
    [ WITH ( <table_option> [ ,...n ] ) ]

[ ; ]
```

Each of the items in the previous code can be expanded, and some of the elements can be further expanded. The items covered in this lesson include the following:

- Database name
- Schema name
- Table name
- Column definition
- Computed column definition
- Table constraint
- Table option

Look at a sample CREATE TABLE statement: the Production.Categories table from the TSQL2012 database. (You'll look at the table constraints in Lesson 2, "Enforcing Data Integrity.")

```
CREATE TABLE Production.Categories(
    categoryid INT IDENTITY(1,1) NOT NULL,
    categoryname NVARCHAR(15) NOT NULL,
    description NVARCHAR(200) NOT NULL)
GO
```

Using the sample Production.Categories table, look at the essentials of what the CREATE TABLE statement contains.

When you create a table, you can specify the database schema; in this case, Production. (You can let SQL Server fill in the database schema with your user name's default schema).

> ***NOTE*** **TWO-PART NAMING**
>
> **SQL Server always assigns the table exactly one database schema. Therefore, you should always reference tables by using two-part names (with both the schema and table name) to avoid errors and make your code more robust.**

You must specify:

- The table name; in this case, Categories.
- The table columns, including:
  - Column names, such as categoryid.
  - Column data types, such as INT.

You can also specify:

- For columns:
  - The lengths of character data types, such as (15) for categoryname.
  - The precision of numeric and some date data types.
  - Optional special types of columns (computed, sparse, IDENTITY, ROWGUIDCOL), such as IDENTITY, in the case of categoryid.
  - The collation of the column (normally used only if you need to specify a non-default collation).
- Constraints, including:
  - Nullability (categoryid is defined with the NOT NULL constraint).
  - Default and check constraints.
  - Optional column collations.
  - Primary key (such as PK_Categories).
  - Foreign key constraints.
  - Unique constraints.
- Possible table storage directions, including:
  - Filegroup (such as ON [PRIMARY], meaning the primary filegroup).
  - Partition schema.
  - Table compression.

It is common to define the table constraints later, after the table is created, using an ALTER TABLE command. You'll take a look at each of these in order, starting with the required elements, in the following sections.

Specifying a Database Schema

Every table belongs to a grouping of objects within a database called a database schema. The *database schema* is a named container (a namespace) that you can use to group tables and other database objects. For the TSQL2012 table Production.Categories, the database schema is Production.

The primary purpose of a database schema is to group many database objects, such as tables, together. In the case of tables, a database schema also allows many tables with the same table name to belong to different schemas. This works because the database schema becomes a part of the table's name and helps identify the table. If you don't supply a database schema name when you create a table, SQL Server will supply one based on your database user name's default schema.

> ***IMPORTANT* DATABASE SCHEMA AND TABLE SCHEMA**
>
> **Do not confuse the term database schema with table schema. A database schema is a database-wide container of objects. A table schema is the definition of a table that includes the CREATE TABLE statement with all the column definitions.**

For example, look at the following query.

```
SELECT TOP (10) categoryname FROM Production.Categories;
```

The name Production.Categories specifies the table name within the database. There could be other objects in the same database name Categories, but only one object with that name can exist in the Production database schema. So to exactly specify the name of a table, you must supply the database schema name.

The following four built-in database schemas cannot be dropped:

- The dbo database schema is the default database schema for new objects created by users having the db_owner or db_ddl_admin roles.
- The guest schema is used to contain objects that would be available to the guest user. This schema is rarely used.
- The INFORMATION_SCHEMA schema is used by the Information Schema views, which provide ANSI standard access to metadata.
- The sys database schema is reserved by SQL Server for system objects such as system tables and views.

An additional set of database schemas are named after the built-in database roles, and though they can be dropped, they are meant to pair up with the database roles. They are also seldom used.

Before SQL Server 2005, when the user names that owned objects were the same as schemas, it was common to assign objects to the dbo owner when they needed to be shared across all users. Beginning with SQL Server 2005, you can create schemas that have no intrinsic relationship to users and can serve to give a finer-grained permissions structure to the tables of a database. For example, in the TSQL2012 database, you will notice four user-defined database schemas: HR, Production, Sales, and Stats.

Notice that when you view a table list in SQL Server Management Studio (SSMS), every table has two parts to its name: the database schema followed by the table name within the schema, such as Production.Categories.

> ***NOTE*** **DATABASE SCHEMAS ARE NOT NESTED**
>
> **There can be only one level of database schema; one schema cannot contain another schema.**

Every database schema must be owned by exactly one authorized database user. That database schema owner can then grant permissions to other users regarding the objects in this schema. For example, the following statement creates the Production database schema.

```
CREATE SCHEMA Production AUTHORIZATION dbo;
GO
```

The schema named Production is actually owned by the user named dbo, not by the dbo database schema. This allows one user (for example, dbo) to own many different database schemas.

EXAM TIP

You can move a table from one schema to another by using the ALTER SCHEMA TRANSFER statement. Assuming there is no object named Categories in the Sales database schema, the following statement moves the Production.Categories table to the Sales database schema.

```
ALTER SCHEMA Sales TRANSFER Production.Categories;
```

To move the table back, issue the following.

```
ALTER SCHEMA Production TRANSFER Sales.Categories;
```

Naming Tables and Columns

You are free to choose a wide variety of names for schemas, tables, and columns. However, there are some important restrictions and best practices, as detailed in this section.

All schema, table, and column names must be valid SQL Server identifiers. Identifiers must be at least one character long and no longer than 128 characters.

There are two types of identifiers: *regular* and *delimited*.

Regular identifiers are names that follow a set of rules and don't need to be surrounded by delimiters like square brackets ([ ]) or quotation marks (the single character "). For regular identifiers, the characters can be:

- Letters as defined in the Unicode Standard 3.2.
- Decimal numbers from either Basic Latin or other national scripts.

The first character must be a letter defined in the Unicode Standard 3.2 or an underscore (_), and cannot be a digit. However, there are two exceptions:

- Variables must begin with an at sign (@).
- Temporary tables or procedures must begin with a number sign (#).

Subsequent identifier characters can include:

- Letters as defined in the Unicode Standard 3.2.
- Numerals from Basic Latin (0 through 9) or other collations.
- The at sign (@), the dollar sign ($), the number sign (#), and the underscore (_).

A regular identifier cannot be a T-SQL reserved word and cannot include embedded spaces or non-alphanumeric characters other than @, $, #, and _. For example, the table named Production.Categories uses two valid regular identifiers: Production as the schema name, and Categories as the table name.

> ***NOTE*** **USE REGULAR IDENTIFIERS WHEN POSSIBLE**
>
> **If you embed special characters other than @, #, and $ in an identifier for a schema, table, or column name, that action makes the identifier delimited, no longer regular. Generally, it is a best practice to use regular identifiers, using just letters, numbers, and underscores. Then users do not need delimiters to refer to the object names. Some T-SQL developers like to embed underscores between names, to help readability. For example, they might write the column categoryid as category_id.**

Delimited identifiers are names that do not adhere to the rules for regular identifiers. There is no restriction on what characters can be embedded in them, but when they do not obey the rules for regular identifiers, you must use either square brackets or quotation marks as delimiters in order to reference them. In T-SQL, square brackets can always be used for delimited identifiers.

Using quotation marks as delimiters is the ANSI SQL standard. However, use of quotation marks as delimiters requires that the SET QUOTED_IDENTIFIER setting is set to ON, which is the SQL Server default. Because it is possible to turn that setting to OFF, using quotation marks is risky. For example, you could create a table as follows.

```
CREATE TABLE Production.[Yesterday's News]
...
```

Or you could write it in the following way.

```
CREATE TABLE Production."Tomorrow's Schedule"
...
```

Because of the embedded space and apostrophe, these are not regular identifiers and they require the use of delimiters.

> **NOTE REGULAR IDENTIFIERS ARE MORE USER-FRIENDLY**
>
> **Even though you can use square brackets as delimiters, it is a best practice to always make sure those names follow the rules for regular identifiers. That way, if one of your users does not use the delimiters in a query, their query will still succeed.**

When choosing the name of schemas, tables, and columns, it is a best practice to follow your organization's or project's naming guidelines.

> **NOTE DO NOT MAKE OBJECT NAMES VERY LONG**
>
> **Don't make schema, table, or column names too long. Organizations often make it part of the naming convention for constraint and index names to include the table name and the names of the columns used as keys in the constraint or index name. Because constraint and index names must also be identifiers, they cannot exceed the maximum identifier length of 128 characters.**

Generally, the best practice is to make your schema, table, and column names short but descriptive. Also, avoid abbreviations unless they are really necessary or commonly understood. For example, the column name categoryid uses the abbreviation id (short for identification), but it is so common that there's little risk of being misunderstood.

Choosing Column Data Types

The data type used for each column is very important. For full information about data types, see Lesson 2, "Working with Data Types and Built-in Functions," in Chapter 2, "Getting Started with the SELECT Statement."

Here are some brief guidelines that you can use for choosing data types for columns:

- Try to use the most efficient data type: one that requires the least amount of disk storage and adequately captures the data, and won't need to be changed later on when the table fills with data.
- When you need to store character strings, if they will likely vary in length, use the NVARCHAR or VARCHAR data types rather than the fixed NCHAR or CHAR. If the column value might be updated often, and especially if it is short, using the fixed length can prevent excessive row movement.

- The DATE, TIME, and DATETIME2 data types can store data more efficiently and with better precision than DATETIME and SMALLDATETIME.
- Use VARCHAR(MAX), NVARCHAR(MAX), and VARBINARY(MAX) instead of the deprecated TEXT, NTEXT, and IMAGE data types.
- Use ROWVERSION instead of the deprecated TIMESTAMP.
- DECIMAL and NUMERIC are the same data type, but generally people prefer DECIMAL because the name is a bit more descriptive. Use DECIMAL and NUMERIC instead of FLOAT or REAL data types unless you really need floating-point precision and are familiar with possible rounding issues.

NULL and Default Values

How to handle unknowns is a difficult problem in database theory and is just as difficult in database design. When you cannot enter data into a particular column of a row, how do you indicate that? T-SQL follows the ANSI SQL standard in allowing one non-value property of a column called NULL. NULL is not the value of a column; it's just a way of saying the value is completely and totally unknown.

You can specify whether a column allows NULL by stating NULL or NOT NULL right after the column's data type. NULL means the column allows NULLs, and NOT NULL means it does not allow NULLs. Use the following guidelines:

- If you know that a value for a column must be optional because sometimes no value is known at the time the row will be inserted, then define the column as NULL.
- If you don't want to allow NULL in the column, but you do want to specify some default value to indicate that the column has not yet been populated, you can specify a DEFAULT constraint by adding the DEFAULT clause right after saying NOT NULL.

For example, you could indicate that the values for the description column in the Production.Categories table are not yet entered by supplying an empty string (two single quotation marks with no space between them: '') as the default value.

```
CREATE TABLE Production.Categories(
    categoryid INT IDENTITY(1,1) NOT NULL,
    categoryname NVARCHAR(15) NOT NULL,
    description NVARCHAR(200) NOT NULL DEFAULT ('')
    ) ON [PRIMARY];
GO
```

Now if the application inserts a row with a new category, the user does not need to add a description immediately but can return later to update the row with the description. For more information about default values, see "Default Constraints" in Lesson 2.

The Identity Property and Sequence Numbers

In T-SQL, the Identity property can be assigned to a column in order to automatically generate a sequence of numbers. You can use it for only one column of a table, and you can specify both seed and increment values for the number sequence generated.

When you define the property in a CREATE TABLE statement, you can specify a seed value (that is, the value to begin with), and then an increment amount (that is, the amount to increment each new sequence number by). The most common values for seed and increment are (1,1) as shown in the following example from the TSQL2012 Production.Categories table.

```
CREATE TABLE Production.Categories(
    categoryid INT IDENTITY(1,1) NOT NULL,
    ...
```

Many of the TSQL2012 tables have primary key columns with identity properties.

SQL Server 2012 introduces an optional way to generate sequence numbers by using sequence objects. You can use sequence objects as an optional way to generate unique numeric values in a table. However, because sequence objects behave differently from the Identity property, they may or may not be a good substitute for the Identity property.

For more information about the Identity property and sequence objects, see Lesson 1, "Using the Sequence Object and IDENTITY Column Property," in Chapter 11, "Other Data Modification Aspects."

Computed Columns

You can also define columns as values that are computed based on expressions. These expressions could be based on the value of other columns in the row or based on T-SQL functions. For example, you might query the data in the table Sales.OrderDetails and realize that two columns can be multiplied together, unitprice and qty, to get the initial cost of the order detail line (before applying the discount). You could compute this in a SELECT statement as follows.

```
SELECT TOP (10) orderid, productid, unitprice, qty,
    unitprice * qty AS initialcost -- expression
FROM Sales.OrderDetails;
```

You can take that expression, unitprice * qty AS initialcost, and embed it in the CREATE TABLE statement as a computed column, as follows.

```
CREATE TABLE Sales.OrderDetails
(
  orderid   INT           NOT NULL,
...
  initialcost AS unitprice * qty -- computed column
);
```

Also, you can make the computed column persisted, meaning that SQL Server will store the computed values with the table's data, and not compute the values on the fly. However, if a computed column is to be persisted, the column cannot make use of any functions that are not deterministic, which means that the expression cannot reference various dynamic functions like GETDATE() or CURRENT_TIMESTAMP. For more information about deterministic functions, see "Deterministic and Nondeterministic Functions" at *http://msdn.microsoft.com/en-us/library/ms178091.aspx*.

Table Compression

You can compress the data in a table, in addition to the indexes, to get more efficient storage, if you use the Enterprise edition of SQL Server 2012 (in addition to SQL Server 2008 and SQL Server 2008 R2.) Table compression has two levels:

- **Row** For row-level compression, SQL Server applies a more compact storage format to each row of a table.
- **Page** Page-level compression includes row-level plus additional compression algorithms that can be performed at the page level.

The following command adds row-level compression to the Production.OrderDetails table as part of the CREATE TABLE statement.

```
CREATE TABLE Sales.OrderDetails
(
  orderid   INT           NOT NULL,
...
  )
    WITH (DATA_COMPRESSION = ROW);
```

To change the command to apply page compression, just state DATA_COMPRESSION = PAGE.

You can also use the ALTER command to alter a table to set its compression.

```
ALTER TABLE Sales.OrderDetails
REBUILD WITH (DATA_COMPRESSION = PAGE);
```

SQL Server provides the sp_estimate_data_compression_savings stored procedure to help you determine whether a table with data in it would benefit from compression. For more information about table compression, see "Data Compression" at *http://msdn.microsoft.com/en-us/library/cc280449.aspx* and "sp_estimate_data_compression_savings (Transact-SQL)" at *http://msdn.microsoft.com/en-us/library/cc280574.aspx*.

Quick Check

1. **Can a table or column name contain spaces, apostrophes, and other nonstandard characters?**
2. **What types of table compression are available?**

Quick Check Answer

1. **Yes, table and column names can be delimited identifiers that contain nonstandard characters.**
2. **You can use either page or row compression on a table. Page compression includes row compression.**

Altering a Table

After you have created a table, you can use the ALTER TABLE command to change the table's structure and add or remove certain table properties, such as table constraints. You can use ALTER TABLE to:

- Add or remove a column, including a computed column. (New columns are placed at the end of the table's column order.)
- Change the data type of a column.
- Change a column's nullability (that is, from NULL to NOT NULL, or vice versa).
- Add or remove a constraint, including the following:
  - Primary key constraint
  - Unique constraint
  - Foreign key constraint
  - Check constraint
  - Default constraint

If you want to change the definition of a constraint or the definition of a computed column, drop the constraint or column with the old definition and add the constraint or computed column back in with the new definition.

You cannot use ALTER TABLE to:

- Change a column name.
- Add an identity property.
- Remove an identity property.

Choosing Table Indexes

You can choose some indexes for a table when creating it, and you can add indexes later when you see how users actually query the data. Some indexes are created automatically with constraints, which is covered in the next lesson. For indexes in general, see Chapter 15.

PRACTICE Creating and Altering Tables

In this practice, you use the ALTER TABLE command to add columns to a table and change data types.

If you encounter a problem completing an exercise, you can install the completed projects from the companion content for this chapter and lesson.

EXERCISE 1 Use ALTER TABLE to Add and Modify Columns

Examine the following CREATE TABLE statement, from the TSQL2012.sql script, that is used to create the Production.Categories table.

```
/* From TSQL2012.sql:
-- Create table Production.Categories
CREATE TABLE Production.Categories
(
  categoryid   INT           NOT NULL IDENTITY,
  categoryname NVARCHAR(15)  NOT NULL,
  description  NVARCHAR(200) NOT NULL,
  CONSTRAINT PK_Categories PRIMARY KEY(categoryid)
);
*/
```

In this exercise, you create a similar table by the name of Production.CategoriesTest, one column at a time. Then you use the SET IDENTITY_INSERT command to insert a new row.

1. Start a new query window in SSMS, and make sure a fresh copy of the TSQL2012 database is on the server. In this exercise, you create an extra table and then drop it in the TSQL2012 database.

2. Create the table with one column. Execute the following statements in order to create your copy of the original table, but just one column to start with.

```
USE TSQL2012;
GO
CREATE TABLE Production.CategoriesTest
(
  categoryid   INT           NOT NULL IDENTITY
);
GO
```

3. Add the categoryname and description columns to match the original table.

```
ALTER TABLE Production.CategoriesTest
    ADD categoryname NVARCHAR(15) NOT NULL;
GO
ALTER TABLE Production.CategoriesTest
    ADD description NVARCHAR(200) NOT NULL;
GO
```

4. Now you attempt an insert into the copy table from the original table, but the Insert will fail. Execute the following.

```
INSERT Production.CategoriesTest (categoryid, categoryname, description)
    SELECT categoryid, categoryname, description
    FROM Production.Categories;
GO
```

5. Try again with IDENTITY_INSERT ON, which allows a row to be inserted with an explicit identity value.

```
SET IDENTITY_INSERT Production.CategoriesTest ON;
INSERT Production.CategoriesTest (categoryid, categoryname, description)
    SELECT categoryid, categoryname, description
    FROM Production.Categories;
GO
SET IDENTITY_INSERT Production.CategoriesTest OFF;
GO
```

6. To clean up, drop the table. You can skip this step if you are going to the next exercise.

```
IF OBJECT_ID(N'Production.CategoriesTest', N'U') IS NOT NULL
    DROP TABLE Production.CategoriesTest;
GO
```

EXERCISE 2 Work with NULL Columns in Tables

In this exercise, you use the table from the previous exercise, and explore the consequences of adding a column that does not and then does allow NULL.

1. Create and populate the table from the previous exercise by executing the following code. You can skip this step if you still have the table in TSQL2012 from the previous exercise.

```
-- Create table Production.CategoriesTest
CREATE TABLE Production.CategoriesTest
(
  categoryid   INT           NOT NULL IDENTITY,
  categoryname NVARCHAR(15)  NOT NULL,
  description  NVARCHAR(200) NOT NULL,
  CONSTRAINT PK_CategoriesTest PRIMARY KEY(categoryid)
);
-- Populate the table Production.CategoriesTest
SET IDENTITY_INSERT Production.CategoriesTest ON;
INSERT Production.CategoriesTest (categoryid, categoryname, description)
    SELECT categoryid, categoryname, description
    FROM Production.Categories;
GO
SET IDENTITY_INSERT Production.CategoriesTest OFF;
GO
```

2. Make the description column larger.

```
ALTER TABLE Production.CategoriesTest
    ALTER COLUMN description NVARCHAR(500) NOT NULL;
GO
```

3. Inspect the table for the existence of any NULLs in the description column. Note there are none:

```
SELECT description
    FROM Production.CategoriesTest
    WHERE categoryid = 8; -- Seaweed and fish
```

4. Try to change a value in the description column to NULL. This fails.

```
UPDATE Production.CategoriesTest
    SET description = NULL
    WHERE categoryid = 8;
GO
```

5. Alter the table and make the description column allow NULL.

```
ALTER TABLE Production.CategoriesTest
    ALTER COLUMN description NVARCHAR(500) NULL ;
GO
```

6. Now retry the update. This works.

```
UPDATE Production.CategoriesTest
    SET description = NULL
    WHERE categoryid = 8;
GO
```

7. Attempt to change the column back to NOT NULL. This fails.

```
ALTER TABLE Production.CategoriesTest
    ALTER COLUMN description NVARCHAR(500) NOT NULL ;
GO
```

8. Retry the update, but give the description back its original value.

```
UPDATE Production.CategoriesTest
    SET description = 'Seaweed and fish'
    WHERE categoryid = 8;
GO
```

9. Change the description column back to NOT NULL. This succeeds.

```
ALTER TABLE Production.CategoriesTest
    ALTER COLUMN description NVARCHAR(500) NOT NULL ;
GO
```

10. To clean up, drop the table.

```
IF OBJECT_ID(N'Production.CategoriesTest', N'U') IS NOT NULL
    DROP TABLE Production.CategoriesTest;
GO
```

Lesson Summary

- Creating a table involves specifying a table schema as a namespace or container for the table.
- Name tables and columns carefully and descriptively.
- Choose the most efficient and accurate data types for columns.
- Choose the appropriate remaining properties of columns, such as the identity property and whether a column should allow NULLs.
- You can specify whether a table should be compressed when creating the table.
- You can use ALTER TABLE to change most properties of columns after a table has been created.

Lesson Review

Answer the following questions to test your knowledge of the information in this lesson. You can find the answers to these questions and explanations of why each answer choice is correct or incorrect in the "Answers" section at the end of this chapter.

1. Which of the following are T-SQL regular identifiers? (Choose all that apply.)
   - **A.** categoryname
   - **B.** category name
   - **C.** category$name
   - **D.** category_name
2. Which data type should be used in place of TIMESTAMP?
   - **A.** VARBINARY
   - **B.** ROWVERSION
   - **C.** DATETIME2
   - **D.** TIME
3. How can you express that the column categoryname allow NULLs?
   - **A.** categoryname PERMIT NULL NVARCHAR(15)
   - **B.** categoryname NVARCHAR(15) ALLOW NULL
   - **C.** categoryname NVARCHAR(15) PERMIT NULL
   - **D.** categoryname NVARCHAR(15) NULL

Lesson 2: Enforcing Data Integrity

Because databases store data in a persistent way, the tables in a database need some way to enforce various types of validations of the data no matter how the data might be changed from external sources. These types of validations go beyond just data types; they cover which columns should have unique values, what ranges of valid values a column might accept, and whether the value of a column should match some column in a different table.

When you embed those methods of data validation inside the definition of the table itself, it is called declarative data integrity. This is implemented using table constraints, and you use ISO standard SQL commands to create those constraints, on a table-by-table basis.

This lesson covers the types of constraints that you can create on tables that help you enforce data integrity.

After this lesson, you will be able to:

- Implement declarative data integrity on your tables.
- Define and use primary key constraints.
- Define and use unique constraints.
- Define and use foreign key constraints.
- Define and use check constraints.
- Define default constraints.

Estimated lesson time: 30 minutes

Using Constraints

The best way to enforce data integrity in SQL Server tables is by creating or declaring constraints on base tables. You apply these constraints to a table and its columns by using the CREATE TABLE or ALTER TABLE statements.

NOTE **DO NOT USE DEPRECATED RULES**

The very first versions of SQL Server did not support constraints and used database "rules" instead, employing the CREATE RULE command. Rules are not as well suited for enforcing data integrity as declarative constraints. Also, rules are deprecated and will be removed in a future version of SQL Server. In any case, you should avoid using rules and use constraints instead.

In SQL Server, all table constraints are database objects, just like tables, views, stored procedures, functions, and so on. Therefore, constraints must have unique names across the database. But because every table constraint is scoped to an individual table, it makes sense to adopt a naming convention that states the type of constraint, the table name, and then, if relevant, the key columns declared in the constraint. For example, the table Production.Categories has its primary key named PK_Categories. When you adopt a naming convention like that, it is easy to tell what the object does from its name.

Primary Key Constraints

Every table in a relational database should have some method of distinguishing each row from all the others. The most common method is to designate a column as the primary key that will have a unique value for each row. Sometimes a combination of columns may be required, but the most common approach is to use a single column.

A column (or combination of columns) within the data of a table that uniquely identifies every row (such as the category name in the TSQL2012 Production.Categories table) is called the natural key or business key of the table. You can use the natural key of a table as its primary key, but database designers most often find it more convenient in the long run to create a special column with a numeric data type (such as integer), which will have a unique but otherwise meaningless value, called a surrogate key. Then the surrogate key serves as the primary key, and the natural key's uniqueness is enforced using a unique constraint.

For example, consider again the TSQL2012 table Production.Categories. The following shows how it is defined in the TSQL2012.sql script.

```
CREATE TABLE Production.Categories
(
  categoryid   INT           NOT NULL IDENTITY,
  categoryname NVARCHAR(15)  NOT NULL,
  description  NVARCHAR(200) NOT NULL,
  CONSTRAINT PK_Categories PRIMARY KEY(categoryid)
);
```

In this table, categoryid is the primary key, which you can tell because of the added CONSTRAINT clause at the end of the CREATE TABLE statement. The name of the constraint is PK_Categories, which is a name that you supply.

Another way of declaring a column as a primary key is to use the ALTER TABLE statement, which you could write as follows.

```
ALTER TABLE Production.Categories
    ADD CONSTRAINT PK_Categories PRIMARY KEY(categoryid);
GO
```

It's important to remember that the columns you choose as primary keys will end up being used in other tables to refer back to the original table. It is a best practice to use the same name for the column in both tables, if at all possible. Also, you can make it easier for people to query the referenced table by using a descriptive column name. In other words, choose a name for the primary key column that flows naturally from the table name. Then it's easier to recognize when that column is a foreign key in other tables. You'll notice, for example, that all the primary keys in the TSQL2012 database are just the table name with "id" on the end. This makes it really easy in other tables to know the table that a foreign key will reference.

To create a primary key on a column, there are a number of requirements:

- The column or columns cannot allow NULL. If the column or columns allow NULL, the constraint command will fail.
- Any data already in the table must have unique values in the primary key column or columns. If there are any duplicates, the ALTER TABLE statement will fail.
- There can be only one primary key constraint at a time in a table. If you try to create two primary key constraints on the same table, the command will fail.

When you create a primary key, SQL Server enforces the constraint behind the scenes by creating a unique index on that column and using the primary key column or columns as the keys of the index.

To list the primary key constraints in a database, you can query the sys.key_constraints table filtering on a type of PK.

```
SELECT *
FROM sys.key_constraints
WHERE type = 'PK';
```

Also you can find the unique index that SQL Server uses to enforce a primary key constraint by querying sys.indexes. For example, the following query shows the unique index declared on the Production.Categories table for the PK_Categories primary key constraint.

```
SELECT *
FROM sys.indexes
WHERE object_id = OBJECT_ID(N'Production.Categories', N'U') AND name = 'PK_Categories';
```

For more information about indexes, see Chapter 15.

Unique Constraints

Unique constraints are very similar to primary key constraints. Often, you will have more than one column or set of columns that uniquely determine rows in a table. For example, if you have a surrogate key defined as the primary key, you will most likely also have a natural key whose uniqueness you would also like to enforce. For natural keys or business unique keys, you can use the unique constraint. (Sometimes people call it a uniqueness constraint, but the technically accurate term is unique constraint.)

For example, in the Production.Categories table, you might also want to enforce that all category names be unique, so you could declare a unique constraint on the categoryname column, with the following.

```
ALTER TABLE Production.Categories
   ADD CONSTRAINT UC_Categories UNIQUE (categoryname);
GO
```

Like the primary key constraint, the unique constraint automatically creates a unique index with the same name as the constraint. The unique index can be either clustered or nonclustered. SQL Server uses that index to enforce the uniqueness of the column or combination of columns.

EXAM TIP

The unique constraint does not require the column to be NOT NULL. You can allow NULL in a column and still have a unique constraint, but only one row can be NULL.

Both primary key and unique constraints have the same size limitations as an index: you can combine no more than 16 columns as the key columns of the index, and there is a maximum combined width of 900 bytes of data across those columns.

NOTE **CONSTRAINTS AND COMPUTED COLUMNS**

You can also create both primary key and unique constraints on computed columns.

Just as with the primary key constraints, you can list unique constraints in a database by querying the sys.key_constraints table filtering on a type of UQ.

```
SELECT *
FROM sys.key_constraints
WHERE type = 'UQ';
```

You can find the unique index that SQL Server uses to enforce a primary key constraint by querying sys.indexes and filtering on the constraint name.

Quick Check

1. **How does SQL Server enforce uniqueness in both primary key and unique constraints?**
2. **Can a primary key on one table have the same name as the primary key in another table in the same database and in the same schema?**

Quick Check Answer

1. **SQL Server uses unique indexes to enforce uniqueness for both primary key and unique constraints.**
2. **No, all table constraints must have unique names withing the schema of a database.**

Foreign Key Constraints

A foreign key is a column or combination of columns in one table that serve as a link to look up data in another table. In the second table, often called a lookup table, the corresponding column or combination of columns have a primary key or unique constraint applied to them, or a unique index. So a value in the first table may be duplicated, but in the second table where you look up the corresponding value, it must be unique. If you know the value in the first table, the foreign key relationship allows you to get related data from the other table by looking up the corresponding data.

For example, there is a column called categoryid in the Production.Products table. The column corresponds to the primary key categoryid in the Production.Categories table. For any specified product in the Products table, you can find related category information by looking it up in the Categories table.

You can use the foreign key constraint to enforce that every entry into the categoryid column of the Production.Products table is a valid categoryid from the Production.Categories table. Here's the code to create the foreign key.

```
USE TSQL2012
GO
ALTER TABLE Production.Products  WITH CHECK
    ADD  CONSTRAINT FK_Products_Categories FOREIGN KEY(categoryid)
    REFERENCES Production.Categories (categoryid)
GO
```

Here's how the command works:

- You always declare the foreign key constraint on the table for which this key is "foreign"—that is, a key from a different table. So that's why you must ALTER the Production.Products table.
- You can decide whether to allow violations when you create the constraint. Creating a constraint WITH CHECK implies that if there is any data in the table already, and if there would be violations of the constraint, then the ALTER TABLE will fail.
- You add the constraint and specify the name of the foreign key constraint. In this case, TSQL2012 uses FK_ as a prefix for foreign keys.
- After entering the type of constraint, FOREIGN KEY, you then in parentheses state the column (or combination of columns) in this table that you are constraining to be validated by a lookup into a different table.
- Then you state what the other table is—that is, what table in the current database that this constraint REFERENCES, along with the column or combination of columns. This column (or columns) is from the referenced table and must be a primary key or unique constraint in the table, or else it may instead have a unique index.

Keep the following rules in mind when creating foreign keys:

- The column or set of columns from each table must have exactly the same data types and collation (if they have a string data type).
- As mentioned earlier, the columns of the referenced table must have a unique index created on them, either implicitly with a primary key or a unique constraint, or explicitly by creating the index.
- You can also create foreign key constraints on computed columns.

Tables are often joined based on foreign keys so that a query can return data that is related between two tables. For example, the following query returns the categoryname of a set of products from the Production.Products table.

```
SELECT P.productname, C.categoryname
FROM Production.Products AS P
JOIN Production.Categories AS C
    ON P.categoryid = C.categoryid;
```

Notice that the query returns the correct categoryname for each product because the JOIN is on the foreign key P.categoryid and its referenced column C.categoryid in Production. Categories.

EXAM TIP

Because joins often occur on foreign keys, it can help query performance to create a nonclustered index on the foreign key in the referencing table. There is already a unique index on the corresponding column in the referenced table, but if the referencing table, like Production.Products, has a lot of rows, it may help SQL Server resolve the join faster if it can use an index on the big table.

Finally, to find a database's foreign keys, you can query the sys.foreign_keys table. The following query finds the row for the FK_Products_Categories table.

```
SELECT *
FROM sys.foreign_keys
WHERE name = 'FK_Products_Categories';
```

Check Constraints

With a check constraint, you declare that the values of a column are constrained in some fashion. The values are already constrained by the data type, so a check constraint adds some additional constraints on the ranges, or set of allowable values. When you create a check constraint, you specify some expression so that SQL Server can constrain the valid values. The expression can reference other columns in the same row of the table and use built-in T-SQL functions.

For example, the TSQL2012 Production.Products table has a check constraint on the unitprice column called CHK_Products_unitprice. Here's how it could be created.

```
ALTER TABLE Production.Products  WITH CHECK
    ADD  CONSTRAINT CHK_Products_unitprice
    CHECK  (unitprice>=0);
GO
```

The unitprice column already has a data type of money, but that does not prevent it from having negative values. However, a negative price makes no sense. You can prevent negative values by creating the constraint on the table, referencing the column, and declaring the expression that must be true: that unitprice be greater than or equal to zero. Being less than zero is not allowed.

Check constraints have a number of advantages:

- Their expressions are similar to the filter expressions in a WHERE clause of a SELECT statement.
- The constraint is in the table, so it is always enforced, as long as WITH CHECK is specified. If a similar constraint were only enforced in the application outside the database, there is always a chance that data might get into the table that violates the allowable values.
- They can perform better than alternative methods of constraining columns, such as triggers.

Some things to watch out for when using check constraints are as follows:

- If the column allows NULL, make sure the expression accounts for potential NULLs. A NULL, for example, is not negative, but it is also not positive. An insert of a NULL passes the constraint unitprice >= 0 and it also passes the constraint unitprice < 0.
- You cannot customize the error message from a check constraint as you can if you implemented the constraint using a trigger.
- A check constraint cannot test the action of an update: you cannot reference the previous value of a column in the check constraint expression. If you need to do that, you must use a trigger. For example, if you want to enforce a constraint that unitprice cannot be increased by more than 25 percent in any update, you must use a trigger.

You can list the check constraints for a table by querying sys.check_constraints, as in the following.

```
SELECT *
FROM sys.check_constraints
WHERE parent_object_id = OBJECT_ID(N'Production.Products', N'U');
```

The parent_object_id is the object_id of the table to which the check constraint belongs.

Default Constraints

The least constraining of all the T-SQL table constraints is the default constraint. In fact, you could say default constraints don't really constrain anything at all; they just supply a default value during an INSERT if no other value is supplied.

Default constraints are most useful when you have a column in a table that does not allow NULL, but you don't want to prevent an INSERT from succeeding if it does not specify a value for the column. However, you can equally apply a default constraint to a column that does allow NULL but you want a default value inserted instead of having a NULL applied when an INSERT doesn't specify the value.

For an example of a default constraint, the unitprice column of the Production.Products table has a default constraint defined as 0. Although you could use an ALTER TABLE to add a default constraint, it is much more common to put it into the CREATE TABLE statement. Here's the example from TSQL2012.

```
CREATE TABLE Production.Products
(
  productid    INT          NOT NULL IDENTITY,
  productname  NVARCHAR(40) NOT NULL,
  supplierid   INT          NOT NULL,
  categoryid   INT          NOT NULL,
  unitprice    MONEY        NOT NULL
    CONSTRAINT DFT_Products_unitprice DEFAULT(0),
  discontinued BIT          NOT NULL
    CONSTRAINT DFT_Products_discontinued DEFAULT(0),
...
);
```

In this case, the default constraint is listed right after the column's data type. Here it is given an explicit name. If you do not provide an explicit name, SQL Server will supply a machine-generated name.

Having default values for the unitprice and discontinued columns means that an INSERT can succeed in adding a new row without having to supply values for those columns. Remember that default constraints, like all other constraints, are schema-wide objects. Their names must be unique across an entire schema. No two tables scoped to the same schema can have default constraints named the same.

You can get a list of default constraints by querying sys.default_constraints. The following query finds all the default constraints for the Production.Products table.

```
SELECT *
FROM sys.default_constraints
WHERE parent_object_id = OBJECT_ID(N'Production.Products', N'U');
```

PRACTICE Enforcing Data Integrity

In this practice, you use the ALTER TABLE command to add and drop constraints to a table, including primary key, unique, and foreign key constraints.

If you encounter a problem completing an exercise, you can install the completed projects from the companion content for this chapter and lesson.

EXERCISE 1 Work with Primary and Foreign Key Constraints

The following is the CREATE TABLE statement for Production.Products, taken from TSQL2012.sql.

```
/*
-- Create table Production.Products
CREATE TABLE Production.Products
(
  productid    INT           NOT NULL IDENTITY,
  productname  NVARCHAR(40)  NOT NULL,
  supplierid   INT           NOT NULL,
  categoryid   INT           NOT NULL,
  unitprice    MONEY         NOT NULL
    CONSTRAINT DFT_Products_unitprice DEFAULT(0),
  discontinued BIT           NOT NULL
    CONSTRAINT DFT_Products_discontinued DEFAULT(0),
  CONSTRAINT PK_Products PRIMARY KEY(productid),
  CONSTRAINT FK_Products_Categories FOREIGN KEY(categoryid)
    REFERENCES Production.Categories(categoryid),
  CONSTRAINT FK_Products_Suppliers FOREIGN KEY(supplierid)
    REFERENCES Production.Suppliers(supplierid),
  CONSTRAINT CHK_Products_unitprice CHECK(unitprice >= 0)
);
*/
```

In this exercise, you test the primary key and foreign key constraints of the table. You use ALTER TABLE to drop, test, and add a foreign key constraint back into the table.

1. Test the primary key using the following.

```
SELECT productname FROM Production.Products
WHERE productid = 1;
SET IDENTITY_INSERT Production.Products ON;
GO
INSERT INTO Production.Products (productid, productname, supplierid, categoryid,
unitprice, discontinued)
     VALUES (1, N'Product TEST', 1, 1, 18, 0);
GO
SET IDENTITY_INSERT Production.Products OFF;
```

2. Insert a new row that lets the Identity property assign a new productid.

```
INSERT INTO Production.Products (productname, supplierid, categoryid, unitprice,
discontinued)
     VALUES (N'Product TEST', 1, 1, 18, 0);
GO
```

3. Delete the test row.

```
DELETE FROM Production.Products WHERE productname = N'Product TEST';
GO
```

4. Try again with an invalid categoryid = 99. The insert fails because of the foreign key constraint.

```
INSERT INTO Production.Products (productname, supplierid, categoryid, unitprice,
discontinued)
     VALUES (N'Product TEST', 1, 99, 18, 0);
GO
```

5. Drop the foreign key constraint.

```
ALTER TABLE Production.Products DROP CONSTRAINT FK_Products_Categories;
GO
```

6. Try the insert now with the invalid categoryid = 99. The insert succeeds.

```
INSERT INTO Production.Products (productname, supplierid, categoryid, unitprice,
discontinued)
     VALUES (N'Product TEST', 1, 99, 18, 0);
GO
```

7. Try to add the foreign key constraint back in using WITH CHECK. The command fails.

```
ALTER TABLE Production.Products  WITH CHECK
    ADD  CONSTRAINT FK_Products_Categories FOREIGN KEY(categoryid)
    REFERENCES Production.Categories (categoryid);
GO
```

8. Update the row so that it has a valid categoryid.

```
UPDATE Production.Products
    SET categoryid = 1
    WHERE productname = N'Product TEST';
GO
```

9. Now try to add the foreign key constraint back to the table. You succeed.

```
ALTER TABLE Production.Products  WITH CHECK
    ADD  CONSTRAINT FK_Products_Categories FOREIGN KEY(categoryid)
    REFERENCES Production.Categories (categoryid);
GO
```

10. Drop the test row from the table.

```
DELETE FROM Production.Products WHERE productname = N'Product TEST';
GO
```

EXERCISE 2 Work with Unique Constraints

In this exercise, you create a unique constraint on the productname column of the TSQL2012 table Production.Products. You test to verify that all names are unique when the constraint is applied.

1. Verify that all productnames in Production.Products are unique.

```
USE TSQL2012;
GO
SELECT productname, COUNT(*) AS productnamecount
FROM Production.Products
GROUP BY productname
HAVING COUNT(*) > 1;
```

2. Inspect the productname for productid = 1; the value is 'Product HHYDP'.

```
SELECT productname
FROM Production.Products
WHERE productid = 1;
```

3. Use the UPDATE statement to test whether there can be a duplicate product name.

```
UPDATE Production.Products
    SET productname = 'Product RECZE'
    WHERE productid = 1;
```

4. Verify that there are duplicates.

```
SELECT productname, COUNT(*) AS productnamecount
FROM Production.Products
GROUP BY productname
HAVING COUNT(*) > 1;
```

5. Now try to add a unique constraint. Note that it fails.

```
ALTER TABLE Production.Products
    ADD CONSTRAINT U_Productname UNIQUE (productname);
```

6. Restore the original product name.

```
UPDATE Production.Products
    SET productname = 'Product HHYDP'
    WHERE productid = 1;
```

7. Try a second time to add the unique constraint.

```
ALTER TABLE Production.Products
    ADD  CONSTRAINT U_Productname UNIQUE (productname);
```

8. To clean up, drop the unique constraint.

```
ALTER TABLE Production.Products
    DROP  CONSTRAINT U_Productname;
```

Lesson Summary

- To help preserve data integrity in database tables, you can declare constraints that persist in the database.
- Constraints ensure that data entered into tables has to obey more complex rules than those defined for data types and nullability.
- Table constraints include primary key and unique constraints, which SQL Server enforces using a unique index. They also include foreign key constraints, which ensures that only data validated from another lookup table is allowed in the original table. And they include check and default constraints, which apply to columns.

Lesson Review

Answer the following questions to test your knowledge of the information in this lesson. You can find the answers to these questions and explanations of why each answer choice is correct or incorrect in the "Answers" section at the end of this chapter.

1. Which of the following columns would be appropriate as a surrogate key? (Choose all that apply.)
   - **A.** The time (in hundredths of a second) that the row was inserted
   - **B.** An automatically increasing integer number
   - **C.** The last four digits of a social security number concatenated with the first eight digits of a user's last name
   - **D.** A uniqueidentifier (GUID) newly selected from SQL Server at the time the row is inserted
2. You want to enforce that a valid supplierid be entered for each productid in the Production.Products table. What is the appropriate constraint to use?
   - **A.** A unique constraint
   - **B.** A default constraint
   - **C.** A foreign key constraint
   - **D.** A primary key constraint
3. What metadata tables give you a list of constraints in a database? (Choose all that apply.)
   - **A.** sys.key_constraints
   - **B.** sys.indexes
   - **C.** sys.default_constraints
   - **D.** sys.foreign_keys

Case Scenarios

In the following case scenarios, you apply what you've learned about SQL Server tables and data integrity. You can find the answers to these questions in the "Answers" section at the end of this chapter.

Case Scenario 1: Working with Table Constraints

As the lead database developer on a new project, you notice that database validation occurs in the client application. As a result, database developers periodically run very costly queries to verify the integrity of the data. You have decided that your team should refactor the database to improve the integrity of the database and shorten the costly nightly validation queries. Answer the following questions about the actions you might take.

1. How can you ensure that certain combinations of columns in a table have a unique value?
2. How can you enforce that values in certain tables are restricted to specified ranges?
3. How can you enforce that all columns that contain values from lookup tables are valid?
4. How can you ensure that all tables have a primary key, even tables that right now do not have any primary key declared?

Case Scenario 2: Working with Unique and Default Constraints

As you examine the database of your current project more closely, you find that there are more data integrity problems than you first realized. Here are some of the problems you found. How would you solve them?

1. Most of the tables have a surrogate key, which you have implemented as a primary key. However, there are other columns or combinations of columns that must be unique, and a table can have only one primary key. How can you enforce that certain other columns or combinations of columns will be unique?
2. Several columns allow NULLs, even though the application is supposed to always populate them. How can you ensure that those columns will never allow NULLs?
3. Often the application must specify specific values for every column when inserting into a row. How can you set up the columns so that if the application does not insert a value, a standard default value will be inserted automatically?

Suggested Practices

To help you successfully master the exam objectives presented in this chapter, complete the following tasks.

Create Tables and Enforce Data Integrity

The following practices extend the code you worked with in the lessons and exercises in this chapter. Continue to develop these in the TSQL2012 database.

- **Practice 1** Use ALTER TABLE to add a new column called **categorystatus** to the test table Production.CategoriesTest from the exercise in Lesson 1. Define the column by using NVARCHAR(15) NOT NULL. If the table has data, adding a NOT NULL column will fail. Now try the same ALTER TABLE command but this time define the column with NVARCHAR(15) NOT NULL DEFAULT '' (two single quotation marks). What is the difference between the two column definitions?
- **Practice 2** Test the check constraint CHK_Products_unitprice in the Production.Products table by using the same kind of logic you used in the Lesson 2 exercise. Try to insert a new row with all valid columns, but use a negative unitprice of -10. Drop the check constraint. Retry the insert. Try to add the check constraint back into the table. Update the inserted row so that it has a positive unitprice. Now try adding the check constraint back into the table. Would you be able to add the check constraint back into the table if there were no rows? Why?

Answers

This section contains the answers to the lesson review questions and solutions to the case scenarios in this chapter.

Lesson 1

1. **Correct Answers: A, C, and D**
   - **A. Correct:** A regular identifier can consist of all alphabetic characters.
   - **B. Incorrect:** A regular identifier cannot contain a space.
   - **C. Correct:** A regular identifier may contain a dollar sign ($).
   - **D. Correct:** A regular identifier may contain an underscore (_).
2. **Correct Answer: B**
   - **A. Incorrect:** VARBINARY is meant to store general purpose binary data and cannot replace TIMESTAMP.
   - **B. Correct:** ROWVERSION is the replacement for the deprecated TIMESTAMP.
   - **C. Incorrect:** DATETIME2 stores date and time data and cannot replace TIMESTAMP.
   - **D. Incorrect:** The TIME data type stores time-formatted data only and cannot replace TIMESTAMP.
3. **Correct Answer: D**
   - **A. Incorrect:** Specifying NULL must come after the data type.
   - **B. Incorrect:** ALLOW NULL is not a valid construct in the CREATE TABLE statement.
   - **C. Incorrect:** PERMIT NULL is not a valid construct in the CREATE TABLE statement.
   - **D. Correct:** You specify NULL right after the data type.

Lesson 2

1. **Correct Answers: B and D**
   - **A. Incorrect:** Surrogate keys should be meaningless, and time is a meaningful number. In addition, there is no guarantee that two rows could not be inserted at nearly the same time.
   - **B. Correct:** An automatically increasing integer value is commonly used as a surrogate key because it does not reflect meaningful data about the row, and it will be unique for every row.
   - **C. Incorrect:** A surrogate key should not have meaningful data such as a portion of a user id and the user's name.
   - **D. Correct:** A uniqueidentifier (GUID) can also be used as a surrogate key when it is uniquely generated for each row.

2. **Correct Answer: C**
   - A. **Incorrect:** A unique constraint only enforces uniqueness and cannot validate that a value exists in another table.
   - B. **Incorrect:** A default constraint only supplies a default value. It cannot validate that a value exists in another table.
   - C. **Correct:** A foreign key constraint validates that a value exists in another table.
   - D. **Incorrect:** A primary key constraint enforces uniqueness and cannot validate that a value exists in another table.
3. **Correct Answers: A, C, and D**
   - A. **Correct:** sys.key_constraints lists all primary key and unique constraints in a database.
   - B. **Incorrect:** sys.indexes does not list constraints.
   - C. **Correct:** sys.default_constraints lists the default constraints in a database.
   - D. **Correct:** sys.foreign_keys lists all the foreign keys in a database.

Case Scenario 1

1. You can ensure that certain columns or combinations of columns in a table are unique by applying primary key and unique constraints. You can also apply a unique index. Normally, it is preferable to use the declared primary key and unique constraints because they are easy to find and recognize within the SQL Server metadata and management tools. If the uniqueness of a row cannot be specified using a constraint or a unique index, you may be able to use a trigger.
2. For simple restrictions of ranges in a table, you can use a check constraint. You can then specify the restriction in the expression value of the constraint.
3. To enforce that lookup values are valid, you should normally use foreign key constraints. Foreign key constraints are declared constraints, and as such are known through metadata to SQL Server and the query optimizer. When joining a table that has a foreign key constraint to its lookup table, it is helpful to add an index on the foreign key column to assist join performance.
4. You cannot actively enforce every table to have a primary key constraint. However, you can query sys.key_constraints to monitor the tables to make sure that every table does include a primary key.

Case Scenario 2

1. You can create a unique constraint on a column or set of columns to ensure their unique values, in addition to the primary key.
2. You can prevent a column from ever having NULLs by altering the table and redefining the column as NOT NULL.
3. You can create a default constraint on a column to ensure that if no value is inserted, a default value will be inserted in its place.

CHAPTER 9

Designing and Creating Views, Inline Functions, and Synonyms

Exam objectives in this chapter:

- Create Database Objects
  - Create and alter views (simple statements).
  - Design views.
- Work with Data
  - Query data by using SELECT statements.

Microsoft SQL Server provides three different ways to present a logical view of a table to user queries without having to expose the physical base table directly. Views behave just like tables but can hide complex logic; inline functions can be used like views but also take parameters; and synonyms are a simple way to refer to database objects under a different name.

In this chapter, you learn to design, create, and modify objects that present data tables for your T-SQL code in indirect ways.

Lessons in this chapter:

- Lesson 1: Designing and Implementing Views and Inline Functions
- Lesson 2: Using Synonyms

Before You Begin

To complete the lessons in this chapter, you must have:

- An understanding of basic database concepts.
- Experience working with SQL Server Management Studio (SSMS).
- Some experience writing T-SQL code.
- Access to a SQL Server 2012 instance with the sample database TSQL2012 installed.

Lesson 1: Designing and Implementing Views and Inline Functions

With views and inline functions, you can present the contents of one or more base data tables to users, and you can encapsulate complex logic such as joins and filters so that the user does not need to remember them. In this lesson, you learn how to create and manage views and inline functions.

After this lesson, you will be able to:

- Use the CREATE VIEW statement to create a view.
- Understand how to design views.
- Use the ALTER VIEW statement to re-create a view.
- Design and implement inline functions.

Estimated lesson time: 45 minutes

Introduction

In SQL Server, you can use *views* to store and re-use queries in the database. Views appear for almost all purposes as tables: You can select from them, and filter the results, just as you do with tables. You can even insert, update, and delete rows through views, though with restrictions.

Every view is defined by a SELECT statement, which can reference multiple base tables as well as other views. So you can also use views as a way of simplifying the underlying complexity required to join multiple tables together, making it easier for users or applications to access the database data. In this lesson, you learn how to create and modify views, as well as modify data through a view.

Views

To create a view, you name the view and then specify the SELECT statement that will constitute the view. For example, the following CREATE VIEW statement, which is called Sales.OrderTotalsByYear, is taken from TSQL2012.sql.

```
USE TSQL2012;
GO
CREATE VIEW Sales.OrderTotalsByYear
  WITH SCHEMABINDING
AS
SELECT
  YEAR(O.orderdate) AS orderyear,
  SUM(OD.qty) AS qty
```

```
FROM Sales.Orders AS O
  JOIN Sales.OrderDetails AS OD
    ON OD.orderid = O.orderid
GROUP BY YEAR(orderdate);
GO
```

You can read from a view just as you would a table. So you can select from it as follows.

```
SELECT orderyear, qty
FROM Sales.OrderTotalsByYear;
```

Here are some things for you to note right away about this view:

- Just as with other CREATE statements such as CREATE TABLE, you can optionally specify a database schema as the container for the view. In this case, the view is created in the Sales schema. As a best practice, you should always reference database objects such as views by using the two-part name, which includes the schema name. (For more information about database schemas, see "Specifying a Database Schema" in Chapter 8, "Creating Tables and Enforcing Data Integrity.")
- This view is created with the view option called SCHEMABINDING, which guarantees that the underlying table structures cannot be altered without dropping the view.
- The body of the view is just a SELECT statement, subject to all the usual rules for SELECT statements.
- You can add new columns to the view by creating new columns in the SELECT statement, by using expressions.
- You can prevent users from seeing some columns of an underlying table by removing the columns from the SELECT statement that defines the view.
- You can rename columns by using column aliases, just as in a SELECT statement.

NOTE **VIEWS PRESENT ABSTRACTED LAYERS TO USERS**

A major use of views in relational databases, for both online transaction processing (OLTP) and data warehouse systems, is to provide a level of abstraction between the end user and the database. When a database requires complex joins of tables, you can make user queries easier by embedding those joins into views. Users query the views and not the tables, giving them a simpler, logical view of the database without them having to know the complex physical details.

Database Views Syntax

Now look at the basic syntax for the CREATE VIEW statement:

```
CREATE VIEW [ schema_name . ] view_name [ (column [ ,...n ] ) ]
[ WITH <view attribute> [ ,...n ] ]
AS select_statement
[ WITH CHECK OPTION ] [ ; ]
```

Here's a step-by-step breakdown:

- Although it doesn't say this in the syntax diagram, the CREATE VIEW statement must be the first statement in a batch. You cannot put other T-SQL statements ahead of it, or make the CREATE VIEW statement conditional by putting it inside an IF statement.
- The view is named just like a table and other database objects (such as procedures and functions).
- You can specify the set of output columns following the view name. For example, you could rewrite the CREATE VIEW statement for Sales.OrderTotalsByYear and specify the column names right after the view name instead of in the SELECT statement, as follows. However, note that it is more difficult now to see what the column names of the view are when reading the SELECT statement.

```
CREATE VIEW Sales.OrderTotalsByYear(orderyear, qty)
  WITH SCHEMABINDING
AS
SELECT
  YEAR(O.orderdate),
  SUM(OD.qty)
FROM Sales.Orders AS O
  JOIN Sales.OrderDetails AS OD
    ON OD.orderid = O.orderid
GROUP BY YEAR(orderdate);
GO
```

NOTE **MAKE A VIEW SELF-DOCUMENTING**

It is a best practice to make your T-SQL code self-documenting. Generally speaking, a view will be more self-documenting if the column names of the view are specified in the SELECT statement and not listed separately in the view.

View Options

You can add any combination of three view options, as follows:

- Using WITH ENCRYPTION, you can specify that the view text should be stored in an obfuscated manner (this is not strong encryption). This makes it difficult for users to discover the SELECT text of the view.
- WITH SCHEMABINDING, as explained earlier, binds the view to the table schemas of the underlying tables: The table cannot have its schema definitions changed unless the view is dropped. This protects the view from having table structures changed and breaking the view.
- WITH VIEW_METADATA, when specified, returns the metadata of the view instead of the base table.

The SELECT and UNION Statements in a View

Note that there is only one SELECT statement in the syntax, and by implication, only one SELECT statement is allowed in a view. That is true because a key requirement is that a view will return only one result set so that the view can always appear to most SQL statements as though it were a table.

However, you can combine SELECT statements that return the same result sets by using a UNION or UNION ALL clause in the SELECT statement. This is discussed further in the section "Partitioned Views" later in this lesson. For more information about the UNION clause, see Lesson 3, "Using Set Operators," in Chapter 4, "Combining Sets."

WITH CHECK OPTION

Finally, you can add a WITH CHECK OPTION to the view. This is an important option. If you define a view with a filter restriction in the WHERE clause of the SELECT statement, and then you modify rows of a table through the view, you could change a value so that the affected row no longer matches the WHERE clause filter. It is even possible to update rows that fall outside the filter. WITH CHECK OPTION prevents such disappearing rows from occurring when you update through the view, and it restricts modifications to only rows that match the filter condition. For more about view updatability, see "Modifying Data Through a View" later in this lesson.

View Names

Every view is a database object, and its name is scoped to the database. Therefore, in a database, every view name, in its database schema, must be unique. The view cannot have the same schema name and object name combination as any other schema-scoped objects in the database, which include:

- Views
- Tables
- Stored procedures
- Functions
- Synonyms

For more about synonyms, see Lesson 2, "Using Synonyms," in this chapter.

View names must be T-SQL identifiers, just as for tables, stored procedures, functions, indexes, and other SQL Server database objects. (For more about T-SQL identifiers, see "Naming Tables and Columns" in Chapter 8.)

Restrictions on Views

Views have a number of restrictions, such as the following:

- You cannot add an ORDER BY to the SELECT statement in a view. A view must appear just like a table, and tables in a relational database contain sets of rows. Sets by themselves are not ordered, although you can apply an order to a result set using ORDER BY. Similarly, tables and views in SQL Server do not have a logical order to their rows, though you can apply one by adding an ORDER BY to the outermost SELECT statement when you access the view.
- You cannot pass parameters to views.
  - Similarly, a view cannot reference a variable inside the SELECT statement. See the section "Inline Functions" for information on how to use functions to simulate passing parameters to a view.
- A view cannot create a table, whether permanent or temporary. In other words, you cannot use the SELECT/INTO syntax in a view.
- A view can reference only permanent tables; a view cannot reference a temporary table.

EXAM TIP

Results of a view are never ordered. You must add your own ORDER BY when you SELECT from the view. You can include an ORDER BY in a view only by adding the TOP operator or the OFFSET FETCH clause to the SELECT clause. Even then, the results of the view will not be ordered. Therefore, an ORDER BY in a view, even when you can enter it, is useless.

Indexed Views

Normally, a view is just a definition by a SELECT statement of how the results should be built: no data is stored. In other words, only the SELECT statement is stored and not any data.

However, it is possible to create a unique clustered index on a view and materialize the data. In that case, more than the view definition is stored. The actual results of the view query are stored on disk, in the clustered index structure. To be indexed, a view must satisfy a number of important restrictions. For more information about *indexed views*, see "Implementing Indexed Views" in Chapter 15, "Implementing Indexes and Statistics."

Querying from Views

When you query from a regular nonmaterialized view, the SQL Server Query Optimizer combines your outer query with the query embedded in the view and processes the combined query. As a result, when you look at query plans based on queries that select from views, you will see the referenced underlying tables of the view in the query plan; the view itself will not be an object in the query plan.

Altering a View

After you have created a view, you can use the ALTER VIEW command to change the view's structure and add or remove the view properties. An ALTER VIEW simply redefines how the view works by reissuing the entire view definition. For example, you could redefine the Sales.OrderTotalsByYear view to add a new column for the region the order was shipped to, the shipregion column, as follows.

```
ALTER VIEW Sales.OrderTotalsByYear
  WITH SCHEMABINDING
AS
SELECT
  O.shipregion,
  YEAR(O.orderdate) AS orderyear,
  SUM(OD.qty) AS qty
FROM Sales.Orders AS O
  JOIN Sales.OrderDetails AS OD
    ON OD.orderid = O.orderid
GROUP BY YEAR(orderdate), O.shipregion;
GO
```

Now you can change the way you select from the view, just as you would with a table, to include the new column; and you can optionally order the results with an ORDER BY, as follows.

```
SELECT shipregion, orderyear, qty
FROM Sales.OrderTotalsByYear
ORDER BY shipregion;
```

Dropping a View

You drop a view in the same way you would a table.

```
DROP VIEW Sales.OrderTotalsByYear;
```

When you need to create a new view and conditionally replace the old view, you must first drop the old view and then create the new view. The following example shows one method.

```
IF OBJECT_ID(N'Sales.OrderTotalsByYear', N'V') IS NOT NULL
    DROP VIEW Sales.OrderTotalsByYear;
GO
CREATE VIEW Sales.OrderTotalsByYear
...
```

The 'V' parameter in the OBJECT_ID() function looks for views in the current database and then returns an object_id if a view with that name is found.

Modifying Data Through a View

You can update, insert, or delete data through a view, rather than directly referencing the underlying tables, but there are numerous restrictions, such as the following:

- DML statements (INSERT, UPDATE, and DELETE) must reference exactly one table at a time, no matter how many tables the view references.

- The view columns must directly reference table columns, and not be expressions or functions surrounding the column value.
  - Accordingly, you cannot modify a view column that has an aggregate function, such as SUM(), MAX(), or MIN(), applied to the table's column.
- You cannot modify a view column that is computed from a UNION/UNION ALL, CROSS JOIN, EXCEPT, or INTERSECT.
- You cannot modify a view column whose values result from grouping, such as DISTINCT, or the GROUP BY and HAVING clause.
- You cannot modify a view that has a TOP operator or OFFSET FETCH in the SELECT statement along with the WITH CHECK OPTION clause.

If you really must update tables through a view, and the view does not meet all the requirements for updatability, you can create an INSTEAD OF trigger on the view and use the trigger to update the underlying tables. For more information on INSTEAD OF triggers, see "INSTEAD OF Triggers" in Chapter 13, "Designing and Implementing T-SQL Routines."

Partitioned Views

SQL Server supports the use of views to partition large tables, on one server, in one or more tables across multiple databases, and across multiple servers. If you are not able to use table partitioning, you can manually partition your tables and create a view that applies a UNION statement across those tables. The result is called a *partitioned view*. If the tables are in one database or at least on one instance of SQL Server, it is called a partitioned view or a local partitioned view. If the tables are spread across multiple SQL Server instances, the view is called a distributed partitioned view.

For a partitioned view, if you want the SQL Server Query Optimizer to take advantage of your partitioning and resolve queries efficiently using partition elimination, your view must satisfy a number of important conditions. After these conditions are met, you can select and modify data through the view in an efficient fashion and with the support of SQL Server. For more information about partitioned views, see "Using Partitioned Views" in Books Online for SQL Server 2012 at *http://msdn.microsoft.com/en-us/library/ms190019.aspx*.

Views and Metadata

Views were designed to appear as tables, and in fact, when you use SQL Server Management Studio (SSMS) and other tools to drill down into a view, notice that it expands into columns with data types just like you see with tables. To ensure that users in a database can see the metadata for views, grant them VIEW DEFINITION on the views in question.

To explore view metadata by using T-SQL, you can query the sys.views catalog view, as follows.

```
USE TSQL2012;
GO
SELECT name, object_id, principal_id, schema_id, type
FROM sys.views;
```

You can also query the INFORMATION_SCHEMA.TABLES system view, but it is slightly more complex.

```
SELECT TABLE_SCHEMA, TABLE_NAME, TABLE_TYPE
FROM INFORMATION_SCHEMA.TABLES
WHERE TABLE_TYPE = 'VIEW';
```

Using sys.views is more informative, and from it, you can join to other catalog views such as sys.sql_modules to get further information.

Quick Check

1. **Must a view consist of only one SELECT statement?**
2. **What types of views are available in T-SQL?**

Quick Check Answer

1. **Technically, yes, but a workaround to this is that you can unite (using the UNION statement) multiple SELECT statements that together produce one result set.**
2. **You can create regular views, which are just stored SELECT statements, or indexed views, which actually materialize the data, in addition to partitioned views.**

Inline Functions

In T-SQL, the only way to filter a view is to add the filter in a WHERE clause when you select from the view. There is no way to pass a parameter to a view in order to filter the rows. However, you can use an *inline table-valued function* to simulate passing a parameter to a view, or in other words, simulate a parameterized view.

An inline table-valued function returns a rowset based on a SELECT statement you coded into the function. In effect, you treat the table-valued function as a table and select from it by using the SELECT FROM statement. For example, you can create an inline function that would operate just like the Sales.OrderTotalsByYear view, with no parameters, as follows.

```
USE TSQL2012;
GO
IF OBJECT_ID (N'Sales.fn_OrderTotalsByYear', N'IF') IS NOT NULL
    DROP FUNCTION Sales.fn_OrderTotalsByYear;
GO
CREATE FUNCTION Sales.fn_OrderTotalsByYear ()
RETURNS TABLE
AS
RETURN
    (
```

```
    SELECT
      YEAR(O.orderdate) AS orderyear,
      SUM(OD.qty) AS qty
    FROM Sales.Orders AS O
      JOIN Sales.OrderDetails AS OD
        ON OD.orderid = O.orderid
    GROUP BY YEAR(orderdate)
    );
GO
```

To create an inline table-valued function:

- Specify parameters. Parameters are optional, but the parentheses that would enclose parameters are not optional.
- Add the clause RETURNS TABLE to signal to SQL Server that this is a table-valued function.
- Following the AS block, enter a single RETURN statement. This acts like an internal function to return the embedded SELECT statement.
- Embed the SELECT statement that will define what you want the function to return as a rowset to the caller.
- The semicolon following the last parenthesis is optional, but if present, it must follow the closing parenthesis.

In an inline table-valued function, the body of the function can only be a SELECT statement; you cannot declare variables and perform other T-SQL commands, as you can with scalar UDFs and multistatement table-valued functions. (For more about the SQL Server T-SQL user-defined functions, see Lesson 3, "Implementing User-Defined Functions," in Chapter 13.

In the previous example, the SELECT statement was just as complex as the original Sales.OrderTotalsByYear view. If you don't need any additional columns from the table, you could actually simplify the function by selecting from the view directly.

```
USE TSQL2012;
GO
IF OBJECT_ID (N'Sales.fn_OrderTotalsByYear', N'IF') IS NOT NULL
    DROP FUNCTION Sales.fn_OrderTotalsByYear;
GO
CREATE FUNCTION Sales.fn_OrderTotalsByYear ()
RETURNS TABLE
AS
RETURN
    (
    SELECT orderyear, qty FROM Sales.OrderTotalsByYear
    );
GO
```

Consider that if you only wanted to see the year 2007, you would just put that in a WHERE clause when selecting from the view.

```
SELECT orderyear, qty
FROM Sales.OrderTotalsByYear
WHERE orderyear = 2007;
```

To make the WHERE clause more flexible, you can declare a variable and then filter based on the variable.

```
DECLARE @orderyear int = 2007;
SELECT orderyear, qty
FROM Sales.OrderTotalsByYear
WHERE orderyear = @orderyear;
```

Keeping this in mind, it is now just a quick step to an inline function. Instead of declaring a variable @orderyear, define the parameter @orderyear in the function while filtering the SELECT statement in the same way as previously.

```
USE TSQL2012;
GO
IF OBJECT_ID (N'Sales.fn_OrderTotalsByYear', N'IF') IS NOT NULL
    DROP FUNCTION Sales.fn_OrderTotalsByYear;
GO
CREATE FUNCTION Sales.fn_OrderTotalsByYear (@orderyear int)
RETURNS TABLE
AS
RETURN
    (
    SELECT orderyear, qty FROM Sales.OrderTotalsByYear
    WHERE orderyear = @orderyear
    );
GO
```

You can query the function and pass the year you want to see, as follows.

```
SELECT  orderyear, qty FROM Sales.fn_OrderTotalsByYear(2007);
```

What you effectively have done is created a parameterized view, using an inline function. The inline function is more flexible than a view, because it returns results based on the parameter value that is supplied. You don't have to add an additional WHERE clause.

Inline Function Options

Inline functions have two significant options, both shared with views:

- You can create a function by using WITH ENCRYPTION, making it difficult for users to discover the SELECT text of the function.
- You can add WITH SCHEMABINDING, which binds the table schemas of the underlying objects, such as tables or views, to the function. The schemas of the referenced objects cannot be altered unless the function is dropped or the WITH SCHEMABINDING option is removed.

Quick Check

1. What type of data does an inline function return?
2. What type of view can an inline function simulate?

Quick Check Answer

1. Inline functions return tables, and accordingly, are often referred to as inline table-valued functions.
2. An inline table-valued function can simulate a parameterized view—that is, a view that takes parameters.

PRACTICE Working with Views and Inline Functions

In this practice, you build your understanding of T-SQL views and use an inline function to simulate a parameterized view.

If you encounter a problem completing an exercise, you can install the completed projects from the companion content for this chapter and lesson.

EXERCISE 1 Build a View for a Report

Assume the following scenario: You have been asked to develop the database interface for a report on the TSQL2012 database. The application needs a view that shows the quantity sold and total sales for all sales, by year, per customer and per shipper. The user would also like to be able to filter the results by upper and lower total quantity.

1. Start with the current Sales.OrderTotalsByYear as shown earlier in this lesson. Type the SELECT statement without the view definition.

```
USE TSQL2012;
GO
SELECT
  YEAR(O.orderdate) AS orderyear,
  SUM(OD.qty) AS qty
FROM Sales.Orders AS O
  JOIN Sales.OrderDetails AS OD
    ON OD.orderid = O.orderid
GROUP BY YEAR(orderdate);
```

Note that the Sales.OrderValues view does contain the computed sales amount, as follows.

```
CAST(SUM(OD.qty * OD.unitprice * (1 - OD.discount))
     AS NUMERIC(12, 2)) AS val
```

2. Combine the two queries.

```
SELECT
  YEAR(O.orderdate) AS orderyear,
  SUM(OD.qty) AS qty,
  CAST(SUM(OD.qty * OD.unitprice * (1 - OD.discount))
     AS NUMERIC(12, 2)) AS val
FROM Sales.Orders AS O
  JOIN Sales.OrderDetails AS OD
    ON OD.orderid = O.orderid
GROUP BY YEAR(orderdate);
```

3. Add the columns for custid to return the customer ID and the shipper ID. Note that you must now change the GROUP BY clause in order to expose those two IDs.

```
SELECT
  O.custid,
  O.shipperid,
  YEAR(O.orderdate) AS orderyear,
  SUM(OD.qty) AS qty,
  CAST(SUM(OD.qty * OD.unitprice * (1 - OD.discount))
     AS NUMERIC(12, 2)) AS val
FROM Sales.Orders AS O
  JOIN Sales.OrderDetails AS OD
    ON OD.orderid = O.orderid
GROUP BY YEAR(O.orderdate), O.custid, O.shipperid;
```

4. So far so good, but you need to show the shipper and customer names in the results for the report. So you need to add JOINs to the Sales.Customers table and to the Sales.Shippers table.

```
SELECT
  YEAR(O.orderdate) AS orderyear,
  SUM(OD.qty) AS qty,
  CAST(SUM(OD.qty * OD.unitprice * (1 - OD.discount))
     AS NUMERIC(12, 2)) AS val
FROM Sales.Orders AS O
  JOIN Sales.OrderDetails AS OD
    ON OD.orderid = O.orderid
  JOIN Sales.Customers AS C
    ON O.custid = C.custid
  JOIN Sales.Shippers AS S
    ON O.shipperid = S.shipperid
GROUP BY YEAR(O.orderdate);
```

5. Add the customer company name (companyname) and the shipping company name (companyname). You must expand the GROUP BY clause to expose those columns.

```
SELECT
  C.companyname AS customercompany,
  S.companyname AS shippercompany,
  YEAR(O.orderdate) AS orderyear,
  SUM(OD.qty) AS qty,
  CAST(SUM(OD.qty * OD.unitprice * (1 - OD.discount))
     AS NUMERIC(12, 2)) AS val
```

```
FROM Sales.Orders AS O
  JOIN Sales.OrderDetails AS OD
    ON OD.orderid = O.orderid
  JOIN Sales.Customers AS C
    ON O.custid = C.custid
  JOIN Sales.Shippers AS S
    ON O.shipperid = S.shipperid
GROUP BY YEAR(O.orderdate), C.companyname, S.companyname;
```

6. Turn this into a view called **Sales.OrderTotalsByYearCustShip**.

```
IF OBJECT_ID (N'Sales.OrderTotalsByYearCustShip', N'V') IS NOT NULL
    DROP VIEW Sales.OrderTotalsByYearCustShip;
GO
CREATE VIEW Sales.OrderTotalsByYearCustShip
  WITH SCHEMABINDING
AS
SELECT
  C.companyname AS customercompany,
  S.companyname AS shippercompany,
  YEAR(O.orderdate) AS orderyear,
  SUM(OD.qty) AS qty,
  CAST(SUM(OD.qty * OD.unitprice * (1 - OD.discount))
     AS NUMERIC(12, 2)) AS val
FROM Sales.Orders AS O
  JOIN Sales.OrderDetails AS OD
    ON OD.orderid = O.orderid
  JOIN Sales.Customers AS C
    ON O.custid = C.custid
  JOIN Sales.Shippers AS S
    ON O.shipperid = S.shipperid
GROUP BY YEAR(O.orderdate), C.companyname, S.companyname;
GO
```

7. Test the view by selecting from it.

```
SELECT customercompany, shippercompany, orderyear, qty, val
FROM Sales.OrderTotalsByYearCustShip
ORDER BY customercompany, shippercompany, orderyear;
```

8. To clean up, drop the view.

```
IF OBJECT_ID(N'Sales.OrderTotalsByYearCustShip', N'V') IS NOT NULL
    DROP VIEW Sales.OrderTotalsByYearCustShip
```

EXERCISE 2 Convert a View into an Inline Function

In this exercise, you convert the view from the previous exercise into an inline function.

9. Change the view into an inline function that filters by low and high values of the total quantity. Add two parameters called **@highqty** and **@lowqty**, both integers, and add a HAVING clause to filter the results. Give the function the name **Sales.fn_OrderTotalsByYearCustShip**.

```
IF OBJECT_ID (N'Sales.fn_OrderTotalsByYearCustShip', N'IF') IS NOT NULL
    DROP FUNCTION Sales.fn_OrderTotalsByYearCustShip;
GO
CREATE FUNCTION Sales.fn_OrderTotalsByYearCustShip (@lowqty int, @highqty int)
RETURNS TABLE
AS
RETURN
     (
    SELECT
      C.companyname AS customercompany,
      S.companyname AS shippercompany,
      YEAR(O.orderdate) AS orderyear,
      SUM(OD.qty) AS qty,
      CAST(SUM(OD.qty * OD.unitprice * (1 - OD.discount))
         AS NUMERIC(12, 2)) AS val
    FROM Sales.Orders AS O
      JOIN Sales.OrderDetails AS OD
          ON OD.orderid = O.orderid
      JOIN Sales.Customers AS C
        ON O.custid = C.custid
      JOIN Sales.Shippers AS S
        ON O.shipperid = S.shipperid
    GROUP BY YEAR(O.orderdate), C.companyname, S.companyname
    HAVING SUM(OD.qty) >= @lowqty AND SUM(OD.qty) <= @highqty
    );
GO
```

10. Test the function.

```
SELECT customercompany, shippercompany, orderyear, qty, val
FROM Sales.fn_OrderTotalsByYearCustShip (100, 200)
ORDER BY customercompany, shippercompany, orderyear;
```

Experiment with other values until you are certain you understand how the function and its filtering are working.

11. To clean up, drop the view and the function.

```
IF OBJECT_ID (N'Sales.OrderTotalsByYearCustShip', N'V') IS NOT NULL
    DROP VIEW Sales.OrderTotalsByYearCustShip;
GO
IF OBJECT_ID (N'Sales.fn_OrderTotalsByYearCustShip', N'IF') IS NOT NULL
    DROP FUNCTION Sales.fn_OrderTotalsByYearCustShip;
GO
```

Lesson Summary

- Views are stored T SQL SELECT statements that can be treated as though they were tables.
- Normally, a view consists of only one SELECT statement, but you can work around this by combining SELECT statements with compatible results using UNION or UNION ALL.
- Views can reference multiple tables and simplify complex joins for users.

- By default, views do not contain any data. Creating a unique clustered index on a view results in an indexed view that materializes data.
- When you select from a view, SQL Server takes your outer SELECT statement and combines it with the SELECT statement of the view definition. SQL Server then executes the combined SELECT statement.
- You can modify data through a view, but only one table at a time, and only columns of certain types.
- You can add WITH CHECK OPTION to a view to prevent any updates through the view that would cause some rows to get values no longer satisfying a WHERE clause of the view.
- Views can refer to tables or views in other databases and in other servers via linked servers.
- Special views called partitioned views can be created if a number of conditions are satisfied, and SQL Server routes suitable queries and updates to the correct partition of the view.
- Inline functions can be used to simulate parameterized views. T-SQL views cannot take parameters. However, an inline table-valued function can return the same data as a view and can accept parameters that can filter the results.

Lesson Review

Answer the following questions to test your knowledge of the information in this lesson. You can find the answers to these questions and explanations of why each answer choice is correct or incorrect in the "Answers" section at the end of this chapter.

1. Which of the following operators work in T-SQL views? (Choose all that apply.)
   - **A.** The WHERE clause
   - **B.** The ORDER BY clause
   - **C.** The UNION or UNION ALL operators
   - **D.** The GROUP BY clause
2. What is the result of WITH SCHEMABINDING in a view?
   - **A.** The view cannot be altered without altering the table.
   - **B.** The tables referred to in the view cannot be altered unless the view's SELECT statement is first altered.
   - **C.** The tables referred to in the view cannot be altered unless the view is first dropped.
   - **D.** The view cannot be altered unless the tables it refers to are first dropped.

3. What is the result of the WITH CHECK OPTION in a view that has a WHERE clause in its SELECT statement?

   A. Data can no longer be updated through the view.
   B. Data can be updated through the view, but primary key values cannot be changed.
   C. Data can be updated through the view, but values cannot be changed that would cause rows to fall outside the filter of the WHERE clause.
   D. Data can be updated through the view, but only columns with check constraints can be changed.

Lesson 2: Using Synonyms

In addition to views, which can provide an abstraction layer for database tables, SQL Server provides synonyms, which can provide an abstraction layer for all schema-scoped database objects. *Synonyms* are names stored in a database that can be used as substitutes for other object names. These names are also scoped to the database, and qualified with a schema name.

After this lesson, you will be able to:

- Create and drop synonyms.
- Understand how synonyms can be used as an abstraction layer.
- Understand similarities and differences between synonyms and other database objects.

Estimated lesson time: 15 minutes

Creating a Synonym

To create a synonym, you simply assign a synonym name and specify the name of the database object it will be assigned to. For example, you could define a synonym called Categories and put it in the dbo schema so that users do not need to remember the schema-object name Production.Categories in their queries. You can issue the following.

```
USE TSQL2012;
GO
CREATE SYNONYM dbo.Categories FOR Production.Categories;
GO
```

Then the end user can select from Categories without needing to specify a schema.

```
SELECT categoryid, categoryname, description
FROM Categories;
```

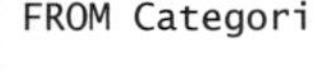

The basic syntax for creating a synonym is quite simple.

```
CREATE SYNONYM schema_name.synonym_name FOR object_name
```

The synonym name is a database object and the name must comply with the following rules for a T-SQL identifier:

- Synonyms do not store any data or any T-SQL code.
- Synonym names must be T-SQL identifiers, just as for other database objects. (For more about T-SQL identifiers, see "Naming Tables and Columns" in Chapter 8.)
- If you don't specify a schema, SQL Server will use the default schema associated with your user name.
- The object_name does not need to actually exist, and SQL Server doesn't test it. This is because of the late-binding behavior of synonyms, which is discussed later in this lesson.
- When you actually use the synonym in a T-SQL statement, SQL Server will check for the object's existence.

Synonyms can be used for the following types of objects:

- Tables (including temporary tables)
- Views
- User-defined functions (scalar, table-valued, inline)
- Stored procedures (T-SQL, extended stored procedures, and replication filter procedures)
- CLR assemblies (stored procedures; table-valued, scalar, and aggregate functions)

For more details about the types of objects that synonyms can be used for, see "CREATE SYNONYM (Transact-SQL)" in Books Online for SQL Server 2012 at *http://msdn.microsoft.com/en-us/library/ms177544.aspx*.

EXAM TIP

Synonyms cannot refer to other synonyms. They can only refer to database objects such as tables, views, stored procedures, and functions. In other words, synonym chaining is not allowed.

You can use synonyms in the T-SQL statements that refer to the types of objects that synonyms can stand for. In addition to EXECUTE for stored procedures, you can use the statements for data manipulation: SELECT, INSERT, UPDATE, and DELETE.

NOTE **USING ALTER WITH SYNONYMS**

You cannot reference a synonym in a DDL statement such as ALTER. Such statements require that you reference the base object instead.

Dropping a Synonym

You can drop a synonym by using the DROP SYNONYM statement.

```
DROP SYNONYM dbo.Categories
```

Because there is no ALTER SYNONYM, to change a synonym, you must drop and recreate it.

Abstraction Layer

Synonyms can refer to objects in other databases, in addition to objects referenced by linked servers. That makes it possible to dramatically simplify queries in your database and potentially remove the need for three-part and four-part references.

For example, suppose the database ReportsDB has a view called Sales.Reports, and it is on the same server as TSQL2012. To query it from TSQL2012, you must write something like the following.

```
SELECT report_id, report_name FROM ReportsDB.Sales.Reports
```

Now suppose you add a synonym, called simply Sales.Reports.

```
CREATE SYNONYM Sales.Reports FOR ReportsDB.Sales.Reports
```

The query is now simplified to the following.

```
SELECT report_id, report_name  FROM Sales.Reports
```

The user no longer has to remember the other database name. This turns out to be even more useful if you are using linked servers. Then you can reduce a four-part name down to two parts and even one part, making life much easier for the end user.

Synonyms and References to Nonexisting Objects

You can create a synonym even if the object referenced does not exist. An advantage is that you can use a single synonym for many different objects, just recreating the synonym for each object as you need it. Or you can create the same synonym in many databases that refer to a single object, and not have to use a three-part reference.

The disadvantage is that there is no such thing as WITH SCHEMABINDING: If you drop an object in a database, it will be dropped whether or not a synonym references it. Any synonyms referencing the object are effectively orphans; they fail to work when someone tries to use them.

Synonym Permissions

To create a synonym, you must have the CREATE SYNONYM permission, which inherits from the CONTROL SERVER permission. After you've created a synonym, you can grant other users permissions such as EXECUTE or SELECT to the synonym, depending on the type of object the synonym stands for.

Comparing Synonyms with Other Database Objects

Synonyms are unusual in that, although they are technically database objects belonging to the same namespace as other database objects, they don't contain any data or any code. It's interesting to compare synonyms with the other database objects.

Some advantages of synonyms over views are as follows:

- Unlike views, synonyms can stand in for many other kinds of objects, not just tables.
- Just as with views, synonyms can provide an abstraction layer, allowing you to present a logical view of a system without having to expose the physical names of the database objects to the end user. If the underlying object is altered, the synonym will not break.

Some disadvantages of synonyms are:

- Unlike views, synonyms cannot simplify complex logic like a view can simplify complex joins. Synonyms are really just names.
- A view can refer to many tables but a synonym can only ever refer to just one object.
- A view can reference another view, but a synonym cannot reference another synonym; synonym chaining is not allowed.

When a view stands in for a table, a user can see the columns and data types of the view. But a synonym does not expose the metadata of the underlying table or view that it stands for. This could be seen as either an advantage or a disadvantage depending on the context:

- If you do not want to expose metadata to the user, this could be an advantage. In SSMS, when the user opens the tree to look at a synonym, the user will not see any columns or data types if the synonym refers to a table or view, nor will the user see any parameters if the synonym refers to a procedure or function.
- If you do want to expose metadata to users as part of user education, then a synonym could be a disadvantage. For example, the user might need external documentation to find out what columns are available.

In most respects, synonyms behave just like other database objects such as tables, views, and T-SQL code objects: For example, you can use the synonym in SELECT statements in place of table names, view names, and inline function names, and you can assign the same sets of permissions to synonyms that you can for tables and views.

Quick Check

1. **Does a synonym store T-SQL or any data?**
2. **Can synonyms be altered?**

Quick Check Answer

1. **No, a synonym is just a name. All that is stored with a synonym is the object it refers to.**
2. **No, to change a synonym, you must drop and recreate it.**

PRACTICE Using Synonyms

In this practice, you use what you've learned about synonyms to create a user interface and to run reports.

If you encounter a problem completing an exercise, you can install the completed projects from the companion content for this chapter and lesson.

EXERCISE 1 Use Synonyms to Provide More Descriptive Names for Reporting

In this exercise, you create a user interface for reporting in the TSQL database.

Assume the following scenario: The TSQL2012 system has been in production for some time now, and you have been asked to provide access for a new reporting application to the database. However, the current view names are not as descriptive as the reporting users would like, so you will use synonyms to make them more descriptive.

1. Start in the TSQL2012 database.

```
USE TSQL2012;
GO
```

2. Create a special schema for reports.

```
CREATE SCHEMA Reports AUTHORIZATION dbo;
GO
```

3. Create a synonym for the Sales.CustOrders view in the TSQL2012 database. Look first at the data.

```
SELECT custid, ordermonth, qty FROM Sales.CustOrders;
```

You have determined that the data actually shows the customer ID, then the total of the qty column, by month. Therefore, create the **TotalCustQtyByMonth** synonym and test it.

```
CREATE SYNONYM Reports.TotalCustQtyByMonth FOR Sales.CustOrders;
SELECT  custid, ordermonth, qty FROM Reports.TotalCustQtyByMonth;
```

4. Create a synonym for the Sales.EmpOrders view by inspecting the data first.

```
SELECT empid, ordermonth, qty, val, numorders FROM Sales.EmpOrders;
```

The data shows employee ID, then the total of the qty and val columns, by month. Therefore, create the **TotalEmpQtyValOrdersByMonth** synonym and test it.

```
CREATE SYNONYM Reports.TotalEmpQtyValOrdersByMonth FOR Sales.EmpOrders;
SELECT empid, ordermonth, qty, val, numorders FROM
    Reports.TotalEmpQtyValOrdersByMonth;
```

5. Inspect the data for Sales.OrderTotalsByYear.

```
SELECT orderyear, qty FROM Sales.OrderTotalsByYear;
```

This view shows the total of the qty value by year, so name the synonym **TotalQtyByYear**.

```
CREATE SYNONYM Reports.TotalQtyByYear FOR Sales.OrderTotalsByYear;
SELECT orderyear, qty FROM Reports.TotalQtyByYear;
```

6. Inspect the data for Sales.OrderValues.

```
SELECT orderid, custid, empid, shipperid, orderdate, requireddate, shippeddate,
    qty, val
FROM Sales.OrderValues;
```

This view shows the total of val and qty for each order, so name the synonym **TotalQtyValOrders**.

```
CREATE SYNONYM Reports.TotalQtyValOrders FOR Sales.OrderValues;
SELECT orderid, custid, empid, shipperid, orderdate, requireddate, shippeddate,
    qty, val
FROM Reports.TotalQtyValOrders;
```

Note that there is no unique key on the combination of columns, minus the orderid column, in the GROUP BY of the Sales.OrderValues view. Right now, the number of rows grouped is also the number of orders, but that is not guaranteed. Your feedback to the development team should be that if this set of columns does define a unique row in the table, they should create a unique constraint (or a unique index) on the table to enforce it.

7. Now inspect the metadata for the synonyms. Note that you can use the SCHEMA_NAME() function to display the schema name without having to join to the sys.schemas table.

```
SELECT name, object_id, principal_id, schema_id, parent_object_id FROM
    sys.synonyms;
SELECT SCHEMA_NAME(schema_id) AS schemaname,  name, object_id, principal_id,
    schema_id, parent_object_id
FROM sys.synonyms;
```

8. Now you can optionally clean up the TSQL database and remove your work.

```
DROP SYNONYM Reports.TotalCustQtyByMonth;
DROP SYNONYM Reports.TotalEmpQtyValOrdersByMonth;
DROP SYNONYM Reports.TotalQtyByYear;
DROP SYNONYM Reports.TotalQtyValOrders;
GO
DROP SCHEMA Reports;
GO
```

EXERCISE 2 Use Synonyms to Simplify a Cross-Database Query

In this exercise, you show how reports could be run from a reporting database by using synonyms that refer to another database.

Assume the following scenario: You want to show the reporting team that they could run their reports from a dedicated reporting database on the server without having to directly query the main TSQL2012 database. You have decided to use synonyms to prototype the strategy.

1. Create a new reporting database called **TSQL2012Reports**:

```
USE master;
GO
CREATE DATABASE TSQL2012Reports;
GO
```

2. In the reporting database, create a schema called **Reports**.

```
USE TSQL2012Reports;
GO
CREATE SCHEMA Reports AUTHORIZATION dbo;
GO
```

3. As an initial test, create the **TotalCustQtyByMonth** synonym to the nonexistent local object Sales.CustOrders and test.

```
CREATE SYNONYM Reports.TotalCustQtyByMonth FOR Sales.CustOrders;
GO
SELECT custid, ordermonth, qty FROM Reports.TotalCustQtyByMonth; -- Fails

GO
DROP SYNONYM Reports.TotalCustQtyByMonth;
GO
```

4. Create the **TotalCustQtyByMonth** synonym referencing the Sales.CustOrders view in the TSQL2012 database and test it.

```
CREATE SYNONYM Reports.TotalCustQtyByMonth FOR TSQL2012.Sales.CustOrders;
GO
SELECT custid, ordermonth, qty FROM Reports.TotalCustQtyByMonth; -- Succeeds
GO
```

5. After you've demonstrated to the reporting team that this scenario can work, clean up and remove the database.

```
DROP SYNONYM Reports.TotalCustQtyByMonth;
GO
DROP SCHEMA Reports;
GO
USE Master;
GO
DROP DATABASE TSQL2012Reports;
GO
```

Lesson Summary

- A synonym is a name that refers to another database object such as a table, view, function, or stored procedure.
- No T-SQL code or any data is stored with a synonym. Only the object referenced is stored with a synonym.
- Synonyms are scoped to a database, and therefore are in the same namespace as the objects they refer to. Consequently, you cannot name a synonym the same as any other database object.
- Synonym chaining is not allowed; a synonym cannot refer to another synonym.
- Synonyms do not expose any metadata of the objects they reference.
- Synonyms can be used to provide an abstraction layer to the user by presenting different names for database objects.
- You can modify data through a synonym, but you cannot alter the underlying object.
- To change a synonym, you must drop and recreate it.

Lesson Review

Answer the following questions to test your knowledge of the information in this lesson. You can find the answers to these questions and explanations of why each answer choice is correct or incorrect in the "Answers" section at the end of this chapter.

1. What types of database objects can have synonyms? (Choose all that apply.)
   - **A.** Stored procedures
   - **B.** Indexes
   - **C.** Temporary tables
   - **D.** Database users
2. Which of the following are true about synonyms? (Choose all that apply.)
   - **A.** Synonyms do not store T-SQL code or data.
   - **B.** Synonyms do not require schema names.
   - **C.** Synonym names can match those of the objects they refer to.
   - **D.** Synonyms can reference objects in other databases or through linked servers.
3. What kind of dependencies do synonyms have on the objects they refer to?
   - **A.** Synonyms can be created WITH SCHEMABINDING to prevent the underlying objects from being altered.
   - **B.** Synonyms can refer to other synonyms.
   - **C.** Synonyms can be created to refer to database objects that do not yet exist.
   - **D.** Synonyms can be created without an initial schema name, which can be added later.

Case Scenarios

In the following case scenarios, you apply what you've learned about views, inline functions, and synonyms. You can find the answers to these questions in the "Answers" section at the end of this chapter.

Case Scenario 1: Comparing Views, Inline Functions, and Synonyms

As the lead database developer on a new project, you need to expose a logical view of the database to applications that produce daily reports. Your job is to prepare a report for the DBA team, showing the advantages and disadvantages of views, inline functions, and synonyms for creating that logical view of the database. What would you recommend using, based on each of the following conditions: views, inline functions, or synonyms?

- The application developers do not want to work with complex joins for their reports. For updating data, they will rely on stored procedures.
- In some cases, you need to be able to change the names of tables or views without having to recode the application.
- In other cases, the application needs to filter report data on the database by passing parameters, but the developers do not want to use stored procedures for retrieving the data.

Case Scenario 2: Converting Synonyms to Other Objects

You have just been assigned the database developer responsibility for a database that makes extensive use of synonyms in place of tables and views. Based on user feedback, you need to replace some of the synonyms. In the following cases, identify what actions you can take that will not cause users or applications to change their code.

1. Some synonyms refer to tables. However, some of the tables must be filtered. You need to leave the synonym in place but somehow filter what the table returns.
2. Some synonyms refer to tables. Sometimes column names of the table can change, but the synonym still needs to return the old column names.
3. Some synonyms refer to views. You need to make it possible for users to see the names and data types of the columns returned by the views when the users browse the database by using SSMS.

Suggested Practices

To help you successfully master the exam objectives presented in this chapter, complete the following tasks.

Design and Create Views, Inline Functions, and Synonyms

The following practices extend the code you worked with in the lessons and exercises in this chapter. Continue to develop these in the TSQL2012 database.

- **Practice 1** Create a simple view on the HR.Employees table, including the filter WHERE country = 'USA' and the WITH CHECK OPTION clause. Insert a new row with a country 'Canada'. Then attempt to change the country value for one of the USA employees to Canada. Do these updates work? Then recreate the view but do not include the WITH CHECK OPTION clause. Retry the changes. Do they work? Can you explain why?
- **Practice 2** Explore creating synonyms for stored procedures and functions. Create a stored procedure that inserts data into the Production.Categories table with parameters that provide values for the new row. Then create a synonym for that stored procedure. Execute the synonym with the parameters and make sure it succeeds. Now execute the synonym without the parameters. What is the error message? Does it refer to the synonym or to the stored procedure? Do you understand why?

Answers

This section contains the answers to the lesson review questions and solutions to the case scenarios in this chapter.

Lesson 1

1. **Correct Answers: A, C, and D**
   - **A. Correct:** A view can contain a WHERE clause.
   - **B. Incorrect:** A view can contain an ORDER BY if the SELECT TOP clause is used, but no actual sorting of the results is guaranteed.
   - **C. Correct:** You can combine SELECT statements in a view with UNION and UNION ALL.
   - **D. Correct:** A view can contain a GROUP BY clause.
2. **Correct Answer: C**
   - **A. Incorrect:** You can always alter a view without altering the underlying table or tables.
   - **B. Incorrect:** Even if you alter the view, if WITH SCHEMABINDING is applied to the view, the underlying tables cannot be altered.
   - **C. Correct:** WITH SCHEMABINDING implies that the underlying table schemas are fixed by the view. To alter the tables, you must first drop the view.
   - **D. Incorrect:** You never need to drop the tables in order to alter a view.
3. **Correct Answer: C**
   - **A. Incorrect:** WITH CHECK OPTION does not prevent updating data through a view.
   - **B. Incorrect:** WITH CHECK OPTION does not restrict all updates to only primary key columns.
   - **C. Correct:** The purpose of WITH CHECK OPTION is to prevent any updates from causing rows to violate the WHERE clause of the view. It also prevents updating any rows that are outside the WHERE clause filter.
   - **D. Incorrect:** WITH CHECK OPTION has no relationship to check constraints of a table.

Lesson 2

1. **Correct Answers: A and C**
   - **A. Correct:** Synonyms can refer to stored procedures.
   - **B. Incorrect:** Synonyms cannot refer to indexes; indexes are not database objects that are scoped by schema names.
   - **C. Correct:** Synonyms can refer to temporary tables.
   - **D. Incorrect:** Database users are not database objects that are scoped by schema names.
2. **Correct Answers: A and D**
   - **A. Correct:** Synonyms are just names, and do not store T-SQL code or any data.
   - **B. Incorrect:** Synonyms are database objects that are scoped to database schemas, just like tables, views, functions, and stored procedures, so they require schema names.
   - **C. Incorrect:** A synonym name (schema name plus object name) cannot be the same as any other schema-scoped database object, including other synonyms.
   - **D. Correct:** Synonyms can reference other database objects using three-part names, and objects through linked servers using four-part names.
3. **Correct Answer: C**
   - **A. Incorrect:** Only views can be created WITH SCHEMABINDING, not synonyms.
   - **B. Incorrect:** Synonyms cannot refer to other synonyms; synonym chaining is not allowed.
   - **C. Correct:** You can create a synonym that refers to a nonexistent object. In order to use the synonym, however, you must ensure that the object exists.
   - **D. Incorrect:** Synonyms always require a schema name.

Case Scenario 1

- To remove the need for developers working with complex joins, you can present them with views and inline functions that hide the complexity of the joins. Because they will use stored procedures to update data, you do not need to ensure that the views are updatable.
- You can change the names or definitions of views and change table names without affecting the application if the application refers to synonyms. You will have to drop and recreate the synonym when the underlying table or view has a name change, and that will have to be done when the application is offline.

- You can use inline functions to provide viewlike objects that can be filtered by parameters. Stored procedures are not required because users can reference the inline function in the FROM clause of a query.

Case Scenario 2

1. To filter the data coming from the table, you can create a view or inline function that filters the data appropriately, and recreate the synonym to reference the view or function.
2. To keep synonyms working even if column names of a table are changed, you can create a view that refers to the tables and recreate the synonym to refer to the view.
3. Synonyms cannot expose metadata. Therefore, when browsing a database in SSMS, users will not see column names and their data types under the synonym. In order to enable users to see the column data types of the underlying data tables, you must replace the synonym with a view.

CHAPTER 10

Inserting, Updating, and Deleting Data

Exam objectives in this chapter

- Modify Data
  - Modify data by using INSERT, UPDATE, and DELETE statements.

This chapter covers certain aspects of data modification. It describes how to insert, update, and delete data by using different T-SQL statements. Chapter 11, "Other Data Modification Aspects," continues the topic by covering more specialized aspects of data modification.

Lessons in this chapter:

Before You Begin

To complete the lessons in this chapter, you must have:

- Experience working with Microsoft SQL Server Management Studio (SSMS).
- Some experience writing T-SQL code.
- Access to a SQL Server 2012 instance with the sample database TSQL2012 installed.
- An understanding of filtering and sorting data.
- An understanding of creating tables and enforcing data integrity.

Lesson 1: Inserting Data

T-SQL supports a number of different methods that you can use to insert data into your tables. Those include statements like INSERT VALUES, INSERT SELECT, INSERT EXEC, and SELECT INTO. This lesson covers these statements and demonstrates how to use them through examples.

After this lesson, you will be able to:

- Insert single and multiple rows into a table by using the INSERT VALUES statement.
- Insert the result of a query into a table by using the INSERT SELECT statement.
- Insert the result of a stored procedure or a dynamic batch into a table by using the INSERT EXEC statement.
- Use a query result to create and populate a table by using the SELECT INTO statement.

Estimated lesson time: 30 minutes

Sample Data

Some of the code examples in this lesson use a table called Sales.MyOrders. Use the following code to create such a table in the sample database TSQL2012.

```
USE TSQL2012;
IF OBJECT_ID(N'Sales.MyOrders', N'U') IS NOT NULL DROP TABLE Sales.MyOrders;
GO

CREATE TABLE Sales.MyOrders
(
  orderid INT NOT NULL IDENTITY(1, 1)
    CONSTRAINT PK_MyOrders_orderid PRIMARY KEY,
  custid  INT NOT NULL,
  empid   INT NOT NULL,
  orderdate DATE NOT NULL
    CONSTRAINT DFT_MyOrders_orderdate DEFAULT (CAST(SYSDATETIME() AS DATE)),
  shipcountry NVARCHAR(15) NOT NULL,
  freight MONEY NOT NULL
);
```

Observe that the orderid column has an IDENTITY property defined with a seed 1 and an increment 1. This property generates the values in this column automatically when rows are inserted. Chapter 11, "Other Data Modification Aspects," covers the IDENTITY column property in detail, in addition to alternative methods to generate surrogate keys like using the sequence object.

Also observe that the orderdate column has a default constraint with an expression that returns the current system's date.

EXAM TIP

Make sure you understand how modification statements are affected by constraints defined in the target table.

INSERT VALUES

With the INSERT VALUES statement, you can insert one or more rows into a target table based on value expressions. Here's an example for a statement inserting one row into the Sales.MyOrderValues table.

```
INSERT INTO Sales.MyOrders(custid, empid, orderdate, shipcountry, freight)
  VALUES(2, 19, '20120620', N'USA', 30.00);
```

Specifying the target column names after the table name is optional but considered a best practice. That's because it allows you to control the source value to target column association, irrespective of the order in which the columns were defined in the table.

Without the target column list, you must specify the values in column definition order. If the underlying table definition changes but the INSERT statements aren't modified accordingly, this can result in either errors, or worse, values written to the wrong columns.

The INSERT VALUES statement does not specify a value for a column with an IDENTITY property because the property generates the value for the column automatically. Observe that the previous statement doesn't specify the orderid column. If you do want to provide your own value instead of letting the IDENTITY property do it for you, you need to first turn on a session option called IDENTITY_INSERT, as follows.

```
SET IDENTITY_INSERT <table> ON;
```

When you're done, you need to remember to turn it off.

Note that in order to use this option, you need quite strong permissions; you need to be the owner of the table or have ALTER permissions on the table.

Besides using the IDENTITY property, there are other ways for a column to get its value automatically in an INSERT statement. A column can have a default constraint associated with it like the orderdate column in the Sales.MyOrders table. If the INSERT statement doesn't specify a value for the column explicitly, SQL Server will use the default expression to generate that value. For example, the following statement doesn't specify a value for orderdate, and therefore SQL Server uses the default expression.

```
INSERT INTO Sales.MyOrders(custid, empid, shipcountry, freight)
  VALUES(3, 11, N'USA', 10.00);
```

Another way to achieve the same behavior is to specify the column name in the names list and the keyword DEFAULT in the respective element in the VALUES list. Here's an INSERT example demonstrating this.

```
INSERT INTO Sales.MyOrders(custid, empid, orderdate, shipcountry, freight)
  VALUES(3, 17, DEFAULT, N'USA', 30.00);
```

If you don't specify a value for a column, SQL Server will first check whether the column gets its value automatically—for example, from an IDENTITY property or a default constraint. If that's not the case, SQL Server will check whether the column allows NULLs, in which case it will assume a NULL. If that's not the case, SQL Server will generate an error.

The INSERT VALUES statement doesn't limit you to inserting only one row; rather, it allows you to insert multiple rows. Simply separate the rows with commas, as follows.

```
INSERT INTO Sales.MyOrders(custid, empid, orderdate, shipcountry, freight) VALUES
  (2, 11, '20120620', N'USA', 50.00),
  (5, 13, '20120620', N'USA', 40.00),
  (7, 17, '20120620', N'USA', 45.00);
```

Note that the entire statement is considered one transaction, meaning that if any row fails to enter the target table, the entire statement fails and no row is inserted.

To see the result of running all INSERT examples in this lesson, query the table by using the following.

```
SELECT *
FROM Sales.MyOrders;
```

> ***IMPORTANT*** **USE OF SELECT ***
>
> **As explained in Chapter 2, "Getting Started with the SELECT Statement," using SELECT * in production code is considered a worst practice. In this chapter, SELECT * is used only for ad hoc querying purposes to examine the contents of tables after applying changes.**

When this code was run on one system, it returned the following output.

```
orderid  custid  empid  orderdate  shipcountry  freight
-------- ------- ------ ---------- ------------ --------
1        2       19     2012-06-20 USA          30.00
2        3       11     2012-04-19 USA          10.00
3        3       17     2012-04-19 USA          30.00
4        2       11     2012-06-20 USA          50.00
5        5       13     2012-06-20 USA          40.00
6        7       17     2012-06-20 USA          45.00
```

Remember that some of the INSERT examples relied on the default expression associated with the orderdate column, so naturally the dates you get will reflect the date when you ran those examples.

INSERT SELECT

The INSERT SELECT statement inserts the result set returned by a query into the specified target table. As with INSERT VALUES, the INSERT SELECT statement supports optionally specifying the target column names. Also, you can omit columns that get their values automatically from an IDENTITY property, default constraint, or when allowing NULLs.

As an example, the following code inserts into the Sales.MyOrders table the result of a query against Sales.Orders returning orders shipped to customers in Norway.

```
SET IDENTITY_INSERT Sales.MyOrders ON;

INSERT INTO Sales.MyOrders(orderid, custid, empid, orderdate, shipcountry, freight)
  SELECT orderid, custid, empid, orderdate, shipcountry, freight
  FROM Sales.Orders
  WHERE shipcountry = N'Norway';

SET IDENTITY_INSERT Sales.MyOrders OFF;
```

The code turns on the IDENTITY_INSERT option against Sales.MyOrders in order to use the original order IDs and not let the IDENTITY property generate those.

Query the table after running this code.

```
SELECT *
FROM Sales.MyOrders;
```

This returned the following output when run on one system.

```
orderid  custid  empid  orderdate  shipcountry  freight
-------- ------- ------ ---------- ------------ --------
1        2       19     2012-06-20 USA          30.00
2        3       11     2012-04-19 USA          10.00
3        3       17     2012-04-19 USA          30.00
4        2       11     2012-06-20 USA          50.00
5        5       13     2012-06-20 USA          40.00
6        7       17     2012-06-20 USA          45.00
10387    70      1      2006-12-18 Norway       93.63
10520    70      7      2007-04-29 Norway       13.37
10639    70      7      2007-08-20 Norway       38.64
10831    70      3      2008-01-14 Norway       72.19
10909    70      1      2008-02-26 Norway       53.05
11015    70      2      2008-04-10 Norway       4.62
```

The last six rows in the output (with the shipcountry Norway) were added by the last INSERT SELECT statement.

In certain conditions, the INSERT SELECT statement can benefit from minimal logging, which could result in improved performance compared to a fully logged operation. The conditions include using a simple or bulk logged recovery model, the TABLOCK hint, and others. For details, see "The Data Loading Performance Guide" at *http://msdn.microsoft.com/en-us/library/dd425070.aspx*.

INSERT EXEC

With the INSERT EXEC statement, you can insert the result set (or sets) returned by a dynamic batch or a stored procedure into the specified target table. Much like the INSERT VALUES and INSERT SELECT statements, INSERT EXEC supports specifying an optional target column list, and allows omitting columns that accept their values automatically.

To demonstrate the INSERT EXEC statement, the following example uses a procedure called Sales.OrdersForCountry, which accepts a ship country as input and returns orders shipped to the input country. Run the following code to create the Sales.OrdersForCountry procedure.

```
IF OBJECT_ID(N'Sales.OrdersForCountry', N'P') IS NOT NULL
  DROP PROC Sales.OrdersForCountry;
GO

CREATE PROC Sales.OrdersForCountry
  @country AS NVARCHAR(15)
AS

SELECT orderid, custid, empid, orderdate, shipcountry, freight
FROM Sales.Orders
WHERE shipcountry = @country;
GO
```

Run the following code to invoke the stored procedure with Portugal as the input country, and insert the result of the procedure into the Sales.MyOrders table.

```
SET IDENTITY_INSERT Sales.MyOrders ON;

INSERT INTO Sales.MyOrders(orderid, custid, empid, orderdate, shipcountry, freight)
  EXEC Sales.OrdersForCountry
    @country = N'Portugal';

SET IDENTITY_INSERT Sales.MyOrders OFF;
```

Here as well, the code turns on the IDENTITY_INSERT option against the target table to allow the INSERT statement to specify the values for the IDENTITY column instead of letting the property assign those.

Query the table after running the INSERT statement.

```
SELECT *
FROM Sales.MyOrders;
```

Here's the output of this code.

```
orderid  custid  empid  orderdate  shipcountry  freight
-------- ------- ------ ---------- ------------ --------
1        2       19     2012-06-20 USA          30.00
2        3       11     2012-04-19 USA          10.00
3        3       17     2012-04-19 USA          30.00
4        2       11     2012-06-20 USA          50.00
5        5       13     2012-06-20 USA          40.00
6        7       17     2012-06-20 USA          45.00
```

```
10328    28    4    2006-10-14 Portugal     87.03
10336    60    7    2006-10-23 Portugal     15.51
10352    28    3    2006-11-12 Portugal     1.30
10387    70    1    2006-12-18 Norway       93.63
10397    60    5    2006-12-27 Portugal     60.26
10433    60    3    2007-02-03 Portugal     73.83
10464    28    4    2007-03-04 Portugal     89.00
10477    60    5    2007-03-17 Portugal     13.02
10491    28    8    2007-03-31 Portugal     16.96
10520    70    7    2007-04-29 Norway       13.37
10551    28    4    2007-05-28 Portugal     72.95
10604    28    1    2007-07-18 Portugal     7.46
10639    70    7    2007-08-20 Norway       38.64
10664    28    1    2007-09-10 Portugal     1.27
10831    70    3    2008-01-14 Norway       72.19
10909    70    1    2008-02-26 Norway       53.05
10963    28    9    2008-03-19 Portugal     2.70
11007    60    8    2008-04-08 Portugal     202.24
11015    70    2    2008-04-10 Norway       4.62
```

> ***TIP*** **INSERT EXEC AND MULTIPLE QUERIES**
>
> **INSERT EXEC works even when the source dynamic batch or stored procedure has more than one query. But that's as long as all queries return result sets that are compatible with the target table definition.**

SELECT INTO

The SELECT INTO statement involves a query (the SELECT part) and a target table (the INTO part). The statement creates the target table based on the definition of the source and inserts the result rows from the query into that table. The statement copies from the source some aspects of the data definition like the column names, types, nullability, and IDENTITY property, in addition to the data itself. Certain aspects of the data definition aren't copied like indexes, constraints, triggers, permissions, and others. If you want to include these aspects, you need to script them from the source and apply them to the target.

The following code shows an example for a SELECT INTO statement that queries the Sales. Orders table returning orders shipped to Norway, creates a target table called Sales.MyOrders, and stores the query's result in the target table.

```
IF OBJECT_ID(N'Sales.MyOrders', N'U') IS NOT NULL DROP TABLE Sales.MyOrders;

SELECT orderid, custid, orderdate, shipcountry, freight
INTO Sales.MyOrders
FROM Sales.Orders
WHERE shipcountry = N'Norway';
```

As mentioned, the SELECT INTO statement creates the target table based on the definition of the source. You don't have direct control over the definition of the target. If you want target columns to be defined different than the source, you need to apply some manipulation.

For example, the source orderid column has an IDENTITY property, and hence the target column is defined with an IDENTITY property as well. If you want the target column not to have the property, you need to apply some kind of manipulation, like orderid + 0 AS orderid. Note that after you apply manipulation, the target column will be defined as allowing NULLs. If you want the target column to be defined as not allowing NULLs, you need to use the ISNULL function, returning a non-NULL value in case the source is a NULL. This is just an artificial expression that lets SQL Server know that the outcome cannot be NULL and, hence, the column can be defined as not allowing NULLs. For example, you could use an expression such as this one: ISNULL(orderid + 0, -1) AS orderid.

Similarly, the source custid column is defined in the source as allowing NULLs. To make the target column be defined as NOT NULL, use the expression ISNULL(custid, -1) AS custid.

If you want the target column's type to be different than the source, you can use the CAST or CONVERT functions. But remember that in such a case, the target column will be defined as allowing NULLs even if the source column disallowed NULLs, because you applied manipulation to the source column. As with the previous examples, you can use the ISNULL function to make SQL Server define the target column as not allowing NULLs. For example, to convert the orderdate column from its source type DATETIME to DATE in the target, and disallow NULLs, use the expression ISNULL(CAST(orderdate AS DATE), '19000101') AS orderdate.

To put it all together, the following code uses a query similar to the previous example, only defining the orderid column without the IDENTITY property as NOT NULL, the custid column as NOT NULL, and the orderdate column as DATE NOT NULL.

```
IF OBJECT_ID(N'Sales.MyOrders', N'U') IS NOT NULL DROP TABLE Sales.MyOrders;

SELECT
  ISNULL(orderid + 0, -1) AS orderid, -- get rid of IDENTITY property
                                      -- make column NOT NULL
  ISNULL(custid, -1) AS custid, -- make column NOT NULL
  empid,
  ISNULL(CAST(orderdate AS DATE), '19000101') AS orderdate,
  shipcountry, freight
INTO Sales.MyOrders
FROM Sales.Orders
WHERE shipcountry = N'Norway';
```

Remember that SELECT INTO does not copy constraints from the source table, so if you need those, it's your responsibility to define them in the target. For example, the following code defines a primary key constraint in the target table.

```
ALTER TABLE Sales.MyOrders
  ADD CONSTRAINT PK_MyOrders PRIMARY KEY(orderid);
```

Query the table to see the result of the SELECT INTO statement.

```
SELECT *
FROM Sales.MyOrders;
```

You get the following output.

```
orderid  custid  empid  orderdate  shipcountry  freight
-------- ------- ------ ---------- ------------ --------
10387    70      1      2006-12-18 Norway       93.63
10520    70      7      2007-04-29 Norway       13.37
10639    70      7      2007-08-20 Norway       38.64
10831    70      3      2008-01-14 Norway       72.19
10909    70      1      2008-02-26 Norway       53.05
11015    70      2      2008-04-10 Norway       4.62
```

One of the benefits of using SELECT INTO is that when the database's recovery model is not set to full, but instead to either simple or bulk logged, the statement uses minimal logging. This can potentially result in a faster insert compared to when full logging is used.

The SELECT INTO statement also has drawbacks. One of them is that you have only limited control over the definition of the target table. Earlier in this lesson, you learned how to control the definition of the target columns indirectly. But some things you simply cannot control—for example the file group of the target table.

Also, remember that SELECT INTO involves both creating a table and populating it with data. This means that both the metadata related to the target table and the data are exclusively locked until the SELECT INTO transaction finishes. As a result, you can run into blocking situations due to conflicts related to both data and metadata access.

When you are done, run the following code for cleanup.

```
IF OBJECT_ID(N'Sales.MyOrders', N'U') IS NOT NULL
  DROP TABLE Sales.MyOrders;
```

Quick Check

1. **Why is it recommended to specify the target column names in INSERT statements?**
2. **What is the difference between SELECT INTO and INSERT SELECT?**

Quick Check Answer

1. **Because then you don't care about the order in which the columns are defined in the table. Also, you won't be affected if the column order is rearranged due to future definition changes, in addition to when columns that get their values automatically are added.**
2. **SELECT INTO creates the target table and inserts into it the result of the query. INSERT SELECT inserts the result of the query into an already existing table.**

PRACTICE Inserting Data

In this practice, you exercise your knowledge of inserting data.

If you encounter a problem completing an exercise, you can install the completed projects from the companion content for this chapter and lesson.

EXERCISE 1 Insert Data for Customers Without Orders

In this exercise, you identify customers who did not place orders and insert the customer's data into a target table. You use both the INSERT SELECT and SELECT INTO statements.

1. Open SSMS and connect to the sample database TSQL2012.
2. Examine the structure of the Sales.Customers table by running the following code.

```
EXEC sp_describe_first_result_set N'SELECT * FROM Sales.Customers;';
```

   In the output of sp_describe_first_result_set, notice the attributes: name, system_type_name, and is_nullable.

3. Create a table called Sales.MyCustomers based on the definition of Sales.Customers. Define a primary key on the column custid. Do not define an IDENTITY property on the custid column. Your create table statement should look like the following.

```
IF OBJECT_ID(N'Sales.MyCustomers', N'U') IS NOT NULL DROP TABLE Sales.MyCustomers;

CREATE TABLE Sales.MyCustomers
(
  custid       INT NOT NULL
    CONSTRAINT PK_MyCustomers PRIMARY KEY,
  companyname  NVARCHAR(40) NOT NULL,
  contactname  NVARCHAR(30) NOT NULL,
  contacttitle NVARCHAR(30) NOT NULL,
  address      NVARCHAR(60) NOT NULL,
  city         NVARCHAR(15) NOT NULL,
  region       NVARCHAR(15) NULL,
  postalcode   NVARCHAR(10) NULL,
  country      NVARCHAR(15) NOT NULL,
  phone        NVARCHAR(24) NOT NULL,
  fax          NVARCHAR(24) NULL
);
```

4. Write an INSERT statement that inserts into the Sales.MyCustomers table customer data from Sales.Customers for customers who did not place orders. Your INSERT statement should look like the following.

```
INSERT INTO Sales.MyCustomers
  (custid, companyname, contactname, contacttitle, address,
   city, region, postalcode, country, phone, fax)
  SELECT
    custid, companyname, contactname, contacttitle, address,
    city, region, postalcode, country, phone, fax
```

```
FROM Sales.Customers AS C
WHERE NOT EXISTS
  (SELECT * FROM Sales.Orders AS O
   WHERE O.custid = C.custid);
```

5. After executing the previous INSERT statement, query the Sales.MyCustomers table to return the IDs of the inserted customers.

   ```
   SELECT custid FROM Sales.MyCustomers;
   ```

   You get the following output.

   ```
   custid
   -----------
   22
   57
   ```

EXERCISE 2 Use the SELECT INTO Statement

In this exercise, you use the SELECT INTO statement to create a table and populate it with data for customers who did not place orders.

1. Achieve the same result as in Exercise 1 but this time by using the SELECT INTO command instead of a CREATE TABLE and INSERT SELECT statements. Your solution should look like the following.

   ```
   IF OBJECT_ID(N'Sales.MyCustomers', N'U') IS NOT NULL DROP TABLE Sales.MyCustomers;

   SELECT
     ISNULL(custid, -1) AS custid,
     companyname, contactname, contacttitle, address,
     city, region, postalcode, country, phone, fax
   INTO Sales.MyCustomers
   FROM Sales.Customers AS C
   WHERE NOT EXISTS
     (SELECT * FROM Sales.Orders AS O
      WHERE O.custid = C.custid);

   ALTER TABLE Sales.MyCustomers
    ADD CONSTRAINT PK_MyCustomers PRIMARY KEY(custid);

   SELECT custid FROM Sales.MyCustomers;
   ```

   The output of the last query should look like the following.

   ```
   custid
   -----------
   22
   57
   ```

Lesson Summary

- T-SQL supports different statements that insert data into tables in your database. Those are INSERT VALUES, INSERT SELECT, INSERT EXEC, SELECT INTO, and others.
- With the INSERT VALUES statement, you can insert one or more rows based on value expressions into the target table.
- With the INSERT SELECT statement, you can insert the result of a query into the target table.
- You can use the INSERT EXEC statement to insert the result of queries in a dynamic batch or a stored procedure into the target table.
- With the statements INSERT VALUES, INSERT SELECT, and INSERT EXEC, you can omit columns that get their values automatically. A column can get its value automatically if it has a default constraint associated with it, or an IDENTITY property, or if it allows NULLs.
- The SELECT INTO statement creates a target table based on the definition of the data in the source query, and inserts the result of the query into the target table.
- It is considered a best practice in INSERT statements to specify the target column names in order to remove the dependency on column order in the target table definition.

Lesson Review

Answer the following questions to test your knowledge of the information in this lesson. You can find the answers to these questions and explanations of why each answer choice is correct or incorrect in the "Answers" section at the end of this chapter.

1. In which case out of the following are you normally not allowed to specify the target column in an INSERT statement?
   - **A.** If the column has a default constraint associated with it
   - **B.** If the column allows NULLs
   - **C.** If the column does not allow NULLs
   - **D.** If the column has an IDENTITY property
2. What are the things that the SELECT INTO statement doesn't copy from the source? (Choose all that apply.)
   - **A.** Indexes
   - **B.** Constraints
   - **C.** The IDENTITY property
   - **D.** Triggers

3. What are the benefits of using the combination of statements CREATE TABLE and INSERT SELECT over SELECT INTO? (Choose all that apply.)
   - **A.** Using the CREATE TABLE statement, you can control all aspects of the target table. Using SELECT INTO, you can't control some of the aspects, like the destination file group.
   - **B.** The INSERT SELECT statement is faster than SELECT INTO.
   - **C.** The SELECT INTO statement locks both data and metadata for the duration of the transaction. This means that until the transaction finishes, you can run into blocking related to both data and metadata. If you run the CREATE TABLE and INSERT SELECT statements in separate transactions, locks against metadata will be released quickly, reducing the probability for and duration of blocking related to metadata.
   - **D.** Using the CREATE TABLE plus INSERT SELECT statements involves less coding than using SELECT INTO.

Lesson 2: Updating Data

T-SQL supports the UPDATE statement to enable you to update existing data in your tables. In this lesson, you learn about both the standard UPDATE statement and also about a few T-SQL extensions to the standard. You also learn about modifying data by using joins. You learn about nondeterministic updates. Finally, you learn about modifying data through table expressions, updating with variables, and how all-at-once operations affect updates.

After this lesson, you will be able to:

- Use the UPDATE statement to modify rows.
- Update data by using joins.
- Describe the circumstances in which you get nondeterministic updates.
- Update data through table expressions.
- Update data by using variables.
- Describe the implications of the all-at-once property of SQL on updates.

Estimated lesson time: 30 minutes

Sample Data

Both the current section, which covers updating data, and the next one, which covers deleting data, use sample data involving tables called Sales.MyCustomers with customer data, Sales.MyOrders with order data, and Sales.MyOrderDetails with order lines data. These tables are made as initial copies of the tables Sales.Customers, Sales.Orders, and Sales.OrderDetails from the TSQL2012 sample database. By working with copies of the original tables, you can safely run code samples that update and delete rows without worrying about making changes to the original tables. Use the following code to create and populate the sample tables.

```
IF OBJECT_ID(N'Sales.MyOrderDetails', N'U') IS NOT NULL
  DROP TABLE Sales.MyOrderDetails;
IF OBJECT_ID(N'Sales.MyOrders', N'U') IS NOT NULL
  DROP TABLE Sales.MyOrders;
IF OBJECT_ID(N'Sales.MyCustomers', N'U') IS NOT NULL
  DROP TABLE Sales.MyCustomers;

SELECT * INTO Sales.MyCustomers FROM Sales.Customers;
ALTER TABLE Sales.MyCustomers
  ADD CONSTRAINT PK_MyCustomers PRIMARY KEY(custid);

SELECT * INTO Sales.MyOrders FROM Sales.Orders;
ALTER TABLE Sales.MyOrders
  ADD CONSTRAINT PK_MyOrders PRIMARY KEY(orderid);

SELECT * INTO Sales.MyOrderDetails FROM Sales.OrderDetails;
ALTER TABLE Sales.MyOrderDetails
  ADD CONSTRAINT PK_MyOrderDetails PRIMARY KEY(orderid, productid);
```

UPDATE Statement

T-SQL supports the standard UPDATE statement, which enables you to update existing rows in a table. The standard UPDATE statement has the following form.

```
UPDATE <target table>
  SET <col 1> = <expression 1>,
      <col 2> = <expression 2>,
      ...,
      <col n> = <expression n>
WHERE <predicate>;
```

You specify the target table name in the UPDATE clause. If you want to filter a subset of rows, you indicate a WHERE clause with a predicate. Only rows for which the predicate evaluates to true are updated. Rows for which the predicate evaluates to false or unknown are not affected. An UPDATE statement without a WHERE clause affects all rows. You assign values to target columns in the SET clause. The source expressions can involve columns from the table, in which case their values before the update are used.

> ***IMPORTANT*** **BEWARE OF UNQUALIFIED UPDATES**
>
> **As mentioned, an unqualified UPDATE statement affects all rows in the target table. You should be especially careful about unintentionally highlighting and executing only the UPDATE and SET clauses of the statement without the WHERE clause.**

As an example, modify rows in the Sales.MyOrderDetails table representing order lines associated with order 10251. Query those rows to examine their state prior to the update.

```
SELECT *
FROM Sales.MyOrderDetails
WHERE orderid = 10251;
```

You get the following output.

```
orderid     productid   unitprice             qty    discount
----------- ----------- --------------------- ------ ---------
10251       22          16.80                 6      0.050
10251       57          15.60                 15     0.050
10251       65          16.80                 20     0.000
```

The following code demonstrates an UPDATE statement that adds a 5 percent discount to these order lines.

```
UPDATE Sales.MyOrderDetails
  SET discount += 0.05
WHERE orderid = 10251;
```

Notice the use of the compound assignment operator discount += 0.05. This assignment is equivalent to discount = discount + 0.05. T-SQL supports such enhanced operators for all binary assignment operators: += (add), -= (subtract), *= (multiply), /= (divide), %= (modulo), &= (bitwise and), |= (bitwise or), ^= (bitwise xor), += (concatenate).

Query again the order lines associated with order 10251 to see their state after the update.

```
SELECT *
FROM Sales.MyOrderDetails
WHERE orderid = 10251;
```

You get the following output showing an increase of 5 percent in the discount.

```
orderid     productid   unitprice             qty    discount
----------- ----------- --------------------- ------ ---------
10251       22          16.80                 6      0.100
10251       57          15.60                 15     0.100
10251       65          16.80                 20     0.050
```

Use the following code to reduce the discount in the aforementioned order lines by 5 percent.

```
UPDATE Sales.MyOrderDetails
  SET discount -= 0.05
WHERE orderid = 10251;
```

These rows should now be back to their original state before the first update.

UPDATE Based on Join

Standard SQL doesn't support using joins in UPDATE statements, but T-SQL does. The idea is that you might want to update rows in a table, and refer to related rows in other tables for filtering and assignment purposes.

As an example, suppose that you want to add a 5 percent discount to order lines associated with orders placed by customers from Norway. The rows you need to modify are in the Sales.MyOrderDetails table. But the information you need to examine for filtering purposes is in rows in the Sales.MyCustomers table. In order to match a customer with its related order lines, you need to join Sales.MyCustomers with Sales.MyOrders, and then join the result with Sales.MyOrderDetails. Note that it's not sufficient to examine the shipcountry column in Sales.MyOrders; instead, you must check the country column in Sales.MyCustomers.

Based on your knowledge of joins from previous chapters, if you wanted to write a SELECT statement returning the order lines that are the target for the update, you would write a query like the following one.

```
SELECT OD.*
FROM Sales.MyCustomers AS C
  INNER JOIN Sales.MyOrders AS O
    ON C.custid = O.custid
  INNER JOIN Sales.MyOrderDetails AS OD
    ON O.orderid = OD.orderid
WHERE C.country = N'Norway';
```

This query generates the following output.

```
orderid     productid   unitprice             qty    discount
----------- ----------- --------------------- ------ ---------
10387       24          3.60                  15     0.000
10387       28          36.40                 6      0.000
10387       59          44.00                 12     0.000
10387       71          17.20                 15     0.000
10520       24          4.50                  8      0.000
10520       53          32.80                 5      0.000
10639       18          62.50                 8      0.000
10831       19          9.20                  2      0.000
10831       35          18.00                 8      0.000
10831       38          263.50                8      0.000
10831       43          46.00                 9      0.000
10909       7           30.00                 12     0.000
10909       16          17.45                 15     0.000
10909       41          9.65                  5      0.000
11015       30          25.89                 15     0.000
11015       77          13.00                 18     0.000
```

In order to perform the desired update, simply replace the SELECT clause from the last query with an UPDATE clause, indicating the alias of the table that is the target for the UPDATE (OD in this case), and the assignment in the SET clause, as follows.

```
UPDATE OD
  SET OD.discount += 0.05
```

```
FROM Sales.MyCustomers AS C
  INNER JOIN Sales.MyOrders AS O
    ON C.custid = O.custid
  INNER JOIN Sales.MyOrderDetails AS OD
    ON O.orderid = OD.orderid
WHERE C.country = N'Norway';
```

Note that you can refer to elements from all tables involved in the statement in the source expressions, but you're allowed to modify only one target table at a time.

Query the affected order lines to examine their state after the update.

```
SELECT OD.*
FROM Sales.MyCustomers AS C
  INNER JOIN Sales.MyOrders AS O
    ON C.custid = O.custid
  INNER JOIN Sales.MyOrderDetails AS OD
    ON O.orderid = OD.orderid
WHERE C.country = N'Norway';
```

You get the following output.

```
orderid     productid   unitprice             qty    discount
----------- ----------- --------------------- ------ ---------
10387       24          3.60                  15     0.050
10387       28          36.40                 6      0.050
10387       59          44.00                 12     0.050
10387       71          17.20                 15     0.050
10520       24          4.50                  8      0.050
10520       53          32.80                 5      0.050
10639       18          62.50                 8      0.050
10831       19          9.20                  2      0.050
10831       35          18.00                 8      0.050
10831       38          263.50                8      0.050
10831       43          46.00                 9      0.050
10909       7           30.00                 12     0.050
10909       16          17.45                 15     0.050
10909       41          9.65                  5      0.050
11015       30          25.89                 15     0.050
11015       77          13.00                 18     0.050
```

Notice the 5 percent increase in the discount of the affected order lines.

To get the previous order lines back to their original state, run an UPDATE statement that reduces the discount by 5 percent.

```
UPDATE OD
  SET OD.discount -= 0.05
FROM Sales.MyCustomers AS C
  INNER JOIN Sales.MyOrders AS O
    ON C.custid = O.custid
  INNER JOIN Sales.MyOrderDetails AS OD
    ON O.orderid = OD.orderid
WHERE C.country = N'Norway';
```

Nondeterministic UPDATE

You should be aware that the proprietary T-SQL UPDATE syntax based on joins can be nondeterministic. The statement is nondeterministic when multiple source rows match one target row. Unfortunately, in such a case, SQL Server doesn't generate an error or even a warning. Instead, SQL Server silently performs a nondeterministic UPDATE where one of the source rows arbitrarily "wins."

> ***TIP*** **USING MERGE INSTEAD OF UPDATE**
>
> **Instead of using the nonstandard UPDATE statement based on joins, you can use the standard MERGE statement. The latter generates an error if multiple source rows match one target row, requiring you to revise your code to make it deterministic. The MERGE statement is covered in Chapter 11.**

As an example, the following query matches customers with their related orders, returning the customers' postal codes, as well shipping postal codes from related orders.

```
SELECT C.custid, C.postalcode, O.shippostalcode
FROM Sales.MyCustomers AS C
  INNER JOIN Sales.MyOrders AS O
    ON C.custid = O.custid
ORDER BY C.custid;
```

This query generates the following output.

```
custid      postalcode shippostalcode
----------- ---------- --------------
1           10092      10154
1           10092      10156
1           10092      10155
1           10092      10154
1           10092      10154
1           10092      10154
2           10077      10182
2           10077      10181
2           10077      10181
2           10077      10180
...
```

Each customer row is repeated in the output per each matching order. This means that each customer's only postal code is repeated in the output as many times as the number of matching orders. It's important for the purposes of this example to remember that there is only one postal code per customer. The shipping postal code is associated with an order, so as you can realize, there may be multiple distinct shipping postal codes per each customer.

With this background in mind, consider the following UPDATE statement.

```
UPDATE C
  SET C.postalcode = O.shippostalcode
FROM Sales.MyCustomers AS C
  INNER JOIN Sales.MyOrders AS O
    ON C.custid = O.custid;
```

There are 89 customers that have matching orders—some with multiple matches. SQL Server doesn't generate an error though; instead it arbitrarily chooses per each target row which source row will be considered for the update, returning the following message.

```
(89 row(s) affected)
```

Query the rows from the Sales.Customers table after the update.

```
SELECT custid, postalcode
FROM Sales.MyCustomers
ORDER BY custid;
```

This generated the following output on one system, but your results could be different.

```
custid      postalcode
----------- ----------
1           10154
2           10182
...
(91 row(s) affected)
```

Note that the table has 91 rows, but because only 89 of those customers have related orders, the previous UPDATE statement affected 89 rows.

As to which source row gets chosen per each target row, the choice isn't exactly random, but arbitrary; in other words, it's optimization-dependent. At any rate, you do not have any logical elements in the language to control this choice. The recommended approach is simply not to use such nondeterministic UPDATE statements. First, figure out logically how to break ties, and after you have this part figured out, you can write a deterministic UPDATE statement that includes tiebreaking logic.

For example, suppose that you want to update the customer's postal code with the shipping postal code from the customer's first order (based on the sort order of orderdate, orderid). You can achieve this using the APPLY operator, as follows.

```
UPDATE C
  SET C.postalcode = A.shippostalcode
FROM Sales.MyCustomers AS C
  CROSS APPLY (SELECT TOP (1) O.shippostalcode
               FROM Sales.MyOrders AS O
               WHERE O.custid = C.custid
               ORDER BY orderdate, orderid) AS A;
```

SQL Server generates the following message.

```
(89 row(s) affected)
```

Query the Sales.MyCustomers table after the update.

```
SELECT custid, postalcode
FROM Sales.MyCustomers
ORDER BY custid;
```

You get the following output.

```
custid      postalcode
----------- ----------
1           10154
2           10180
...

(91 row(s) affected)
```

If you want to use the most-recent order as the source for the update, simply use descending sort order in both columns: ORDER BY orderdate DESC, orderid DESC.

UPDATE and Table Expressions

With T-SQL, you can modify data through table expressions like CTEs and derived tables. This capability can be useful, for example, when you want to be able to see which rows are going to be modified and with what data before you actually apply the update.

Suppose that you need to modify the country and postalcode columns of the Sales.MyCustomers table with the data from the respective rows from the Sales.Customers table. But you want to be able to run the code as a SELECT statement first in order to see the data that you're about to update. You could first write a SELECT query, as follows.

```
SELECT TGT.custid,
  TGT.country AS tgt_country, SRC.country AS src_country,
  TGT.postalcode AS tgt_postalcode, SRC.postalcode AS src_postalcode
FROM Sales.MyCustomers AS TGT
  INNER JOIN Sales.Customers AS SRC
    ON TGT.custid = SRC.custid;
```

This query generates the following output.

```
custid      tgt_country     src_country     tgt_postalcode src_postalcode
----------- --------------- --------------- -------------- --------------
1           Germany         Germany         10154          10092
2           Mexico          Mexico          10180          10077
3           Mexico          Mexico          10211          10097
4           UK              UK              10238          10046
5           Sweden          Sweden          10269          10112
6           Germany         Germany         10302          10117
7           France          France          10329          10089
8           Spain           Spain           10359          10104
9           France          France          10369          10105
10          Canada          Canada          10130          10111
```

But to actually perform the update, you now need to replace the SELECT clause with an UPDATE clause, as follows.

```
UPDATE TGT
  SET TGT.country = SRC.country,
      TGT.postalcode = SRC.postalcode
FROM Sales.MyCustomers AS TGT
  INNER JOIN Sales.Customers AS SRC
    ON TGT.custid = SRC.custid;
```

As an alternative, you will probably find it easier to define a table expression based on the last query, and issue the modification through the table expression. The following code demonstrates how this can be achieved using a common table expression (CTE).

```
WITH C AS
(
  SELECT TGT.custid,
    TGT.country AS tgt_country, SRC.country AS src_country,
    TGT.postalcode AS tgt_postalcode, SRC.postalcode AS src_postalcode
  FROM Sales.MyCustomers AS TGT
    INNER JOIN Sales.Customers AS SRC
      ON TGT.custid = SRC.custid
)
UPDATE C
  SET tgt_country = src_country,
      tgt_postalcode = src_postalcode;
```

Behind the scenes, the Sales.MyCustomers table gets modified. But with this solution, you can always highlight just the inner SELECT query and run it independently just to see the data involved in the update without actually applying it.

You can achieve the same thing using a derived table, as follows.

```
UPDATE D
  SET tgt_country = src_country,
      tgt_postalcode = src_postalcode
FROM (
       SELECT TGT.custid,
         TGT.country AS tgt_country, SRC.country AS src_country,
         TGT.postalcode AS tgt_postalcode, SRC.postalcode AS src_postalcode
       FROM Sales.MyCustomers AS TGT
         INNER JOIN Sales.Customers AS SRC
           ON TGT.custid = SRC.custid
     ) AS D;
```

Notice that you need to use the FROM clause to define the derived table, and then specify the derived table name in the UPDATE clause.

Back to UPDATE statements based on joins: Earlier in this lesson, you saw the following statement.

```
UPDATE TGT
  SET TGT.country = SRC.country,
      TGT.postalcode = SRC.postalcode
FROM Sales.MyCustomers AS TGT
  INNER JOIN Sales.Customers AS SRC
    ON TGT.custid = SRC.custid;
```

Interestingly, if you write an UPDATE statement with a table A in the UPDATE clause and a table B (but not A) in the FROM clause, you get an implied cross join between A and B. If you also add a filter with a predicate involving elements from both tables, you get a logical equivalent to an inner join. Based on this logic, the following statement achieves the same result as the previous statement.

```
UPDATE Sales.MyCustomers
  SET MyCustomers.country = SRC.country,
      MyCustomers.postalcode = SRC.postalcode
FROM Sales.Customers AS SRC
WHERE MyCustomers.custid = SRC.custid;
```

This code is equivalent to the following use of an explicit cross join with a filter.

```
UPDATE TGT
  SET TGT.country = SRC.country,
      TGT.postalcode = SRC.postalcode
FROM Sales.MyCustomers AS TGT
  CROSS JOIN Sales.Customers AS SRC
WHERE TGT.custid = SRC.custid;
```

And this code is logically equivalent to the aforementioned UPDATE with the explicit inner join.

The ability to update data through table expressions is also handy when you want to modify rows with expressions that are normally disallowed in the SET clause. For example, window functions are not supported in the SET clause. The workaround is to invoke the window function in the inner query's SELECT list and to assign a column alias to the result column. Then in the outer UPDATE statement, you can refer to the column alias as a source expression in the SET clause.

UPDATE Based on a Variable

Sometimes you need to modify a row and also collect the result of the modified columns into variables. You can handle such a need with a combination of UPDATE and SELECT statements, but this would require two visits to the row. T-SQL supports a specialized UPDATE syntax that allows achieving the task by using one statement and one visit to the row.

As an example, run the following query to examine the current state of the order line associated with order 10250 and product 51.

```
SELECT *
FROM Sales.MyOrderDetails
WHERE orderid = 10250
  AND productid = 51;
```

This code generates the following output.

```
orderid     productid   unitprice             qty    discount
----------- ----------- --------------------- ------ ---------
10250       51          42.40                 35     0.150
```

Suppose that you need to modify the row, increasing the discount by 5 percent, and collect the new discount into a variable called @newdiscount. You can achieve this using a single UPDATE statement, as follows.

```
DECLARE @newdiscount AS NUMERIC(4, 3) = NULL;

UPDATE Sales.MyOrderDetails
  SET @newdiscount = discount += 0.05
WHERE orderid = 10250
  AND productid = 51;

SELECT @newdiscount;
```

As you can see, the UPDATE and WHERE clauses are similar to those you use in normal UPDATE statements. But the SET clause uses the assignment @newdiscount = discount += 0.05, which is equivalent to using @newdiscount = discount = discount + 0.05. The statement assigns the result of discount + 0.05 to discount, and then assigns the result to the variable @ newdiscount.

The last SELECT statement in the code generates the following output.

```
------
0.200
```

When you're done, issue the following code to undo the last change.

```
UPDATE Sales.MyOrderDetails
  SET discount -= 0.05
WHERE orderid = 10250
  AND productid = 51;
```

UPDATE All-at-Once

Earlier in this Training Kit, in Chapter 1, "Querying Foundations," and Chapter 3, "Filtering and Sorting Data," a concept called all-at-once was discussed. Those chapters explained that this concept means that all expressions that appear in the same logical query processing phase are evaluated conceptually at the same point in time.

The all-at-once concept also has implications on UPDATE statements. To demonstrate those implications, this section uses a table called T1. Use the following code to create the table T1 and insert a row into it.

```
IF OBJECT_ID(N'dbo.T1', N'U') IS NOT NULL DROP TABLE dbo.T1;

CREATE TABLE dbo.T1
(
  keycol INT NOT NULL
    CONSTRAINT PK_T1 PRIMARY KEY,
  col1 INT NOT NULL,
  col2 INT NOT NULL
);

INSERT INTO dbo.T1(keycol, col1, col2) VALUES(1, 100, 0);
```

Next, examine the following code but don't run it yet.

```
DECLARE @add AS INT = 10;

UPDATE dbo.T1
  SET col1 += @add, col2 = col1
WHERE keycol = 1;

SELECT * FROM dbo.T1;
```

Can you guess what should be the value of col2 in the modified row after the update? If you guessed 110, you were not thinking of the all-at-once property of SQL. Based on this property, all assignments use the original values of the row as the source values, irrespective of their order of appearance. So the assignment col2 = col1 doesn't get the col1 value after the change, but rather before the change—namely 100. To verify this, run the previous code.

You get the following output.

```
keycol      col1        col2
----------- ----------- -----------
1           110         100
```

When you're done, run the following code for cleanup.

```
IF OBJECT_ID(N'dbo.T1', N'U') IS NOT NULL DROP TABLE dbo.T1;
```

Quick Check

1. Which table rows are updated in an UPDATE statement without a WHERE clause?
2. Can you update rows in more than one table in one UPDATE statement?

Quick Check Answer

1. All table rows.
2. No, you can use columns from multiple tables as the source, but update only one table at a time.

PRACTICE Updating Data

In this practice, you exercise your knowledge of updating data.

If you encounter a problem completing an exercise, you can install the completed projects from the companion content for this chapter and lesson.

EXERCISE 1 Update Data by Using Joins

In this exercise, you update data based on joins.

1. Open SSMS and connect to the sample database TSQL2012.
2. Use the following code to create the table Sales.MyCustomers and populate it with a couple of rows representing customers with IDs 22 and 57.

```
IF OBJECT_ID(N'Sales.MyCustomers', N'U') IS NOT NULL DROP TABLE Sales.MyCustomers;

CREATE TABLE Sales.MyCustomers
(
  custid       INT NOT NULL
    CONSTRAINT PK_MyCustomers PRIMARY KEY,
  companyname  NVARCHAR(40) NOT NULL,
  contactname  NVARCHAR(30) NOT NULL,
  contacttitle NVARCHAR(30) NOT NULL,
  address      NVARCHAR(60) NOT NULL,
  city         NVARCHAR(15) NOT NULL,
  region       NVARCHAR(15) NULL,
  postalcode   NVARCHAR(10) NULL,
  country      NVARCHAR(15) NOT NULL,
  phone        NVARCHAR(24) NOT NULL,
  fax          NVARCHAR(24) NULL
);

INSERT INTO Sales.MyCustomers
  (custid, companyname, contactname, contacttitle, address,
   city, region, postalcode, country, phone, fax)
  VALUES(22, N'', N'', N'', N'', N'', N'', N'', N'', N'', N''),
        (57, N'', N'', N'', N'', N'', N'', N'', N'', N'', N'');
```

3. Write an UPDATE statement that overwrites the values of all nonkey columns in the Sales.MyCustomers table with those from the respective rows in the Sales.Customers table. Your solution should look like the following.

```
UPDATE TGT
  SET   TGT.companyname  = SRC.companyname ,
        TGT.contactname  = SRC.contactname ,
        TGT.contacttitle = SRC.contacttitle,
        TGT.address      = SRC.address     ,
        TGT.city         = SRC.city        ,
        TGT.region       = SRC.region      ,
        TGT.postalcode   = SRC.postalcode  ,
        TGT.country      = SRC.country     ,
        TGT.phone        = SRC.phone       ,
        TGT.fax          = SRC.fax
FROM Sales.MyCustomers AS TGT
  INNER JOIN Sales.Customers AS SRC
    ON TGT.custid = SRC.custid;
```

EXERCISE 2 Update Data by Using a CTE

In this exercise, you update data indirectly by using a CTE.

1. You are given the same task as in Exercise 1, step 3; namely, update the values of all nonkey columns in the Sales.MyCustomers table with those from the respective rows in the Sales.Customers table. But this time you want to be able to examine the data that needs to be modified before actually applying the update. Implement the task by using a CTE. Your solution should look like the following.

```
WITH C AS
(
  SELECT
    TGT.companyname  AS tgt_companyname , SRC.companyname  AS src_companyname ,
    TGT.contactname  AS tgt_contactname , SRC.contactname  AS src_contactname ,
    TGT.contacttitle AS tgt_contacttitle, SRC.contacttitle AS src_contacttitle,
    TGT.address      AS tgt_address     , SRC.address      AS src_address     ,
    TGT.city         AS tgt_city        , SRC.city         AS src_city        ,
    TGT.region       AS tgt_region      , SRC.region       AS src_region      ,
    TGT.postalcode   AS tgt_postalcode  , SRC.postalcode   AS src_postalcode  ,
    TGT.country      AS tgt_country     , SRC.country      AS src_country     ,
    TGT.phone        AS tgt_phone       , SRC.phone        AS src_phone       ,
    TGT.fax          AS tgt_fax         , SRC.fax          AS src_fax
  FROM Sales.MyCustomers AS TGT
    INNER JOIN Sales.Customers AS SRC
      ON TGT.custid = SRC.custid
)
UPDATE C
  SET    tgt_companyname  = src_companyname ,
         tgt_contactname  = src_contactname ,
         tgt_contacttitle = src_contacttitle,
         tgt_address      = src_address     ,
         tgt_city         = src_city        ,
         tgt_region       = src_region      ,
         tgt_postalcode   = src_postalcode  ,
         tgt_country      = src_country     ,
         tgt_phone        = src_phone       ,
         tgt_fax          = src_fax;
```

   You can use the inner SELECT query with the join both before and after issuing the actual update to ensure that you achieved the desired result.

Lesson Summary

- T-SQL supports the standard UPDATE statement as well as a few extensions to the standard.
- You can modify data in one table based on data in another table by using an UPDATE based on joins. Remember though that if multiple source rows match one target row, the update won't fail; instead, it will be nondeterministic. You should generally avoid such updates.

- T-SQL supports updating data by using table expressions. This capability is handy when you want to be able to see the result of the query before you actually update the data. This capability is also handy when you want to modify rows with expressions that are normally disallowed in the SET clause, like window functions.
- If you want to modify a row and query the result of the modification, you can use a specialized UPDATE statement with a variable that can do this with one visit to the row.

Lesson Review

Answer the following questions to test your knowledge of the information in this lesson. You can find the answers to these questions and explanations of why each answer choice is correct or incorrect in the "Answers" section at the end of this chapter.

1. How do you modify a column value in a target row and collect the result of the modification in one visit to the row?
   - **A.** By using an UPDATE based on a join
   - **B.** By using an UPDATE based on a table expression
   - **C.** By using an UPDATE with a variable
   - **D.** The task cannot be achieved with only one visit to the row.
2. What are the benefits of using an UPDATE statement based on joins? (Choose all that apply.)
   - **A.** You can filter the rows to update based on information in related rows in other tables.
   - **B.** You can update multiple tables in one statement.
   - **C.** You can collect information from related rows in other tables to be used in the source expressions in the SET clause.
   - **D.** You can use data from multiple source rows that match one target row to update the data in the target row.
3. How can you update a table, setting a column to the result of a window function?
   - **A.** By using an UPDATE based on a join
   - **B.** By using an UPDATE based on a table expression
   - **C.** By using an UPDATE with a variable
   - **D.** The task cannot be achieved.

Lesson 3: Deleting Data

T-SQL supports two statements that you can use to delete rows from a table: DELETE and TRUNCATE. This lesson describes these statements, the differences between them, and different aspects of working with them.

After this lesson, you will be able to:

- Use the DELETE and TRUNCATE statements to delete rows from a table.
- Use a DELETE statement based on joins.
- Use a DELETE statement based on table expressions.

Estimated lesson time: 30 minutes

Sample Data

This section uses the same sample data that was used in Lesson 2. As a reminder, the sample data involves the tables Sales.MyCustomers, Sales.MyOrders, and Sales.MyOrderDetails, which are initially created as copies of the tables Sales.Customers, Sales.Orders, and Sales.OrderDetails, respectively. Use the following code to recreate tables and repopulate them with sample data.

```
IF OBJECT_ID(N'Sales.MyOrderDetails', N'U') IS NOT NULL
  DROP TABLE Sales.MyOrderDetails;
IF OBJECT_ID(N'Sales.MyOrders', N'U') IS NOT NULL
  DROP TABLE Sales.MyOrders;
IF OBJECT_ID(N'Sales.MyCustomers', N'U') IS NOT NULL
  DROP TABLE Sales.MyCustomers;

SELECT * INTO Sales.MyCustomers FROM Sales.Customers;
ALTER TABLE Sales.MyCustomers
  ADD CONSTRAINT PK_MyCustomers PRIMARY KEY(custid);

SELECT * INTO Sales.MyOrders FROM Sales.Orders;
ALTER TABLE Sales.MyOrders
  ADD CONSTRAINT PK_MyOrders PRIMARY KEY(orderid);

SELECT * INTO Sales.MyOrderDetails FROM Sales.OrderDetails;
ALTER TABLE Sales.MyOrderDetails
  ADD CONSTRAINT PK_MyOrderDetails PRIMARY KEY(orderid, productid);
```

DELETE Statement

With the DELETE statement, you can delete rows from a table. You can optionally specify a predicate to restrict the rows to be deleted. The general form of a DELETE statement looks like the following.

```
DELETE FROM <table>
WHERE <predicate>;
```

If you don't specify a predicate, all rows from the target table are deleted. As with unqualified updates, you need to be especially careful about accidentally deleting all rows by highlighting only the DELETE part of the statement, missing the WHERE part.

The following example deletes all order lines containing product ID 11 from the Sales.MyOrderDetails table.

```
DELETE FROM Sales.MyOrderDetails
WHERE productid = 11;
```

When you run this code, SQL Server returns the following message, indicating that 38 rows were deleted.

```
(38 row(s) affected)
```

The tables used by the examples in this chapter are very small, but in a more realistic production environment, the volumes of data are likely to be much bigger. A DELETE statement is fully logged and as a result, large deletes can take a long time to complete. Such large deletes can cause the transaction log to increase in size dramatically during the process. They can also result in lock escalation, meaning that SQL Server escalates fine-grained locks like row locks to a full-blown table lock. Such escalation may result in blocking access to all table data by other processes.

To prevent the aforementioned problems from happening, you can split your large delete into smaller chunks. You can achieve this by using a DELETE statement with a TOP option that limits the number of affected rows in a loop. Here's an example for implementing such a solution.

```
WHILE 1 = 1
BEGIN
  DELETE TOP (1000) FROM Sales.MyOrderDetails
  WHERE productid = 12;

  IF @@rowcount < 1000 BREAK;
END
```

As you can see, the code uses an infinite loop (WHILE 1 = 1 is always true). In each iteration, a DELETE statement with a TOP option limits the number of affected rows to no more than 1,000 at a time. Then the IF statement checks if the number of affected rows is less than 1,000; in such a case, the last iteration deleted the last chunk of qualifying rows. After the last chunk of rows has been deleted, the code breaks from the loop. With this sample data, there are only 14 qualifying rows in total. So if you run this code, it will be done after one round; it will then break from the loop, and return the following message.

```
(14 row(s) affected)
```

But with a very large number of qualifying rows, say, many millions, you'd very likely be better off with such a solution.

TRUNCATE Statement

The TRUNCATE statement deletes all rows from the target table. Unlike the DELETE statement, it doesn't have an optional filter, so it's all or nothing. As an example, the following statement truncates the table Sales.MyOrderDetails.

```
TRUNCATE TABLE Sales.MyOrderDetails;
```

After executing the statement, the target table is empty.

The DELETE and TRUNCATE statements have a number of important differences between them:

- The DELETE statement writes significantly more to the transaction log compared to the TRUNCATE statement. For DELETE, SQL Server records in the log the actual data that was deleted. For TRUNCATE, SQL Server records information only about which pages were deallocated. As a result, the TRUNCATE statement tends to be substantially faster.
- The DELETE statement doesn't attempt to reset an identity property if one is associated with a column in the target table. The TRUNCATE statement does. If you use TRUNCATE and would prefer not to reset the property, you need to store the current identity value plus one in a variable (using the IDENT_CURRENT function), and reseed the property with the stored value after the truncation.
- The DELETE statement is supported if there's a foreign key pointing to the table in question as long as there are no related rows in the referencing table. TRUNCATE is not allowed if a foreign key is pointing to the table—even if there are no related rows in the referencing table, and even if the foreign key is disabled.
- The DELETE statement is allowed against a table involved in an indexed view. A TRUNCATE statement is disallowed in such a case.
- The DELETE statement requires DELETE permissions on the target table. The TRUNCATE statement requires ALTER permissions on the target table.

When you need to delete all rows from a table, it is usually preferred to use TRUNCATE because it is significantly faster than DELETE. However, it does require stronger permissions, and is more restricted.

DELETE Based on a Join

T-SQL supports a proprietary DELETE syntax based on joins similar to the UPDATE syntax described in Lesson 2. The idea is to enable you to delete rows from one table based on information that you evaluate in related rows in other tables.

As an example, suppose that you want to delete all orders placed by customers from the United States. The country is a property of the customer—not the order. So even though the target for the DELETE statement is the Sales.MyOrders table, you need to examine the country column in the related customer row in the Sales.MyCustomers table. You can achieve this by using a DELETE statement based on a join, as follows.

```
DELETE FROM O
FROM Sales.MyOrders AS O
  INNER JOIN Sales.MyCustomers AS C
    ON O.custid = C.custid
WHERE C.country = N'USA';
```

The FROM clause defining the JOIN table operator is logically evaluated first. The join matches orders with their respective customers. Then the WHERE clause filters only the rows where the customer's country is the USA. This filter results in keeping only orders placed by customers from the USA. Then the DELETE clause indicates the alias of the side of the join that is the actual target of the delete—O for Orders in this case. This statement generates the following output indicating that 122 rows were deleted.

```
(122 row(s) affected)
```

You can implement the same task by using a subquery instead of a join, as the following example shows.

```
DELETE FROM Sales.MyOrders
WHERE EXISTS
  (SELECT *
   FROM Sales.MyCustomers
   WHERE MyCustomers.custid = MyOrders.custid
     AND MyCustomers.country = N'USA');
```

This statement gets optimized the same as the one that uses a join, so in this case, there's no performance motivation to use one version over the other. But you should note that the subquery version is considered standard, whereas the join version isn't. So if standard compliance is a priority, you would want to stick to the subquery version. Otherwise, some people feel more comfortable phrasing such a task by using a join, and others by using a subquery; it's a personal thing.

DELETE Using Table Expressions

Like with updates, T-SQL supports deleting rows by using table expressions. The idea is to use a table expression such as a CTE or a derived table to define the rows that you want to delete, and then issue a DELETE statement against the table expression. The rows get deleted from the underlying table, of course.

As an example, suppose that you want to delete the 100 oldest orders (based on orderdate, orderid ordering). The DELETE statement supports using the TOP option directly, but it doesn't support an ORDER BY clause. So you don't have any control over which rows the TOP filter will pick. As a workaround, you can define a table expression based on a SELECT query with the TOP option and an ORDER BY clause controlling which rows get filtered. Then you can issue a DELETE against the table expression. Here's how the complete code looks.

```
WITH OldestOrders AS
(
  SELECT TOP (100) *
  FROM Sales.MyOrders
  ORDER BY orderdate, orderid
)
DELETE FROM OldestOrders;
```

This code generates the following output, indicating that 100 rows were deleted.

```
(100 row(s) affected)
```

When you're done, run the following code for cleanup.

```
IF OBJECT_ID(N'Sales.MyOrderDetails', N'U') IS NOT NULL
  DROP TABLE Sales.MyOrderDetails;
IF OBJECT_ID(N'Sales.MyOrders', N'U') IS NOT NULL
  DROP TABLE Sales.MyOrders;
IF OBJECT_ID(N'Sales.MyCustomers', N'U') IS NOT NULL
  DROP TABLE Sales.MyCustomers;
```

Quick Check

1. **Which rows from the target table get deleted by a DELETE statement without a WHERE clause?**
2. **What is the alternative to a DELETE statement without a WHERE clause?**

Quick Check Answer

1. **All target table rows.**
2. **The TRUNCATE statement. But there are a few differences between the two that need to be considered.**

PRACTICE Deleting and Truncating Data

In this practice, you exercise your knowledge of deleting data using the DELETE and TRUNCATE statements.

If you encounter a problem completing an exercise, you can install the completed projects from the companion content for this chapter and lesson.

EXERCISE 1 Delete Data by Using Joins

In this exercise, you delete rows based on a join.

1. Open SSMS and connect to the sample database TSQL2012.
2. Run the following code to create the tables Sales.MyCustomers and Sales.MyOrders as initial copies of the Sales.Customers and Sales.MyOrders tables, respectively.

```
IF OBJECT_ID(N'Sales.MyOrders', N'U') IS NOT NULL
  DROP TABLE Sales.MyOrders;
IF OBJECT_ID(N'Sales.MyCustomers', N'U') IS NOT NULL
  DROP TABLE Sales.MyCustomers;

SELECT * INTO Sales.MyCustomers FROM Sales.Customers;
ALTER TABLE Sales.MyCustomers
  ADD CONSTRAINT PK_MyCustomers PRIMARY KEY(custid);

SELECT * INTO Sales.MyOrders FROM Sales.Orders;
ALTER TABLE Sales.MyOrders
  ADD CONSTRAINT PK_MyOrders PRIMARY KEY(orderid);

ALTER TABLE Sales.MyOrders
  ADD CONSTRAINT FK_MyOrders_MyCustomers
  FOREIGN KEY(custid) REFERENCES Sales.MyCustomers(custid);
```

3. Write a DELETE statement that deletes rows from the Sales.MyCustomers table if the customer has no related orders in the Sales.MyOrders table. Use a DELETE statement based on a join to implement the task. Your solution should look like the following.

```
DELETE FROM TGT
FROM Sales.MyCustomers AS TGT
  LEFT OUTER JOIN Sales.MyOrders AS SRC
    ON TGT.custid = SRC.custid
WHERE SRC.orderid IS NULL;
```

4. Use the following query to count the number of customers remaining in the table.

```
SELECT COUNT(*) AS cnt FROM Sales.MyCustomers;
```

You get 89.

EXERCISE 2 Truncate Data

In this exercise, you truncate data.

1. Use TRUNCATE statements to clear first the Sales.MyOrders table and then the Sales.MyCustomers table. Your code should look like this.

```
TRUNCATE TABLE Sales.MyOrders;
TRUNCATE TABLE Sales.MyCustomers;
```

   The second statement fails with the following error.

```
Msg 4712, Level 16, State 1, Line 1
Cannot truncate table 'Sales.MyCustomers' because it is being referenced by a
FOREIGN KEY constraint.
```

2. Explain why the error happened and come up with a solution.

   The error happened because a TRUNCATE statement is disallowed when the target table is referenced by a foreign key constraint, even if there are no related rows in the referencing table. The solution is to drop the foreign key, truncate the target table, and then create the foreign key again.

```
ALTER TABLE Sales.MyOrders
  DROP CONSTRAINT FK_MyOrders_MyCustomers;

TRUNCATE TABLE Sales.MyCustomers;

ALTER TABLE Sales.MyOrders
  ADD CONSTRAINT FK_MyOrders_MyCustomers
  FOREIGN KEY(custid) REFERENCES Sales.MyCustomers(custid);
```

3. When you're done, run the following code for cleanup.

```
IF OBJECT_ID(N'Sales.MyOrders', N'U') IS NOT NULL
  DROP TABLE Sales.MyOrders;
IF OBJECT_ID(N'Sales.MyCustomers', N'U') IS NOT NULL
  DROP TABLE Sales.MyCustomers;
```

Lesson Summary

- With the DELETE statement, you can delete rows from a table, and optionally limit the rows to delete by using a filter based on a predicate. You can also limit the rows to delete using the TOP filter, but then you cannot control which rows get chosen.
- With the TRUNCATE statement, you can delete all rows from the target table. This statement doesn't support a filter. The benefit of TRUNCATE over DELETE is that the former uses optimized logging, and therefore tends to be much faster than the latter. However, TRUNCATE has more restrictions than DELETE and requires stronger permissions.

- T-SQL supports a DELETE syntax based on joins, enabling you to delete rows from one table based on information in related rows in other tables.
- T-SQL also supports deleting rows through table expressions like CTEs and derived tables.

Lesson Review

Answer the following questions to test your knowledge of the information in this lesson. You can find the answers to these questions and explanations of why each answer choice is correct or incorrect in the "Answers" section at the end of this chapter.

1. How do you delete rows from a table for which a ROW_NUMBER computation is equal to 1?
   A. You refer to the ROW_NUMBER function in the DELETE statement's WHERE clause.
   B. You use a table expression like a CTE or derived table computing a column based on the ROW_NUMBER function, and then issue a filtered DELETE statement against the table expression.
   C. You use a table expression like a CTE or derived table computing a column based on the ROW_NUMBER function, and then issue a filtered TRUNCATE statement against the table expression.
   D. The task cannot be achieved.
2. Which of the following is applicable to a DELETE statement? (Choose all that apply.)
   A. The statement writes more to the transaction log than TRUNCATE.
   B. The statement resets an IDENTITY property.
   C. The statement is disallowed when a foreign key points to the target table.
   D. The statement is disallowed when an indexed view based on the target table exists.
3. Which of the following is applicable to a TRUNCATE statement? (Choose all that apply.)
   A. The statement writes more to the transaction log than DELETE.
   B. The statement resets an IDENTITY property.
   C. The statement is disallowed when a foreign key points to the target table.
   D. The statement is disallowed when an indexed view based on the target table exists.

Case Scenarios

In the following case scenarios, you apply what you've learned about inserting, updating, and deleting data. You can find the answers to these questions in the "Answers" section at the end of this chapter.

Case Scenario 1: Using Modifications That Support Optimized Logging

You are a consultant for the IT department of a large retail company. The company has a nightly process that first clears all rows from a table by using a DELETE statement, and then populates the table with the result of a query against other tables. The result contains a few dozen million rows. The process is extremely slow. You are asked to provide recommendations for improvements.

1. Provide recommendations for improving the delete part of the process.
2. Provide recommendations for improving the insert part of the process.

Case Scenario 2: Improving a Process That Updates Data

The same company that hired you to consult about its inefficient nightly process from the first scenario hires you again. They ask for your advice regarding the following update processes:

1. The database has a table holding about 100 million rows. About a third of the existing rows need to be updated. Can you provide recommendations as to how to handle the update in order not to cause unnecessary performance problems in the system?
2. There's an UPDATE statement that modifies rows in one table based on information from related rows in another table. The UPDATE statement currently uses a separate subquery for each column that needs to be modified, obtaining the value of the respective column from the related row in the source table. The statement also uses a subquery to filter only rows that have matches in the source table. The process is very slow. Can you suggest ways to improve it?

Suggested Practices

To help you successfully master the topics presented in this chapter, complete the following tasks.

DELETE vs. TRUNCATE

This practice helps you realize the significant performance difference between the DELETE and TRUNCATE statements. Use your knowledge of cross joins, the SELECT INTO statement, and the DELETE and TRUNCATE statements to observe the performance difference between fully logged versus minimally logged deletions.

- **Practice 1** The first task in the performance test you're about to run is to prepare sample data. You use the SELECT INTO statement for this purpose. Remember that in order for the SELECT INTO statement to benefit from minimal logging, you need to set the recovery model of the database to simple or bulk logged. You need to create a test table and fill it with enough data for the performance test. A few million rows should be sufficient. To achieve this, you can perform a cross join between one of the tables in the sample database TSQL2012 (for example, Sales.Orders) and the table dbo.Nums. You can use a filter against the Nums.n column to control the number of rows to generate in the result. If you filter n <= 2000, you get 2000 copies of the other table in the join. Use the SELECT INTO statement to create the target table and populate it with the result of the query.
- **Practice 2** Delete all rows from the target table by using the DELETE statement and take note of how long it took the statement to finish.
- **Practice 3** Recreate the sample data. Then use the TRUNCATE statement to delete all rows from the target table. Compare the performance of the two methods.

Answers

This section contains the answers to the lesson review questions and solutions to the case scenarios in this chapter.

Lesson 1

1. **Correct Answer: D**
   - **A. Incorrect:** If you want, you are allowed to not specify the column and let the default constraint generate the value, but it's not like you have to skip it. If you want, you can indicate your own value.
   - **B. Incorrect:** Again, if you want, you are allowed to not specify the column and let SQL Server assign a NULL to the column, but it's not like you have to skip it. If you want, you can indicate your own value.
   - **C. Incorrect:** If the column doesn't allow NULLs and doesn't somehow get its value automatically, you actually must specify it.
   - **D. Correct:** If the column has an IDENTITY property, you must normally skip it in the INSERT statement and let the property assign the value. To provide your own value, you need to turn on the IDENTITY_INSERT option, but that's not what happens normally.
2. **Correct Answers: A, B, and D**
   - **A. Correct:** SELECT INTO doesn't copy indexes.
   - **B. Correct:** SELECT INTO doesn't copy constraints.
   - **C. Incorrect:** SELECT INTO does copy an IDENTITY property.
   - **D. Correct:** SELECT INTO doesn't copy triggers.
3. **Correct Answers: A and C**
   - **A. Correct:** SELECT INTO has limited control over the definition of the target, unlike the alternative that has full control.
   - **B. Incorrect:** The INSERT SELECT statement generally isn't faster than SELECT INTO. In fact, there are more cases where SELECT INTO can benefit from minimal logging.
   - **C. Correct:** SELECT INTO locks both data and metadata, and therefore can cause blocking related to both. If the CREATE TABLE and INSERT SELECT are executed in different transactions, you hold locks on metadata only for a very short period.
   - **D. Incorrect:** It's exactly the other way around—SELECT INTO involves less coding because you don't need to define the target table.

Lesson 2

1. **Correct Answer: C**
   - **A. Incorrect:** The support for joins in an update is not what allows only one visit to the row.
   - **B. Incorrect:** The support for updates based on table expressions is not what allows only one visit to the row.
   - **C. Correct:** An UPDATE with a variable can both modify a column value and collect the result into a variable using one visit to the row.
   - **D. Incorrect:** The task can be achieved as explained in answer C.
2. **Correct Answers: A and C**
   - **A. Correct:** The join can be used to filter the updated rows.
   - **B. Incorrect:** You cannot update multiple tables in one UPDATE statement.
   - **C. Correct:** The join gives you access to information in other tables that can be used in the source expressions for the assignments.
   - **D. Incorrect:** When multiple source rows match one target row, you get a nondeterministic update in which only one source row is used. Also, the fact that such an update doesn't fail should be considered a disadvantage—not a benefit.
3. **Correct Answer: B**
   - **A. Incorrect:** An UPDATE based on a join cannot refer to window functions in the SET clause.
   - **B. Correct:** With an UPDATE based on table expressions, you can invoke a window function in the inner query's SELECT list. You can then refer to the alias you assigned to the result column in the outer UPDATE statement's SET clause.
   - **C. Incorrect:** An UPDATE with a variable cannot refer to window functions in the SET clause.
   - **D. Incorrect:** The task can be achieved as described in answer B.

Lesson 3

1. **Correct Answer: B**
   - **A. Incorrect:** You cannot refer to the ROW_NUMBER function directly in the DELETE statement's WHERE clause.
   - **B. Correct:** Using a table expression you can create a result column based on the ROW_NUMBER function, and then refer to the column alias in the outer statement's filter.
   - **C. Incorrect:** The TRUNCATE statement doesn't have a filter.
   - **D. Incorrect:** The task can be achieved as described in answer B.

2. **Correct Answer: A**

   A. **Correct:** The DELETE statement writes more to the transaction log than TRUNCATE.

   B. **Incorrect:** The DELETE statement does not reset an IDENTITY property.

   C. **Incorrect:** A DELETE statement is allowed even when there's a foreign key pointing to the table, as long as there are no rows related to the deleted ones.

   D. **Incorrect:** A DELETE statement is allowed when an indexed view based on the target table exists.

3. **Correct Answers: B, C and D**

   A. **Incorrect:** The TRUNCATE statement uses optimized logging, whereas DELETE doesn't.

   B. **Correct:** The TRUNCATE statement resets an IDENTITY property.

   C. **Correct:** The TRUNCATE statement is disallowed when a foreign key pointing to the table exists.

   D. **Correct:** The TRUNCATE statement is disallowed when an indexed view based on the table exists.

Case Scenario 1

1. Regarding the delete process, if the entire table needs to be cleared, the customer should consider using the TRUNCATE statement, which is minimally logged.

2. Regarding the insert process, it could be that it's currently very slow because it doesn't benefit from minimal logging. The customer should evaluate the feasibility of using minimally logged inserts like the SELECT INTO statement (which would require dropping the target table first), the INSERT SELECT statement with the TABLOCK option, and others. Note that the recovery model of the database needs to be simple or bulk logged, so the customer should evaluate whether this is acceptable in terms of the organization's requirements for recovery capabilities.

Case Scenario 2

1. The customer should consider developing a process that handles the large update in chunks. If done in one big transaction, the process will very likely result in a significant increase in the transaction log size. The process will also likely result in lock escalation leading to blocking problems.

2. The customer should consider using an UPDATE statement based on a join instead of the existing use of subqueries. The amount of code will be significantly reduced, and the performance will likely improve. Each subquery requires a separate visit to the related row. So using multiple subqueries to obtain values from multiple columns will result in multiple visits to the data. With a join, through one visit to the matching row, you can obtain any number of column values that you need.

CHAPTER 11

Other Data Modification Aspects

Exam objectives in this chapter:

- Modify Data
  - Modify data by using INSERT, UPDATE, and DELETE statements.
  - Combine datasets.

Chapter 10, "Inserting, Updating, and Deleting Data," covered the three fundamental data modification statements: INSERT, UPDATE, and DELETE. This chapter covers additional aspects of data modification such as the sequence object and the IDENTITY column property, the MERGE statement, and the OUTPUT option.

Lessons in this chapter:

- Lesson 1: Using the Sequence Object and IDENTITY Column Property
- Lesson 2: Merging Data
- Lesson 3: Using the OUTPUT Option

Before You Begin

To complete the lessons in this chapter, you must have:

- Experience working with Microsoft SQL Server Management Studio (SSMS).
- Some experience writing T-SQL code.
- An understanding of data types.
- An understanding of combining sets.
- An understanding of data modification statements.
- Access to a SQL Server 2012 instance with the sample database TSQL2012 installed.

Lesson 1: Using the Sequence Object and IDENTITY Column Property

The *IDENTITY column property* and the *sequence object* are both features that you can use to generate a sequence of numbers automatically. The numbers are usually used as surrogate keys in tables for entities like orders, products, employees, and customers. The IDENTITY property is a very old feature in the product and has a number of limitations and restrictions. The sequence object was introduced in SQL Server 2012 and overcomes many of the limitations of IDENTITY. This lesson starts by covering the IDENTITY property and then describes the sequence object.

After this lesson, you will be able to:

- Use the IDENTITY column property and the sequence object.
- Describe the advantages of the sequence object over the IDENTITY property.

Estimated lesson time: 40 minutes

Using the IDENTITY Column Property

IDENTITY is a property of a column in a table. The property automatically assigns a value to the column upon insertion. You can define it for columns with any numeric type that has a scale of 0. This means all integer types, but also NUMERIC/DECIMAL with a scale of 0. When defining the property, you can optionally specify a seed and an increment. If you don't, the defaults are 1 and 1. Only one column in a table can have an IDENTITY property.

EXAM TIP

An important technique in multiple choice questions in the exam is to first eliminate answers that are obviously incorrect. For example, suppose you get a question and a few possible answers that contain code samples. And suppose one of the answers contains code defining a table that has two columns with an IDENTITY property or two PRIMARY KEY constraints. You can quickly eliminate such answers from consideration. This way, you can spend more time on fewer answers.

Here's a code example that creates a table called Sales.MyOrders with a column called orderid that has an IDENTITY property with a seed of 1 and an increment of 1.

```
USE TSQL2012;
IF OBJECT_ID(N'Sales.MyOrders', N'U') IS NOT NULL DROP TABLE Sales.MyOrders;
GO

CREATE TABLE Sales.MyOrders
```

```
(
  orderid INT NOT NULL IDENTITY(1, 1)
    CONSTRAINT PK_MyOrders_orderid PRIMARY KEY,
  custid  INT NOT NULL
    CONSTRAINT CHK_MyOrders_custid CHECK(custid > 0),
  empid   INT NOT NULL
    CONSTRAINT CHK_MyOrders_empid CHECK(empid > 0),
  orderdate DATE NOT NULL
);
```

When you insert rows into the table, don't specify a value for the IDENTITY column because it gets its values automatically. For example, the following code inserts three rows and does not specify values for the orderid column.

```
INSERT INTO Sales.MyOrders(custid, empid, orderdate) VALUES
  (1, 2, '20120620'),
  (1, 3, '20120620'),
  (2, 2, '20120620');

SELECT * FROM Sales.MyOrders;
```

After the insertion, the query returns the following output.

```
orderid     custid      empid       orderdate
----------- ----------- ----------- ----------
1           1           2           2012-06-20
2           1           3           2012-06-20
3           2           2           2012-06-20
```

For cases in which you insert rows into the table and you want to specify your own values for the orderid column, you need to set a session option called SET IDENTITY_INSERT <*table*> to ON. Note that there's no option that you can set to update an IDENTITY column.

T-SQL provides a number of functions that you can use to query the last identity value generated—for example, in case you need it when you insert related rows into another table:

- The SCOPE_IDENTITY function returns the last identity value generated in your session in the current scope.
- The @@IDENTITY function returns the last identity value generated in your session regardless of scope.
- The IDENT_CURRENT function accepts a table as input and returns the last identity value generated in the input table regardless of session.

As an example, the following code queries all three functions in the same session that ran the last INSERT statement.

```
SELECT
  SCOPE_IDENTITY()                AS SCOPE_IDENTITY,
  @@IDENTITY                      AS [@@IDENTITY],
  IDENT_CURRENT('Sales.MyOrders') AS IDENT_CURRENT;
```

There was no activity after the last INSERT statement, either in the current session or in others; hence, all three functions return the same values.

```
SCOPE_IDENTITY  @@IDENTITY  IDENT_CURRENT
--------------- ----------- --------------
3               3           3
```

Next, open a new query window and run the query again. This time, you get the following result.

```
SCOPE_IDENTITY  @@IDENTITY  IDENT_CURRENT
--------------- ----------- --------------
NULL            NULL        3
```

Because you're issuing the query in a different session than the one that generated the identity value, both SCOPE_IDENTITY and @@IDENTITY return NULLs. As for IDENT_CURRENT, it returns the last value generated in the input table irrespective of session.

As for the difference between SCOPE_IDENTITY and @@IDENTITY, suppose that you have a stored procedure P1 with three statements:

- An INSERT that generates a new identity value
- A call to a stored procedure P2 that also has an INSERT statement that generates a new identity value
- A statement that queries the functions SCOPE_IDENTITY and @@IDENTITY

The SCOPE_IDENTITY function will return the value generated by P1 (same session and scope). The @@IDENTITY function will return the value generated by P2 (same session irrespective of scope).

If you need to delete all rows from a table, you should be aware of a specific difference between doing so by using a DELETE without a WHERE clause versus by using a TRUNCATE statement. The former doesn't affect the current identity value, whereas the latter resets it to the initial seed. For example, run the following code to clear the Sales.MyOrders table by using a TRUNCATE statement.

```
TRUNCATE TABLE Sales.MyOrders;
```

Next, query the current identity value in the table.

```
SELECT IDENT_CURRENT('Sales.MyOrders') AS [IDENT_CURRENT];
```

You get 1 as the result. To reseed the current identity value, use the DBCC CHECKIDENT command, as follows.

```
DBCC CHECKIDENT('Sales.MyOrders', RESEED, 4);
```

To see that the value was reseeded, issue an INSERT statement and query the table.

```
INSERT INTO Sales.MyOrders(custid, empid, orderdate) VALUES(2, 2, '20120620');
SELECT * FROM Sales.MyOrders;
```

You get the following output.

```
orderid     custid     empid       orderdate
----------- ---------- ----------- ----------
4           2          2           2012-06-20
```

It is important to understand that there are certain things that the IDENTITY property doesn't guarantee. It doesn't guarantee uniqueness. Remember that you can enter explicit values if you turn on the IDENTITY_INSERT option. Also, you can reseed the property value. To guarantee uniqueness you must use a constraint like PRIMARY KEY or UNIQUE.

Also, the IDENTITY property doesn't guarantee that there will be no gaps between the values. If an INSERT statement fails, the current identity value is not changed back to the original one, so the unused value is lost. The next insertion will have a value after the one that wasn't used. To demonstrate this, run the following INSERT statement.

```
INSERT INTO Sales.MyOrders(custid, empid, orderdate) VALUES(3, -1, '20120620');
```

This statement violates the CHECK constraint defined on the table with the predicate empid > 0. This code generates the following error.

```
Msg 547, Level 16, State 0, Line 1
The INSERT statement conflicted with the CHECK constraint "CHK_MyOrders_empid". The
conflict occurred in database "TSQL2012", table "Sales.MyOrders", column 'empid'.
The statement has been terminated.
```

The IDENTITY property generated a new identity value of 5 for the INSERT statement; however, SQL Server did not undo the change to the current identity value due to the failure. Next, issue another INSERT statement.

```
INSERT INTO Sales.MyOrders(custid, empid, orderdate) VALUES(3, 1, '20120620');
```

This time, the insertion succeeds. Query the table.

```
SELECT * FROM Sales.MyOrders;
```

You get the following output.

```
orderid     custid     empid       orderdate
----------- ---------- ----------- ----------
4           2          2           2012-06-20
6           3          1           2012-06-20
```

Observe that the value 5 that was generated for the failed INSERT statement wasn't used and now you have a gap between the values. For this reason, the IDENTITY column property is not an adequate sequencing solution in cases where you cannot allow gaps. One such example is for invoicing systems; gaps between invoice numbers are not allowed. In such cases, you need to create an alternative solution, such as storing the last-used value in a table.

The IDENTITY property has no cycling support. This means that after you reach the maximum value in the type, the next insertion will fail due to an overflow error. To get around this, you need to reseed the current identity value before such an attempt is made.

Using the Sequence Object

SQL Server 2012 introduces the sequence object. Unlike the IDENTITY column property, a sequence is an independent object in the database. The sequence object doesn't suffer from many of the limitations of the IDENTITY property, which include the following:

- The IDENTITY property is tied to a particular column in a particular table. You cannot remove an existing property from a column or add it to an existing column. The column has to be defined with the property.
- Sometimes you need keys to not conflict across different tables. But IDENTITY is table-specific.
- Sometimes you need to generate the value before using it. With the IDENTITY property, this is not possible. You have to insert the row and only then collect the new value with a function.
- You cannot update an IDENTITY column.
- The IDENTITY property doesn't support cycling.
- A TRUNCATE statement resets the identity value.

The sequence object doesn't suffer from these limitations. This section explains how to work with the object and shows how it doesn't suffer from the same restrictions as IDENTITY.

You create a sequence object as an independent object in the database. It's not tied to a particular column in a particular table. You use the CREATE SEQUENCE command to create a sequence. At a minimum, you just need to specify a name for the object, as follows.

```
CREATE SEQUENCE <schema>.<object>;
```

Like IDENTITY, all numeric types with a scale of 0 are supported. But if you don't indicate a type explicitly, SQL Server will assume BIGINT by default. If you need a different type, you need to ask for it explicitly by adding AS *<type>* after the sequence name.

There are a number of properties that you can set, all with default options in case you don't provide your own. The following are some of the properties and their default values:

- **INCREMENT BY** Increment value. The default is 1.
- **MINVALUE** The minimum value to support. The default is the minimum value in the type. For example, for an INT type, it will be -2147483648.
- **MAXVALUE** The maximum value to support. The default is the maximum value in the type.
- **CYCLE | NO CYCLE** Defines whether to allow the sequence to cycle or not. The default is NO CYCLE.
- **START WITH** The sequence start value. The default is MINVALUE for an ascending sequence (positive increment) and MAXVALUE for a descending one.

Here's an example you can use to define a sequence that will help generate order IDs.

```
CREATE SEQUENCE Sales.SeqOrderIDs AS INT
  MINVALUE 1
  CYCLE;
```

Observe that the definition sets the minimum value to 1 (and therefore also the start value to 1), and specifies that the sequence should allow cycling. The more common thing to see people doing when they want the sequence to start with 1 is to set the START WITH property to 1. However, this won't change the minimum value from -2147483648. This will turn out to be a problem if the sequence allows cycling. After you hit the last value in the type, the next value generated won't be 1; instead, it will be -2147483648. Therefore, the smarter thing to do if you need your sequence to generate only positive values is to set the MINVALUE to 1. This will implicitly set the START WITH value to 1 as well.

Note that in real-life cases, normally you would not allow a sequence generating order IDs to cycle, but here the cycling sequence is defined just for demonstration purposes.

To request a new value from the sequence, use the NEXT VALUE FOR *<sequence name>* function. For example, run the following code three times.

```
SELECT NEXT VALUE FOR Sales.SeqOrderIDs;
```

You get the values 1, 2, and 3. This function can be called in INSERT VALUES and INSERT SELECT statements, a SET clause of an UPDATE statement, an assignment to a variable, a DEFAULT constraint expression, and other places. Examples are provided later in this lesson.

You cannot change the data type of an existing sequence, but you can change all of its properties by using the ALTER SEQUENCE command. For example, if you want to change the current value, you can do so with the following code.

```
ALTER SEQUENCE Sales.SeqOrderIDs
  RESTART WITH 1;
```

To see for yourself how to use sequence values when inserting rows into a table, recreate the Sales.MyOrders table by running the following code.

```
IF OBJECT_ID(N'Sales.MyOrders', N'U') IS NOT NULL DROP TABLE Sales.MyOrders;
GO

CREATE TABLE Sales.MyOrders
(
  orderid INT NOT NULL
    CONSTRAINT PK_MyOrders_orderid PRIMARY KEY,
  custid  INT NOT NULL
    CONSTRAINT CHK_MyOrders_custid CHECK(custid > 0),
  empid   INT NOT NULL
    CONSTRAINT CHK_MyOrders_empid CHECK(empid > 0),
  orderdate DATE NOT NULL
);
```

Observe that this time the orderid column doesn't have an IDENTITY property.

Here's an example of using the NEXT VALUE FOR function in an INSERT VALUES statement that inserts three rows into the table.

```
INSERT INTO Sales.MyOrders(orderid, custid, empid, orderdate) VALUES
  (NEXT VALUE FOR Sales.SeqOrderIDs, 1, 2, '20120620'),
  (NEXT VALUE FOR Sales.SeqOrderIDs, 1, 3, '20120620'),
  (NEXT VALUE FOR Sales.SeqOrderIDs, 2, 2, '20120620');
```

As mentioned, you can also use the function in INSERT SELECT statements. In such a case, you can optionally add an OVER clause with an ORDER BY list to control the order in which the sequence values are assigned to the result rows.

```
INSERT INTO Sales.MyOrders(orderid, custid, empid, orderdate)
  SELECT
    NEXT VALUE FOR Sales.SeqOrderIDs OVER(ORDER BY orderid),
    custid, empid, orderdate
  FROM Sales.Orders
  WHERE custid = 1;
```

This is a T-SQL extension to the standard.

To see the values generated by both statements, query the table.

```
SELECT * FROM Sales.MyOrders;
```

You get the following output.

```
orderid     custid     empid       orderdate
----------- ---------- ----------- ----------
1           1          2           2012-06-20
2           1          3           2012-06-20
3           2          2           2012-06-20
4           1          6           2007-08-25
5           1          4           2007-10-03
6           1          4           2007-10-13
7           1          1           2008-01-15
8           1          1           2008-03-16
9           1          3           2008-04-09
```

You can also use the NEXT VALUE FOR function in a DEFAULT constraint, and this way let the constraint generate the values automatically when you insert rows. Use the following code to define such a DEFAULT constraint for the orderid column.

```
ALTER TABLE Sales.MyOrders
  ADD CONSTRAINT DFT_MyOrders_orderid
    DEFAULT(NEXT VALUE FOR Sales.SeqOrderIDs) FOR orderid;
```

Next, run the following INSERT statement, omitting the orderid column.

```
INSERT INTO Sales.MyOrders(custid, empid, orderdate)
  SELECT
    custid, empid, orderdate
  FROM Sales.Orders
  WHERE custid = 2;
```

This time, the order ID values were generated automatically. This feature is an extension to the standard that makes it easy to provide an alternative to the IDENTITY property. This alternative is in fact more flexible than IDENTITY because it only assigns a default value if one wasn't specified explicitly in the INSERT statement.

The sequence object also supports a caching option that controls how often the current sequence value is written to disk versus written to memory. For example, a sequence with a CACHE 100 defined for it will write to disk once every 100 changes. SQL Server keeps two members in memory, holding the current sequence value and how many values are left. So it will write only to memory 100 times, and only when it runs out of those 100 values will it write the current value plus 100 to disk. The benefit is better performance for allocation of sequence values. The risk is losing a range up to the size of the cache value in case there's an unordered shutdown of the service.

Note that, as with IDENTITY, the sequence object doesn't guarantee that there won't be gaps. If SQL Server creates a new sequence value in a transaction and the transaction fails, the change to the sequence value is not undone. So if you're working with the sequence object, you have to accept the possibility of having gaps anyway.

There's a very big performance difference between using NO CACHE versus CACHE <*some value*>. With NO CACHE, SQL Server has to write to disk for every request of a new sequence value. With some caching, the performance is much better. The default cache value is 50 at the date of this writing, but Microsoft doesn't publish the default because they reserve the right to change it in the future.

Here's an example of changing the cache value to 100.

```
ALTER SEQUENCE Sales.SeqOrderIDs
  CACHE 100;
```

T-SQL also supports a stored procedure called sp_sequence_get_range that you can use to allocate an entire range of sequence values of a requested size. You provide the requested range size by using the input parameter @range_size and collect the first value in the allocated range by using the output parameter @range_first_value. Then you can assign the values in the allocated range as you want. The sequence itself gets modified only once by advancing it from its current value to the current value plus @range_size. For details about other supported parameters of the stored procedure, see the Books Online for SQL Server 2012 article "sp_sequence_get_range (Transact-SQL)" at *http://msdn.microsoft.com/en-us/library/ff878352.aspx*.

SQL Server provides a view called sys.sequences that you can use to query the properties of sequences defined in the current database.

Going back to the list of limitations of the IDENTITY property mentioned earlier, here are the benefits of the sequence object:

- The sequence object is not tied to a particular column in a particular table. You can, if you want, assign a new value by using a DEFAULT constraint. You can add such a constraint to or remove it from an existing column.
- Because the sequence is an independent object in the database, you can use the same sequence to generate keys that are used in different tables. This way, the keys won't conflict across tables.
- You can generate a sequence value before using it by storing the result of the NEXT VALUE FOR function in a variable.
- You can UPDATE columns with the result of the NEXT VALUE FOR function.
- The sequence object supports cycling.
- A TRUNCATE statement doesn't reset the current value of a sequence object because the sequence is independent of the tables that use it.

Make sure that you keep on hand the Sales.MyOrders table because it's used by subsequent lessons in this chapter.

Quick Check

1. **How many columns with an IDENTITY property are supported in one table?**
2. **How do you obtain a new value from a sequence?**

Quick Check Answer

1. **One.**
2. **With the NEXT VALUE FOR function.**

PRACTICE Using the Sequence Object

In this practice, you generate keys by using the sequence object.

If you encounter a problem completing an exercise, you can install the completed projects from the companion content for this chapter and lesson.

EXERCISE 1 Create a Sequence with Default Options

In this exercise, you create a sequence object with default options and query its properties.

1. Open SSMS and connect to the sample database TSQL2012.

2. Run the following code to create a sequence called dbo.Seq1. You specify only the schema and object names and rely on defaults for all of the sequence properties.

```
CREATE SEQUENCE dbo.Seq1;
```

3. Issue the following code against the sys.sequences view to query the sequence properties.

```
SELECT
  TYPE_NAME(system_type_id) AS type,
  start_value, minimum_value, current_value, increment, is_cycling
FROM sys.sequences
WHERE object_id = OBJECT_ID(N'dbo.Seq1', N'SO');
```

This code generates the following output.

```
type    start_value          minimum_value
------- -------------------- --------------------
bigint  -9223372036854775808 -9223372036854775808

current_value        increment  is_cycling
-------------------- ---------- ----------
-9223372036854775808 1          0
```

Observe that SQL Server used the BIGINT data type by default, the lowest value supported by the type (-9223372036854775808) as both the minimum and current values, the highest value supported by the type as the maximum value, 1 as the increment, and no cycling.

EXERCISE 2 Create a Sequence with Nondefault Options

In this exercise, you create a sequence with nondefault options.

1. Start with the sequence named dbo.Seq1 that you created in Exercise 1. In this exercise you will alter the data type of the sequence from the default BIGINT to INT, in addition to making it start with 1 and supporting cycling. However, unlike all other properties, the data type of an existing sequence cannot be altered. You have to recreate the sequence. Run the following code to drop and recreate the sequence.

```
IF OBJECT_ID(N'dbo.Seq1', N'SO') IS NOT NULL DROP SEQUENCE dbo.Seq1;
CREATE SEQUENCE dbo.Seq1 AS INT
  START WITH 1 CYCLE;
```

This code creates a sequence with an INT data type, indicating 1 as the start value, and creates support for cycling. Query the properties of the sequence.

```
SELECT
  TYPE_NAME(system_type_id) AS type,
  start_value, minimum_value, current_value, increment, is_cycling
FROM sys.sequences
WHERE object_id = OBJECT_ID(N'dbo.Seq1', N'SO');
```

You get the following output.

```
type start_value  minimum_value
---- ------------ -------------
int  1            -2147483648

current_value  increment  is_cycling
-------------- ---------- ----------
1              1          1
```

Observe that although the sequence was defined with a start value of 1, the minimum value was still set to the lowest value in the type (-2147483648 in the case of INT) by default.

2. To see what happens after you get to the maximum value, first alter the current sequence value to the maximum supported by the type by using the following code.

```
ALTER SEQUENCE dbo.Seq1 RESTART WITH 2147483647;
```

Then run the following code twice.

```
SELECT NEXT VALUE FOR dbo.Seq1;
```

You first get 2147483647, and then get -2147483648—not 1—because the minimum sequence is defined as -2147483648.

3. If you want to create a sequence that cycles and supports only positive values, you need to set the MINVALUE property to 1. Run the following code to achieve this.

```
IF OBJECT_ID(N'dbo.Seq1', N'SO') IS NOT NULL DROP SEQUENCE dbo.Seq1;
CREATE SEQUENCE dbo.Seq1 AS INT
  MINVALUE 1 CYCLE;
```

4. Query the sequence properties by running the following code.

```
SELECT
  TYPE_NAME(system_type_id) AS type,
  start_value, minimum_value, current_value, increment, is_cycling
FROM sys.sequences
WHERE object_id = OBJECT_ID(N'dbo.Seq1', N'SO');
```

You get the following output.

```
type start_value  minimum_value
---- ------------ -------------
int  1            1

current_value  increment  is_cycling
-------------- ---------- ----------
1              1          1
```

Notice that both the minimum value and the start value were set to 1.

5. To see what happens when you reach the maximum value, first run the following code.

```
ALTER SEQUENCE dbo.Seq1 RESTART WITH 2147483647;
```

Then run the following code twice to request two new sequence values.

```
SELECT NEXT VALUE FOR dbo.Seq1;
```

You first get 2147483647, and then you get 1.

Lesson Summary

- SQL Server provides two features to help you generate a sequence of keys: the IDENTITY column property and the sequence object.
- The IDENTITY column property is defined with a seed and an increment. When you insert a new row into the target table, you don't specify a value for the IDENTITY column; instead, SQL Server generates it for you automatically.
- To get the newly generated identity value, you can query the functions SCOPE_IDENTITY, @@IDENTITY, and IDENT_CURRENT. The first returns the last identity value generated by your session and scope. The second returns the last identity value generated by your session. The third returns the last identity value generated in the input table.
- The sequence object is an independent object in the database. It is not tied to a specific column in a specific table.
- The sequence object supports defining the start value, increment value, minimum and maximum supported values, cycling, and caching.
- You use the NEXT VALUE FOR function to request a new value from the sequence. You can use this function in INSERT and UPDATE statements, DEFAULT constraints, and assignments to variables.
- The sequence object circumvents many of the restrictions of the IDENTITY property.

Lesson Review

Answer the following questions to test your knowledge of the information in this lesson. You can find the answers to these questions and explanations of why each answer choice is correct or incorrect in the "Answers" section at the end of this chapter.

1. Which function do you use to return the last identity value generated in a specific table?

   A. MAX

   B. SCOPE_IDENTITY

   C. @@IDENTITY

   D. IDENT_CURRENT

2. What are the advantages of using a sequence object instead of IDENTITY? (Choose all that apply.)
   - **A.** The IDENTITY property doesn't guarantee that there won't be gaps and the sequence object does.
   - **B.** The IDENTITY property cannot be added to or removed from an existing column; a DEFAULT constraint with a NEXT VALUE FOR function can be added to or removed from an existing column.
   - **C.** A new identity value cannot be generated before issuing an INSERT statement, whereas a sequence value can.
   - **D.** You cannot provide your own value when inserting a row into a table with an IDENTITY column without special permissions. You can specify your own value for a column that normally gets its values from a sequence object.
3. In an INSERT SELECT statement, how do you generate sequence values in specific order?
   - **A.** Use the OVER clause in the NEXT VALUE FOR function.
   - **B.** Specify an ORDER BY clause at the end of the query.
   - **C.** Use TOP (100) PERCENT and ORDER BY in the query.
   - **D.** Use TOP (9223372036854775807) and ORDER BY in the query.

Lesson 2: Merging Data

With the MERGE statement, you can merge data from a source table into a target table. The statement has many practical uses in both online transaction processing (OLTP) scenarios and in data warehousing ones. As an example of an OLTP use case, suppose that you have a table that isn't updated directly by your application; instead, you get the delta of changes periodically from an external system. You first load the delta of changes into a staging table, and then use the staging table as the source for the merge operation into the target.

As an example for a data warehousing scenario, suppose that you maintain aggregated views of the data in your data warehouse. Using the MERGE statement, you can apply changes that happen to detail rows into the aggregated form.

These are just a couple of typical use cases; there are many more. This lesson describes the MERGE statement and its different options, and demonstrates its use through examples. The examples in this lesson use the table Sales.MyOrders and the sequence Sales.SeqOrderIDs that you created in the previous lesson.

After this lesson, you will be able to:

- Use the MERGE statement to merge data from a source into a target.
- Define a predicate that identifies whether a source row is matched by a target row.
- Define an action to take against the target when a source row is matched by a target.
- Define an action to take against the target when a source row is not matched by a target.
- Define an action to take against the target when a target row is not matched by a source row.
- Describe the difference between the role of the ON clause used by a MERGE statement and an ON clause used by a join.

Estimated lesson time: 40 minutes

Using the MERGE Statement

With the MERGE statement, you can MERGE data from a source table or table expression into a target table. The general form of the MERGE statement is as follows.

```
MERGE INTO <target table> AS TGT
USING <SOURCE TABLE> AS SRC
  ON <merge predicate>
WHEN MATCHED [AND <predicate>]                   -- two clauses allowed:
   THEN <action>                                 --   one with UPDATE one with DELETE
WHEN NOT MATCHED [BY TARGET] [AND <predicate>] -- one clause allowed:
   THEN INSERT...                                --   if indicated, action must be INSERT
WHEN NOT MATCHED BY SOURCE [AND <predicate>]    -- two clauses allowed:
  THEN <action>;                                 --   one with UPDATE one with DELETE
```

The following are the clauses of the statement and their roles.

- **MERGE INTO *<target table>*** This clause defines the target table for the operation. You can alias the table in this clause if you want.
- **USING *<source table>*** This clause defines the source table for the operation. You can alias the table in this clause if you want. Note that the USING clause is designed similar to a FROM clause in a SELECT query, meaning that in this clause you can define table operators like joins, refer to a table expression like a derived table or a common table expression (CTE), or even refer to a table function like OPENROWSET. The outcome of the USING clause is eventually a table result, and that table will be considered the source of the merge operation.

- **ON <*merge predicate*>** In this clause, you specify a predicate that matches rows between the source and the target and defines whether a source row is or isn't matched by a target row. Note that this clause isn't a filter like the ON clause in a join. You have a chance to see the importance of this fact in the exercise for this lesson.
- **WHEN MATCHED [AND <*predicate*>] THEN <*action*>** This clause defines an action to take when a source row is matched by a target row. Because a target row exists, an INSERT action isn't allowed in this clause. The two actions that are allowed are UPDATE and DELETE. If you want to apply different actions in different conditions, you can specify two WHEN MATCHED clauses, each with a different additional predicate to determine when to apply an UPDATE and when to apply a DELETE.
- **WHEN NOT MATCHED [BY TARGET] [AND <*predicate*>] THEN <*action*>** This clause defines what action to take when a source row is not matched by a target row. Because a target row does not exist, the only action allowed in this clause (if you choose to include this clause in the statement) is INSERT. Using UPDATE or DELETE holds no meaning when a target row doesn't exist. You can still add an additional predicate that must be true in order to perform the action.
- **WHEN NOT MATCHED BY SOURCE [AND <*predicate*>] THEN <*action*>** This clause defines an action to take when a target row exists, but it is not matched by a source row. Because a target row exists, you can apply either an UPDATE or a DELETE, but not an INSERT. If you want, you can have two such clauses with different additional predicates that define when to use an UPDATE and when to use a DELETE.

As mentioned, to demonstrate examples of the MERGE statement, this lesson uses the Sales.MyOrders table and the Sales.SeqOrderIDs sequence from the previous lesson. If you still have them in the database, use the following code to clear the table and reset the sequence.

```
TRUNCATE TABLE Sales.MyOrders;
ALTER SEQUENCE Sales.SeqOrderIDs RESTART WITH 1;
```

If the table and sequence don't exist in the database, use the following code to create them.

```
IF OBJECT_ID(N'Sales.MyOrders', N'U') IS NOT NULL DROP TABLE Sales.MyOrders;
IF OBJECT_ID(N'Sales.SeqOrderIDs', N'SO') IS NOT NULL DROP SEQUENCE Sales.SeqOrderIDs;

CREATE SEQUENCE Sales.SeqOrderIDs AS INT
  MINVALUE 1
  CYCLE;

CREATE TABLE Sales.MyOrders
(
  orderid INT NOT NULL
    CONSTRAINT PK_MyOrders_orderid PRIMARY KEY
    CONSTRAINT DFT_MyOrders_orderid
      DEFAULT(NEXT VALUE FOR Sales.SeqOrderIDs),
  custid  INT NOT NULL
    CONSTRAINT CHK_MyOrders_custid CHECK(custid > 0),
```

```
  empid    INT NOT NULL
    CONSTRAINT CHK_MyOrders_empid CHECK(empid > 0),
  orderdate DATE NOT NULL
);
```

Suppose that you need to define a stored procedure that accepts as input parameters attributes of an order. If an order with the input order ID already exists in the Sales.MyOrders table, you need to update the row, setting the values of the nonkey columns to the new ones. If the order ID doesn't exist in the target table, you need to insert a new row. Because this Training Kit doesn't cover stored procedures until a later chapter, the examples in this lesson use local variables for now. A MERGE statement in a stored procedure simply refers to the procedure's input parameters instead of the local variables.

The first things to identify in a MERGE statement are the target and the source tables. The target is easy—it's the Sales.MyOrders table. The source is supposed to be a table or table expression, but in this case, it's just a set of input parameters making an order. To turn the inputs into a table expression, you can use one of two options: a SELECT without a FROM clause or the VALUES table value constructor.

Here's an example for a query against a table expression defined from input variables based on a SELECT statement without a FROM clause.

```
DECLARE
  @orderid   AS INT  = 1,
  @custid    AS INT  = 1,
  @empid     AS INT  = 2,
  @orderdate AS DATE = '20120620';

SELECT *
FROM (SELECT @orderid, @custid, @empid, @orderdate )
      AS SRC( orderid,  custid,  empid,  orderdate );
```

Here's an example of doing the same thing with the VALUES table value constructor.

```
DECLARE
  @orderid   AS INT  = 1,
  @custid    AS INT  = 1,
  @empid     AS INT  = 2,
  @orderdate AS DATE = '20120620';

SELECT *
FROM (VALUES(@orderid, @custid, @empid, @orderdate))
      AS SRC( orderid,  custid,  empid,  orderdate);
```

Either way, you defined a table expression based on input variables that together make a single order. The SELECT statement against the table expression returns the following output.

```
orderid     custid      empid       orderdate
----------- ----------- ----------- ----------
1           1           2           2012-06-20
```

The MERGE statement expects a table or table expression as input, and that input table could be based on one of the demonstrated options. For example, the following code implements what some people refer to as upsert logic (update where exists, insert where not exists). The code uses the Sales.MyOrders table as the target table and the table value constructor from the previous example as the source table.

```
DECLARE
  @orderid   AS INT  = 1,
  @custid    AS INT  = 1,
  @empid     AS INT  = 2,
  @orderdate AS DATE = '20120620';

MERGE INTO Sales.MyOrders WITH (HOLDLOCK) AS TGT
USING (VALUES(@orderid, @custid, @empid, @orderdate))
       AS SRC( orderid,  custid,  empid,  orderdate)
  ON SRC.orderid = TGT.orderid
WHEN MATCHED THEN UPDATE
  SET TGT.custid    = SRC.custid,
      TGT.empid     = SRC.empid,
      TGT.orderdate = SRC.orderdate
WHEN NOT MATCHED THEN INSERT
  VALUES(SRC.orderid, SRC.custid, SRC.empid, SRC.orderdate);
```

Observe that the MERGE predicate compares the source order ID with the target order ID. When a match is found (the source order ID is matched by a target order ID), the MERGE statement performs an UPDATE action that updates the values of the nonkey columns in the target to those from the respective source row.

When a match isn't found (the source order ID is not matched by a target order ID), the MERGE statement inserts a new row with the source order information into the target.

***IMPORTANT* AVOIDING MERGE CONFLICTS**

Suppose that a certain key K doesn't yet exist in the target table. Two processes, P1 and P2, run a MERGE statement such as the previous one at the same time with the same source key K. It is normally possible for the MERGE statement issued by P1 to insert a new row with the key K between the points in time when the MERGE statement issued by P2 checks whether the target already has that key and inserts rows. In such a case, the MERGE statement issued by P2 will fail due to a primary key violation. To prevent such a failure, use the hint SERIALIZABLE or HOLDLOCK (both have equivalent meanings) against the target as shown in the previous statement. For details about the serializable isolation level see Chapter 12, "Implementing Transactions, Error Handling, and Dynamic SQL."

Remember that you cleared the Sales.MyOrders table at the beginning of this lesson. So if you run the previous code for the first time, it will perform an INSERT action against the target. If you run it a second time, it will perform an UPDATE action.

TIP MERGE REQUIRES ONLY ONE CLAUSE AT MINIMUM

The MERGE statement doesn't require you to always specify the WHEN MATCHED and WHEN NOT MATCHED clauses; at a minimum, you are required to specify only one clause, and it could be any of the three WHEN clauses. For example, a MERGE statement that specifies only the WHEN MATCHED clause is a standard alternative to an UPDATE statement based on a join, which isn't standard.

Regarding the second run of the code, notice that it's a waste to issue an UPDATE action when the source and target rows are completely identical. An update costs you resources and time, and furthermore, if there are any triggers or auditing activity taking place, they will consider the target row as updated. There is a way to avoid such an update when there's no real value change. Remember that each WHEN clause in the MERGE statement allows an additional predicate that must be true in order for the respective action to be applied. You can add a predicate that says that at least one of the nonkey column values in the source and the target must be different in order to apply the UPDATE action. Your code would look like the following.

```
DECLARE
  @orderid   AS INT  = 1,
  @custid    AS INT  = 1,
  @empid     AS INT  = 2,
  @orderdate AS DATE = '20120620';

MERGE INTO Sales.MyOrders WITH (HOLDLOCK) AS TGT
USING (VALUES(@orderid, @custid, @empid, @orderdate))
       AS SRC( orderid,  custid,  empid,  orderdate)
  ON SRC.orderid = TGT.orderid
WHEN MATCHED AND (   TGT.custid    <> SRC.custid
                  OR TGT.empid     <> SRC.empid
                  OR TGT.orderdate <> SRC.orderdate) THEN UPDATE
  SET TGT.custid    = SRC.custid,
      TGT.empid     = SRC.empid,
      TGT.orderdate = SRC.orderdate
WHEN NOT MATCHED THEN INSERT
  VALUES(SRC.orderid, SRC.custid, SRC.empid, SRC.orderdate);
```

Now the code updates the target row only when the source order ID is equal to the target order ID, and at least one of the other columns have different values in the source and the target. If the source order ID is not found in the target, the statement will insert a new row like before.

IMPORTANT **MERGE PREDICATE AND NULLS**

When checking whether the target column value is different than the source column value, the preceding MERGE statement uses a simple inequality operator (<>). In this example, neither the target nor the source columns can be NULL. But if NULLs are possible in the data, you need to add logic to deal with those, and consider a case when one side is NULL and the other isn't as true. For example, say the custid column allowed NULLs. You would use the following predicate.

```
TGT.custid <> SRC.custid OR (TGT.custid IS NULL AND SRC.custid IS NOT
NULL) OR (TGT.custid IS NOT NULL AND SRC.custid IS NULL).
```

If you execute the previous example now, it should report that 0 rows were affected.

What's interesting about the USING clause where you define the source for the MERGE operation is that it's designed like the FROM clause in a SELECT statement. This means that you can define table operators like JOIN, APPLY, PIVOT, and UNPIVOT; and use table expressions like derived tables, CTEs, views, inline table functions, and even table functions like OPENROWSET and OPENXML. You can refer to real tables, temporary tables, or table variables as the source. Ultimately, the USING clause returns a table result, and that table result is used as the source for the MERGE statement.

T-SQL extends standard SQL by supporting a third clause called WHEN NOT MATCHED BY SOURCE. With this clause, you can define an action to take against the target row when the target row exists but is not matched by a source row. The allowed actions are UPDATE and DELETE. For example, suppose that you want to add such a clause to the last example to indicate that if a target row exists and it is not matched by a source row, you want to delete the target row. Here's how your MERGE statement would look (this time using a table variable with multiple orders as the source).

```
DECLARE @Orders AS TABLE
(
  orderid   INT  NOT NULL PRIMARY KEY,
  custid    INT  NOT NULL,
  empid     INT  NOT NULL,
  orderdate DATE NOT NULL
);

INSERT INTO @Orders(orderid, custid, empid, orderdate) VALUES
  (2, 1, 3, '20120612'),
  (3, 2, 2, '20120612'),
  (4, 3, 5, '20120612');

MERGE INTO Sales.MyOrders AS TGT
USING @Orders AS SRC
  ON SRC.orderid = TGT.orderid
WHEN MATCHED AND (   TGT.custid    <> SRC.custid
                  OR TGT.empid     <> SRC.empid
                  OR TGT.orderdate <> SRC.orderdate) THEN UPDATE
```

```
  SET TGT.custid    = SRC.custid,
      TGT.empid     = SRC.empid,
      TGT.orderdate = SRC.orderdate
WHEN NOT MATCHED THEN INSERT
  VALUES(SRC.orderid, SRC.custid, SRC.empid, SRC.orderdate)
WHEN NOT MATCHED BY SOURCE THEN
  DELETE;
```

Before you ran this statement, only one row in the table had order ID 1. So the statement inserted the three rows with order IDs 2, 3, and 4, and deleted the row that had order ID 1. Query the current state of the table.

```
SELECT *
FROM Sales.MyOrders;
```

You get the following output with the three remaining rows.

```
orderid     custid      empid       orderdate
----------- ----------- ----------- ----------
2           1           3           2012-06-12
3           2           2           2012-06-12
4           3           5           2012-06-12
```

Quick Check

1. What is the purpose of the ON clause in the MERGE statement?
2. What are the possible actions in the WHEN MATCHED clause?
3. How many WHEN MATCHED clauses can a single MERGE statement have?

Quick Check Answer

1. The ON clause determines whether a source row is matched by a target row, and whether a target row is matched by a source row. Based on the result of the predicate, the MERGE statement knows which WHEN clause to activate and as a result, which action to take against the target.
2. UPDATE and DELETE.
3. Two—one with an UPDATE action and one with a DELETE action.

PRACTICE Using the MERGE Statement

In this practice, you exercise your knowledge of the MERGE statement.

If you encounter a problem completing an exercise, you can install the completed projects from the companion content for this chapter and lesson.

EXERCISE 1 Use the MERGE Statement

In this exercise, you use the MERGE statement to merge data from a source table into a target table.

1. Open SSMS and connect to the sample database TSQL2012.
2. Run the following code to create the Sales.MyOrders table.

```
IF OBJECT_ID(N'Sales.MyOrders', N'U') IS NOT NULL DROP TABLE Sales.MyOrders;
IF OBJECT_ID(N'Sales.SeqOrderIDs', N'SO') IS NOT NULL DROP SEQUENCE Sales.SeqOrderIDs;

CREATE SEQUENCE Sales.SeqOrderIDs AS INT
  MINVALUE 1
  CYCLE;

CREATE TABLE Sales.MyOrders
(
  orderid INT NOT NULL
    CONSTRAINT PK_MyOrders_orderid PRIMARY KEY
    CONSTRAINT DFT_MyOrders_orderid
      DEFAULT(NEXT VALUE FOR Sales.SeqOrderIDs),
  custid  INT NOT NULL
    CONSTRAINT CHK_MyOrders_custid CHECK(custid > 0),
  empid   INT NOT NULL
    CONSTRAINT CHK_MyOrders_empid CHECK(empid > 0),
  orderdate DATE NOT NULL
);
```

3. Write a MERGE statement that merges data from the Sales.Orders table into the Sales.MyOrders table. To check whether or not a source row is matched by a target row, compare the source orderid column with the target orderid column. If the source row is matched by a target row, update the nonkey columns in the target with the data from the source row. If the source row isn't matched by a target row, insert a new row with the information from the source. Do not update target rows that are identical to the respective source rows. Implement and execute the following MERGE statement.

```
MERGE INTO Sales.MyOrders AS TGT
USING Sales.Orders AS SRC
  ON  SRC.orderid = TGT.orderid
WHEN MATCHED AND (   TGT.custid    <> SRC.custid
                  OR TGT.empid     <> SRC.empid
                  OR TGT.orderdate <> SRC.orderdate) THEN UPDATE
  SET TGT.custid    = SRC.custid,
      TGT.empid     = SRC.empid,
      TGT.orderdate = SRC.orderdate
WHEN NOT MATCHED THEN INSERT
  VALUES(SRC.orderid, SRC.custid, SRC.empid, SRC.orderdate);
```

Do not drop the Sales.MyOrders table, because you will use it in Exercise 2.

EXERCISE 2 Understand the Role of the ON Clause in a MERGE Statement

In this exercise, you use the MERGE statement and learn about the special role that the ON clause plays. You will realize that unlike in a join table operator, in a MERGE statement the ON clause does not filter rows; instead, it only defines matches and nonmatches, and accordingly, which action to take against the target.

1. Run the following code to populate the Sales.MyOrders table with orders from the Sales.Orders table that were shipped to countries other than Norway.

```
TRUNCATE TABLE Sales.MyOrders;

INSERT INTO Sales.MyOrders(orderid, custid, empid, orderdate)
  SELECT orderid, custid, empid, orderdate
  FROM Sales.Orders
  WHERE shipcountry <> N'Norway';
```

2. Merge orders that were shipped to Norway from the Sales.Orders table into the Sales. MyOrders table. If a source order is matched by a target order and at least one of the nonkey attributes is different, you need to update the target row. If a source row isn't matched by a target row, you need to insert the order into the target table. Remember, merge only orders shipped to Norway. Thinking incorrectly that the ON clause serves a filtering purpose, you might try implementing a MERGE statement with the predicate shipcountry = N'Norway' as part of the ON clause, as follows.

```
MERGE INTO Sales.MyOrders AS TGT
USING Sales.Orders AS SRC
  ON  SRC.orderid = TGT.orderid
  AND shipcountry = N'Norway'
WHEN MATCHED AND (   TGT.custid    <> SRC.custid
                  OR TGT.empid     <> SRC.empid
                  OR TGT.orderdate <> SRC.orderdate) THEN UPDATE
  SET TGT.custid    = SRC.custid,
      TGT.empid     = SRC.empid,
      TGT.orderdate = SRC.orderdate
WHEN NOT MATCHED THEN INSERT
  VALUES(SRC.orderid, SRC.custid, SRC.empid, SRC.orderdate);
```

If you try running this code, you get the following error.

```
Msg 2627, Level 14, State 1, Line 1
Violation of PRIMARY KEY constraint 'PK_MyOrders_orderid'. Cannot insert duplicate
key in object 'Sales.MyOrders'. The duplicate key value is (10248).
The statement has been terminated.
```

Explain the reason for the error.

The reason is that the ON clause doesn't filter rows; it only determines whether a source row is matched by a target or not, and whether a target row is matched by a source row. Based on the outcome of the predicate, the right WHEN clause is activated and the respective action takes place. So in this case, orders shipped to countries other than Norway are simply considered nonmatches; then the WHEN NOT

MATCHED clause is activated, and an INSERT action is applied. Because the target already has the orders that were shipped to countries other than Norway, the attempt to insert those orders fails due to a primary key violation.

3. As one possible solution, filter the relevant rows in a table expression like a CTE or a derived table. This way, the source data consists of only orders shipped to Norway. Implement the following code, which uses a CTE.

```
WITH SRC AS
(
  SELECT *
  FROM Sales.Orders
  WHERE shipcountry = N'Norway'
)
MERGE INTO Sales.MyOrders AS TGT
USING SRC
  ON  SRC.orderid = TGT.orderid
WHEN MATCHED AND (   TGT.custid    <> SRC.custid
                  OR TGT.empid     <> SRC.empid
                  OR TGT.orderdate <> SRC.orderdate) THEN UPDATE
  SET TGT.custid    = SRC.custid,
      TGT.empid     = SRC.empid,
      TGT.orderdate = SRC.orderdate
WHEN NOT MATCHED THEN INSERT
  VALUES(SRC.orderid, SRC.custid, SRC.empid, SRC.orderdate);
```

This should run successfully and report that six rows were affected.

Now implement the same approach by using a derived table as the source, using the following code.

```
MERGE INTO Sales.MyOrders AS TGT
USING ( SELECT *
        FROM Sales.Orders
        WHERE shipcountry = N'Norway' ) AS SRC
  ON  SRC.orderid = TGT.orderid
WHEN MATCHED AND (   TGT.custid    <> SRC.custid
                  OR TGT.empid     <> SRC.empid
                  OR TGT.orderdate <> SRC.orderdate) THEN UPDATE
  SET TGT.custid    = SRC.custid,
      TGT.empid     = SRC.empid,
      TGT.orderdate = SRC.orderdate
WHEN NOT MATCHED THEN INSERT
  VALUES(SRC.orderid, SRC.custid, SRC.empid, SRC.orderdate);
```

Lesson Summary

- With the MERGE statement, you can merge data from a source table or table expression into a target table.
- You specify the target table in the MERGE INTO clause and the source table in the USING clause. The USING clause is designed similar to the FROM clause in a SELECT

statement, meaning that you can use table operators, table expressions, table functions, and so on.

- You specify a MERGE predicate in the ON clause that defines whether a source row is matched by a target row and whether a target row is matched by a source row. Remember that the ON clause is not used to filter data; instead, it is used only to determine matches and nonmatches, and accordingly, to determine which action to take against the target.
- You define different WHEN clauses that determine which action to take against the target depending on the outcome of the predicate. You can define actions to take when a source row is matched by a target row, when a source row is not matched by a target row, and when a target row is not matched by a source row.

Lesson Review

Answer the following questions to test your knowledge of the information in this lesson. You can find the answers to these questions and explanations of why each answer choice is correct or incorrect in the "Answers" section at the end of this chapter.

1. Which WHEN clauses are required in a MERGE statement at minimum?
   - **A.** At minimum, the WHEN MATCHED and WHEN NOT MATCHED clauses are required.
   - **B.** At minimum, only one clause is required, and it can be any of the WHEN clauses.
   - **C.** At minimum, the WHEN MATCHED clause is required.
   - **D.** At minimum, the WHEN NOT MATCHED clause is required.
2. What can you specify as the source data in the USING clause? (Choose all that apply.)
   - **A.** A regular table, table variable, or temporary table
   - **B.** A table expression like a derived table or a CTE
   - **C.** A stored procedure
   - **D.** A table function like OPENROWSET or OPENXML
3. Which clause of the MERGE statement isn't standard?
   - **A.** The WHEN MATCHED clause
   - **B.** The WHEN NOT MATCHED clause
   - **C.** The WHEN NOT MATCHED BY SOURCE clause
   - **D.** All MERGE clauses are standard.

Lesson 3: Using the OUTPUT Option

T-SQL supports an OUTPUT clause for modification statements, which you can use to return information from modified rows. You can use the output for purposes like auditing or archiving. This lesson covers the OUTPUT clause with the different types of modification statements and demonstrates using the clause through examples. The lesson uses the Sales.MyOrders table and Sales.SeqOrderIDs sequence from the previous lessons in the examples of this lesson, so make sure you still have them around.

After this lesson, you will be able to:

- Use the OUTPUT clause in modification statements.
- Return the result of the OUTPUT clause to the caller.
- Use the INTO clause to store the result in a table.
- Describe the special considerations of using the OUTPUT clause in a MERGE statement.
- Filter output rows with composable DML.

Estimated lesson time: 30 minutes

Working with the OUTPUT Clause

The design of the OUTPUT clause is very similar to that of the SELECT clause in the sense that you can specify expressions and assign them with result column aliases. One difference from the SELECT clause is that, in the OUTPUT clause, when you refer to columns from the modified rows, you need to prefix the column names with the keywords *inserted* or *deleted*. Use inserted when the rows are inserted rows and deleted when they are deleted rows. In an UPDATE statement, inserted represents the state of the rows after the update and deleted represents the state before the update.

You can have the OUTPUT clause return a result set back to the caller much like a SELECT does. Or you can add an INTO clause to direct the output rows into a target table. In fact, you can have two OUTPUT clauses if you like—the first with INTO directing the rows into a table, and the second without INTO, returning a result set from the query. If you do use the INTO clause, the target cannot participate in either side of a foreign key relationship and cannot have triggers defined on it.

As mentioned, this lesson uses the Sales.MyOrders table and Sales.SeqOrderIDs sequence from the previous lesson in the examples. Run the following code to clear the table and reset the sequence start value to 1.

```
TRUNCATE TABLE Sales.MyOrders;
ALTER SEQUENCE Sales.SeqOrderIDs RESTART WITH 1;
```

If the table and sequence don't exist in the database, use the following code to create them.

```
IF OBJECT_ID(N'Sales.MyOrders', N'U') IS NOT NULL DROP TABLE Sales.MyOrders;
IF OBJECT_ID(N'Sales.SeqOrderIDs', N'SO') IS NOT NULL DROP SEQUENCE Sales.SeqOrderIDs;

CREATE SEQUENCE Sales.SeqOrderIDs AS INT
  MINVALUE 1
  CYCLE;

CREATE TABLE Sales.MyOrders
(
  orderid INT NOT NULL
    CONSTRAINT PK_MyOrders_orderid PRIMARY KEY
    CONSTRAINT DFT_MyOrders_orderid
      DEFAULT(NEXT VALUE FOR Sales.SeqOrderIDs),
  custid  INT NOT NULL
    CONSTRAINT CHK_MyOrders_custid CHECK(custid > 0),
  empid   INT NOT NULL
    CONSTRAINT CHK_MyOrders_empid CHECK(empid > 0),
  orderdate DATE NOT NULL
);
```

INSERT with OUTPUT

The OUTPUT clause can be used in an INSERT statement to return information from the inserted rows. An example for a very practical use case is when you have a multirow INSERT statement that generates new keys by using the IDENTITY property or a sequence, and you need to know which new keys were generated.

For example, suppose that you need to query the Sales.Orders table and insert orders shipped to Norway to the Sales.MyOrders table. You are not going to use the original order IDs in the target rows; instead, let the sequence object generate those for you. But you need to get back information from the INSERT statement about which order IDs were generated, in addition to additional columns from the inserted rows. To achieve this, simply add an OUTPUT clause to the INSERT statement right before the query. List the columns that you need to return from the inserted rows and prefix them with the keyword inserted, as follows.

```
INSERT INTO Sales.MyOrders(custid, empid, orderdate)
  OUTPUT
    inserted.orderid, inserted.custid, inserted.empid, inserted.orderdate
  SELECT custid, empid, orderdate
  FROM Sales.Orders
  WHERE shipcountry = N'Norway';
```

This code generates the following output.

```
orderid     custid      empid       orderdate
----------- ----------- ----------- ----------
1           70          1           2006-12-18
2           70          7           2007-04-29
3           70          7           2007-08-20
4           70          3           2008-01-14
5           70          1           2008-02-26
6           70          2           2008-04-10
```

You can see that the sequence object generated the order IDs 1 through 6 for the new rows. If you need to store the result in a table instead of returning it back to the caller, add an INTO clause with the target table name, as follows.

```
INSERT INTO Sales.MyOrders(custid, empid, orderdate)
  OUTPUT
    inserted.orderid, inserted.custid, inserted.empid, inserted.orderdate
    INTO SomeTable(orderid, custid, empid, orderdate)
  SELECT custid, empid, orderdate
  FROM Sales.Orders
  WHERE shipcountry = N'Norway';
```

Don't run this code; the table SomeTable doesn't exist in the database—it is just an example.

As mentioned, if you use the INTO clause, the target table cannot participate in either side of a foreign key relationship and cannot have triggers defined on it.

DELETE with OUTPUT

You can use the OUTPUT clause to return information from deleted rows in a DELETE statement. You need to prefix the columns that you refer to with the keyword deleted.

The following example deletes the rows from the Sales.MyOrders table where the employee ID is equal to 1. Using the OUTPUT clause, the code returns the order IDs of the deleted orders.

```
DELETE FROM Sales.MyOrders
  OUTPUT deleted.orderid
WHERE empid = 1;
```

This code generates the following output.

```
orderid
-----------
1
5
```

Remember that if you need to persist the output rows in a table—for example, for archiving purposes—you can add an INTO clause with the target table name.

UPDATE with OUTPUT

You can use the OUTPUT clause to return information from modified rows in an UPDATE statement. With updated rows, you have access to both the old and the new images of the modified rows. To refer to columns from the original state of the row before the update, prefix the column names with the keyword deleted. To refer to columns from the new state of the row after the update, prefix the column names with the keyword inserted.

As an example, the following UPDATE statement adds a day to the order date of all orders that were handled by employee 7.

```
UPDATE Sales.MyOrders
  SET orderdate = DATEADD(day, 1, orderdate)
  OUTPUT
    inserted.orderid,
    deleted.orderdate AS old_orderdate,
    inserted.orderdate AS neworderdate
WHERE empid = 7;
```

The code uses the OUTPUT clause to return the order IDs of the modified rows, in addition to the order dates—both before and after the update. This code generates the following output.

```
orderid     old_orderdate neworderdate
----------- ------------- ------------
2           2007-04-29    2007-04-30
3           2007-08-20    2007-08-21
```

MERGE with OUTPUT

You can use the OUTPUT clause with the MERGE statement, but there are special considerations with this statement. Remember that one MERGE statement can apply different actions against the target table. And suppose that when returning output rows, you need to know which action (INSERT, UPDATE, or DELETE) affected the output row. For this purpose, SQL Server provides you with the $action function. This function returns a string ('INSERT', 'UPDATE', or 'DELETE') indicating the action.

As explained before, you can refer to columns from the deleted rows with the deleted prefix and to columns from the inserted rows with the inserted prefix. Rows affected by an INSERT action have values in the inserted row and NULLs in the deleted row. Rows affected by a DELETE action have NULLs in the inserted row and values in the deleted row. Rows affected by an UPDATE action have values in both. So, for example, if you want to return the key of the affected row (assuming the key itself wasn't modified), you can use the expression COALESCE(inserted.orderid, deleted.orderid).

The following example demonstrates the use of the MERGE statement with the OUTPUT clause, returning the output of the $action function to indicate which action affected the row, and the key of the modified row.

```
MERGE INTO Sales.MyOrders AS TGT
USING (VALUES(1,         70,      1,        '20061218'),
             (2,         70,      7,        '20070429'),
             (3,         70,      7,        '20070820'),
             (4,         70,      3,        '20080114'),
             (5,         70,      1,        '20080226'),
             (6,         70,      2,        '20080410'))
       AS SRC(orderid,  custid,  empid,  orderdate )
  ON SRC.orderid = TGT.orderid
WHEN MATCHED AND (   TGT.custid    <> SRC.custid
                  OR TGT.empid     <> SRC.empid
                  OR TGT.orderdate <> SRC.orderdate) THEN UPDATE
  SET TGT.custid    = SRC.custid,
      TGT.empid     = SRC.empid,
      TGT.orderdate = SRC.orderdate
WHEN NOT MATCHED THEN INSERT
  VALUES(SRC.orderid, SRC.custid, SRC.empid, SRC.orderdate)
WHEN NOT MATCHED BY SOURCE THEN
  DELETE
OUTPUT
  $action AS the_action,
  COALESCE(inserted.orderid, deleted.orderid) AS orderid;
```

This code generates the following output.

```
the_action orderid
---------- -----------
INSERT     1
INSERT     5
UPDATE     2
UPDATE     3
```

The output shows that two rows were inserted and two were updated.

TIP **MERGE AND OUTPUT**

In INSERT, UPDATE, and DELETE statements, you can only refer to columns from the target table in the OUTPUT clause. In a MERGE statement you can refer to columns from both the target and the source.

At this point, run the following code to clear the Sales.MyOrders table.

```
TRUNCATE TABLE Sales.MyOrders;
```

Composable DML

Suppose you need to capture output from a modification statement, but you are interested only in a subset of the output rows and not all of them. T-SQL has a solution for this in the form of what some platforms refer to as *composable DML* (data manipulation language).

With T-SQL, you can define something that looks like a derived table based on a modification with an OUTPUT clause. Then you can have an outer INSERT SELECT statement against a target table, with the source table being this special derived table. The outer INSERT SELECT can have a WHERE clause that filters the output rows from the derived table, inserting only the rows that satisfy the search condition into the target. The outer INSERT SELECT statement cannot have other elements besides WHERE like table operators, GROUP BY, HAVING, and so on.

As an example of *composable DML*, consider the previous MERGE statement. Suppose that you need to capture only the rows affected by an INSERT action in a table variable for further processing. You can achieve this by using the following code.

```
DECLARE @InsertedOrders AS TABLE
(
  orderid   INT  NOT NULL PRIMARY KEY,
  custid    INT  NOT NULL,
  empid     INT  NOT NULL,
  orderdate DATE NOT NULL
);

INSERT INTO @InsertedOrders(orderid, custid, empid, orderdate)
  SELECT orderid, custid, empid, orderdate
  FROM (MERGE INTO Sales.MyOrders AS TGT
        USING (VALUES(1,         70,      1,       '20061218'),
                     (2,         70,      7,       '20070429'),
                     (3,         70,      7,       '20070820'),
                     (4,         70,      3,       '20080114'),
                     (5,         70,      1,       '20080226'),
                     (6,         70,      2,       '20080410'))
               AS SRC(orderid,  custid,  empid,  orderdate )
          ON SRC.orderid = TGT.orderid
        WHEN MATCHED AND (   TGT.custid    <> SRC.custid
                          OR TGT.empid     <> SRC.empid
                          OR TGT.orderdate <> SRC.orderdate) THEN UPDATE
          SET TGT.custid    = SRC.custid,
              TGT.empid     = SRC.empid,
              TGT.orderdate = SRC.orderdate
        WHEN NOT MATCHED THEN INSERT
          VALUES(SRC.orderid, SRC.custid, SRC.empid, SRC.orderdate)
        WHEN NOT MATCHED BY SOURCE THEN
          DELETE
        OUTPUT
          $action AS the_action, inserted.*) AS D
  WHERE the_action = 'INSERT';

SELECT *
FROM @InsertedOrders;
```

Notice the derived table D that is defined based on the MERGE statement with the OUTPUT clause. The OUTPUT clause returns, among other things, the result of the $action function, naming the target column the_action. The code uses an INSERT SELECT statement with the source being the derived table D and the target table being the table variable @InsertedOrders. The WHERE clause in the outer query filters only the rows that have the INSERT action.

When you run the previous code for the first time, you get the following output.

```
orderid     custid      empid       orderdate
----------- ----------- ----------- ----------
1           70          1           2006-12-18
2           70          7           2007-04-29
3           70          7           2007-08-20
4           70          3           2008-01-14
5           70          1           2008-02-26
6           70          2           2008-04-10
```

Run it for the second time. It should return an empty set this time.

```
orderid     custid      empid       orderdate
----------- ----------- ----------- ----------
```

When you're done, run the following code for cleanup.

```
IF OBJECT_ID(N'Sales.MyOrders', N'U') IS NOT NULL DROP TABLE Sales.MyOrders;
IF OBJECT_ID(N'Sales.SeqOrderIDs', N'SO') IS NOT NULL DROP SEQUENCE Sales.SeqOrderIDs;
```

Quick Check

1. **How many OUTPUT clauses can a single statement have?**
2. **How do you determine which action affected the OUTPUT row in a MERGE statement?**

Quick Check Answer

1. **Two—one with INTO and one without INTO.**
2. **Use the $action function.**

PRACTICE Using the OUTPUT Clause

In this practice, you exercise your knowledge of the OUTPUT clause.

If you encounter a problem completing an exercise, you can install the completed projects from the companion content for this chapter and lesson.

EXERCISE 1 Use OUTPUT in an UPDATE Statement

In this exercise, you use the OUTPUT clause in an UPDATE statement and compare columns before and after the change.

1. Open SSMS and connect to the sample database TSQL2012.
2. You need to apply an update to products in category 1 that are supplied by supplier 16. You first issue the following query against the Production.Products table to examine the products that you're about to update.

```
SELECT productid, productname, unitprice
FROM Production.Products
WHERE categoryid = 1
  AND supplierid = 16;
```

   You get the following output.

```
productid  productname    unitprice
---------- -------------- ----------
34         Product SWNJY  14.00
35         Product NEVTJ  18.00
67         Product XLXQF  14.00
```

3. Write an UPDATE statement that modifies the products in category 1 that are supplied by supplier 16, increasing their unit prices by 2.5. Include an OUTPUT clause that returns the product ID, product name, old price, new price, and percent difference between the new and old prices. Your UPDATE statement should look like the following.

```
UPDATE Production.Products
  SET unitprice += 2.5
  OUTPUT
    inserted.productid,
    inserted.productname,
    deleted.unitprice AS oldprice,
    inserted.unitprice AS newprice,
    CAST(100.0 * (inserted.unitprice - deleted.unitprice)
                 / deleted.unitprice AS NUMERIC(5, 2)) AS pct
WHERE categoryid = 1
  AND supplierid = 16;
```

   This statement generates the following output with the requested information.

```
productid  productname    oldprice  newprice  pct
---------- -------------- --------- --------- ------
34         Product SWNJY  14.00     16.50     17.86
35         Product NEVTJ  18.00     20.50     13.89
67         Product XLXQF  14.00     16.50     17.86
```

4. To get back to the original values, write an inverse UPDATE statement, reducing the unit prices by 2.5. Include the same output information as in the previous statement. Your code should look like the following.

```
UPDATE Production.Products
  SET unitprice -= 2.5
  OUTPUT
    inserted.productid,
    inserted.productname,
    deleted.unitprice AS oldprice,
    inserted.unitprice AS newprice,
    CAST(100.0 * (inserted.unitprice - deleted.unitprice)
                 / deleted.unitprice AS NUMERIC(5, 2)) AS pct
WHERE categoryid = 1
  AND supplierid = 16;
```

This statement generates the following output.

```
productid  productname    oldprice  newprice  pct
---------- -------------- --------- --------- ------
34         Product SWNJY  16.50     14.00     -15.15
35         Product NEVTJ  20.50     18.00     -12.20
67         Product XLXQF  16.50     14.00     -15.15
```

EXERCISE 2 Use Composable DML

In this exercise, you use composable DML. You delete rows from a table and archive in another table a subset of the deleted rows.

1. Create the tables and sample for this exercise by running the following code.

```
IF OBJECT_ID(N'Sales.MyOrdersArchive', N'U') IS NOT NULL
  DROP TABLE Sales.MyOrdersArchive;
IF OBJECT_ID(N'Sales.MyOrders', N'U') IS NOT NULL
  DROP TABLE Sales.MyOrders;

CREATE TABLE Sales.MyOrders
(
  orderid INT NOT NULL
    CONSTRAINT PK_MyOrders PRIMARY KEY,
  custid  INT NOT NULL,
  empid   INT NOT NULL,
  orderdate DATE NOT NULL
);

INSERT INTO Sales.MyOrders(orderid, custid, empid, orderdate)
  SELECT orderid, custid, empid, orderdate
  FROM Sales.Orders;
```

```
CREATE TABLE Sales.MyOrdersArchive
(
  orderid INT NOT NULL
    CONSTRAINT PK_MyOrdersArchive PRIMARY KEY,
  custid  INT NOT NULL,
  empid   INT NOT NULL,
  orderdate DATE NOT NULL
);
```

2. Write a statement against the Sales.MyOrders table that deletes orders placed before the year 2007. Use composable DML to archive deleted orders that were placed by the customers that have IDs of 17 and 19. Implement and execute the following statement.

```
INSERT INTO Sales.MyOrdersArchive(orderid, custid, empid, orderdate)
  SELECT orderid, custid, empid, orderdate
  FROM (DELETE FROM Sales.MyOrders
          OUTPUT deleted.*
        WHERE orderdate < '20070101') AS D
  WHERE custid IN (17, 19);
```

3. Query the Sales.MyOrdersArchive table to see which rows got archived.

```
SELECT *
FROM Sales.MyOrdersArchive;
```

You get the following output.

```
orderid     custid      empid       orderdate
----------- ----------- ----------- ----------
10363       17          4           2006-11-26
10364       19          1           2006-11-26
10391       17          3           2006-12-23
```

4. When you're done, run the following code for cleanup.

```
IF OBJECT_ID(N'Sales.MyOrdersArchive', N'U') IS NOT NULL
  DROP TABLE Sales.MyOrdersArchive;
IF OBJECT_ID(N'Sales.MyOrders', N'U') IS NOT NULL
  DROP TABLE Sales.MyOrders;
```

Lesson Summary

- With the OUTPUT clause, you can return information from modified rows in modification statements.
- The OUTPUT clause is designed like the SELECT clause, allowing you to form expressions and assign the result columns with column aliases.
- The result of the OUTPUT clause can be sent back to the caller as a result set from a query or stored in a target table by using the INTO clause.

- When you refer to columns from the modified rows, you prefix the column names with the keyword inserted for inserted rows and deleted for deleted rows.
- In a MERGE statement, you can use the $action function to return a string that represents the action that affected the target row.
- Use the composable DML feature to filter output rows that you want to store in a target table.

Lesson Review

Answer the following questions to test your knowledge of the information in this lesson. You can find the answers to these questions and explanations of why each answer choice is correct or incorrect in the "Answers" section at the end of this chapter.

1. When referring in the OUTPUT clause to columns from the inserted rows, when should you prefix the columns with the keyword inserted?
   - **A.** Always
   - **B.** Never
   - **C.** Only when the statement is UPDATE
   - **D.** Only when the statement is MERGE
2. What is the restriction in regard to the table specified as the target of an OUTPUT INTO clause? (Choose all that apply.)
   - **A.** The table can only be a table variable.
   - **B.** The table can only be a temporary table.
   - **C.** The table cannot participate in either side of a foreign key relationship.
   - **D.** The table cannot have triggers defined on it.
3. Which of the following is only possible when using the MERGE statement in regard to the OUTPUT clause?
   - **A.** Referring to columns from the source table
   - **B.** Referring to both the keywords deleted and inserted
   - **C.** Assigning aliases to output columns
   - **D.** Using composable DML

Case Scenarios

In the following case scenarios, you apply what you've learned about the data modification aspects that were covered in this chapter. You can find the answers to these questions in the "Answers" section at the end of this chapter.

Case Scenario 1: Providing an Improved Solution for Generating Keys

You're a member of the database administrator (DBA) group in a company that manufactures hiking gear. Most tables in the company's OLTP database currently use an IDENTITY property but require more flexibility. For example, often the application needs to generate the new key before using it. Sometimes the application needs to update the key column, overwriting it with new values. Also, the application needs to produce keys that do not conflict across multiple tables.

1. Suggest an alternative to using the IDENTITY column property.
2. Explain how the alternative solution solves the existing problems.

Case Scenario 2: Improving Modifications

You work in the database group of a company that has recently upgraded the database from SQL Server 2000 to SQL Server 2005 and then to SQL Server 2012. The code is still SQL Server 2000–compatible. There are issues with modifications submitted by the application to the database.

The application uses a procedure that accepts as inputs attributes of a row. The procedure then uses logic that checks whether the key already exists in the target table, and if it does, updates the target row. If it doesn't, the procedure inserts a new row into the target. The problem is that occasionally the procedure fails due to a primary key violation. This happens when the existence check doesn't find a row, but between that check and the insertion, someone else managed to insert a new row with the same key.

The application has a monthly process that archives data that it needs to purge. Currently, the application first copies data that needs to be deleted to the archive table in one statement and then deletes those rows in another statement. Both statements use a filter that is based on a date column called dt. You need to filter the rows where dt is earlier than a certain date. The problem is that sometimes rows representing late arrivals are inserted into the table between the copying and the deletion of rows, and the deletion process ends up deleting rows that were not archived.

You are tasked with finding solutions to the existing problems.

1. Can you suggest a solution to the existing problem with the procedure that updates the row when the source key exists in the target and inserts a row if it doesn't?
2. Can you suggest a solution to the problem with the archiving process that prevents deleting rows that were not archived?

Suggested Practices

To help you successfully master the exam objectives presented in this chapter, complete the following tasks.

Compare Old and New Features

In the following suggested practices you will test how much you remember from what you've read in this chapter. Try to implement the suggested practices only from your memory. Only after completing the task, go over the chapter's text to see if you missed anything.

- **Practice 1** Form a list of the advantages of the sequence object compared to the IDENTITY column property.
- **Practice 2** Form a list of the advantages of the MERGE statement compared to using separate statements for the different cases (WHEN MATCHED, WHEN NOT MATCHED, WHEN NOT MATCHED BY SOURCE).
- **Practice 3** Form a list of the advantages of the OUTPUT clause over techniques that do not make use of the OUTPUT clause to achieve similar results. Use auditing and archiving as the example tasks.

Answers

This section contains the answers to the lesson review questions and solutions to the case scenarios in this chapter.

Lesson 1

1. **Correct Answer: D**
   - **A. Incorrect:** The maximum value in the table is not necessarily the last identity value generated.
   - **B. Incorrect:** The SCOPE_IDENTITY function is not table specific; it's session specific and scope specific.
   - **C. Incorrect:** The @@IDENTITY function is not table specific; it's session specific.
   - **D. Correct:** The IDENT_CURRENT function accepts a table name as input and returns the last identity value generated in that table.
2. **Correct Answers: B, C, and D**
   - **A. Incorrect:** Both do not guarantee there won't be gaps.
   - **B. Correct:** One of the advantages of using a sequence object instead of IDENTITY is that you can attach a DEFAULT constraint that has a call to the NEXT VALUE FOR function to an existing column, or remove such a constraint from a column.
   - **C. Correct:** You can generate a new sequence value before using it by assigning the value to a variable and later using the variable in an INSERT statement. This cannot be done with IDENTITY.
   - **D. Correct:** You can specify your own value for a column that has an IDENTITY property, but this requires turning on the session option IDENTITY_INSERT, which in turn requires special permissions. The sequence object is more flexible. You can insert your own values into a column that normally gets its value from a sequence object. And that's without needing to turn on any special options and without needing special permissions.
3. **Correct Answer: A**
   - **A. Correct:** Using the OVER clause, you can control the order of assignment of sequence values in an INSERT SELECT statement.
   - **B. Incorrect:** Adding an ORDER BY clause at the end of a query is not an assurance that sequence values will be generated in the same order.
   - **C. Incorrect:** Using a TOP option with an ORDER BY clause is not an assurance that sequence values will be generated in the same order.
   - **D. Incorrect:** Using a TOP option with an ORDER BY clause is not an assurance that sequence values will be generated in the same order.

Lesson 2

1. **Correct Answer: B**
   - **A. Incorrect:** Only one clause is required at minimum.
   - **B. Correct:** Only one clause is required at minimum, and it can be any of the WHEN clauses.
   - **C. Incorrect:** There's no specific WHEN clause that is required; instead, any one clause at minimum is required.
   - **D. Incorrect:** There's no specific WHEN clause that is required; instead, any one clause at minimum is required.
2. **Correct Answers: A, B, and D**
   - **A. Correct:** Tables, table variables, and temporary tables are allowed.
   - **B. Correct:** Table expressions are allowed.
   - **C. Incorrect:** Stored procedures aren't allowed as the source in a MERGE statement.
   - **D. Correct:** Table functions are allowed.
3. **Correct Answer: C**
   - **A. Incorrect:** The WHEN MATCHED clause is standard.
   - **B. Incorrect:** The WHEN NOT MATCHED clause is standard.
   - **C. Correct:** The WHEN NOT MATCHED BY SOURCE clause isn't standard.
   - **D. Incorrect:** The WHEN NOT MATCHED BY SOURCE clause isn't standard.

Lesson 3

1. **Correct Answer: A**
   - **A. Correct:** When referring to elements from inserted rows, you must always prefix the column with the keyword inserted.
   - **B. Incorrect:** There are no cases where you can omit the keyword inserted—even if the statement is just an INSERT.
   - **C. Incorrect:** It's true that you need to prefix inserted elements in an UPDATE statement with the keyword inserted, but not just in an UPDATE statement.
   - **D. Incorrect:** It's true that you need to prefix inserted elements in a MERGE statement with the keyword inserted, but not just in a MERGE statement.
2. **Correct Answers: C and D**
   - **A. Incorrect:** Other table types are also supported.
   - **B. Incorrect:** Other table types are also supported.
   - **C. Correct:** The target table cannot take part in a foreign key relationship.
   - **D. Correct:** The target table cannot have triggers defined on it.

3. **Correct Answer: A**

   A. **Correct:** Only in a MERGE statement's OUTPUT clause can you refer to elements from the source table.

   B. **Incorrect:** This can be done in an UPDATE statement too.

   C. **Incorrect:** Aliasing of target columns in the OUTPUT clause is allowed in all statements.

   D. **Incorrect:** Composable DML supports all statements.

Case Scenario 1

1. You can address all of the existing problems with the IDENTITY property by using the sequence object instead.
2. With the sequence object, you can generate values before using them by invoking the NEXT VALUE FOR function and storing the result in a variable. Unlike with the IDENTITY property, you can update a column that normally gets its values from a sequence object. Also, because a sequence object is not tied to a specific column in a specific table, but instead is an independent object in the database, you can generate values from one sequence and use them in different tables.

Case Scenario 2

1. A recommended solution is to use the MERGE statement. Define the source for the MERGE statement as a derived table based on the VALUES clause, with a row made of the input parameters for the procedure. Specify the table hint HOLDLOCK or SERIALIZABLE against the target to prevent conflicts such as the ones that currently exist in the system. Then use the WHEN MATCHED clause to issue an UPDATE action if the target row exists, and the WHEN NOT MATCHED clause to issue an INSERT action if the target row doesn't exist.
2. One option is to work with the SERIALIZABLE isolation level, handling both the statement that copies the rows to the archive environment and the statement that deletes the rows in one transaction. But a simpler solution is to do both tasks in one statement—a DELETE with an OUTPUT INTO clause. This ensures that only rows that are copied to the archive table are deleted. And if for whatever reason the copying of the rows to the archive table fails, the delete operation also fails, because both activities are part of the same transaction.

CHAPTER 12

Implementing Transactions, Error Handling, and Dynamic SQL

Exam objectives in this chapter:

- Work with Data
  - Query data by using SELECT statements.
- Troubleshoot & Optimize
  - Optimize queries.
  - Manage transactions.
  - Implement error handling.

Microsoft SQL Server is a relational database that strictly enforces transactional behavior on database changes in order to protect data integrity. This chapter presents the T-SQL code behind transactions, and extends that code to handling errors and using dynamic SQL.

Lessons in this chapter:

- Lesson 1: Managing Transactions and Concurrency
- Lesson 2: Implementing Error Handling
- Lesson 3: Using Dynamic SQL

Before You Begin

To complete the lessons in this chapter, you must have:

- An understanding of basic database concepts.
- Experience working with SQL Server Management Studio (SSMS).
- Some experience writing T-SQL code.
- Access to a SQL Server 2012 instance with the sample database TSQL2012 installed.

Lesson 1: Managing Transactions and Concurrency

The SQL Server 2012 relational database management system (RDBMS) maintains transactional control over all changes to database data. The strict adherence to transactional control in SQL Server ensures that the integrity of database data will never be compromised by partially completed transactions, constraint violations, interference from other transactions, or service interruptions.

After this lesson, you will be able to:

- Define the ACID properties of transactions.
- Describe and set SQL Server 2012 transaction modes and types.
- Describe lock modes, blocking, and deadlocking.
- Describe and set transaction isolation levels.
- Describe efficient transaction coding guidelines.

Estimated lesson time: 50 minutes

Understanding Transactions

A *transaction* is a logical unit of work. Either all the work completes as a whole unit, or none of it does. Transactions are common in our daily lives. For example, purchasing something is commonly considered a transaction. When you pay money for something but don't receive the object, the transaction is stopped and you expect to receive your money back. Paying with your money and receiving what you purchased form a logical unit of work. Either both steps succeed together, or both steps must fail together.

For SQL Server, all changes to database data take place in the context of a transaction. In other words, all operations that in any way write to the database are treated by SQL Server as transactions. This includes:

- All data manipulation language (DML) statements such as INSERT, UPDATE, and DELETE.
- All data definition language (DDL) statements such as CREATE TABLE and CREATE INDEX.

Technically, even single SELECT statements are a type of transaction in SQL Server; these are called read-only transactions. Because these are not part of DML and DDL transactions, they won't be covered in this book. For information about read-only transactions, see the topic "sys.dm_tran_database_transactions" in Books Online for SQL Server 2012 at *http://msdn.microsoft.com/en-us/library/ms186957(v=sql.110).aspx.*

The terms *commit* and *rollback* are used in this book to refer to the act of controlling the result of transactions in SQL Server. When the work of a transaction has been approved by the user, SQL Server completes the transaction's changes by committing them. If an unrecoverable error occurs or the user decides not to commit, then the transaction is rolled back.

ACID Properties of Transactions

In relational databases, the ACID acronym is used to describe the properties of transactions. The ACID properties are:

- **Atomicity** Every transaction is an atomic unit of work, meaning that all database changes in the transaction succeed or none of them succeed.
- **Consistency** Every transaction, whether successful or not, leaves the database in a consistent state as defined by all object and database constraints. If an inconsistent state results, SQL Server will roll back the transaction to maintain a consistent state.
- **Isolation** Every transaction looks as though it occurs in isolation from other transactions in regard to database changes. The degree of isolation can vary based on isolation level.
- **Durability** Every transaction endures through an interruption of service. When service is restored, all committed transactions are rolled forward (committed changes to the database are completed) and all uncommitted transactions are rolled back (uncommitted changes are removed).

SQL Server ensures all these ACID properties through a variety of mechanisms. To maintain atomicity, SQL Server treats every data DML or DDL command individually and will not allow any command to only partially succeed. Consider, for example, an UPDATE statement that would update 500 rows in a table at the point in time that the transaction begins. The command will not finish until exactly all those 500 rows are updated. If something prevents that command from updating all 500 rows, SQL Server will abort the command and roll back the transaction.

If more than one command is present in a transaction, SQL Server will normally not allow the entire transaction to be committed unless both statements succeed. (If XACT_ABORT is OFF, which is the default, you can insert code to decide whether to roll back the transaction or commit it. See the sections on TRY/CATCH and XACT_ABORT later in this lesson for more information.)

For consistency, SQL Server ensures that all constraints in the database are enforced. If your transaction attempts to insert a row that has an invalid foreign key, for example, then SQL Server will detect that a constraint would be violated, and generate an error message. You can add logic to decide whether or not to roll back the transaction.

To enforce transactional isolation, SQL Server ensures that when a transaction makes multiple changes to the database, none of the objects being changed by that transaction are allowed to be changed by any other transactions. In other words, one transaction's changes are isolated from any other transaction activities. If two transactions want to change the same data, one of them must wait until the other transaction is finished.

SQL Server accomplishes transactional isolation by means of locking as well as row versioning. SQL Server locks objects (for example, rows and tables) to prevent other transactions from interfering with that transaction's activity. (Locking is covered later in this lesson.)

Isolation can vary considerably based on how much isolation is provided for a transaction when it reads data. This variation is provided by setting isolation levels (described later in this lesson).

SQL Server maintains transactional durability by using the database transaction log. Every database change (data modification statement or DDL statement) is first written to the transaction log, with the original version of the data (in the case of updates and deletes). When a transaction is committed and all consistency checks pass, the fact that the transaction has been successfully committed is written to the transaction log. For example, if the database server shuts down unexpectedly just after the fact of successful commit has been written to the transaction log, when SQL Server starts up the database, the transaction will be rolled forward and any unwritten changes to the database will be finished.

On the other hand, if the database server shuts down unexpectedly before the fact of successful commit could be written to the log, when SQL Server starts up the database, the transaction will be rolled back and any database changes undone.

In SQL Server, every database, including every system database, has a transaction log to enforce transaction durability. You cannot turn off a database's transaction log or remove it. Although some operations can somewhat reduce transaction logging, all database changes are always written first to the transaction log.

MORE INFO **SQL SERVER AND TRANSACTION DURABILITY**

For detailed information about how the transaction log implements durability, see the Books Online for SQL Server 2008 R2 article "Write-Ahead Transaction Log" at *http://msdn.microsoft.com/en-us/library/ms186259(SQL.105).aspx*.

Quick Check

1. **Why is it important for SQL Server to maintain the ACID quality of transactions?**
2. **How does SQL Server implement transaction durability?**

Quick Check Answer

1. **To ensure that the integrity of database data will not be compromised.**
2. **By first writing all changes to the database transaction log before making changes to the database data.**

Types of Transactions

SQL Server has two basic types of transactions:

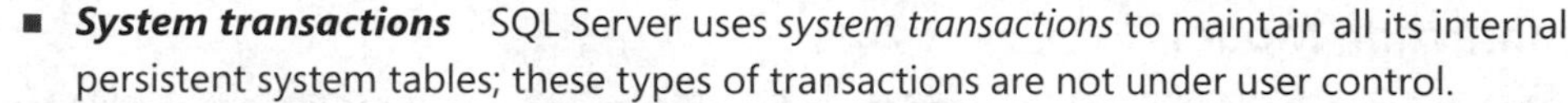

- ***System transactions*** SQL Server uses *system transactions* to maintain all its internal persistent system tables; these types of transactions are not under user control.

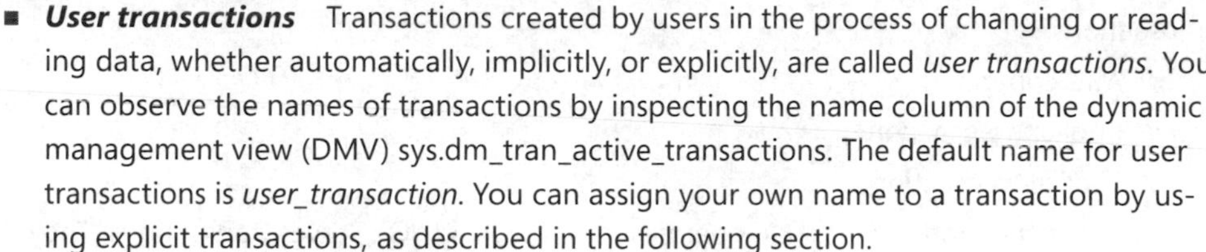

- ***User transactions*** Transactions created by users in the process of changing or reading data, whether automatically, implicitly, or explicitly, are called *user transactions*. You can observe the names of transactions by inspecting the name column of the dynamic management view (DMV) sys.dm_tran_active_transactions. The default name for user transactions is *user_transaction*. You can assign your own name to a transaction by using explicit transactions, as described in the following section.

The remainder of this lesson deals only with user transactions, not system transactions.

Transaction Commands

The commands described in this section govern what code is included in an explicit transaction and how the transaction behaves.

Every transaction consists of a T-SQL BEGIN TRANSACTION statement, which marks the start of the transaction in your code. The actual command can also be written as BEGIN TRAN. A name can be assigned to the transaction.

You must end the transaction at some point by committing it or rolling it back. To commit a transaction, issue the COMMIT TRANSACTION command, which you can also write as COMMIT TRAN, COMMIT WORK, or just COMMIT. To roll back a transaction, issue the ROLLBACK TRANSACTION command, or alternatively, ROLLBACK TRAN, ROLLBACK WORK, or just ROLLBACK.

Transactions can be nested—that is, you can place transactions within transactions, and they can span across batches of T-SQL code.

Transaction Levels and States

You can detect the transaction level or state by using two system functions:

- @@TRANCOUNT can be queried to find the level of transaction.
  - A level of 0 indicates that at this point, the code is not within a transaction.
  - A level > 0 indicates that there is an active transaction, and a number > 1 indicates the nesting level of nested transactions.
- XACT_STATE() can be queried to find the state of the transaction.
  - A state of 0 indicates that there is no active transaction.
  - A state of 1 indicates that there is an uncommitted transaction, and it can be committed, but the nesting level is not reported.
  - A state of -1 indicates that there is an uncommitted transaction, but it cannot be committed due to a prior fatal error.

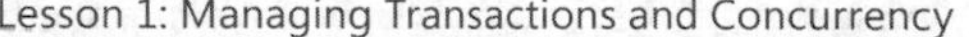

These two functions complement each other: @@TRANCOUNT does not report uncommittable transactions and XACT_STATE() does not report the transaction nesting level.

Transaction Modes

There are three *modes* for user transactions in SQL Server—that is, three ways of working with transactions:

- Autocommit
- Implicit transaction
- Explicit transaction

These are the modes your code operates in when using SQL Server transactions. They do not change transaction behavior.

AUTOCOMMIT MODE

In the autocommit mode, single data modification and DDL T-SQL statements are executed in the context of a transaction that will be automatically committed when the statement succeeds, or automatically rolled back if the statement fails.

The *autocommit mode* is the default transaction management mode. The simple state diagram in Figure 12-1 illustrates the autocommit mode.

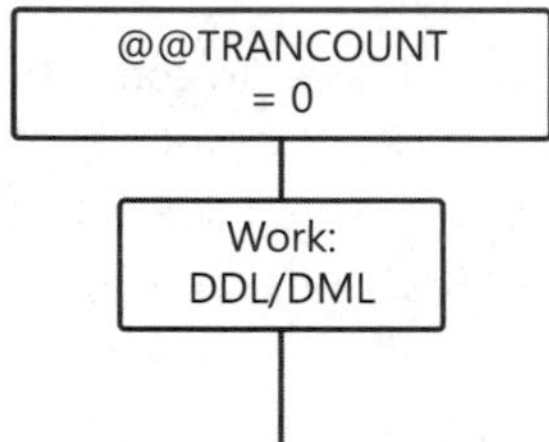

FIGURE 12-1 A transaction in autocommit mode with no COMMIT required.

In the autocommit mode, you do not issue any surrounding transactional commands such as BEGIN TRAN, ROLLBACK TRAN, or COMMIT TRAN. Further, the @@TRANCOUNT value (for the user session) is not normally detectable for that command, though it would be in a data modification statement trigger. Whatever changes you make to the database are automatically handled, statement by statement, as transactions. Remember, autocommit is the default operation of SQL Server.

IMPLICIT TRANSACTION MODE

In the *implicit transaction mode*, when you issue one or more DML or DDL statements, or a SELECT statement, SQL Server starts a transaction, increments @@TRANCOUNT, but does not automatically commit or roll back the statement. You must issue a COMMIT or ROLLBACK interactively to finish the transaction, even if all you issued was a SELECT statement.

Implicit transaction mode is not the SQL Server default. You enter that mode by issuing the following command.

```
SET IMPLICIT_TRANSACTIONS ON;
```

You can also issue the following command. However, this command just effectively issues the first command for you.

```
SET ANSI_DEFAULTS ON;
```

As soon as you do any work—that is, make changes to the database data—a transaction automatically begins. Figure 12-2 illustrates how this works.

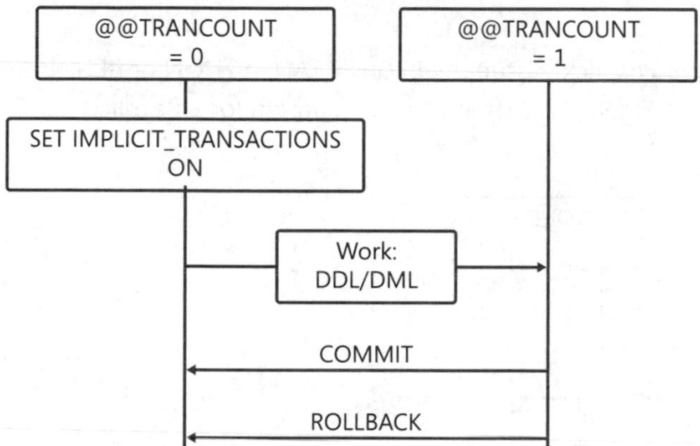

FIGURE 12-2 An implicit transaction using COMMIT or ROLLBACK.

As soon as you enter any command to change data, the value of @@TRANCOUNT becomes equal to 1, indicating that you are one level deep in the transaction. You must then manually issue a COMMIT or a ROLLBACK statement to finish the transaction. If you issue more DML or DDL statements, they also become part of the transaction.

Some advantages to using implicit transactions are:

- You can roll back an implicit transaction after the command has been completed.
- Because you must explicitly issue the COMMIT statement, you may be able to catch mistakes after the command is finished.

Some disadvantages to using implicit transactions are:

- Any locks taken out by your command are held until you complete the transaction. Therefore, you could end up blocking other users from doing their work.
- Because this is not the standard method of using SQL Server, you must constantly remember to set it for your session.
- The implicit transaction mode does not work well with explicit transactions because it causes the @@TRANCOUNT value to increment to 2 unexpectedly.
- If you forget to commit an implicit transaction, you may leave locks open.

Note that implicit transactions can span batches.

MORE INFO IMPLICIT TRANSACTIONS

For more details about implicit transactions, see the Books Online for SQL Server 2012 article "SET IMPLICIT_TRANSACTIONS (Transact-SQL)" at _http://msdn.microsoft.com/en-us/library/ms187807.aspx_.

EXPLICIT TRANSACTION MODE

An *explicit transaction* occurs when you explicitly issue the BEGIN TRANSACTION or BEGIN TRAN command to start a transaction. Figure 12-3 shows a state diagram for an explicit transaction.

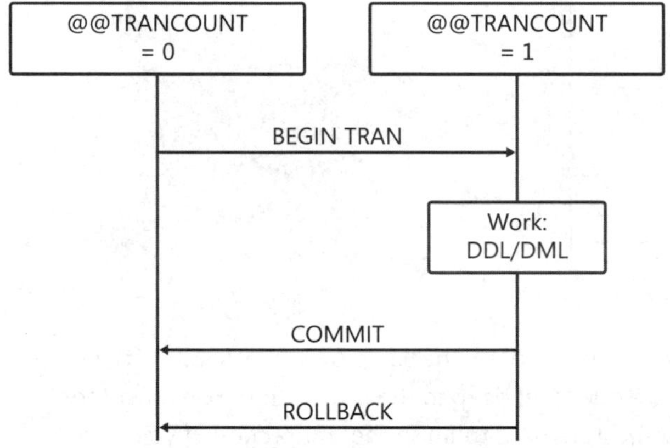

FIGURE 12-3 An explicit transaction with COMMIT or ROLLBACK.

In an explicit transaction, as soon as you issue the BEGIN TRAN command, the value of @@TRANCOUNT is incremented by 1. Then you issue your DML or DDL commands, and when ready, issue COMMIT or ROLLBACK.

You can run explicit transactions interactively or in code such as stored procedures.

Explicit transactions can be used in implicit transaction mode, but if you start an explicit transaction when running your session in implicit transaction mode, the value of @@TRANCOUNT will increment from 0 to 2 immediately after the BEGIN TRAN command. This effectively becomes a nested transaction. As a result, it is not considered a good practice to let @@TRANCOUNT increase beyond 1 when using implicit transactions.

What happens if any of your data modification or DDL statements encounter an error? Some errors cause the entire transaction to roll back, but others, such as foreign key violations do not cause all the statements to roll back. To ensure that your transactions behave correctly, you need to add error handling to your code.

EXAM TIP

Note that transactions can span batches. This includes both implicit transactions and explicit transactions—that is, GO statements. However, it is often a best practice to make sure that each transaction takes place in one batch.

Nested Transactions

When explicit transactions are nested—that is, placed within each other—they are called *nested transactions*. The behavior of COMMIT and ROLLBACK changes when you nest transactions.

Figure 12-4 shows a two-level nested transaction with only COMMIT statements executed.

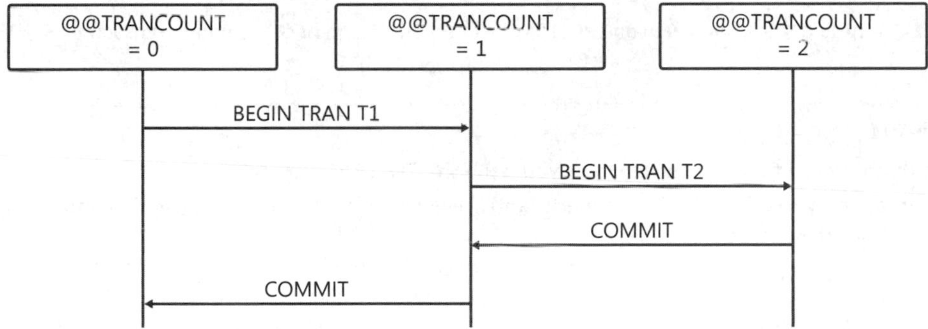

FIGURE 12-4 The final outermost COMMIT statement in a nested transaction.

EXAM TIP

An inner COMMIT statement has no real effect on the transaction, only decrementing @@TRANCOUNT by 1. Just the outermost COMMIT statement, the one executed when @@TRANCOUNT = 1, actually commits the transaction.

Figure 12-5 shows a two-level nested transaction with the ROLLBACK command issued at the outermost level.

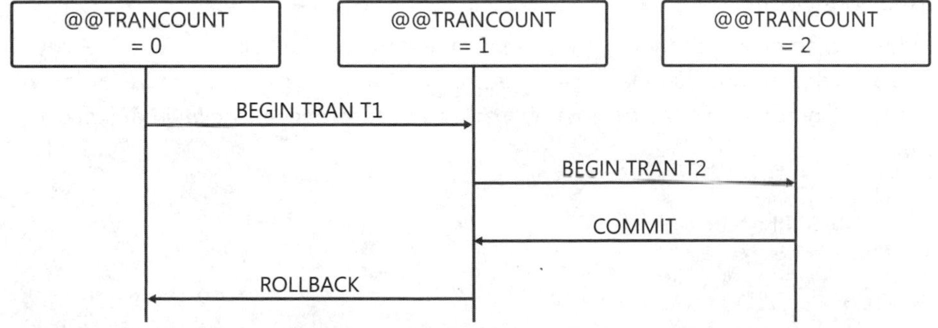

FIGURE 12-5 A final ROLLBACK statement rolling back the entire transaction.

As previously mentioned, the inner COMMIT statement has no effect other than to reduce the @@TRANCOUNT value.

Finally, Figure 12-6 shows a nested transaction where a ROLLBACK is issued before any COMMIT statements.

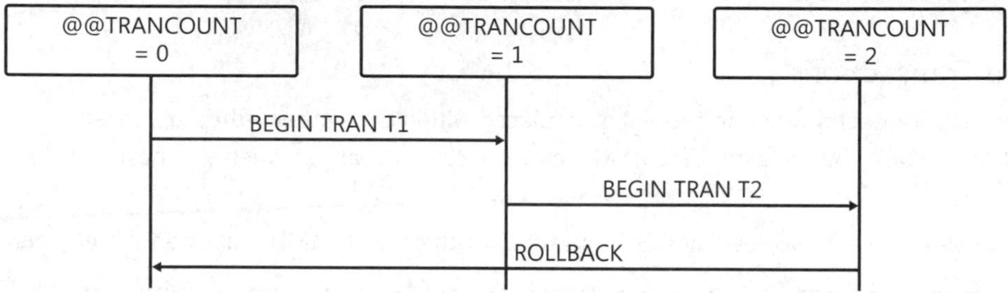

FIGURE 12-6 A nested transaction with one ROLLBACK statement rolling back the entire transaction.

EXAM TIP

Note that it doesn't matter at what level you issue the ROLLBACK command. A transaction can contain only one ROLLBACK command, and it will roll back the entire transaction and reset the @@TRANCOUNT counter to 0.

Marking a Transaction

You can name an explicit transaction by putting the name after the BEGIN TRAN statement. Transaction names must follow the rules for SQL Server identifiers; however, SQL Server only recognizes the first 32 characters as a unique name and ignores any remaining characters, so keep all transaction names to 32 characters or less in length. The transaction name is displayed in the name column of sys.dm_tran_active_transactions, as shown in the following example.

```
USE TSQL2012;
SELECT * FROM sys.dm_tran_active_transactions
```

Note that SQL Server only records transaction names for the outermost transaction. If you have nested transactions, any names for the nested transactions are ignored.

Named transactions are used for placing a mark in the transaction log in order to specify a point to which one or more databases can be restored. When the transaction is recorded in the database's transaction log, the transaction mark is also recorded, as shown in the following example.

```
USE TSQL2012;
BEGIN TRAN Tran1 WITH MARK;
    -- <transaction work>
COMMIT TRAN; -- or ROLLBACK TRAN
-- <other work>
```

If you need to restore the database to the transaction mark later, you can run the following code.

```
RESTORE DATABASE TSQ2012 FROM DISK = 'C:\SQLBackups\TSQL2012.bak'
    WITH NORECOVERY;
GO
RESTORE LOG TSQL2012 FROM DISK = 'C:\SQLBackups\TSQL2012.trn'
    WITH STOPATMARK = 'Tran1';
GO
```

Note the following about using WITH MARK:

- You must use the transaction name with STOPATMARK.
- You can place a description after the clause WITH MARK, but SQL Server ignores it.
- You can restore to just before the transaction with STOPBEFOREMARK.
- You can recover the dataset by restoring with either WITH STOPATMARK or STOPBEFOREMARK.
- You can add RECOVERY to the WITH list, but it has no effect.

Additional Transaction Options

Numerous additional remaining options for transactions are available that are somewhat more specialized. They include:

- ***Savepoints*** These are locations within transactions that you can use to roll back a selective subset of work.
  - You can define a savepoint by using the SAVE TRANSACTION <*savepoint name*> command.
  - The ROLLBACK statement must reference the savepoint. Otherwise, if the statement is unqualified, it will roll back the entire transaction.
- ***Cross-database transactions*** A transaction may span two or more databases on a single SQL Server instance without any additional work on the user's part.
  - SQL Server preserves the ACID properties of cross-database transactions without any additional considerations.
  - However, there are limitations on database mirroring when using cross-database transactions. A cross-database transaction may not be preserved after a failover of one of the databases.
- ***Distributed transactions*** It is possible to make a transaction span more than one server, by using a linked server. In that case, the transaction is known as a distributed (as opposed to local) transaction.
  - After a transaction spans multiple servers by using a linked server, the transaction is considered a distributed transaction and SQL Server invokes the Distributed Transaction Coordinator (MSDTC).
  - A transaction restricted to one database, or to a cross-database transaction, is considered a *local* transaction, as opposed to a *distributed* transaction, which crosses SQL Server instance boundaries.

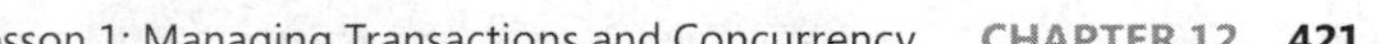

Quick Check

1. **How many ROLLBACKs must be executed in a nested transaction to roll it back?**
2. **How many COMMITs must be executed in a nested transaction to ensure that the entire transaction is committed?**

Quick Check Answer

1. **Only one ROLLBACK. A ROLLBACK always rolls back the entire transaction, no matter how many levels the transaction has.**
2. **One COMMIT for each level of the nested transaction. Only the last COMMIT actually commits the entire transaction.**

MORE INFO **IMPLICIT AND EXPLICIT TRANSACTIONS**

For more details about implicit transactions, see the Books Online for SQL Server 2012 article "SET IMPLICIT_TRANSACTIONS" at *http://msdn.microsoft.com/en-us/library/ms187807.aspx*.

Basic Locking

To preserve the isolation of transactions, SQL Server implements a set of locking protocols. At the basic level, there are two general modes of locking:

- **Shared locks** Used for sessions that read data—that is, for readers
- **Exclusive locks** Used for changes to data—that is, writers

NOTE **ADVANCED LOCKING MODES**

There are more advanced modes called update, intent, and schema locks used for special purposes.

When a session sets out to change data, SQL Server will attempt to secure an exclusive lock on the objects in question. These exclusive locks always occur in the context of a transaction, even if only in the autocommit mode and the session does not start an explicit transaction. When a session has an exclusive lock on an object, such as a row, table, or some system object, no other transaction can change that data until this transaction either commits or rolls back. Except in special isolation levels, other sessions cannot even read exclusively locked objects.

Lock Compatibility

When a session is just reading data, by default SQL Server will issue very brief shared locks on the resource, such as a row or table. Two or more sessions can read the same objects because shared locks are compatible with other shared locks. However, when a session has a resource locked exclusively, no other session can read the resource, in addition to not being able to write to the resource.

Table 12-1 summarizes the basic lock compatibility between shared and exclusive locks.

TABLE 12-1 Shared and exclusive lock compatibility

	Granted	
Requested	*Exclusive (X)*	*Shared (S)*
Exclusive	No	No
Shared	No	Yes

> ***NOTE*** **BASIC LOCK COMPATIBILITY**
>
> **Only shared locks are compatible with each other. An exclusive lock is not compatible with any other kind of lock.**

What kinds of resources are there? There are numerous kinds of resources, but the most granular for SQL Server is the row of a table. However, SQL Server may also need to place a lock on an entire page or on an entire table.

Blocking

A *block* occurs when one session has an exclusive lock on a resource, preventing another session from obtaining any kind of lock on the resource. In a transaction, exclusive locks are held to the end of the transaction, so if the first session is performing a transaction, the second session will have to wait until the first session either commits or rolls back the transaction. No two sessions can write to the same resource (such as a table or row) at the same time, so writers can block writers.

It's not just two requests for an exclusive lock on the same resource that results in blocking. An exclusive lock can also block a request to read the same data, if the reader is requesting a shared lock, because an exclusive lock is also incompatible with a shared lock. In a transaction operating with the default READ COMMITTED isolation level, shared locks are released as soon as the data is read, and they are not held to the end of the transaction except in higher isolation levels.

Deadlocking

A *deadlock* results from mutual blocking between two or more sessions. Sometimes locking sequences between sessions cannot be resolved simply by waiting for one transaction to finish. This occurs due to a cyclical relationship between two or more commands. SQL Server detects this cycle as a deadlock between two sessions, aborts one of the transactions, and returns error message 1205 to the client.

Quick Check

1. Can readers (shared locks) block readers?
2. Can readers block writers (exclusive locks)?

Quick Check Answer

1. No, because shared locks are compatible with other shared locks.
2. Yes, even if only momentarily, because any exclusive lock request has to wait until the shared lock is released.

You can create a deadlock and then resolve it by using the steps shown in Table 12-2. First, start SSMS and open two empty query windows. Place the code for session 1 in one query window and the code for session 2 in the other query window. Then execute each of the two sessions step by step, going back and forth between the two query windows as required. Note that each transaction has a lock on a resource that the other transaction is also requesting a lock on.

TABLE 12-2 Two transactions making the same table changes in the opposite order result in a deadlock

Session 1	Session 2
`USE TSQL2012;` `BEGIN TRAN;`	`USE TSQL2012;` `BEGIN TRAN;`

`UPDATE HR.Employees`
`SET Region = N'10004'`
`WHERE empid = 1`	

	`UPDATE Production.Suppliers`
	`SET Fax = N'555-1212'`
	`WHERE supplierid = 1`

`UPDATE Production.Suppliers`
`SET Fax = N'555-1212'`
`WHERE supplierid = 1`	

<blocked>	`UPDATE HR.Employees`
	`SET phone = N'555-9999'`
	`WHERE empid = 1`

	<blocked>
A deadlock results; one transaction finishes and the other transaction is aborted and error message 1205 is sent to client. Be sure to issue a ROLLBACK for the transaction that succeeded, as shown in the next row.	
`IF @@TRANCOUNT > 0 ROLLBACK`	`IF @@TRANCOUNT > 0 ROLLBACK`

Table 12-3 shows that if both transactions were to do their updates to the tables in the same order, no deadlocking would occur. To see this, open two new empty query windows in SSMS and execute the code in Table 12-3 step by step. Place the code for session 1 in the first query window and the code for session 2 in the second query window. Then execute the code step by step, going back and forth between each window. The session 1 transaction finishes because it is never blocked. The session 2 transaction is blocked until session 1 finishes. But the session 2 transaction never locks a resource that session 1 needs.

TABLE 12-3 When the transactions of two sessions make the same changes but now in the same order, no deadlock results

Session 1	Session 2
`USE TSQL2012;` `BEGIN TRAN;`	`USE TSQL2012;` `BEGIN TRAN;`

`UPDATE HR.Employees`
`SET Region = N'10004'`
`WHERE empid = 1`	

	`UPDATE HR.Employees`
	`SET phone = N'555-9999'`
	`WHERE empid = 1`

	<blocked>

`UPDATE Production.Suppliers`
`SET Fax = N'555-1212'`
`WHERE supplierid = 1`	

`COMMIT TRAN;`	
	<unblocked>

	`UPDATE Production.Suppliers`
	`SET Fax = N'555-1212'`
	`WHERE supplierid = 1`

	`COMMIT TRAN;`

Quick Check

1. **If two transactions never block each other, can a deadlock between them result?**
2. **Can a SELECT statement be involved in a deadlock?**

Quick Check Answer

1. **No. In order to deadlock, each transaction must already have locked a resource the other transaction wants, resulting in mutual blocking.**
2. **Yes. If the SELECT statement locks some resource that keeps a second transaction from finishing, and the SELECT cannot finish because it is blocked by the same transaction, the deadlock cycle results.**

MORE INFO **TROUBLESHOOTING DEADLOCKS**

There is a wealth of information on the complexities of troubleshooting deadlocks. To get started, see the Books Online for SQL Server 2008 R2 article "Detecting and Ending Deadlocks" at *http://msdn.microsoft.com/en-us/library/ms178104(SQL.105).aspx.*

Transaction Isolation Levels

Among the ACID properties of transactions, SQL Server never compromises the atomicity, consistency, and durability requirements of a database transaction. However, the degree of isolation can vary for readers depending on settings that their session applies.

During the time a transaction is changing some data, SQL Server never allows that data to be changed by any other transaction until the first transaction finishes, nor can your transaction change any data that other transactions are changing until they finish. Therefore, some blocking and deadlocking is always possible when transactions change data. Writers always block writers, and exclusive locks in one transaction are never compatible with exclusive locks in another.

But blocking and deadlocking can be increased or reduced based on varying the degree of isolation of the transaction ACID properties. SQL Server allows your transaction to read other transactions' data or allows data to be changed by other transactions that the current transaction only reads, based on the setting of what is called the *transaction isolation level.*

The most commonly used isolation levels are:

- **READ COMMITTED** This is the default isolation level. All readers in that session will only read data changes that have been committed. So all the SELECT statements will attempt to acquire shared locks, and any underlying data resources that are being changed by a different session, and therefore have exclusive locks, will block the READ COMMITTED session.
- **READ UNCOMMMITED** This isolation level allows readers to read uncommitted data. This setting removes the shared locks taken by SELECT statements so that readers no longer are blocked by writers. However, the results of a SELECT statement could read uncommitted data that was changed during a transaction and then later was rolled back to its initial state. This is called *reading dirty data.*
- **READ COMMITTED SNAPSHOT** This is actually not a new isolation level; it is an optional way of using the default READ COMMITTED isolation level, the default isolation level in Windows Azure SQL Database. This isolation level has the following traits:
  - Often abbreviated as RCSI, it uses tempdb to store original versions of changed data. These versions are only stored as long as they are needed to allow readers

(that is, SELECT statements) to read underlying data in its original state. As a result, SELECT statements no longer need shared locks on the underlying resource while only reading (originally) committed data.

- The READ COMMITTED SNAPSHOT option is set at the database level and is a persistent database property.
- RCSI is not a separate isolation level; it is only a different way of implementing READ COMMITTED, preventing writers from blocking readers.
- RCSI is the default isolation level for Windows Azure SQL Database.

Sometimes you may actually want greater isolation for transactions, beyond the default isolation level of READ COMMITTED. The following remaining isolation levels enforce stricter controls over what data can be read between transactions. Because they can result in even more blocking, or more overhead, they are not used nearly as often as the weaker isolation levels.

- **REPEATABLE READ** This isolation level, also set per session, guarantees that whatever data is read in a transaction can be re-read later in the transaction. Updates and deletes of rows already selected are prevented. As a result, shared locks are kept until the end of a transaction. However, the transaction may see new rows added after its first read; this is called a *phantom read*.
- **SNAPSHOT** This isolation level also uses row versioning in tempdb (as does RCSI). It is enabled as a persistent database property and then set per transaction. A transaction using the SNAPSHOT isolation level will be able to repeat any reads, and it will not see any phantom reads. New rows may be added to a table, but the transaction will not see them. Because it uses row versioning, the SNAPSHOT isolation level does not require shared locks on the underlying data.
- **SERIALIZABLE** This isolation level is the strongest level and is set per session. At this level, all reads are repeatable and new rows are not allowed in the underlying tables that would satisfy the conditions of the SELECT statements in the transaction.

EXAM TIP

Isolation levels are set per session. If you do not set a different isolation level in your session, all your transactions will execute using the default isolation level, READ COMMITTED. For on-premise SQL Server instances, this is READ COMMITTED. In Windows Azure SQL Database, the default isolation level is READ COMMITTED SNAPSHOT.

✔ Quick Check

1. If your session is in the READ COMMITTED isolation level, is it possible for one of your queries to read uncommitted data?
2. Is there a way to prevent readers from blocking writers and still ensure that readers only see committed data?

Quick Check Answer

1. Yes, if the query uses the WITH (NOLOCK) or WITH (READUNCOMMITTED) table hint. The session value for the isolation level does not change, just the characteristics for reading that table.
2. Yes, that is the purpose of the READ COMMITTED SNAPSHOT option within the READ COMMITTED isolation level. Readers see earlier versions of data changes for current transactions, not the currently uncommitted data.

PRACTICE Implementing Transactions

In this practice, you implement a number of transactions by using SQL Server 2012 Management Studio and the TSQL2012 database. For some of the transactions, you run T-SQL statements in side-by-side sessions, going back and forth between two sessions. You execute the scripts in such a way that you can see what effect they have on each other.

If you encounter a problem completing an exercise, you can install the completed projects from the companion content for this chapter and lesson.

EXERCISE 1 Work with Transaction Modes

In this exercise, you work with the basic transaction modes.

1. Work with an implicit transaction first by opening SSMS and opening an empty query window. Execute the following code. Execute each command step by step, in sequence. Note the output of @@TRANCOUNT.

```
USE TSQL2012;
SET IMPLICIT_TRANSACTIONS ON;
SELECT @@TRANCOUNT; -- 0
SET IDENTITY_INSERT Production.Products ON;
-- Issue DML or DDL command here
INSERT INTO Production.Products(productid, productname, supplierid, categoryid,
 unitprice, discontinued)
    VALUES(101, N'Test2: New productid', 1, 1, 18.00, 0);
SELECT @@TRANCOUNT; -- 1
COMMIT TRAN;
SET IDENTITY_INSERT Production.Products OFF;
SET IMPLICIT_TRANSACTIONS OFF;
-- Remove the inserted row
DELETE FROM Production.Products WHERE productid = 101; -- Note the row is deleted
```

2. Next, you work with an explicit transaction. Execute the following code. Note the value of @@TRANCOUNT.

```
USE TSQL2012;
SELECT @@TRANCOUNT; -- 0
BEGIN TRAN;
    SELECT @@TRANCOUNT; -- 1
    SET IDENTITY_INSERT Production.Products ON;
    INSERT INTO Production.Products(productid, productname, supplierid,
categoryid,     unitprice, discontinued)
        VALUES(101, N'Test2: New productid', 1, 1, 18.00, 0);
    SELECT @@TRANCOUNT; -- 1
    SET IDENTITY_INSERT Production.Products OFF;
COMMIT TRAN;
-- Remove the inserted row
DELETE FROM Production.Products WHERE productid = 101; -- Note the row is deleted
```

3. To work with a nested transaction by using COMMIT TRAN, execute the following code. Note that the value of @@TRANCOUNT increments to 2.

```
USE TSQL2012;
SELECT @@TRANCOUNT; -- = 0
BEGIN TRAN;
    SELECT @@TRANCOUNT; -- = 1
    BEGIN TRAN;
        SELECT @@TRANCOUNT; -- = 2
        -- Issue data modification or DDL commands here
    COMMIT
    SELECT @@TRANCOUNT; -- = 1
COMMIT TRAN;
SELECT @@TRANCOUNT; -- = 0
```

4. To work with a nested transaction by using ROLLBACK TRAN, execute the following code. Note that the value of @@TRANCOUNT increments to 2 but only one ROLLBACK is required.

```
USE TSQL2012;
SELECT @@TRANCOUNT; -- = 0
BEGIN TRAN;
    SELECT @@TRANCOUNT; -- = 1
    BEGIN TRAN;
        SELECT @@TRANCOUNT; -- = 2
        -- Issue data modification or DDL command here
    ROLLBACK; -- rolls back the entire transaction at this point
SELECT @@TRANCOUNT; -- = 0
```

EXERCISE 2 Work with Blocking and Deadlocking

In this exercise, you work with two common scenarios: blocking and deadlocking.

1. In this step, you work with writers blocking writers. Open SSMS and two empty query windows. Execute the code side by side as shown in Table 12-4. Execute each step in sequence. When locks are incompatible, the session requesting the incompatible lock must wait and is considered to be in a *blocked* state. Session 1 obtains an exclusive

lock on the row being changed. At nearly the same time or shortly thereafter, Session 2 tries to update the same row. Session 1 has not released its exclusive lock on the row *because in a transaction, all exclusive locks are held until the end of the transaction.* Therefore, Session 2 has to wait until Session 1 either commits or rolls back, and the lock on the row is released, for its update to finish.

> ***NOTE*** **WRITERS BLOCK WRITERS**
>
> **An exclusive lock is incompatible with a similar exclusive lock request.**

TABLE 12-4 Two sessions with incompatible exclusive locks

Session 1	Session 2
`USE TSQL2012;` `BEGIN TRAN;`	`USE TSQL2012;`

`UPDATE HR.Employees`
`SET postalcode = N'10004'`
`WHERE empid = 1;`
	`UPDATE HR.Employees`
	`SET phone = N'555-9999'`
	`WHERE empid = 1;`

<more work>	<blocked>
`COMMIT TRAN;`	
	<results returned>

`-- Cleanup:`
`UPDATE HR.Employees`
`SET postalcode = N'10003'`
`WHERE empid = 1;`	

2. This step works with writers blocking readers. Open SSMS and two empty query windows. Execute the code side by side as shown in Table 12-5. Execute each step in sequence. In this case, Session 2 must get a shared lock on the row in HR.Employees that Session 1 has locked exclusively. Because shared locks are incompatible with exclusive locks on the same resource, Session 2 must wait until Session 1 releases the lock by finishing its transaction.

> ***NOTE*** **WRITERS BLOCK READERS**
>
> **An exclusive lock is also incompatible with a shared lock request.**

TABLE 12-5 Two sessions illustrating incompatibility between an exclusive lock and a shared lock request

Session 1	Session 2
`USE TSQL2012;` `BEGIN TRAN;`	`USE TSQL2012;`

`UPDATE HR.Employees`
`SET postalcode = N'10005'`
`WHERE empid = 1`
	`SELECT lastname, firstname`
	`FROM HR.Employees`

	<blocked>
`COMMIT TRAN;`	
	<results returned>

`-- Cleanup:`
`UPDATE HR.Employees`
`SET postalcode = N'10003'`
`WHERE empid = 1;`	

EXERCISE 3 Work with Transaction Isolation Levels

In this exercise, you work with the most common isolation levels by using the TSQL2012 database and experiencing the isolation levels' effect on blocking between two sessions.

1. In this step, you work with READ COMMITTED. Open SSMS and two empty query windows. Execute the code side by side as shown in Table 12-6. Execute each step in sequence. Note that the SELECT statement in Session 2 is blocked, but is freed as soon as Session 1 completes its transaction.

TABLE 12-6 READ COMMITTED resulting in writers blocking readers

Session 1	Session 2

`USE TSQL2012;`
`BEGIN TRAN;`
	`USE TSQL2012;`
	`SET TRANSACTION ISOLATION`
	`LEVEL READ COMMITTED;`

`UPDATE HR.Employees`
`SET postalcode = N'10006'`
`WHERE empid = 1;`	

	`SELECT lastname, firstname` `FROM HR.Employees;`
	<blocked>
`COMMIT TRAN;`	
	<results returned>

`-- Cleanup:`
`UPDATE HR.Employees`
`SET postalcode = N'10003'`
`WHERE empid = 1;`	

2. This step works with READ UNCOMMITTED. In the READ COMMITTED isolation level, even a reader may have to wait for a transaction to finish, causing blocking and even deadlocking in busy systems. One way to reduce that blocking is to allow readers to read uncommitted data by using the READ UNCOMMITTED isolation level. Open SSMS and two empty query windows. Execute the code side by side as shown in Table 12-7. Execute each step in sequence. Note that the SELECT statement in Session 2 now reads uncommitted data.

TABLE 12-7 READ UNCOMMITTED resulting in reading uncommitted data that may be later rolled back

Session 1	Session 2
USE TSQL2012; BEGIN TRAN;	USE TSQL2012; SET TRANSACTION ISOLATION LEVEL READ UNCOMMITTED;
UPDATE HR.Employees SET region = N'1004' WHERE empid = 1;	
	SELECT lastname, firstname, region FROM HR.Employees
	<results returned: region = 1004 for empid = 1>
ROLLBACK TRAN;	
<region for empid = 1 rolled back to original value>	SELECT lastname, firstname, region FROM HR.Employees;
	<results returned: region = original value for empid = 1>
-- Cleanup: UPDATE HR.Employees SET region = N'1003' WHERE empid = 1;	

3. This step uses a table hint to implement READ UNCOMMITTED in a single command. Instead of applying this isolation level to an entire session, you can apply it at the individual command, per table, by using the READUNCOMMITTED table hint. Replace the SELECT command in the code for the previous step with the following, which has the WITH (READUNCOMMITTED) table hint. Then modify the statement to use WITH (NOLOCK).

```
SELECT lastname, firstname
FROM HR.Employees WITH (READUNCOMMITTED);
```

> **NOTE NOLOCK IS DEPRECATED**
>
> The NOLOCK table hint is deprecated and will not be allowed in UPDATE and DELETE statements in a future version of SQL Server. Other than in this exercise, use the READUNCOMMITTED table hint instead.

4. In this step, you use READ COMMITTED SNAPSHOT. SQL Server 2005 introduced a more elegant way to reduce locking and blocking so that writers might no longer block readers. Open SSMS and two empty query windows. Execute the code side by side as shown in Table 12-8. Execute each step in sequence. Note that the SELECT statement in Session 2 is no longer blocked but now reads committed data.

TABLE 12-8 RCSI resulting in reading previously committed data without requiring shared locks

Session 1	Session 2

`USE TSQL2012;`
`ALTER DATABASE TSQL2012 SET`
`READ_COMMITTED_SNAPSHOT ON;`
	`Use master;`

`BEGIN TRAN;`	`USE TSQL2012;`

`UPDATE HR.Employees`
`SET postalcode = N'10007'`
`WHERE empid = 1;`	

	`SELECT lastname, firstname, postalcode`
	`FROM HR.Employees`
	`WHERE empid = 1;`

	<Results returned show postalcode in original state for empid = 1>
`ROLLBACK TRAN;`	
<postalcode for empid = 1 rolled back to original value>	

`-- Cleanup:`
`UPDATE HR.Employees`
`SET postalcode = N'10003'`
`WHERE empid = 1;`	

> ***MORE INFO* SQL SERVER ROW VERSIONING AND ISOLATION LEVELS**
>
> For more details on how SQL Server implements row versioning for the READ COMMITTED SNAPSHOT option of READ COMMITTED, and the SNAPSHOT isolation level, see the Books Online for SQL Server 2008 R2 article "Understanding Row Versioning-Based Isolation Levels" at *http://msdn.microsoft.com/en-us/library/ms189050(SQL.105).aspx.*

Lesson Summary

- All SQL Server data changes occur in the context of a transaction. Executing a ROLLBACK command at any level in the transaction immediately rolls back the entire transaction.
- Every COMMIT statement reduces the value of @@TRANCOUNT by 1, and only the outermost COMMIT statement commits the entire nested transaction.
- SQL Server uses locking to enforce the isolation of transactions.
- A deadlock can result between two or more sessions if each session has acquired incompatible locks that the other session needs to finish its statement. When SQL Server sees a deadlock, it chooses one of the sessions and terminates the batch.
- SQL Server enforces the isolation level ACID property with varying degrees of strictness.
- The READ COMMITTED isolation level is the default isolation level for on-premise SQL Server.
- The READ COMMITTED SNAPSHOT isolation option (RCSI) of the default isolation level allows read requests to access previously committed versions of exclusively locked data. This can greatly reduce blocking and deadlocking. RCSI is the default isolation level in Windows Azure SQL Database.
- The READ UNCOMMITTED isolation level allows a session to read uncommitted data, known as "dirty reads."

Lesson Review

Answer the following questions to test your knowledge of the information in this lesson. You can find the answers to these questions and explanations of why each answer choice is correct or incorrect in the "Answers" section at the end of this chapter.

1. Which of the following T-SQL statements automatically occur in the context of a transaction? (Choose all that apply.)
   - **A.** An ALTER TABLE command
   - **B.** A PRINT command
   - **C.** An UPDATE command
   - **D.** A SET command

2. How do the COMMIT and ROLLBACK commands work with nested transactions in T-SQL? (Choose all that apply.)
   - **A.** A single COMMIT commits the entire nested transaction.
   - **B.** A single ROLLBACK rolls back the entire nested transaction.
   - **C.** A single COMMIT commits only one level of the nested transaction.
   - **D.** A single ROLLBACK rolls back only one level of the nested transaction.

3. Which of the following strategies can help reduce blocking and deadlocking by reducing shared locks? (Choose all that apply.)
   - **A.** Add the READUNCOMMITTED table hint to queries.
   - **B.** Use the READ COMMTTED SNAPSHOT option.
   - **C.** Use the REPEATABLE READ isolation level.
   - **D.** Use the SNAPSHOT isolation level.

Lesson 2: Implementing Error Handling

When writing T-SQL that performs data changes, whether through data modification commands or DDL commands, and especially when contained in explicit transactions and/or stored procedures, you should include error handling. SQL Server 2012 supplies a nearly full set of structured error handling commands that can anticipate almost all conditions. This lesson starts by describing T-SQL error messages and then proceeds into error handling techniques.

After this lesson, you will be able to:

- Describe the parts of a T-SQL error message.
- Describe how unstructured error handling is implemented.
- Describe how to implement the TRY/CATCH block and the THROW statement
- Describe how to implement error handling in transactions.

Estimated lesson time: 40 minutes

Detecting and Raising Errors

When SQL Server encounters an error while executing T-SQL code, SQL Server will generate an error condition and take action. You need to prepare for possible errors in your T-SQL code and handle them so that you do not lose control over your code.

In addition, inside your own routines, you may need to test for situations that SQL Server would not consider erroneous but that are clearly errors from your code's standpoint. For example, if a certain table has no rows, you may not want to continue with your code. In such cases, you need to raise errors of your own and handle those errors as well.

T-SQL provides you with ways of detecting SQL Server errors and raising errors of your own. When SQL Server generates an error condition, the system function @@ERROR will have a positive integer value indicating the error number.

If the T-SQL code is not in a TRY/CATCH block, the error message will be passed through to the client and cannot be intercepted in T-SQL code.

In addition to the error messages that SQL Server raises when it encounters an error, you can raise your own errors by using two commands:

- The older RAISERROR command
- The SQL Server 2012 THROW command

Either of these commands can be used to generate your own errors in your T-SQL code.

Analyzing Error Messages

The following is a sample error message from SQL Server 2012.

```
Msg 547, Level 16, State 0, Line 11
The INSERT statement conflicted with the FOREIGN KEY constraint "FK_Products_
 Categories".
The conflict occurred in database "TSQL2012", table "Production.Categories", column
 'categoryid'.
```

Note that error messages in SQL Server have four parts:

- **Error number** The error number is an integer value.
  - SQL Server error messages are numbered from 1 through 49999.
  - Custom error messages are numbered 50001 and higher.
  - The error number 50000 is reserved for a custom message that does not have a custom error number.
- **Severity level** SQL Server defines 26 severity levels numbered from 0 through 25.
  - As a general rule, errors with a severity level of 16 or higher are logged automatically to the SQL Server log and the Windows Application log.
  - Errors with a severity level from 19 through 25 can be specified only by members of the sysadmin fixed server role.
  - Errors with a severity level from 20 through 25 are considered fatal and cause the connection to be terminated and any open transactions to be rolled back.
  - Errors with severity level 0 through 10 are informational only.
- **State** This is an integer with a maximum value of 127, used by Microsoft for internal purposes.
- **Error message** The error message can be up to 255 Unicode characters long.
  - SQL Server error messages are listed in sys.messages.
  - You can add your own custom error messages by using sp_addmessage.

MORE INFO **SEVERITY LEVELS**

For more details on error severity levels, see the Books Online for SQL Server 2012 article "Database Engine Error Severities" at *http://msdn.microsoft.com/en-us/library/ms164086.aspx*.

RAISERROR

The RAISERROR command uses the following syntax.

```
RAISERROR ( { msg_id | msg_str | @local_variable }
{ ,severity ,state }
[ ,argument [ ,...n ] ] )
[ WITH option [ ,...n ] ]
```

The message (a message ID, string, or string variable), along with the severity and state, are required. The message can be a simple string, as shown in the following example.

```
RAISERROR ('Error in usp_InsertCategories stored procedure', 16, 0);
```

You can also use a printf style formatting in the string, as follows.

```
RAISERROR ('Error in %s stored procedure', 16, 0, N'usp_InsertCategories');
```

In addition, you can use a variable, as in the following.

```
GO
DECLARE @message AS NVARCHAR(1000) = 'Error in %s stored procedure';
RAISERROR (@message, 16, 0, N'usp_InsertCategories');
```

And you can add formatting outside RAISERROR by using the FORMATMESSAGE function.

```
GO
DECLARE @message AS NVARCHAR(1000) = 'Error in %s stored procedure';
SELECT @message = FORMATMESSAGE (@message, N'usp_InsertCategories');
RAISERROR (@message, 16, 0);
```

> ***NOTE*** **SIMPLE FORM OF RAISERROR NO LONGER ALLOWED**
>
> **A very simple RAISERROR int, 'string', was permitted in earlier versions of SQL Server but is no longer allowed in SQL Server 2012.**

Some more advanced features of RAISERROR include the following:

- You can issue purely informational messages (similar to PRINT) by using a severity level of 0 through 9.
- You can issue RAISERROR with a severity level > 18 if you use the WITH LOG option and if you have the SQL Server sysadmin role. SQL Server will then terminate the connection when the error is raised.
- You can use RAISERROR with NOWAIT to send messages immediately to the client. The message does not wait in the output buffer before being sent.

THROW

The THROW command behaves mostly like RAISERROR, with some important exceptions. The basic syntax of THROW is the following.

```
THROW [ { error_number | @local_variable },
{ message | @local_variable },
{ state | @local_variable }
] [ ; ]
```

THROW has many of the same components as RAISERROR but with the following significant differences:

- THROW does not use parentheses to delimit parameters.
- THROW can be used without parameters, but only in the CATCH block of a TRY/CATCH construct.
- When parameters are supplied, error_number, message, and state are all required.
- The error_number does not require a matching defined message in sys.messages.
- The message parameter does not allow formatting, but you can use FORMATMESSAGE() with a variable to get the same effect.
- The state parameter must be an integer that ranges from 0 to 255.
- Any parameter can be a variable.
- There is no severity parameter; the severity is always set to 16.
- THROW always terminates the batch except when it is used in a TRY block.

EXAM TIP

The statement *before* the THROW statement must be terminated by a semicolon (;). This reinforces the best practice to terminate all T-SQL statements with a semicolon.

As an example, you can issue a simple THROW as follows.

```
THROW 50000, 'Error in usp_InsertCategories stored procedure', 0;
```

Because THROW does not allow formatting of the message parameter, you can use FORMATMESSAGE(), as follows.

```
GO
DECLARE @message AS NVARCHAR(1000) = 'Error in %s stored procedure';
SELECT @message = FORMATMESSAGE (@message, N'usp_InsertCategories');
THROW 50000, @message, 0;
```

There are some additional important differences between THROW and RAISERROR. For example, RAISERROR does not normally terminate a batch.

```
RAISERROR ('Hi there', 16, 0);
PRINT 'RAISERROR error'; -- Prints

GO
```

However, THROW does terminate the batch.

```
THROW 50000, 'Hi there', 0;
PRINT 'THROW error'; -- Does not print

GO
```

Here are a couple more important differences between THROW and RAISERROR:

- You cannot issue THROW with a NOWAIT command in order to cause immediate buffer output.
- You cannot issue THROW using a severity level higher than 16 by using the WITH LOG clause as you can with RAISERROR.

TRY_CONVERT and TRY_PARSE

You can use two functions to preempt or detect potential errors so that your code can avoid unexpected errors. TRY_CONVERT attempts to cast a value as a target data type, and if it succeeds, returns the value, returning NULL if the test fails. The following example tests two values of the datetime data type, which does not accept dates earlier than 1753-01-01 as valid dates.

```
SELECT TRY_CONVERT(DATETIME, '1752-12-31');
SELECT TRY_CONVERT(DATETIME, '1753-01-01');
```

The first statement returns a NULL, signaling that the conversion will not work. The second statement returns the converted datetime value as a datetime data type. TRY_CONVERT has a format similar to the existing CONVERT function, so you can also pass a style in the case of string conversions.

With TRY_PARSE, you can take an input string containing data of an indeterminate data type and convert it to a specific data type if possible, and return NULL if it is not. The following example attempts to parse two strings.

```
SELECT TRY_PARSE('1' AS INTEGER);
SELECT TRY_PARSE('B' AS INTEGER);
```

The first string converts to an integer, so the TRY_PARSE function returns the value as an integer. The second string, 'B', will not convert to an integer, so the function returns NULL. The TRY_PARSE function follows the syntax of the PARSE and CAST functions.

Quick Check

1. How can you add custom error messages?
2. What is severity level 0 used for?

Quick Check Answer

1. You can use the system stored procedure sp_addmessage to add your own custom error messages.
2. When you issue a RAISERROR with severity level 0, only an informational message is sent. If you add WITH NOWAIT, the message will be sent without waiting in the output buffer.

Handling Errors After Detection

There are essentially two error handling methods available: unstructured and structured. With unstructured error handling, you must handle each error as it happens by accessing the @@ERROR function. With structured error handling, you can designate a central location (the CATCH block) to handle errors.

Unstructured Error Handling Using @@ERROR

Unstructured error handling consists of testing individual statements for their error status immediately after they execute. You do this by querying the @@ERROR system function. When SQL Server executes any T-SQL statement, it records an error status of the command result in @@ERROR. If an error occurs, you can query @@ERROR to find the error number. If the statement succeeded, @@ERROR will be 0, and if the statement fails, @@ERROR will contain the error number.

Unfortunately, just querying the @@ERROR function, even in an IF clause, causes it to be reset to a new number, because @@ERROR always reports the error status of the command last executed. Therefore, it is not possible to test the value of @@ERROR inside the error handling code. Instead, it is better to add code that captures @@ERROR in a variable, and then test the variable.

Because you must check @@ERROR after each data modification or DML statement, unstructured error handling has a fundamental problem. Because it does not provide a central place to handle errors, you must provide error handling through custom coding.

It is possible to add code of your own to add a degree of structure to the error handling. However, custom code for unstructured error handling can quickly become complex. What you need is a built-in central place to handle errors.

Using XACT_ABORT with Transactions

There is another option for trapping errors that is one step toward structured error handling: SET XACT_ABORT (where XACT stands for "transaction"). XACT_ABORT works with all types of code and affects the entire batch. You can make an entire batch fail if any error occurs by beginning it with SET XACT_ABORT ON. You set XACT_ABORT per session. After it is set to ON, all remaining transactions in that setting are subject to it until it is set to OFF.

SET XACT_ABORT has some advantages. It causes a transaction to roll back based on any error with severity > 10. However, XACT_ABORT has many limitations, such as the following:

- You cannot trap for the error or capture the error number.
- Any error with severity level > 10 causes the transaction to roll back.
- None of the remaining code in the transaction is executed. Even the final PRINT statements of the transaction are not executed.
- After the transaction is aborted, you can only infer what statements failed by inspecting the error message returned to the client by SQL Server.

As a result, XACT_ABORT does not provide you with error handling capability. You need TRY/CATCH.

Structured Error Handling Using TRY/CATCH

SQL Server 2005 added the TRY/CATCH construct to provide structured error handling to SQL Server. With TRY/CATCH:

- You wrap the code that you want to test for errors in a TRY block.
  - Every TRY block must be followed by a CATCH block where you handle errors.
  - Both blocks must be paired, and both blocks must be in the same T-SQL batch.
- If an error condition is detected in a T-SQL statement inside the TRY block, control is passed to its corresponding CATCH block for error handling.
  - The remaining T-SQL statements in the TRY block are not executed.
  - After you process the error in the CATCH block, control is transferred to the first T-SQL statement following the END CATCH statement.
  - If no error is detected in the TRY block, control is transferred past the CATCH block to the first T-SQL statement following END CATCH.
- When SQL Server encounters an error in the TRY block, no message is sent to the client.
  - This contrasts sharply with unstructured error handling, where an error message is always sent to the client and cannot be intercepted.
  - Even a RAISERROR in the TRY block with a severity level from 11 to 19 will not generate a message to the client, but instead transfers control to the CATCH block.

By using TRY/CATCH blocks, you no longer need to trap individual statements for errors. Almost all errors cause the code path to fall into the CATCH block.

Here are some rules for using TRY/CATCH:

- Errors with severity greater than 10 and less than 20 within the TRY block result in transferring control to the CATCH block.
- Errors with a severity level of 20 and greater that do not close connections are also handled by the CATCH block.
- Compile errors and some runtime errors involving statement level compilation abort the batch immediately and do not pass control to the CATCH block.
- If an error is encountered in the CATCH block, the transaction is aborted and the error is returned to the calling application unless the CATCH block is nested within another TRY block.
- Within the CATCH block, you can commit or roll back the current transaction unless the transaction cannot be committed and must be rolled back. To test for the state of a transaction, you can query the XACT_STATE function.
- A TRY/CATCH block does not trap errors that cause the connection to be terminated, such as a fatal error or a sysadmin executing the KILL command.
- You also cannot trap errors that occur due to compilation errors, syntax errors, or non-existent objects. Therefore, you cannot use TRY/CATCH to test for an object's existence.
- You can nest TRY/CATCH blocks; in other words, you can place an inner TRY/CATCH block inside an outer TRY block. An error within the nested TRY block transfers execution to the corresponding nested CATCH block.

You can use the following set of functions within the CATCH block to report on errors:

- **ERROR_NUMBER** Returns the error number
- **ERROR_MESSAGE** Returns the error message
- **ERROR_SEVERITY** Returns the severity of the error
- **ERROR_LINE** Returns the line number of the batch where the error occurred
- **ERROR_PROCEDURE** The function, trigger, or procedure name that was executing when the error occurred
- **ERROR_STATE** The state of the error

You can encapsulate calls to these functions in a stored procedure, along with additional information (such as the database and server name, and perhaps the time and date), and then call the stored procedure from the various CATCH blocks.

```
BEGIN CATCH
    -- Error handling
    SELECT ERROR_NUMBER() AS errornumber
        , ERROR_MESSAGE() AS errormessage
        , ERROR_LINE() AS errorline
        , ERROR_SEVERITY() AS errorseverity
        , ERROR_STATE() AS errorstate;
END CATCH;
```

REAL WORLD ANTICIPATING ERRORS

When you handle errors in a CATCH block, the number of errors that can occur is quite large, so it is difficult to anticipate all of them. Also, the types of transactions or procedures involved might be specialized. Some T-SQL developers prefer to just return the values of the error functions as in the previous SELECT statement. This can be most useful for utility stored procedures. In other contexts, some T-SQL developers use a stored procedure that can be called from the CATCH block and that will provide a common response for certain commonly encountered errors.

THROW vs. RAISERROR in TRY/CATCH

In the TRY block, you can use either RAISERROR or THROW (with parameters) to generate an error condition and transfer control to the CATCH block. A RAISERROR in the TRY block must have a severity level from 11 to 19 to transfer control to the CATCH block.

Whether you use RAISERROR or THROW in the TRY block, SQL Server will not send an error message to the client.

In the CATCH block, you have three options: RAISERROR, THROW with parameters, or THROW without parameters.

You can use a RAISERROR in the CATCH block to report the original error back to the client, or to raise an additional error that you want to report. The original error number cannot be re-raised. It must be a custom error message number or, in this case, the default error number 50000. To return the original error number, you could add it to the msg_str parameter of the RAISERROR statement.

Execution of the CATCH block continues after the RAISERROR statement.

You can use a THROW statement with parameters, like RAISERROR, to re-raise the error in the CATCH block. However, THROW with parameters always raises errors with a custom error number and a severity level of 16, so you don't get the exact information. THROW with parameters terminates the batch, so commands following it are not executed.

A THROW without parameters can be used to re-raise the original error message and send it back to the client. This is by far the best method for reporting the error back to the caller. Now you get the original message sent back to the client, and under your control, though it does terminate the batch immediately.

EXAM TIP

You must take care that the THROW with or without parameters is the last statement you want executed in the CATCH block, because it terminates the batch and does not execute any remaining commands in the CATCH block.

Using XACT_ABORT with TRY/CATCH

XACT_ABORT behaves differently when used in a TRY block. Instead of terminating the transaction as it does in unstructured error handling, XACT_ABORT transfers control to the CATCH block, and as expected, any error is fatal. The transaction is left in an uncommittable state (and XACT_STATE() returns a –1). Therefore, you cannot commit a transaction inside a CATCH block if XACT_ABORT is turned on; you must roll it back.

The XACT_STATE() values are:

- **1** An open transaction exists that can be either committed or rolled back.
- **0** There is no open transaction; it is equivalent to @@TRANCOUNT = 0.
- **-1** An open transaction exists, but it is not in a committable state. The transaction can only be rolled back.

Within the CATCH block, you can determine the current transaction nesting level with the @@TRANCOUNT system function.

If you have nested transactions, you can retrieve the state of the innermost transaction with the XACT_STATE function.

Quick Check

1. **What are the main advantages of using a TRY/CATCH block over the traditional trapping for @@ERROR?**
2. **Can a TRY/CATCH block span batches?**

Quick Check Answer

1. **The main advantage is that you have one place in your code that errors will be trapped, so you only need to put error handling in one place.**
2. **No, you must have one set of TRY/CATCH blocks for each batch of code.**

PRACTICE Working with Error Handling

In this practice, you implement code that writes to the database and tests for errors, allowing you to explore unstructured and structured error handling. You use SSMS and the TSQL2012 database.

If you encounter a problem completing an exercise, you can install the completed projects from the companion content for this chapter and lesson.

EXERCISE 1 Work with Unstructured Error Handling

In this exercise, you work with unstructured error handling, using the @@ERROR function.

1. This step uses @@ERROR. In the following code, you test the value of the @@ERROR statement immediately after a data modification statement takes place. Open SSMS and open an empty query window. Execute the entire batch of T-SQL code. Note the error message that SQL Server sends back to the client application, SQL Server Management Studio.

```
USE TSQL2012;
GO
DECLARE @errnum AS int;
BEGIN TRAN;
SET IDENTITY_INSERT Production.Products ON;
INSERT INTO Production.Products(productid, productname, supplierid, categoryid,
    unitprice, discontinued)
    VALUES(1, N'Test1: Duplicate productid', 1, 1, 18.00, 0);
SET @errnum = @@ERROR;
IF @errnum <> 0 -- Handle the error
    BEGIN
        PRINT 'Insert into Production.Products failed with error ' + CAST(@errnum
    AS VARCHAR);
    END;
GO
IF @@TRANCOUNT <> 0 ROLLBACK TRANSACTION
```

2. In this step, you work with unstructured error handling in a transaction. In the following code, you have two INSERT statements in a batch and wrap them in a transaction in order to roll back the transaction if either statement fails. The first INSERT fails, but the second succeeds because SQL Server, by default, will not roll back a transaction with a duplicate primary key error. When the code runs, note that the first INSERT fails, due to a primary key violation, and the transaction is rolled back. However, the second INSERT succeeds because the unstructured error handling does not transfer control of the program in a way that would avoid the second INSERT. To achieve better control, you must add significant coding to get around this problem. Open SSMS and open an empty query window. Execute the entire batch of T-SQL code.

```
USE TSQL2012;
GO
DECLARE @errnum AS int;
BEGIN TRAN;
    SET IDENTITY_INSERT Production.Products ON;
    -- Insert #1 will fail because of duplicate primary key
    INSERT INTO Production.Products(productid, productname, supplierid,
     categoryid, unitprice, discontinued)
        VALUES(1, N'Test1: Duplicate productid', 1, 1, 18.00, 0);
    SET @errnum = @@ERROR;
    IF @errnum <> 0
```

```
        BEGIN
            IF @@TRANCOUNT > 0 ROLLBACK TRAN;
            PRINT 'Insert #1 into Production.Products failed with error ' +
             CAST(@errnum AS VARCHAR);
        END;
    -- Insert #2 will succeed
    INSERT INTO Production.Products(productid, productname, supplierid,
     categoryid,unitprice, discontinued)
        VALUES(101, N'Test2: New productid', 1, 1, 18.00, 0);
    SET @errnum = @@ERROR;
    IF @errnum <> 0
        BEGIN
            IF @@TRANCOUNT > 0 ROLLBACK TRAN;
            PRINT 'Insert #2 into Production.Products failed with error ' +
             CAST(@errnum AS VARCHAR);
        END;
    SET IDENTITY_INSERT Production.Products OFF;
    IF @@TRANCOUNT > 0 COMMIT TRAN;
-- Remove the inserted row
DELETE FROM Production.Products WHERE productid = 101;
PRINT 'Deleted ' + CAST(@@ROWCOUNT AS VARCHAR) + ' rows';
```

EXERCISE 2 Use XACT_ABORT to Handle Errors

In this exercise, you work with the XACT_ABORT setting as a method of error handling.

1. In this step, you use XACT_ABORT and encounter an error. In the following code, you verify that XACT_ABORT will abort a batch if SQL Server encounters an error in a data modification statement. Open SSMS and open an empty query window. Execute both batches of T-SQL code. Note the error message that SQL Server sends back to the client application, SQL Server Management Studio.

```
USE TSQL2012;
GO
SET XACT_ABORT ON;
PRINT 'Before error';
SET IDENTITY_INSERT Production.Products ON;
INSERT INTO Production.Products(productid, productname, supplierid, categoryid,
 unitprice, discontinued)
    VALUES(1, N'Test1: Duplicate productid', 1, 1, 18.00, 0);
SET IDENTITY_INSERT Production.Products OFF;
PRINT 'After error';
GO
PRINT 'New batch';
SET XACT_ABORT OFF;
```

2. This step uses THROW with XACT_ABORT. In the following code, you verify that XACT_ABORT will abort a batch if you throw an error. Open SSMS and open an empty query window. Note that executing THROW with XACT_ABORT ON causes the batch to be terminated. Execute both batches of T-SQL code.

```
USE TSQL2012;
GO
```

```
SET XACT_ABORT ON;
PRINT 'Before error';
THROW 50000, 'Error in usp_InsertCategories stored procedure', 0;
PRINT 'After error';
GO
PRINT 'New batch';
SET XACT_ABORT OFF;
```

3. In this step, you use XACT_ABORT in a transaction. Execute the following code as an entire batch. Notice that XACT_ABORT in a transaction will not allow the second INSERT statement to be executed and no row is deleted in the second batch. Note that the IF @errnum clause will not be executed because of the XACT_ABORT setting. Open SSMS and open an empty query window. Execute each batch of T-SQL code in sequence.

```
USE TSQL2012;
GO
DECLARE @errnum AS int;
SET XACT_ABORT ON;
BEGIN TRAN;
    SET IDENTITY_INSERT Production.Products ON;
    -- Insert #1 will fail because of duplicate primary key
    INSERT INTO Production.Products(productid, productname, supplierid,
     categoryid, unitprice, discontinued)
        VALUES(1, N'Test1: Duplicate productid', 1, 1, 18.00, 0);
    SET @errnum = @@ERROR;
    IF @errnum <> 0
        BEGIN
            IF @@TRANCOUNT > 0 ROLLBACK TRAN;
            PRINT 'Error in first INSERT';
        END,
    -- Insert #2 no longer succeeds
    INSERT INTO Production.Products(productid, productname, supplierid,
     categoryid, unitprice, discontinued)

        VALUES(101, N'Test2: New productid', 1, 1, 18.00, 0);
    SET @errnum = @@ERROR;
    IF @errnum <> 0
        BEGIN
            -- Take actions based on the error
            IF @@TRANCOUNT > 0 ROLLBACK TRAN;
            PRINT 'Error in second INSERT';
        END;
    SET IDENTITY_INSERT Production.Products OFF;
    IF @@TRANCOUNT > 0 COMMIT TRAN;
GO

DELETE FROM Production.Products WHERE productid = 101;
PRINT 'Deleted ' + CAST(@@ROWCOUNT AS VARCHAR) + ' rows';
SET XACT_ABORT OFF;
GO
SELECT XACT_STATE(), @@TRANCOUNT;
```

EXERCISE 3 Work with Structured Error Handling by Using TRY/CATCH

1. In this step, you start out with TRY/CATCH. The following code has two INSERT statements in a single batch, wrapped in a transaction. The first INSERT fails, but the second will succeed because SQL Server by default will not abort a transaction with a duplicate primary key error. When the code runs, note that the first INSERT fails, due to a duplicate key violation, and the transaction is rolled back. However, no error is sent to the client, and execution transfers to the CATCH block. The error is handled and the transaction is rolled back. Open SSMS and open an empty query window. Execute the entire batch of T-SQL code.

```
USE TSQL2012;
GO
BEGIN TRY
BEGIN TRAN;
    SET IDENTITY_INSERT Production.Products ON;
    INSERT INTO Production.Products(productid, productname, supplierid,
     categoryid, unitprice, discontinued)
        VALUES(1, N'Test1: Duplicate productid', 1, 1, 18.00, 0);
    INSERT INTO Production.Products(productid, productname, supplierid,
     categoryid, unitprice, discontinued)
        VALUES(101, N'Test2: New productid', 1, 1, 18.00, 0);
    SET IDENTITY_INSERT Production.Products OFF;
COMMIT TRAN;
END TRY
BEGIN CATCH
    IF ERROR_NUMBER() = 2627 -- Duplicate key violation
        BEGIN
            PRINT 'Primary Key violation';
        END
    ELSE IF ERROR_NUMBER() = 547 -- Constraint violations
        BEGIN
            PRINT 'Constraint violation';
        END
    ELSE
        BEGIN
            PRINT 'Unhandled error';
        END;
    IF @@TRANCOUNT > 0 ROLLBACK TRANSACTION;
END CATCH;
```

2. Revise the CATCH block by using variables to capture error information and re-raise the error using RAISERROR.

```
USE TSQL2012;
GO
SET NOCOUNT ON;
DECLARE @error_number AS INT, @error_message AS NVARCHAR(1000), @error_severity AS
INT;
BEGIN TRY
BEGIN TRAN;
    SET IDENTITY_INSERT Production.Products ON;
    INSERT INTO Production.Products(productid, productname, supplierid,
```

```
     categoryid, unitprice, discontinued)
        VALUES(1, N'Test1: Duplicate productid', 1, 1, 18.00, 0);
    INSERT INTO Production.Products(productid, productname, supplierid,
     categoryid, unitprice, discontinued)
        VALUES(101, N'Test2: New productid', 1, 1, 18.00, 0);
    SET IDENTITY_INSERT Production.Products OFF;
    COMMIT TRAN;
END TRY
BEGIN CATCH
    SELECT XACT_STATE() as 'XACT_STATE', @@TRANCOUNT as '@@TRANCOUNT';
    SELECT @error_number = ERROR_NUMBER(), @error_message = ERROR_MESSAGE(),
     @error_severity = ERROR_SEVERITY();
    RAISERROR (@error_message, @error_severity, 1);
    IF @@TRANCOUNT > 0 ROLLBACK TRANSACTION;
END CATCH;
```

3. Next, use a THROW statement without parameters to re-raise (re-throw) the original error message and send it back to the client. This is by far the best method for reporting the error back to the caller.

```
USE TSQL2012;
GO
BEGIN TRY
BEGIN TRAN;
    SET IDENTITY_INSERT Production.Products ON;
    INSERT INTO Production.Products(productid, productname, supplierid,
     categoryid, unitprice, discontinued)
        VALUES(1, N'Test1: Duplicate productid', 1, 1, 18.00, 0);
    INSERT INTO Production.Products(productid, productname, supplierid,
     categoryid, unitprice, discontinued)
        VALUES(101, N'Test2: New productid', 1, 1, 18.00, 0);
    SET IDENTITY_INSERT Production.Products OFF;
COMMIT TRAN;
END TRY
BEGIN CATCH
    SELECT XACT_STATE() as 'XACT_STATE', @@TRANCOUNT as '@@TRANCOUNT';
    IF @@TRANCOUNT > 0 ROLLBACK TRANSACTION;
    THROW;
END CATCH;
GO
SELECT XACT_STATE() as 'XACT_STATE', @@TRANCOUNT as '@@TRANCOUNT';
```

Lesson Summary

- SQL Server 2012 uses both RAISERROR and the THROW command to generate errors.
- You can query the @@ERROR system function to determine whether an error has occurred and what the error number is.
- You can use the SET XACT_ABORT ON command to force a failure of a transaction and abort a batch when an error occurs.
- Unstructured error handling does not provide a single place in your code to handle errors.

- The TRY/CATCH block provides each batch of T-SQL code with a CATCH block in which to handle errors.
- The THROW command can be used to re-throw errors.
- There is a complete set of error functions to capture information about errors.

Lesson Review

Answer the following questions to test your knowledge of the information in this lesson. You can find the answers to these questions and explanations of why each answer choice is correct or incorrect in the "Answers" section at the end of this chapter.

1. What is the advantage of using THROW in a CATCH block?
   - **A.** THROW in a CATCH block does not require parameters and so is easier to write.
   - **B.** THROW re-throws the original error so that the original error can be handled.
   - **C.** THROW causes an error severity of level 16 automatically.
   - **D.** The statement before a THROW requires a semicolon.
2. Which of the following functions can be used in a CATCH block to return information about the error? (Choose all that apply.)
   - **A.** @@ERROR
   - **B.** ERROR_NUMBER()
   - **C.** ERROR_MESSAGE()
   - **D.** XACT_STATE()
3. How does SET XACT_ABORT ON affect a transaction?
   - **A.** If a T-SQL error with a severity level > 16 occurs, the transaction will be aborted.
   - **B.** If a T-SQL error with a severity level > 10 occurs, the transaction will be aborted.
   - **C.** If a T-SQL error with a severity level > 16 occurs, some statements of the transaction may still be executed.
   - **D.** If a T-SQL error with a severity level > 10 occurs, some statements of the transaction may still be executed.

Lesson 3: Using Dynamic SQL

Dynamic SQL refers to the technique of using T-SQL code to generate and potentially execute other T-SQL. With dynamic SQL, you write T-SQL code that will dynamically construct a different set of T-SQL code and then often send that code, batch by batch, to SQL Server for execution. The upshot is that you are using T-SQL to generate and execute T-SQL.

After this lesson, you will be able to:

- Describe the value of using T-SQL to generate T-SQL.
- Describe how to use the EXECUTE command to execute dynamic SQL.
- Describe how SQL injection can be used to add unwanted commands to dynamic SQL.
- Describe how to use the sp_executesql command to parameterize dynamic SQL and reduce the risk of SQL injection.

Estimated lesson time: 40 minutes

Dynamic SQL Overview

Often, you have tasks in your T-SQL code that require values to be supplied dynamically when the code runs, and not beforehand, so you supply the values in variables. But there are numerous cases where variables cannot be substituted for literals in T-SQL code.

For example, suppose you want to count the rows in the Production.Products table of the TS2012 database.

```
USE TSQL2012;
GO
SELECT COUNT(*) AS ProductRowCount FROM [Production].[Products];
```

Now suppose you want to substitute a variable for the table and schema name so that you can execute this same statement against any number of tables. A simple variable substitution will not work.

```
USE TSQL2012;
GO
DECLARE @tablename AS NVARCHAR(261) = N'[Production].[Products]';
SELECT COUNT(*) FROM @tablename;
```

> ***NOTE*** **PLANNING FOR SQL IDENTIFIER LENGTH**
>
> **This code uses NVARCHAR(261) to make sure the string variable is sufficiently long to handle two SQL Server identifiers (128 characters) plus the dot separator and brackets.**

But concatenate that variable with a string literal, and you can print out the command.

```
USE TSQL2012;
GO
DECLARE @tablename AS NVARCHAR(261) = N'[Production].[Products]';
PRINT N'SELECT COUNT(*) FROM ' + @tablename;
```

Or you can use the SELECT statement to get the same effect but in a result set.

```
DECLARE @tablename AS NVARCHAR(261) = N'[Production].[Products]';
SELECT N'SELECT COUNT(*) FROM ' + @tablename;
```

In each case, the result is valid T-SQL.

```
SELECT COUNT(*) AS ProductRowCount FROM [Production].[Products];
```

You can copy this to a query window and execute it manually, or you can embed it and execute it immediately using the EXECUTE command or sp_executesql, to execute it directly.

```
DECLARE @tablename AS NVARCHAR(261) = N'[Production].[Products]';
EXECUTE(N'SELECT COUNT(*) AS TableRowCount FROM ' + @tablename);
```

Dynamic SQL encompasses both the generation of new T-SQL code and the immediate execution of the generated code.

Uses for Dynamic SQL

Dynamic SQL is useful because T-SQL will not permit the direct replacement of many parts of commands with variables, including:

- The database name in the USE statement.
- Table names in the FROM clause.
- Column names in the SELECT, WHERE, GROUP BY, and HAVING clauses, in addition to the ORDER BY clause.
- Contents of lists such as in the IN and PIVOT clauses.

If you must use variables for these parts of commands, you must use dynamic SQL.

Some common scenarios for dynamic SQL include:

- Generating code to automate administrative tasks.
- Iterating through all databases on a server, through various types of objects in a database, and through object metadata such as column names or indexes.
- Building stored procedures with many optional parameters that build resulting queries based on which parameters have values. For example, a search procedure might accept name, address, city, and state, but the user passes in only a value for name. The procedure then needs to build a SELECT command that filters only by name and not the other parameters.
- Constructing parameterized ad hoc queries that can reuse previously cached execution plans (see the section "Using sp_executesql" later in this lesson).
- Constructing commands that require elements of the code based on querying the underlying data; for example, constructing a PIVOT query dynamically when you don't know ahead of time which literal values should appear in the IN clause of the PIVOT operator.

Generating T-SQL Strings

When you generate T-SQL statements, you are working with strings and must pay special attention to the way you delimit those strings. In SQL Server 2012, by default, you must use the single quotation mark (that is, the apostrophe) to delimit strings. This is due to the QUOTED_IDENTIFIER setting.

When SET QUOTED_IDENTIFIER is ON, which is the default, you delimit string literals by using single quotation marks, and use double quotation marks only to delimit T-SQL identifiers (in addition to square brackets).

If you set QUOTED_IDENTIFIER to OFF, then along with single quotation marks, you can also use double quotation marks to delimit strings. But then you must use square brackets to delimit T-SQL identifiers.

EXAM TIP

You should leave QUOTED_IDENTIFIER set to ON because that is the ANSI standard and the SQL Server default.

But using only single quotation marks as string delimiters leads to a problem: What do you do about embedded single quotation marks? For example, how can you search the TSQL2012 Sales.Customers table for the address "5678 rue de l'Abbaye"? You can try the following.

```
USE TSQL2012;
GO
SELECT custid, companyname, contactname, contacttitle, address FROM [Sales].[Customers]
WHERE address = N'5678 rue de l'Abbaye';
```

Note the error message.

```
Msg 156, Level 15, State 1, Line 1
Incorrect syntax near the keyword 'AS'.
Msg 105, Level 15, State 1, Line 3
Unclosed quotation mark after the character string '
'.
```

SQL Server has interpreted the search string to be *5678 rue de l* because it sees the second single quotation mark as the terminator of the string. The remaining part of the string, *Abbaye*' is treated as a syntax error. In order to handle embedded single quotation marks, you must change the intended single quotation mark into two single embedded quotation marks in order to get the output of one single quotation mark.

```
SELECT custid, companyname, contactname, contacttitle, address FROM [Sales].[Customers]
WHERE address = N'5678 rue de l''Abbaye';
```

This gives the desired result. When SQL Server sees the two single quotation marks inside a string and evaluates them, it translates the two single quotation marks into one single quotation mark.

Unfortunately, embedding two single quotation marks for every intended output single quotation mark makes it difficult to read and understand dynamic SQL when dealing with delimited strings. For example, to print the previous command by using a PRINT statement, you would have to use something like the following.

```
PRINT N'SELECT custid, companyname, contactname, contacttitle, address
FROM [Sales].[Customers]
WHERE address = N''5678 rue de l''''Abbaye'';';
```

An alternative is to use the QUOTENAME function, which can hide the complexity of the embedded quotation marks. You can use QUOTENAME to automatically double up the number of quotation marks. For example, the following:

```
PRINT QUOTENAME(N'5678 rue de l''Abbaye', '''');
```

results in this.

```
'5678 rue de l''Abbaye'
```

> ***NOTE*** **MANAGEMENT STUDIO OUTPUT LIMIT**
>
> **SQL Server can generate very large dynamic SQL strings, but SQL Server Management Studio will not show more than 8,000 bytes in its output to the Text window, whether you generate the output by using a PRINT statement or a SELECT statement. To show more than 8,000 bytes, you must break up the long string into substrings less than or equal to 8,000 bytes and generate them individually.**

After you generate the strings you want to execute, you can either generate the results and execute them yourself, or send the string directly to SQL Server. This is called executing the dynamic SQL, and two methods are available: the EXECUTE statement and the sp_executesql stored procedure.

The EXECUTE Command

The simplest method provided by SQL Server for executing dynamic SQL is the EXECUTE statement, which can be written as EXECUTE or abbreviated as EXEC. From this point on, this lesson uses the shorter form, EXEC.

The EXEC statement has several uses, only one of which involves dynamic SQL:

- Executing stored procedures
- Impersonating users or logins
- Querying a linked server
- Executing dynamic SQL generated strings

In this lesson, the last option, executing dynamic SQL strings, is the focus.

Although not strictly speaking a function, the dynamic SQL form of EXEC accepts a character string as input in parentheses. Here are some things to note about the EXEC command:

- The input string must be a single T-SQL batch. The string can contain many T-SQL commands, but the string cannot contain GO delimiters.
- You can use string literals, string variables, or a concatenation of the two.
  - The string variables can have any string data type, regular or Unicode characters.
  - The string variables can have (MAX) length definitions.

The following example of the EXEC command illustrates the potential value of using dynamic SQL. The following returns to the original example at the beginning of the lesson, but this time enhances it to use string variables.

```
USE TSQL2012;
GO
DECLARE @SQLString AS NVARCHAR(4000)
    , @tablename AS NVARCHAR(261) = '[Production].[Products]';
SET @SQLString = 'SELECT COUNT(*) AS TableRowCount FROM ' + @tablename;
EXEC(@SQLString);
```

Although the EXEC command accepts a single variable, it also accepts a concatenation of two or more string variables.

```
USE TSQL2012;
GO
DECLARE @SQLString AS NVARCHAR(MAX)
    , @tablename AS NVARCHAR(261) = '[Production].[Products]';
SET @SQLString = 'SELECT COUNT(*) AS TableRowCount FROM '
EXEC(@SQLString + @tablename);
```

Quick Check

1. **Can you generate and execute dynamic SQL in a different database than the one your code is in?**
2. **What are some objects that cannot be referenced in T-SQL by using variables?**

Quick Check Answer

1. **Yes, because the USE <*database*> command can be inserted into a dynamic SQL batch.**
2. **Objects that you cannot use variables for in T-SQL commands include the database name in a USE statement, the table name in a FROM clause, column names in the SELECT and WHERE clauses, and lists of literal values in the IN() and PIVOT() functions.**

SQL Injection

Using dynamic SQL in applications that send user input to the database can be subject to SQL injection, where a user enters something that was not intended to be executed. SQL injection is a large topic; there are many types of SQL injection, and it can occur at the client level and at the server level. Your job as a T-SQL developer is to protect against any SQL injection exposure in your T-SQL code.

Hackers have learned that by inserting just a single quotation mark, they can sometimes cause applications to report back an error message to the user, indicating that the command has been assembled by using dynamic SQL and may be hackable. All the hacker does is type in a single quotation mark (').

The resulting message from SQL Server is as follows.

```
Msg 105, Level 15, State 1, Line 1
Unclosed quotation mark after the character string '''.
Msg 102, Level 15, State 1, Line 1
Incorrect syntax near '''.
```

The telltale message is "Unclosed quotation mark after the character string." This tells the hacker that he or she can add a delimiter and extra code, if the string accepts longer input. That clues the hacker into realizing that inserting a single quotation mark may have terminated a string early, so that a "dangling" string delimiter, a hidden single quotation mark, was detected by SQL Server. So now all the hacker has to type is a single line comment after the single quotation mark to make SQL Server ignore the trailing single quotation mark. The hacker types **' --** .

If that succeeds in removing the error message, then the hacker knows that another T-SQL command can be injected into the string, as in the following.

```
' SELECT TOP 1 name FROM sys.tables --
```

Of course, the input string must allow enough characters to support the injected command, but that is something the hacker will eventually find out.

More dangerous than a SELECT statement is a DELETE or DROP statement that could be used to maliciously affect data.

There are many methods of preventing SQL injection, and it is quite a large topic. From the standpoint of a T-SQL developer, one of the most important methods is to parameterize the dynamic SQL generation and execution by using sp_executesql.

> ***MORE INFO*** **SQL INJECTION**
>
> **For more details on SQL Injection, see the Books Online for SQL Server 2012 article "SQL Injection" at *http://msdn.microsoft.com/en-us/library/ms161953(SQL.105).aspx.***

 **Quick Check**

1. **How can a hacker detect that SQL injection may be possible?**
2. **Where is the injected code inserted?**

Quick Check Answer

1. **By inserting a single quotation mark and observing an error message.**
2. **Between an initial single quotation mark, which terminates the data input string, and a final comment mark, which disables the internal terminating single quotation mark.**

Using sp_executesql

The sp_executesql system stored procedure was introduced as an alternative to using the EXEC command for executing dynamic SQL. It both generates and executes a dynamic SQL string.

The sp_executesql system stored procedure supports parameters. The parameters must be passed as Unicode.

Output parameters are supported. Because of parameters, sp_executesql is more secure and can help prevent some types of SQL injection. The sp_executesql parameters cannot be used to replace required string literals such as table and column names.

The syntax for sp_executesql is as follows.

```
sp_executesql [ @statement = ] statement
[   { , [ @params = ] N'@parameter_name data_type [ OUT | OUTPUT ][ ,...n ]' }
     { , [ @param1 = ] 'value1' [ ,...n ] }]
```

The @statement input parameter is basically an NVARCHAR(MAX). You submit a statement in the form of a Unicode string in the @statement parameter, and embed parameters in that statement that you would like to have substituted in the final string. You list those parameter names with their data types in the @params string, and then put the values in the @param1 list, @param2 list, and so on.

So you can rewrite the command that counts rows from a dynamically generated table as follows by using the @tablename parameter.

```
USE TSQL2012;
GO
DECLARE @SQLString AS NVARCHAR(4000), @address AS NVARCHAR(60);
SET @SQLString = N'
SELECT custid, companyname, contactname, contacttitle, address
FROM [Sales].[Customers]
WHERE address = @address';
SET @address = N'5678 rue de l''Abbaye';
EXEC sp_executesql
    @statement = @SQLString
    , @params = N'@address NVARCHAR(60)'
    , @address = @address;
```

EXAM TIP

The ability to parameterize means that sp_excutesql avoids simple concatenations like those used in the EXEC statement. As a result, it can be used to help prevent SQL injection.

The sp_executesql stored procedure can sometimes provide better query performance than the EXEC command because its parameterization aids in reusing cached execution plans. Because sp_executesql forces you to parameterize, often the actual query string will be the same and only the parameter values will change. Then SQL Server can keep the overall string constant and reuse the query plan created for the original call of that distinct string to sp_executesql. Plan reuse is not guaranteed because there are other factors that SQL Server takes into account, but you do increase the chances for plan reuse.

Quick Check

1. **How can you pass information from sp_executesql to the caller?**
2. **How does sp_executesql help stop SQL injection?**

Quick Check Answer

1. **Use one or more OUTPUT parameters. You can also persist the data in a permanent or temporary table, but the most direct method is through the OUTPUT parameter.**
2. **You can use sp_executesql to parameterize user input, which can prevent any injected code from being executed.**

PRACTICE Writing and Testing Dynamic SQL

In this practice, you write and test dynamic SQL code. You use SSMS and the TSQL2012 database.

If you encounter a problem completing an exercise, you can install the completed projects from the companion content for this chapter and lesson.

EXERCISE 1 Generate T-SQL Strings and Use QUOTENAME

In this exercise, you use QUOTENAME to simplify the process of generating T-SQL strings. A quick way to see the benefit of QUOTENAME is when using a variable.

1. In this step, you use a variable to generate T-SQL strings. Open SSMS and open an empty query window. Execute the following batch of T-SQL code. Note that the resulting string that is printed does not have the correct delimiters.

```
USE TSQL2012;
GO
DECLARE @address AS NVARCHAR(60) = '5678 rue de l''Abbaye';
PRINT N'SELECT *
FROM [Sales].[Customers]
WHERE address = '+ @address;
```

2. Now embed the variable with QUOTENAME before concatenating it to the PRINT statement. Note that the resulting string is now successful.

```
USE TSQL2012;
GO
DECLARE @address AS NVARCHAR(60) = '5678 rue de l''Abbaye';
PRINT N'SELECT *
FROM [Sales].[Customers]
WHERE address = '+ QUOTENAME(@address, '''') + ';';
```

EXERCISE 2 Prevent SQL Injection

In this exercise, you simulate SQL injection by using T-SQL, and practice how to prevent it by using the sp_executesql stored procedure. You pass a parameter to a stored procedure to simulate how a hacker would send in input from a screen.

1. Open SSMS and load the following stored procedure script into a query window. The procedure uses dynamic SQL to return a list of customers based on address. The exercise uses an address because it is a longer character string that could permit additional SQL commands to be appended to it.

```
USE TSQL2012;
GO
IF OBJECT_ID(N'Sales.ListCustomersByAddress', N'P') IS NOT NULL
    DROP PROCEDURE Sales.ListCustomersByAddress;
GO
CREATE PROCEDURE Sales.ListCustomersByAddress
    @address NVARCHAR(60)
AS
    DECLARE @SQLString AS NVARCHAR(4000);
SET @SQLString = N'
SELECT companyname, contactname
FROM Sales.Customers WHERE address = ''' + @address + '''';
    -- PRINT @SQLString;
EXEC(@SQLString);
RETURN;
GO
```

2. The stored procedure works as expected when the input parameter @address is normal. In a separate query window, execute the following.

```
USE TSQL2012;
GO
EXEC Sales.ListCustomersByAddress @address = N'8901 Tsawassen Blvd.';
```

3. To simulate the hacker passing in a single quotation mark, call the stored procedure with two single quotation marks as a delimited string. Note the error message from SQL Server.

```
USE TSQL2012;
GO
EXEC Sales.ListCustomersByAddress @address = N'''';
```

4. Now insert a comment marker after the single quotation mark so that the final string delimiter is ignored.

```
USE TSQL2012;
GO
EXEC Sales.ListCustomersByAddress @address = N''' -- ';
```

5. All that remains is to inject the malicious code. The user actually types **SELECT 1 -- '**, which you can simulate as follows. The SELECT 1 command actually gets executed by SQL Server after execution of the first SELECT command. The hacker can now insert any command, provided it is within the length of the accepted string.

```
USE TSQL2012;
GO
EXEC Sales.ListCustomersByAddress @address = N''' SELECT 1 -- ';
```

6. Now revise the stored procedure to use sp_executesql and bring in the address as a parameter to the stored procedure, as follows.

```
USE TSQL2012;
GO
IF OBJECT_ID(N'Sales.ListCustomersByAddress', N'P') IS NOT NULL
    DROP PROCEDURE Sales.ListCustomersByAddress;
GO
CREATE PROCEDURE Sales.ListCustomersByAddress
    @address AS NVARCHAR(60)
AS
DECLARE @SQLString AS NVARCHAR(4000);
SET @SQLString = N'
SELECT companyname, contactname
FROM Sales.Customers WHERE address = @address';
EXEC sp_executesql
    @statement = @SQLString
    , @params = N'@address NVARCHAR(60)'
    , @address = @address;
RETURN;
GO
```

7. Now enter a valid address by using the revised stored procedure. Note that there is no message indicating that there is an unclosed quotation mark. The single quotation mark as a parameter to the stored procedure and to sp_executesql guarantees it will only be treated as a single string.

```
USE TSQL2012;
GO
EXEC Sales.ListCustomersByAddress @address = N'8901 Tsawassen Blvd.';
```

8. Execute again the remaining steps to ensure that no unexpected data is returned.

```
USE TSQL2012;
GO
EXEC Sales.ListCustomersByAddress @address = N'''';
EXEC Sales.ListCustomersByAddress @address = N''' -- ';
EXEC Sales.ListCustomersByAddress @address = N''' SELECT 1 -- ';
```

EXERCISE 3 Use Output Parameters with sp_executesql

In this exercise, you use sp_executesql to return a value by using an output parameter. Sometimes it is convenient to bring back results in a variable from dynamic SQL. That is not possible with the EXEC statement, but sp_executesql can do that through output parameters.

1. Open SSMS and enter the following script into a query window. The script uses the EXEC command to count the number of rows. Note that it is not possible to return that count value back directly. Apart from storing it in a temporary table or some other persistent mechanism, EXEC simply cannot communicate back to the caller. You can see the count value in the output of SSMS, but cannot capture it in a variable.

```
USE TSQL2012;
GO
DECLARE @SQLString AS NVARCHAR(4000);
SET @SQLString = N'SELECT COUNT(*) FROM Production.Products';
EXEC(@SQLString);
```

2. You can use sp_executesql to capture and return values back to the caller by using output parameters. In the following code, you specify the keyword OUTPUT both in the parameter declaration and in the parameter assignment.

```
USE TSQL2012;
GO
DECLARE @SQLString AS NVARCHAR(4000)
    , @outercount AS int;
SET @SQLString = N'SET @innercount = (SELECT COUNT(*) FROM Production.Products)';
EXEC sp_executesql
    @statment = @SQLString
    , @params = N'@innercount AS int OUTPUT'
    , @innercount = @outercount OUTPUT;
SELECT @outercount AS  'RowCount';
```

Lesson Summary

- Dynamic SQL can be used to generate and execute T-SQL code in cases where the T-SQL statements must be constructed at run time.
- SQL injection refers to the potential for applications to accept input that injects unwanted code that dynamic SQL executes.
- The sp_executesql stored procedure can be used to help prevent SQL injection by forcing the relevant parts of dynamic SQL to be parameterized.

Lesson Review

Answer the following questions to test your knowledge of the information in this lesson. You can find the answers to these questions and explanations of why each answer choice is correct or incorrect in the "Answers" section at the end of this chapter.

1. Which of the following techniques can be used to inject unwanted code into dynamic SQL when user input is concatenated with valid SQL commands?
   - **A.** Insert a comment string of two dashes, then the malicious code, and then a single quotation mark.
   - **B.** Insert a single quotation mark, then the malicious code, and then a comment string of two dashes.
   - **C.** Insert the malicious code followed by a single quotation mark and a comment string of two dashes.
2. What are the advantages of sp_executesql over the EXECUTE() command? (Choose all that apply.)
   - **A.** sp_executesql can parameterize search arguments and help prevent SQL injection.
   - **B.** sp_executesql uses Unicode strings.
   - **C.** sp_executesql can return data through output parameters.
3. Which of the following are true about the SET QUOTED_IDENTIFIER statement? (Choose all that apply.)
   - **A.** When set to ON, QUOTED_IDENTIFIER allows you to use double quotation marks to delimit T-SQL identifiers such as table and column names.
   - **B.** When set to OFF, QUOTED_IDENTIFIER allows you to use double quotation marks to delimit T-SQL identifiers such as table and column names.
   - **C.** When set to ON, QUOTED_IDENTIFIER allows you to use double quotation marks to delimit strings.
   - **D.** When set to OFF, QUOTED_IDENTIFIER allows you to use double quotation marks to delimit strings.

Case Scenarios

In the following case scenarios, you apply what you've learned about transactions, error handling, and dynamic SQL. You can find the answers to these questions in the "Answers" section at the end of this chapter.

Case Scenario 1: Implementing Error Handling

As a database developer on a key project for your company, you have been asked to refactor a set of stored procedures in your production database server. You have observed that the stored procedures have practically no error handling, and when they do have it, it is ad hoc and unstructured. None of the stored procedures are using transactions. You need to put a plan together to justify your activity.

1. When should you recommend using explicit transactions?
2. When should you recommend using a different isolation level?
3. What type of error handling should you recommend?
4. What plans should you include for refactoring dynamic SQL?

Case Scenario 2: Implementing Transactions

You have just been assigned to a new project as the database developer on the team. The application will use stored procedures for performing some of the financial operations. You have decided to use T-SQL transactions. Answer the following questions about what you would recommend in the specified situations.

1. In some transactions that update tables, after a session reads a particular value from another table, it is critical that the other table's value not change until the transaction is finished. What is the appropriate transaction isolation level to accomplish this?
2. You will use T-SQL scripts to deploy new objects such as tables, views, or T-SQL code to the database. If any kind of T-SQL error occurs, you want the entire deployment script to quit. How can you accomplish this without adding complex error handling?
3. One of the stored procedures will transfer money from one account to another. During that transfer period, neither account can have any data changed, inserted, or deleted for the range of values read by the transaction. What is the appropriate transaction isolation level to accomplish this?

Suggested Practices

To help you successfully master the exam objectives presented in this chapter, complete the following tasks.

Implement Error Handling

Use the TS2012 database to perform the following actions.

- **Practice 1** Create a transaction to update the TSQL2012 Production.Products table, incrementing the unitprice column by 5 for productid = 100. Use THROW with parameters to raise an error if no rows are updated.
- **Practice 2** Add a TRY/CATCH block to the transaction.
- **Practice 3** In the CATCH block, report all the error information back to the client by using the error functions, roll back the transaction, and re-raise the error using THROW.

Answers

This section contains the answers to the lesson review questions and solutions to the case scenarios in this chapter.

Lesson 1

1. **Correct Answers: A and C**
   - **A. Correct:** An ALTER TABLE command is a DDL command that changes metadata and always executes as a transaction.
   - **B. Incorrect:** A PRINT command does not change data, and therefore does not execute by itself in a transaction.
   - **C. Correct:** An UPDATE statement changes data and executes as a transaction.
   - **D. Incorrect:** A SET statement only affects session settings and does not change data, and therefore does not execute as a transaction.
2. **Correct Answer: B**
   - **A. Incorrect:** A single COMMIT commits only the innermost level of the transaction and will not commit the entire nested transaction.
   - **B. Correct:** A single ROLLBACK will roll back the entire outer transaction of a nested transaction.
   - **C. Incorrect:** A single COMMIT commits data only at the outermost level of a nested transaction.
   - **D. Incorrect:** A single ROLLBACK does not roll back just one level of the transaction; instead, it rolls back the entire transaction.
3. **Correct Answers: A, B, and D**
   - **A. Correct:** Adding a READUNCOMMITTED table hint causes no shared locks to be used by the statement.
   - **B. Correct:** The READ COMMITTED SNAPSHOT option reads committed data from versions, not by acquiring shared locks.
   - **C. Incorrect:** The REPEATABLE READ isolation level actually holds shared locks until the end of a transaction, and therefore can actually increase blocking and deadlocking.
   - **D. Correct:** The SNAPSHOT isolation level also reduces shared locks by reading committed data from committed versions and not by using shared locks, so it also can reduce blocking and deadlocking.

Lesson 2

1. **Correct Answer: B**

   A. **Incorrect:** Although it is true that THROW does not take parameters in a CATCH block, that is not necessarily an advantage.

   B. **Correct:** The THROW statement in a CATCH block can re-throw an error and thereby allow you to report on an error in the TRY block without having to have stored any prior information. This makes it possible to do all error handling in the CATCH block.

   C. **Incorrect:** THROW always results in a severity level of 16, but that is not necessarily an advantage. RAISERROR is more flexible by allowing a range of severity levels.

   D. **Incorrect:** Requiring a semicolon on the previous T-SQL statement is perhaps a good coding requirement, but it is not a benefit provided by the THROW command.

2. **Correct Answers: A, B, C, and D**

   A. **Correct:** The value of @@ERROR changes with each successful command, so if it is accessed in the very first statement of the CATCH block, you can get the original error message.

   B. **Correct:** ERROR_NUMBER() returns the error number of the original error that led to control being passed to the CATCH block.

   C. **Correct:** ERROR_MESSAGE() returns the text of the original error.

   D. **Correct:** XACT_STATE() tells you the state of the transaction in a CATCH block, in particular whether the transaction is committable.

3. **Correct Answer: B**

   A. **Incorrect:** If a T-SQL error with severity level > 16 occurs, the transaction will not be aborted.

   B. **Correct:** A T-SQL error with severity level > 10 causes the transaction to be aborted.

   C. **Incorrect:** When a transaction is aborted by XACT_ABORT, no other statements in the transaction will be executed.

   D. **Incorrect:** When a transaction is aborted by XACT_ABORT, no other statements in the transaction will be executed.

Lesson 3

1. **Correct Answer: B**

   A. Incorrect: The comment string must come last and the embedded single quotation mark must come first.

   B. Correct: The initial single quotation mark terminates the input string, and the final comment removes the effect of the terminating single quotation mark. Then the malicious code can be inserted in between them.

   C. Incorrect: The malicious code must come after the first single quotation mark and before the final comment marks.

2. **Correct Answers: A and C**

   A. Correct: Parameterization is the key advantage of sp_executesql over the EXEC() statement because it ensures that any injected code will only be seen as a string parameter value, and not as executable code.

   B. Incorrect: Although sp_executesql does require Unicode strings as parameters, this fact is not necessarily an advantage. The EXECUTE command accepts both Unicode and non-Unicode, and therefore could be considered more flexible.

   C. Correct: The use of output parameters solves a serious limitation of the EXECUTE command. EXECUTE cannot return information to the calling session directly.

3. **Correct Answers: A and D**

   A. Correct: When you set QUOTED_IDENTIFIER to ON, you can use double quotation marks to delimit T-SQL identifiers such as table and column names.

   B. Incorrect: When you set QUOTED_IDENTIFIER to OFF, you cannot use double quotation marks to delimit T-SQL identifiers such as table and column names.

   C. Incorrect: When you set QUOTED_IDENTIFIER to ON, you cannot use double quotation marks to delimit strings.

   D. Correct: When you set QUOTED_IDENTIFIER to OFF, you can use double quotation marks to delimit strings.

Case Scenario 1

1. Whenever more than one data change occurs in a stored procedure, and it is important that the data changes be treated as a logical unit of work, you should add transaction logic to the stored procedure.
2. You need to adapt the isolation levels to the requirements for transactional consistency. You should investigate the current application and the database for instances of blocking and especially deadlocking. If you find deadlocks, and establish that they are not due to mistakes in T-SQL coding, you can use various methods of lowering the isolation level in order to make deadlocks less likely. However, be aware that some transactions may require higher levels of isolation.
3. You should use TRY/CATCH blocks in every stored procedure where errors might occur, and encourage your team to standardize on that usage. By funneling all errors to the CATCH block, you can handle errors in just one place in the code.
4. Check the stored procedures for the use of dynamic SQL, and where possible, replace calls to the EXECUTE command with the sp_executesql stored procedure.

Case Scenario 2

1. To ensure that whenever data is read in a transaction the data will not change until the end of the transaction, you can use the REPEATABLE READ transaction isolation level. This is the least restrictive level that will satisfy the requirements.
2. When you deploy new database objects by using T-SQL scripts, you can wrap the batches in a single transaction and use SET XACT_ABORT ON right after the BEGIN TRANSACTION statement. Then if any T-SQL error occurs, the entire transaction will abort and you will not have to add complex error handling.
3. To ensure that, for the range of values read by the transaction, none of the rows being read can be changed and that no new rows may be inserted and none deleted, you can use the SERIALIZABLE isolation level. This is the most restrictive isolation level and can lead to a lot of blocking, so you need to ensure that the transactions complete as quickly as possible.

CHAPTER 13

Designing and Implementing T-SQL Routines

Exam objectives in this chapter:

- Create Database Objects
  - Create and alter DML triggers.
- Modify Data
  - Create and alter stored procedures (simple statements).
  - Work with functions.

T-SQL code can be stored within Microsoft SQL Server databases by using T-SQL routines such as stored procedures, triggers, and functions. This helps make your T-SQL code more portable, because it stays with the database and these routines will be restored from a database backup along with the database data. These routines can then be executed from the database as well. In this chapter, you learn about creating reusable T-SQL routines in stored procedures, triggers, and user-defined functions.

Lessons in this chapter:

- Lesson 1: Designing and Implementing Stored Procedures
- Lesson 2: Implementing Triggers
- Lesson 3: Implementing User-Defined Functions

Before You Begin

To complete the lessons in this chapter, you must have:

- An understanding of basic database concepts.
- Experience working with SQL Server Management Studio (SSMS).
- Some experience writing T-SQL code.
- Access to a SQL Server 2012 instance with the sample database TSQL2012 installed.

Lesson 1: Designing and Implementing Stored Procedures

Stored procedures are routines that reside in a database and encapsulate code. SQL Server permits several types of stored procedures, such as the following:

- T-SQL stored procedures written in T-SQL code
- CLR stored procedures stored as Microsoft .NET assemblies in the database
- Extended stored procedures, which make calls to externally compiled data definition languages (DLLs)

The lessons in this chapter introduce you to T-SQL stored procedures. All references in this chapter to stored procedures refer to T-SQL stored procedures. Any references to CLR or extended stored procedures are called out explicitly. This lesson focuses on the design and implementation of stored procedures.

After this lesson, you will be able to:

- Create basic T-SQL stored procedures.
- Write a stored procedure to meet a specific set of requirements.
- Apply branching logic in a stored procedure.
- Define the different types of stored procedure results.
- Describe how stored procedures can be used for the data access layer of an application.

Estimated lesson time: 50 minutes

Understanding Stored Procedures

A T-SQL stored procedure consists of a single batch of T-SQL code. Stored procedures have a number of important features, such as the following:

- They can be called from T-SQL code by using the EXECUTE command.
- You can pass data to them through input parameters, and receive data back through output parameters.
- They can return result sets of queries to the client application.
- They can modify data in tables.
- They can create, alter, and drop tables and indexes.

Using T-SQL stored procedures in a SQL Server database has a number of advantages, such as the following:

- To encapsulate T-SQL code
  - A single stored procedure can be called from many places, and with parameters that adapt the code to different initial conditions.
- To make a database more secure
  - Rather than give the user access to database tables directly, you can grant permissions to a stored procedure.
  - Stored procedures can help prevent SQL injection by parameterizing dynamic SQL.
- To present a more versatile data access layer to users and applications
  - The stored procedure allows the user to bypass complex logic to get desired results.
  - Underlying physical structures of database tables may change, and the stored procedure may be modified, but because the user sees the same procedure and parameters, the user does not need to know about the changes.
- To help improve performance by creating execution plans that can be reused
  - By passing in parameters, you can reuse the cached plan of a stored procedure for many different parameter values, preventing the need to recompile the T-SQL code.
  - Stored procedures can reduce network traffic. If the application had to do all the work, intermediate results would have to be passed back to the application over the network. Similarly, if the application does all the work, it must send every T-SQL command to the SQL Server over the network.

Stored procedures can be used for encapsulating application logic that deals with data, and for administrative functions such as backup and restore. In fact, almost all T-SQL statements can be included in a stored procedure. However, keep the following in mind:

- You cannot use the USE *<database name>* command.
- You cannot use a CREATE statement with any of the following object types: AGGREGATE, RULE, DEFAULT, CREATE, FUNCTION, TRIGGER, PROCEDURE, or VIEW.
- You can create, alter, and drop a table and an index by using the CREATE, ALTER, and DROP statements.

Consider the following T-SQL code, which queries the TSQL2012 database to find all the orders placed by a customer with a customer ID of 37 in the second quarter of 2007.

```
USE TSQL2012;
GO
SELECT orderid, custid, shipperid, orderdate, requireddate, shippeddate
FROM Sales.Orders
WHERE custid = 37
    AND orderdate >= '2007-04-01'
    AND orderdate < '2007-07-01';
```

This query is limited because it has literal values in the WHERE clause. To make the code a little more general, you can use variables in place of those literals values, such as in the following.

```
USE TSQL2012;
GO
DECLARE  @custid   AS INT,
    @orderdatefrom AS DATETIME,
    @orderdateto   AS DATETIME;
SET @custid = 37;
SET @orderdatefrom = '2007-04-01';
SET @orderdateto = '2007-07-01';
SELECT orderid, custid, shipperid, orderdate, requireddate, shippeddate
FROM Sales.Orders
WHERE custid = @custid
    AND orderdate >= @orderdatefrom
    AND orderdate < @orderdateto;
GO
```

Notice that all you've done is declare three variables for the literal values, and assigned them values before executing the query. When you execute the batch of T-SQL code against the original TSQL2012 Sales.Orders table, you will see three rows returned. Now examine how this code might look when it is further encapsulated in a stored procedure.

```
IF OBJECT_ID(N'Sales.GetCustomerOrders', N'P') IS NOT NULL
    DROP PROC Sales.GetCustomerOrders;
GO
CREATE PROC Sales.GetCustomerOrders
    @custid   AS INT,
    @orderdatefrom AS DATETIME = '19000101',
    @orderdateto   AS DATETIME = '99991231',
    @numrows  AS INT = 0 OUTPUT
AS
BEGIN
    SET NOCOUNT ON;
    SELECT orderid, custid, shipperid, orderdate, requireddate, shippeddate
    FROM Sales.Orders
    WHERE custid = @custid
        AND orderdate >= @orderdatefrom
        AND orderdate < @orderdateto;
    SET @numrows = @@ROWCOUNT;
    RETURN;
END
GO
```

After you execute the previous code and create the stored procedure, you can call the stored procedure as follows.

```
DECLARE @rowsreturned AS INT;
EXEC Sales.GetCustomerOrders
  @custid    = 37,
  @orderdatefrom = '20070401',
  @orderdateto  = '20070701',
  @numrows   = @rowsreturned OUTPUT;
SELECT @rowsreturned AS "Rows Returned";
GO
```

The result is the same set of rows of data, but you also get the number of rows back in a special OUTPUT parameter. Examine this procedure and the way it was called step by step in order to draw out the essential features of a T-SQL stored procedure.

Testing for the Existence of a Stored Procedure

If you try to create a stored procedure and it already exists, your CREATE command will fail. If the stored procedure already exists, you can alter the stored procedure, but if you try to alter a stored procedure that does not exist, the ALTER command will fail. The first part of the script solves this problem by placing a conditional DROP of the stored procedure before trying to create it.

```
IF OBJECT_ID(N'Sales.GetCustomerOrders', N'P') IS NOT NULL
    DROP PROC Sales.GetCustomerOrders;
GO
```

You can check for the existence of a database object such as a stored procedure in many ways. For example, you can check the metadata in sys.objects. However, using the OBJECT_ID() function is probably the least verbose.

Stored Procedure Parameters

Stored procedures take parameters that have a syntax very similar to the DECLARE syntax for variables. Take a look at the CREATE PROCEDURE statement.

```
CREATE PROC Sales.GetCustomerOrders
    @custid   AS INT,
    @orderdatefrom AS DATETIME = '19000101',
    @orderdateto   AS DATETIME = '99991231',
    @numrows  AS INT = 0 OUTPUT
AS
BEGIN
    SET NOCOUNT ON;
    SELECT orderid, custid, shipperid, orderdate, requireddate, shippeddate
    FROM [Sales].[Orders]
    WHERE custid = @custid
        AND orderdate >= @orderdatefrom
        AND orderdate < @orderdateto;
    SET @numrows = @@ROWCOUNT;
    RETURN;
END
```

You can write either CREATE PROCEDURE or use the abbreviation CREATE PROC when creating the stored procedure. Then you must follow with the stored procedure name.

Note the following regarding stored procedure parameters:

- You don't have to put parameters in a stored procedure, but if you want to add them, they must be listed right after the beginning of the procedure.
- Parameters can be required or optional.

    - If you do not provide a default initialization, the parameter is required. In the previous code, @custid is a required parameter.
    - If you do provide a default initialization, the parameter is optional. In the previous code, @orderdatefrom and @orderdateto are optional parameters. If an optional parameter is not given a value when the procedure is called, the default value will be used in the rest of the procedure.
- Stored procedure parameters are treated as variables for the rest of the procedure.
- You can initialize the parameter values in the same way that you can with variables.
- The OUTPUT keyword specifies a special parameter that returns values back to the caller.
    - Output parameters are always optional parameters.
- The AS command is required after the list of the parameters.

BEGIN/END

You can surround the code in a stored procedure by using a BEGIN/END block. Though this is not required, using a BEGIN/END block can help clarify the code.

SET NOCOUNT ON

You can embed the setting of NOCOUNT to ON inside the stored procedure to remove messages like (3 row(s) affected) being returned every time the procedure executes.

EXAM TIP

The NOCOUNT setting of ON or OFF stays with the stored procedure when it is created. Placing a SET NOCOUNT ON at the beginning of every stored procedure prevents the procedure from returning that message to the client. In addition, SET NOCOUNT ON can improve the performance of frequently executed stored procedures because there is less network communication required when the "rows(s) affected" message is not returned to the client.

RETURN and Return Codes

A stored procedure ends when the T-SQL batch ends, but you can cause the procedure to exit at any point by using the RETURN command. You can use more than one RETURN command in a procedure. RETURN stops the execution of the procedure and returns control back to the caller. Statements after the RETURN statement are not executed.

RETURN by itself causes SQL Server to send a status code back to the caller. The statuses are 0 for successful and a negative number if there is an error. However, the error numbers are not reliable, so you should not rely on them. Use the SQL Server error numbers from @@ERROR or from ERROR_NUMBER() in a CATCH block instead.

You can send your own return codes back to the caller by inserting an integer value after the RETURN statement. However, if you want to send information back to the caller, it is considered a better practice to use an OUTPUT parameter instead.

Executing Stored Procedures

To execute a stored procedure from T-SQL, you use an EXECUTE statement, or EXEC for short. If a stored procedure does not have any input parameters, you use EXEC followed by the stored procedure name, as in the following.

```
EXEC sp_configure;
```

This code executes the system stored procedure sp_configure. Because it is a system stored procedure in the master database, it can be executed from any database.

If the execution of a stored procedure is the first statement in a batch of T-SQL code or the only statement selected in a query window, you do not need the EXEC statement. However, if the stored procedure is the second or later statement, you must precede it with EXEC or EXECUTE.

EXAM TIP

Always include the EXEC command when calling a stored procedure. That will avoid getting unexpected and confusing errors. If the statement is no longer the first statement in the batch, it will still run.

Input Parameters

When the stored procedure has input parameters, you can pass in a parameter value either by putting it in the correct position or by associating the value with the name of the parameter. For example, in the previous section, you created a stored procedure that was named Sales.GetCustomerOrders in the TSQL2012 database. To call the procedure by passing in a parameter by position, just type the following.

```
EXEC Sales.GetCustomerOrders 37, '20070401', '20070701';
```

Note that you can ignore the optional OUTPUT parameter.

Now call the procedure by listing the parameter by name, as in the following.

```
EXEC Sales.GetCustomerOrders  @custid   = 37,   @orderdatefrom = '20070401',
 @orderdateto  = '20070701';
```

When you pass the parameter values by using the parameter names, you can put the named parameters in any order. For example, when calling the Sales.GetCustomerOrders stored procedure, you could put @custid later than the date parameters. (Ignore the optional OUTPUT parameter for now. Output parameters are covered in the next section.)

```
EXEC Sales.GetCustomerOrders
    @orderdatefrom = '20070401',
    @orderdateto  = '20070701',
    @custid   = 37;
GO
```

However, when you pass the parameter values by position, you must use the exact position of the parameters as defined in the CREATE PROCEDURE statement.

```
EXEC Sales.GetCustomerOrders 37, '20070401', '20070701';
GO
```

EXAM TIP

It is a best practice to name the parameters when you call stored procedures. Although passing parameter values by position may be more compact, it is also more error prone. If you pass parameters by name and the parameter order changes in the stored procedure, your call of the procedure will still work.

Note that because the date parameters are optional, you could drop them entirely from the procedure call, as follows.

```
EXEC Sales.GetCustomerOrders
  @custid   = 37;
GO
```

Output Parameters

To use output parameters, you add the keyword OUTPUT (which can be abbreviated as OUT) after the parameter when you declare it in the CREATE PROC statement.

```
CREATE PROC Sales.GetCustomerOrders
    @custid   AS INT,
    @orderdatefrom AS DATETIME = '19000101',
    @orderdateto   AS DATETIME = '99991231',
    @numrows AS INT = 0 OUTPUT
AS <rest of procedure>
```

To retrieve data from the output parameter, you must also use the keyword OUTPUT when you call the stored procedure, and you must provide a variable to capture the value when it comes back. If you don't have the OUTPUT keyword in the procedure value, no value will be returned in the variable. For example, the following code shows NULL in @rowsreturned because there is no OUTPUT keyword following the @numrows parameter line.

```
DECLARE @rowsreturned AS INT;
EXEC Sales.GetCustomerOrders
  @custid   = 37,
  @orderdatefrom = '20070401',
  @orderdateto   = '20070701',
  @numrows   = @rowsreturned;
SELECT @rowsreturned AS 'Rows Returned';
GO
```

When you add the OUTPUT keyword, the procedure call works as expected.

```
DECLARE @rowsreturned AS INT;
EXEC Sales.GetCustomerOrders
  @custid   = 37,
  @orderdatefrom = '20070401',
```

```
  @orderdateto  = '20070701',
  @numrows  = @rowsreturned OUTPUT;
SELECT @rowsreturned AS 'Rows Returned';
GO
```

Branching Logic

T-SQL offers several statements that you can use to control the flow of your code. These constructs can be used in T-SQL scripts, and they are commonly used in stored procedures. When you use branching logic, you enable your code to handle complex situations that require different actions based on inputs. The control flow statements include the following:

- IF/ELSE
- WHILE (with BREAK and CONTINUE)
- WAITFOR
- GOTO
- RETURN (normally inside T-SQL routines)

The last section already covered the RETURN statement, which is a common component of a stored procedure. This part of Lesson 1 focuses on the remaining control flow statements.

IF/ELSE

The IF/ELSE construct gives you the ability to conditionally execute code. You enter an expression after the IF keyword, and if the expression evaluates as true, the statement or block of statements after the IF statement will be executed. You can use the optional ELSE to add a different statement or block of statements that will be executed if the expression in the IF statement evaluates to false. The following shows an example.

```
DECLARE @var1 AS INT, @var2 AS INT;
SET @var1 = 1;
SET @var2 = 2;
IF @var1 = @var2
    PRINT 'The variables are equal';
ELSE
    PRINT 'The variables are not equal';
GO
```

When the IF or ELSE statements are used without BEGIN/END blocks, they each only deal with one statement. Beware of code like the following.

```
DECLARE @var1 AS INT, @var2 AS INT;
SET @var1 = 1;
SET @var2 = 1;
IF @var1 = @var2
    PRINT 'The variables are equal';
ELSE
    PRINT 'The variables are not equal';
    PRINT '@var1 does not equal @var2';
GO
```

Even though the second PRINT statement is indented to make it look like it will only execute if the variables are equal, in fact it is outside the scope of the IF condition. To bring it in scope, put both PRINT statements inside a BEGIN/END block, as in the following.

```
DECLARE @var1 AS INT, @var2 AS INT;
SET @var1 = 1;
SET @var2 = 1;
IF @var1 = @var2 BEGIN
        PRINT 'The variables are equal';
        PRINT '@var1 equals @var2';
    END
ELSE
    BEGIN
        PRINT 'The variables are not equal';
        PRINT '@var1 does not equal @var2';
    END
GO
```

WHILE

With the WHILE construct, you can create loops inside T-SQL in order to execute a statement block as long as a condition continues to evaluate to true. You can use the WHILE construct in cursors or you can use it by itself. The keyword WHILE is followed by a condition that evaluates to either true or false. If the condition evaluates to true when it's first tested, the control of execution enters the loop, finishes the commands inside the loop the first time, and then tests the condition. Each time the loop is repeated, the WHILE condition is retested. As soon as the condition evaluates to false, the loop ends and execution control passes to the next statement following the WHILE loop.

> ***MORE INFO*** **CURSORS AND THE WHILE STATEMENT**
>
> **For information about using the WHILE loop inside a T-SQL cursor, see Chapter 16, "Understanding Cursors, Sets, and Temporary Tables."**

The following example of a WHILE loop just counts up from 1 to 10 and quits.

```
SET NOCOUNT ON;
DECLARE @count AS INT = 1;
WHILE @count <= 10
    BEGIN
        PRINT CAST(@count AS NVARCHAR);
        SET @count += 1;
    END;
```

The previous code casts the integer @count to NVARCHAR so that the output is more readable. The SET statement in the body of the loop increments the value of @count by one so that the condition after the WHILE keyword will eventually evaluate to false. If the condition never evaluates to false, the WHILE loop can run forever, producing what is called an "infinite loop."

EXAM TIP

When you code a WHILE loop, it is critical to ensure that something happens in the loop that will eventually make the WHILE condition evaluate to false so that the WHILE loop will terminate. Always check the body of the WHILE loop and make sure that a counter is incremented or a value changes so that the loop will always terminate under all conditions.

Inside the WHILE loop, you can use a BREAK statement to end the loop immediately and a CONTINUE statement to cause execution to jump back to the beginning of the loop. For example, look at the following code.

```
GO
SET NOCOUNT ON;
DECLARE @count AS INT = 1;
WHILE @count <= 100
    BEGIN
        IF @count = 10
            BREAK;
        IF @count = 5
            BEGIN
                SET @count += 2;
                CONTINUE;
            END
        PRINT CAST(@count AS NVARCHAR);
        SET @count += 1;
    END;
```

When you execute this, you should see the following output.

```
1
2
3
4
7
8
9
```

The numbers 5 and 6 are skipped because of the CONTINUE branch; the output ends at 9 and does not reach 10 because of the BREAK statement. BREAK and CONTINUE statements usually are not needed, because you can add conditional logic inside the loop to accomplish the same thing.

EXAM TIP

Even though a BEGIN/END block is optional in a WHILE loop if you only have one statement, it is a best practice to include it. The BEGIN/END block helps you organize your code, makes it easier to read, and makes it easier to modify in the future. Any statement block in a WHILE loop with more than one statement requires the BEGIN/END construct.

What is critical when you are iterating through some values with a WHILE loop is that you base the iteration on a unique value. For example, in the following code, the WHILE loop displays each categoryid of the entire Production.Categories table.

```
DECLARE @categoryid AS INT;
SET @categoryid = (SELECT MIN(categoryid) FROM Production.Categories);
WHILE @categoryid IS NOT NULL
BEGIN
  PRINT CAST(@categoryid AS NVARCHAR);
  SET @categoryid = (SELECT MIN(categoryid) FROM Production.Categories
    WHERE categoryid > @categoryid);
END;
GO
```

You should see output very similar to the following.

```
1
2
3
4
5
6
7
8
```

In the case of a categoryid, which is the primary key of the table, you know that every value will be unique. Now suppose you want to iterate through the category names. You could just revise the preceding code, replacing the variable and column names, and adjusting the data type of the new @categoryname variable.

```
DECLARE @categoryname AS NVARCHAR(15);
SET @categoryname = (SELECT MIN(categoryname) FROM Production.Categories);
WHILE @categoryname IS NOT NULL
BEGIN
  PRINT @categoryname;
  SET @categoryname = (SELECT MIN(categoryname) FROM Production.Categories
    WHERE categoryname > @categoryname);
END;
GO
```

You should see output like the following.

```
Beverages
Condiments
Confections
Dairy Products
Grains/Cereals
Meat/Poultry
Produce
Seafood
```

In this case, there are eight rows and eight distinct category names. But that just happens by accident: in the actual Production.Categories table, there is no enforcement of the uniqueness of the category name, so there could be duplicates.

What's important to see is that when the WHILE condition tests elements that might contain duplicates, it only captures the value they have in common and skips past the rest. So for example, no matter how many duplicate category names the Production.Categories table has, the preceding WHILE loop will only show their distinct values.

To get all the rows, you must choose a column that is guaranteed to be unique. That could be categoryname if there were a unique constraint or a unique index on the column, or it could be the categoryid, which is the primary key, and therefore guaranteed to be unique.

WAITFOR

The WAITFOR command does not exactly change control flow or cause branching, but it fits here because it can cause execution of statements to pause for a specified period of time. WAITFOR has three options: WAITFOR DELAY, WAITFOR TIME, and WAITFOR RECEIVE. (WAITFOR RECEIVE is used only with Service Broker.)

WAITFOR DELAY causes the execution to delay for a requested duration. For example, the following WAITFOR DELAY pauses code execution for 20 seconds.

```
WAITFOR DELAY '00:00:20';
```

WAITFOR TIME, on the other hand, pauses execution to wait for a specific time. For example, the following code waits until 11:46.

```
WAITFOR TIME '23:46:00';
```

GOTO

With the GOTO construct, you can cause your code to jump to a defined T-SQL label. All the intervening T-SQL code is skipped when the jump occurs. For example, in the following code, the second PRINT statement is skipped.

```
PRINT 'First PRINT statement';
GOTO MyLabel;
PRINT 'Second PRINT statement';
MyLabel:
PRINT 'End';
```

It is not recommended to use the GOTO statement because it can quickly lead to code that is complex and convoluted ("spaghetti code"), and other T-SQL constructs do the job better.

Developing Stored Procedures

When you develop stored procedures, you need to keep in mind a number of things that affect how the procedure behaves.

Stored Procedure Results

Stored procedures can return result sets back to the client, based on a query that is executed within the procedure. In fact, they can send back more than one result set. For example, the following code shows a simple procedure that returns two result sets, each result set having just one row.

```
IF OBJECT_ID(N'Sales.ListSampleResultsSets', N'P') IS NOT NULL
  DROP PROC Sales.ListSampleResultsSets;
GO
CREATE PROC Sales.ListSampleResultsSets
AS
    BEGIN
        SELECT TOP (1) productid, productname, supplierid,
            categoryid, unitprice, discontinued
        FROM Production.Products;
        SELECT TOP (1) orderid, productid, unitprice, qty, discount
        FROM Sales.OrderDetails;
    END
GO
EXEC Sales.ListSampleResultsSets
```

Other types of results that a stored procedure can return are values in OUTPUT parameters and return codes sent back from the RETURN statement, both of which were covered earlier in this lesson.

Calling Other Stored Procedures

You can call other stored procedures from within stored procedures. In fact, this is a common way to encapsulate and reuse code. However, you need to observe the following when calling other procedures:

- If you create a temporary table in one stored procedure—for example, call it Proc1—that temporary table is visible to all other stored procedures called from Proc1. However, that temporary table is not visible to any procedures that call Proc1.
- Variables declared in Proc1 and Proc1's parameters are not visible to any of the procedures called by Proc1.

Stored Procedures and Error Handling

To protect your stored procedures from errors, you can use the TRY/CATCH block with the THROW statement, just as you can with any T-SQL script. For instructions on how to use stored procedures and TRY/CATCH, see Lesson 2, "Implementing Error Handling," in Chapter 12, "Implementing Transactions, Error Handling, and Dynamic SQL."

Dynamic SQL in Stored Procedures

Just as in T-SQL scripts, you can use dynamic SQL inside stored procedures. When stored procedures using dynamic SQL are exposed to external users, you need to ensure that you protect your code from SQL injection. For information on how dynamic SQL works and how to prevent SQL injection, see Lesson 3, "Using Dynamic SQL," in Chapter 12.

Quick Check

1. **What are the two types of parameters for a T-SQL stored procedure?**
2. **Can a stored procedure span multiple batches of T-SQL code?**

Quick Check Answer

1. **A T-SQL stored procedure can have input and output parameters.**
2. **No, a stored procedure can only contain one batch of T-SQL code.**

PRACTICE Implementing Stored Procedures

In this practice, you write two types of stored procedures, applying what you learned about stored procedures in this lesson.

If you encounter a problem completing an exercise, you can install the completed projects from the companion content for this chapter and lesson.

EXERCISE 1 Create a Stored Procedure to Perform Administrative Tasks

In this exercise, you develop a stored procedure to perform database backups. You start with a script and a WHILE loop, and then gradually refine the code to finally create a stored procedure with a parameter that indicates the type of database to back up.

1. Develop a WHILE loop that will iterate through a set of nonsystem databases. The PRINT statement is a placeholder for the backup command. Run the loop in SSMS to test that it prints out the nonsystem database names.

```
DECLARE @databasename AS NVARCHAR(128);
SET @databasename = (SELECT MIN(name) FROM sys.databases WHERE name NOT IN
  ('master', 'model', 'msdb', 'tempdb'));
WHILE @databasename IS NOT NULL
BEGIN
  PRINT @databasename;
  SET @databasename = (SELECT MIN(name) FROM sys.databases WHERE name NOT IN
   ('master', 'model', 'msdb', 'tempdb') AND name > @databasename);
END
GO
```

2. In the next few steps, you develop a file name for the database backup file, in the format *<database name>_<yyyymmdd>_<hhmmss>*.bak. Use the current date and time and use the CONVERT() function to convert it to a string.

```
SELECT CONVERT(NVARCHAR, GETDATE(), 120)
```

3. Now use the REPLACE() function to remove the dashes from the date and colons from the time, and insert an underscore in place of the space.

```
SELECT REPLACE(REPLACE(REPLACE(CONVERT(NVARCHAR,
    GETDATE(), 120), ' ', '_'), ':', ''), '-', '');
```

4. You can now add the BACKUP DATABASE command in place of the PRINT statement. For simplicity, just do a FULL backup of the database to one file. The backup file name is the name of the database, followed by the time string, and then the .bak extension. To create the time string, use the CONVERT() and REPLACE() functions from steps 2 and 3 and put the result in the variable @timecomponent.

```
DECLARE @databasename AS NVARCHAR(128)
  , @timecomponent AS NVARCHAR(50)
  , @sqlcommand AS NVARCHAR(1000);
SET @databasename = (SELECT MIN(name) FROM sys.databases WHERE name
    NOT IN ('master', 'model', 'msdb', 'tempdb'));
WHILE @databasename IS NOT NULL
BEGIN
  SET @timecomponent = REPLACE(REPLACE(REPLACE(CONVERT(NVARCHAR,
    GETDATE(), 120), ' ', '_'), ':', ''), '-', '');
  SET @sqlcommand = 'BACKUP DATABASE ' + @databasename + ' TO DISK =
      ''C:\Backups\' + @databasename + '_' + @timecomponent + '.bak''';
  PRINT @sqlcommand;
  --EXEC(@sqlcommand);
  SET @databasename = (SELECT MIN(name) FROM sys.databases WHERE name
    NOT IN ('master', 'model', 'msdb', 'tempdb') AND name > @databasename);
END;
GO
```

5. Now convert the script to a stored procedure.

```
IF OBJECT_ID(N'dbo.BackupDatabases', N'P') IS NOT NULL
  DROP PROCEDURE dbo.BackupDatabases
GO
CREATE PROCEDURE dbo.BackupDatabases
AS
BEGIN
  DECLARE @databasename AS NVARCHAR(128)
    , @timecomponent AS NVARCHAR(50)
    , @sqlcommand AS NVARCHAR(1000);
  SET @databasename = (SELECT MIN(name) FROM sys.databases
    WHERE name NOT IN ('master', 'model', 'msdb', 'tempdb'));
  WHILE @databasename IS NOT NULL
    BEGIN
      SET @timecomponent = REPLACE(REPLACE(REPLACE(
          CONVERT(NVARCHAR, GETDATE(), 120), ' ', '_'), ':', ''), '-', '');
      SET @sqlcommand = 'BACKUP DATABASE ' + @databasename + ' TO DISK =
          ''C:\Backups\' + @databasename + '_' + @timecomponent + '.bak''';
      PRINT @sqlcommand;
      --EXEC(@sqlcommand);
      SET @databasename = (SELECT MIN(name) FROM sys.databases WHERE name
          NOT IN ('master', 'model', 'msdb', 'tempdb') AND name > @databasename);
```

```
  END;
  RETURN;
END;
GO
```

6. After you run the code in step 5 to create the procedure, test it. The procedure should print out a set of BACKUP DATABASE commands, one for each database.

```
EXEC dbo.BackupDatabases
```

7. Finally, add a parameter called **@databasetype** to the procedure; if the value of the parameter is 'user', back up all user databases; if the value is 'system', back up all system databases.

```
IF OBJECT_ID(N'dbo.BackupDatabases', N'P') IS NOT NULL
  DROP PROCEDURE dbo.BackupDatabases;
GO
CREATE PROCEDURE dbo.BackupDatabases
  @databasetype AS NVARCHAR(30)
AS
BEGIN
  DECLARE @databasename AS NVARCHAR(128)
  , @timecomponent AS NVARCHAR(50)
  , @sqlcommand AS NVARCHAR(1000);
  IF @databasetype NOT IN ('User', 'System')
    BEGIN
      THROW 50000, 'dbo.BackupDatabases: @databasetype must be User or System', 0;
      RETURN;
    END;
  IF @databasetype = 'System'
    SET @databasename = (SELECT MIN(name) FROM sys.databases WHERE name IN
       ('master', 'model', 'msdb'));
  ELSE
    SET @databasename = (SELECT MIN(name) FROM sys.databases WHERE name NOT IN
       ('master', 'model', 'msdb', 'tempdb'));
  WHILE @databasename IS NOT NULL
    BEGIN
      SET @timecomponent = REPLACE(REPLACE(REPLACE(CONVERT(
          NVARCHAR, GETDATE(), 120), ' ', '_'), ':', ''), '-', '');
      SET @sqlcommand = 'BACKUP DATABASE ' + @databasename + ' TO DISK =
          ''C:\Backups\' + @databasename + '_' + @timecomponent + '.bak''';
      PRINT @sqlcommand;
      --EXEC(@sqlcommand);
      IF @databasetype = 'System'
        SET @databasename = (SELECT MIN(name) FROM sys.databases WHERE name IN
            ('master', 'model', 'msdb') AND name > @databasename);
      ELSE
        SET @databasename = (SELECT MIN(name) FROM sys.databases WHERE name NOT IN
            ('master', 'model', 'msdb', 'tempdb') AND name > @databasename);
  END;
  RETURN;
END
GO
```

8. Now test the procedure. If you pass no parameters, or pass a parameter other than 'user' or 'system', you should see an error message. If you pass the correct parameters, you should see the backup commands printed out.

```
EXEC dbo.BackupDatabases;
GO
EXEC dbo.BackupDatabases 'User';
GO
EXEC dbo.BackupDatabases 'System';
GO
EXEC dbo.BackupDatabases 'Unknown'
```

9. When you are satisfied that the stored procedure is working, you can remove the comment from the EXEC command, and comment out the PRINT command, in order to back up your databases.

EXERCISE 2 Develop an INSERT Stored Procedure for the Data Access Layer

In this exercise, you develop a basic INSERT stored procedure that could be used by an application to insert data into the TSQL2012 database. You then add parameter testing and error handling to the stored procedure.

1. Open SSMS and open an empty query window. Load or key in the following code to create the stored procedure. Note that the INSERT statement is completely unprotected.

```
-- Version 1 A simple insert stored procedure
USE TSQL2012;
GO
IF OBJECT_ID(N'Production.InsertProducts', N'P') IS NOT NULL
  DROP PROCEDURE Production.InsertProducts
GO
CREATE PROCEDURE Production.InsertProducts
  @productname AS NVARCHAR(40)
  , @supplierid AS INT
  , @categoryid AS INT
  , @unitprice AS MONEY = 0
  , @discontinued AS BIT = 0
AS
BEGIN
  INSERT Production.Products (productname, supplierid, categoryid,
     unitprice, discontinued)
    VALUES (@productname, @supplierid, @categoryid, @unitprice,
       @discontinued);
  RETURN;
END;
GO
```

2. To test the procedure, execute it by using valid parameters as shown in the following code. Inspect the results, and then remove the test row.

```
EXEC Production.InsertProducts
  @productname = 'Test Product'
  , @supplierid = 10
  , @categoryid = 1
  , @unitprice  = 100
  , @discontinued = 0;
GO
-- Inspect the results
SELECT * FROM Production.Products WHERE productname = 'Test Product';
GO
-- Remove the new row
DELETE FROM Production.Products WHERE productname = 'Test Product';
```

3. Now test the stored procedure by using an invalid parameter value. Note that you get a SQL Server error message.

```
EXEC Production.InsertProducts
  @productname = 'Test Product'
  , @supplierid = 10
  , @categoryid = 1
  , @unitprice  = -100
  , @discontinued = 0
```

4. Now add error handling to the procedure by adding a TRY/CATCH block. Load or key in the following code to a query window, and execute it to create the stored procedure.

```
-- Version 2 with error handling
IF OBJECT_ID(N'Production.InsertProducts', N'P') IS NOT NULL
  DROP PROCEDURE Production.InsertProducts
GO
CREATE PROCEDURE Production.InsertProducts
  @productname AS NVARCHAR(40)
  , @supplierid AS INT
  , @categoryid AS INT
  , @unitprice AS MONEY = 0
  , @discontinued AS BIT = 0
AS
BEGIN
BEGIN TRY
  INSERT Production.Products (productname, supplierid, categoryid,
    unitprice, discontinued)
  VALUES (@productname, @supplierid, @categoryid,
    @unitprice, @discontinued);
END TRY
BEGIN CATCH
  THROW;
  RETURN;
END CATCH;
END;
GO
```

5. Again, test the stored procedure by using an invalid unitprice parameter.

```
EXEC Production.InsertProducts
  @productname = 'Test Product'
  , @supplierid = 10
  , @categoryid = 1
  , @unitprice  = -100
  , @discontinued = 0
```

6. Now add parameter testing to the stored procedure. Load or key in the following.

```
-- Version 3 With parameter testing
IF OBJECT_ID(N'Production.InsertProducts', N'P') IS NOT NULL
  DROP PROCEDURE Production.InsertProducts
GO
CREATE PROCEDURE Production.InsertProducts
  @productname AS NVARCHAR(40)
  , @supplierid AS INT
  , @categoryid AS INT
  , @unitprice AS MONEY = 0
  , @discontinued AS BIT = 0
AS
BEGIN
  DECLARE @ClientMessage NVARCHAR(100);
  BEGIN TRY
    -- Test parameters
    IF NOT EXISTS(SELECT 1 FROM Production.Suppliers
      WHERE supplierid = @supplierid)
      BEGIN
        SET @ClientMessage = 'Supplier id '
            + CAST(@supplierid AS VARCHAR) + ' is invalid';
        THROW 50000, @ClientMessage, 0;
      END
    IF NOT EXISTS(SELECT 1 FROM Production.Categories
        WHERE categoryid = @categoryid)
      BEGIN
        SET @ClientMessage = 'Category id '
           + CAST(@categoryid AS VARCHAR) + ' is invalid';
        THROW 50000, @ClientMessage, 0;
      END;
    IF NOT(@unitprice >= 0)
      BEGIN
        SET @ClientMessage = 'Unitprice '
          + CAST(@unitprice AS VARCHAR) + ' is invalid. Must be >= 0.';
        THROW 50000, @ClientMessage, 0;
      END;
    -- Perform the insert
    INSERT Production.Products (productname, supplierid, categoryid,
      unitprice, discontinued)
    VALUES (@productname, @supplierid, @categoryid, @unitprice, @discontinued);
  END TRY
  BEGIN CATCH
    THROW;
  END CATCH;
END;
GO
```

7. Test the stored procedure by using a unitprice parameter out of range.

```
EXEC Production.InsertProducts
  @productname = 'Test Product'
  , @supplierid = 10
  , @categoryid = 1
  , @unitprice  = -100
  , @discontinued = 0
```

8. Test the stored procedure by using a different invalid parameter, in this case an invalid supplierid.

```
EXEC Production.InsertProducts
  @productname = 'Test Product'
  , @supplierid = 100
  , @categoryid = 1
  , @unitprice  = 100
  , @discontinued = 0
```

9. Drop the stored procedure.

Lesson Summary

- T-SQL stored procedures are modules of T-SQL code that are stored in a database and can be executed by using the T-SQL EXECUTE command.
- Stored procedures can be used to encapsulate code on the server side, thereby reducing network overhead from applications; to present a data access layer to applications; and to perform maintenance and administrative tasks.
- Stored procedures can be defined by using parameters. Input parameters are sent to the stored procedure for the procedure's internal use. Output parameters can be used to return information to the caller of the procedure.
- Within the stored procedure, parameters are defined by using the same syntax as T-SQL variables, and they can be referenced and manipulated within the procedure just like variables.
- Every stored procedure consists of only one batch of T-SQL code.
- Stored procedures can call other stored procedures.
- Whenever a RETURN is executed, execution of the stored procedure ends and control returns to the caller.
- Stored procedures can return more than one result set to the caller.

Lesson Review

Answer the following questions to test your knowledge of the information in this lesson. You can find the answers to these questions and explanations of why each answer choice is correct or incorrect in the "Answers" section at the end of this chapter.

1. Which of the following T-SQL statements can be used to cause branching within a stored procedure? (Choose all that apply.)
   - **A.** WHILE
   - **B.** BEGIN/END
   - **C.** IF/ELSE
   - **D.** GO
2. A stored procedure calls another stored procedure. The calling stored procedure has created temporary tables, declared variables, and passes parameters to the called stored procedure. What data can the called stored procedure see from the caller?
   - **A.** The called procedure can see the variables, temporary tables, and passed parameters of the caller.
   - **B.** The called procedure can see the temporary tables but not the variables and passed parameters of the caller.
   - **C.** The called procedure can see the passed parameters and temporary tables but not the variables of the caller.
   - **D.** The called procedure cannot see any objects created by the calling procedure.
3. How can you use output parameters in T-SQL stored procedures? (Choose all that apply.)
   - **A.** You can pass data into a procedure by using an output parameter, but you cannot receive information back from it.
   - **B.** You can pass data into a procedure by using an output parameter, and any change made to the parameter will be passed back to the calling routine.
   - **C.** You cannot pass data into a procedure by using an output parameter; it is only used for passing data back to the caller.
   - **D.** You cannot pass data into a procedure by using an output parameter, nor can you receive data back from a procedure from an output parameter.

Lesson 2: Implementing Triggers

A *trigger* is a special kind of stored procedure that is associated with selected data manipulation language (DML) events on a table or view. A trigger cannot be explicitly executed. Rather, a trigger is fired when a DML event occurs that the trigger is associated with, such as

INSERT, UPDATE, or DELETE. Whenever the event takes place, the trigger fires and the trigger's code runs.

SQL Server supports the association of triggers with two kinds of events:

- Data manipulation events (DML triggers)
- Data definition events (DDL triggers) such as CREATE TABLE

This lesson is concerned exclusively with DML triggers.

After this lesson, you will be able to:

- Create and alter T-SQL AFTER and INSTEAD OF triggers.
- Describe the inserted and deleted tables used by triggers.
- Describe how nested triggers work.
- Use the UPDATED function in a trigger.
- Handle multiple rows in a trigger.
- Describe the impact triggers can have on performance.

Estimated lesson time: 30 minutes

DML Triggers

A *DML trigger* is a T-SQL batch associated with a table that is defined to respond to a particular DML event such as an INSERT, UPDATE, or DELETE, or a combination of those events. SQL Server supports two kinds of DML triggers:

- **AFTER** This trigger fires after the event it is associated with finishes and can only be defined on permanent tables.
- **INSTEAD OF** This trigger fires instead of the event it is associated with and can be defined on permanent tables and views.

A trigger executes only once for each DML statement, no matter how many rows may be affected. The schema of the trigger must be the same as the schema of the table or view the trigger is associated with.

You can use DML triggers for auditing, enforcing complex integrity rules, and more.

Both types of DML triggers execute as part of the transaction associated with the INSERT, UPDATE, or DELETE statement. A trigger is considered part of the transaction that includes the event that caused the trigger to fire.

Issuing a ROLLBACK TRAN command within the trigger's code causes a rollback of all changes that took place in the trigger, in addition to rolling back the original DML statement to which the trigger is attached. However, using a ROLLBACK TRAN in a trigger can have some unwanted side effects. Instead, you can issue THROW or RAISERROR and control the failure by using your standard error handling routines.

The normal exit from a trigger is to use the RETURN statement, just as in a stored procedure.

In the T-SQL code for both types of DML triggers, you can access tables that are named *inserted* and *deleted*. These tables contain the rows that were affected by the modification that caused the trigger to fire. The inserted table holds the new image of the affected rows in the case of INSERT and UPDATE statements. The deleted table holds the old image of the affected rows in the case of DELETE and UPDATE statements. In the case of INSTEAD OF triggers, the inserted and deleted tables contain the rows that would be affected by the DML statement.

AFTER Triggers

AFTER triggers can only be defined for tables. In an AFTER trigger, the trigger code executes after the DML statement has passed all constraints, such as a primary or foreign key constraint, a unique constraint, or a check constraint. If the constraint is violated, the statement fails and the trigger is not executed.

To see how an AFTER trigger works, you can start by inserting an AFTER trigger snippet from SSMS. Open a new query window, right-click, choose Insert Snippet, and then navigate to Create Trigger and press Enter. The following is inserted into your query window.

```
CREATE TRIGGER TriggerName
    ON [dbo].[TableName]
    FOR DELETE, INSERT, UPDATE
    AS
    BEGIN
    SET NOCOUNT ON
    END
```

First, make sure it's an AFTER trigger. In a trigger definition, AFTER is the default type of trigger when you specify FOR. But you can replace FOR with either AFTER or INSTEAD OF to determine the type of trigger.

EXAM TIP

When an INSERT, UPDATE, or DELETE occurs and no rows are affected, there is no point in proceeding with the trigger. You can improve the performance of the trigger by testing whether @@ROWCOUNT is 0 in the very first line of the trigger. It must be the first line because @@ROWCOUNT will be set back to 0 by any additional statement. When the AFTER trigger begins, @@ROWCOUNT will contain the number of rows affected by the outer INSERT, UPDATE, or DELETE statement.

Now add an existence test to the OBJECT_ID() function, using 'TR' as the object type. Define it on the TSQL2012 Sales.OrderDetails table, and call it **Sales.tr_SalesOrderDetailsDML**.

```
IF OBJECT_ID(N'Sales.tr_SalesOrderDetailsDML', N'TR') IS NOT NULL
    DROP TRIGGER Sales.tr_SalesOrderDetailsDML;
GO
CREATE TRIGGER Sales.tr_SalesOrderDetailsDML
ON Sales.OrderDetails
AFTER DELETE, INSERT, UPDATE
AS
BEGIN
  IF @@ROWCOUNT = 0 RETURN; -- Must be 1st statement
  SET NOCOUNT ON;
END;
```

Now add SELECT statements on the inserted and deleted tables.

```
IF OBJECT_ID(N'Sales.tr_SalesOrderDetailsDML', N'TR') IS NOT NULL
    DROP TRIGGER Sales.tr_SalesOrderDetailsDML;
GO
CREATE TRIGGER Sales.tr_SalesOrderDetailsDML
ON Sales.OrderDetails
AFTER DELETE, INSERT, UPDATE
AS
BEGIN
  IF @@ROWCOUNT = 0 RETURN;
  SET NOCOUNT ON;
  SELECT COUNT(*) AS InsertedCount FROM Inserted;
  SELECT COUNT(*) AS DeletedCount FROM Deleted;END;
```

The main purpose of this trigger is to give you feedback regarding how many rows are in the inserted and deleted tables. Notice that you've defined it for INSERT, UPDATE, and DELETE.

EXAM TIP

It is not a good practice to return result sets from triggers. In SQL Server 2012 and earlier versions, returning a rowset from a trigger is allowed, but it cannot be relied on. You can also disable it with the sp_configure option called Disallow Results From Triggers. In addition, the ability to return result sets from a trigger is deprecated and will be dropped in the next version of SQL Server after SQL Server 2012.

Now modify the trigger to do some work. Notice that the Production.Categories table does not have a unique constraint or a unique index on the categoryname column. The following code enforces uniqueness by using an AFTER trigger. You will define the trigger for both INSERT and UPDATE.

```
IF OBJECT_ID(N'Production.tr_ ProductionCategories_categoryname', N'TR') IS NOT NULL
    DROP TRIGGER Production.tr_ProductionCategories_categoryname;
GO
CREATE TRIGGER Production.tr_ProductionCategories_categoryname
ON Production.Categories
AFTER INSERT, UPDATE
AS
```

```
BEGIN
  IF @@ROWCOUNT = 0 RETURN;
  SET NOCOUNT ON;
  IF EXISTS (SELECT COUNT(*)
        FROM Inserted AS I
        JOIN Production.Categories AS C
          ON I.categoryname = C.categoryname
        GROUP BY I.categoryname
        HAVING COUNT(*) > 1 )

    BEGIN
      THROW 50000, 'Duplicate category names not allowed', 0;
    END;
END;
GO
```

Now test it with the following INSERT command.

```
INSERT INTO Production.Categories (categoryname,description)
     VALUES ('TestCategory1', 'Test1 description v1');
```

This INSERT command works once but not a second time, because that would cause a duplicate row. Now try an UPDATE command.

```
UPDATE Production.Categories
  SET categoryname = 'Beverages' WHERE categoryname = 'TestCategory1';
```

The UPDATE command also fails because it would cause a duplicate. To clean up the table, just issue the following.

```
DELETE FROM Production.Categories WHERE categoryname = 'TestCategory1';
```

In this example, you test the join between the inserted rows and the actual table, but only *after* the insert has taken place—because this is an AFTER trigger! So you can use a regular join, and the new rows from the inserted table will match up with the rows freshly inserted into the base table. If the distinct count of the category name is greater than 1, you know you inserted a duplicate. Also, by looking at the count of all rows, you handle the case when multiple rows are inserted or updated.

Nested AFTER Triggers

AFTER triggers can be nested—that is, you can have a trigger on Table A that updates Table B. Then Table B may have a trigger that is executed as well. The maximum depth of nested trigger executions is 32. If the nesting is circular (Table A's trigger fires Table B's trigger, which fires Table C's trigger, which fires Table A's trigger, and so on), the maximum level of 32 will be reached and the trigger execution will stop.

Nested triggers is a configuration option for the entire SQL Server instance. It is on by default, but you can disable it for the server. You can check the setting by using the sp_configure stored procedure.

```
EXEC sp_configure 'nested triggers';
```

To turn the nested triggers option off at the server level, issue the following command.

```
EXEC sp_configure 'nested triggers', 0;
```

You must then issue the RECONFIGURE statement to make the setting take place. Because this is not an advanced setting, you do not need to set Show Advanced Options on by using sp_configure.

INSTEAD OF Triggers

The INSTEAD OF trigger executes a batch of T-SQL code instead of the INSERT, UPDATE, or DELETE statement. You can reissue the statement later in the code.

Although INSTEAD OF triggers can be created against both tables and views, they are commonly used with views. The reason is that when you send an UPDATE statement against a view, only one base table can be updated at a time. In addition, the view may have aggregations or functions on columns that prevent a direct update. An INSTEAD OF trigger can take that UPDATE statement against the view and instead of executing it, replace it with two or more UPDATE statements against the base tables of the view.

For example, take the AFTER trigger from the previous section and rewrite it as an INSTEAD OF trigger. For simplicity, just define it for INSERT.

```
IF OBJECT_ID(N'Production.tr_ProductionCategories_categoryname', N'TR') IS NOT NULL
  DROP TRIGGER Production.tr_ProductionCategories_categoryname;
GO
CREATE TRIGGER Production.tr_ProductionCategories_categoryname
ON Production.Categories
INSTEAD OF INSERT
AS
BEGIN
  SET NOCOUNT ON;
  IF EXISTS (SELECT COUNT(*)
        FROM Inserted AS I
        LEFT JOIN Production.Categories AS C
          ON I.categoryname = C.categoryname
        GROUP BY I.categoryname
        HAVING COUNT(*) > 0 )    BEGIN
      THROW 50000, 'Duplicate category names not allowed', 0;

    END;
  ELSE
    INSERT Production.Categories (categoryname, description)
      SELECT categoryname, description FROM Inserted;
END;
GO
-- Cleanup
IF OBJECT_ID(N'Production.tr_ProductionCategories_categoryname', N'TR') IS NOT NULL
  DROP TRIGGER Production.tr_ProductionCategories_categoryname;
```

DML Trigger Functions

You can use two functions in your trigger code to get information about what is going on:

- **UPDATE()** You can use this function to determine whether a particular column has been referenced by an INSERT or UPDATE statement. For example, you can insert the following inside the trigger.

```
IF UPDATE(qty)
  PRINT 'Column qty affected';
```

  The following statement would make UPDATE(qty) true.

```
UPDATE Sales.OrderDetails
  SET qty = 99
  WHERE orderid = 10249 AND productid = 16;
```

  The UPDATE() function returns true even if the column value is set to itself in an UPDATE statement. It is only testing whether the column is referenced.

- **COLUMNS_UPDATED()** You can use this function if you know the sequence number of the column in the table. It requires you to use the bitwise AND operation (&) to see whether a column was updated.

Quick Check

1. **What are the two types of DML triggers that can be created?**
2. **If an AFTER trigger discovers an error, how does it prevent the DML command from completing?**

Quick Check Answer

1. **You can create AFTER and INSTEAD OF DML-type triggers.**
2. **An AFTER trigger issues a THROW or RAISERROR command to cause the transaction of the DML command to roll back.**

PRACTICE Writing DML Triggers

In this practice, you write two AFTER triggers. First, you learn to explore the inserted and deleted tables, and then you enforce a business rule by using a trigger.

If you encounter a problem completing an exercise, you can install the completed projects from the companion content for this chapter and lesson.

EXERCISE 1 Inspect the Inserted and Deleted Tables

In this exercise, you use an AFTER trigger to inspect the contents of the inserted and deleted tables that are visible when a trigger executes.

NOTE **RESULT SETS FROM TRIGGERS DEPRECATED**

As mentioned previously, the ability to return result sets from triggers is a deprecated feature and will not be available in future versions of SQL Server. Also, the feature can be disabled in sp_configure, so to do this exercise, make sure Disallow Results From Triggers is disabled.

1. Recreate the trigger on the Sales.OrderDetails table as follows.

```
USE TSQL2012
GO
IF OBJECT_ID(N'Sales.tr_SalesOrderDetailsDML', Ns'TR') IS NOT NULL
  DROP TRIGGER Sales.tr_SalesOrderDetailsDML;
GO
CREATE TRIGGER Sales.tr_SalesOrderDetailsDML
ON Sales.OrderDetails
AFTER DELETE, INSERT, UPDATE
AS
BEGIN
  IF @@ROWCOUNT = 0 RETURN;
  SET NOCOUNT ON;
  SELECT COUNT(*) AS InsertedCount FROM Inserted;
  SELECT COUNT(*) AS DeletedCount FROM Deleted;
END;
```

2. Ensure that some selected data values can be entered. The following rows do not exist in the default TSQL2012 database, so delete them if they are there.

```
DELETE FROM  Sales.OrderDetails
WHERE orderid = 10249 and productid in (15, 16);
GO
```

3. Now add some data to the table. When you insert these two rows, you should see two rows in the inserted table and none in the deleted table. (If you execute the following INSERT statement twice in a row, you'll get a primary key violation and won't see any output of the trigger because it will not be executed.)

```
INSERT INTO Sales.OrderDetails (orderid,productid,unitprice,qty,discount)
  VALUES (10249, 16, 9.00, 1, 0.60) ,
  (10249, 15, 9.00, 1, 0.40);
GO
```

4. Update one of those two rows. You should see one row in the inserted table (the new data) and one row in the deleted table (the old data).

```
UPDATE Sales.OrderDetails
  SET unitprice = 99
  WHERE orderid = 10249 AND productid = 16;
GO
```

5. Now delete those two rows. You should see no rows in the inserted table and two rows in the deleted table.

```
DELETE FROM  Sales.OrderDetails
WHERE orderid = 10249 and productid in (15, 16);
```

6. Finally, drop the trigger.

```
IF OBJECT_ID(N'Sales.tr_SalesOrderDetailsDML', N'TR') IS NOT NULL
  DROP TRIGGER Sales.tr_SalesOrderDetailsDML;
GO
```

EXERCISE 2 Write an AFTER Trigger to Enforce a Business Rule

In this exercise, you create an AFTER trigger to enforce a business rule against the Sales.OrderDetails table in the TSQL2012 database.

1. You need to write a trigger to enforce the following: if any item in the Sales.OrderDetails table has a unitprice less than 10, it cannot have a discount greater than .5. First create the basic trigger on the Sales.OrderDetails table as follows. (Note that variables are used to capture and test the unitprice and discount values.)

```
USE TSQL2012;
GO
-- Step 1: Basic trigger
IF OBJECT_ID(N'Sales.OrderDetails_AfterTrigger', N'TR') IS NOT NULL
  DROP Trigger Sales.OrderDetails_AfterTrigger;
GO
CREATE TRIGGER Sales.OrderDetails_AfterTrigger ON Sales.OrderDetails
AFTER INSERT, UPDATE
AS
BEGIN
  IF @@ROWCOUNT = 0 RETURN;
  SET NOCOUNT ON;
  -- Perform the check
  DECLARE @unitprice AS money, @discount AS NUMERIC(4,3);
  SELECT @unitprice = unitprice FROM inserted;
  SELECT @discount = discount FROM inserted;
  IF @unitprice < 10 AND @discount > .5
    BEGIN
      THROW 50000, 'Discount must be <= .5 when unitprice < 10', 0;
    END;

END;
GO
```

2. Next, test the trigger on two rows. The trigger finds the violating row, which has a unitprice of 9.00 and a discount of 0.60.

```
INSERT INTO Sales.OrderDetails (orderid,productid,unitprice,qty,discount)
  VALUES (10249, 16, 9.00, 1, 0.60) ,
  (10249, 15, 9.00, 1, 0.40);
```

3. Now try the same insert with the order of the rows reversed. This time, the violating row is not found.

```
INSERT INTO Sales.OrderDetails (orderid,productid,unitprice,qty,discount)
  VALUES (10249, 15, 9.00, 1, 0.40),
  (10249, 16, 9.00, 1, 0.60) ;
```

4. Delete the wrongly inserted rows.

```
DELETE FROM Sales.OrderDetails WHERE orderid = 10249 AND productid IN (15, 16);
GO
```

5. Revise the trigger to capture and test all the rows.

```
IF OBJECT_ID(N'Sales.OrderDetails_AfterTrigger', N'TR') IS NOT NULL
  DROP Trigger Sales.OrderDetails_AfterTrigger;
GO
CREATE TRIGGER Sales.OrderDetails_AfterTrigger ON Sales.OrderDetails
AFTER INSERT, UPDATE
AS
BEGIN
  IF @@ROWCOUNT = 0 RETURN;
  SET NOCOUNT ON;
  -- Check all rows
  IF EXISTS(SELECT * FROM inserted AS I WHERE unitprice < 10 AND discount > .5)
    BEGIN
      THROW 50000, 'Discount must be <= .5 when unitprice < 10', 0;
    END
END
GO
```

6. Re-run the same test on multiple rows.

```
INSERT INTO Sales.OrderDetails (orderid,productid,unitprice,qty,discount)
  VALUES (10249, 15, 9.00, 1, 0.40),
  (10249, 16, 9.00, 1, 0.60) ;
```

Now the trigger should capture the violating row or rows no matter how many rows you insert or update.

7. As a last step, drop the trigger.

```
IF OBJECT_ID(N'Sales.OrderDetails_AfterTrigger', N'TR') IS NOT NULL
  DROP Trigger Sales.OrderDetails_AfterTrigger;
GO
```

Lesson Summary

- A DML trigger is a T-SQL batch of code, similar to a stored procedure, that is associated with a table and sometimes a view. You can use DML triggers for auditing, enforcing complex integrity rules, and more.

- Triggers execute when a particular DML event such as an INSERT, UPDATE, or DELETE occurs.
- SQL Server supports two kinds of DML triggers: AFTER triggers and INSTEAD OF triggers. Both types of DML triggers execute as part of the transaction associated with the INSERT, UPDATE, or DELETE statement.
- In the T-SQL code for both types of DML triggers, you can access tables that are named *inserted* and *deleted*. These tables contain the rows that were affected by the modification that caused the trigger to fire.

Lesson Review

Answer the following questions to test your knowledge of the information in this lesson. You can find the answers to these questions and explanations of why each answer choice is correct or incorrect in the "Answers" section at the end of this chapter.

1. How do the inserted and deleted tables work with a DML statement in an AFTER trigger?
   - **A.** For a DELETE statement, the inserted table contains new rows and the deleted table contains the deleted rows.
   - **B.** The inserted table only contains rows from the INSERT statement, and the deleted table contains only rows from the DELETE statement.
   - **C.** For an INSERT statement, the inserted table contains new rows and the deleted table is empty.
   - **D.** For an UPDATE statement, the inserted table is empty and the deleted table contains all the changed rows.
2. Which of the following statements are true about an INSTEAD OF trigger? (Choose all that apply.)
   - **A.** INSTEAD OF triggers can be created on views.
   - **B.** INSTEAD OF triggers execute instead of AFTER triggers.
   - **C.** INSTEAD OF triggers can only be declared for UPDATE statements.
   - **D.** INSTEAD OF triggers execute code in place of the original DML statement.
3. How can you turn off nested triggers on a SQL Server instance by using T-SQL?
   - **A.** Use the sp_configure stored procedure followed by 'nested triggers' and 'OFF'.
   - **B.** Use the sp_configure stored procedure followed by 'nested triggers' and 0.
   - **C.** Use the sp_configure stored procedure followed by 'nested triggers' and 'OFF', followed by the RECONFIGURE statement.
   - **D.** Use the sp_configure stored procedure followed by 'nested triggers' and 0, followed by the RECONFIGURE statement.

Lesson 3: Implementing User-Defined Functions

User-defined functions are T-SQL or CLR routines that can accept parameters and return either scalar values or tables. This lesson focuses on T-SQL user-defined functions. Built-in system functions for SQL Server 2012 are covered in Chapter 2, "Getting Started with the SELECT Statement."

After this lesson, you will be able to:

- Create and alter user-defined functions (UDFs).
- Describe scalar and table values.
- Use deterministic and nondeterministic functions.

Estimated lesson time: 20 minutes

Understanding User-Defined Functions

The purpose of a user-defined function (UDF) is to encapsulate reusable T-SQL code and return a scalar value or a table to the caller.

Like stored procedures, UDFs can accept parameters, and the parameters can be accessed inside the function as variables. Unlike stored procedures, UDFs are embedded in T-SQL statements, and they execute as part of a T-SQL command. UDFs cannot be executed by using the EXECUTE command.

UDFs access SQL Server data, but they cannot perform any DDL—that is, they cannot create tables, and they cannot make modifications to tables, indexes, or other objects, or change any data in permanent tables by using a DML statement.

There are two major types of UDFs: scalar and table-valued. The scalar function returns a single value back to the caller, whereas the table-valued function returns a table. Both scalar UDFs and table-valued UDFs can consist of a single line of T-SQL code, or of multiple lines.

Table-valued UDFs return a table. Table-valued functions can appear in the FROM clause of a T-SQL query. A table-valued UDF with a single line of code is called an inline table-valued UDF. A table-valued UDF with multiple lines of code is called a multistatement table-valued UDF.

Note that when referencing the type of a function, whether from the type column of sys.objects or from the type parameter of the OBJECT_ID() function, there are three abbreviations for functions:

- FN = SQL scalar function
- IF = SQL inline table-valued function
- TF = SQL table-valued-function

Scalar UDFs

Scalar UDFs are called scalar because they return a single value. Scalar UDFs can appear anywhere in the query where an expression that returns a single value can appear (for example, in the SELECT column list). All the code within the scalar UDF must be enclosed in a BEGIN/END block.

In SSMS, if you right-click in a query window, choose Insert Snippet, and insert the snippet for a scalar function, you see the output as follows.

```
CREATE FUNCTION dbo.FunctionName
(
    @param1 int,
    @param2 int
)
RETURNS INT
AS
BEGIN
    RETURN @param1 + @param2
END
```

Take this snippet output and create a simple scalar function to compute the extension of price times quantity in the Sales table. Take the unitprice column and the qty column and return the result of multiplying them together. Make the following changes to the snippet code:

- Assign the name **Sales.fn_extension** to the UDF.
- Prepend a conditional DROP statement.
- Add parameters for both the unitprice and qty columns of the Sales.OrderDetails table.
- Insert the multiplication operator as the computation.

```
IF OBJECT_ID(N'Sales.fn_extension', N'FN') IS NOT NULL
    DROP FUNCTION Sales.fn_extension
GO
CREATE FUNCTION Sales.fn_extension
(
  @unitprice AS MONEY,
  @qty AS INT
)
RETURNS MONEY
AS
BEGIN
    RETURN @unitprice * @qty
END;
GO
```

Note that you can add additional lines to a scalar UDF just by inserting additional lines between the BEGIN/END statements. To call the function, simply invoke it inside a T-SQL query, such as a SELECT statement. Here's one example, using the function in the SELECT list.

```
SELECT Orderid, unitprice, qty, Sales.fn_extension(unitprice, qty) AS extension
FROM Sales.OrderDetails;
```

Here's another example, using the function in the WHERE clause to limit the output to extensions that are > 1,000.

```
SELECT Orderid, unitprice, qty, Sales.fn_extension(unitprice, qty) AS extension
FROM Sales.OrderDetails
WHERE Sales.fn_extension(unitprice, qty) > 1000;
```

Table-Valued UDFs

A table-valued UDF returns a table rather than a single value to the caller. As a result, it can be called in a T-SQL query wherever a table is expected, which is in the FROM clause.

An inline table-valued function is the only type of UDF that can be written without a BEGIN/END block.

A multistatement table-valued UDF has a RETURN statement at the end of the function body.

An Inline Table-Valued UDF

An inline table-valued UDF contains a single SELECT statement that returns a table. To see how an inline table-valued UDF works, insert the following SSMS snippet for an inline table-valued function that cannot by itself be executed.

```
CREATE FUNCTION dbo.FunctionName
(
    @param1 int,
    @param2 char(5)
)
RETURNS TABLE AS RETURN
(
    SELECT @param1 AS c1,
           @param2 AS c2
)
```

Now modify the function to return only those rows from Sales.OrderDetails that have a quantity between two values. Prepend a drop statement, assign the name **Sales.fn_FilteredExtension**, and add parameters for the low and high qty values.

```
IF OBJECT_ID(N'Sales.fn_FilteredExtension', N'IF') IS NOT NULL
    DROP FUNCTION Sales.fn_FilteredExtension;
GO
CREATE FUNCTION Sales.fn_FilteredExtension
(
  @lowqty AS SMALLINT,
  @highqty AS SMALLINT
 )
RETURNS TABLE AS RETURN
(
    SELECT orderid, unitprice, qty
    FROM Sales.OrderDetails
    WHERE qty BETWEEN @lowqty AND @highqty
);
GO
```

To call the function, embed it in the FROM clause of a SELECT statement, but be sure to supply the required parameters. In the following example, you see the rows that have a qty between 10 and 20.

```
SELECT orderid, unitprice, qty
FROM Sales.fn_FilteredExtension (10,20);
```

Note that because an inline table-valued function does not perform any other operations, the optimizer treats an inline table-valued function just like a view. You can even use INSERT, UPDATE, and DELETE against it, just as you would a view. For that reason, you can think of inline table-valued functions as parameterized views.

Also note how the function sets up the return table from a SELECT statement by using a single statement.

```
RETURNS TABLE AS RETURN
(
<SELECT …>
);
```

It's this ability to return the results of a single SELECT that makes this an *inline* table-valued UDF.

Multistatement Table-Valued UDF

To construct a multistatement table-valued UDF, the syntax has to change a bit. Look at the following SSMS code snippet for a table-valued UDF.

```
CREATE FUNCTION dbo.FunctionName
(
    @param1 int,
    @param2 char(5)
)
RETURNS @returntable TABLE
(
    c1 int,
    c2 char(5)
)
AS
BEGIN
    INSERT @returntable
         SELECT @param1, @param2
    RETURN
END;
GO
```

Note the differences. In a table-valued UDF, you must define the table to be returned as a table variable and insert data into the table variable. The RETURN statement just ends the function and is not used to send any data back to the caller.

Take the previous inline table-valued UDF Sales.fn_FilteredExtension and convert it to a multistatement table-valued UDF.

```
IF OBJECT_ID(N'Sales.fn_FilteredExtension2', N'TF') IS NOT NULL
    DROP FUNCTION Sales.fn_FilteredExtension2;
GO
CREATE FUNCTION Sales.fn_FilteredExtension2
(
  @lowqty AS SMALLINT,
  @highqty AS SMALLINT
 )
RETURNS @returntable TABLE
(
    orderid  INT,
    unitprice  MONEY,
    qty  SMALLINT
)
AS
BEGIN
  INSERT @returntable
    SELECT orderid, unitprice, qty
    FROM Sales.OrderDetails
    WHERE qty BETWEEN @lowqty AND @highqty
  RETURN
END;
GO
```

Now use the multistatement table-valued UDF Sales.fnFilteredExtension2.

```
SELECT orderid, unitprice, qty
FROM Sales.fn_FilteredExtension2 (10,20);
```

Limitations on UDFs

The user creating the function needs CREATE FUNCTION privileges in the database.

UDFs cannot do the following:

- Apply any schema or data changes in the database.
- Change the state of a database or SQL Server instance.
- Create or access temporary tables.
- Call stored procedures.
- Execute dynamic SQL.
- Produce side effects. For example, both the RAND() and NEWID() functions rely on information from the previous invocation. Relying on previous information is a "side effect" that is not allowed.

UDF Options

You can specify five options with UDFs:

- **ENCRYPTION** As with stored procedures and triggers, this is really an obfuscation of the source code and not a complete encryption.
- **SCHEMABINDING** This binds the schemas of all referenced objects.
- **RETURNS NULL ON NULL INPUT** If this is set, any NULL parameters cause a scalar UDF to return NULL without executing the body of the function.
- **CALLED ON NULL INPUT** This is the default, and it implies that a scalar function body will execute even if NULL is passed as a parameter.
- **EXECUTE AS** This executes under various contexts.

UDFs can also be nested. For example, a table-valued UDF may call a scalar UDF in the course of its work, and of course, a scalar UDF might call another scalar UDF.

UDF Performance Considerations

How a function is used can have a dramatic impact on the performance of the queries that you execute. Specifically, scalar UDFs need to be very efficient because they are executed once for every row in a result set or sometimes for an entire table.

A scalar UDF in the SELECT list, when applied to column values, is executed for every single row retrieved.

A scalar UDF in the WHERE clause that restricts a result set is executed once for every row in the referenced table.

Use of scalar UDFs prevent queries from being parallelized.

Quick Check

1. **What are the two types of table-valued UDFS?**
2. **What type of UDF returns only a single value?**

Quick Check Answer

1. **You can create inline or multistatement table-valued UDFs.**
2. **A scalar UDF returns only a single value.**

PRACTICE Writing User-Defined Functions

In this practice, you write two UDFs: a scalar UDF and an inline table-valued UDF.

If you encounter a problem completing an exercise, you can install the completed projects from the companion content for this chapter and lesson.

EXERCISE 1 Write a Scalar UDF to Compute a Discounted Cost

In this exercise, you write a scalar UDF that determines the cost of an item after applying the discount on the Sales.OrderDetails table.

1. Start by writing a query to determine the cost of an item after applying the discount. The Sales.SalesOrder table has three columns used in the computation: unitprice (the price per unit), qty (the number of units sold), and discount (the fraction to reduce total cost by).

```
SELECT orderid
   , productid
   , unitprice
   , qty
   , discount
FROM Sales.OrderDetails;
```

2. The product of these two is the extended cost—that is, the total cost for all those units for that order detail. Add that to the query.

```
SELECT orderid
   , productid
   , unitprice
   , qty
   , discount
   , unitprice * qty AS totalcost
FROM Sales.OrderDetails
```

3. The discount is a fraction, indicating what ratio to deduct. If you multiply either the unitprice or the totalcost by (1 - discount), that gives you the cost after the discount is applied. For this example, apply the discount to the computed totalcost.

```
SELECT orderid
   , productid
   , unitprice
   , qty
   , discount
   , unitprice * qty as totalcost
   , (unitprice * qty) * (1 - discount) as costafterdiscount
FROM Sales.OrderDetails;
```

4. Now you have enough to insert this into a function. The function needs three parameters: @unitprice, @qty, and @discount.

```
IF OBJECT_ID(N'Sales.fn_CostAfterDiscount', N'FN') IS NOT NULL
  DROP FUNCTION Sales.fn_CostAfterDiscount;
GO
CREATE FUNCTION Sales.fn_CostAfterDiscount(
  @unitprice AS MONEY,
  @qty AS SMALLINT,
  @discount AS NUMERIC(4,3)
) RETURNS MONEY
AS
BEGIN
  RETURN (@unitprice * @qty) * (1 - @discount);
END;
GO
```

5. Inspect the results.

```
SELECT Orderid
   , unitprice
   , qty
   , discount
   , Sales.fn_CostAfterDiscount(unitprice, qty, discount) AS costafterdiscount
FROM Sales.OrderDetails;
```

6. Drop the function.

```
IF OBJECT_ID(N'Sales.fn_CostAfterDiscount', N'FN') IS NOT NULL
  DROP FUNCTION Sales.fn_CostAfterDiscount;
GO
```

EXERCISE 2 Create Table-Valued UDFs

In this exercise, you write an inline table-valued UDF.

1. You must write a function that returns a table of the Sales.OrderDetails rows filtered by a low and high value of the quantity and also by adding a column for the extension. The extension is just the unitprice * qty. Here is the basic SELECT statement without any filter.

```
SELECT orderid, unitprice, qty, (unitprice * qty) AS extension
  FROM Sales.OrderDetails;
```

2. To add the filter, you could use a couple of variables, such as the following.

```
DECLARE @lowqty AS SMALLINT = 10
  , @highqty AS SMALLINT = 20;
SELECT orderid, unitprice, qty, (unitprice * qty) AS extension
FROM Sales.OrderDetails
WHERE qty BETWEEN @lowqty AND @highqty;
```

3. Now you have enough for the function. Start with the following SSMS snippet for an inline table-valued function.

```
CREATE FUNCTION dbo.FunctionName
(
    @param1 int,
    @param2 char(5)
)
RETURNS TABLE AS RETURN
(
    SELECT @param1 AS c1,
         @param2 AS c2
)
```

4. Use the variables as the parameters, and assign the name **fn_FilteredExtension**. Remember to remove the assigned values from the variables when making them parameters.

```
IF OBJECT_ID(N'Sales.fn_FilteredExtension', N'IF') IS NOT NULL
  DROP FUNCTION Sales.fn_FilteredExtension;
GO
CREATE FUNCTION Sales.fn_FilteredExtension
(
  @lowqty AS SMALLINT,
  @highqty AS SMALLINT
 )
RETURNS TABLE AS RETURN
(
    SELECT orderid, unitprice, qty, (unitprice * qty) AS extension
  FROM Sales.OrderDetails
  WHERE qty BETWEEN @lowqty AND @highqty
);
GO
```

5. Now test the function.

```
SELECT *
FROM Sales.fn_FilteredExtension (10,20);
```

6. Finally, drop the function.

```
IF OBJECT_ID(N'Sales.fn_FilteredExtension', N'IF') IS NOT NULL
  DROP FUNCTION Sales.fn_FilteredExtension;
GO
```

Lesson Summary

- User-defined functions (UDFs) encapsulate reusable T-SQL code and return a scalar value or a table to the caller.
- Like stored procedures, UDFs can accept parameters, and the parameters can be accessed inside the function as variables. Unlike stored procedures, UDFs are embedded in T-SQL statements, and they execute as part of a T-SQL command. UDFs cannot be executed by using the EXECUTE command.

- UDFs access SQL Server data, but they cannot perform any DDL—that is, they cannot make modifications to tables, indexes, or other objects, or change the data tables by using DML.
- There are two major types of UDFs: scalar and table-valued. The scalar UDF returns a single value back to the caller and can be invoked in numerous places, including a SELECT list and a WHERE clause. The table-valued function returns a table and can appear in a FROM clause. Both scalar UDFs and table-valued UDFs can consist of a single line or of multiple lines of T-SQL code.

Lesson Review

Answer the following questions to test your knowledge of the information in this lesson. You can find the answers to these questions and explanations of why each answer choice is correct or incorrect in the "Answers" section at the end of this chapter.

1. Which of the following is true about scalar UDFs?
   - **A.** Scalar UDFs are both inline and multistatement.
   - **B.** Scalar UDFs return the result of a SELECT statement.
   - **C.** Scalar UDFs can be invoked in a SELECT list or a WHERE clause.
   - **D.** Scalar UDFs can be invoked in the FROM clause of a SELECT statement.
2. Which of the following are true about table-valued UDFs?
   - **A.** Table-valued UDFs can return scalar values or tables.
   - **B.** Table-valued UDFs always involve multiple T-SQL statements.
   - **C.** Table-valued UDFs can be invoked in a SELECT list or a WHERE clause.
   - **D.** Table-valued UDFs can be invoked in the FROM clause of a SELECT statement.
3. Which sentence best describes the difference between an inline table-valued UDF and a multistatement table-valued UDF?
   - **A.** An inline table-valued UDF defines the schema of a table variable, with column names and data types, and inserts data into the table variable.
   - **B.** An inline table-valued UDF defines the schema of a permanent table, with column names and data types, and then inserts data into that table.
   - **C.** A multistatement table-valued UDF defines the schema of a table variable, with column names and data types, and inserts data into the table variable.
   - **D.** A multistatement table-valued UDF defines the schema of a permanent table, with column names and data types, and then inserts data into that table.

Case Scenarios

In the following case scenarios, you apply what you've learned about coding stored procedures, triggers, and user-defined functions. You can find the answers to these questions in the "Answers" section at the end of this chapter.

Case Scenario 1: Implementing Stored Procedures and UDFs

You have been assigned to a new project. As the lead database developer, you notice that almost all data validation against the database occurs in the client software. Sometimes fatal bugs in the client software have caused database inconsistency, and you want to refactor the system by using stored procedures to help protect the database. Answer the following questions about what actions you can take to improve the reliability of the application.

1. What steps can be taken to prevent duplicates or inconsistencies on unique keys and mismatched foreign keys?
2. How can you present a standard interface from the application code to the database?
3. The client developers would like to put parameters on views but T-SQL doesn't allow them. What can you use in place of parameterized views?
4. There is one large table that is searched often based on three different columns, but the user can choose any of the columns and leave the others blank. How can you use stored procedures to make this searching more efficient?

Case Scenario 2: Implementing Triggers

You have been asked to review the T-SQL code of an existing database application and recommend improvements. Answer the following questions about recommendations you can make about the design.

1. You notice that the system uses a lot of triggers to enforce foreign key constraints, and the triggers are error-prone and difficult to debug. What changes can you recommend to reduce the use of triggers?
2. You also observe that there are some complex operations that use nested triggers, which have never been made to work correctly in the application. What action can you recommend to eliminate the use of nested triggers?
3. The application must often insert data into a main table and several subsidiary tables in the same action, making the application code very complex. What can you recommend as a way of moving some of that complexity into the database and out of the application?

4. There is an important table that requires some simple logging actions to take place after any changes to the data. The logging is to a custom table built especially to meet application requirements. What recommendation might you make to help implement such a logging action?

Suggested Practices

To help you successfully master the exam objectives presented in this chapter, complete the following tasks.

Use Stored Procedures, Triggers, and UDFs

The following practices extend the code you worked with in the lessons and exercises in this chapter. Continue to develop these in the TSQL2012 database.

- **Practice 1** Add a TRY/CATCH block for error handling to the Backup stored procedure dbo.BackupDatabases that you created in Lesson 1, Exercise 1.
- **Practice 2** Add a TRY/CATCH block for error handling to the AFTER trigger Sales.OrderDetails_AfterTrigger that you created in Lesson 2, Exercise 2.
- **Practice 3** Modify the inline table-valued UDF Sales.fn_FilteredExtension that you created in Lesson 3, Exercise 2 to be a multistatement table-valued UDF.

Answers

This section contains the answers to the lesson review questions and solutions to the case scenarios in this chapter.

Lesson 1

1. **Correct Answers: A and C**
   - **A. Correct:** A WHILE statement starts a looping structure.
   - **B. Incorrect:** BEGIN and END do not cause branching. They are only used to group statements together.
   - **C. Correct:** IF and ELSE cause code execution to branch based on a condition in the IF clause.
   - **D. Incorrect:** A GO statement is just a batch terminator. It has no effect on code execution as such.
2. **Correct Answer: C**
   - **A. Incorrect:** The variables of the calling procedure cannot be seen by the called procedure.
   - **B. Incorrect:** Temporary tables are visible, but passed parameters are also visible.
   - **C. Correct:** The called procedure can see temporary tables and parameters passed to it from the calling procedure.
   - **D. Incorrect:** The called procedure can see temporary tables and passed parameters from the calling procedure.
3. **Correct Answer: B**
   - **A. Incorrect:** You can use an output parameter to receive information back from a stored procedure.
   - **B. Correct:** You can both pass data into a stored procedure and retrieve information back from it, by using an output parameter.
   - **C. Incorrect:** An output parameter is not used only for passing data back to the caller of the stored procedure. It is also used to pass data from the caller to a stored procedure.
   - **D. Incorrect:** You can both pass data into a stored procedure and retrieve information back from it, by using an output parameter.

Lesson 2

1. **Correct Answer: C**
   - **A. Incorrect:** In the case of a DELETE statement, there are no new or changed rows, so the inserted table is empty.
   - **B. Incorrect:** The inserted and deleted tables also contain rows for the UPDATE statement, not just the INSERT and DELETE statements.
   - **C. Correct:** An INSERT statement has all inserted rows in the inserted table but no rows in the deleted table.
   - **D. Incorrect:** For an UPDATE statement that updates rows in a table, the rows being changed will be in the inserted table with their new values, and in the deleted table with their old values.
2. **Correct Answers: A and D**
   - **A. Correct:** You can create INSTEAD OF triggers on views to reroute inserts or updates to the underlying base tables.
   - **B. Incorrect:** INSTEAD OF triggers execute instead of their DML statements, not instead of AFTER triggers.
   - **C. Incorrect:** INSTEAD OF triggers can be declared for all DML statements: INSERT, UPDATE, and DELETE.
   - **D. Correct:** With INSTEAD OF triggers, you can substitute the trigger code in place of the original DML statement.
3. **Correct Answer: D**
   - **A. Incorrect:** 'OFF' is not a valid value for the second parameter of sp_configure.
   - **B. Incorrect:** The 'nested triggers' option requires an additional RECONFIGURE statement.
   - **C. Incorrect:** 'OFF' is not a valid value for the second parameter of sp_configure.
   - **D. Correct:** After issuing the sp_configure stored procedure followed by 'nested triggers' and 0, you must also execute the RECONFIGURE statement.

Lesson 3

1. **Correct Answer: C**
   - **A. Incorrect:** Scalar UDFs are never inline. Only table-valued UDFs can be inline.
   - **B. Incorrect:** The results of a SELECT statement would be a table, and scalar UDFs do not return tables.
   - **C. Correct:** You can invoke a scalar UDF in a SELECT list or in the conditions of a WHERE clause, anywhere a scalar value would be valid.
   - **D. Incorrect:** A FROM clause requires a table and scalar UDFs cannot return tables.

2. **Correct Answer: D**
   - **A. Incorrect:** Table-valued UDFs only return tables.
   - **B. Incorrect:** Inline table-valued UDFs consist of only one T-SQL statement. Even multistatement table-valued UDFs only require one T-SQL statement.
   - **C. Incorrect:** Invoking in a SELECT list or a WHERE clause would require a scalar value, and table-valued UDFs only return tables.
   - **D. Correct:** The FROM clause requires a table and table-valued UDFs return tables.
3. **Correct Answer: C**
   - **A. Incorrect:** An inline table-valued UDF does not define the schema of the table structure it returns.
   - **B. Incorrect:** An inline table-valued UDF cannot create a permanent table.
   - **C. Correct:** A multistatement table-valued UDF defines an explicit schema of a table variable, and then inserts data into the table variable.
   - **D. Incorrect:** A multistatement table-valued UDF cannot create a permanent table.

Case Scenario 1

1. To prevent inconsistency in the database, ensure that the proper constraints are in place: primary key and unique key constraints on tables, check constraints on columns, and foreign key constraints between tables. Other more complex business rules can be enforced by using triggers.
2. To present a standard interface to the database, use data tier stored procedures—that is, use standard insert, update, and delete stored procedures for every table. The client software should only be allowed to change data in tables by using those stored procedures.
3. You can use table-valued functions in place of views, and define parameters to match the requirements of the application developers. You can then call the function from inside a stored procedure that accepts those parameters and send the results back to the client.
4. Consider making a search stored procedure that consists of a driver, and have it call sub-procedures, one for each combination of parameter. Those sub-procedures will always have the same query plan, so the procedures will not need to be recompiled.

Case Scenario 2

1. Foreign key constraints can be implemented by using triggers, but the code can become complex and error prone. You can recommend instead that the database developers implement true referential integrity by using T-SQL declared foreign key constraints rather than triggers.
2. You can recommend that the application disable nested triggers on the development server so that the database developers can get used to the idea of completing all necessary actions within only one level of a trigger. That should help simplify the trigger code and improve the ability to debug it.
3. When the application inserts data into one table, and must also insert into other subsidiary tables in the same action, you can recommend that the database developers use an INSTEAD OF trigger to execute. In that trigger, multiple inserts can be made before inserting into the main table.
4. To support simple logging, you can recommend that the database developers use a DML AFTER trigger. This type of trigger executes after an INSERT, UPDATE, or DELETE statement and it can write to the logging table.

CHAPTER 14

Using Tools to Analyze Query Performance

Exam objectives in this chapter:

- Troubleshoot & Optimize
  - Optimize queries.

Writing queries requires basic T-SQL knowledge; writing well-performing queries needs much more advanced knowledge. However, Microsoft SQL Server 2012 helps you in this learning process. SQL Server exposes information about query execution, like amount of disk IO and CPU time needed to execute the query, detailed execution steps, missing indexes and indexes that are not used, and much more. In this chapter, you learn how to use the query execution information exposed by SQL Server.

Lessons in this chapter:

- Lesson 1: Getting Started with Query Optimization
- Lesson 2: Using SET Session Options and Analyzing Query Plans
- Lesson 3: Using Dynamic Management Objects

Before You Begin

To complete the lessons in this chapter, you must have:

- An understanding of relational database concepts.
- Experience working with SQL Server Management Studio (SSMS).
- Some experience writing T-SQL code.
- Access to a SQL Server 2012 instance with the sample database TSQL2012 installed.

Lesson 1: Getting Started with Query Optimization

People are not very keen on waiting. They get nervous in a traffic jam. They are not too satisfied if they have to sit without a drink for a while in a bar. Similarly, they want their applications to be as responsive as possible. End users perceive performance problems through waiting.

SQL Server does a great job optimizing the execution of your queries. However, the SQL Server Query Optimizer is not perfect. Actually, as you will soon see, finding a reasonable execution plan is an extremely complex process. You can help the optimizer with appropriate database and application architecture, properly written queries, good indexing, query execution hints, and more. In order to select the best option for improving performance of your queries, you need to understand how SQL Server executes them. SQL Server exposes this information in many different ways. In this lesson, you learn about query optimization basics and get an overview of simple tools that can help you with optimization, namely with SQL Trace, SQL Server Profiler, and SQL Server Extended Events. You get more familiar with other tools in the next two lessons of this chapter.

After this lesson, you will be able to:

- Understand query optimization problems.
- Describe the SQL Server Query Optimizer.
- Use SQL Trace and SQL Server Profiler.
- Use SQL Server Extended Events.

Estimated lesson time: 40 minutes

Query Optimization Problems and the Query Optimizer

Except for very simple queries, a query can be executed in many different ways. How many ways? Well, the number of different ways of execution or execution plans grows exponentially with query complexity. For example, analyze the following pseudo-query very superficially. (Note that this query, of course, would not run if you executed it.)

```
SELECT A.col5, SUM(C.col6) AS col6sum
FROM TableA AS A
 INNER JOIN TableB AS B
   ON A.col1 = B.col1
 INNER JOIN TableC AS C
   ON B.col2 = c.col2
WHERE A.col3 = constant1
  AND B.col4 = constant2
GROUP BY A.col5;
```

Start with the FROM part. Which tables should SQL Server join first, TableA and TableB or TableB and TableC? And in each join, which of the two tables joined should be the left and which one the right table? The number of all possibilities is six, if the two joins are evaluated linearly, one after another. With evaluation of multiple joins at the same time, the number of all possible combinations for processing the joins is already 12. The actual formula for possible combinations of join evaluation is n!, or n factorial, for linear evaluation, and (2n -2)!/(n-1)! for parallel evaluation of possible joins. In addition, SQL Server can perform a join in different ways. It can use any of the following join algorithms:

- Nested Loops
- Merge
- Hash
- Bitmap Filtering Optimized Hash (also called Star join optimization)

This already gives four options for each join. So far, there are 6 x 4 = 24 different options for only the FROM part of this query. But the real situation is even worse. SQL Server can execute a hash join in three different ways. As mentioned, this is just a quick superficial analysis of pseudo-query execution, and for this introduction to query optimization problems, such details are not needed.

In the WHERE clause, two expressions are connected with a logical AND operator. The logical AND operator is commutative, so SQL Server can evaluate the second expression first. Again, there are two choices. Altogether, there are already 6 x 4 x 2 = 48 choices. And again, the real situation is much worse. Because in the pseudo-query all joins are inner joins and because expressions in the WHERE clause are commutative, SQL Server can even start executing the query with any of the expressions of the WHERE clause, then switch to the FROM clause and perform first a join, evaluate the second expression from the WHERE clause, and so on. So the number of possible plans is already much higher than 48.

For this superficial overview, continue with the GROUP BY clause. SQL Server can execute this part in two ways, as an ordered group or as a hash group. Therefore, the number of options for executing the pseudo-query is already 6 x 4 x 2 x 2 = 96.

You can stop analyzing options for executing the pseudo-query. The important conclusion is that you can see that the number of different possible execution plans for a query grows factorially with query complexity. You can quickly get billions of possible execution plans. SQL Server has to decide which one to use in a very short time. You wouldn't want to wait, for example, for a whole day for SQL Server to find out the best possible plan and then execute your queries in 5 seconds instead of in 15 seconds. Now you can imagine the complexity of the problems the SQL Server Query Optimizer has to solve with any single query.

Before continuing with the query optimization process, this lesson briefly introduces how SQL Server executes a query. Figure 1 shows this process.

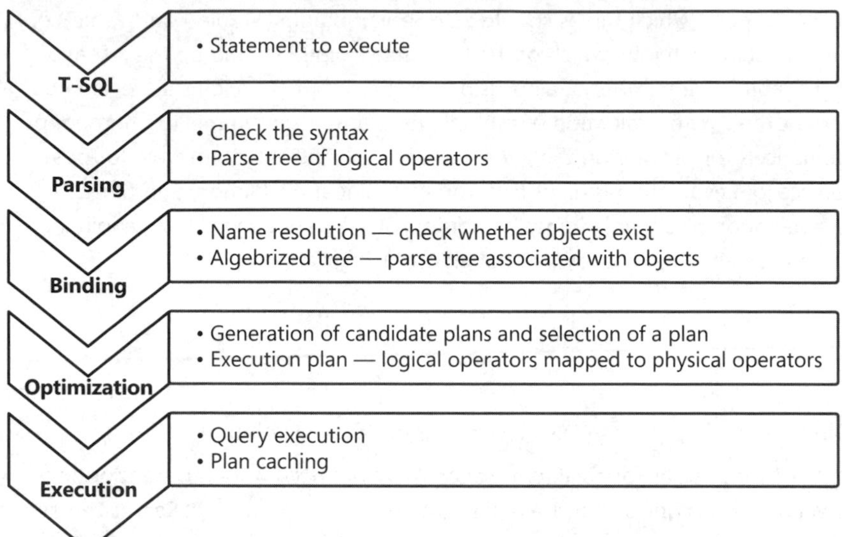

FIGURE 14-1 Query execution phases.

Query execution starts with your T-SQL query. During the *parsing* phase, SQL Server checks whether your query is syntactically correct. The result of this phase, if the query passed the syntax check, is a tree of *logical* operators known as a *parse tree*. In the next phase, the *binding* phase, SQL Server resolves the object names in the query. This means that it binds objects to logical operators. Of course, objects must exist for this phase to be finished successfully. The result of this phase is the *algebrized tree*, which is a tree of logical operators bound to actual objects.

The process for finding and evaluating different options—that is, different execution plans—to execute the query takes place during the *optimization* phase. This is the phase in which the Query Optimizer performs the vast majority of its work. In this phase, SQL Server generates candidate execution plans and evaluates them. It selects the best plan for the next phase. The result of this phase is the actual *execution plan*, which is a single tree with *physical* operators.

All of the steps so far are performed by the *relational engine*. The relational engine is an internal component that works on a logical level. The actual execution is performed by the *storage engine*. Of course, both parts are indivisible, implemented in a single service. The storage engine carries out the physical operations. In short, the Query Optimizer has to make the transformation from logical to physical operators. Of course, the Query Optimizer can use only physical operators that the storage engine can execute. For example, a logical operator can be a join operator; a physical operator can be a Merge Join operation.

The result of the final phase, the *execution phase*, is your desired result set. In addition, the result of the execution phase might also be a cached plan. SQL Server can cache an execution plan in order to have it ready for the next execution, thus avoiding doing the optimization again. Of course, SQL Server has to compile the code to binary code before execution; therefore, compiled plans are cached.

The SQL Server Query Optimizer is a *cost-based* optimizer. It assigns a number called cost to each possible plan. A higher cost means a more complex plan, and a more complex plan means a slower query. Theoretically, SQL Server should generate all possible plans and then select the one with the lowest cost. The *search space* for a given query is the set of all possible execution plans. Because the number of possible plans grows in a factorial way with query complexity, it is impossible to generate and check all possible plans for complex queries. The Query Optimizer balances between plan quality and time needed for the optimization. Therefore, the Query Optimizer cannot guarantee that the best possible plan is always selected.

SQL Server calculates the cost of an operation by determining the algorithm used by a physical operator and by estimating the number of rows that have to be processed. The estimation of the number of rows is also called *cardinality estimation*. The cost expresses usage of physical resources such as the amount of disk I/O, CPU time, and memory needed for execution. After the Query Optimizer gets the cost for all operators in a plan, it can calculate the cost of the whole plan.

Calculating the cost in advance can be quite tricky. The Query Optimizer needs some information for the estimation of the number of rows processed by each physical operator. The Query Optimizer gets this information from optimizer *statistics*. SQL Server maintains statistics about the total number of rows and distribution of the number of rows over key values of an index for each index. In addition, SQL Server can generate statistics for a column even if the column is not indexed. You can also generate and maintain statistics manually. You learn more about indexes and statistics in Chapter 15, "Implementing Indexes and Statistics."

Caching the selected execution plan in the *plan cache* can speed up the next execution of the same query or of an equivalent query from the execution perspective. SQL Server actually tries to parameterize your queries in order to have one plan for multiple equivalent queries. Equivalent queries are queries that can be executed in the same way. For example, the following two pseudo-queries can use the same execution plan.

```
SELECT col1 FROM TableA WHERE col2 = 3;

SELECT col1 FROM TableA WHERE col2 = 5;
```

SQL Server transforms queries like this into a parameterized query like the following pseudo-query.

```
SELECT col1 FROM TableA WHERE col2 = ?;
```

Of course, you can also write your own parameterized queries in your stored procedures. Then you pass parameters during stored procedure calls. In addition, you can use the sys.sp_executesql system procedure to parameterize ad hoc queries. Using stored procedures is considered a best practice, because auto-parameterization has many limitations that prevent many queries from getting parameterized.

SQL Server caches the execution plan separately from the actual value—that is, the *execution context*. This way, SQL Server can reuse the same execution plan many times. However, using a cached plan might not always be the best solution. For example, the number of rows in a table might grow substantially. All plans that include scans of that table, which might be fast enough for a small table, could suddenly become suboptimal.

Plans in cache can also become obsolete because metadata changes in a database. For example, an index could be added to a table or a constraint could be altered.

The Query Optimizer sometimes has to guess the cardinality estimation because it cannot detect for sure what it is from your parameters. This problem is known as a *parameter sniffing* problem. Parameter sniffing is a process where SQL Server tries to guess, or *sniff*, the current parameter value during compilation, and passes it to the Query Optimizer.

SQL Server does a great job in optimizing queries and maintains cached plans. However, there are many possibilities when something goes wrong and the best plan is not selected, such as in the following scenarios:

- The selected plan is not the best because the search space of the execution plans was too big.
- Statistical information is not present or updated, which leads to wrong cardinality estimation.
- A cached plan is suboptimal for the current parameter value.
- Parameter sniffing leads to inaccurate cardinality estimation.
- The Query Optimizer underestimates or overestimates the cost of an algorithm implemented in a physical operator.
- Hardware changes could better accommodate a different plan. For example, somebody could add CPUs to the box, and a plan that uses more CPU time could be more appropriate.

Of course, because of the complexity of the problem, more factors can exist that lead to a suboptimal plan. Therefore, there is always room for query optimization. In order to realize what went wrong, you have to be able to retrieve the information about estimated plans and actual execution plans used, about index usage, about statistical information, and more. SQL Server exposes this information in many ways. In the rest of this chapter, you learn how to retrieve the information needed for query optimization.

Quick Check

- **What is the result of the parsing phase of query execution?**

Quick Check Answer

- **The result of this phase, if the query passed the syntax check, is a tree of logical operators known as a parse tree.**

SQL Server Extended Events, SQL Trace, and SQL Server Profiler

Any monitoring has some impact on the system you are monitoring. If you are monitoring a system that already has performance problems, you could slow it down even more. This means you want to have as lightweight a monitoring system as possible. SQL Server Extended Events is a very lightweight performance monitoring system. With the Extended Events infrastructure, you can even correlate data from SQL Server with data from the operating system and applications. The complete Extended Events system is quite sophisticated. However, because SQL Server 2012 Extended Events provides two GUIs—the New Session Wizard and New Session UI—you can easily create a monitoring session and exploit Extended Events benefits quickly.

An Extended Events *package* is a container for all extended events objects. These objects include:

- **Events** These are your points of interest for monitoring. You can use events for monitoring or to trigger synchronous or asynchronous actions.
- **Targets** These are event consumers. You can use targets that write to a file, store event data in a memory buffer, or aggregate event data. Targets can process data synchronously or asynchronously.
- **Actions** These are responses to an event. They are bound to an event. Actions can capture a stack dump and inspect data, store information in a local variable, aggregate event data, or even append data to event data. For example, in SQL Server, you can use the execution plan detection action to detect execution plans.
- **Predicates** These are sets of logical rules to filter captured events. In order to minimize the impact of a monitoring session on your system, it is important that you capture only events you need.
- **Types** These help interpret the data collected. The data is actually a collection of bytes, and types give this data context. A type is provided for events, actions, targets, predicates, and types themselves.
- **Maps** These are SQL Server internal tables that map internal numeric values to meaningful strings.

SQL Server audit, which provides a database administrator (DBA) with lightweight auditing, is also based on Extended Events. SQL Server audit is outside the scope of this book. You learn a bit more about using Extended Events in the practice for this lesson.

SQL Trace is an internal SQL Server mechanism for capturing events. SQL Trace is deprecated in future versions. This means that it will still be available in the life cycle of SQL Server 2012 and the next version of SQL Server; however, after the next version, SQL Trace might be discontinued.

You can create *traces* through a set of SQL Server system stored procedures. You can create traces manually or through the SQL Server Profiler UI. You trace SQL Server *events*. A source for a trace event can be a T-SQL batch or some other SQL Server event, such as a deadlock. After an event occurs, the trace gathers the event information. Event information is then passed to a queue. Before passing to the queue, events are filtered according to your *filters*. From the queue, the trace information can go to a file or a SQL Server table, or it can be used by applications, such as SQL Server Profiler.

SQL Server Profiler is a rich application that serves as a UI for SQL Trace. With SQL Server Profiler, you can create and manage traces, and you can analyze results of your traces. You can replay events from a saved trace step by step. To start a server-side trace, you can script a trace you created through the SQL Server Profiler UI, and then execute the script directly on your SQL Server instance.

Note that there are some drawbacks to using SQL Server Profiler, such as the following:

- You increase the monitoring impact on your SQL Server instance compared to when you use SQL Trace only, due to the overhead SQL Server Profiler is producing.
- When you use the SQL Server Profiler UI on a computer with the SQL Server instance you are monitoring, SQL Server Profiler competes for the same resources.
- When you use SQL Server Profiler remotely, all events must travel over a network, which slows down other network operations.
- SQL Server Profiler shows events in a grid, which can consume a lot of memory when you capture many events.
- You or somebody else might inadvertently close the Profiler and stop the trace when you need to capture the events for a longer time.

Therefore, when monitoring an instance used in production, you should use SQL Trace.

Because SQL Server Profiler is, like SQL Trace, deprecated in future versions of SQL Server, you should switch to Extended Events in the near future. However, you can still use SQL Server Profiler for learning purposes. For example, it is extremely simple to start a trace with SQL Server Profiler and check what commands an application sends to SQL Server. This way, you can learn things about an application, T-SQL commands, and SQL Server system procedures.

The following provides a list of terms used by both SQL Trace and SQL Server Profiler:

- **Event** An event is an action within SQL Server. For example, an action can be a logon failure, T-SQL batch, start of a stored procedure, and more.
- **EventClass** This is the type of an event. The event class defines the data that an event can report.
- **EventCategory** Event categories define groupings of events.

- **DataColumn** A data column is an attribute of an event. If you save a trace to a table, an event is represented by a row in the table, and attributes of events are columns in the table.
- **Template** A template is a saved trace definition. SQL Server Profiler comes with a couple of predefined templates that can speed up the creation of a trace.
- **Filter** Filters limit the events traced. You can put a filter on any event column. In order to minimize the impact of monitoring on your SQL Server instance, you should filter out any event you do not need in your current trace.
- **Trace** A trace is a collection of events, columns, filters, and data returned.

EXAM TIP

You should use SQL Server Extended Events instead of SQL Trace and SQL Server Profiler because Extended Events is more lightweight and SQL Trace and SQL Server Profiler are deprecated in future versions of SQL Server.

PRACTICE Using Extended Events

In this practice, you create an Extended Events session. You also execute a T-SQL statement and observe the results.

If you encounter a problem completing an exercise, you can install the completed projects from the companion content for this chapter and lesson.

EXERCISE 1 Prepare a T-SQL Statement and Create an Extended Events Session

In this exercise, you prepare a T-SQL statement that you are going to analyze, and you create and start an Extended Events session with the help of the wizard.

1. Start SSMS and connect to your SQL Server instance.
2. Open a new query window by clicking the New Query button.
3. Change the context to the TSQL2012 database.
4. Write the following query and execute it to test whether it works.

```
SELECT C.custid, C.companyname,
 O.orderid, O.orderdate
FROM Sales.Customers AS C
 INNER JOIN Sales.Orders AS O
   ON C.custid = O.custid
ORDER BY C.custid, O.orderid;
```

5. In SSMS Object Explorer, expand the Management folder. Expand Extended Events. Right-click the Sessions folder and select New Session Wizard.
6. On the Introduction page, read the information and click Next.
7. On the Set Session Properties page, name the session **TK461Ch14**. Click Next.
8. On the Choose Template page, select the Do Not Use A Template option. Click Next.
9. On the Select Events To Capture page, type the string **sql** in the Event Library text box to filter events that have this string in their name. Select the sql_statement_completed event and move it to the Selected Events pane, as shown in Figure 14-2. Click Next.

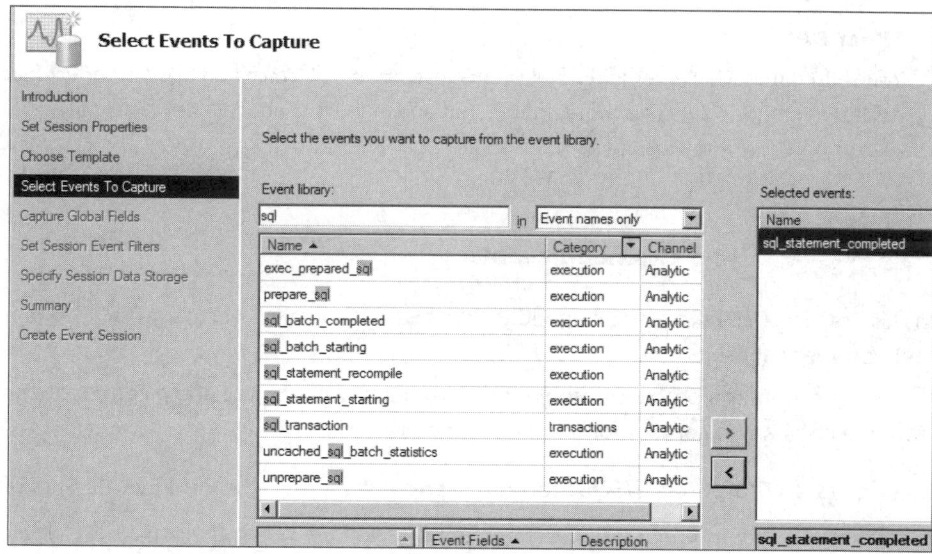

FIGURE 14-2 Selecting events to capture.

10. On the Capture Global Fields page, review the global fields (actions) that are common to all events. Specific fields for the selected event are available automatically, so you do not need to select any of the global events. Click Next.
11. On the Set Session Event Filters page, create a filter that filters the sqlserver.database_name to be equal to the value TSQL2012; and for the sqlserver.sql_text field operator, use like_i_sql_unicode_string to filter the statements that are like the string SELECT C.custid, C.companyname%. Click inside cells for the AndOr, Field, and Operator columns in the grid to select appropriate values. Your filter should look like the one shown in Figure 14-3. Click Next.

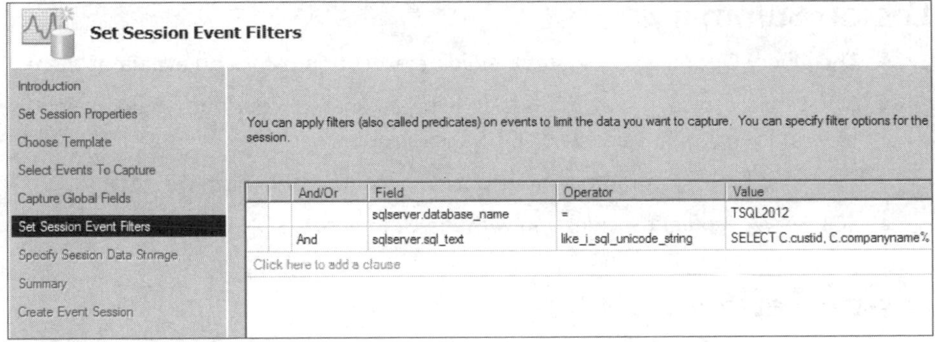

FIGURE 14-3 Setting session event filters.

12. On the Specify Session Data Storage page, select the Work With Only The Most Recent Data (Ring_Buffer Target) check box. Click Next.
13. On the Summary page, review the summary information and click Finish.
14. On the last page, the Create Event Session page, select both check boxes: Start the event session immediately after session creation and watch the live data on the screen as it is captured. Click Close. The Extended Events Live Data window should open in SSMS.

EXERCISE 2 Use the Extended Events Session

In this exercise, you use the Extended Events session you prepared in the previous exercise. You also script the session to understand how to create it with T-SQL.

1. Switch to the query window that has your query.
2. Execute the query.
3. Switch back to the Extended Events Live Data window and observe the results. Note the fields collected.
4. Close the Extended Events Live Data window.
5. In SSMS Object Explorer, expand the Sessions folder of Extended Events. Besides your sessions, some default sessions are already defined.
6. Right-click your TK461Ch14 session and script it as a CREATE DDL statement to a new query window. Observe the CREATE EVENT SESSION statement.
7. Close the query window with the CREATE EVENT SESSION statement. To clean up, right-click your TK461Ch14 session and select Delete.

Lesson Summary

- The Query Optimizer generates candidate execution plans and evaluates them.
- SQL Server provides many tools that help you analyze your queries, including Extended Events, SQL Trace, and SQL Server Profiler.
- Extended Events is a more lightweight monitoring mechanism than SQL Trace.
- SQL Server Profiler provides you with the UI to access SQL Trace.

Lesson Review

Answer the following questions to test your knowledge of the information in this lesson. You can find the answers to these questions and explanations of why each answer choice is correct or incorrect in the "Answers" section at the end of this chapter.

1. What are the actions of the optimization phase of query execution? (Choose all that apply.)

- **A.** Generation of the algebrized tree
- **B.** Generation of candidate plans
- **C.** Selection of the best candidate plan
- **D.** Caching the plan
- **E.** Query execution

2. In which phase of query execution does SQL Server check whether the objects referred to by the query exist?

- **A.** In the parsing phase
- **B.** In the binding phase
- **C.** In the optimization phase
- **D.** In the execution phase

3. Which of the following is not a part of an Extended Events package?

- **A.** Predicates
- **B.** Targets
- **C.** Sources
- **D.** Actions

Lesson 2: Using SET Session Options and Analyzing Query Plans

As you learned in the previous lesson, query optimization is a complex process. You can improve the performance of your queries with a proper design, appropriate indexes, updated statistics, query hints, and more. SQL Server exposes information about its own activity in many different ways. In the previous lesson, you learned about tools that you can use to trace the activity over time, such as Extended Events, SQL Trace, and SQL Server Profiler. In this lesson, you learn how to make a detailed analysis of a single query with the help of SET session options and exposed execution plans.

After this lesson, you will be able to:

- Use the SET session options to analyze your queries.
- Read the estimated and the actual execution plans.

Estimated lesson time: 40 minutes

SET Session Options

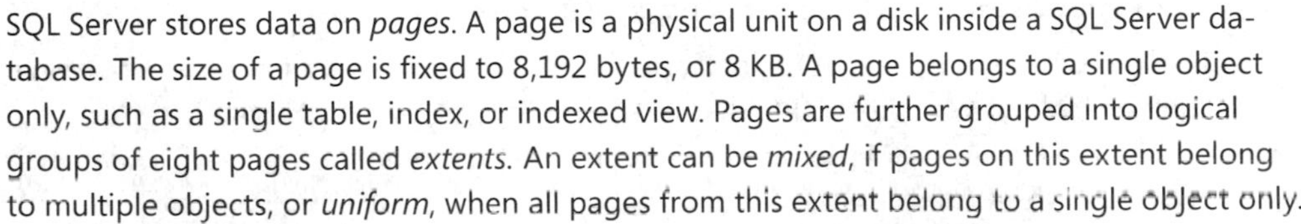

SQL Server stores data on *pages*. A page is a physical unit on a disk inside a SQL Server database. The size of a page is fixed to 8,192 bytes, or 8 KB. A page belongs to a single object only, such as a single table, index, or indexed view. Pages are further grouped into logical groups of eight pages called *extents*. An extent can be *mixed*, if pages on this extent belong to multiple objects, or *uniform*, when all pages from this extent belong to a single object only.

You learn a bit more about page content in a table or in an index in Chapter 15. For this chapter, it is enough to remember that one of the targets of optimizing a query is to lower disk I/O. This means you want to lower the number of pages SQL Server has to read.

You can get information about the number of pages per table accessed by queries if you turn statistics IO on. You can do this on a session level with the SET STATISTICS IO T-SQL command. A session level option means that the option stays unchanged for the complete session, until you disconnect from SQL Server, unless you turn it off. You can turn it off with the same statement.

The following code checks the number of pages that Sales.Customers and Sales.Orders occupy in the TSQL2012 database.

```
DBCC DROPCLEANBUFFERS;
SET STATISTICS IO ON;
SELECT * FROM Sales.Customers;
SELECT * FROM Sales.Orders;
```

Note that DBCC DROPCLEANBUFFERS clears data from the cache. SQL Server caches data besides query and procedure plans. In order to show the IO statistics, it is good to have no data in the cache. However, you should clean the cache on a production server with a lot of caution. SQL Server caches data in order to speed up queries; because a piece of data is cached, the next time it is needed, SQL Server can retrieve it from memory and not from a disk, and thus execute a query that needs this data much faster. Here are the results.

```
(91 row(s) affected)
Table 'Customers'. Scan count 1, logical reads 5, physical reads 1, read-ahead reads 10,
lob logical reads 0, lob physical reads 0, lob read-ahead reads 0.

(830 row(s) affected)
Table 'Orders'. Scan count 1, logical reads 21, physical reads 1, read-ahead reads 19,
lob logical reads 0, lob physical reads 0, lob read-ahead reads 0.
```

The meaning of the information returned is as follows:

- **Scan count** The number of index or table scans performed.
- **Logical reads** The number of pages read from the data cache. When you read a whole table as in the queries from the example, this number gives you an estimate about table size.
- **Physical reads** The number of pages read from the disk. This number is lower than the actual number of pages because many pages are cached.
- **Read-ahead reads** The number of pages SQL Server reads ahead.
- **Lob logical reads** The number of large object (LOB) pages read from the data cache. LOBs are columns of types VARCHAR(MAX), NVARCHAR(MAX), VARBINARY(MAX), TEXT, NTEXT, IMAGE, XML, or large CLR data types, including the system CLR spatial types GEOMETRY and GEOGRAPHY.
- **Lob physical reads** The number of large object-type pages read from disk.
- **Lob read-ahead reads** The number of large object pages SQL Server reads ahead.

For a starting point, you can orient on logical reads. Logical reads give you a first and rough estimation of the effectiveness of a query. However, you should not use this information without thinking and additional knowledge.

Look at the following two queries.

```
SELECT C.custid, C.companyname,
    O.orderid, O.orderdate
    FROM Sales.Customers AS C
    INNER JOIN Sales.Orders AS O
        ON C.custid = O.custid;

    SELECT C.custid, C.companyname,
    O.orderid, O.orderdate
    FROM Sales.Customers AS C
    INNER JOIN Sales.Orders AS O
        ON C.custid = O.custid
    WHERE O.custid < 5;
```

Statistics IO for the first query shows only two logical reads for the Sales.Customers table, although it shows 60 logical reads for the second query. However, the second query filters rows for customers with custid lower than 5 only, so it should perform less IO, right? Well, SQL Server counts every touch of a table, even if pages needed are already cached. However, when pages are in the cache, touching them is not expensive. Here's a brief explanation of the numbers: SQL Server used a Nested Loops join algorithm in the second query, and Sales.Customers was the inner table in this join. You learn more details about joins in Chapter 17, "Understanding Further Optimization Aspects." For now, it is enough to know that it is important not to rely on statistics IO only when analyzing query performance. Fortunately, you have many additional options.

The next SET session command that is useful for analyzing performance is SET STATISTICS TIME. The following code turns this option on. Note the DBCC DROPCLEANBUFFERS command. This command drops cached plans from the cache. Again, you should be very careful about using this command in production.

```
SET STATISTICS TIME ON;
DBCC DROPCLEANBUFFERS;
```

Then the following code executes the first query from the previous example.

```
SELECT C.custid, C.companyname,
 O.orderid, O.orderdate
FROM Sales.Customers AS C
 INNER JOIN Sales.Orders AS O
  ON C.custid = O.custid;
```

The results can differ slightly from execution to execution. For example, the results during one of the test executions were the following.

```
SQL Server parse and compile time:
   CPU time = 0 ms, elapsed time = 0 ms.
 SQL Server Execution Times:
   CPU time = 0 ms,  elapsed time = 92 ms.
```

You can see that the statistics time returned includes CPU time and total (elapsed) time needed for an operation. In addition, you can see the actual execution time and the time needed for preexecution phases, including parsing, binding, optimization, and compilation. At this point, it's time to drop cached plans again.

```
DBCC DROPCLEANBUFFERS;
```

If you execute the second query from the example, you get different results.

```
DBCC DROPCLEANBUFFERS;
SELECT C.custid, C.companyname,
 O.orderid, O.orderdate
FROM Sales.Customers AS C
 INNER JOIN Sales.Orders AS O
  ON C.custid = O.custid
WHERE O.custid < 5;
```

The results are as follows.

```
SQL Server Execution Times:
   CPU time = 0 ms,  elapsed time = 1 ms.
 SQL Server Execution Times:
   CPU time = 15 ms,  elapsed time = 10 ms.
```

Now you can see that the second query was faster. However, you have even more sophisticated tools for investigating how SQL Server executes a query.

Execution Plans

You can get the most exhaustive information about how a query is executing by analyzing its execution plan. SQL Server exposes *estimated* and *actual* plans. If you display an estimated plan only, the query is not executed. Actual and estimated plans usually don't differ; however, in some cases, an estimated plan cannot give you completely exact information like an actual plan does. For example, if you create and query a temporary table in the same batch, SQL Server cannot optimize the data access to the temporary table because it is not created at the time of optimization yet. In addition, SQL Server postpones optimization of dynamic SQL because it is not clear what to execute and how to optimize this dynamic SQL until execution time. However, for large queries that execute for a long time, estimated plans can be very useful. You probably don't want to execute a query that reads a billion rows on a production system just to get the actual execution plan.

You can get both the estimated and the actual plan in three forms: as text, as XML, or graphically. SQL Server returns the plan in XML format natively. SSMS presents this XML in graphical format. Text presentations of plans are deprecated and will be removed in future versions of SQL Server. You can turn on and off text plans with the following T-SQL SET session commands:

- SET SHOWPLAN_TEXT and SET SHOWPLAN_ALL for estimated plans
- SET STATISTICS PROFILE for actual plans

You can turn on and off XML plans with the following commands:

- SET SHOWPLAN_XML for estimated plans
- SET STATISTICS XML for actual plans

You can turn graphical and actual plans on and off from SSMS in the following ways:

- Right-click in the Query Editor window and select either the Display Estimated Execution Plan option or the Include Actual Execution Plan option.
- Press Ctrl+L for the Display Estimated Execution Plan option or press Ctrl+M for the Include Actual Execution Plan option.

- Select either of these two options from the Query menu.
- Click the Display Estimated Execution Plan and Include Actual Execution Plan buttons on the SQL Editor toolbar.

Here is an example of a query.

```
SELECT C.custid, MIN(C.companyname) AS companyname,
 COUNT(*) AS numorders
FROM Sales.Customers AS C
 INNER JOIN Sales.Orders AS O
  ON C.custid = O.custid
WHERE O.custid < 5
GROUP BY C.custid
HAVING COUNT(*) > 6;
```

This query produces the actual execution plan shown in Figure 14-4.

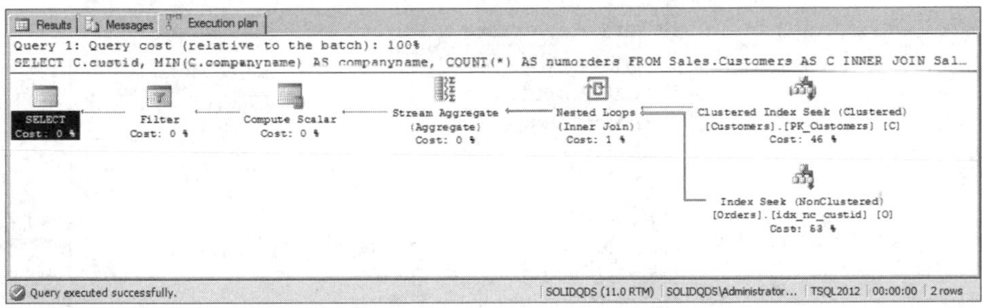

FIGURE 14-4 Graphical execution plan.

You can see the physical operators used during the execution. You read the execution plan from right to left, from top to bottom. SQL Server started the execution of this query with a clustered index seek in the Sales.Customers table, and then with a nonclustered index seek in the Sales.Orders table. Then SQL Server joined the results from previous operations with a Nested Loops join, and so on. You can also see the relative cost of each operator in the total query cost expressed as a percentage of the total query cost. In this example, the first two operators contribute 99 percent (46% + 53%) to the total cost of the query. You can quickly focus on the most expensive operators.

The arrows show you the data flow from one physical operator to another. The thickness of an arrow corresponds to the relative number of rows passed from an operator to an operator. By pausing on an operator or over an arrow, you get much more detailed information. Figure 14-5 shows detailed information for the Nested Loops operator.

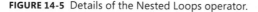

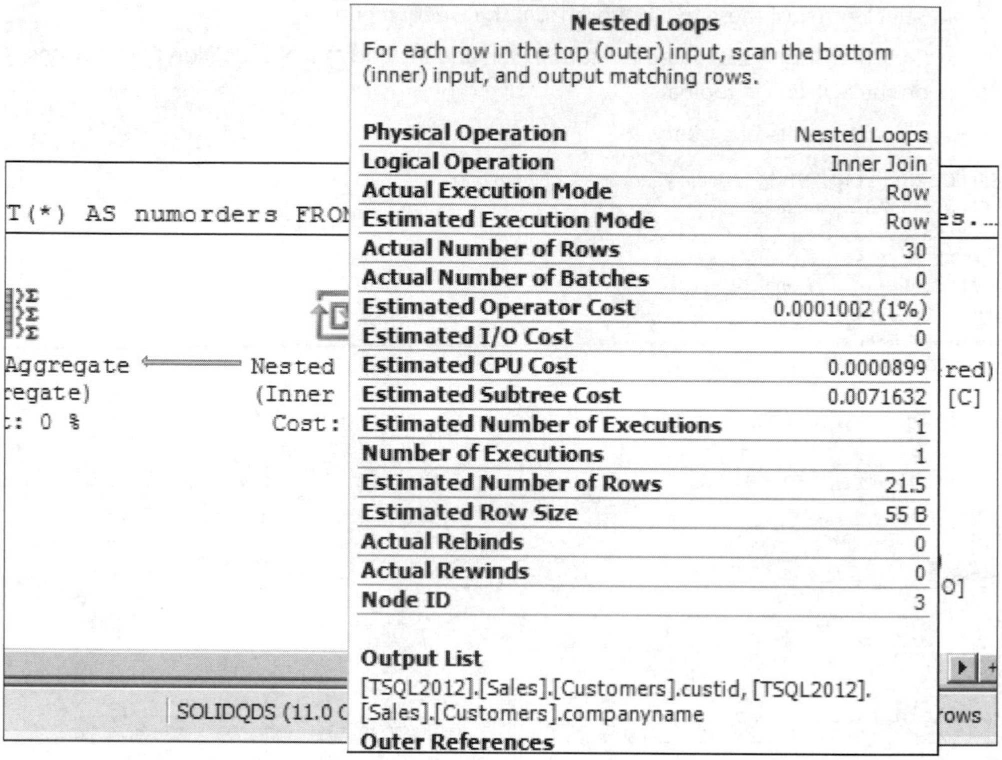

Nested Loops

For each row in the top (outer) input, scan the bottom (inner) input, and output matching rows.

Physical Operation	Nested Loops
Logical Operation	Inner Join
Actual Execution Mode	Row
Estimated Execution Mode	Row
Actual Number of Rows	30
Actual Number of Batches	0
Estimated Operator Cost	0.0001002 (1%)
Estimated I/O Cost	0
Estimated CPU Cost	0.0000899
Estimated Subtree Cost	0.0071632
Estimated Number of Executions	1
Number of Executions	1
Estimated Number of Rows	21.5
Estimated Row Size	55 B
Actual Rebinds	0
Actual Rewinds	0
Node ID	3

Output List

[TSQL2012].[Sales].[Customers].custid, [TSQL2012].[Sales].[Customers].companyname

Outer References

FIGURE 14-5 Details of the Nested Loops operator.

From the details, you can see both the physical and logical operators used. You can see the estimated number of rows (21.5 in the example) and the actual number of rows (30). This way, you can quickly notice errors in cardinality estimation. You can see the estimated operator cost and the estimated cost of the complete subtree up to this point. The cost of the operator is used to calculate the percentage of the total cost. You can get the total estimated cost for the query if you pause on the last operator in the plan and read the estimated subtree cost. You can get even more details of each operator if you open the Properties window. You can open it from the View menu or press F4.

Note that the execution plan is in XML form and SSMS is responsible for graphical presentation. You can right-click in the graphical plan and show it as XML by selecting the Show Execution Plan XML option. You can save the plan for later analysis with the Save Execution Plan As option. The execution plan is saved in XML format in a file with the extension sqlplan.

For information on all possible operators that can appear in an execution plan, see the Books Online for SQL Server 2008 R2 article "Graphical Execution Plan Icons (SQL Server Management Studio)" at *http://msdn.microsoft.com/en-us/library/ms175913(v=SQL.105).aspx*. Table 14-1 shows some of the most common operators, including their icons in the graphical plan, their names, and a short description of each.

TABLE 14-1 Common execution plan operators

Icon	Operator	Description
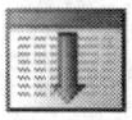	Table Scan	Scan of a whole table stored as a heap. A table can be organized as a heap or as a clustered index.
	Clustered Index Scan	Scan of a whole table stored as a clustered index. Indexes are stored as balanced trees.
	Clustered Index Seek	SQL Server seeks for the first value in the seek argument (for example, a column value in the WHERE clause) in a clustered index and then performs a partial scan.
	Index Scan	Scan of a whole nonclustered index.
	Index Seek	SQL Server seeks for the first value in the seek argument (for example, a column value in the WHERE clause) in a nonclustered index and then performs a partial scan.
	RID Lookup	Lookup for a single row in a table stored as a heap by using its row identifier (RID).
	Key Lookup	Lookup for a single row in a table stored as a clustered index by using the key of the index.
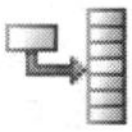	Hash Match Join	Joins that use the Hash algorithm.
	Merge Join	Joins that use the Merge algorithm.
	Nested Loops	Joins that use the Nested Loops algorithm.
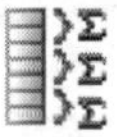	Stream Aggregate	Aggregation of ordered rows.
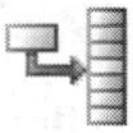	Hash Match Aggregate	Hash algorithm used for aggregating. Note that the icon is the same as the icon for the Hash Match Join; however, in an execution plan, text below the icons gives you information about whether the operator performed a join or an aggregate.
	Filter	Filters rows based on a predicate (for example, a predicate of the WHERE clause).
	Sort	Sort of incoming rows.

It's preferable to see some of these operators in a transactional environment and to see others in data warehousing environments. None of the operators is good or bad. You will understand more about when which operator is preferred after Chapter 15 and Chapter 17. You also get more information about heaps and clustered and nonclustered indexes in Chapter 15.

Quick Check

1. **How would you quickly measure the amount of disk IO a query is performing?**
2. **How can you get an estimated execution plan in XML format for further analysis?**

Quick Check Answers

1. **You should use the SET STATISTICS IO command.**
2. **You can use the SET SHOWPLAN_XML command.**

PRACTICE Using SET Session Options and Execution Plans

In this practice, you use a graphical execution plan and SET session options. You also explore an additional execution plan option: a missing index warning.

If you encounter a problem completing an exercise, you can install the completed projects from the companion content for this chapter and lesson.

EXERCISE 1 Prepare the Data

In this exercise, you create a new table with data and index it.

1. If you closed SSMS, start it and connect to your SQL Server instance.
2. Open a new query window by clicking the New Query button.
3. Change the context to the TSQL2012 database.
4. Write the following query to create a new table from the Sales.Orders table and multiply the number of rows from the original table 30 times.

```
SELECT N1.n * 100000 + O.orderid AS norderid,
       O.*
INTO dbo.NewOrders
FROM Sales.Orders AS O
 CROSS JOIN (VALUES(1),(2),(3),(4),(5),(6),(7),(8),(9),
  (10),(11),(12),(13),(14),(15),(16),
  (17),(18),(19),(20),(21),(22),(23),
  (24),(25),(26),(27),(28),(29),(30)) AS N1(n);
```

5. Create a nonclustered index named **idx_nc_orderid** on the new table. Index the orderid column. Use the following code.

```
CREATE NONCLUSTERED INDEX idx_nc_orderid
 ON dbo.NewOrders(orderid);
```

EXERCISE 2 Analyze a Query

In this exercise, you analyze a query that queries the table you created in the previous exercise.

1. Turn the statistics IO and statistics time on.

```
SET STATISTICS IO ON;
SET STATISTICS TIME ON;
```

2. Execute the following query.

```
SELECT norderid
FROM dbo.NewOrders
WHERE norderid = 110248
ORDER BY norderid;
```

3. Note that the query uses only the norderid column, whereas the index you created included the orderid column only. Check the CPU and elapsed time needed for parsing, compilation, and execution. Check the number of logical reads. Remember the numbers, and then turn the statistics IO and statistics time off.

```
SET STATISTICS IO OFF;
SET STATISTICS TIME OFF;
```

4. Include the actual execution plan when you execute the query by clicking the Include Actual Execution Plan button. Execute the same query again.

```
SELECT norderid
FROM dbo.NewOrders
WHERE norderid = 110248
ORDER BY norderid;
```

5. In the SSMS query window, in the results pane, click the Execution Plan tab. Analyze the execution plan. It should look like the one shown in Figure 14-6.

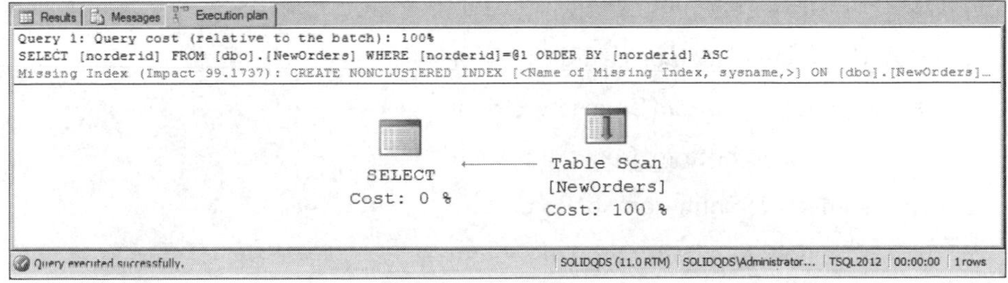

FIGURE 14-6 Execution plan with a missing index warning.

6. Note the missing index warning. Right-click it and select the Missing Index Details option to script the index creation statement.
7. Create the missing index by using the following code.

```
CREATE NONCLUSTERED INDEX idx_nc_norderid
 ON dbo.NewOrders(norderid);
```

8. Execute the query again. Observe the new execution plan. If you want, you can also check the logical IO and elapsed time.
9. Turn off the actual execution plan.
10. Clean up the database by using the following code.

```
DROP TABLE dbo.NewOrders;
```

Lesson Summary

- You can use SET session options to analyze your queries.
- You can use graphical execution plans to get detailed information about how SQL Server executes a query.
- You can display an estimated or an actual execution plan.
- In a graphical execution plan, you can get detailed properties of each operator.

Lesson Review

Answer the following questions to test your knowledge of the information in this lesson. You can find the answers to these questions and explanations of why each answer choice is correct or incorrect in the "Answers" section at the end of this chapter.

1. Which SET session options are useful for query optimization? (Choose all that apply.)
   - **A.** SET STATISTICS IO
   - **B.** SET STATISTICS EXECUTION_DETAILS
   - **C.** SET IDENTITY_INSERT
   - **D.** SET STATISTICS TIME
2. How do you read a graphical execution plan?
   - **A.** From top to bottom, from left to right
   - **B.** From top to bottom, from right to left
   - **C.** From left to right, from top to bottom
   - **D.** From right to left, from top to bottom

3. Which commands turn on an XML plan? (Choose all that apply.)
   - **A.** SET EXECUTION_XML ON
   - **B.** SET SHOWPLAN_XML ON
   - **C.** SET XML PLAN ON
   - **D.** SET STATISTICS XML ON

Lesson 3: Using Dynamic Management Objects

Even with Extended Events, SQL Trace, SQL Server Profiler, SET session options, and the execution plans of the SQL Server toolset to help you, the options for optimizing your queries are still not exhausted. SQL Server constantly monitors itself and gathers information useful for monitoring the health of an instance, finds problems such as missing indexes, and optimizes queries. SQL Server exposes this information through *dynamic management objects (DMOs)*. These objects include *dynamic management views* and *dynamic management functions*. Functions, which are different than views, accept parameters. All DMOs are in the sys system schema; DMO names start with the string dm_. Some of the information from DMOs shows the current state of an instance, whereas other information is cumulative from the start of an instance.

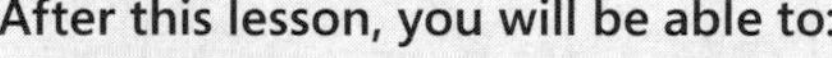

After this lesson, you will be able to:

- Understand dynamic management objects.
- Use dynamic management objects to tune queries.

Estimated lesson time: 35 minutes

Introduction to Dynamic Management Objects

Imagine that you get complaints from end users about SQL Server performance. You have to start investigating the problem immediately. How would you start? In a production system, end users can submit thousands of queries per hour. Which query would you analyze first? You could try to start an Extended Events monitoring session. You could use SQL Trace. In both cases, you would have to wait for quite a while before you gather enough data to start analysis and find the most problematic queries. And what if the problematic queries are not executed soon again after you start your monitoring session? You could only hope that you would be able to catch the problems in a reasonable time.

This is the point at which DMOs become extremely helpful. With DMOs, a lot of the data that you need is already gathered. All you need to do is query appropriate DMOs with regular T-SQL queries and extract useful information. DMOs are not materialized in any database; DMOs are virtual objects that give you access to the data SQL Server collects in memory.

Although DMOs are really useful, they have some drawbacks. The most important issue you should take care of is when the last restart of the instance you are inspecting occurred. Cumulative information is useless if the instance was restarted recently.

More than 130 DMOs are available for querying in SQL Server 2012. For details, see the Books Online for SQL 2012 article "Dynamic Management Views and Functions (Transact-SQL)" at *http://msdn.microsoft.com/en-us/library/ms188754.aspx*. In this lesson, you learn about some of the most important ones for query and index tuning.

The Most Important DMOs for Query Tuning

DMOs are grouped into many categories. For analyzing query performance, the most useful groups include:

- **SQL Server Operating System (SQLOS)–related DMOs** The SQLOS manages operating system resources that are specific to SQL Server.
- **Execution-related DMOs** These DMOs provide you with insight into queries that have been executed, including their query text, execution plan, number of executions, and more.
- **Index-related DMOs** These DMOs provide useful information about index usage and missing indexes.

You can start an analyzing session by gathering some system information. From the sys.dm_os_sys_info SQLOS-related dynamic management view, you can get basic information about your instance, as the following query shows.

```
SELECT cpu_count AS logical_cpu_count,
 cpu_count / hyperthread_ratio AS physical_cpu_count,
 CAST(physical_memory_kb / 1024. AS int) AS physical_memory__mb,
 sqlserver_start_time
FROM sys.dm_os_sys_info;
```

The query returns information about the number of logical CPUs, physical CPUs, physical memory, and the time at which SQL Server was started. The last information tells you whether it makes sense to analyze cumulative information or not.

The SQLOS-related sys.dm_os_waiting_tasks DMO gives you information about sessions that are currently waiting on something. For example, the sessions could be blocked by another session because of locking. You can join this DMO to the execution-related sys.dm_exec_sessions DMO to get information about the user, host, and application that are waiting. You can also use the is_user_process flag from the sys.dm_exec_sessions DMO to filter out system sessions. The following query gives this information.

```
SELECT S.login_name, S.host_name, S.program_name,
 WT.session_id, WT.wait_duration_ms, WT.wait_type,
 WT.blocking_session_id, WT.resource_description
FROM sys.dm_os_waiting_tasks AS WT
 INNER JOIN sys.dm_exec_sessions AS S
  ON WT.session_id = S.session_id
WHERE s.is_user_process = 1;
```

The sys.dm_exec_requests execution-related DMO returns information about currently executing requests. It includes a column called sql_handle, which is a hash map of the T-SQL batch text that is executed. You can use this handle to retrieve the complete text of the batch with the help of the execution-related sys.dm_exec_sql_text dynamic management function that accepts this handle as a parameter. The following query joins information about current requests, their waits, and text of their SQL batch with the sys.dm_exec_sessions dynamic management view to also get user, host, and application info.

```
SELECT S.login_name, S.host_name, S.program_name,
 R.command, T.text,
 R.wait_type, R.wait_time, R.blocking_session_id
FROM sys.dm_exec_requests AS R
 INNER JOIN sys.dm_exec_sessions AS S
  ON R.session_id = S.session_id
 OUTER APPLY sys.dm_exec_sql_text(R.sql_handle) AS T
WHERE S.is_user_process = 1;
```

You can retrieve a lot of information about executed queries from the execution-related sys.dm_exec_query_stats DMO. You can retrieve information about disk IO per query, CPU consumption per query, elapsed time per query, and more. With the help of the sys.dm_exec_sql_text DMO, you can retrieve the text of the query as well. You can extract specific query text from batch text with the help of the statement_start_offset and statement_end_offset columns from the sys.dm_exec_query_stats DMO. The extraction is somewhat tricky. The following query lists five queries that used the most logical disk IO with their query text extracted from the batch text.

```
SELECT TOP (5)
 (total_logical_reads + total_logical_writes) AS total_logical_IO,
 execution_count,
 (total_logical_reads/execution_count) AS avg_logical_reads,
 (total_logical_writes/execution_count) AS avg_logical_writes,
 (SELECT SUBSTRING(text, statement_start_offset/2 + 1,
    (CASE WHEN statement_end_offset = -1
          THEN LEN(CONVERT(nvarchar(MAX),text)) * 2
          ELSE statement_end_offset
     END - statement_start_offset)/2)
   FROM sys.dm_exec_sql_text(sql_handle)) AS query_text
FROM sys.dm_exec_query_stats
ORDER BY (total_logical_reads + total_logical_writes) DESC;
```

Many useful index-related DMOs are available. You can find missing indexes with the help of the sys.dm_db_missing_index_details, sys.dm_db_missing_index_columns, sys.dm_db_missing_index_groups, and sys.dm_db_missing_index_group_stats DMOs. Note that having too many indexes is bad as well; although queries do not use them, SQL Server has to maintain them. With the help of sys.indexes catalog view and sys.dm_db_index_usage_stats dynamic management view, you can find indexes that are not used. You use the index-related DMOs in the practice for this lesson.

 **Quick Check**

- **Which DMO gives you detailed text of queries executed?**

Quick Check Answer

- **You can retrieve the text of batches and queries executed from the sys.dm_exec_sql_text DMO.**

PRACTICE Using Index-Related DMOs

In this practice, you use the index-related DMOs. You also learn how important is to have a representative sample of queries collected before using DMOs that return cumulative values.

If you encounter a problem completing an exercise, you can install the completed projects from the companion content for this chapter and lesson.

EXERCISE 1 Find Unused Indexes

In this exercise, you find unused indexes.

1. Restart your SQL Server instance. (Note: don't do this on a production server.) If you did not close SSMS, you can do this from the Object Explorer by right-clicking your instance and selecting the Restart option. You can also use the SQL Server Configuration Manager for this task.
2. Connect to your instance with SSMS. Open a new query window by clicking the New Query button.
3. Change the context to the TSQL2012 database.
4. Find nonclustered indexes that were not used from the last start of the instance by using the following query.

```
SELECT OBJECT_NAME(I.object_id) AS objectname,
 I.name AS indexname,
 I.index_id AS indexid
FROM sys.indexes AS I
 INNER JOIN sys.objects AS O
  ON O.object_id = I.object_id
WHERE I.object_id > 100
  AND I.type_desc = 'NONCLUSTERED'
  AND I.index_id NOT IN
       (SELECT S.index_id
        FROM sys.dm_db_index_usage_stats AS S
        WHERE S.object_id=I.object_id
          AND I.index_id=S.index_id
          AND database_id = DB_ID('TSQL2012'))
ORDER BY objectname, indexname;
```

Note the results. The query returned all nonclustered indexes from the TSQL2012 database. Of course, because you just restarted your instance, SQL Server did not gather any index usage data yet. This shows you how important it is to have a representative sample when analyzing cumulative data.

EXERCISE 2 Find Missing Indexes

In this exercise, you find missing indexes.

1. Quickly create the table and the index on that table from the practice for the previous lesson, but use 10 times less data. Then index it and execute the query that could benefit from an additional index. Here is the code.

```
SELECT N1.n * 100000 + O.orderid AS norderid,
       O.*
INTO dbo.NewOrders
FROM Sales.Orders AS O
 CROSS JOIN (VALUES(1),(2),(3)) AS N1(n);
GO
CREATE NONCLUSTERED INDEX idx_nc_orderid
 ON dbo.NewOrders(orderid);
GO
SELECT norderid
FROM dbo.NewOrders
WHERE norderid = 110248
ORDER BY norderid;
GO
```

2. Find missing indexes by using index-related DMOs. Use the following query.

```
SELECT MID.statement AS [Database.Schema.Table],
 MIC.column_id AS ColumnId,
 MIC.column_name AS ColumnName,
 MIC.column_usage AS ColumnUsage,
 MIGS.user_seeks AS UserSeeks,
 MIGS.user_scans AS UserScans,
 MIGS.last_user_seek AS LastUserSeek,
 MIGS.avg_total_user_cost AS AvgQueryCostReduction,
 MIGS.avg_user_impact AS AvgPctBenefit
FROM sys.dm_db_missing_index_details AS MID
 CROSS APPLY sys.dm_db_missing_index_columns (MID.index_handle) AS MIC
 INNER JOIN sys.dm_db_missing_index_groups AS MIG
    ON MIG.index_handle = MID.index_handle
 INNER JOIN sys.dm_db_missing_index_group_stats AS MIGS
    ON MIG.index_group_handle=MIGS.group_handle
ORDER BY MIGS.avg_user_impact DESC;
```

3. Analyze the information you got.
4. After you finish analysis, clean up the database by using the following code.

```
DROP TABLE dbo.NewOrders;
```

5. Exit SSMS.

Lesson Summary

- Dynamic management objects help you to immediately gather the information collected by SQL Server.
- For query analysis, use SQLOS, execution-related, and index-related DMOs.
- Not only do index-related DMOs provide useful information about index usage, they also provide information about missing indexes.

Lesson Review

Answer the following questions to test your knowledge of the information in this lesson. You can find the answers to these questions and explanations of why each answer choice is correct or incorrect in the "Answers" section at the end of this chapter.

1. Which DMO gives you information about index usage?
   - **A.** sys.dm_exec_query_stats
   - **B.** sys.dm_exec_query_text
   - **C.** sys.dm_db_index_usage_stats
   - **D.** sys.indexes
2. What is the most important drawback of DMOs?
   - **A.** You must have enough data collected from the last restart of SQL Server.
   - **B.** DMOs are complex to use.
   - **C.** DMOs are not available in the Standard edition of SQL Server.
   - **D.** You have to recreate DMOs before each analysis.
3. How can you find the text of the query executed by using DMOs?
   - **A.** This info is provided in the sys.dm_exec_query_stats dynamic management view.
   - **B.** By querying the sys.dm_exec_sql_text dynamic management function.
   - **C.** The sys.dm_exec_query_plan dynamic management function returns the query text.
   - **D.** You cannot find the query text through DMOs.

Case Scenarios

In the following case scenarios, you apply what you've learned about SQL Server tools that are useful for analyzing queries in order to optimize them. You can find the answers to these questions in the "Answers" section at the end of this chapter.

Case Scenario 1: Analysis of Queries

You got an urgent call from a manager of a company where you are maintaining SQL Server. The manager complains that their SQL Server database has been unresponsive for a couple of hours. Your task is to optimize one query only, but as soon as possible. However, you need to find the most problematic query. You connect to the SQL Server instance. You realize there are hundreds of concurrent users, and neither Extended Events nor a SQL Trace session is running. You also find out that SQL Server has been running without interruption for six months.

1. How do you start analysis in this situation?
2. When you find the most problematic query, how do you proceed?

Case Scenario 2: Constant Monitoring

You need to monitor your SQL Server instance constantly in order to detect potential bottlenecks. Your SQL Server instance is used heavily. You should not overload it with monitoring procedures.

1. Which tool would you use for monitoring?
2. How would you minimize the impact of the tool?

Suggested Practices

To help you successfully master the exam objectives presented in this chapter, complete the following tasks.

Learn More About Extended Events, Execution Plans, and Dynamic Management Objects

You can find a lot of information about Extended Events, execution plans, and dynamic management objects in SQL Server Books Online.

- **Practice 1** In order to understand SQL Server Extended Events thoroughly, read the information provided in the Books Online for SQL Server 2012 article "Extended Events" at *http://msdn.microsoft.com/en-us/library/bb630282(SQL.110).aspx.*
- **Practice 2** In order to understand execution plans thoroughly, read the information provided in the Books Online for SQL Server 2012 article "Showplan Logical and Physical Operators Reference" at *http://msdn.microsoft.com/en-us/library/ms191158.aspx.*
- **Practice 3** In order to understand SQL Server DMOs thoroughly, read the information provided in the Books Online for SQL Server 2012 article "Dynamic Management Views and Functions (Transact-SQL) at *http://msdn.microsoft.com/en-us/library/ms188754.aspx.*

Answers

This section contains answers to the lesson review questions and solutions to the case scenarios in this chapter.

Lesson 1

1. **Correct Answers: B and C**
   - **A. Incorrect:** An algebrized tree is generated in the binding phase.
   - **B. Correct:** In the optimization phase, SQL Server generates candidate plans.
   - **C. Correct:** During the optimization phase, SQL Server selects an execution plan from the set of candidate plans.
   - **D. Incorrect:** The plan is cached in the execution phase.
   - **E. Incorrect:** A query is executed in the execution phase.
2. **Correct Answer: B**
   - **A. Incorrect:** In the parsing phase, SQL Server checks for syntax correctness.
   - **B. Correct:** SQL Server resolves object names and binds them to logical operators in the binding phase.
   - **C. Incorrect:** In the optimization phase, SQL Server generates candidate plans and selects the execution plan.
   - **D. Incorrect:** In the execution phase, SQL Server executes the query and caches the execution plan.
3. **Correct Answer: C**
   - **A. Incorrect:** Predicates are objects in an Extended Events package.
   - **B. Incorrect:** Targets are objects in an Extended Events package.
   - **C. Correct:** Sources are not a part of an Extended Events package.
   - **D. Incorrect:** Actions are objects in an Extended Events package.

Lesson 2

1. **Correct Answers: A and D**
   - **A. Correct:** The SET STATISTICS IO session option is useful for analyzing query performance.
   - **B. Incorrect:** There is no SET STATISTICS EXECUTION_DETAILS option.
   - **C. Incorrect:** You use the SET IDENTITY_INSERT option to provide a value for the column that has an identity property.
   - **D. Correct:** The SET STATISTICS TIME session option is useful for analyzing query performance.

2. **Correct Answer: D**
   - **A. Incorrect:** You read execution plans from right to left, from top to bottom.
   - **B. Incorrect:** You read execution plans from right to left, from top to bottom.
   - **C. Incorrect:** You read execution plans from right to left, from top to bottom.
   - **D. Correct:** You read execution plans from right to left, from top to bottom.
3. **Correct Answers: B and D**
   - **A. Incorrect:** There is no SET EXECUTION_XML command.
   - **B. Correct:** You use the SET SHOWPLAN_XML command to turn on the estimated XML plans.
   - **C. Incorrect:** There is no SET XML PLAN command.
   - **D. Correct:** You use the SET STATISTICS XML command to turn on the actual XML plans.

Lesson 3

1. **Correct Answer: C**
   - **A. Incorrect:** The sys.dm_exec_query_stats DMO gives you statistics about queries, not indexes.
   - **B. Incorrect:** The sys.dm_exec_query_text DMO gives you the text of the batches and queries.
   - **C. Correct:** The sys.dm_db_index_usage_stats DMO gives you information about index usage.
   - **D. Incorrect:** sys.indexes is a catalog view, not a DMO.
2. **Correct Answer: A**
   - **A. Correct:** Not having enough data is the most important drawback of DMOs.
   - **B. Incorrect:** Although some queries that use DMOs can become quite complex, you can easily overcome this by learning more about T-SQL and DMOs.
   - **C. Incorrect:** DMOs are available in all editions.
   - **D. Incorrect:** DMOs are system objects; you cannot drop or create them.
3. **Correct Answer: B**
   - **A. Incorrect:** There is no query text provided from the sys.dm_exec_query_stats DMO.
   - **B. Correct:** You can get the query text by querying the sys.dm_exec_sql_text dynamic management function.
   - **C. Incorrect:** There is no query text provided from the sys.dm_exec_query_plan DMO.
   - **D. Incorrect:** You can get the query text by querying the sys.dm_exec_sql_text dynamic management function.

Case Scenario 1

1. You should use execution-related DMOs to find the most problematic query.
2. You could use a graphical estimated execution plan for this query to find the operators that have the highest cost. You could also check whether there are any missing indexes reported by index-related DMOs that this query could benefit from.

Case Scenario 2

1. You should use SQL Server Extended Events as a very lightweight performance monitoring system.
2. You should monitor a few of the most important events only for your case. You should capture only fields you need. You should also filter the session events to include only the events you really need.

CHAPTER 15

Implementing Indexes and Statistics

Exam objectives in this chapter:

- Create Database Objects
  - Create and alter views (simple statements).
- Troubleshoot & Optimize
  - Optimize queries.

In Chapter 14, "Using Tools to Analyze Query Performance", you learned about the tools that help you find performance problems. Indexes are mentioned in that chapter many times. This is not a coincidence. Proper indexing is necessary for good performance of your databases. In order to create appropriate indexes, you need to understand how Microsoft SQL Server stores data in tables and indexes, and how it then accesses this data. You learn about this in the longest lesson in this chapter, Lesson 1, "Implementing Indexes."

No indexes can help you if you write inefficient queries. In Lesson 2, "Using Search Arguments," you learn how to write arguments that SQL Server can use for seeks over indexes. However, even if you have indexes and proper searchable arguments, SQL Server might still decide not to use an index. This might happen because statistical information about the index is not present or is outdated. In Lesson 3, "Understanding Statistics," you learn how to get information about statistics and maintain it.

Lessons in this chapter:

- Lesson 1: Implementing Indexes
- Lesson 2: Using Search Arguments
- Lesson 3: Understanding Statistics

Before You Begin

To complete the lessons in this chapter, you must have:

- An understanding of relational database concepts.
- Experience working with SQL Server Management Studio (SSMS).
- Some experience writing T-SQL code.
- Access to a SQL Server 2012 instance with the sample database TSQL2012 installed.

Lesson 1: Implementing Indexes

SQL Server internally organizes data in a data file in pages. A page is an 8 KB unit and belongs to a single object; for example, to a table or an index. A page is the smallest unit of reading and writing. Pages are further organized into extents. An *extent* consists of eight consecutive pages. Pages from an extent can belong to a single object or to multiple objects. If the pages belong to multiple objects, then the extent is called a *mixed* extent; if the pages belong to a single object, then the extent is called a *uniform* extent. SQL Server stores the first eight pages of an object in mixed extents. When an object exceeds eight pages, SQL Server allocates additional uniform extents for this object. With this organization, small objects waste less space and big objects are less fragmented.

Although the previous information provides a brief introduction to the *physical* structure of SQL Server, from a database developer perspective, logical structures are much more important. This lesson focuses on logical structures.

After this lesson, you will be able to:

- Understand how SQL Server uses pages and extents.
- Describe heaps and balanced trees.
- Create clustered and nonclustered indexes.
- Create indexed views.

Estimated lesson time: 60 minutes

Heaps and Balanced Trees

Pages are physical structures. SQL Server organizes data in pages in logical structures.

SQL Server organizes tables as heaps or as *balanced trees*. A table organized as a balanced tree is also known as a clustered table or a clustered index. (You can use these two terms interchangeably.)

Indexes are always organized as balanced trees. Other indexes, such as indexes that do not contain all of the data and serve as pointers to table rows for quick seeks, are called *non-clustered indexes.*

Heaps

A *heap* is a quite simple structure. Data in a heap is not organized in any logical order. A heap is just a bunch of pages and extents.

SQL Server traces which pages and extents belong to an object through special system pages called Index Allocation Map (IAM) pages. Every table or index has at least one IAM page, called *first IAM*. A single IAM page can point to approximately 4 GB of space. Large objects can have more than one IAM page. IAM pages for an object are organized as a *doubly linked list*; each page has a pointer to its descendant and antecedent. SQL Server stores pointers to first IAM pages in its own internal system tables.

Figure 15-1 shows what an exemplary table for storing customers' orders looks like when it is organized as a heap.

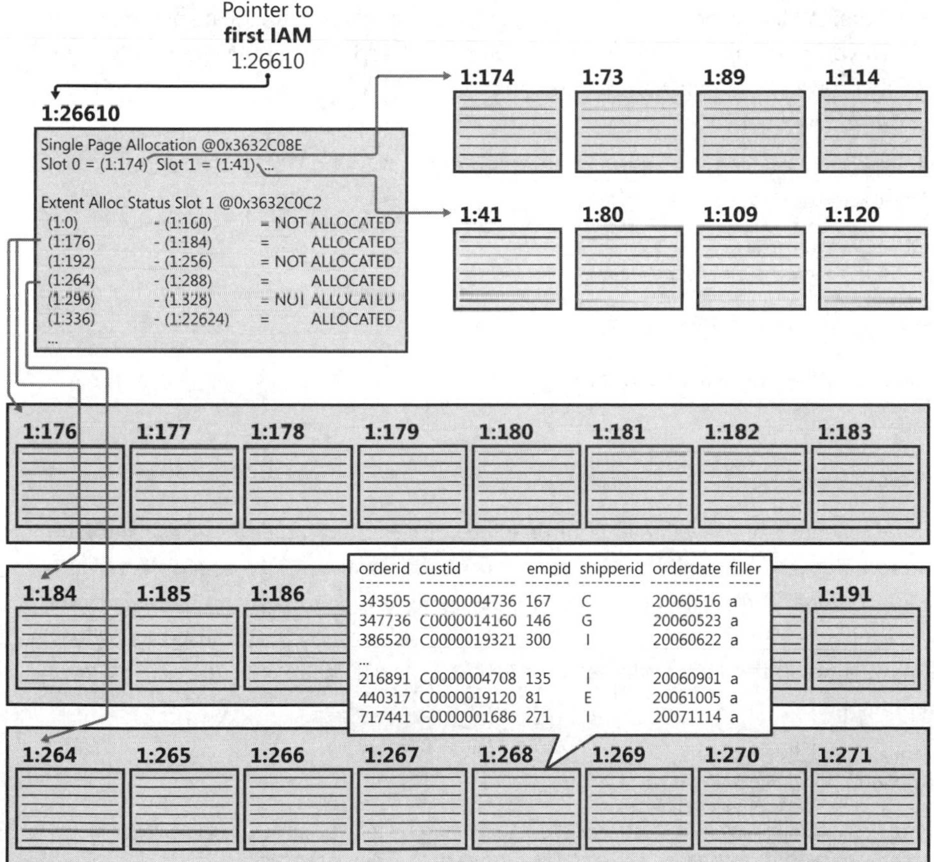

FIGURE 15-1 A table organized as a heap.

SQL Server can find data in a heap only by scanning the whole heap. SQL Server uses IAM pages to scan heaps in physical order, or *allocation* order. Even if your query wants to retrieve only a single row, SQL Server has to scan the entire heap. SQL Server stores new rows anywhere in a heap. It can store a new row in an existing page if the page is not full, or allocate a new page or extent for the object where you are inserting the new row. Of course, this means that heaps can become very fragmented over time.

You can better understand SQL Server structures through examples. The following code creates a table organized as a heap.

```
USE tempdb;
GO
CREATE TABLE dbo.TestStructure
(
id INT NOT NULL,
filler1 CHAR(36) NOT NULL,
filler2 CHAR(216) NOT NULL
);
```

If you do not create a clustered index explicitly or implicitly through primary key or unique constraints, then a table is organized as a heap. SQL Server does not allocate any pages for a table when you create it. It allocates the first page, and also the first IAM page, when you insert the first row in the table. You can find general information about tables and indexes in the sys.indexes catalog view.

The following query retrieves basic information about the dbo.TestStructure table that was created from the previous code.

```
SELECT OBJECT_NAME(object_id) AS table_name,
 name AS index_name, type, type_desc
FROM sys.indexes
WHERE object_id = OBJECT_ID(N'dbo.TestStructure', N'U');
```

The results of the query are as follows.

```
table_name     index_name  type  type_desc
-------------  ----------  ----  ---------
TestStructure  NULL        0     HEAP
```

The type column stores a value of 0 for heaps, 1 for clustered tables (indexes), and 2 for nonclustered indexes. You can find out how many pages are allocated for an object from the sys.dm_db_index_physical_stats dynamic management function or with the help of the dbo.sp_spaceused system procedure, as shown in the following code. Because this code is reused many times in this lesson, this lesson refers to it as the "heap allocation check" for easy identification.

```
SELECT index_type_desc, page_count,
 record_count, avg_page_space_used_in_percent
FROM sys.dm_db_index_physical_stats
    (DB_ID(N'tempdb'), OBJECT_ID(N'dbo.TestStructure', N'U'), NULL, NULL , 'DETAILED');
EXEC dbo.sp_spaceused @objname = N'dbo.TestStructure', @updateusage = true;
```

The output of these two commands is as follows.

```
index_type_desc  page_count  record_count  avg_page_space_used_in_percent
---------------  ----------  ------------  ------------------------------
HEAP             0           0             0

name           rows  reserved  data  index_size  unused
-------------  ----  --------  ----  ----------  ------
TestStructure  0     0 KB      0 KB  0 KB        0 KB
```

You can see that the table is empty, and an empty table does not occupy any space. Note the last column in the output of the first query, the avg_space_used_in_percent column. This column shows internal fragmentation. *Internal fragmentation* means that pages are not full. The more rows you have stored on a single page, the fewer pages SQL Server must read to retrieve these rows, and the less memory it uses for cached pages for the same number of rows. In heaps, you do not get much internal fragmentation, because SQL Server stores new rows in existing pages, as you already know, if there is enough space there. Now insert the first row.

```
INSERT INTO dbo.TestStructure
(id, filler1, filler2)
VALUES
(1, 'a', 'b');
```

If you run the heap allocation check code again, you get the following results.

```
index_type_desc  page_count  record_count  avg_page_space_used_in_percent
---------------  ----------  ------------  ------------------------------
HEAP             1           1             3.24932048430937

name           rows  reserved  data  index_size  unused
-------------  ----  --------  ----  ----------  ------
TestStructure  1     16 KB     8 KB  8 KB        0 KB
```

The table occupies one page with one row. Average page space used is low because there is only a single row in the page. The results of the dbo.sp_spaceused procedure show that the table has two pages reserved, one page for the data and one for the first IAM page. You can see that SQL Server allocates only a page and not an extent for the table. Now fill the page by using the following code.

```
DECLARE @i AS int = 1;
WHILE @i < 30
BEGIN
SET @i = @i + 1;
INSERT INTO dbo.TestStructure
(id, filler1, filler2)
VALUES
(@i, 'a', 'b');
END;
```

After you run the heap allocation, check the code again. You get the following results.

```
index_type_desc  page_count  record_count  avg_page_space_used_in_percent
---------------  ----------  ------------  ------------------------------
HEAP               1         30             98.1961947121324

name           rows  reserved  data  index_size  unused
-------------  ----  --------  ----  ----------  ------
TestStructure  30    16 KB     8 KB  8 KB        0 KB
```

There is still only one page allocated; however, this page has no internal fragmentation because the page cannot accommodate any additional rows. Try to insert an additional row.

```
INSERT INTO dbo.TestStructure
(id, filler1, filler2)
VALUES
(31, 'a', 'b');
```

The heap allocation check code returns the following output.

```
index_type_desc  page_count  record_count  avg_page_space_used_in_percent
---------------  ----------  ------------  ------------------------------
HEAP               2         31             50.7227575982209

name           rows  reserved  data   index_size  unused
-------------  ----  --------  -----  ----------  ------
TestStructure  31    24 KB     16 KB  8 KB        0 KB
```

Now you can see that a single additional page from a mixed extent was allocated. Of course, internal fragmentation has risen, because the second page is nearly empty. Fill up eight pages by using the following code.

```
DECLARE @i AS int = 31;
WHILE @i < 240
BEGIN
SET @i = @i + 1;
INSERT INTO dbo.TestStructure
(id, filler1, filler2)
VALUES
(@i, 'a', 'b');
END;
```

The results of the heap allocation check code are as follows.

```
index_type_desc  page_count  record_count  avg_page_space_used_in_percent
---------------  ----------  ------------  ------------------------------
HEAP               8         240            98.1961947121324

name           rows  reserved  data   index_size  unused
-------------  ----  --------  -----  ----------  ------
TestStructure  240   72 KB     64 KB  8 KB        0 KB
```

Eight pages are full. What happens if you insert a new row? Try it out with the following code.

```
INSERT INTO dbo.TestStructure
(id, filler1, filler2)
VALUES
(241, 'a', 'b');
```

The results of the heap allocation check code are as follows.

```
index_type_desc  page_count  record_count  avg_page_space_used_in_percent
---------------  ----------  ------------  ------------------------------
HEAP             9           241           87.6465530022239

name           rows  reserved  data   index_size  unused
-------------  ----  --------  -----  ----------  ------
TestStructure  241   136 KB    72 KB  8 KB        56 KB
```

NOTE **IDENTICAL RESULTS ARE NOT GUARANTEED**

With a different database configuration—for example, if you have two or more data files—your results might slightly differ.

Now you can see that although the table occupies only 9 pages, 16 data pages plus the first IAM page are reserved for the table. As the results of the dbo.sp_spaceused procedure show, SQL Server reserved 136 KB for the table, which means 17 pages; 56 KB are still unused. The unused 56 KB of space means that 7 pages from a uniform extent are still empty. The first 8 pages stay on the mixed extents. Because the table is already bigger than 8 pages, SQL Server allocates uniform extents for additional space needed.

Clustered Indexes

You organize a table as a balanced tree when you create a clustered index. The structure is called a balanced tree because it resembles an inverse tree. Every balanced tree has a single root page and at least one or more leaf pages. In addition, it can have zero or more intermediate levels. All data in a clustered table is stored in leaf pages. Data is stored in logical order of the clustering key. A *clustering key* can consist of a single column, or of multiple columns. If the key consists of multiple columns, then this is a *composite key*. You can have up to 16 columns in a key; the size of all columns together in a composite key must not exceed 900 bytes. Note that data is stored logically and is not physically ordered. SQL Server still uses IAM pages to follow the physical allocation.

IMPORTANT A CLUSTERED INDEX IS A TABLE

When you create a clustered index, you are not making a copy of data; instead, you reorganize the table. In addition, do not suppose that the data is physically sorted; if you need an ordered output of a query, you have to include the ORDER BY clause.

Pages above leaf level point to leaf-level pages. A row in a page above leaf level contains a clustering key value and a pointer to a page where this value starts in logically ordered leaf level. If a single page can point to all leaf-level pages, then only a root page is allocated. If more than one page is needed to point to leaf-level pages, SQL Server creates the first intermediate-level pages, which point to leaf-level pages. The root page rows point to intermediate-level pages. If the root page cannot point to all first-level intermediate pages, SQL Server creates a new intermediate level. Pages on the same level are organized as a doubly linked list; therefore, SQL Server can find the previous and the next page in logical order for any specific page. In addition to balanced tree pages, SQL Server uses IAM pages to track physical allocation of the balanced tree pages.

You can use a column or columns with unique or nonunique values for a key of a clustered index. However, SQL Server internally always maintains uniqueness of the clustering key. It adds a *uniquifier* value, which is a sequential integer, to the repeating values. The first value is stored without a uniquifier; the first repeating value gets a uniquifier with a value of one, the second with two, and so on. You will understand why clustering key values must be unique internally when you learn about nonclustered indexes later in this lesson.

Figure 15-2 shows the clustered structure of the exemplary table for customers' orders. Note that the order date (the od column in the figure) is used for the clustering key. Because the column is not unique, the uniquifier is added to the repeating values (the unq column in the figure).

SQL Server can seek for a row in a clustered index. To find a specific row in the table represented in Figure 15-2, SQL Server has to read three pages only. If the table was organized as a heap, SQL Server would need to read the whole table, which would be comparable to reading all pages on the leaf level of the clustered index. Of course, if you request all rows, SQL Server scans the leaf level of the clustered index as well. A clustered index scan can be done in logical order or, when the logical order is not needed, in physical or allocation order. In addition, SQL Server can perform a partial scan if sequential rows in the order of the clustering key are requested by your query. These are some of the advantages of clustered indexes over heaps.

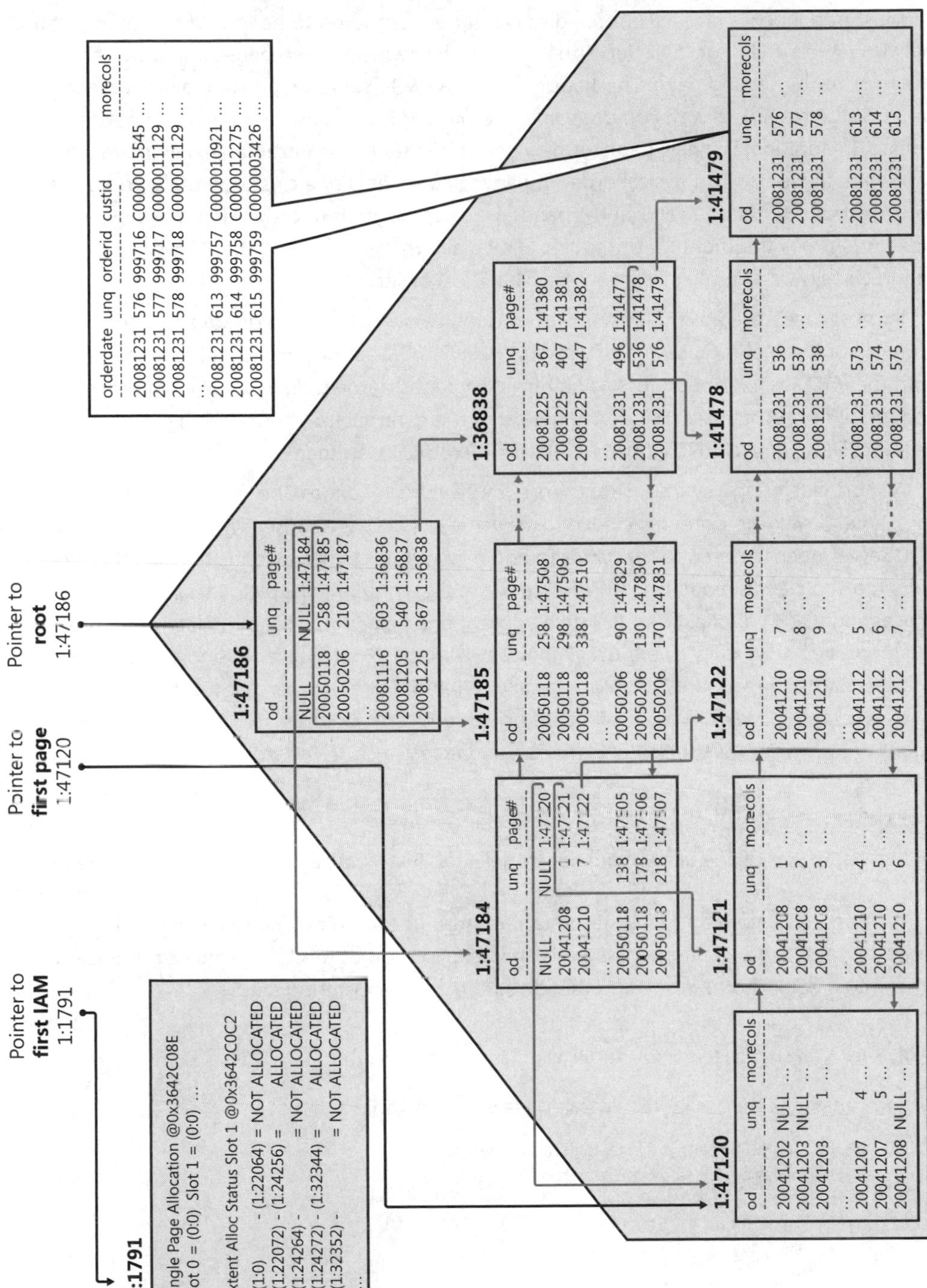

FIGURE 15-2 A table organized as a balanced tree.

Clustered indexes also have some disadvantages compared to heaps. When you insert a new row into a full page, SQL Server has to split the page into two pages and move half of the rows to the second page. This happens because SQL Server needs to maintain the logical order of the rows. This way, you get some internal fragmentation, which you cannot get in a heap. In addition, the new page (or new uniform extent for a large table) can be reserved anywhere in a data file. Physical order of pages and extents of a clustered table do not need to correspond to the logical order. If pages are physically out of order, then the clustered table is *logically* fragmented. This is also known as *external* fragmentation. External fragmentation can slow down full or partial scans in logical order.

In most cases, the advantages of clustered tables overwhelm the disadvantages. You can control the internal fragmentation with the FILLFACTOR option for the leaf-level pages and with the PAD_INDEX option for the higher-level pages of the CREATE INDEX statement. You can rebuild or reorganize an index to get rid of the external fragmentation by using the ALTER INDEX...REORGANIZE or ALTER INDEX...REBUILD statements.

A short clustering key means that more rows can fit on pages above the leaf level. Therefore, fewer levels are potentially needed. Fewer levels means a more efficient index because SQL Server needs to read fewer pages to find a row. A uniquifier extends the key; therefore, having a short and unique key is preferred for seeks. This is very typical for online transaction processing (OLTP) applications. For such applications, selecting a sequential integer as the clustering key is typically a very good choice. However, in data warehousing scenarios, many queries read huge amounts of data, typically ordered. For example, many data warehouse queries search for rows in order of a date or datetime column. If this is the case, then you might prefer to support such a partial scan, and create a clustered index on the date column.

EXAM TIP

Make sure you clearly understand how to select a clustering key in different environments.

You can learn more about clustered tables through examples. The following code truncates the table created and populated in the heap section of this lesson and reorganizes the table into a balanced tree by using the id column as the clustering key.

```
TRUNCATE TABLE dbo.TestStructure;
CREATE CLUSTERED INDEX idx_cl_id ON dbo.TestStructure(id);
```

You can check the sys.indexes catalog view for this table again.

```
SELECT OBJECT_NAME(object_id) AS table_name,
 name AS index_name, type, type_desc
FROM sys.indexes
WHERE object_id = OBJECT_ID(N'dbo.TestStructure', N'U');
```

This query returns the following output.

```
table_name     index_name  type  type_desc
-------------  ----------  ----  ---------
TestStructure  idx_cl_id   1     CLUSTERED
```

As you can see, the type has changed to 1 and the heap does not exist anymore. When you create a clustered index, you actually reorganize the table. Now fill 621 pages of this table by using unique values for the clustering key.

```
DECLARE @i AS int = 0;
WHILE @i < 18630
BEGIN
SET @i = @i + 1;
INSERT INTO dbo.TestStructure
(id, filler1, filler2)
VALUES
(@i, 'a', 'b');
END;
```

Note that if you know that the values have to be unique, you should create a primary key or a unique constraint on the table. You could also create a unique index; however, because uniqueness is constraining the values, you should use constraints instead.

You can check some basic information about the index by querying the sys.dm_db_index_physical_stats dynamic management function. The following piece of code is reused multiple times in this part of the lesson, so further references to this code will be to the "clustered index allocation check" code.

```
SELECT index_type_desc, index_depth, index_level, page_count,
 record_count, avg_page_space_used_in_percent
FROM sys.dm_db_index_physical_stats
    (DB_ID(N'tempdb'), OBJECT_ID(N'dbo.TestStructure', N'U'), NULL, NULL , 'DETAILED');
```

The result of the clustered index allocation check code is as follows.

```
index_type_desc index_depth index_level page_count record_count avg_pg_spc_used_in_pct
--------------- ----------- ----------- ---------- ------------ ---------------------
CLUSTERED INDEX 2           0           621        18630        98.1961947121324
CLUSTERED INDEX 2           1           1          621          99.7158388930072
```

NOTE COLUMN NAMES IN THE OUTPUT

In the results shown, some column names are slightly shortened from the actual output column names in order to fit the output on the book page.

You can see that the index has two levels only, the leaf level and the root page. The root page has 621 rows that point to 621 leaf pages. There is no internal fragmentation in this case. Now insert one more row.

```
INSERT INTO dbo.TestStructure
(id, filler1, filler2)
VALUES
(18631, 'a', 'b');
```

By running the clustered index allocation check code, you get the following output.

```
index_type_desc index_depth index_level page_count record_count avg_pg_spc_used_in_pct
--------------- ----------- ----------- ---------- ------------ ----------------------
CLUSTERED INDEX 3           0           622        18631        98.0435507783543
CLUSTERED INDEX 3           1           2          622          49.9258710155671
CLUSTERED INDEX 3           2           1          2            0.296515937731653
```

Now the index has three levels. Because a new page was allocated on the leaf level, the original root page could not reference all leaf pages anymore. SQL Server added an intermediate level with two pages pointing to 622 leaf pages, and a new root page pointing to the two intermediate-level pages.

In order to demonstrate the influence of the uniquifier, the following code truncates the table and fills 423 pages by using nonunique values for the clustering key.

```
TRUNCATE TABLE dbo.TestStructure;
DECLARE @i AS int = 0;
WHILE @i < 8908
BEGIN
SET @i = @i + 1;
INSERT INTO dbo.TestStructure
(id, filler1, filler2)
VALUES
(@i % 100, 'a', 'b');
END;
```

If you run the clustered index allocation check code, you get the following output.

```
index_type_desc index_depth index_level page_count record_count avg_pg_spc_used_in_pc
--------------- ----------- ----------- ---------- ------------ ----------------------
CLUSTERED INDEX 2           0           423        8908         70.9815171732147
CLUSTERED INDEX 2           1           1          423          99.8393872003954
```

Note that the root page can refer to 423 leaf-level pages only. To fill two levels of the index, only 8,908 rows were needed, whereas with unique values for the clustering key in the previous case, SQL Server could accommodate 18,630 rows in two levels.

To prove that, add another row.

```
INSERT INTO dbo.TestStructure
(id, filler1, filler2)
VALUES
(8909 % 100, 'a', 'b');
```

The clustered index allocation check code returns the following output.

```
index_type_desc index_depth index_level page_count record_count avg_pg_spc_used_in_pc
--------------- ----------- ----------- ---------- ------------ ---------------------
CLUSTERED INDEX 3           0           424        8909         70.8220039535458
CLUSTERED INDEX 3           1           2          424          50.0370644922165
CLUSTERED INDEX 3           2           1          2            0.395354583642204
```

You can see that SQL Server has to add an additional level to the index much earlier when the values of the key are not unique.

So far, the values of the clustering key were sequential. What happens if they are not? The following code truncates the dbo.TestStructure table, drops the existing clustered index, and creates a new one by using the filler1 column as the clustering key, and then inserts 9,000 rows in the table with unique sequential values in the clustering key.

```
TRUNCATE TABLE dbo.TestStructure;
DROP INDEX idx_cl_id ON dbo.TestStructure;
CREATE CLUSTERED INDEX idx_cl_filler1 ON dbo.TestStructure(filler1);
DECLARE @i AS int = 0;
WHILE @i < 9000
BEGIN
SET @i = @i + 1;
INSERT INTO dbo.TestStructure
(id, filler1, filler2)
VALUES
(@i, FORMAT(@i,'0000'), 'b');
END;
```

Now check the fragmentation. The following code, referred to as the "fragmentation check" code later in this part, checks the internal fragmentation (the avg_page_space_used_in_percent column) and the external fragmentation (the avg_fragmentation_in_percent column).

```
SELECT index_level, page_count,
 avg_page_space_used_in_percent, avg_fragmentation_in_percent
FROM sys.dm_db_index_physical_stats
    (DB_ID(N'tempdb'), OBJECT_ID(N'dbo.TestStructure', N'U'), NULL, NULL , 'DETAILED');
```

The output of the fragmentation check code in this case is as follows.

```
index_level page_count avg_page_space_used_in_percent avg_fragmentation_in_percent
----------- ---------- ------------------------------ ----------------------------
0           300        98.1961947121324               1.66666666666667
1           3          55.5720286632073               0
2           1          1.64319248826291               0
```

> **NOTE** **IDENTICAL RESULTS ARE NOT GUARANTEED**
>
> **The values for the avg_page_space_used_in_percent and the avg_fragmentation_in_percent columns might slightly differ in your results.**

You can see that the index has three levels. There is no internal fragmentation on the leaf level; in addition, there is nearly no external fragmentation. All pages on the leaf level are full and the physical order is nearly the same as the logical order. Now truncate the table and fill it with random values in the filler1 column. The following code uses the NEWID() T-SQL function that generates GUIDs and stores the GUIDs in the filler1 column.

```
TRUNCATE TABLE dbo.TestStructure;
DECLARE @i AS int = 0;
WHILE @i < 9000
BEGIN
SET @i = @i + 1;
INSERT INTO dbo.TestStructure
(id, filler1, filler2)
VALUES
(@i, CAST(NEWID() AS CHAR(36)), 'b');
END;
```

GUIDs generated by the NEWID() function are nearly random. If you run the fragmentation check code again, you get the following output.

```
index_level page_count avg_page_space_used_in_percent avg_fragmentation_in_percent
----------- ---------- ------------------------------ ----------------------------
0           432        68.1842599456387               98.6111111111111
1           4          60.0197677291821               50
2           1          2.19915987150976               0
```

> **NOTE** **IDENTICAL RESULTS ARE NOT GUARANTEED**
>
> **The values for the avg_page_space_used_in_percent and the avg_fragmentation_in_percent columns might slightly differ in your results.**

You can see that the leaf-level pages have only 68 percent of the space filled with rows. This is because SQL Server performed multiple page splits. In addition, the external fragmentation is around 99 percent; almost no page is physically in correct logical order. You can see that using GUIDs for clustering keys can lead to quite inefficient indexes. External fragmentation mainly slows down scans, which should not be that frequent in OLTP environments; however, they are very important in the data warehousing area. Internal fragmentation is a problem in both scenarios because the table is much bigger than it would be with a sequential key.

You can get rid of the fragmentation if you rebuild or reorganize the index. Reorganizing an index is a slower but less intrusive process than rebuilding an index. As a general guideline, you should reorganize an index when the external fragmentation is less than 30 percent and rebuild it if it is greater than 30 percent. The following code rebuilds the index.

```
ALTER INDEX idx_cl_filler1 ON dbo.TestStructure REBUILD;
```

If you would prefer to reorganize the table, you should just replace the keyword REBUILD with the keyword REORGANIZE. If you run the fragmentation check code after the rebuild, you see from the output that there is almost no fragmentation anymore.

```
index_level page_count avg_page_space_used_in_percent avg_fragmentation_in_percent
----------- ---------- ------------------------------ ----------------------------
0           300        98.1961947121324               0.666666666666667
1           2          83.3703978255498               0
2           1          1.08722510501606               0
```

> ***NOTE*** **IDENTICAL RESULTS ARE NOT GUARANTEED**
>
> **The values for the avg_page_space_used_in_percent and the avg_fragmentation_in_percent columns might slightly differ in your results.**

Quick Check

- **What kind of clustering key would you select for an OLTP environment?**

Quick Check Answer

- **For an OLTP environment, a short, unique, and sequential clustering key might be the best choice.**

Implementing Nonclustered Indexes

Nonclustered indexes have a very similar structure to clustered ones. Actually, the root and the intermediate levels look the same as in a clustered index. The leaf level is different because it does not hold all of the data. What is stored on the leaf level of a nonclustered index depends on the underlying table organization, whether it is organized as a heap or as a balanced tree. You can have up to 999 nonclustered indexes on a single table.

The leaf level of a nonclustered index contains the index keys and *row locators*. Again, you can have up to 16 columns in a key, and the size of all columns together in a composite key must not exceed 900 bytes. A row locator points to a row in the underlying table. If the table is a heap, then the row locator is called row identifier (RID). This is an 8-byte pointer containing the database file ID and page ID of the target row, and the target row ID on that page.

Figure 15-3 shows a nonclustered index on a heap. It uses the same example of the customers' orders table as other figures in this chapter so far. The orderid column is used for the key of the index.

In order to seek for a row, SQL Server needs to traverse the index to the leaf level, and then read the appropriate page from the heap and retrieve the row from the page. The operation of retrieving the row from the heap is called *RID lookup*. If your query is very selective and searches for one row or a small amount of rows only, then index seek with RID lookup is very efficient. Because pages on the same level of an index are connected in a doubly linked list, SQL Server can also perform a partial or full ordered scan on a nonclustered index, and then perform RID lookups without starting the path from the root page for every row. However, as the number of rows the query retrieves increases, the RID lookup becomes much more expensive, because the cost of RID lookup is typically one page per row.

If a table is organized as a balanced tree, then the row locator is the clustering key. This means that when SQL Server seeks for a row, it has to traverse all levels on a nonclustered index and then also all levels of a clustered index. This operation is called a *key lookup*. At first glimpse, this sounds worse than retrieving a single page from a heap. However, because in this case the row locator is pointing to a logical structure and not to a physical structure, it does not matter where the row in the table is physically located. This means that you can freely reorganize or rebuild the clustered index; as long as you do not change the clustering key, SQL Server does not have to update the nonclustered indexes. If a row moves in a heap, SQL Server needs to update all nonclustered indexes to reflect the new position. SQL Server has an optimization for updates of a heap; if a row has to move to another page, SQL Server leaves a forwarding pointer to a new location in the original page, so SQL Server still does not have to update all nonclustered indexes. However, even with this optimization, it is still a good practice to organize tables as balanced trees. If the clustering key is narrow—for example a 4-byte integer—then SQL Server can also accommodate more rows on a leaf-level page than when RID is used as the row locator.

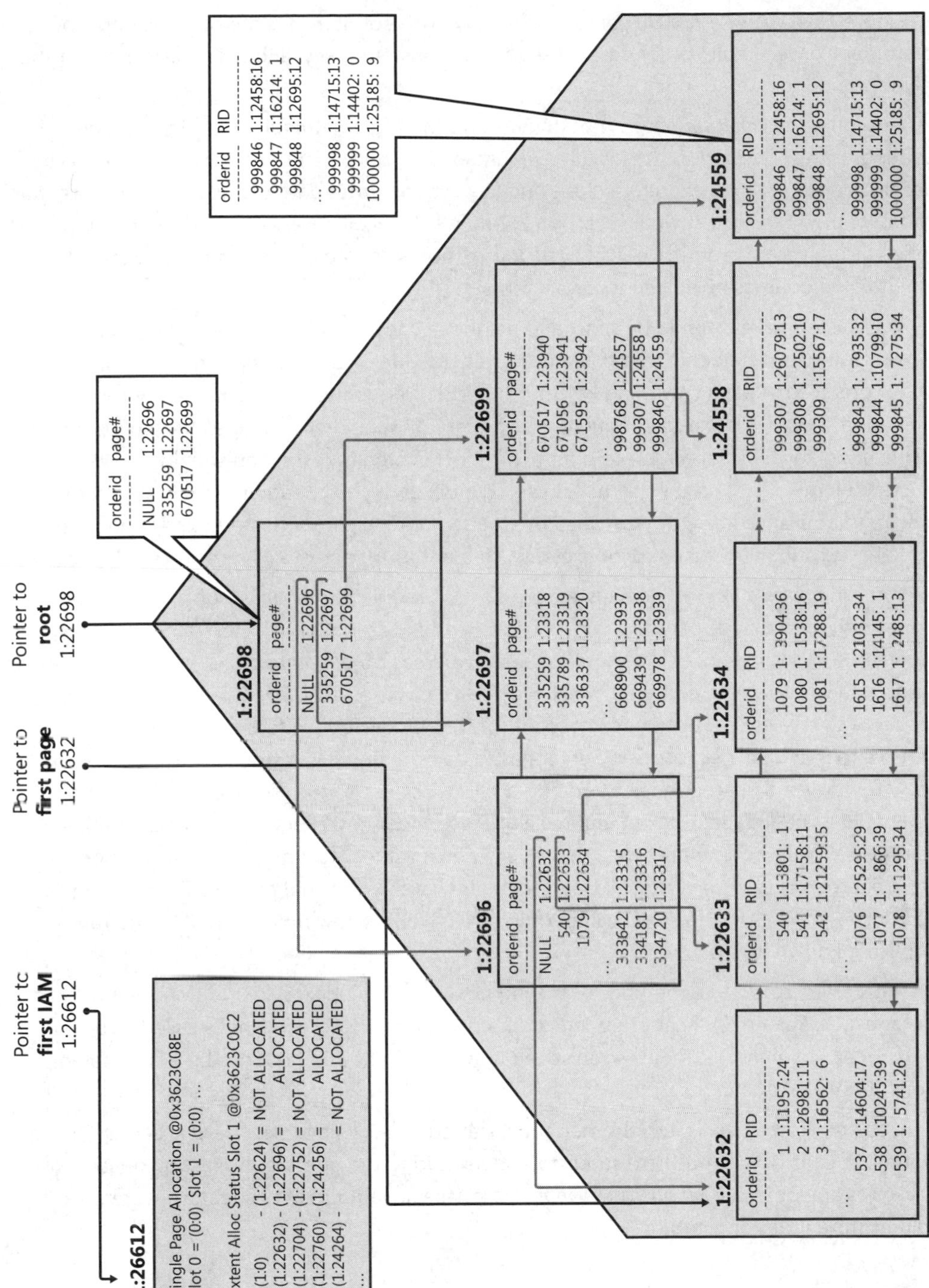

FIGURE 15-3 Nonclustered index on a heap.

Figure 15-4 shows a nonclustered index on a clustered table. It is the same example of the customers' orders table; order date is used for the clustering key, and order ID is used for the key of the nonclustered index.

Note that the clustering key is not unique, and therefore a uniquifier is added to the repeating values. The key of the nonclustered index is unique. If a query searches for a specific order ID (a single row) and gets a clustering key with an order date that is equal for more than one row, then SQL Server would return a wrong result set. SQL Server would return all the rows with the same order date. This is, of course, not acceptable. Therefore, SQL Server has to maintain uniqueness of clustering keys internally.

The clustering key should be short and unique because it appears in all nonclustered indexes. However, note again that this is not a general rule; in data warehousing scenarios, you might prefer to select a clustering key that supports frequent partial scans. In any case, the clustering should not change frequently, or preferably should not change at all. If you update a clustering key, SQL Server has to update all nonclustered indexes. You should also create a clustered index first, and then all nonclustered indexes. If you change the table structure from a heap to a balanced tree or vice-versa by creating or dropping a clustered index and the table has existing nonclustered indexes, SQL Server has to recreate all nonclustered indexes.

You can create a filtered nonclustered index. A filtered index spans a subset of column values only, and thus applies to a subset of table rows. Filtered nonclustered indexes are useful when some values in a column occur rarely, whereas other values occur frequently. In such cases, you would create a filtered index over the rare values only. SQL Server uses this index for seeks of rare values, but performs scans for frequent values. Filtered indexes are inexpensive to maintain, because SQL Server has to update them for changes in the rare values only. You create a filtered index by adding a WHERE clause to the CREATE INDEX statement. You could use a filtered index to enforce a filtered uniqueness. For example, imagine that a column has NULLs in multiple rows; however, known values must be unique. You cannot create a filtered primary key or unique constraint; however, you could create a filtered unique nonclustered index from known values only, which would allow multiple NULLs and reject duplicate known values.

SQL Server 2012 has a method for storing nonclustered indexes. In addition to regular row storage, SQL Server 2012 can store index data column by column in what's called a *columnstore index*. Columnstore indexes can speed up data warehousing queries by a large factor, from 10 to even 100 times.

A columnstore index is just another nonclustered index on a table. The SQL Server Query Optimizer considers using the columnstore index during the query optimization phase just as it does any other index. All you have to do to take advantage of this feature is create a columnstore index on a table.

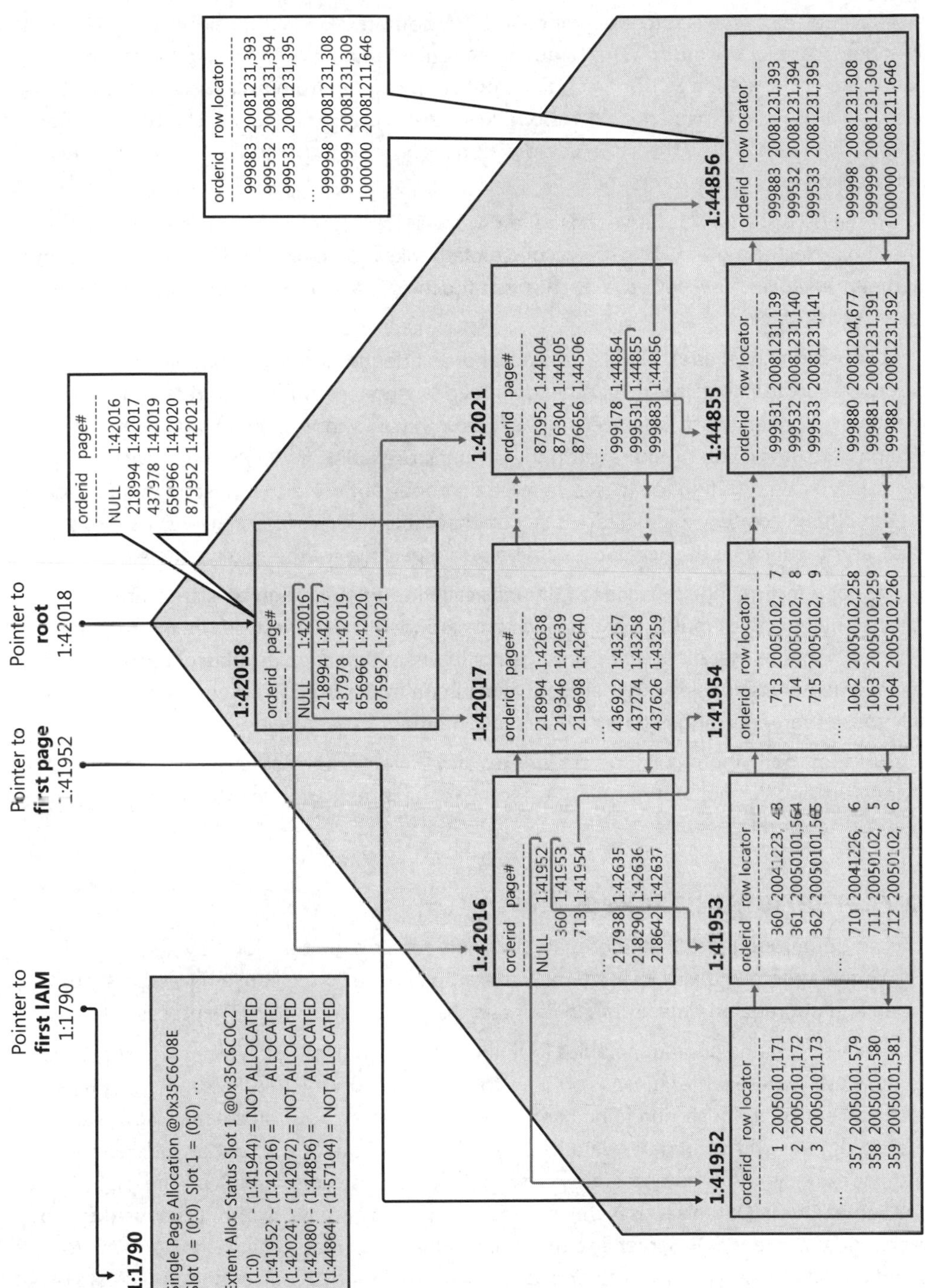

FIGURE 15-4 Nonclustered index on a clustered table.

A columnstore index is stored compressed. The compression factor can be up to 10 times the original size of the index. When a query references a single column that is a part of a columnstore index, then SQL Server fetches only that column from disk; it doesn't fetch entire rows as with row storage. This also reduces disk I/O and memory cache consumption. Columnstore indexes use their own compression algorithm; you cannot use Row or Page compression on a columnstore index.

On the other hand, SQL Server has to return rows. Therefore, rows must be reconstructed when you execute a query. This row reconstruction takes some time and uses some CPU and memory resources. Very selective queries that touch only a few rows might not benefit from columnstore indexes.

Columnstore indexes accelerate data warehouse queries, not OLTP workloads. Because of the row reconstruction issues and other overhead when you update compressed data, tables containing a columnstore index become read only. If you want to update a table by using a columnstore index, you must first drop the columnstore index. If you use table partitioning, you can switch a partition to a different table that does not use a columnstore index, update the data there, create a columnstore index on that table (which has a smaller subset of the data), and then switch the new table data back to a partition of the original table.

The columnstore index is divided into units called segments. Segments are stored as large objects and consist of multiple pages. *Segments* are the unit of transfer from disk to memory. Each segment has metadata that stores the minimum and maximum value of each column for that segment. This enables early segment elimination in the storage engine. SQL Server loads only those segments requested by a query into memory.

You learn more about columnstore indexes and their efficient usage in Chapter 17, "Understanding Further Optimization Aspects," You test regular nonclustered indexes in the practice for this lesson.

Implementing Indexed Views

You can optimize queries that aggregate data and perform multiple joins by permanently storing the aggregated and joined data. For example, you could create a new table by using joined and aggregated data and then maintain that table during your ETL process.

However, creating additional tables for joined and aggregated data is not a best practice, because using these tables means you have to change report queries. Fortunately, you can use another option for storing joined and aggregated tables. You can create a view with a query that joins and aggregates data. Then you can index the view to get an *indexed view*. With indexing, you are materializing a view. In the Enterprise edition of SQL Server 2012, the SQL Server Query Optimizer uses the indexed view automatically—without the need for you to change the query. SQL Server also maintains indexed views automatically. However, to speed up data loads, you can drop or disable the index before a load and then recreate or rebuild it after the load.

> **MORE INFO FEATURES SUPPORTED BY SQL SERVER 2012 EDITIONS**
>
> For more information on indexed view usage and other features supported by different editions of SQL Server 2012, see the Books Online for SQL Server article "Features Supported by the Editions of SQL Server 2012" at *http://msdn.microsoft.com/en-us/library/cc645993(SQL.110).aspx*.

Indexed views have many limitations, restrictions, and prerequisites, and you should refer to Books Online for SQL Server for details about them. However, you can create a simple test that shows how indexed views can be useful. The following query aggregates the qty column of the Sales.OrderDetails table over the shipcountry column of the Sales.Orders table in the TSQL2012 sample database. The code also sets STATISTICS IO to ON to measure the I/O.

```
USE TSQL2012;
SET STATISTICS IO ON;
-- Aggregate query with a join
SELECT O.shipcountry, SUM(OD.qty) AS totalordered
FROM Sales.OrderDetails AS OD
 INNER JOIN Sales.Orders AS O
  ON OD.orderid = O.orderid
GROUP BY O.shipcountry;
```

The query makes 11 logical reads in the Sales.OrderDetails table and 21 logical reads in the Sales.Orders table. You can create a view from this query and index it, as shown in the following code.

```
-- Create a view from the query
CREATE VIEW Sales.QuantityByCountry
WITH SCHEMABINDING
AS
SELECT O.shipcountry, SUM(OD.qty) AS total_ordered,
 COUNT_BIG(*) AS number_of_rows
FROM Sales.OrderDetails AS OD
 INNER JOIN Sales.Orders AS O
  ON OD.orderid = O.orderid
GROUP BY O.shipcountry;
GO
-- Index the view
CREATE UNIQUE CLUSTERED INDEX idx_cl_shipcountry
ON Sales.QuantityByCountry(shipcountry);
GO
```

Note that the view must be created with the SCHEMABINDING option if you want to index it. In addition, you must use the COUNT_BIG aggregate function. For details, see the prerequisites for indexed views article "Create Indexed Views" in Books Online for SQL Server 2012 at *http://msdn.microsoft.com/en-us/library/ms191432.aspx*. Nevertheless, after you create the view and the index, execute the aggregate query again and measure the I/O. This time, the query makes only two logical reads in the Sales.QuantityByCountry view.

After you analyze the indexed view, you should set the STATISTICS IO to OFF and clean up your TSQL2012 database by running the following code.

```
SET STATISTICS IO OFF;
DROP VIEW Sales.QuantityByCountry;
```

PRACTICE Analyzing Nonclustered Indexes

In this practice, you analyze nonclustered indexes.

If you encounter a problem completing an exercise, you can install the completed projects from the companion content for this chapter and lesson.

EXERCISE 1 Implement a Nonclustered Index on a Heap

In this exercise, you create a nonclustered index on a heap.

1. Start SSMS and connect to your SQL Server instance.
2. Open a new query window by clicking the New Query button.
3. Change the context to the tempdb database. Set the NOCOUNT option to ON to stop the message that shows the count of the number of rows affected by a command. Inserts are much faster this way. Use the following code.

   ```
   USE tempdb;
   SET NOCOUNT ON;
   ```

4. Create a table named **dbo.TestStructure** that has the same structure as the table used for testing the heap and the clustered index structure. Use the following code.

   ```
   CREATE TABLE dbo.TestStructure
   (
   id      INT       NOT NULL,
   filler1 CHAR(36)  NOT NULL,
   filler2 CHAR(216) NOT NULL
   );
   GO
   ```

5. Note that the table is organized as a heap because you did not create a clustered index. Create a nonclustered index on the filler1 column by using the following code.

   ```
   CREATE NONCLUSTERED INDEX idx_nc_filler1 ON dbo.TestStructure(filler1);
   ```

6. Query the sys.indexes catalog view to confirm that the table is stored as a heap and that the nonclustered index exists.

   ```
   SELECT OBJECT_NAME(object_id) AS table_name,
    name AS index_name, type, type_desc
   FROM sys.indexes
   WHERE object_id = OBJECT_ID(N'dbo.TestStructure', N'U');
   ```

7. Insert 24,472 rows into the table. Create sequential values for the id and filler1 columns. Use the following code.

```
DECLARE @i AS int = 0;
WHILE @i < 24472
BEGIN
SET @i = @i + 1;
INSERT INTO dbo.TestStructure
(id, filler1, filler2)
VALUES
(@i, FORMAT(@i,'00000'), 'b');
END;
```

8. Use the sys.dm_db_index_physical_stats dynamic management function to check how many levels the nonclustered index has and how many pages and rows are on each level. Also check the heap. You can use the following code.

```
SELECT index_type_desc, index_depth, index_level,
 page count, record_count
FROM sys.dm_db_index_physical_stats
    (DB_ID(N'tempdb'), OBJECT_ID(N'dbo.TestStructure', N'U'), NULL, NULL , 'DETAILED');
```

9. You should have two levels of the nonclustered index. Now insert another row.

```
INSERT INTO dbo.TestStructure
(id, filler1, filler2)
VALUES
(24473, '24473', 'b');
```

10. Check the number of levels of the nonclustered index and the heap again.

```
SELECT index_type_desc, index_depth, index_level,
 page_count, record_count
FROM sys.dm_db_index_physical_stats
    (DB_ID(N'tempdb'), OBJECT_ID(N'dbo.TestStructure', N'U'), NULL, NULL , 'DETAILED');
```

Now you should have three levels in the nonclustered index.

EXERCISE 2 Implement a Nonclustered Index on a Clustered Table

In this exercise, you change the physical structure of the table in the previous exercise from a heap to a clustered index. You observe the difference between a nonclustered index on a heap and a nonclustered index on a clustered table.

1. Truncate the table you created in the previous exercise and create a clustered index on the id column.

```
TRUNCATE TABLE dbo.TestStructure;
CREATE CLUSTERED INDEX idx_cl_id ON dbo.TestStructure(id);
GO
```

2. Query the sys.indexes catalog view to confirm that the table is stored as a balanced tree and that the nonclustered index exists.

```
SELECT OBJECT_NAME(object_id) AS table_name,
 name AS index_name, type, type_desc
FROM sys.indexes
WHERE object_id = OBJECT_ID(N'dbo.TestStructure', N'U');
```

3. Insert 28,864 rows into the table. Create sequential values for the id and filler1 columns. Use the following code.

```
DECLARE @i AS int = 0;
WHILE @i < 28864
BEGIN
SET @i = @i + 1;
INSERT INTO dbo.TestStructure
(id, filler1, filler2)
VALUES
(@i, FORMAT(@i,'00000'), 'b');
END;
```

4. Check the number of levels of the nonclustered index and the clustered index.

```
SELECT index_type_desc, index_depth, index_level,
 page_count, record_count
FROM sys.dm_db_index_physical_stats
    (DB_ID(N'tempdb'), OBJECT_ID(N'dbo.TestStructure', N'U'), NULL, NULL , 'DETAILED');
```

5. The clustered index should have three levels and the nonclustered two. You could accommodate more rows on each page of the nonclustered index on a clustered index than in the nonclustered index on a heap because the clustering key is shorter than the RID. Now add one more row.

```
INSERT INTO dbo.TestStructure
(id, filler1, filler2)
VALUES
(28865, '28865', 'b');
```

6. Check the number of levels of the nonclustered index and the clustered index again.

```
SELECT index_type_desc, index_depth, index_level,
 page_count, record_count
FROM sys.dm_db_index_physical_stats
    (DB_ID(N'tempdb'), OBJECT_ID(N'dbo.TestStructure', N'U'), NULL, NULL , 'DETAILED');
```

   Now the nonclustered index should have three levels.

7. Clean up the tempdb database.

```
DROP TABLE dbo.TestStructure;
```

8. Close the query window.

Lesson Summary

- You can store a table as a heap or as a balanced tree. If the table is stored as a balanced tree, it is clustered; this is also known as a clustered index.
- You can create a nonclustered index on a heap or on a clustered table.
- You can also index a view.

Lesson Review

Answer the following questions to test your knowledge of the information in this lesson. You can find the answers to these questions and explanations of why each answer choice is correct or incorrect in the "Answers" section at the end of this chapter.

1. What levels can an index have? (Choose all that apply.)
   - **A.** Intermediate level
   - **B.** Heap level
   - **C.** Root level
   - **D.** Leaf level
2. How many clustered indexes can you create on a table?
   - **A.** 999
   - **B.** 16
   - **C.** 1
   - **D.** 900
3. What is the row locator when a table is stored as a balanced tree?
   - **A.** RID.
   - **B.** Columnstore index key.
   - **C.** Clustering key.
   - **D.** A table is never stored as a balanced tree.

Lesson 2: Using Search Arguments

Indexes are useful only if queries use them. You need to know which types of queries can benefit from indexes, and which types of queries do not use indexes, even if indexes exist. In addition, you need to write correct predicates when filtering rows in order to enable the SQL Server Query Optimizer to use indexes.

After this lesson, you will be able to:

- Support queries with indexes.
- Use appropriate search arguments in queries.

Estimated lesson time: 35 minutes

Supporting Queries with Indexes

Writing efficient queries starts by including the WHERE clause to filter rows. The WHERE clause is one of the most important parts of a query that can benefit from an index. You can check whether an index was used by displaying the estimated or actual execution plan. You can also track index usage by querying the sys.dm_db_index_usage_stats dynamic management view. Remember that information provided in dynamic management objects is cumulative from the last start of SQL Server.

The following query shows index usage in the TSQL2012 database. Note that the query was executed right after restarting SQL Server.

```
SELECT OBJECT_NAME(S.object_id) AS table_name,
 I.name AS index_name,
 S.user_seeks, S.user_scans, s.user_lookups
FROM sys.dm_db_index_usage_stats AS S
 INNER JOIN sys.indexes AS i
  ON S.object_id = I.object_id
   AND S.index_id = I.index_id
WHERE S.object_id = OBJECT_ID(N'Sales.Orders', N'U');
```

This query is going to be used in further examples in this lesson; therefore, for ease of reference, future references are to the "index usage" query. The index usage query does not return any rows because SQL Server does not have any information about index usage collected yet. The next query does not include a WHERE clause; it retrieves all rows from the Sales.Orders table.

```
SELECT orderid, custid, shipcity
FROM Sales.Orders;
```

The execution plan for this query shows that SQL Server used a clustered index scan. The whole table was scanned, although there are many indexes on the Sales.Orders table. Note that the scan was unordered, or an allocation scan, as Figure 15-5 shows. The Ordered property of the operator is set to False. Remember that order is not guaranteed if you do not include the ORDER BY clause.

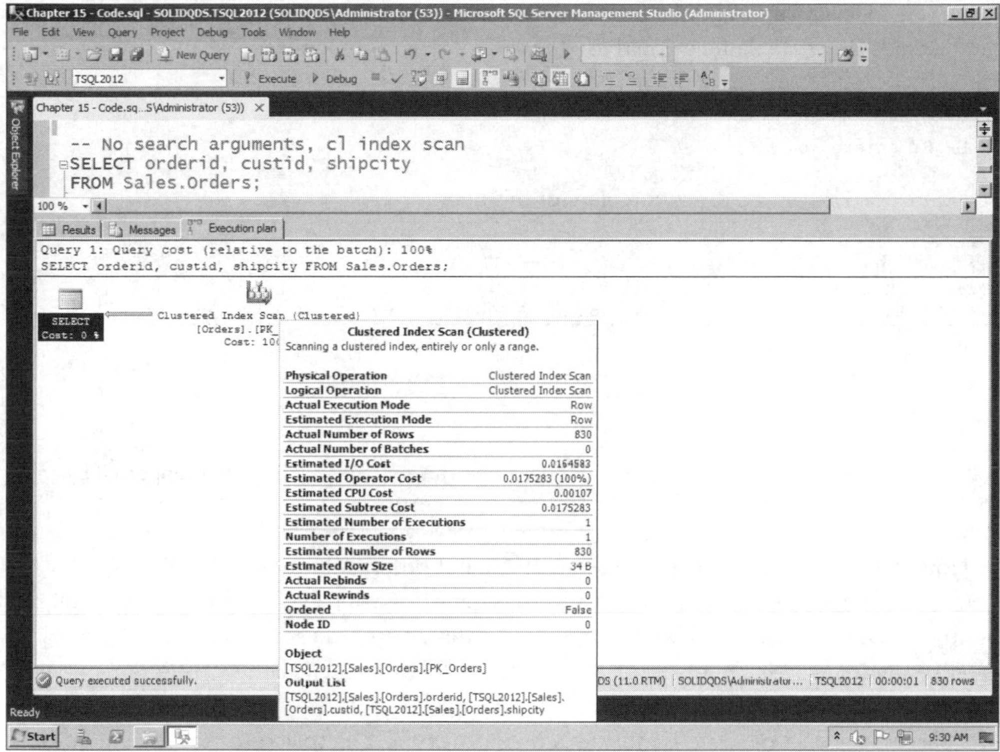

FIGURE 15-5 Unordered clustered index scan.

Adding a WHERE clause to the query does not guarantee that an index is going to be used. The clause has to be supported by an appropriate index, and it must be selective enough. If the query returns too many rows, it is less expensive for SQL Server to perform a table or clustered index scan than to do a nonclustered index seek and then RID or key lookups. For example, although the following query is quite selective, SQL Server still uses the clustered index scan because the WHERE predicate is not supported by an index. There is no index that would have the shipcity column for its key.

```
SELECT orderid, custid, shipcity
FROM Sales.Orders
WHERE shipcity = N'Vancouver';
```

The JOIN clause of a query can benefit from appropriate indexes as well. You will learn more about joins and supporting joins with indexes in Chapter 17.

If your query aggregates data and uses the GROUP BY clause, you should consider supporting this clause with an index. SQL Server can aggregate data by using a hash or a stream aggregate operator. The stream aggregate is faster; however, it needs sorted input. An aggregate query can benefit from an index even if it does not include the GROUP BY clause. For example, if you use the MIN() aggregation function and you have an appropriate index, then SQL Server can seek for the first value of an index only, and does not have to scan the entire table. The following aggregate query is not supported by in index because there is no index on the Sales.Orders table that would use the shipregion column for the key.

```
SELECT shipregion, COUNT(*) AS num_regions
FROM Sales.Orders
GROUP BY shipregion;
```

Figure 15-6 shows the execution plan for this query.

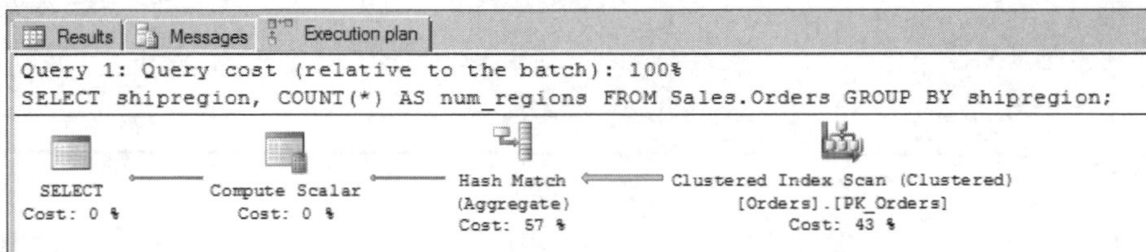

FIGURE 15-6 Hash Match (Aggregate) operator used when an aggregate query is not supported by an index.

Note that the results of the previous query are not ordered. Including the GROUP BY clause in a query does not guarantee a sorted result set. Again, if you need a sorted result, use the ORDER BY clause. However, if you include this clause, you should consider supporting it with an index as well. If there is no appropriate index for the ORDER BY clause, SQL Server must sort data before returning it. Sorting large datasets could be a big performance hit on SQL Server. The data needs to be sorted in memory or must be spilled to tempdb if it does not fit in memory. The following query uses an ORDER BY clause that is not supported by an index.

```
SELECT shipregion
FROM Sales.Orders
ORDER BY shipregion;
```

The execution plan for this query includes the Sort operator, as shown in Figure 15-7.

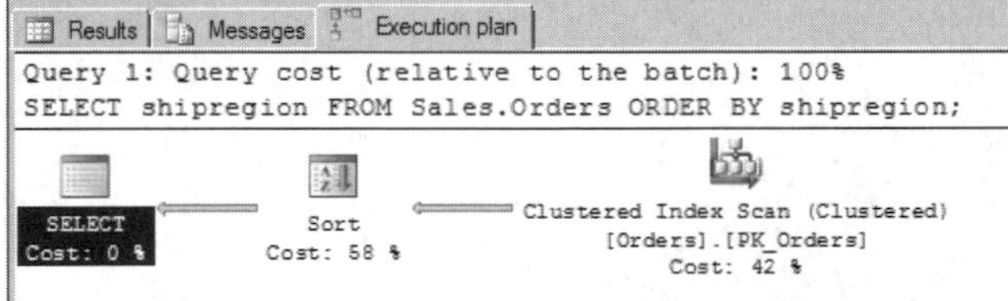

FIGURE 15-7 SQL Server using the Sort operator to sort the output.

Running the index usage query again returns the following output.

```
table_name  index_name  user_seeks  user_scans  user_lookups
----------  ----------  ----------  ----------  ------------
Orders      PK_Orders   0           4           0
```

All four queries executed in this lesson so far used a clustered index scan. It is time to start supporting the queries with appropriate indexes. The next piece of code creates a nonclustered index by using the shipregion column.

```
CREATE NONCLUSTERED INDEX idx_nc_shipregion ON Sales.Orders(shipregion);
```

If you execute the query that aggregates data and the query that requests sorted data again, like the following code shows, you get different execution plans.

```
-- Query that aggregates the data
SELECT shipregion, COUNT(*) AS num_regions
FROM Sales.Orders
GROUP BY shipregion;
-- Query that sorts the output
SELECT shipregion
FROM Sales.Orders
ORDER BY shipregion;
```

The execution plan for the first query uses the Stream Aggregate operator, and the execution plan for the second query does not include a Sort operator, as Figure 15-8 shows.

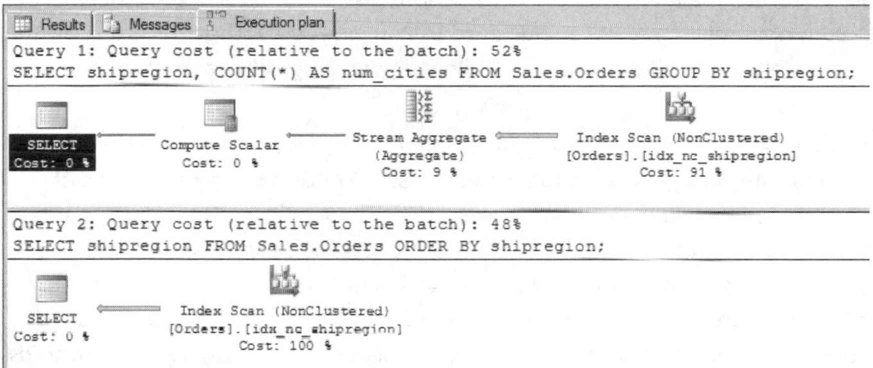

FIGURE 15-8 Execution plans for GROUP BY and ORDER BY queries supported by an index.

Running the index usage query returns the following output.

```
table_name  index_name          user_seeks  user_scans  user_lookups
----------  ------------------  ----------  ----------  ------------
Orders      idx_nc_shipregion   0           2           0
Orders      PK_Orders           0           4           0
```

Note that the idx_nc_shipregion nonclustered index was used for two scans, and there was no additional usage of the clustered index. You could also see this from the execution plans in Figure 15-8. SQL Server found all data for the query in the nonclustered index, and did not have to perform a RID or key lookup. If SQL Server finds all data in nonclustered indexes, then the query is *covered* by the nonclustered indexes, and the indexes are *covering* indexes. Covered queries are very efficient.

You could try to add more columns to a nonclustered index key to cover more queries. However, with a longer key, the index would become less efficient. There is another option in SQL Server 2012. You can also include a column in a nonclustered index on the leaf level only and not as a part of the key. You do this by using the INCLUDE clause of the CREATE INDEX statement. The included column is not part of the key, and SQL Server does not use it for seeks. Included columns help cover queries. However, you should be careful and not include too many columns. For example, if you included all columns of a table, you would actually copy the table.

The idx_nc_shipregion index is not useful for further examples in this lesson, so it's dropped in the following code.

```
DROP INDEX idx_nc_shipregion ON Sales.Orders;
```

Search Arguments

Including the WHERE clause in a query, even if the predicate is very selective and supported by an index, does not guarantee that SQL Server is going to use an index. You need to write an appropriate predicate to allow the Query Optimizer to take advantage of the indexes. The Query Optimizer is not omnipotent. It can decide to use an index only when the arguments in the predicate are searchable. You have to learn how to write appropriate search arguments (SARGs).

To write an appropriate SARG, you must ensure that a column that has an index on it appears in the predicate alone, not as a function parameter. SARGs must take the form of *column inclusive_operator <value>* or *<value> inclusive_operator column*. The column name is alone on one side of the expression, and the constant or calculated value appears on the other side. Inclusive operators include the operators =, >, <, =>, <=, BETWEEN, and LIKE. However, the LIKE operator is inclusive only if you do not use a wildcard % or _ at the beginning of the string you are comparing the column to. For example, the following query returns orders for the dates July 10, 2006, and July 11, 2006.

```
SELECT orderid, custid, orderdate, shipname
FROM Sales.Orders
WHERE DATEDIFF(day, '20060709', orderdate) <= 2
 AND DATEDIFF(day, '20060709', orderdate) > 0;
```

The query returns two rows only; therefore, the WHERE predicate is very selective. There is a nonclustered index on the orderdate column. However, SQL Server did not use the index, as the execution plan in Figure 15-9 shows.

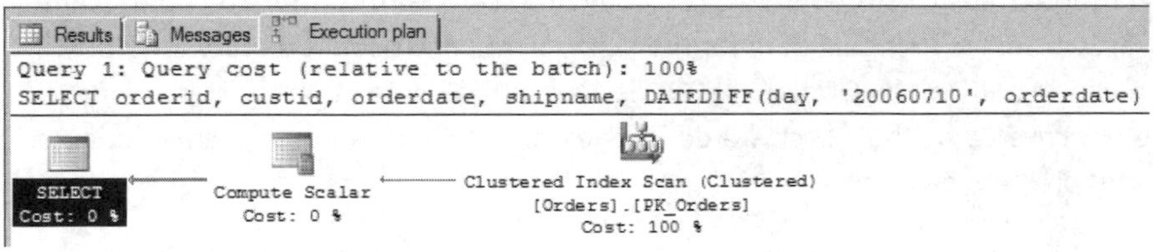

```
Results | Messages | Execution plan
Query 1: Query cost (relative to the batch): 100%
SELECT orderid, custid, orderdate, shipname, DATEDIFF(day, '20060710', orderdate)

SELECT      <- Compute Scalar <- Clustered Index Scan (Clustered)
Cost: 0 %      Cost: 0 %         [Orders].[PK_Orders]
                                 Cost: 100 %
```

FIGURE 15-9 Query in which the predicate is not a SARG.

The orderdate in the predicate does not appear alone; it is instead an argument of a function. You can rewrite such a query many times. The following query produces the same result, but this time the predicate is a SARG.

```
SELECT orderid, custid, orderdate, shipname
FROM Sales.Orders
WHERE DATEADD(day, 2, '20060709') >= orderdate
 AND '20060709' < orderdate;
```

In Figure 15-10, you can see that SQL Server used the idx_nc_orderdate index for seeks and then performed key lookups

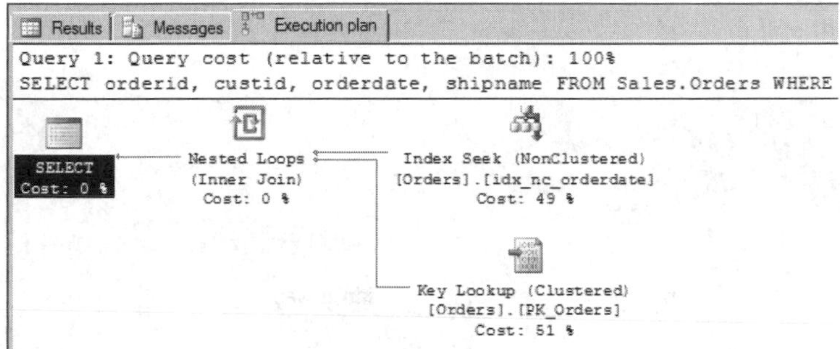

FIGURE 15-10 Query in which the predicate is a SARG.

You could rewrite the query in more different ways. You could use the IN operator to include the list of the dates for which you want the query to retrieve the orders. You could also use the equals operator for each date, and connect the two equals predicates with the logical OR operator. Actually, these two queries would be internally treated as the same; the Query Optimizer converts the IN operator to OR with a separate comparison to each element from the IN operator list. The following two queries return the same two rows and are internally treated as equal.

```
SELECT orderid, custid, orderdate, shipname
FROM Sales.Orders
WHERE orderdate IN ('20060710', '20060711');

SELECT orderid, custid, orderdate, shipname
FROM Sales.Orders
WHERE orderdate = '20060710'
 OR orderdate = '20060711';
```

You can see that SQL Server executed both queries by using the same execution plan, as shown in Figure 15-11.

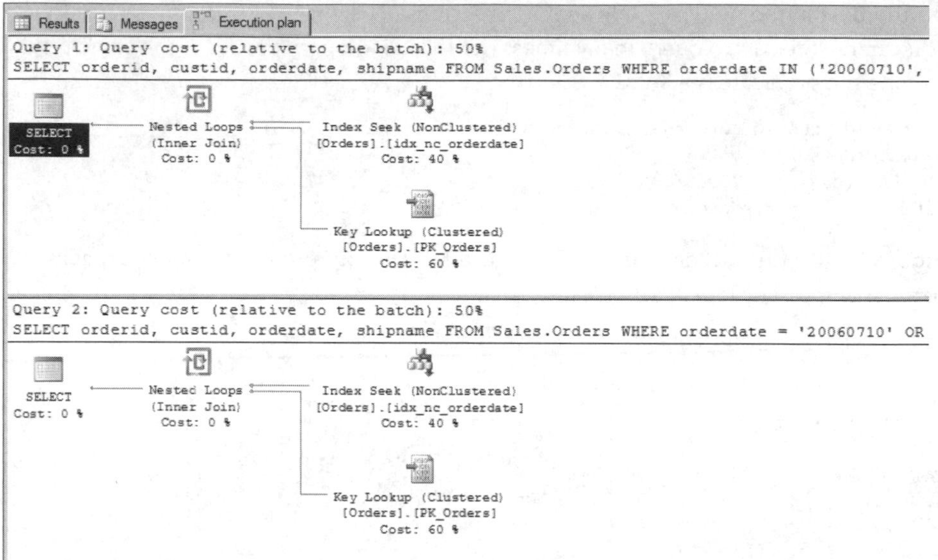

FIGURE 15-11 SQL Server executing the IN and the OR operators in the same way.

Using the AND operator in the WHERE clause predicate means that each part of the predicate limits the result set even more than the previous part. For example, if the first condition limits a query to five rows, then the next condition connected to the first one with the logical AND operator limits the query to five rows at most. The Query Optimizer understands how the logical AND operator works, and can use appropriate indexes.

However, the logical OR operator is inclusive. For example, if the first condition in a predicate would limit the query to 5 rows and the next condition connected to the first condition with the logical OR operator would limit the query to 6 rows, then the result set could have anything between 6 and 11 rows. If the two conditions use two different columns, then SQL Server conservatively takes the worst case and estimates that the query would return 11 rows. Having multiple conditions in a predicate connected with the OR operator lowers the possibility for SQL Server to use indexes. You should consider rewriting the predicate to a logically equivalent predicate that uses the AND operator.

Quick Check

- **Which clauses of a query should you consider supporting with an index?**

Quick Check Answer

- **The list of the clauses you should consider supporting with an index includes, but is not limited to, the WHERE, JOIN, GROUP BY, and ORDER BY clauses.**

PRACTICE Using the OR and AND Logical Operators

In this practice, you use the OR and AND logical operators to connect two conditions of a predicate of a query, and then you check the execution plans.

If you encounter a problem completing an exercise, you can install the completed projects from the companion content for this chapter and lesson.

EXERCISE 1 Support the OR Logical Operators

In this exercise, you test the influence of the OR logical operator on query execution. You are going to support queries with appropriate indexes.

1. If you closed SSMS, start it and connect to your SQL Server instance.
2. Open a new query window by clicking the New Query button.
3. Change the context to the TSQL2012 database.
4. Create a nonclustered index on the Sales.Orders table on the shipcity column.

```
CREATE NONCLUSTERED INDEX idx_nc_shipcity ON Sales.Orders(shipcity);
```

5. Retrieve the orderid, custid, and shipcity columns for the city of Vancouver.

```
SELECT orderid, custid, shipcity
FROM Sales.Orders
WHERE shipcity = N'Vancouver';
```

6. The query is selective, because it returns three rows only. Check whether the nonclustered index you just created was used by using the following code.

```
SELECT OBJECT_NAME(S.object_id) AS table_name,
 I.name AS index_name,
 S.user_seeks, S.user_scans, s.user_lookups
FROM sys.dm_db_index_usage_stats AS S
 INNER JOIN sys.indexes AS i
  ON S.object_id = I.object_id
   AND S.index_id = I.index_id
WHERE S.object_id = OBJECT_ID(N'Sales.Orders', N'U')
 AND I.name = N'idx_nc_shipcity';
```

You should get a single row showing the index was used for a seek.

7. Turn on the actual execution plan. Now retrieve the same columns for the customer with an ID of 42.

```
SELECT orderid, custid, shipcity
FROM Sales.Orders
WHERE custid = 42;
```

Note that the same three rows were returned. SQL Server used the idx_nc_custid nonclustered index this time, as you can see from the execution plan. The index uses the custid column for its key.

8. Retrieve the same result set again. However, now include both conditions, the city Vancouver and the customer ID of 42, in the WHERE clause, connected with the OR operator, like the following code shows.

```
SELECT orderid, custid, shipcity
FROM Sales.Orders
WHERE custid = 42
 OR shipcity = N'Vancouver';
```

9. Again, the same three rows were retrieved. However, you can see from the execution plan that this time SQL Server scanned the clustered index. By pausing on the Clustered Index Scan operator in the plan, you can see the estimated and actual number of rows, as shown in Figure 15-12.

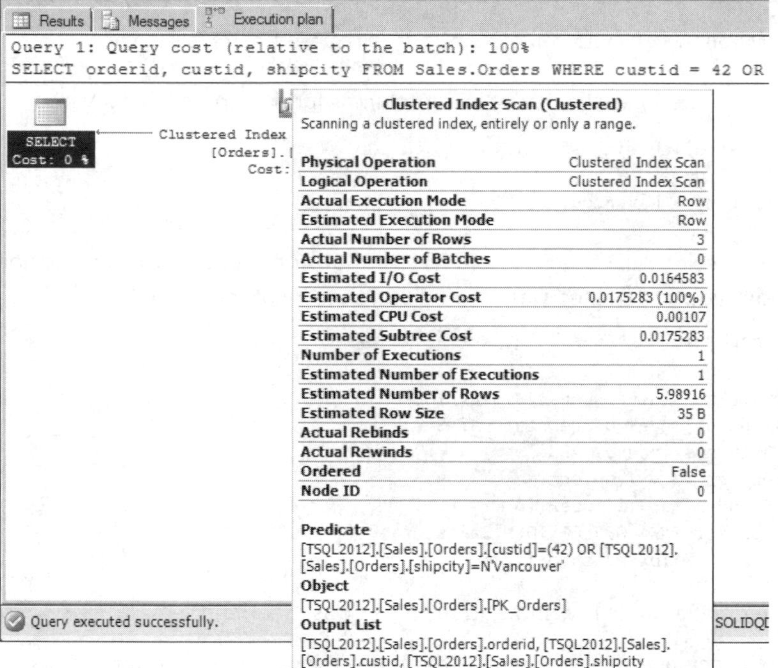

FIGURE 15-12 Estimated and actual number of rows for the Clustered Index Scan operator.

You can see that the estimated number of rows is about six, and SQL Server decided to scan the clustered index.

EXERCISE 2 Support the AND Logical Operator

In this exercise, you test the influence of the AND logical operator on query execution. You also create an index that has an included column.

1. Change the last query from the previous exercise by replacing the OR operator with the AND operator.

   ```
   SELECT orderid, custid, shipcity
   FROM Sales.Orders
   WHERE custid = 42
    AND shipcity = N'Vancouver';
   ```

   Of course, you are still retrieving the same three rows. However, from the execution plan, you can see that SQL Server used the idx_nc_custid nonclustered index this time.

2. Drop the nonclustered index on the Sales.Orders table on the shipcity column.

   ```
   DROP INDEX idx_nc_shipcity ON Sales.Orders;
   ```

3. Create a nonclustered index on the Sales.Orders table on the shipcity column again. This time, include the custid column. Use the following code.

   ```
   CREATE NONCLUSTERED INDEX idx_nc_shipcity_i_custid ON Sales.Orders(shipcity)
   INCLUDE (custid);
   ```

4. Again execute the query that includes both conditions, the city Vancouver and the customer ID of 42, in the WHERE clause, connected with the OR operator.

   ```
   SELECT orderid, custid, shipcity
   FROM Sales.Orders
   WHERE custid = 42
    OR shipcity = N'Vancouver';
   ```

5. You should get a nonclustered index scan. The query is covered by the index with the included column you just created. However, SQL Server still used a scan, because of the OR operator. Change the OR operator to AND again and execute the query.

   ```
   SELECT orderid, custid, shipcity
   FROM Sales.Orders
   WHERE custid = 42
    AND shipcity = N'Vancouver';
   ```

   This time, SQL Server should use the Index Seek operator to seek for the first occurrence of the city of Vancouver and then perform a partial scan.

6. Turn off the actual execution plan and drop the index you created.

   ```
   DROP INDEX idx_nc_shipcity_i_custid ON Sales.Orders;
   ```

Lesson Summary

- You support different parts of queries with indexes.
- Consider supporting the WHERE, JOIN, GROUP BY, ORDER BY, and SELECT clauses of queries with appropriate indexes.
- You write appropriate search arguments by not including key columns of indexes in expressions.

Lesson Review

Answer the following questions to test your knowledge of the information in this lesson. You can find the answers to these questions and explanations of why each answer choice is correct or incorrect in the "Answers" section at the end of this chapter.

1. How can you support the SELECT clause of a query by using a nonclustered index that is already used for the WHERE clause?
   - **A.** You could use SELECT *.
   - **B.** You could modify the index that is already used to include the columns from the select list that are not part of the key.
   - **C.** You could add column aliases.
   - **D.** There is no way to support the SELECT clause with indexes.
2. Where does SQL Server sort the data, if a sort is needed?
   - **A.** In the current database
   - **B.** In the master database
   - **C.** In the msdb database
   - **D.** SQL Server sorts data in memory, or spills the data to tempdb if it does not fit in memory.
3. You create an index to support the WHERE clause of a query. However, SQL Server does not use the index. What are the possible reasons? (Choose all that apply.)
   - **A.** The arguments in the predicate are not searchable.
   - **B.** SQL Server does not consider using an index to support the WHERE clause.
   - **C.** The predicate is not selective enough.
   - **D.** You are in the context of the tempdb database, and SQL Server does not use indexes in this database.

Lesson 3: Understanding Statistics

You might have asked yourself when reading and testing the code from the previous lesson how SQL Server knows in advance whether a query is selective enough to perform an index seek. There is no magic behind it; SQL Server maintains statistics of the distribution of key values in special system statistical pages. The Query Optimizer uses these statistics to estimate the cardinality, or number of rows, in the query result set. You learn about statistics in this lesson.

After this lesson, you will be able to:

- Understand SQL Server statistics.
- Manually maintain statistics.

Estimated lesson time: 25 minutes

Auto-Created Statistics

By default, SQL Server creates statistics automatically. SQL Server creates statistics for each index, and for single columns used as searchable arguments in queries. There are three database options that influence the automatic creation of the statistics:

- **AUTO_CREATE_STATISTICS** When this option is set to on, SQL Server creates statistics automatically. This option is on by default, and you should leave this option on in the vast majority of cases.
- **AUTO_UPDATE_STATISTICS** This option, when turned on, enables SQL Server to automatically update statistics when there are enough changes in the underlying tables and indexes. With this option on, SQL Server also updates an out-of-date statistic during query optimization. SQL Server checks for outdated statistics before compiling a query and before executing a cached query. In general, you should leave this option turned on.
- **AUTO_UPDATE_STATISTICS_ASYNC** This option determines whether SQL Server uses synchronous or asynchronous statistics updates during query optimization. If the statistics are updated asynchronously, SQL Server cannot use them for the optimization of the query that triggered the update; however, SQL Server does not wait for the statistics update during the optimization phase. You should turn this option on only if your queries wait for synchronous updates of statistics too frequently and this causes performance problems. This option is turned off by default, and changing this option has no effect unless AUTO_UPDATE_STATISTICS is set to ON

Each statistics object is stored in a statistics binary large object and is created on one or more columns. The statistics include a histogram with the distribution of values in the first column. Statistics objects on multiple columns store additional statistical information about the correlation of values among the columns. These correlation statistics are also called densities. They are derived from the number of distinct rows of combinations of values of columns of a composite index.

There is a limit for the number of steps in histograms. A statistic can have maximally 200 steps. The statistics object also includes a header with metadata about the statistics, and a density vector to measure cross-column correlation. SQL Server computes an estimated number of rows that a query returns, or a cardinality estimate, with any of the data in the statistics object.

You can get information about statistics by querying the sys.stats and sys.stats_columns catalog views. You can get detailed information about statistics with the DBCC SHOW_STATISTICS command. You can manually maintain statistics with the CREATE, DROP, and UPDATE statistics commands. You can also use the sys.sp_updatestats system procedure to manually update statistics for all tables in a database. For example, the following code uses a cursor on the sys.stats catalog view to loop over all automatically created statistics for the columns that are not used as index keys for the Sales.Orders table, dynamically concatenates the DROP STATISTICS command, and drops these statistics.

```
DECLARE @statistics_name AS NVARCHAR(128), @ds AS NVARCHAR(1000);
DECLARE acs_cursor CURSOR FOR
SELECT name AS statistics_name
FROM sys.stats
WHERE object_id = OBJECT_ID(N'Sales.Orders', N'U')
  AND auto_created = 1;
OPEN acs_cursor;
FETCH NEXT FROM acs_cursor INTO @statistics_name;
WHILE @@FETCH_STATUS = 0
BEGIN
 SET @ds = N'DROP STATISTICS Sales.Orders.' + @statistics_name +';';
 EXEC(@ds);
 FETCH NEXT FROM acs_cursor INTO @statistics_name;
END;
CLOSE acs_cursor;
DEALLOCATE acs_cursor;
```

IMPORTANT **UPDATING STATISTICS FOR ALL TABLES IN A DATABASE**

Using the sys.sp_updatestats system procedure to manually update statistics for all tables in a database can take a long time and use a lot of resources; therefore, be careful when you use this command in a large database. You should use it only during off-peak hours.

Now only the statistics for the indexes should exist, as the following query shows.

```
SELECT OBJECT_NAME(object_id) AS table_name,
 name AS statistics_name, auto_created
FROM sys.stats
WHERE object_id = OBJECT_ID(N'Sales.Orders', N'U');
```

The result of this query is as follows.

```
table_name  statistics_name       auto_created
----------  --------------------  -----------
Orders      PK_Orders             0
Orders      idx_nc_custid         0
Orders      idx_nc_empid          0
Orders      idx_nc_shipperid      0
Orders      idx_nc_orderdate      0
Orders      idx_nc_shippeddate    0
Orders      idx_nc_shippostalcode 0
```

The auto_created column gets a value of 1 for statistics that SQL Server generates automatically for single columns used as searchable arguments during query execution. Before showing the statistics, the following line of code rebuilds the idx_nc_empid and the Sales. Orders table to ensure that SQL Server updated the statistics.

```
ALTER INDEX idx_nc_empid ON Sales.Orders REBUILD;
```

The following command shows the histogram of the idx_nc_empid statistics.

```
DBCC SHOW_STATISTICS(N'Sales.Orders',N'idx_nc_empid') WITH HISTOGRAM;
```

The result of this command is as follows.

```
RANGE_HI_KEY RANGE_ROWS    EQ_ROWS       DISTINCT_RANGE_ROWS  AVG_RANGE_ROWS
------------ ------------- ------------- -------------------- --------------
1            0             123           0                    1
2            0             96            0                    1
3            0             127           0                    1
4            0             156           0                    1
5            0             42            0                    1
6            0             67            0                    1
7            0             72            0                    1
8            0             104           0                    1
9            0             43            0                    1
DBCC execution completed. If DBCC printed error messages, contact your system
administrator.
```

There are only nine steps in the histogram because the empid column has only nine distinct values. If you execute the DBCC SHOW_STATISTICS command without the WITH HISTOGRAM option, you get all statistics information, including the header and the density vector. From the header, you can get useful information like when the statistics were last updated, as the following query does.

```
DBCC SHOW_STATISTICS(N'Sales.Orders',N'idx_nc_empid') WITH STAT_HEADER;
```

Partial output of this query (only the seven leftmost columns) is as follows.

```
Name         Updated             Rows Rows Sampled Steps  Density Average key length
------------ ------------------- ---- ------------ -----  ------- ------------------
idx_nc_empid Mar 24 2012  1:57PM 830  830          9      0       8
```

You can also get information like when the statistics were last updated by using the STATS_DATE() system function.

As mentioned, SQL Server automatically creates statistics for searchable nonkey columns during query execution. To test this, start with the following code that adds a nonclustered index to the Sales.Orders table.

```
CREATE NONCLUSTERED INDEX idx_nc_custid_shipcity ON Sales.Orders(custid, shipcity);
```

The following query retrieves three rows for the customer with the ID of 42 from the Sales.Orders table.

```
SELECT orderid, custid, shipcity
FROM Sales.Orders
WHERE custid = 42;
```

Now check whether the auto-created statistics exist. The following query returns zero rows, meaning that there are no auto-created statistics for the Sales.Orders table yet. SQL Server had enough information through the index statistics from idx_nc_custid_shipcity to execute the previous query.

```
SELECT OBJECT_NAME(object_id) AS table_name,
 name AS statistics_name
FROM sys.stats
WHERE object_id = OBJECT_ID(N'Sales.Orders', N'U')
  AND auto_created = 1;
```

Now select the same three rows from the Sales.Orders table; however, this time use the shipcity column as a SARG and limit output to the city of Vancouver.

```
SELECT orderid, custid, shipcity
FROM Sales.Orders
WHERE shipcity = N'Vancouver';
```

The following query checks whether the auto-created statistics exist, and also adds information about the columns for which the statistics were created.

```
SELECT OBJECT_NAME(s.object_id) AS table_name,
 S.name AS statistics_name, C.name AS column_name
FROM sys.stats AS S
 INNER JOIN sys.stats_columns AS SC
  ON S.stats_id = SC.stats_id
 INNER JOIN sys.columns AS C
  ON S.object_id= C.object_id AND SC.column_id = C.column_id
WHERE S.object_id = OBJECT_ID(N'Sales.Orders', N'U')
  AND auto_created = 1;
```

The output of this query is as follows.

```
table_name  statistics_name            column_name
----------  -------------------------  -----------
Orders      _WA_Sys_0000000B_20C1E124  shipcity
```

You can see that SQL Server created statistics for the shipcity column. All auto-created statistics names start with string _WA_Sys_. To clean up, delete the index you created for this test.

```
DROP INDEX idx_nc_custid_shipcity ON Sales.Orders;
```

If you want, you could also drop all auto-created statistics again.

Manually Maintaining Statistics

There are only a few possible reasons to create statistics manually. One example is when a query predicate contains multiple columns that have cross-column relationships; statistics on the multiple columns can help improve the query plan. Statistics on multiple columns contain cross-column densities that are not available in single-column statistics. However, if the columns are already in the same index, the multicolumn statistics object already exists, so you should not create an additional one manually.

Similarly to filtered indexes, you can also create filtered statistics. Statistics created by SQL Server automatically are always created on all rows of a table. If queries frequently select from a subset of rows that has a unique data distribution, filtered statistics can improve query plans.

Sometimes you can get a warning in the execution plan that a particular statistic is missing. You can create this statistic manually. However, before creating it manually, you should verify that AUTO_CREATE_STATISTICS and AUTO_UPDATE_STATISTICS database options are on and that the database is not read-only. If the database is read-only, the Query Optimizer cannot save statistics.

Consider updating statistics manually in the following circumstances:

- When query execution times are slow, and you know that the queries are written correctly and supported with appropriate indexes. Before you use query hints, update the statistics. SQL Server does not consider using the index with outdated statistics. Check also whether auto-updating statistics is turned off for the database.
- When insert operations occur on ascending or descending key columns. Statistics are not updated for every single row; therefore, the number of rows inserted might be too small to trigger a statistics update. If queries select from the recently added rows, the current statistics might not have cardinality estimates for these new values. In addition, bulk inserting rows to a table or truncating a table can change the distribution of data a lot. Queries executed immediately after these operations might get a suboptimal execution plan because the statistics were not updated automatically yet.
- After an upgrade from a previous version of SQL Server. Statistics information can change with a new version of SQL Server; to be on the safe side, you should update the statistics for the upgraded databases.

 **Quick Check**

- **How would you quickly update statistics for the whole database after an upgrade?**

Quick Check Answer

- **You should use the sys.sp_updatestats system procedure.**

PRACTICE Manually Maintaining Statistics

In this practice, you manually maintain statistics.

If you encounter a problem completing an exercise, you can install the completed projects from the companion content for this chapter and lesson.

EXERCISE 1 Disable Statistics Auto-Creation

In this exercise, you disable statistics auto-creation.

1. If you closed SSMS, start it and connect to your SQL Server instance.
2. Open a new query window by clicking the New Query button.
3. Change the context to the TSQL2012 database.
4. To have a clean start, drop all auto-created statistics for the Sales.Orders table. Use the following code.

```
DECLARE @statistics_name AS NVARCHAR(128), @ds AS NVARCHAR(1000);
DECLARE acs_cursor CURSOR FOR
SELECT name AS statistics_name
FROM sys.stats
WHERE object_id = OBJECT_ID(N'Sales.Orders', N'U')
  AND auto_created = 1;
OPEN acs_cursor;
FETCH NEXT FROM acs_cursor INTO @statistics_name;
WHILE @@FETCH_STATUS = 0
BEGIN
 SET @ds = N'DROP STATISTICS Sales.Orders.' + @statistics_name +';';
 EXEC(@ds);
 FETCH NEXT FROM acs_cursor INTO @statistics_name;
END;
CLOSE acs_cursor;
DEALLOCATE acs_cursor;
```

5. Disable statistics auto-creation for the TSQL2012 database by using the ALTER DATABASE command.

```
ALTER DATABASE TSQL2012
 SET AUTO_CREATE_STATISTICS OFF WITH NO_WAIT;
```

EXERCISE 2 **Observe the Effects When Statistics Auto-Creation Is Disabled**

In this exercise, you observe the effects on index usage when statistics auto-creation is disabled.

1. Add a composite nonclustered index on the Sales.Orders table by using the custid and shipcity columns for the key.

```
CREATE NONCLUSTERED INDEX idx_nc_custid_shipcity
 ON Sales.Orders(custid, shipcity);
```

2. Turn on the actual execution plan. Use the following query to select the three orders where the shipcity is Vancouver.

```
SELECT orderid, custid, shipcity
FROM Sales.Orders
WHERE shipcity = N'Vancouver';
```

3. Check the execution plan. You should get either a Clustered Index Scan operator with a warning sign on it, or an Index Scan (NonClustered) operator, again with a warning sign on it. You can open the Properties window from the View menu or by pressing the F4 key to check the warnings property. Click the three dots at the end of the text of the Warnings property to get a pop-up window for this property, as Figure 15-13 shows.

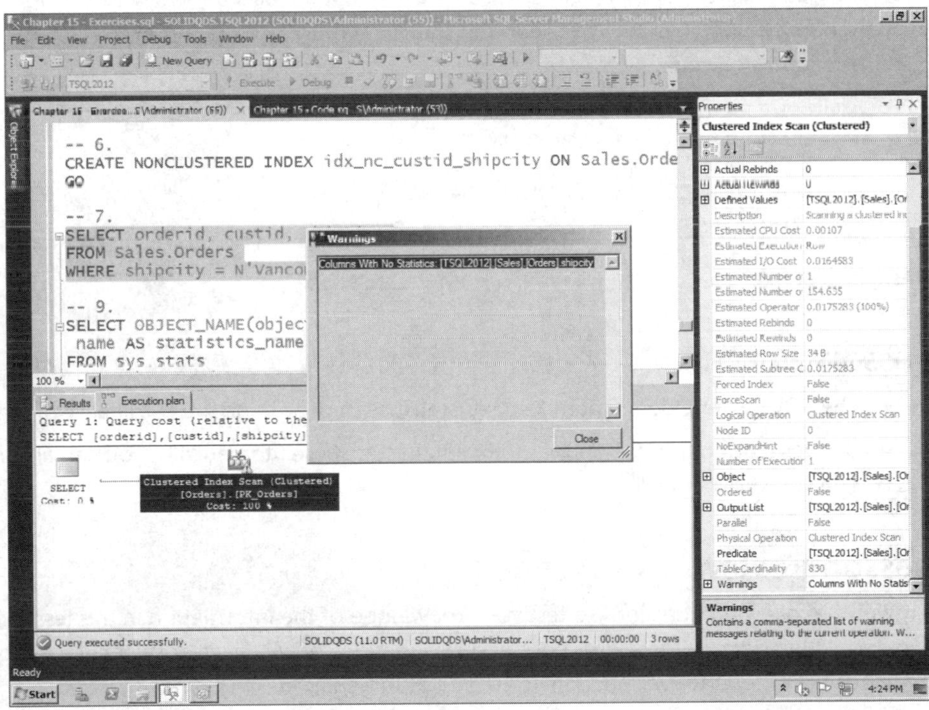

FIGURE 15-13 Missing statistics warning.

4. Check whether any auto-created statistics exist for the Sales.Orders table by using the following query.

```
SELECT OBJECT_NAME(object_id) AS table_name,
 name AS statistics_name
FROM sys.stats
WHERE object_id = OBJECT_ID(N'Sales.Orders', N'U')
  AND auto_created = 1;
```

5. The query should not return any rows. You can create the missing statistics manually. In addition to creating the statistics, you should also clear the cached plan in order to prevent SQL Server from reusing it. Use the following code.

```
CREATE STATISTICS st_shipcity ON Sales.Orders(shipcity);
DBCC FREEPROCCACHE;
```

6. Execute the same query that searches for orders from Vancouver again.

```
SELECT orderid, custid, shipcity
FROM Sales.Orders
WHERE shipcity = N'Vancouver';
```

7. Check the execution plan. You shouldn't get any warning this time.
8. To clean up, turn auto-creating statistics to on, update all statistics in the TSQL2012 database, and drop the index and the statistics you created in this exercise. You can use the following code.

```
DROP STATISTICS Sales.Orders.st_shipcity;
DROP INDEX idx_nc_custid_shipcity ON Sales.Orders;
ALTER DATABASE TSQL2012
SET AUTO_CREATE_STATISTICS ON WITH NO_WAIT;
EXEC sys.sp_updatestats;
```

9. Exit SSMS.

Lesson Summary

- The SQL Server Query Optimizer uses statistics to determine the cardinality of a query.
- Besides leaving it to SQL Server to maintain statistics automatically, you can also maintain statistics manually.

Lesson Review

Answer the following questions to test your knowledge of the information in this lesson. You can find the answers to these questions and explanations of why each answer choice is correct or incorrect in the "Answers" section at the end of this chapter.

1. How can SQL Server estimate the cardinality of a query?
   - **A.** SQL Server stores the cardinality information on leaf-level pages of indexes.
   - **B.** SQL Server quickly executes the query on 10 percent of sample data.
   - **C.** SQL Server cannot estimate the cardinality of a query if you do not provide a table hint.
   - **D.** SQL Server uses statistics to estimate the cardinality of a query.
2. Which of the following is not a reason to update statistics manually?
   - **A.** You just rebuilt an index.
   - **B.** You bulk-inserted a large amount of data to a table and want to query this table immediately after the insert.
   - **C.** You upgraded the database.
   - **D.** Query execution times are slow; however, you know that the queries are written correctly and supported with appropriate indexes.
3. What is the limit for the number of steps in statistic histograms?
   - **A.** 10 steps per histogram
   - **B.** 200 histograms per column
   - **C.** 200 pages per histogram
   - **D.** 200 steps per histogram

Case Scenarios

In the following case scenarios, you apply what you've learned about implementing indexes and statistics. You can find the answers to these questions in the "Answers" section at the end of this chapter.

Case Scenario 1: Table Scans

Database administrators from a company where you are maintaining a SQL Server database complain that SQL Server scans entire tables for most of the queries, although the queries are very selective. The performance is not acceptable. You need to help them improve the performance.

1. What physical structures should you check?
2. Would you check some code as well?

Case Scenario 2: Slow Updates

End users from a company where you are responsible for the database optimization complain that data updates are slow, even when updating a single row. Seeking for the updated row is supported by appropriate indexes. SELECT queries are performing well. This is what you expected, because you created nonclustered indexes on all columns used in these queries. You need to improve the performance of the database for updates as well.

1. What would you suspect to be the reason for slow updates?
2. How would you investigate for possible problems?

Suggested Practices

To help you successfully master the exam objectives presented in this chapter, complete the following tasks.

Learn More About Indexes and How Statistics Influence Query Execution

Using proper indexing and maintaining statistics are very important DBA tasks. You can learn about these two tasks by performing the next two practices.

- **Practice 1** In order to understand how statistical information influences query execution, create a test database with a test table in it. Turn automatic statistics creation and maintenance off for that database. Create a clustered index and one or more nonclustered indexes on that table. Fill the table with test data. Execute test queries and check whether SQL Server used the indexes. Manually create statistics and execute the queries again. Check whether SQL Server used the indexes this time. Add more rows to the table and execute the queries again. After checking index usage, manually update the statistics. Execute queries for the last time and check index usage.
- **Practice 2** Create a table with at least 10 columns. Insert 1,000,000 rows in a loop and measure the time needed for these inserts. Create a nonclustered index on each column. Insert 1,000,000 rows in a loop and measure the time needed for these inserts. You should be able to notice the difference and realize that index maintenance takes some SQL Server resources.

Answers

This section contains answers to the lesson review questions and solutions to the case scenarios in this chapter.

Lesson 1

1. **Correct Answers: A, C, and D**
   - **A. Correct:** An index can have zero or more intermediate levels.
   - **B. Incorrect:** A heap is a separate structure, not a level of an index.
   - **C. Correct:** Every index has the root level, with a single root page.
   - **D. Correct:** The lowest level of an index is the leaf level.
2. **Correct Answer: C**
   - **A. Incorrect:** You can create up to 999 nonclustered indexes on a table.
   - **B. Incorrect:** You can have up to 16 columns in a composite key.
   - **C. Correct:** There can be only one clustered index, because this is the table itself, organized as a balanced tree.
   - **D. Incorrect:** The size of the columns in a key must not exceed 900 bytes.
3. **Correct Answer: C**
   - **A. Incorrect:** RID is used for heaps.
   - **B. Incorrect:** Columns in a columnstore index are not used as row locators.
   - **C. Correct:** The clustering key is the row locator when a table is stored as a balanced tree.
   - **D. Incorrect:** A clustered table is stored as a balanced tree.

Lesson 2

1. **Correct Answer: B**
   - **A. Incorrect:** Using SELECT * is a very bad practice and of course does not help SQL Server to use indexes at all.
   - **B. Correct:** You could modify the index that is already used to include the columns from the SELECT list that are not part of the key.
   - **C. Incorrect:** Adding column aliases has no influence on index usage.
   - **D. Incorrect:** You can support the SELECT clause with indexes.

2. **Correct Answer: D**

   A. **Incorrect:** SQL Server sorts data in memory, or spills the data to tempdb if it does not fit in memory.

   B. **Incorrect:** SQL Server sorts data in memory, or spills the data to tempdb if it does not fit in memory.

   C. **Incorrect:** SQL Server sorts data in memory, or spills the data to tempdb if it does not fit in memory.

   D. **Correct:** SQL Server sorts data in memory, or spills the data to tempdb if it does not fit in memory.

3. **Correct Answers: A and C**

   A. **Correct:** SQL Server does not use an index to support the WHERE clause if the arguments in the predicate are not searchable.

   B. **Incorrect:** SQL Server supports the WHERE clause with indexes.

   C. **Correct:** SQL Server might decide not to use an index to support the WHERE clause if the query is not selective enough.

   D. **Incorrect:** SQL Server considers using indexes in the context of the tempdb database just like in the context of any other database.

Lesson 3

1. **Correct Answer: D**

   A. **Incorrect:** There is no cardinality information on leaf-level pages of indexes.

   B. **Incorrect:** SQL Server does not execute a query in advance on sample data.

   C. **Incorrect:** SQL Server can estimate the cardinality of a query.

   D. **Correct:** SQL Server uses statistics to estimate the cardinality of a query.

2. **Correct Answer: A**

   A. **Correct:** When you rebuild an index, SQL Server updates the statistics automatically.

   B. **Incorrect:** You should update statistics for a table after you bulk-inserted a large amount of data to the table and want to query this table immediately.

   C. **Incorrect:** You should update statistics for the complete database after an upgrade.

   D. **Incorrect:** You should update statistics when queries execute slowly and you know that the queries are written correctly and supported with appropriate indexes.

3. **Correct Answer: D**
   - **A. Incorrect:** You can have up to 200 steps in a histogram.
   - **B. Incorrect:** You have one histogram per statistics.
   - **C. Incorrect:** There is a limit of steps per histogram.
   - **D. Correct:** You can have up to 200 steps in a histogram.

Case Scenario 1

1. You should check whether the queries are supported by indexes. In addition, you should check whether the statistics for the indexes are created and updated.
2. You should check whether the queries use appropriate search arguments.

Case Scenario 2

1. Too many indexes might slow updates. You probably created many indexes that are useless; however, because SQL Server has to maintain them, the updates are slow.
2. You can query the sys.dm_db_index_usage_stats dynamic management object to find which indexes are used for seeks and which are used for updates only.

CHAPTER 16

Understanding Cursors, Sets, and Temporary Tables

Exam objectives in this chapter:

- Troubleshoot & Optimize
  - Evaluate the use of row-based operations vs. set-based operations.

This chapter covers two main topics. It starts with a lesson about the differences between row-by-row operations and set-based operations. It then continues with a lesson about the use of temporary objects like local temporary tables and table variables, explaining when you should consider using each kind.

Lessons in this chapter:

- Lesson 1: Evaluating the Use of Cursor/Iterative Solutions vs. Set-Based Solutions
- Lesson 2: Using Temporary Tables vs. Table Variables

Before You Begin

To complete the lessons in this chapter, you must have:

- Experience working with Microsoft SQL Server Management Studio (SSMS).
- Access to a SQL Server 2012 instance with the sample database TSQL2012 installed.
- An understanding of filtering and sorting data.
- An understanding of combining sets.
- An understanding of grouping and windowing.
- An understanding of creating tables and enforcing data integrity.
- An understanding of modifying data.
- An understanding of indexing.

Lesson 1: Evaluating the Use of Cursor/Iterative Solutions vs. Set-Based Solutions

This lesson describes the differences between iterative solutions and set-based solutions for querying tasks. Unless T-SQL is completely new to you, you've probably heard people recommend the use of set-based solutions over iterative solutions. This lesson explains what set-based solutions are and the reason they are recommended. It also explains the circumstances in which you should consider using iterative constructs.

After this lesson, you will be able to:

- Evaluate the use of iterative solutions for operations that have to be done per row.
- Use cursors to perform operations per row.
- Perform operations per row without a cursor.
- Describe why set-based solutions to querying tasks are usually preferable to iterative solutions.

Estimated lesson time: 40 minutes

The Meaning of "Set-Based"

The term *set-based* is used to describe an approach to handle querying tasks and is based on principles from the relational model. Remember that the relational model is based in part on mathematical set theory. Set-based solutions use T-SQL queries, which operate on the input tables as sets of rows. Such solutions are contrasted with iterative solutions that use cursors or other iterative constructs to handle one row at a time.

According to set theory, a set should be considered as a whole. This means that your attention should be focused on the set and not on its individual elements. With iterative solutions, you break this principle by operating on one element (row) at a time. Also, a set has no particular order to its elements. So when you use set-based solutions, you cannot make any assumptions about the order of the data. Similarly, unless you add an ORDER BY clause to the query, you're not guaranteed that the data will be returned in any particular order. With iterative solutions, you process one row at a time and you can do so in a specific order.

As mentioned, it is generally recommended to use set-based solutions by default, and leave iterative solutions to exceptional cases. One of the reasons for this recommendation is that, as explained in Chapter 1, "Foundations of Querying," set theory is the foundation of the relational model, which in turn is the foundation of SQL—the standard language that T-SQL is based on. By using iterative solutions, you're going against the principles of the foundations of the language.

When you use set-based solutions, you provide your request as a declarative plain language query. In your request, you focus on the "what" part of the request and let the database engine worry about the "how" part. With iterative solutions, you need to implement both the what and the how parts in your code. As a result, iterative solutions tend to be much longer than set-based ones and harder to follow and maintain.

Another reason why you should stick to set-based solutions is a very pragmatic one—performance. Iterative constructs in T-SQL are very slow. For one thing, loops in T-SQL are much slower than those in other programming languages such as in Microsoft .NET code. Secondly, each record fetch from a cursor by using the FETCH NEXT command has quite a high overhead associated with it. There's no such overhead when SQL Server processes a set-based solution, even if internally the execution plan for the query involves iterations. As a result, if you know how to tune queries, you are often able to achieve much better performance compared to using iterative solutions. This is demonstrated in an example later in this lesson.

It should be noted that there are exceptional cases where iterative solutions perform better than set-based ones—even with all of the extra overhead for the row-by-row operations. This could happen when the optimizer doesn't manage to produce an efficient plan for the query, and you cannot find ways to tune the query better. With iterative solutions, you do have more control because you are responsible for the how part. So if you understand well how to process the data efficiently one row at a time, you could sometimes achieve better results than what the optimizer achieved for the set-based solution. But again, such cases are the exception, not the norm.

Iterations for Operations That Must Be Done Per Row

It should be understood that some tasks simply have to be handled by using iterative solutions. Consider management tasks that need to be done per object in a set, such as a set of databases, tables, or indexes. You need to query a catalog view or other system object to return the set of objects in question, iterate through the result rows one at a time, and then perform the task at hand per object. An example of such a management task is rebuilding indexes that have a higher level of fragmentation than a specific percentage that you decide on.

As another example of a task that requires an iterative solution, suppose that you have a stored procedure that performs some work for an input customer. The work involves multiple statements implemented in the procedure's body. The logic cannot be implemented for multiple customers at once; it can be implemented only for a single customer.

The following code defines such a procedure, called Sales.ProcessCustomer.

```
USE TSQL2012;

IF OBJECT_ID(N'Sales.ProcessCustomer', N'P') IS NOT NULL
  DROP PROC Sales.ProcessCustomer;
GO

CREATE PROC Sales.ProcessCustomer
(
  @custid AS INT
)
AS

PRINT 'Processing customer ' + CAST(@custid AS VARCHAR(10));
GO
```

The PRINT statement represents the part that would normally implement the work for the input customer. Suppose that you now need to write code that executes the stored procedure for each customer from the Sales.Customers table. You have to iterate through the customer rows one at a time, obtain the customer ID, and execute the procedure with that ID as input.

You can implement a solution by using a cursor. You first use the DECLARE command to declare the cursor based on a query that returns all customer IDs from the Sales.Customers table. You can use the FAST_FORWARD option to make it a read-only, forward-only cursor.

> ***MORE INFO*** **CURSOR TYPES AND OPTIONS**
>
> **For details about the different cursor types and options, see the Books Online for SQL Server 2012 article "DECLARE CURSOR (Transact-SQL)" at *http://msdn.microsoft.com/en-us/library/ms180169.aspx.***

Next, you use the OPEN command to open the cursor. Then you use the FETCH NEXT command to fetch the customer ID from the first cursor record into a variable. You then iterate through the cursor records by using a WHILE loop while the @@FETCH_STATUS function returns 0. The possible return values from the function are: 0 when the previous fetch was successful, -1 when the row is beyond the result set, and -2 when the row fetched is missing. In each iteration of the loop, you execute the Sales.ProcessCustomer procedure by using the current customer ID as input and then fetch the next cursor record. When the loop is done, you use the CLOSE command to close the cursor and the DEALLOCATE command to deallocate it. Here's the complete code implementing this solution.

```
SET NOCOUNT ON;

DECLARE @curcustid AS INT;

DECLARE cust_cursor CURSOR FAST_FORWARD FOR
  SELECT custid
  FROM Sales.Customers;
```

```
OPEN cust_cursor;

FETCH NEXT FROM cust_cursor INTO @curcustid;

WHILE @@FETCH_STATUS = 0
BEGIN
  EXEC Sales.ProcessCustomer @custid = @curcustid;

  FETCH NEXT FROM cust_cursor INTO @curcustid;
END;

CLOSE cust_cursor;

DEALLOCATE cust_cursor;
GO
```

EXAM TIP

During the exam, make sure you carefully read and understand exactly what the requirements of the questions are. It's easy to fall into the trap of trying to choose the answer representing the best or most efficient way to achieve the task at hand, but that's not always what the question is about. It could be that the correct answer to the question isn't what you would consider the most efficient way to achieve the task.

You can also achieve the same task by using another iterative solution, but one that doesn't use a cursor. You can use a query with a TOP (1) option ordered by the custid column to return the minimum customer ID. Then loop while the last query does not return a NULL. In each iteration of the loop, execute the stored procedure by using the current customer ID as input. To get the next customer ID, issue a query with a TOP (1) option, where the custid column is greater than the previous one, ordered by custid. Here's how the complete solution looks.

```
SET NOCOUNT ON;

DECLARE @curcustid AS INT;

SET @curcustid = (SELECT TOP (1) custid
                  FROM Sales.Customers
                  ORDER BY custid);

WHILE @curcustid IS NOT NULL
BEGIN
  EXEC Sales.ProcessCustomer @custid = @curcustid;

  SET @curcustid = (SELECT TOP (1) custid
                    FROM Sales.Customers
                    WHERE custid > @curcustid
                    ORDER BY custid);
END;
GO
```

Some people think that the last solution is set-based because it doesn't explicitly declare and use a cursor object. However, recall that one of the principles implemented by set-based solutions is that they treat the set as a whole as opposed to handling one element at a time. This principle is violated here. Also, set-based solutions do not rely on the order of the data, and this one does.

In terms of performance, the first solution (with the cursor) doesn't really need any special indexes to support it. The second solution (without the cursor) does. You need an index on the custid column. If you don't have one, each query with the TOP option will end up scanning all table rows and apply a TOP N sort in the plan. In other words, without an index, the second solution will perform badly. Even with an index in place, the second solution does more I/O operations than the first because it needs to perform a seek operation in the index per row.

You may have considered another option; to retrieve the minimum and maximum customer IDs from the table, form a loop that keeps incrementing the current customer ID by 1 until it is equal to the maximum. If at any point gaps appear between existing customer IDs (due to deletions or aspects related to the generation of the keys), your code will end up trying to process customer IDs that don't exist in your table. In short, this approach isn't recommended even if currently there are no gaps between keys.

Cursor vs. Set-Based Solutions for Data Manipulation Tasks

As mentioned earlier, as a rule, you should use set-based solutions for querying tasks and consider iterative solutions only for exceptional cases. As explained earlier, set-based solutions tend to be more concise and also usually provide better performance. This section demonstrates how to solve a querying task by using both approaches.

To generate the sample data for the task in this section, you need to use a helper function called GetNums that accepts two integer inputs called @low and @high, and that returns a result set that has a sequence of integers between the two inputs. Use the following code to define the GetNums function:

```
IF OBJECT_ID(N'dbo.GetNums', N'IF') IS NOT NULL DROP FUNCTION dbo.GetNums;
GO
CREATE FUNCTION dbo.GetNums(@low AS BIGINT, @high AS BIGINT) RETURNS TABLE
AS
RETURN
  WITH
    L0   AS (SELECT c FROM (VALUES(1),(1)) AS D(c)),
    L1   AS (SELECT 1 AS c FROM L0 AS A CROSS JOIN L0 AS B),
    L2   AS (SELECT 1 AS c FROM L1 AS A CROSS JOIN L1 AS B),
    L3   AS (SELECT 1 AS c FROM L2 AS A CROSS JOIN L2 AS B),
    L4   AS (SELECT 1 AS c FROM L3 AS A CROSS JOIN L3 AS B),
    L5   AS (SELECT 1 AS c FROM L4 AS A CROSS JOIN L4 AS B),
    Nums AS (SELECT ROW_NUMBER() OVER(ORDER BY (SELECT NULL)) AS rownum
             FROM L5)
  SELECT @low + rownum - 1 AS n
  FROM Nums
  ORDER BY rownum
  OFFSET 0 ROWS FETCH FIRST @high - @low + 1 ROWS ONLY;
GO
```

The task in this section involves querying a table called Transactions that holds information about bank account transactions. The table has three columns: actid (account ID), tranid (incrementing transaction ID), and val (transaction val—positive for a deposit and negative for a withdrawal). The following code creates the Transactions table and fills it with 1,000,000 rows representing 100 accounts, each with 10,000 transactions.

```
IF OBJECT_ID(N'dbo.Transactions', N'U') IS NOT NULL DROP TABLE dbo.Transactions;

CREATE TABLE dbo.Transactions
(
  actid  INT   NOT NULL,                -- partitioning column
  tranid INT   NOT NULL,                -- ordering column
  val    MONEY NOT NULL,                -- measure
  CONSTRAINT PK_Transactions PRIMARY KEY(actid, tranid)
);

DECLARE
  @num_partitions     AS INT = 100,
  @rows_per_partition AS INT - 10000;

TRUNCATE TABLE dbo.Transactions;

INSERT INTO dbo.Transactions WITH (TABLOCK) (actid, tranid, val)
  SELECT NP.n, RPP.n,
    (ABS(CHECKSUM(NEWID())%2)*2-1) * (1 + ABS(CHECKSUM(NEWID())%5))
  FROM dbo.GetNums(1, @num_partitions) AS NP
    CROSS JOIN dbo.GetNums(1, @rows_per_partition) AS RPP;
GO
```

Your task is to implement a solution that computes per each transaction the account balance at that point. The account balance after a specified transaction is computed as the running total of all transaction values from the beginning of the activity in the account and through the current transaction.

The following code implements an iterative solution by using a cursor.

```
SET NOCOUNT ON;
DECLARE @Result AS TABLE
(
  actid   INT,
  tranid  INT,
  val     MONEY,
  balance MONEY
);

DECLARE
  @actid    AS INT,
  @prvactid AS INT,
  @tranid   AS INT,
  @val      AS MONEY,
  @balance  AS MONEY;
```

```
DECLARE C CURSOR FAST_FORWARD FOR
  SELECT actid, tranid, val
  FROM dbo.Transactions
  ORDER BY actid, tranid;

OPEN C

FETCH NEXT FROM C INTO @actid, @tranid, @val;

SELECT @prvactid = @actid, @balance = 0;

WHILE @@fetch_status = 0
BEGIN
  IF @actid <> @prvactid
    SELECT @prvactid = @actid, @balance = 0;

  SET @balance = @balance + @val;

  INSERT INTO @Result VALUES(@actid, @tranid, @val, @balance);

  FETCH NEXT FROM C INTO @actid, @tranid, @val;
END

CLOSE C;

DEALLOCATE C;

SELECT * FROM @Result;
GO
```

The cursor is based on a query that returns the rows from the Transactions table sorted by actid and tranid. The code iterates through the transactions one at a time. As long as the actid value doesn't change, the code adds the current transaction value to what accumulated so far in a variable called *@balance*, and stores a row with the current transaction information and the balance in a table variable called *@Result*. If the current actid value is different than the previous (meaning that the current transaction is the first for a new account), the @balance variable is reset to 0. When the code is done iterating, it queries the *@Result* table variable to return all transactions along with the computed balances after each transaction.

Due to the slowness of iterations in T-SQL and the high overhead of each record fetch from the cursor, it took this code 66 seconds to complete in the system it was run on. And that's after printing was suppressed for the rows in the output by right-clicking an empty area in the query pane and then choosing Query Options | Results | Grid and selecting the Discard Results After Execution check box.

The following is a set-based solution for the same task, using the enhanced window aggregate functions in SQL Server 2012, which were covered in Chapter 5, "Grouping and Windowing."

```
SELECT actid, tranid, val,
  SUM(val) OVER(PARTITION BY actid
               ORDER BY tranid
               ROWS UNBOUNDED PRECEDING) AS balance
FROM dbo.Transactions;
```

The SUM window aggregate function aggregates the values of all transactions placed in the same account (PARTITION BY actid) from the first transaction in the account and through the current transaction (ORDER BY tranid ROWS UNBOUNDED PRECEDING). What's interesting is that this query is optimized by using a single scan of the data. It does not incur the high overhead that is associated with the cursor-based solution. This query finished in four seconds on the system that ran it.

The key to the efficiency of this solution is that there's a difference between the rows that are supposed to be processed conceptually and what the SQL Server Query Optimizer does in practice. Conceptually, for each row, the window function generates a frame of all rows that represent transactions belonging to the same account, from the beginning of the activity in the account and through the current transaction. But in practice, the optimizer realizes that it can simply scan the data once, and to compute the current running total, it can simply add the value of the current row to the running total that was computed for the previous row. This means that this solution has linear scaling. That is, if the number of rows per account increases by a factor of *f*, the work also increases by a factor of *f*. Therefore, the run time will be affected in a similar manner.

Note that some set-based solutions don't scale that well either. Consider for example the following set-based solution for the same task.

```
SELECT T1.actid, T1.tranid, T1.val,
  SUM(T2.val) AS balance
FROM dbo.Transactions AS T1
  JOIN dbo.Transactions AS T2
    ON T2.actid = T1.actid
   AND T2.tranid <= T1.tranid
GROUP BY T1.actid, T1.tranid, T1.val;
```

Conceptually, this solution matches to each row from the instance of Transactions aliased as T1 all rows that have the same actid value as the current row and a tranid value that is less than or equal to the current row. The problem is that unlike the solution with the window function, the plan for this query also physically processes that many rows. Here the optimizer doesn't use a fast-track optimization that scans the data only once. You end up with quadratic (N2) scaling. That is, if the number of rows per account increases by a factor of *f*, the work increases by a factor of f^2, and the run time similarly increases. This query took 46 minutes and 53 seconds to complete on the system.

The solution using the window function is not supported prior to SQL Server 2012. So in previous versions, a cursor-based solution is actually faster, unless the number of rows per account is very, very small. But in SQL Server 2012, the set-based solution using the window function is much faster and has linear scaling, so it is of course the recommended one.

Quick Check

1. **What are the commands that are required to work with a cursor?**
2. **When using the FAST_FORWARD option in the cursor declaration command, what does it mean regarding the cursor properties?**

Quick Check Answer

1. **DECLARE, OPEN, FETCH in a loop, CLOSE, and DEALLOCATE.**
2. **That the cursor is read-only, forward-only.**

PRACTICE Evaluating Cursor-Based vs. Set-Based Solutions

In this practice, you evaluate the use of cursor/iterative solutions versus set-based solutions.

If you encounter a problem completing an exercise, you can install the completed projects from the companion content for this chapter and lesson.

EXERCISE 1 Compute an Aggregate by Using a Cursor

In this exercise, you use the dbo.Transactions table from the lesson. You observe the computing performance of the maximum value (val column) per account (actid column) by using a cursor-based solution.

1. Open SSMS and connect to the sample database TSQL2012.
2. Create an index on the actid and val columns to support the maximum aggregate computation.

```
USE TSQL2012;
CREATE INDEX idx_actid_val ON dbo.Transactions(actid, val);
```

3. Write a cursor-based solution to handle the task at hand. You can use the cursor example from the lesson as the basis for your code to iterate through the rows in the Transactions table. However, this time, compute the maximum transaction value per account. Your solution should look like the following.

```
SET NOCOUNT ON;
DECLARE @Result AS TABLE
(
  actid INT,
  mx    MONEY
);
```

```
DECLARE
  @actid     AS INT,
  @val       AS MONEY,
  @prevactid AS INT,
  @prevval   AS MONEY;

DECLARE tx_cursor CURSOR FAST_FORWARD FOR
  SELECT actid, val
  FROM dbo.Transactions
  ORDER BY actid, val;

OPEN tx_cursor;

FETCH NEXT FROM tx_cursor INTO @actid, @val;

SELECT @prevactid = @actid, @prevval = @val;

WHILE @@FETCH_STATUS = 0
BEGIN
  IF @actid <> @prevactid
    INSERT INTO @Result(actid, mx)
      VALUES(@prevactid, @prevval);

  SELECT @prevactid = @actid, @prevval = @val;

  FETCH NEXT FROM tx_cursor INTO @actid, @val;
END

IF @prevactid IS NOT NULL
  INSERT INTO @Result(actid, mx)
    VALUES(@prevactid, @prevval);

CLOSE tx_cursor;

DEALLOCATE tx_cursor;

SELECT actid, mx
FROM @Result;
GO
```

4. Take note of the run time of the solution on your system. When this solution ran on the test computer, it took 21 seconds to complete. Most of the run time was due to iterations and cursor overhead.

EXERCISE 2 Compute an Aggregate by Using a Set-Based Solution

In this exercise, you handle the same task as in the previous exercise, but this time with a set-based solution. You then compare the performance of the two solutions.

1. Write a set-based solution to the task presented in the previous exercise. The set-based solution in this case is a very simple grouped query. Your code should look like the following.

```
SELECT actid, MAX(val) AS mx
FROM dbo.Transactions
GROUP BY actid;
```

2. Take note of the run time of the set-based solution in your system and compare it to the performance of the cursor-based solution. When this query ran on the test computer, it took less than a second to complete. Recall that the cursor-based solution ran for 21 seconds.

Lesson Summary

- You can use one of two main approaches to handle querying tasks; one is using set-based solutions and the other is using iterative solutions.
- Set-based solutions essentially use SQL queries that follow principles from the relational model. They interact with the input tables (sets) as a whole, as opposed to interacting with one row at a time. They also don't assume that the data will be consumed or returned in a particular order.
- Some tasks have to be handled with iterative solutions, such as management tasks that need to be handled per object or a stored procedure that you need to execute per row in a table.
- Regarding querying tasks, generally it is recommended to use set-based solutions as your default choice, and reserve the use of iterative solutions for exceptional cases.

Lesson Review

Answer the following questions to test your knowledge of the information in this lesson. You can find the answers to these questions and explanations of why each answer choice is correct or incorrect in the "Answers" section at the end of this chapter.

1. When you fetch rows from a cursor, how do you know when there are no more rows to fetch?
   - **A.** When the @@FETCH_STATUS function returns 0
   - **B.** When the @@FETCH_STATUS function returns -1
   - **C.** When the @@FETCH_STATUS function returns -2
   - **D.** When the @@FETCH_STATUS function generates an error

2. Why is it important to prefer set-based solutions for querying tasks instead of iterative ones? (Choose all that apply.)
   - **A.** Because set-based solutions are based on the relational model, which is the foundation of T-SQL
   - **B.** Because set-based solutions always provide better performance than iterative solutions
   - **C.** Because set-based solutions usually involve less code than iterative solutions
   - **D.** Because set-based solutions enable you to rely on the order of data
3. When you need to operate on one row at a time, what are the alternatives to using a cursor?
   - **A.** Using the FOR EACH looping construct.
   - **B.** Retrieving the minimum and maximum keys, and then looping with a counter that starts with the minimum and keeps being incremented by 1 in each iteration until it reaches the maximum.
   - **C.** Using a TOP (1) query ordered by the key to fetch the first row. Then use a loop while the last key returned is not NULL. In each iteration of the loop, process the current row and then use a TOP (1) query where the key is greater than the last, ordered by the key, to fetch the next row.
   - **D.** Define a per-row SELECT trigger.

Lesson 2: Using Temporary Tables vs. Table Variables

SQL Server supports a number of options that you can use to store data temporarily. You can use temporary tables and table variables. This lesson describes these object types and the differences between them.

After this lesson, you will be able to:

- Describe the difference in scope between temporary tables and table variables.
- Describe DDL and indexing support for temporary objects.
- Describe the physical representation of temporary tables, table variables, and table expressions.
- Describe transactional support for temporary objects.
- Describe how statistics are handled for temporary objects.

Estimated lesson time: 40 minutes

Scope

SQL Server supports two types of temporary tables—local and global—as well as table variables. This section describes the differences in terms of scope, or visibility, between the three types of objects.

Local temporary tables are named with a single number sign as a prefix; for example, #T1. They are visible only to the session that created them. Different sessions can actually create temporary tables with the same name, and each session will see only its own table. Behind the scenes, SQL Server adds unique suffixes to make the names unique in the database, but this is transparent to the sessions.

Local temporary tables are visible throughout the level that created them, across batches, and in all inner levels of the call stack. So if you create a temporary table in a specific level in your code and then execute a dynamic batch or a stored procedure, the inner batch can access the temporary table. If you don't drop the temporary table explicitly, it is destroyed when the level that created it terminates.

Global temporary tables are named with two number signs as a prefix; for example, ##T1. They are visible to all sessions. They are destroyed when the session that created them terminates and there are no active references to them.

Table variables are declared, as opposed to being created. They are named with the at sign (@) as a prefix; for example, *@T1*. They are visible only to the batch that declared them and are destroyed automatically at the end of the batch. They are not visible across batches in the same level, and are also not visible to inner levels in the call stack.

The following code demonstrates that local temporary tables are visible across batches in the same level in addition to in inner levels in the call stack.

```
CREATE TABLE #T1
(
  col1 INT NOT NULL
);

INSERT INTO #T1(col1) VALUES(10);

EXEC('SELECT col1 FROM #T1;');
GO

SELECT col1 FROM #T1;
GO

DROP TABLE #T1;
GO
```

The code runs successfully without any errors.

The following code demonstrates that table variables aren't visible to inner levels in the call stack.

```
DECLARE @T1 AS TABLE
(
  col1 INT NOT NULL
);

INSERT INTO @T1(col1) VALUES(10);

EXEC('SELECT col1 FROM @T1;');
GO
```

The attempt to refer to the table variable from the dynamic batch generates the following error.

```
Msg 1087, Level 15, State 2, Line 1
Must declare the table variable "@T1".
```

The following code demonstrates that table variables are not visible even across batches in the same level.

```
DECLARE @T1 AS TABLE
(
  col1 INT NOT NULL
);

INSERT INTO @T1(col1) VALUES(10);
GO

SELECT col1 FROM @T1;
GO
```

The SELECT query against the table variable fails with the following error.

```
Msg 1087, Level 15, State 2, Line 2
Must declare the table variable "@T1".
```

DDL and Indexes

This section covers data definition language (DDL) and indexing aspects of temporary tables and table variables. It covers aspects of constraint naming and the ability to define indexes on temporary objects.

You should be aware of what could be a surprising thing to some people regarding the use of constraint names in temporary tables. As it turns out, constraint names are considered object names in the schema, and object names must be unique per schema—not per table. So two tables cannot have constraints with the same name in the same schema.

Temporary tables are created in tempdb in the dbo schema. As already mentioned, you can create two temporary tables with the same name in different sessions, because SQL Server internally adds a unique suffix to each. But if you create temporary tables in different sessions with the same constraint name, only one will be created and the other attempts will fail.

As an example, try creating the following temporary table in two different sessions.

```
CREATE TABLE #T1
(
  col1 INT  NOT NULL,
  col2 INT  NOT NULL,
  col3 DATE NOT NULL,
  CONSTRAINT PK_#T1 PRIMARY KEY(col1)
);
```

The first attempt succeeds, but the second attempt fails with the following error.

```
Msg 2714, Level 16, State 5, Line 1
There is already an object named 'PK_#T1' in the database.
Msg 1750, Level 16, State 0, Line 1
Could not create constraint. See previous errors.
```

The reason for the failure is that the code names the primary key constraint PK_#T1, and SQL Server does not allow two occurrences of the same constraint name within the same schema.

Run the following code to drop the table in the session where the table creation attempt was successful.

```
DROP TABLE #T1;
```

If you define a constraint without naming it, SQL Server internally creates a unique name for it. The recommendation therefore is not to name constraints in temporary tables. Here's the revised table definition, this time without naming the constraint.

```
CREATE TABLE #T1
(
  col1 INT  NOT NULL,
  col2 INT  NOT NULL,
  col3 DATE NOT NULL,
  PRIMARY KEY(col1)
);
```

Run this code from two different sessions. Note that both attempts are successful this time.

With SQL Server, you can create indexes on temporary tables after the table is created. For example, the following code creates an index on the table #T1 you just created.

```
CREATE UNIQUE NONCLUSTERED INDEX idx_col2 ON #T1(col2);
```

You can also alter the table definition and apply definition changes, like adding a constraint or a column.

When you're done, run the following code to drop the table #T1 in all sessions where you created it.

```
DROP TABLE #T1;
```

With table variables, SQL Server doesn't allow explicit naming of constraints—not even in a single session. Try running the following code to attempt to declare a table variable that has a named constraint.

```
DECLARE @T1 AS TABLE
(
  col1 INT  NOT NULL,
  col2 INT  NOT NULL,
  col3 DATE NOT NULL,
  CONSTRAINT PK_@T1 PRIMARY KEY(col1)
);
```

The attempt fails with the following error.

```
Msg 156, Level 15, State 2, Line 6
Incorrect syntax near the keyword 'CONSTRAINT'.
```

Try again without naming the constraint.

```
DECLARE @T1 AS TABLE
(
  col1 INT  NOT NULL,
  col2 INT  NOT NULL,
  col3 DATE NOT NULL,
  PRIMARY KEY(col1)
);
```

This time the table is declared successfully.

SQL Server doesn't allow the creation of indexes on a table variable after the table is declared. However, recall that when you define a primary key constraint, SQL Server enforces its uniqueness by using a unique clustered index by default. When you define a unique constraint, SQL Server enforces its uniqueness by using a unique nonclustered index by default. So if you want to define indexes on a table variable, you can do so indirectly by defining constraints. The following example demonstrates this by declaring a table variable that has both a primary key and a unique constraint, creating clustered and nonclustered indexes, respectively.

```
DECLARE @T1 AS TABLE
(
  col1 INT  NOT NULL,
  col2 INT  NOT NULL,
  col3 DATE NOT NULL,
  PRIMARY KEY(col1),
  UNIQUE(col2)
);
```

Physical Representation in tempdb

There's a common misconception that only temporary tables have a physical representation in tempdb and that table variables reside only in memory. This isn't true. Both temporary tables and table variables have a physical representation in tempdb.

You can find entries in the sys.objects view for the internal tables that SQL Server creates in tempdb to implement your temporary tables and table variables. As an example, the following code creates a temporary table called #T1 and then queries the sys.objects view in tempdb looking for table names starting with #.

```
CREATE TABLE #T1
(
  col1 INT NOT NULL
);

INSERT INTO #T1(col1) VALUES(10);

SELECT name FROM tempdb.sys.objects WHERE name LIKE '#%';

DROP TABLE #T1;
GO
```

This code generated the following output in the test system:

```
name
----------
#T1_____________________________________________________________________________________________________________________000000000018
```

As mentioned earlier, SQL Server internally adds a suffix to the user-assigned table names to prevent name conflicts in case multiple sessions create a temporary table with the same name.

The following code demonstrates how to declare a table variable and then query the sys.objects view.

```
DECLARE @T1 AS TABLE
(
  col1 INT NOT NULL
);

INSERT INTO @T1(col1) VALUES(10);

SELECT name FROM tempdb.sys.objects WHERE name LIKE '#%';
```

When this code ran on the test system, it produced the following output.

```
name
----------
#BD095663
```

As you can see, SQL Server created a table in tempdb to implement the table variable you declared.

A common question is whether table expressions such as common table expressions (CTEs) also get persisted like temporary tables and table variables. The answer is no. When SQL Server optimizes a query against a table expression, it unnests the inner query's logic and interacts directly with the underlying tables. This means that unlike temporary tables and table variables, table expressions have no physical side to them.

Transactions

Temporary tables and table variables differ in how they interact with transactions. Temporary tables are similar to regular tables in this respect. Changes applied to a temporary table are undone if the transaction rolls back. The following example demonstrates this behavior.

```
CREATE TABLE #T1
(
  col1 INT NOT NULL
);

BEGIN TRAN

  INSERT INTO #T1(col1) VALUES(10);

ROLLBACK TRAN

SELECT col1 FROM #T1;

DROP TABLE #T1;
GO
```

The code creates a temporary table, opens a transaction, inserts a row, rolls back the transaction, and queries the table. This code generates the following output, which shows that the work in the transaction was undone.

```
col1
-----------
```

As with normal variables, changes applied to table variables in a transaction are not undone if the transaction rolls back. The following test demonstrates this behavior.

```
DECLARE @T1 AS TABLE
(
  col1 INT NOT NULL
);

BEGIN TRAN

  INSERT INTO @T1(col1) VALUES(10);

ROLLBACK TRAN

SELECT col1 FROM @T1;
```

This code generates the following output, which shows that the work done in the transaction wasn't undone.

```
col1
-----------
10
```

Note that a single statement against a table variable must be atomic, so if the statement fails before completion, the partial change is undone. But if the single statement finishes and a user transaction is rolled back, such a change isn't undone. This is quite useful for error handling if you need to log information in a transaction that you roll back.

Statistics

When it comes to performance, there's a very important difference between temporary tables and table variables. SQL Server maintains distribution statistics (*histograms*) for temporary tables but not for table variables. This means that, generally speaking, you tend to get more optimal plans for temporary tables. This comes at the cost of maintaining histograms, and at the cost of recompilations that are associated with histogram refreshes.

To demonstrate, the following provides an example in which the existence of a histogram leads to an optimal plan, and the lack of a histogram leads to a suboptimal plan. To measure the I/O costs of the queries in your session, run the following code.

```
SET STATISTICS IO ON;
```

Use the following code to create a temporary table and populate it with a million rows.

```
CREATE TABLE #T1
(
  col1 INT  NOT NULL,
  col2 INT  NOT NULL,
  col3 DATE NOT NULL,
  PRIMARY KEY(col1),
  UNIQUE(col2)
);

INSERT INTO #T1(col1, col2, col3)
  SELECT n, n * 2, CAST(SYSDATETIME() AS DATE)
  FROM dbo.GetNums(1, 1000000);
```

The code defines a primary key constraint with col1 as the key, creating a clustered index behind the scenes. It also defines a unique constraint with col2 as the key, creating a non clustered index behind the scenes. Turn on the Include Actual Query Plan option by pressing Ctrl + M in SSMS, and then run the following code.

```
SELECT col1, col2, col3
FROM #T1
WHERE col2 <= 5;
```

SQL Server creates the plan shown in Figure 16-1 for this query.

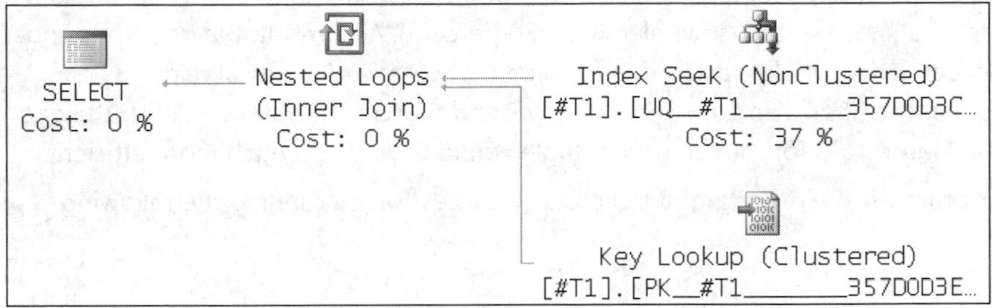

FIGURE 16-1 A plan for a temporary table.

This plan is very efficient. The optimizer examined the histogram on col2 and estimated that a very small number of rows are supposed to be filtered. The plan decided to use the index on col2 because the filter is very selective. Only a small number of key lookups are required to obtain the respective data rows. For such a selective filter, this plan is preferable to one that does a full clustered index scan. The STATISTICS IO option reports that only nine logical reads were required to process this plan.

Run the following code to drop the temporary table.

```
DROP TABLE #T1;
```

Use the following code to run a similar test, but this time use a table variable.

```
DECLARE @T1 AS TABLE
(
  col1 INT  NOT NULL,
  col2 INT  NOT NULL,
  col3 DATE NOT NULL,
  PRIMARY KEY(col1),
  UNIQUE(col2)
);

INSERT INTO @T1(col1, col2, col3)
  SELECT n, n * 2, CAST(SYSDATETIME() AS DATE)
  FROM dbo.GetNums(1, 1000000);

SELECT col1, col2, col3
FROM @T1
WHERE col2 <= 5;
GO
```

The plan for this query is shown in Figure 16-2.

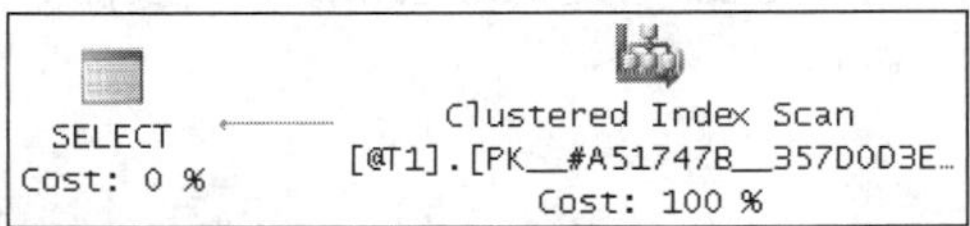

FIGURE 16-2 A plan for a table variable.

Unlike with temporary tables, SQL Server doesn't maintain histograms for table variables. Not being able to accurately estimate the selectivity of the filter, the optimizer relies on hard-coded estimates that assume fairly low selectivity (30 percent). As a result, the optimizer ends up choosing to perform a whole clustered index scan that costs 2,485 logical reads. It just doesn't realize that the filter is actually very selective, and that a plan more similar to the one shown earlier in Figure 16-1 for the temporary table would have been much more efficient.

You can now turn off the reporting of I/O costs in the session by running the following code.

```
SET STATISTICS IO OFF;
```

The conclusion from this example is that when the plan efficiency depends on existence of histograms, you should use temporary tables. Table variables are fine to use in two general cases. One is when the volume of data is so small, like a page or two, that the efficiency of the plan isn't important. The other case is when the plan is trivial. A *trivial plan* means that there's only one sensible plan and the optimizer doesn't really need histograms to come up with this conclusion. An example for such a plan is a range scan in a clustered index or a covering index. Such a plan is not dependent on selectivity of the filter—it's simply always a better option than a full scan.

Quick Check

1. **How do you create a local temporary table, and how do you create a global one?**
2. **Can you name constraints in local temporary tables and in table variables?**

Quick Check Answer

1. **You name a local temporary table by using a single number sign as a prefix and a global one with two number signs as a prefix.**
2. **You can name constraints in local temporary tables, although it's not recommended because it can generate name conflicts. You cannot name constraints in table variables.**

PRACTICE Choosing an Optimal Temporary Object

In this practice, you exercise your knowledge of temporary objects.

If you encounter a problem completing an exercise, you can install the completed projects from the companion content for this chapter and lesson.

EXERCISE 1 Compare Current Counts of Orders to Previous Yearly Counts of Orders by Using CTEs

In this exercise, you are given a task and use a CTE to solve it. The task involves querying the Sales.Orders table to compute the count of orders per year. You need to return the current year's order count for each year, and the difference between the current and the previous year's counts. The solution needs to be compatible with SQL Server 2005 and SQL Server 2008, so you cannot rely on features added in SQL Server 2012.

1. Open SSMS and connect to the TSQL2012 sample database.
2. Write a query that computes the count of orders per year and request to include the actual execution plan by pressing Ctrl+M in SSMS. Your query should look like the following.

```
SELECT YEAR(orderdate) AS orderyear, COUNT(*) AS numorders
FROM Sales.Orders
GROUP BY YEAR(orderdate);
```

SQL Server generates the plan shown in Figure 16-3 for this query.

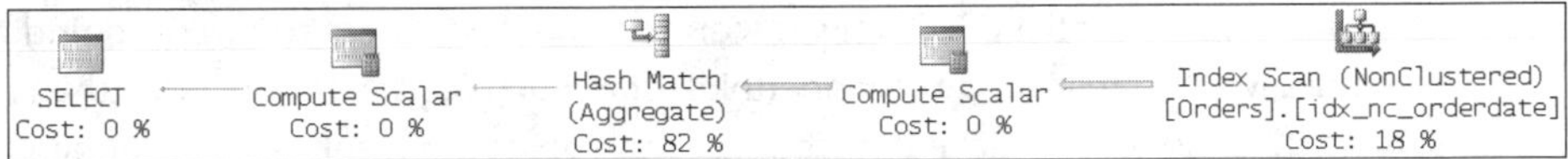

FIGURE 16-3 A plan for a grouped query.

The plan shows that the index idx_nc_orderdate is scanned to obtain all order dates and then the data is grouped and aggregated.

3. Write a solution for the task at hand by using a CTE. Namely, define a CTE based on the query in step 2. In the outer query, join two instances of the CTE to match each year's row with the respective previous year's row. Then compute the difference between the current and previous yearly counts. Your solution should look like the following.

```
WITH YearlyCounts AS
(
  SELECT YEAR(orderdate) AS orderyear, COUNT(*) AS numorders
  FROM Sales.Orders
  GROUP BY YEAR(orderdate)
)
SELECT C.orderyear, C.numorders, C.numorders - P.numorders AS diff
FROM YearlyCounts AS C
  INNER JOIN YearlyCounts AS P
    ON C.orderyear = P.orderyear + 1;
```

4. Examine the execution plan shown in Figure 16-4, which SQL Server generated for this query.

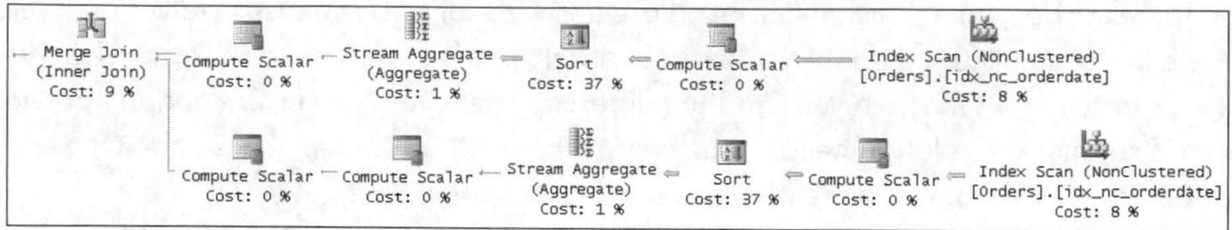

FIGURE 16-4 A plan for the solution using CTEs.

Notice that the work involving scanning the index, in addition to grouping and aggregating the data, was done twice.

EXERCISE 2 Compare Current Counts of Orders to Previous Yearly Counts of Orders by Using Table Variables

In this exercise, you handle the same task as in the previous exercise, but this time by using a table variable.

1. The solution that used a CTE involved scanning the data twice. You want to find a solution that avoids duplicating the work (think of a much bigger Orders table than in the sample database). To achieve this, you need to persist the result of the grouped query in a temporary table or table variable, and then join two instances of the temporary object. Because the result set that needs to be persisted in this case is so small, a table variable would do. Your solution should look like the following.

```
DECLARE @YearlyCounts AS TABLE
(
  orderyear INT NOT NULL,
  numorders INT NOT NULL,
  PRIMARY KEY(orderyear)
);

INSERT INTO @YearlyCounts(orderyear, numorders)
  SELECT YEAR(orderdate) AS orderyear, COUNT(*) AS numorders
  FROM Sales.Orders
  GROUP BY YEAR(orderdate);

SELECT C.orderyear, C.numorders, C.numorders - P.numorders AS diff
FROM @YearlyCounts AS C
  INNER JOIN @YearlyCounts AS P
    ON C.orderyear = P.orderyear + 1;
```

2. Examine the plan SQL Server generates for this solution, which is shown in Figure 16-5.

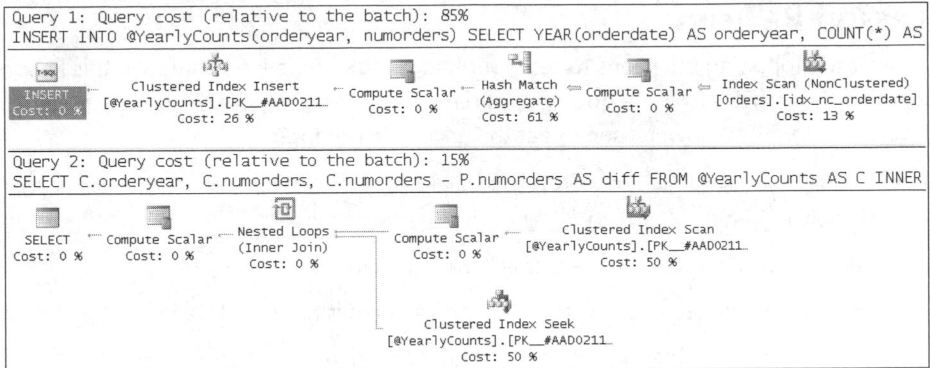

FIGURE 16-5 A plan for a solution using table variables.

Notice that the work that involves scanning, grouping, and aggregating the data is done only once (the top part of the plan). The result is stored in a table variable. Then the bottom part of the plan shows the join between the two instances of the small table variable.

Lesson Summary

- You can use temporary tables and table variables when you need to temporarily store data such as an intermediate result set of a query.
- Temporary tables and table variables differ in a number of ways, including scope, DDL and indexing, interaction with transactions, and distribution statistics.
- Local temporary tables are visible in the level that created them, across batches, and also in inner levels in the call stack. Table variables are visible only to the batch that declared them.
- You can apply a DDL to a temporary table after it is created, including creating indexes and other DDL changes. You cannot apply DDL changes to a table variable after it is declared. You can get indexes indirectly in a table variable through primary key and unique constraints.
- Changes applied to a temporary table in a transaction are undone if the transaction is rolled back. Changes against a table variable are not undone if the user transaction is rolled back.
- SQL Server maintains distribution statistics on temporary tables but not on table variables. As a result, the plans for queries using temporary tables tend to be more optimized compared to those for queries using table variables.

Lesson Review

Answer the following questions to test your knowledge of the information in this lesson. You can find the answers to these questions and explanations of why each answer choice is correct or incorrect in the "Answers" section at the end of this chapter.

1. Which of the following cases is suitable for using table variables? (Choose all that apply.)
   - **A.** When the tables are very small and the plan is trivial
   - **B.** When the tables are very small and the plan is nontrivial
   - **C.** When the tables are large and the plan is trivial
   - **D.** When the tables are large and the plan is nontrivial
2. Can you have indexes on table variables?
   - **A.** No
   - **B.** Yes, by running the CREATE INDEX command
   - **C.** Yes, indirectly by defining primary key and unique constraints
   - **D.** Yes, by defining foreign keys
3. You are tasked with implementing a trigger. As part of the trigger's code in specific conditions, you need to roll back the transaction. However, you need to copy the data from the inserted and deleted tables in the trigger into audit tables to keep track of what was supposed to be changed. How can you achieve this?
   - **A.** Roll back the transaction, and then copy the data from the inserted and deleted tables into the audit tables.
   - **B.** Copy the data from the inserted and deleted tables into the audit tables and then roll back the transaction.
   - **C.** Copy the rows from the inserted and deleted tables into temporary tables, roll back the transaction, and then copy the data from the temporary tables into the audit tables.
   - **D.** Copy the rows from the inserted and deleted tables into table variables, roll back the transaction, and then copy the data from the table variables into the audit tables.

Case Scenarios

In the following case scenarios, you apply what you've learned about cursors, sets, and temporary tables. You can find the answers to these questions in the "Answers" section at the end of this chapter.

Case Scenario 1: Performance Improvement Recommendations for Cursors and Temporary Objects

You are hired as a consultant by a startup company who develops an application that uses SQL Server as the database. The company is currently facing performance and scalability problems. You examine the company's code and identify a number of things.

Almost all solutions use cursors. When you examine the solutions you see that they are not the types that have to be implemented with iterative logic.

Some solutions store intermediate results in table variables and then query the table variables. Large numbers of rows are stored in the table variables.

1. Can you provide recommendations concerning the fact that most solutions use cursors?
2. Can you provide recommendations concerning the use of table variables?
3. Can you explain to the customer what the circumstances are in which cursors and table variables should be used?

Case Scenario 2: Identifying Inaccuracies in Answers

At a conference, you attend a lecture about T-SQL. At the end of the lecture, the speaker conducts a Q&A session. Following are questions members of the audience present to the speaker and the speaker's answers. Identify the inaccuracies in the speaker's responses.

1. **Q:** From a performance perspective, what are the differences between temporary tables and table variables?

   A: There are no differences. Microsoft just wants to give you a dozen different ways to do the same thing.

2. **Q:** I have a multirow UPDATE trigger that sets the value of a column called lastmod in the modified rows to the value returned by the function SYSDATETIME(). The trigger uses a cursor against the inserted table to handle one row at a time. The trigger performs badly. Any suggestions on how to improve the trigger's performance?

   A: Instead of using a cursor, write a set-based solution that uses a WHILE loop and a TOP query to iterate through the keys one at a time.

3. **Q:** Can you give an example for which table expressions are useful?

   A: One example is when you want to persist the result of an expensive query and then need to refer to that result a number of times.

Suggested Practices

To help you successfully master the exam objectives presented in this chapter, complete the following tasks.

Identify Differences

In this practice, you test your memory of the differences between the different temporary objects and between relational and iterative solutions to querying tasks.

- **Practice 1** Without looking back at the text of the lesson, try to fill Table 16-1 with the characteristics of temporary tables, table variables, and table expressions with respect to the listed items. When you're done, go over the sections in the lesson to check whether you were right and correct the items where you weren't.

TABLE 16-1 Comparing temporary objects

	Temporary table	Table variable	Table expression
Scope			
Can apply DDL after creation/declaration?			
Can have indexes?			
Affected by ROLLBACK?			
Has distribution statistics?			
Has physical presence in tempdb?			
Suitable for what table size?			

- **Practice 2** Again, from memory, list the differences between relational and iterative solutions to querying tasks.

Answers

This section contains the answers to the lesson review questions and solutions to the case scenarios in this chapter.

Lesson 1

1. **Correct Answer: B**
   - **A. Incorrect:** 0 means that the last fetch was successful. There could be more rows.
   - **B. Correct:** -1 means that the row is beyond the result set.
   - **C. Incorrect:** -2 means that the row fetched is missing. There still could be more rows.
   - **D. Incorrect:** The function shouldn't generate any errors.
2. **Correct Answers: A and C**
   - **A. Correct:** Set-based solutions are based on principles from the relational model, and this model is the foundation of SQL (the standard language) and T-SQL (the dialect in SQL Server).
   - **B. Incorrect:** Although it is not common, sometimes iterative solutions are faster than set-based ones.
   - **C. Correct:** Because set-based solutions are declarative and iterative solutions are imperative, set-based solutions tend to involve less code.
   - **D. Incorrect:** Set-based solutions cannot make any assumptions regarding the order of the data because sets are unordered.
3. **Correct Answer: C**
   - **A. Incorrect:** T-SQL doesn't support a FOR EACH loop.
   - **B. Incorrect:** In case there are gaps between keys, this approach will result in an attempt to treat nonexistent keys.
   - **C. Correct:** This approach with the TOP option does give you a correct alternative to a cursor. However, you need to think about the fact that it is more I/O-intensive.
   - **D. Incorrect:** There are no SELECT triggers or per-row triggers in T-SQL.

Lesson 2

1. **Correct Answers: A, B, and C**
   - **A. Correct:** Table variables are suitable when the tables are very small.
   - **B. Correct:** Table variables are suitable when the tables are very small.
   - **C. Correct:** When the plan is trivial, table variables are still suitable even if they are large.
   - **D. Incorrect:** When the tables are large and the plan is nontrivial, temporary tables are preferable.
2. **Correct Answer: C**
   - **A. Incorrect:** You can have indexes on table variables.
   - **B. Incorrect:** The CREATE INDEX command is not supported against table variables.
   - **C. Correct:** You can get indexes indirectly by defining primary key and unique constraints.
   - **D. Incorrect:** Foreign keys do not create indexes; besides, they are not supported on temporary tables and table variables.
3. **Correct Answer: D**
   - **A. Incorrect:** After you roll back the transaction in the trigger, the inserted and deleted tables are emptied.
   - **B. Incorrect:** The rollback causes the copying to the audit tables to be undone.
   - **C. Incorrect:** Changes against temporary tables are undone after you roll back a transaction.
   - **D. Correct:** Changes against table variables aren't undone if you roll back a transaction, so this solution works correctly.

Case Scenario 1

1. The customer should evaluate the use of set-based solutions instead of cursor-based ones. If most of their solutions are using cursors, there could be a problem with a lack of knowledge and understanding of relational concepts. It would probably be a good idea to recommend to the company that its developers take training on the subject.
2. When large numbers of rows need to be stored in the temporary object, the optimizer's ability to produce accurate selectivity estimates becomes more important for the efficiency of the plan. The one exception is when the plans are trivial. SQL Server does not maintain distribution statistics (histograms) on table variables, so with those, the estimates tend to be inaccurate. Inaccurate estimates can lead to suboptimal plans. The customer should examine the query plans and look for bad estimates. And if

they find them, they should evaluate whether to use temporary tables in those cases instead. SQL Server does maintain histograms for temporary tables, and therefore the execution plans for those tend to be more optimal.

3. In some cases, it's appropriate to use table variables—for example, when the amount of data is very small, like a page or two. In such a case, the efficiency of the plan is simply not important. Also, when the table is large but the plan is trivial, the optimizer doesn't need histograms in order to choose an efficient plan. The fact that table variables don't have histograms does give you some benefits. You don't pay the costs associated with maintaining them. You also don't pay for recompilations of the execution plans that are related to refreshes of the histograms.

   As for cursors, in some cases, you have to run a process per each row from a table. For example, for maintenance purposes you might need to perform some work per each index, table, database, or other object. Cursors are designed for such purposes. As for data manipulation, there could be cases where the SQL Server Query Optimizer doesn't do a good job optimizing a query, and you cannot find a way to help the optimizer generate an efficient plan. With cursors, despite the higher overhead, sometimes you can achieve better results because you do have more control. But such cases are the exception rather than the norm.

Case Scenario 2

1. There are performance-related differences between temporary tables and table variables. One important difference is the fact that SQL Server maintains distribution statistics (histograms) against temporary tables but not against table variables. This means that with temporary tables, the optimizer can usually make better selectivity estimates. So the plans involving temporary tables tend to be more optimal than plans involving table variables.

2. Using a loop-based solution with a TOP query instead of a cursor neither makes the solution set-based nor necessarily more efficient than the existing cursor-based solution. You're still handling the rows one at a time. A better approach would be to use a single UPDATE or MERGE statement that joins the inserted table with the underlying table, and update all target rows by using one set-based operation.

3. The result of the table expression's inner query doesn't get persisted in a work table. SQL Server unnests all references to table expressions and interacts with the underlying objects directly. Multiple references get unnested multiple times, so the work is repeated. If you want to persist the result of an expensive query to avoid repeating the work, you should consider using temporary tables or table variables. An example of the usefulness of table expressions is when you need to refer to a column alias that was generated in the SELECT list in clauses that are logically processed before the SELECT, like WHERE, GROUP BY, and HAVING.

CHAPTER 17

Understanding Further Optimization Aspects

Exam objectives in this chapter:

- Troubleshoot & Optimize
  - Optimize queries.

In Chapter 15, "Implementing Indexes and Statistics," you learned internals about indexes and statistics in Microsoft SQL Server. In Chapter 14, "Using Tools to Analyze Query Performance," you learned about the tools that help you analyze how a query was executed. In this chapter, you learn how SQL Server finds the data your query requests. SQL Server has different access methods for data retrieval. In addition, SQL Server implements different join algorithms. You learn about those and their strengths and weaknesses in this chapter.

SQL Server can reuse a query plan, even if the subsequent query is not the same. For example, the subsequent query can change a value for a search condition in the WHERE clause of the query. SQL Server tries to parameterize ad hoc queries in order to enable execution plan reuse. Besides this auto-parameterization, you can parameterize your queries as well—for example, by using them in stored procedures.

You can influence query execution by using *hints* in SQL Server. Hints are orders about how to execute a query. You can use *table hints*, which are hints for which you specify how to use a specific table in a query; and *query hints*, which are hints on a query level, for which you specify, for example, which join algorithms should be used for a specific query. You can also use *join hints* for a single join only. Finally, you can prescribe the complete query execution by using plan guides.

Lessons in this chapter:

- Lesson 1: Understanding Plan Iterators
- Lesson 2: Using Parameterized Queries and Batch Operations
- Lesson 3: Using Optimizer Hints and Plan Guides

Before You Begin

To complete the lessons in this chapter, you must have:

- An understanding of relational database concepts.
- Experience working with SQL Server Management Studio (SSMS).
- Some experience writing T-SQL code.
- Access to a SQL Server 2012 instance with the sample database TSQL2012 installed.

Lesson 1: Understanding Plan Iterators

As you already know from Chapter 14, SQL Server executes a query by using a set of physical operators. Because these operators iterate through rowsets, they are also called *iterators*. In this lesson, you learn details about some of the most important iterators: those used to access data, perform joins, and do other activities in order to retrieve the desired results.

After this lesson, you will be able to:

- Understand different SQL Server access methods.
- Describe join algorithms.
- Understand other important plan iterators.

Estimated lesson time: 50 minutes

Access Methods

If a table is organized as a heap and does not have any nonclustered indexes, then the only access method available to SQL Server is a *table scan*. The scan is performed in no specific logical order; SQL Server uses Index Allocation Map (IAM) pages to do the scan in physical *allocation order*. SQL Server can use the allocation order scan when a table is clustered as well. An allocation order scan is faster if a table is less physically fragmented; the scan is slower if the physical fragmentation is higher. Allocation order scans are not affected by the logical fragmentation. The following code creates a heap by selecting all rows in the Sales.OrderDetails table from the TSQL2012 database and places them into a new table.

```
SELECT orderid, productid, unitprice, qty, discount
INTO Sales.OrderDetailsHeap
FROM Sales.OrderDetails;
```

Even if you select only a few columns from this table, and even if you use a very selective WHERE clause that limits the result set to a single row like the following query shows, SQL Server uses the Table Scan iterator to retrieve the data.

```
SELECT orderid, productid
FROM Sales.OrderDetailsHeap
WHERE orderid = 10248
  AND productid = 11;
```

Figure 17-1 shows the execution plan for this query.

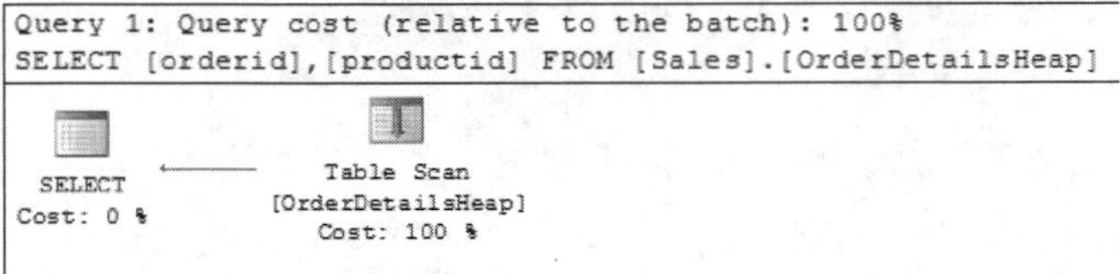

FIGURE 17-1 The Table Scan iterator and access method.

SQL Server may use an allocation order scan for a clustered table if the table has more than 64 pages and the query does not request any specific order and the isolation level is Read Uncommitted or you are working in a readonly environment. When SQL Server scans a clustered index, it can also scan in the logical order of the index by using the *index order scan*. In each of these cases, the Clustered Index Scan iterator is used. SQL Server uses the index leaf–level's linked list to perform an index order scan. Index order scans are affected negatively by both logical and physical fragmentation. The following query does not request any specific ordered result; you can see that the Clustered Index Scan operator's Ordered property is False, meaning that SQL Server didn't have to return the data ordered, as Figure 17-2 shows.

```
SELECT orderid, productid, unitprice
FROM Sales.OrderDetails;
```

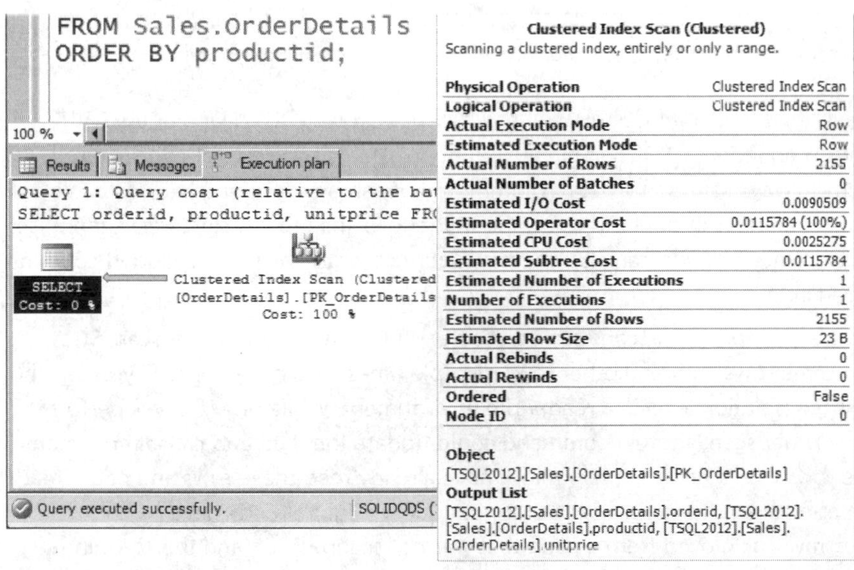

FIGURE 17-2 Clustered Index Scan with a non-ordered rowset returned.

A nonclustered index can cover a query. *Covering* a query means that SQL Server can find all data needed for the query in a nonclustered index and does not need to do any lookups in the base table. SQL Server uses the Index Scan iterator to scan a nonclustered index. As with the Clustered Index Scan iterator, SQL Server can perform an allocation or an index order scan when scanning a nonclustered index. The following query produces a nonclustered index scan and returns the data by using the index order, as Figure 17-3 shows.

```
SELECT orderid, productid
FROM Sales.OrderDetails
ORDER BY productid;
```

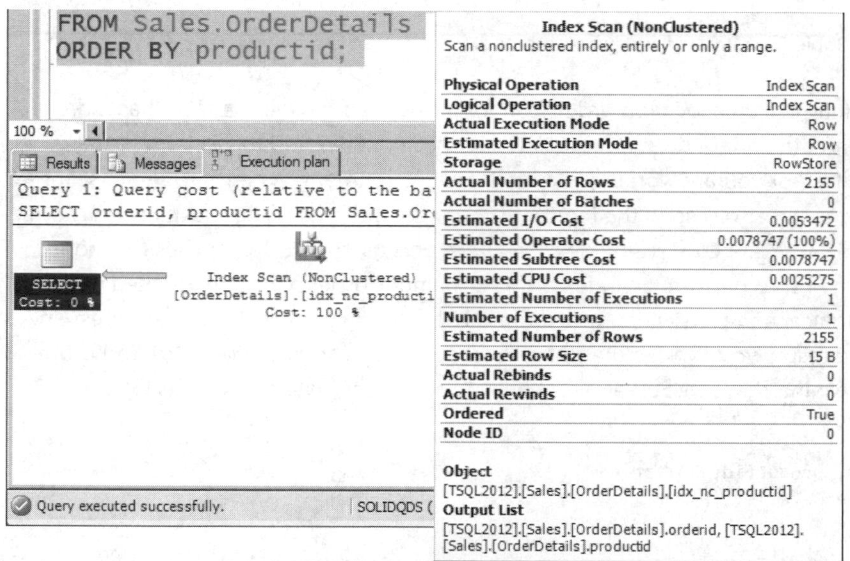

FIGURE 17-3 Index Scan (NonClustered) operator with the data returned in index order.

In some cases, the SQL Server Query Optimizer can even decide to cover a query with multiple nonclustered indexes. SQL Server can join nonclustered indexes. All nonclustered indexes of a table always have some data in common that can be used for a join. If a table is organized as a heap, then this data is the row identifier (RID); if a table is clustered, then this is the clustering key. Note that you can also improve query coverage by using included columns in a nonclustered index.

Note that the allocation order scans can be unsafe. With an allocation order scan, SQL Server can skip some rows and read other rows multiple times. This can happen if you use the Read Uncommitted isolation level in a read-write environment. While one query is performing an allocation order scan, another command could update the data and cause movement of one or more rows. The scanning query might have already read these rows and could read the rows again after the movement. Or the scanning query might already have passed the page to which a row was moved from a page that was not scanned yet, and the scanning query never reads this row. A row can move because of multiple causes. For example, a command might update a variable-length column and replace a short value with a long one. A page might be full, and thus the updated row has to move to another page. A set of rows can move if there are inserts in a clustered table and a page split occurs; approximately half of the rows are moved to the new page. You should be very careful when using the Read Uncommitted isolation level in a read-write environment.

When you scan an index, SQL Server is not limited to a full scan. If you limit a rowset returned by a query and the scan is ordered, then SQL Server can seek for the first value of the rowset needed and then perform a partial scan of subsequent values in the logical order of an index. SQL Server can use a seek and partial scan for both clustered indexes and covering nonclustered indexes. Consider the following query.

```
SELECT orderid, productid, unitprice
FROM Sales.OrderDetails
WHERE orderid BETWEEN 10250 AND 10390
ORDER BY orderid, productid;
```

The query produced the execution plan shown in Figure 17-4. Note that the operator used was Clustered Index Seek; however, from the properties, you can see that the Actual Number Of Rows property value is 377. Therefore, after the first order needed was found, SQL Server did not use seek for subsequent orders; instead, it performed a partial scan.

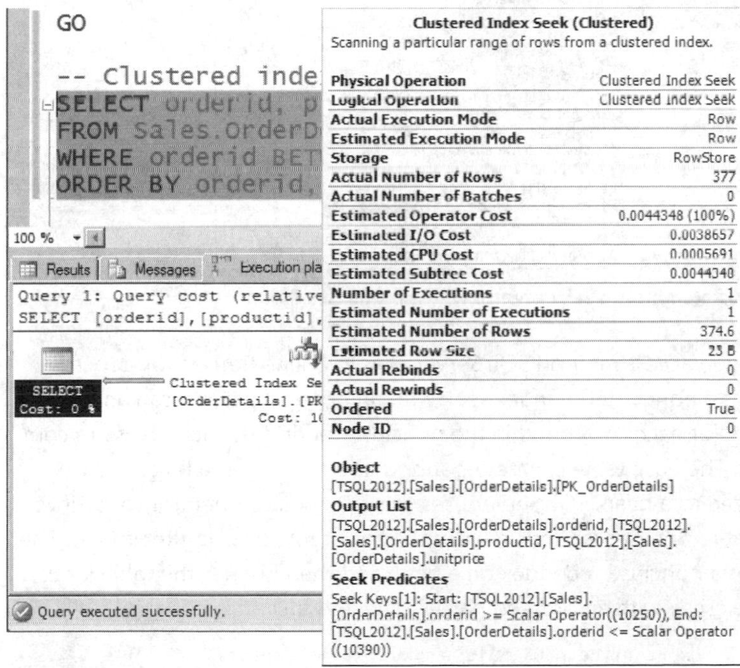

FIGURE 17-4 Clustered Index Seek operator with a partial scan, data ordered.

As mentioned, SQL Server can use the same access method, the index seek, and then a partial ordered scan for a covering nonclustered index, like the following query shows.

```
SELECT orderid, productid
FROM Sales.OrderDetails
WHERE productid BETWEEN 10 AND 30
ORDER BY productid;
```

Figure 17-5 shows the execution plan for this query. Note that the Index Seek operator was used and that the Actual Number Of Rows property value is 593.

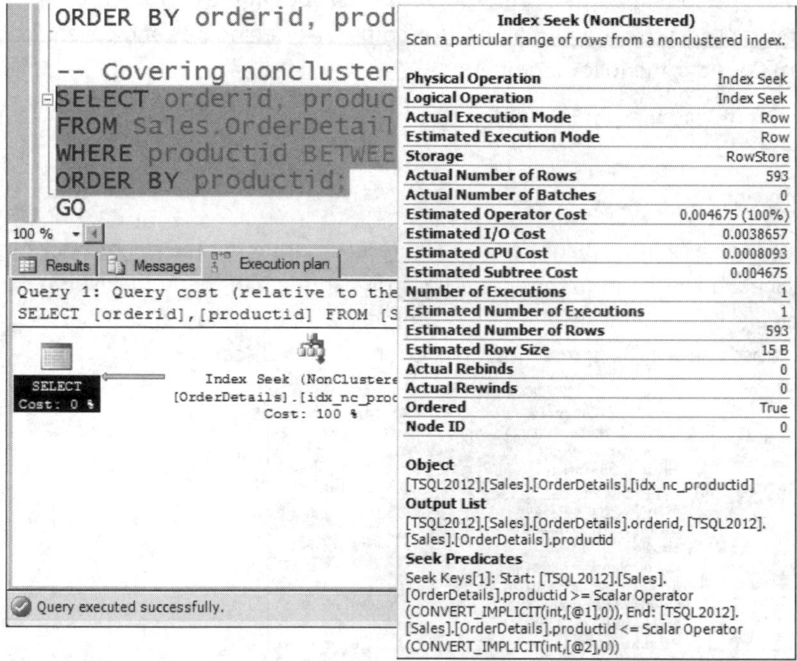

FIGURE 17-5 Covering nonclustered Index Seek operator with a partial scan, data ordered.

Maybe the most common access method SQL Server uses in online transaction processing (OLTP) environments is a nonclustered index seek with an ordered partial scan and then a lookup into the base table for each row found in the nonclustered index. Such plans are common for selective queries. The base table can be organized as a heap or as a balanced tree. When the table is organized as a heap, SQL Server uses the RID Lookup operator to retrieve the rows from the base table. SQL Server finds rows in the base table by using their RIDs. The next piece of code creates a nonclustered index on a heap and then queries the table by using the nonclustered index seek with an ordered partial scan and RID lookup.

```
CREATE NONCLUSTERED INDEX idx_nc_qtyheap ON Sales.OrderDetailsHeap(qty);
SELECT orderid, productid, unitprice, qty
FROM Sales.OrderDetailsHeap
WHERE qty = 52;
```

This query produced the execution plan shown in Figure 17-6.

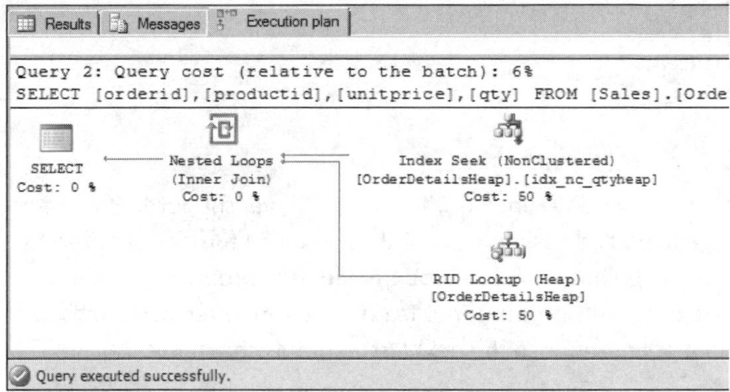

FIGURE 17-6 Index Seek (NonClustered) operator with a partial scan and a RID Lookup operator.

If a table is clustered, then SQL Server uses the Key Lookup operator instead of the RID Lookup operator. The following code creates a nonclustered index on a clustered table and then queries the data by using a nonclustered index seek with an ordered partial scan and a key lookup.

```
CREATE NONCLUSTERED INDEX idx_nc_qty ON Sales.OrderDetails(qty);
SELECT orderid, productid, unitprice, qty
FROM Sales.OrderDetails
WHERE qty = 52;
```

Figure 17-7 shows the execution plan produced by the previous query.

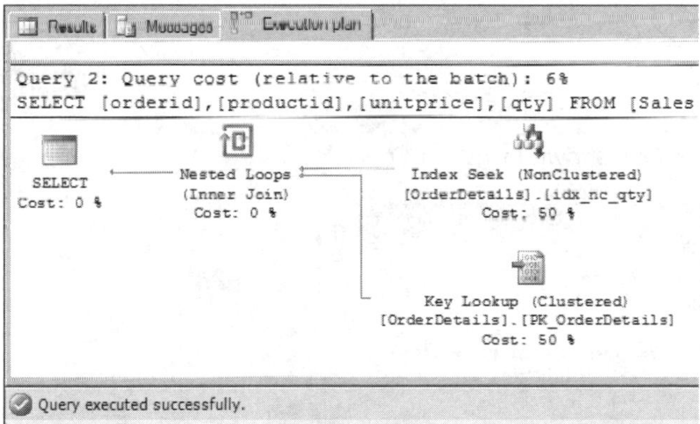

FIGURE 17-7 Index Seek (NonClustered) operator with a partial scan and a Key Lookup operator.

In very rare cases, SQL Server can also decide to use an unordered nonclustered index scan and then perform either key or RID lookups in the base table. In order to get such a plan, a query must be selective enough, no optimal covering nonclustered index can be included, and the index used must not maintain the sought keys in order.

The following code cleans up the TSQL2012 database after testing different access methods.

```
DROP INDEX idx_nc_qtyheap ON Sales.OrderDetailsHeap;
DROP INDEX idx_nc_qty ON Sales.OrderDetails;
DROP TABLE Sales.OrderDetailsHeap;
```

Join Algorithms

When performing joins, SQL Server uses different algorithms. SQL Server supports three basic algorithms: nested loops, merge joins, and hash joins. A hash join can be furher optimized by using *bitmap filtering*; a bitmap filtered hash join could be treated as the fourth algorithm, or as an enhancement of the third, the hash algorithm. You learn about the three basic joins in this section, and about hash join optimization in the next lesson of this chapter.

The *nested loops algorithm* is a very simple and, in many cases, efficient algorithm. SQL Server uses one table for the outer loop, typically the table with fewer rows. For each row in this outer input, SQL Server seeks for matching rows in the second table, which is the inner table. SQL Server uses the join condition to find the matching rows. The join can be a *non-equijoin*, meaning that the Equals operator does not need to be part of the join predicate. If the inner table has no supporting index for a seek, then SQL Server scans the inner input for each row of the outer input. This is not an efficient scenario. A nested loops join is efficient when SQL Server can perform an index seek in the inner input. The following query uses the Nested Loops iterator to join the Sales.Orders and the Sales.OrderDetails tables. Note that the query filters orders to create smaller inputs; without the WHERE clause, SQL Server would use the merge join algorithm.

```
SELECT O.custid, O.orderdate, OD.orderid, OD.productid,OD.qty
FROM Sales.Orders AS O
 INNER JOIN Sales.OrderDetails AS OD
  ON O.orderid = OD.orderid
WHERE O.orderid < 10250;
```

The query produces the execution plan shown in Figure 17-8.

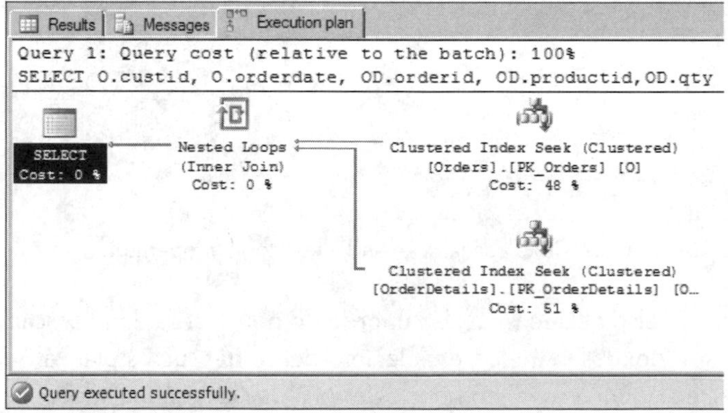

FIGURE 17-8 The Nested Loops iterator.

Merge join is a very efficient join algorithm. However, it has its own limitations. It needs at least one equijoin predicate and sorted inputs from both sides. This means that the merge join should be supported by indexes on both tables involved in the join. In addition, if one input is much smaller than another, then the nested loops join could be more efficient than a merge join.

In a one-to-one or one-to-many scenario, the merge join scans both inputs only once. It starts by finding the first rows on both sides. If the end of input is not reached, the merge join checks the join predicate to determine whether the rows match. If the rows match, they are added to the output. Then the algorithm checks the next rows from the other side and adds them to the output as long as they match the predicate. If the rows from the inputs do not match, then the algorithm reads the next row from the side with the lower value. It reads from this side and compares the row to the row from the other side until the value is bigger than the value from the other side. Then it continues reading from the other side, and so on. In a many-to-many scenario, the merge join algorithm uses a worktable to put the rows from one input side aside for reusage when duplicate matching rows from the other input exist.

The following query uses the Merge Join iterator to join the Sales.Orders and the Sales.OrderDetails tables. The query uses an equijoin. Both inputs are supported by a clustered index.

```
SELECT O.custid, O.orderdate, OD.orderid, OD.productid, OD.qty
FROM Sales.Orders AS O
 INNER JOIN Sales.OrderDetails AS OD
  ON O.orderid = OD.orderid;
```

The query produces the plan shown in Figure 17-9.

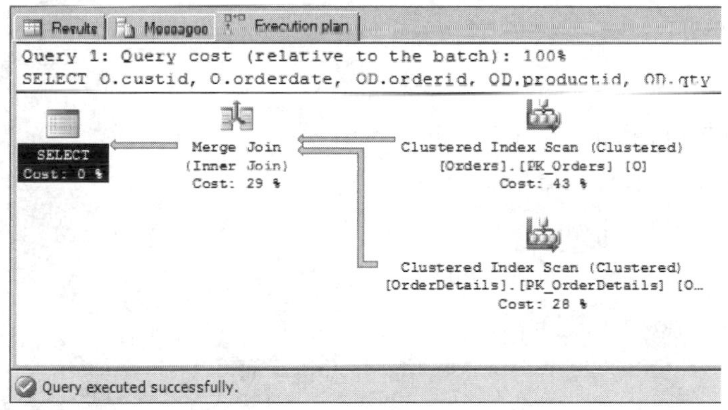

FIGURE 17-9 The Merge Join iterator.

If none of the inputs is supported by an index and an equijoin predicate is used, then the hash join algorithm might be the most efficient one. It uses a searching structure named a *hash table*. This is not a searching structure you can build, like a balanced tree used for indexes. SQL Server builds the hash table internally. It uses a hash function to split the rows from the smaller input into buckets. This is the *build* phase. SQL Server uses the smaller input for building the hash table because SQL Server wants to keep the hash table in memory. If it needs to get spilled to disk, then the algorithm might become much slower. The hash function creates buckets of approximately equal size.

After the hash table is built, SQL Server applies the hash function on each of the rows from the other input. It checks to see into which bucket the row fits. Then it scans through all rows from the bucket. This phase is called the *probe* phase.

A hash join is a kind of compromise between creating a full balanced tree index and then using a different join algorithm, and performing a full scan of one side's input for each row of the other input. At least in the first phase, a seek of the appropriate bucket is used. You might think that the hash join algorithm is not efficient. It is true that in a single-thread mode it is usually slower than merge and nested loops join algorithms that are supported by existing indexes. However, SQL Server can split rows from the probe input in advance, and perform partial joins in multiple threads. The hash join is actually very scalable. This kind of optimization of a hash join is called a *bitmap filtered hash join*. It is typically used in a data warehousing scenario, where you can have large inputs for a query and few concurrent users, so SQL Server can execute a query in parallel. Although a regular hash join can be executed in parallel as well, the bitmap filtered hash join is even more efficient, because SQL Server can use bitmaps for early elimination of rows not used in the join from the bigger table involved in the join.

The following two queries create two heaps that don't have an index from the Sales.Orders and the Sales.OrderDetails tables.

```
SELECT orderid, productid, unitprice, qty, discount
INTO Sales.OrderDetailsHeap
FROM Sales.OrderDetails;
SELECT orderid, custid, orderdate
INTO Sales.OrdersHeap
FROM Sales.Orders;
```

The next query uses the hash join algorithm to join the tables.

```
SELECT O.custid, O.orderdate, OD.orderid, OD.productid, OD.qty
FROM Sales.OrdersHeap AS O
 INNER JOIN Sales.OrderDetailsHeap AS OD
  ON O.orderid = OD.orderid;
```

This query produces the plan shown in Figure 17-10.

The following code cleans up the TSQL2012 database after testing different join algorithms.

```
DROP TABLE Sales.OrderDetailsHeap;
DROP TABLE Sales.OrdersHeap;
```

EXAM TIP

Only a nested loops join algorithm supports non-equijoins.

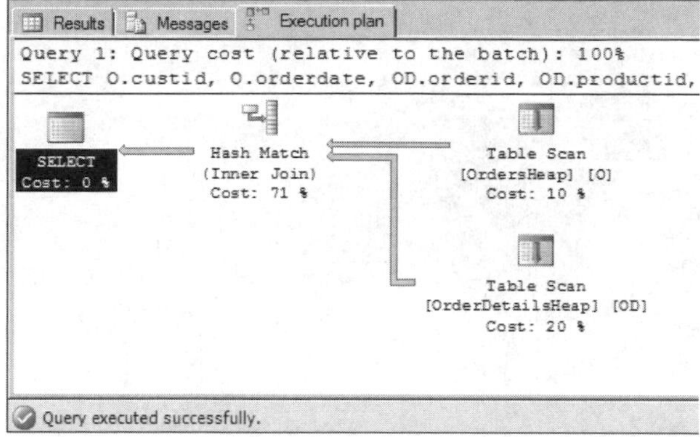

FIGURE 17-10 The Hash Match (Inner Join) iterator— the iterator that performs the hash join.

Other Plan Iterators

Many other execution plan iterators are available. In this section, three additional important iterators are introduced.

> ***MORE INFO*** **EXECUTION PLAN OPERATORS AND ICONS**
>
> **For the complete list of execution plan operators and graphical execution plan icons used in SQL Server 2012, see the Books Online for SQL Server 2012 article "Showplan Logical and Physical Operators Reference" at *http://msdn.microsoft.com/en-us/library/ms191158.aspx*.**

SQL Server uses the Sort operator whenever it has to sort an input. There might be many reasons to sort the input. For example, SQL Server might decide to sort an input so it can use the merge join algorithm. A very typical example of Sort operator usage is for queries that request an ordered rowset when the order is not supported by an index. The sort operation could be very expensive; for good performance, you should make sure that the Sort operator is used for small inputs only. The following query requests an ordered rowset. The rowset should be ordered by the qty column of the Sales.OrderDetails table. However, the table has no index on this column.

```
SELECT orderid, productid, qty
FROM Sales.OrderDetails
ORDER BY qty;
```

Figure 17-11 shows the execution plan for this query. Note that the cost of the Sort operator is around 81 percent of the total query cost.

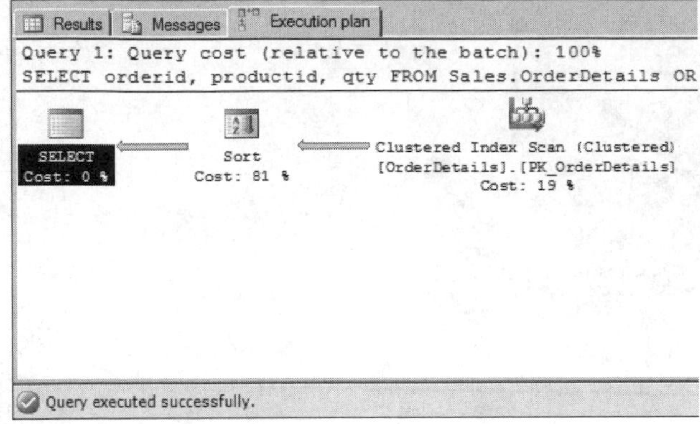

FIGURE 17-11 The Sort iterator.

SQL Server uses two different algorithms for calculating aggregations. If an input is ordered by the columns used in the GROUP BY clause, then SQL Server uses the *stream aggregation* algorithm, which is implemented in the Stream Aggregate operator. Stream aggregation is very efficient. SQL Server might even decide to sort the input before performing the aggregation in order to make it possible to use the Stream Aggregate operator.

The following query uses the Stream Aggregate operator. Note that it groups rows from the Sales.OrderDetails table by the productid column. A nonclustered index over this column exists. In addition, because the query does not require any other column, the index is covering.

```
SELECT productid, COUNT(*) AS num
FROM Sales.OrderDetails
GROUP BY productid;
```

Figure 17-12 shows the execution plan for this query.

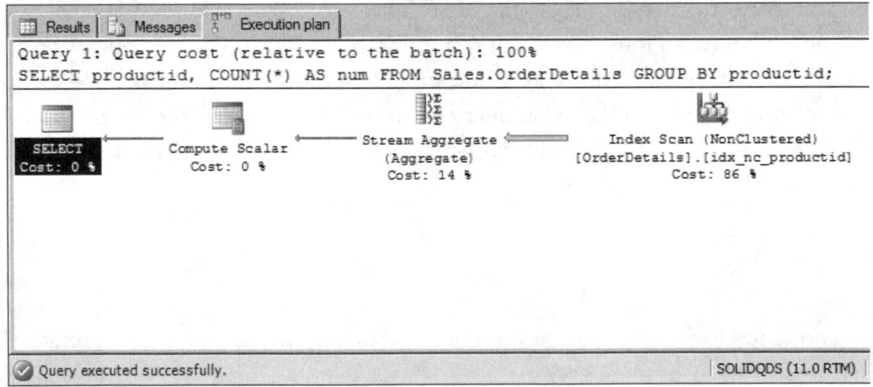

FIGURE 17-12 The Stream Aggregate iterator.

If the input for the aggregation is not ordered and the input is so big that sorting it would be inefficient, then SQL Server uses the *hash aggregation* algorithm. The operator used for this kind of aggregation is the Hash Match Aggregate operator. The icon is the same as the icon for the Hash Match Join operator. The hash aggregation algorithm builds the hash table from the input like it builds it for a hash join. However, the buckets are used to store the groups.

Similarly to a hash join, hash aggregation is scalable as well. Like the stream aggregation algorithm, the hash aggregation algorithm can compute multiple groups simultaneously in multiple threads. The following query groups rows from the Sales.OrderDetails table by the qty column; the aggregation is not supported by an index.

```
SELECT qty, COUNT(*) AS num
FROM Sales.OrderDetails
GROUP BY qty;
```

Figure 17-13 shows the execution plan for this query. Note that SQL Server used the Hash Match (Aggregate) operator. Note also that the relative hash aggregation cost is much higher than the stream aggregation shown earlier in Figure 17-12. While the stream aggregation contributed approximately 14 percent to the total cost of the query, the hash aggregation contributed approximately 71 percent.

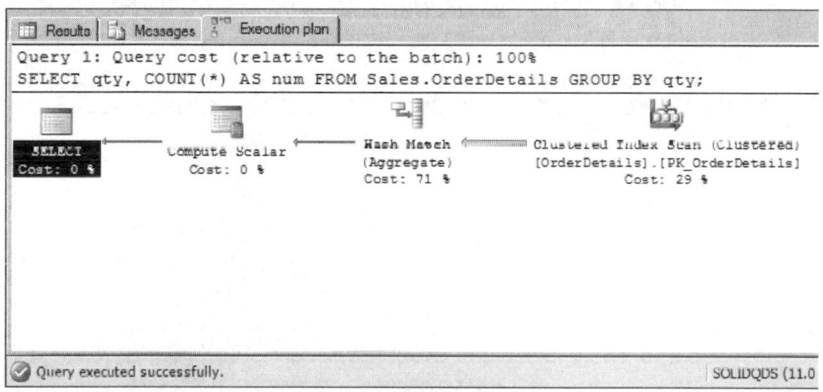

FIGURE 17-13 The Hash Match (Aggregate) iterator.

PRACTICE Determining Execution Plan Iterators

In this practice, you analyze a couple of queries.

If you encounter a problem completing an exercise, you can install the completed projects from the companion content for this chapter and lesson.

EXERCISE 1 Try to Predict the Execution Plan

In this exercise, you execute a couple of different queries in the context of the TSQL2012 database. Before you execute the queries, you try to determine which iterators SQL Server would use. You also execute the queries and check the actual execution plan.

1. Start SSMS and connect to your SQL Server instance.
2. Open a new query window by clicking the New Query button.
3. Change the context to the TSQL2012 database.
4. Analyze the columns and the indexes of the Sales.Customers and the Sales.Orders tables. Look at the following query.

   ```
   SELECT C.custid, C.companyname, C.address, C.city,
    O.orderid, O.orderdate
   FROM Sales.Customers AS C
    INNER JOIN Sales.Orders AS O
     ON C.custid = O.custid;
   ```

   What operators would you expect in the execution plan? What join algorithm should SQL Server use? Would you expect to see the Sort iterator in the execution plan?

5. Turn on the actual execution plan and execute the query. Figure 17-14 shows the execution plan for this query.

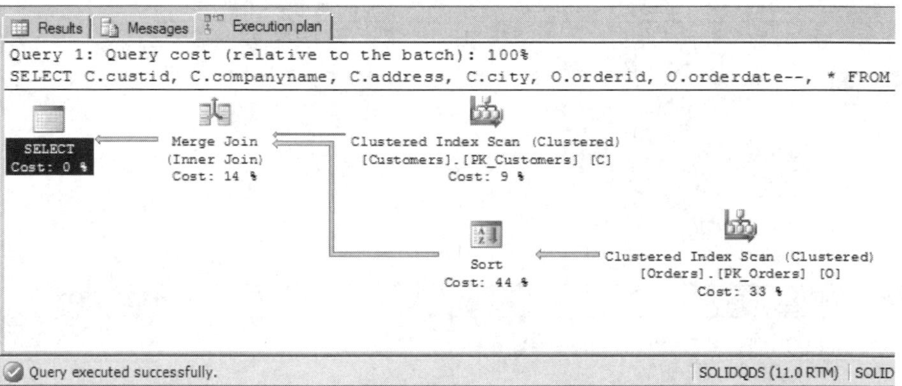

FIGURE 17-14 The actual execution plan for the query from step 4.

You probably correctly expected that SQL Server would scan the clustered Sales.Customers table. You might have expected that a nonclustered index over the custid column on the Sales.Orders would be used. However, the query includes the orderdate column as well, and this nonclustered index would not cover the query. Therefore, SQL Server would need to use the Key Lookup operator. The Query Optimizer decided that it is cheaper to perform a clustered index scan over the Sales.Orders table, sort the rows, and then use the merge join algorithm.

The next query does not include the orderdate column. What kind of execution plan operators would you expect for this query?

```
SELECT C.custid, C.companyname, C.address, C.city,
 O.orderid
FROM Sales.Customers AS C
 INNER JOIN Sales.Orders AS O
  ON C.custid = O.custid;
```

6. Execute the query and check the execution plan. As you probably expected, SQL Server scanned the nonclustered index on the custid column of the Sales.Orders table, and then used the Merge Join iterator to join the data. Figure 17-15 shows the execution plan for this query.

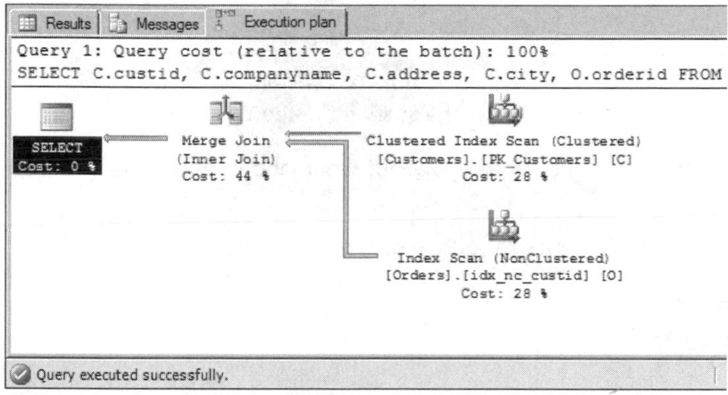

FIGURE 17-15 The actual execution plan for the query from step 5.

EXERCISE 2 Analyze the Execution Plan

In this exercise, you execute a couple of different queries in the context of the TSQL2012 database and analyze the actual execution plans.

1. Execute the following query and check the execution plan. Note that the query is quite selective; there are not many orders for customers from Berlin.

```
SELECT C.custid, C.companyname, C.address, C.city,
 O.orderid, O.orderdate
FROM Sales.Customers AS C
 INNER JOIN Sales.Orders AS O
  ON C.custid = O.custid
WHERE C.city = N'Berlin';
```

Because the query is very selective, SQL Server decided that the Key Lookup operator would not be too expensive. Note that even with only six rows returned, with only six key lookups, the cost of the Key Lookup operator is approximately 74 percent of the total query cost, as Figure 17-16 shows.

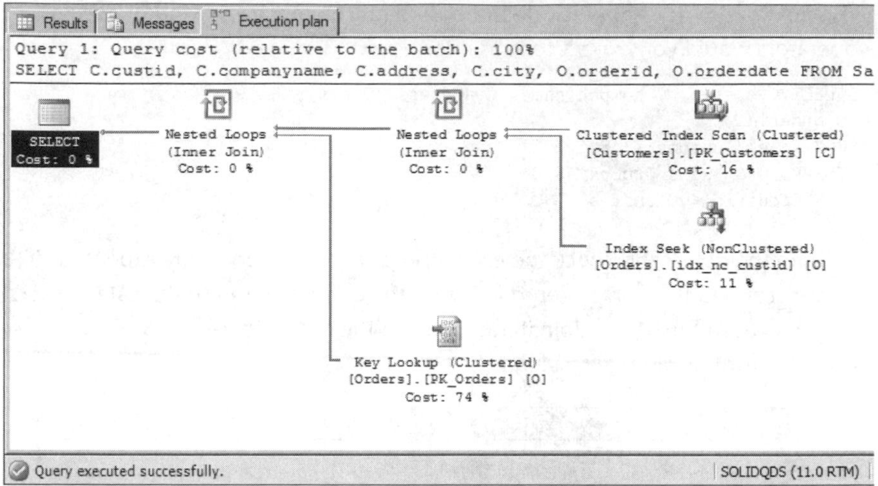

FIGURE 17-16 The actual execution plan for the query from step 1.

2. Check the following query and try to figure out what kind of execution plan SQL Server would use.

```
SELECT C.city, MIN(O.orderid) AS minorderid
FROM Sales.Customers AS C
 INNER JOIN Sales.Orders AS O
  ON C.custid = O.custid
GROUP BY C.city;
```

Note that the query is covered by two nonclustered indexes. There is a nonclustered index over the city column for the Sales.Customers table, which also includes the custid column from the clustered primary key, and there is a nonclustered index over the custid column for the Sales.Orders table. Because the input for the aggregation is ordered, SQL Server uses the Stream Aggregate iterator. Figure 17-17 shows the execution plan for this query.

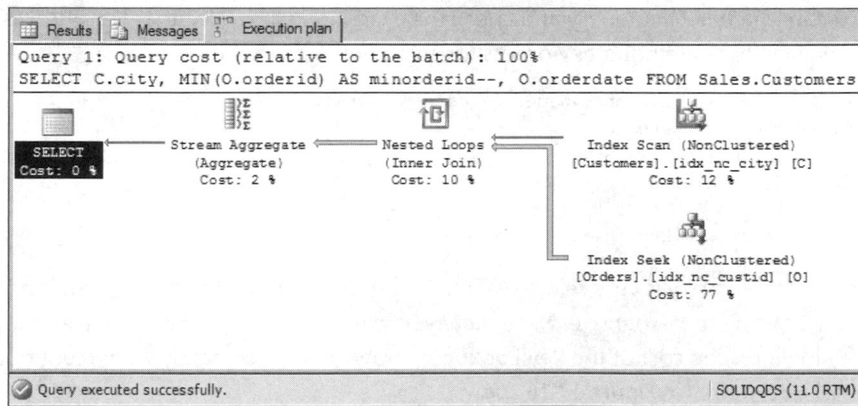

FIGURE 17-17 The actual execution plan for the query from step 2.

3. Close the query window.

Lesson Summary

- SQL Server uses many different data access methods.
- SQL Server uses different join and aggregation algorithms.
- There are no "good" and "bad" iterators. Any iterator can be the best choice for a specific query and specific data.

Lesson Review

Answer the following questions to test your knowledge of the information in this lesson. You can find the answers to these questions and explanations of why each answer choice is correct or incorrect in the "Answers" section at the end of this chapter.

1. What aggregation algorithms does SQL Server use? (Choose all that apply.)
   - **A.** Merge aggregation
   - **B.** Stream aggregation
   - **C.** Hash aggregation
   - **D.** Nested loops aggregation
2. Which operator is used when SQL Server performs a nonclustered index seek to find a row, but then also needs data from the underlying table, which is organized as a clustered index?
   - **A.** RID Lookup
   - **B.** Clustered Index Scan
   - **C.** Merge Join
   - **D.** Key Lookup
3. What is the scan called when SQL Server scans a clustered index in logical order of the index?
   - **A.** Allocation order scan
   - **B.** Clustered index scan
   - **C.** Index order scan
   - **D.** Index order seek

Lesson 2: Using Parameterized Queries and Batch Operations

As you learned in Chapter 14, the SQL Server Query Optimizer has a lot of work to do to determine a good execution plan. After the plan is built, SQL Server caches it in order to make it available for possible reuse. SQL Server tries to *parameterize* your queries, and thus makes it more likely that a plan will be reused. You can help SQL Server by parameterizing your queries by yourself.

In an OLTP environment, most of the optimization work is about lowering the disk I/O. In data warehousing scenarios, queries typically read a lot of data, and thus perform scans anyway. However, data warehousing queries are often parallelized. This way, the CPU might become a bottleneck. SQL Server 2012 introduced *batch processing*, which lowers the CPU burden. It is especially useful with columnstore indexes.

After this lesson, you will be able to:

- Understand query parameterization.
- Understand row and batch processing.
- Use batch processing iterators.

Estimated lesson time: 40 minutes

Parameterized Queries

SQL Server parameterizes ad hoc queries automatically. However, SQL Server is very conservative with plan reuse. It does not want to use a wrong plan. SQL Server decides to reuse a plan only when it is sure that the cached plan is the correct one for a query. Changes in parameter data type, in some SET options, in security context, and more, can produce a new plan when you would expect reuse of an existing cached plan.

You can get information about cached plans and the number of times the plans were reused by querying the sys.dm_exec_query_stats dynamic management function. You can get the exact text of the query from the sys.dm_exec_sql_text dynamic management function. When you are testing plan caching and reuse, you can use the DBCC FREEPROCCACHE T-SQL command to clear the cache. You use it in a very simple way, as shown in the following code.

```
DBCC FREEPROCCACHE;
```

IMPORTANT **USING THE DBCC FREEPROCCACHE COMMMAD IN PRODUCTION**

The DBCC FREEPROCCACHE T-SQL command is very useful for testing. However, you should be very careful about using it in a production environment. If you clear the cache of a production server, SQL Server has to optimize and compile all new subsequent queries, stored procedures, functions, and triggers. Users could experience a huge performance impact.

The following three queries each retrieve a single order from the Sales.Orders table in the TSQL2012 database. They all use the orderid column as a parameter for the WHERE clause. The table has a primary key defined on the orderid column. Therefore, SQL Server knows that each query returns a single row only. However, the first two queries use an integer data type for the parameter, whereas the third one defines the parameter as a decimal number data type.

```
-- Parameter INT
SELECT orderid, custid, empid, orderdate
FROM Sales.Orders
WHERE orderid = 10248;
-- Parameter INT
SELECT orderid, custid, empid, orderdate
FROM Sales.Orders
WHERE orderid = 10249;
-- Parameter DECIMAL
SELECT orderid, custid, empid, orderdate
FROM Sales.Orders
WHERE orderid = 10250.0;
```

You can check the plans in the cache and the number of executions by using the following query.

```
SELECT qs.execution_count AS cnt,
 qt.text
FROM sys.dm_exec_query_stats AS qs
 CROSS APPLY sys.dm_exec_sql_text(qs.sql_handle) AS qt
WHERE qt.text LIKE N'%Orders%'
  AND qt.text NOT LIKE N'%qs.execution_count%'
ORDER BY qs.execution_count;
```

Because this query is used in further examples in this lesson, this lesson refers to it as the "plan reuse" query for future reference. The plan reuse query returns the following output.

```
cnt  text
---  ----
1    (@1 numeric(6,1))SELECT [orderid],[custid],[empid],[orderdate] FROM
      [Sales].[Orders] WHERE [orderid]=@1
2    (@1 smallint)SELECT [orderid],[custid],[empid],[orderdate] FROM [Sales].[Orders]
      WHERE [orderid]=@1
```

You can see that SQL Server parameterized the queries. It reused the execution plan where the parameter was an integer number. When the parameter was a decimal number, SQL Server generated a new plan.

To demonstrate how SQL Server is conservative with plan reuse, the following three queries use the custid in the WHERE clause. The first query returns a single row, the second two rows, and the third 31 rows. SQL Server cannot be sure about the selectivity of the custid column in the Sales.Orders table.

```
-- One row
SELECT orderid, custid, empid, orderdate
FROM Sales.Orders
WHERE custid = 13;
GO
-- Two rows
SELECT orderid, custid, empid, orderdate
FROM Sales.Orders
WHERE custid = 33;
GO
-- 31 rows
SELECT orderid, custid, empid, orderdate
FROM Sales.Orders
WHERE custid = 71;
GO
```

If you cleared the cache before executing the previous three queries, then the plan reuse query returns the following output.

```
cnt  text
---  ----
1    SELECT orderid, custid, empid, orderdate FROM Sales.Orders WHERE custid = 33;
1    SELECT orderid, custid, empid, orderdate FROM Sales.Orders WHERE custid = 13;
1    SELECT orderid, custid, empid, orderdate FROM Sales.Orders WHERE custid = 71;
```

Note that the queries were not parameterized.

> ***MORE INFO*** **WHY SQL SERVER SOMETIMES DOES NOT PARAMETERIZE QUERIES**
>
> **There are many other reasons why SQL Server does not parameterize the queries; for an exhaustive list, see Appendix A of the MSDN article "Plan Caching in SQL Server 2008" at *http://msdn.microsoft.com/en-us/library/ee343986(SQL.100).aspx.* (Although this article is written for SQL Server 2008, it is still valid for SQL Server 2012.)**

To demonstrate further what influences plan reuse, the following two queries are the same as the first two queries from the first example in this section, when the plan was reused. However, a SET option that could influence the query result is changed before the second query.

```
-- Query that is parameterized
SELECT orderid, custid, empid, orderdate
FROM Sales.Orders
WHERE orderid = 10248;
-- Changing a SET option
SET CONCAT_NULL_YIELDS_NULL OFF;
```

```
-- Query that could use the same plan
SELECT orderid, custid, empid, orderdate
FROM Sales.Orders
WHERE orderid = 10249;
-- Restoring the SET option
SET CONCAT_NULL_YIELDS_NULL ON;
```

If you cleared the cache before executing the previous three queries, then the plan reuse query returns the following output.

```
cnt  text
---  ----
1    (@1 smallint)SELECT [orderid],[custid],[empid],[orderdate] FROM [Sales].[Orders]
      WHERE [orderid]=@1
1    (@1 smallint)SELECT [orderid],[custid],[empid],[orderdate] FROM [Sales].[Orders]
      WHERE [orderid]=@1
```

Although SQL Server parameterized the queries, it did not reuse the first plan.

You might think that SQL Server is too conservative about plan reuse. However, the situation is not that bad. Most of the queries come from applications, and applications typically always generate their queries in the same way, with the same options. In addition, you can help SQL Server by using the sys.sp_executesql system procedure to execute a parameterized dynamic SQL. Actually, you should consider using the sys.sp_executesql system procedure as a much better practice than using ad hoc queries.

In the following example, a parameterized query is created as a SQL string, and then executed twice by using different parameters. The first time the parameter is an integer, and the second time it is a decimal data type.

```
DECLARE @v INT;
DECLARE @s NVARCHAR(500);
DECLARE @p NVARCHAR(500);
-- Build the SQL string
SET @s = N'
SELECT orderid, custid, empid, orderdate
FROM Sales.Orders
WHERE orderid = @orderid';
SET @p = N'@orderid INT';
-- Parameter integer
SET @v = 10248;
EXECUTE sys.sp_executesql @s, @p, @orderid = @v;
-- Parameter decimal
SET @v = 10249.0;
EXECUTE sp_executesql @s, @p, @orderid = @v;
```

If you cleared the cache before calling the sys.sp_executesql procedure twice, then the plan reuse query returns the following output.

```
cnt  text
---  ----
2    (@orderid INT) SELECT orderid, custid, empid, orderdate FROM Sales.Orders WHERE
      orderid = @orderid
```

Note that although the second call implicitly used a decimal parameter, SQL Server knew that the parameter is actually an integer number, because it was explicitly defined as an integer for the sys.sp_executesql procedure. Of course, the value had to be implicitly convertible to the INTEGER data type or the second query would fail.

Using dynamic SQL is not a good practice. In order to enforce plan reuse, you should use programmatic objects such as stored procedures. The following code creates a procedure that wraps the query that retrieves a single order in a stored procedure.

```
CREATE PROCEDURE Sales.GetOrder
(@orderid INT)
AS
SELECT orderid, custid, empid, orderdate
FROM Sales.Orders
WHERE orderid = @orderid;
```

You can call the procedure twice, by using a parameter implicitly passed one time as an integer and one time as a decimal number.

```
EXEC Sales.GetOrder @orderid = 10248;
EXEC Sales.GetOrder @orderid = 10249.0;
```

If you cleared the cache before calling the stored procedure twice, then the plan reuse query returns the following output.

```
cnt  text
---  ----
2    CREATE PROCEDURE Sales.GetOrder (@orderid INT) AS SELECT orderid, custid, empid,
      orderdate
      FROM Sales.Orders WHERE orderid = @orderid;
```

You can see that the plan was successfully reused. Stored procedures enforce plan reuse. However, sometimes you might prefer that the subsequent stored procedure calls do not use a cached plan. A procedure might return a different amount of rows based on a parameter value. For some values, a query inside the procedure might be very selective, and for other values not selective at all. Therefore, you might want to have a different execution plan for each call. You can force SQL Server to recompile a stored procedure if you create it with the WITH RECOMPILE option. In addition, you can force recompilation on a query level. Instead of recompiling the complete procedure, you can recompile only the critical statements. You learn about procedure recompilation in the practice for this lesson, and about query recompilation in the next lesson of this chapter.

After testing the procedure, you should clean up the TSQL2012 database.

```
DROP PROCEDURE Sales.GetOrder;
```

Batch Processing

In Lesson 1, you learned about three base join algorithms that SQL Server uses. You also learned that the hash join can be further optimized by performing partial joins in multiple threads, and even more with early elimination of the rows used in a join from a bigger table with bitmap filters. This is the bitmap filtered hash join. You already know that it is typically used in a data warehousing scenario, where you can have large inputs for a query and few concurrent users so that SQL Server can execute a query in parallel. This kind of join is sometimes also called a *star join*, named after the typical data warehousing schema that resembles a star with one central table on the many side of relationships and multiple related surrounding tables on the one side of the relationships. The following code creates four tables in a very simple Star Schema, and populates them with a large amount of rows. It uses an auxiliary tabular function that returns a table of numbers used for population of the data warehouse tables.

```
-- Data distribution settings for DW
DECLARE
  @dim1rows AS INT = 100,
  @dim2rows AS INT = 50,
  @dim3rows AS INT = 200;
-- First dimension
CREATE TABLE dbo.Dim1
(
  key1  INT NOT NULL CONSTRAINT PK_Dim1 PRIMARY KEY,
  attr1 INT NOT NULL,
  filler BINARY(100) NOT NULL DEFAULT (0x)
);
-- Second dimension
CREATE TABLE dbo.Dim2
(
  key2  INT NOT NULL CONSTRAINT PK_Dim2 PRIMARY KEY,
  attr1 INT NOT NULL,
  filler BINARY(100) NOT NULL DEFAULT (0x)
);
-- Third dimension
CREATE TABLE dbo.Dim3
(
  key3  INT NOT NULL CONSTRAINT PK_Dim3 PRIMARY KEY,
  attr1 INT NOT NULL,
  filler BINARY(100) NOT NULL DEFAULT (0x)
);
-- Fact table
CREATE TABLE dbo.Fact
(
  key1 INT NOT NULL CONSTRAINT FK_Fact_Dim1 FOREIGN KEY REFERENCES dbo.Dim1,
  key2 INT NOT NULL CONSTRAINT FK_Fact_Dim2 FOREIGN KEY REFERENCES dbo.Dim2,
  key3 INT NOT NULL CONSTRAINT FK_Fact_Dim3 FOREIGN KEY REFERENCES dbo.Dim3,
  measure1 INT NOT NULL,
  measure2 INT NOT NULL,
  measure3 INT NOT NULL,
  filler  BINARY(100) NOT NULL DEFAULT (0x),
  CONSTRAINT PK_Fact PRIMARY KEY(key1, key2, key3)
);
```

```
-- Populating the first dimension
INSERT INTO dbo.Dim1(key1, attr1)
  SELECT n, ABS(CHECKSUM(NEWID())) % 20 + 1
  FROM dbo.GetNums(1, @dim1rows);
-- Populating the second dimension
INSERT INTO dbo.Dim2(key2, attr1)
  SELECT n, ABS(CHECKSUM(NEWID())) % 10 + 1
  FROM dbo.GetNums(1, @dim2rows);
-- Populating the third dimension
INSERT INTO dbo.Dim3(key3, attr1)
  SELECT n, ABS(CHECKSUM(NEWID())) % 40 + 1
  FROM dbo.GetNums(1, @dim3rows);
-- Populating the fact table
INSERT INTO dbo.Fact WITH (TABLOCK)
    (key1, key2, key3, measure1, measure2, measure3)
  SELECT N1.n, N2.n, N3.n,
    ABS(CHECKSUM(NEWID())) % 1000000 + 1,
    ABS(CHECKSUM(NEWID())) % 1000000 + 1,
    ABS(CHECKSUM(NEWID())) % 1000000 + 1
  FROM dbo.GetNums(1, @dim1rows) AS N1
    CROSS JOIN dbo.GetNums(1, @dim2rows) AS N2
    CROSS JOIN dbo.GetNums(1, @dim3rows) AS N3;
```

Figure 17-18 shows the schema for these four tables. Note that the schema resembles a star. This is why it is called a *Star Schema*.

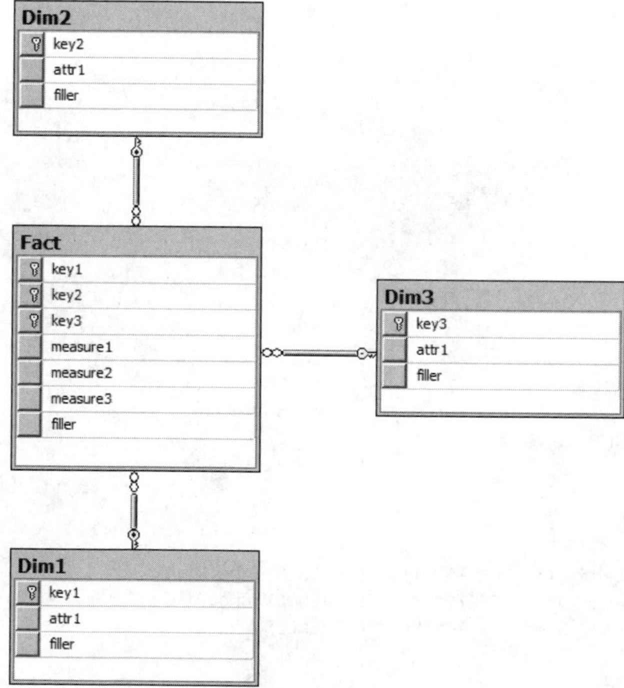

FIGURE 17-18 A Star Schema example.

The following query joins all four tables and aggregates the data. STATISTICS IO and STATISTICS TIME are measured as well.

```
-- Measuring IO and time
SET STATISTICS IO ON;
SET STATISTICS TIME ON;
-- Query demonstrating star join
SELECT D1.attr1 AS x, D2.attr1 AS y, D3.attr1 AS z,
  COUNT(*) AS cnt, SUM(F.measure1) AS total
FROM dbo.Fact AS F
 INNER JOIN dbo.Dim1 AS D1
    ON F.key1 = D1.key1
 INNER JOIN dbo.Dim2 AS D2
    ON F.key2 = D2.key2
 INNER JOIN dbo.Dim3 AS D3
    ON F.key3 = D3.key3
WHERE D1.attr1 <= 10
  AND D2.attr1 <= 15
  AND D3.attr1 <= 10
GROUP BY D1.attr1, D2.attr1, D3.attr1;
```

The query was executed on a computer that has a quad-core processor with hyper-threading. SQL Server used eight logical processors. Figure 17-19 shows the partial execution plan of this query. Note that the query was executed in parallel (the Parallelism iterator), the hash join was used (the Hash Match iterator), and a bitmap filter was used in one case before the join was performed (the Bitmap operator). Note also that there are two other properties for the iterators in SQL Server 2012. In Figure 17-19, you can see the Actual Execution Mode and the Estimated Execution Mode properties for the Hash Match (Inner Join) operator. The value for these two properties is Row.

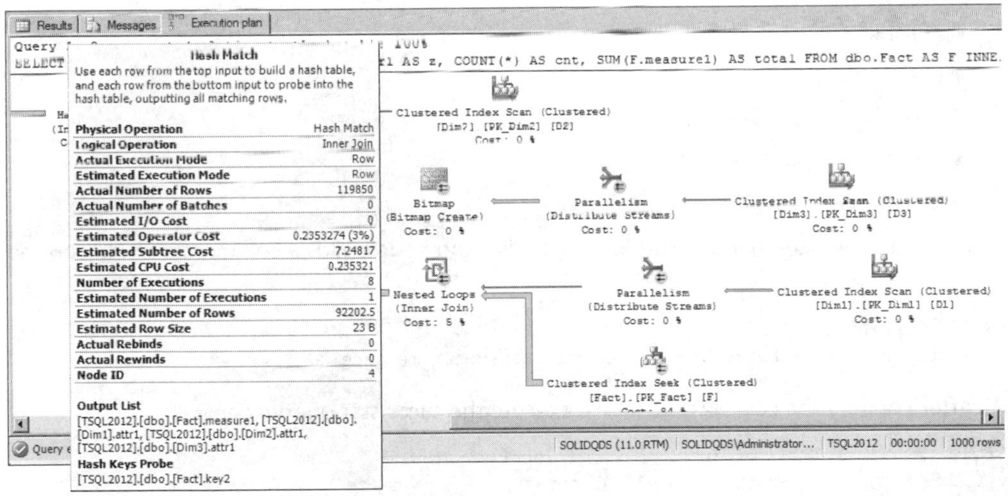

FIGURE 17-19 Partial plan of a star join query.

The abbreviated STATISTICS IO and STATISTICS TIME results for this query are as follows.

```
Table 'Dim2'. Scan count 1, logical reads 2, …
Table 'Dim3'. Scan count 1, logical reads 5, …
Table 'Dim1'. Scan count 1, logical reads 4, …
Table 'Worktable'. Scan count 0, logical reads 0, …
Table 'Fact'. Scan count 47, logical reads 8152, …
Table 'Worktable'. Scan count 0, logical reads 0, …
 SQL Server Execution Times:
   CPU time = 671 ms,  elapsed time = 255 ms.
```

Note the huge amount of logical read in the dbo.Fact table. In addition, note that the CPU time was nearly three times bigger than the elapsed time for this query. Because the query was processed in parallel, the CPU burden was very high, and the CPU could become a bottleneck for this scenario. Imagine what would happen if the table were compressed as well. Then SQL Server would also need to decompress it. You could also create a columnstore index on the table. Then SQL Server would need to recreate rows for the output. Altogether, the CPU can become a bottleneck in data warehousing scenarios.

SQL Server 2012 brings a solution to the CPU burden problem. It introduces iterators that process batches of rows at a time, not just row by row. This way, the CPU needs to deal with metadata for a row only once per batch. Batch processing is orthogonal to columnstore indexes; it can support row storage as well. However, best results come with columnstore indexes. With columnstore indexes, SQL Server can sometimes perform batch operations directly on compressed data, thus skipping the uncompressing action as well. SQL Server 2012 can mix batch and row operators and can dynamically switch from batch to row mode.

The following operators support batch mode processing in SQL Server 2012:

- Filter
- Project
- Scan
- Local hash (partial) aggregation
- Hash inner join
- Batch hash table build

In order to test the batch operations, the following code builds a columnstore index on the dbo.Fact table.

```
CREATE COLUMNSTORE INDEX idx_cs_fact
  ON dbo.Fact(key1, key2, key3, measure1, measure2, measure3);
```

After creating the columnstore index, execute the same star query again.

```
SELECT D1.attr1 AS x, D2.attr1 AS y, D3.attr1 AS z,
  COUNT(*) AS cnt, SUM(F.measure1) AS total
FROM dbo.Fact AS F
 INNER JOIN dbo.Dim1 AS D1
    ON F.key1 = D1.key1
 INNER JOIN dbo.Dim2 AS D2
    ON F.key2 = D2.key2
```

```
   INNER JOIN dbo.Dim3 AS D3
      ON F.key3 = D3.key3
WHERE D1.attr1 <= 10
  AND D2.attr1 <= 15
  AND D3.attr1 <= 10
GROUP BY D1.attr1, D2.attr1, D3.attr1;
```

Figure 17-20 shows the partial execution plan for this execution of the star query. Note that the query uses the Columnstore Index Scan operator. In addition, as you can see from the properties of one of the Hash Match (Inner Join) operators, SQL Server used the batch execution mode.

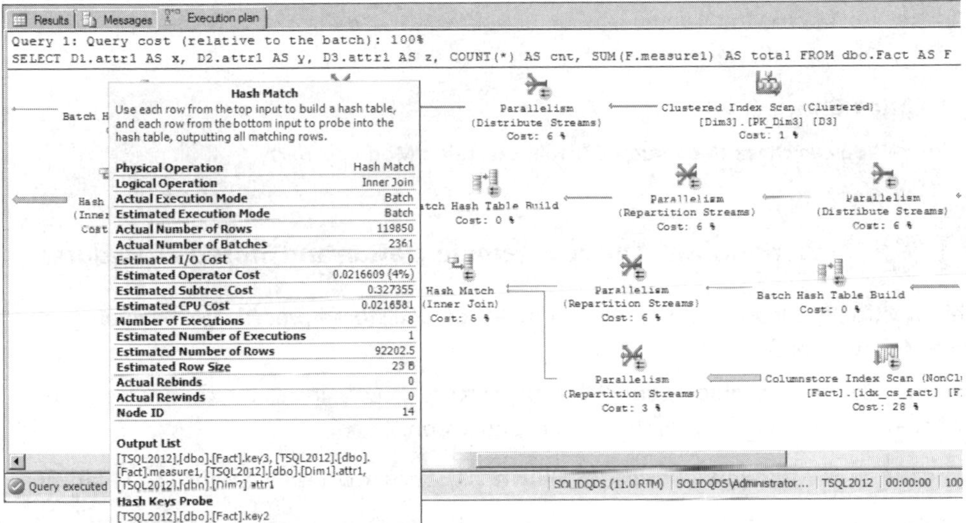

FIGURE 17-20 Partial plan of a star join query that uses a columnstore index and batch processing.

Also check the abbreviated STATISTICS IO and TIME results for this execution.

```
Table 'Dim3'. Scan count 1, logical reads 5, …
Table 'Dim2'. Scan count 1, logical reads 2, …
Table 'Dim1'. Scan count 1, logical reads 4, …
Table 'Fact'. Scan count 8, logical reads 993,…
Table 'Worktable'. Scan count 0, logical reads 0, …
Table 'Worktable'. Scan count 0, logical reads 0, …
 SQL Server Execution Times:
   CPU time = 63 ms,  elapsed time = 186 ms.
```

You can see that the number of logical I/Os in the dbo.Fact table is much lower than it was for the first execution, when the columnstore index did not exist. The elapsed time is smaller than it was for the first execution of the query. However, note especially the CPU time. It is approximately 10 times smaller than it was when the query was executed when the batch processing mode was not used.

The following code cleans up the TSQL2012 database and sets the STATISTICS IO and TIME to OFF.

```
SET STATISTICS IO OFF;
SET STATISTICS TIME OFF;
DROP TABLE dbo.Fact;
DROP TABLE dbo.Dim1;
DROP TABLE dbo.Dim2;
DROP TABLE dbo.Dim3;
```

Quick Check

- **How would you determine whether SQL Server used the batch processing mode for a specific iterator?**

Quick Check Answer

- **You can check the iterator's Actual Execution Mode property.**

PRACTICE Working with Query Parameterization and Stored Procedures

In this practice, you learn how to force recompilation of a stored procedure when you don't want to see plan reuse.

If you encounter a problem completing an exercise, you can install the completed projects from the companion content for this chapter and lesson.

EXERCISE 1 Work with Queries for Which SQL Server Does Not Reuse the Plan

In this exercise, you write two queries for which SQL Server will not reuse the plans.

1. If you closed SSMS, start it and connect to your SQL Server instance.
2. Open a new query window by clicking the New Query button.
3. Change the context to the TSQL2012 database.
4. Execute the following query and check the execution plan.

   ```
   SELECT orderid, custid, empid, orderdate
   FROM Sales.Orders
   WHERE custid = 13;
   ```

   You should see the Index Seek and Key Lookup operators in the plan.
5. Change the parameter and execute the following query with Actual Execution Plan turned on.

   ```
   SELECT orderid, custid, empid, orderdate
   FROM Sales.Orders
   WHERE custid = 71;
   ```

   This time you should see the Clustered Index Scan iterator.

EXERCISE 2 Examine Stored Procedure Recompilation

In this exercise, you create a stored procedure so that SQL Server will reuse the procedure plan. However, you will realize that the plan should not be reused, and therefore, you will use the WITH RECOMPILE option to force procedure recompilation.

1. Create a parameterized procedure from the query used in the previous exercise.

```
CREATE PROCEDURE Sales.GetCustomerOrders
(@custid INT)
AS
SELECT orderid, custid, empid, orderdate
FROM Sales.Orders
WHERE custid = @custid;
```

2. Clear the cache by using the DBCC FREEPROCCACHE command. (Be sure that you don't do this on a production server.)

3. Execute the procedure twice in the same batch, once for customer 13 and once for customer 71.

```
EXEC Sales.GetCustomerOrders @custid = 13;
EXEC Sales.GetCustomerOrders @custid = 71;
```

   You should get the same execution plan, the plan with the Index Seek and Key Lookup operators, for both queries. The first call of the procedure produced this plan; all subsequent calls use the same plan.

4. Alter the procedure to force recompilation on each call.

```
ALTER PROCEDURE Sales.GetCustomerOrders
(@custid INT)
WITH RECOMPILE
AS
SELECT orderid, custid, empid, orderdate
FROM Sales.Orders
WHERE custid = @custid;
```

5. Note that because you altered the procedure, you do not need to clear the cache. SQL Server does not use a cached plan of a procedure you just altered. Execute the procedure twice in the same batch, once for customer 13 and once for customer 71.

```
EXEC Sales.GetCustomerOrders @custid = 13;
EXEC Sales.GetCustomerOrders @custid = 71;
```

   This time you should get a different plan for each call.

6. Clean up the TSQL 2012 database.

```
DROP PROCEDURE Sales.GetCustomerOrders;
```

Lesson Summary

- SQL Server parameterizes queries for better execution plan reusage.
- You can also parameterize queries yourself.
- Batch processing mode, new to SQL Server 2012, can improve the performance of data warehousing queries substantially, especially by lowering the CPU usage.
- Batch processing goes well with columnstore indexes.

Lesson Review

Answer the following questions to test your knowledge of the information in this lesson. You can find the answers to these questions and explanations of why each answer choice is correct or incorrect in the "Answers" section at the end of this chapter.

1. What are possible reasons that SQL Server does not reuse an existing cached plan? (Choose all that apply.)
   - **A.** Because a SET option that influences the query result was changed
   - **B.** Because the query is manually parameterized in a stored procedure, and no recompilation option is used
   - **C.** Because SQL Server cannot determine the selectivity of the parameterized predicate
   - **D.** Because a different data type was used for a parameter in the parameterized predicate
2. What is the main advantage of batch mode processing?
   - **A.** It lowers the disk I/O.
   - **B.** It speeds up network transfer.
   - **C.** It lowers the CPU burden.
   - **D.** It uses less memory.
3. Which of the following SET commands would prevent execution plan reusage?
   - **A.** SET STATISTICS IO ON
   - **B.** SET STATISTICS PROFILE ON
   - **C.** SET CONCAT_NULL_YIELDS_NULL OFF
   - **D.** SET STATISTICS IO OFF

Lesson 3: Using Optimizer Hints and Plan Guides

The SQL Server Query Optimizer cannot always find the best possible execution plans. In some cases, you can order a better plan by using the *optimizer hints*. In order to use the hints, you need to change the query. In addition, you have another option to influence the query execution—the *plan guides*. You can use the plan guides when you don't want to or can't change the query text—for example, when you need to optimize the queries created by an application of a third-party provider. SQL Server uses the plan guides to attach query hints or a fixed query plan to queries.

After this lesson, you will be able to:

- Understand and use the optimizer hints.
- Understand and use the plan guides.

Estimated lesson time: 30 minutes

Optimizer Hints

Optimizer hints have a somewhat unfortunate name. They are not just hints; they are actually directives for the query execution. You can use them with the SELECT statement and the data modification language statements. There are three kinds of hints: *table hints*, *query hints*, and *join hints*.

IMPORTANT **USE OPTIMIZER HINTS CAREFULLY**

When you use a hint, you change the query. SQL Server must execute the query or part of the query always in the same way. The query could be part of an application, so it could be difficult to change it. The data distribution might change over time, and although the hint might have improved the performance in the past, it might harm the performance over time. Use all other means, such as creating appropriate indexes, creating and updating statistics, and even using plan guides before moving to the hints. Use hints as the last resort, and after you use them, validate whether they are still useful from time to time.

You specify query hints as part of the OPTION clause of the SELECT, INSERT, UPDATE, DELETE, and MERGE statements. You cannot use query hints in subqueries, only in the outermost query. If multiple queries are involved in the UNION operation, you can specify the OPTION clause only after the last query. You cannot specify query hints in an INSERT statement except when a SELECT clause is used inside the statement.

The following query hints are supported by SQL Server 2012:

- { HASH | ORDER } GROUP
- { CONCAT | HASH | MERGE } UNION
- { LOOP | MERGE | HASH } JOIN
- EXPAND VIEWS
- FAST *number_rows*
- FORCE ORDER
- IGNORE_NONCLUSTERED_COLUMNSTORE_INDEX
- KEEP PLAN
- KEEPFIXED PLAN
- MAXDOP *number_of_processors*
- MAXRECURSION *number*
- OPTIMIZE FOR (*@variable_name* { UNKNOWN | = *literal_constant* } [,...*n*])
- OPTIMIZE FOR UNKNOWN
- PARAMETERIZATION { SIMPLE | FORCED }
- RECOMPILE
- ROBUST PLAN
- USE PLAN N'*xml_plan*'
- TABLE HINT (*exposed_object_name* [, *<table_hint>* [[,]...*n*]]

> ***MORE INFO*** **QUERY HINTS DETAILS**
>
> **It is out of the scope of this book to go into details for each of the hints. However, you will get familiar with some of them and how to use them through sample code and through the practice for this lesson. For a detailed explanation of each of the query hints, see the Books Online for SQL Server 2012 article "Query Hints (Transact-SQL)" at *http://msdn.microsoft.com/en-us/library/ms181714.aspx.***

The following two queries return the same aggregated rowset; the first one allows SQL Server to decide which aggregation technique to use—SQL Server decides to use the hash aggregation—whereas the second one forces the stream aggregation.

```
-- Hash match aggregate
SELECT qty, COUNT(*) AS num
FROM Sales.OrderDetails
GROUP BY qty;
-- Forcing stream aggregate
SELECT qty, COUNT(*) AS num
FROM Sales.OrderDetails
GROUP BY qty
OPTION (ORDER GROUP);
```

Figure 17-21 shows the execution plan for both queries together because they were executed in a batch.

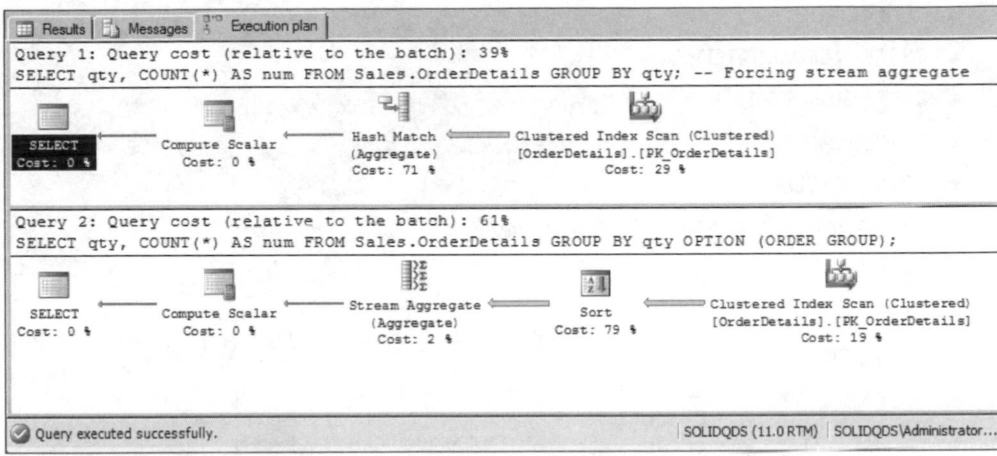

FIGURE 17-21 The plan for a hash aggregation and a forced stream aggregation.

In the second query, SQL Server used the Stream Aggregate operator. However, because this operator expects ordered input, SQL Server also added the Sort operator to the plan. Although the stream aggregation might be faster than the hash aggregation, the second query might be slower because of the additional sort operation.

You can give SQL Server a hint for a single table in a query. Table hints influence locking and the access method for a single table or view only. You can use the table hints in the FROM clause, and introduce them by using the WITH keyword. SQL Server supports the following table hints:

- NOEXPAND
- INDEX (*index_value* [,...*n*]) | INDEX = (*index_value*)
- FORCESEEK [(*index_value* (*index_column_name* [,...]))]
- FORCESCAN
- FORCESEEK
- KEEPIDENTITY
- KEEPDEFAULTS
- IGNORE_CONSTRAINTS
- IGNORE_TRIGGERS
- HOLDLOCK
- NOLOCK
- NOWAIT
- PAGLOCK

- READCOMMITTED
- READCOMMITTEDLOCK
- READPAST
- READUNCOMMITTED
- REPEATABLEREAD
- ROWLOCK
- SERIALIZABLE
- SPATIAL_WINDOW_MAX_CELLS = *integer*
- TABLOCK
- TABLOCKX
- UPDLOCK
- XLOCK

> ***MORE INFO*** **TABLE HINTS DETAILS**
>
> **For a detailed explanation of each of the table hints, see the Books Online for SQL Server 2012 article "Table Hints (Transact-SQL)" at *http://msdn.microsoft.com/en-us/library/ms187373.aspx.***

Maybe the most popular optimizer hint is the table hint that forces a specific index usage. The following two queries show an example of leaving it to SQL Server to choose the access method and of forcing usage of a nonclustered index.

```
-- Clustered index scan
SELECT orderid, productid, qty
FROM Sales.OrderDetails
WHERE productid BETWEEN 10 AND 30
ORDER BY productid;
-- Forcing a nonclustered index usage
SELECT orderid, productid, qty
FROM Sales.OrderDetails WITH (INDEX(idx_nc_productid))
WHERE productid BETWEEN 10 AND 30
ORDER BY productid;
```

Figure 17-22 shows the execution plan for this batch.

SQL Server 2012 also supports the following join hints in the FROM clause:

- LOOP
- HASH
- MERGE
- REMOTE

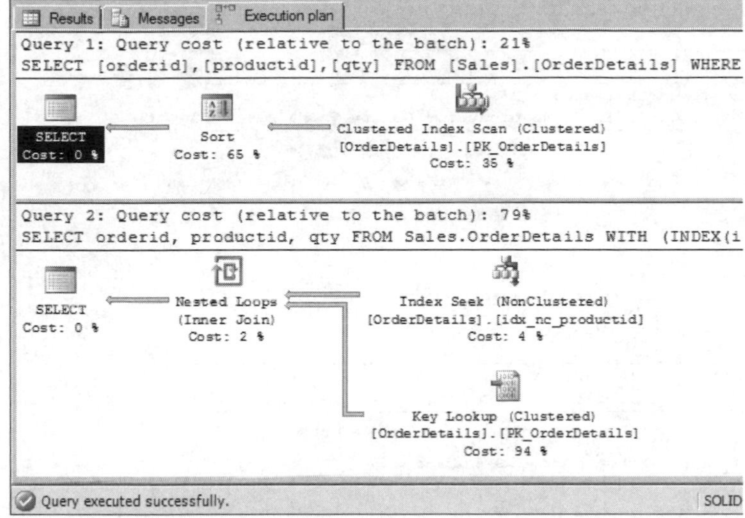

FIGURE 17-22 A plan for a scan and a forced nonclustered index seek.

MORE INFO **JOIN HINT DETAILS**

For a detailed explanation of each of the join hints, see the Books Online for SQL Server 2012 article "Join Hints (Transact-SQL)" at *http://msdn.microsoft.com/en-us/library/ms173815.aspx*.

The following two queries return the same result set again. For the first query, the selection of the join algorithm is left to SQL Server—SQL Server decides to use a nested loops join—and the second query forces a merge join.

```
-- Nested loops join
SELECT O.custid, O.orderdate, OD.orderid, OD.productid,OD.qty
FROM Sales.Orders AS O
 INNER JOIN Sales.OrderDetails AS OD
  ON O.orderid = OD.orderid
WHERE O.orderid < 10250;
-- Forced merge join
SELECT O.custid, O.orderdate, OD.orderid, OD.productid,OD.qty
FROM Sales.Orders AS O
 INNER MERGE JOIN Sales.OrderDetails AS OD
  ON O.orderid = OD.orderid
WHERE O.orderid < 10250;
```

Figure 17-23 shows the execution plan for this batch.

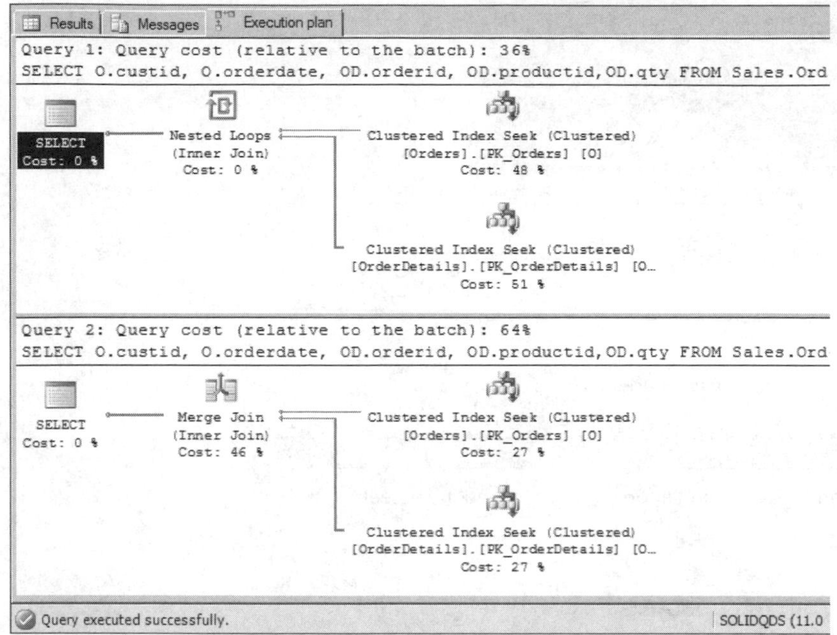

FIGURE 17-23 A plan for a nested loops and a forced merge join.

Plan Guides

In the plan guide, you can specify either the OPTION clause or a specific query plan for the statement you want to optimize. You also specify the T-SQL statement for which the plan guide is intended. The SQL Server Query Optimizer matches the executing T-SQL statement with the statement specified in the plan guide and then uses the guide to create the execution plan. Note that you cannot use plan guides in SQL Server 2012 Express edition.

You can create the following types of plan guides:

- OBJECT plan guides are used by the Query Optimizer to match queries inside stored procedures, scalar user-defined functions, multistatement table-valued user-defined functions, and DML triggers.
- SQL plan guides are used by the Query Optimizer to match stand-alone queries or queries in ad hoc batches.
- TEMPLATE plan guides are used by the Query Optimizer to match stand-alone queries that can be parameterized to a specified form. You can force parameterization with template guides.

You create plan guides by using the sys.sp_create_plan_guide system procedure. You can disable, enable, or drop a plan guide by using the sys.sp_control_plan_guide system procedure. You can create a plan guide from a cached query plan by using the sys.sp_create_plan_guide_from_handle system procedure. You can validate a plan by using the sys.fn_validate_plan_guide system function. A plan guide might become invalid because of a database schema change. You can use the sys.sp_get_query_template system procedure to get the parameterized form of a query. This procedure is especially useful to get the parameterized query for the TEMPLATE plan guide.

Consider the following stored procedure.

```
CREATE PROCEDURE Sales.GetCustomerOrders
(@custid INT)
AS
SELECT orderid, custid, empid, orderdate
FROM Sales.Orders
WHERE custid = @custid;
```

For the vast majority of customers—for example, a customer that has a custid equal to 71—the query in the procedure is not very selective; therefore, a table or clustered index scan would be the most appropriate to use. However, for some rare customers with only a few orders—for example, a customer that has a custid equal to 13—an index seek with a lookup would be better. If a user executes the procedure for customer 13 first, then the procedure plan in the cache would not be appropriate for most of the further executions. By creating a plan guide that uses a query hint that forces optimization of the query in the procedure for the customer that has a custid equal to 71, you are optimizing the stored procedure execution for most of the customers. The following code creates the plan guide.

```
EXEC sys.sp_create_plan_guide
 @name = N'Cust71',
 @stmt = N'
  SELECT orderid, custid, empid, orderdate
  FROM Sales.Orders
  WHERE custid = @custid;',
 @type = N'OBJECT',
 @module_or_batch = N'Sales.GetCustomerOrders',
 @params = NULL,
 @hints = N'OPTION (OPTIMIZE FOR (@custid = 71))';
```

If you execute the procedure by using different parameters after you cleaned the cache to make sure that an older plan for this procedure is not present in the cache, SQL Server always optimizes the query for the custid value 71, and thus uses a clustered index scan. This is true even if you execute the query with value 13 for the custid first, like the following code shows.

```
-- Clearing the cache
DBCC FREEPROCCACHE;
-- Executing the procedure with different parameters
EXEC Sales.GetCustomerOrders @custid = 13;
EXEC Sales.GetCustomerOrders @custid = 71;
```

Figure 17-24 shows the execution plan for this batch. You can see that in both executions, the Clustered Index Scan iterator was used.

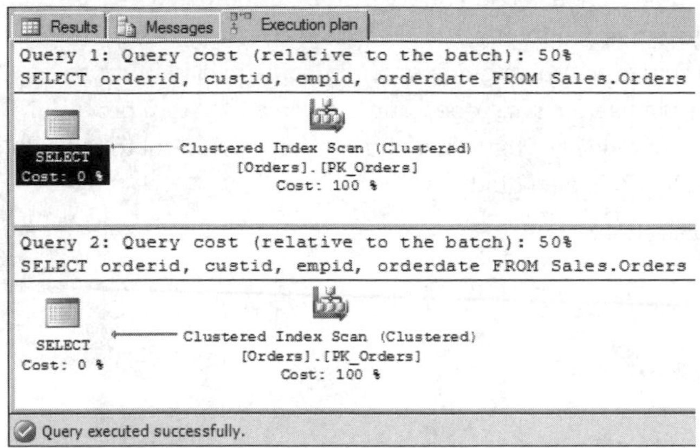

FIGURE 17-24 A plan for two executions of a stored procedure that uses a plan guide.

You can always get a list of all plan guides in a database by querying the sys.plan_guides catalog view. You can also list all of the hints used in each plan guide, like the following query shows.

```
SELECT plan_guide_id, name,       scope_type_desc, is_disabled,
 query_text, hints
FROM sys.plan_guides;
```

The following code cleans up the TSQL2012 database.

```
EXEC sys.sp_control_plan_guide N'DROP', N'Cust71';
DROP PROCEDURE Sales.GetCustomerOrders;
```

Quick Check

- **Why might you prefer using plan guides instead of optimizer hints?**

Quick Check Answer

- **With plan guides, you do not need to change the query text.**

PRACTICE Using Optimizer Hints

In this practice, you see an example of when an optimizer hint might be useful.

If you encounter a problem completing an exercise, you can install the completed projects from the companion content for this chapter and lesson.

EXERCISE 1 Create a Procedure with the RECOMPILE Query Hint

In this exercise, you create a procedure with a query that uses the RECOMPILE query hint.

1. If you closed SSMS, start it and connect to your SQL Server instance.
2. Open a new query window by clicking the New Query button.
3. Change the context to the TSQL2012 database.
4. Create a procedure to get all orders for a single customer, similar to the one you created in the practice for the previous lesson. However, this time use the OPTION clause to force recompilation for a single statement in the procedure. Note that a real procedure might include multiple statements, and recompiling the complete procedure might not be the best option. Using a plan guide might also not be the best option, because the plan from the guide might not be the most efficient plan for all possible values for the query parameter. A query hint might be the best option in this case. Use the following code to create the procedure.

```
CREATE PROCEDURE Sales.GetCustomerOrders
(@custid INT)
AS
SELECT orderid, custid, empid, orderdate
FROM Sales.Orders
WHERE custid = @custid
OPTION (RECOMPILE);
```

EXERCISE 2 Test the Procedure with the RECOMPILE Query Hint

In this exercise, you test the procedure with a query that uses the RECOMPILE query hint.

1. Execute the procedure you created in the previous exercise twice by using two different values for the @custid parameter. Use values 13 and 71.

```
EXEC Sales.GetCustomerOrders @custid = 13;
EXEC Sales.GetCustomerOrders @custid = 71;
```

You should get two different execution plans, as Figure 17-25 shows.

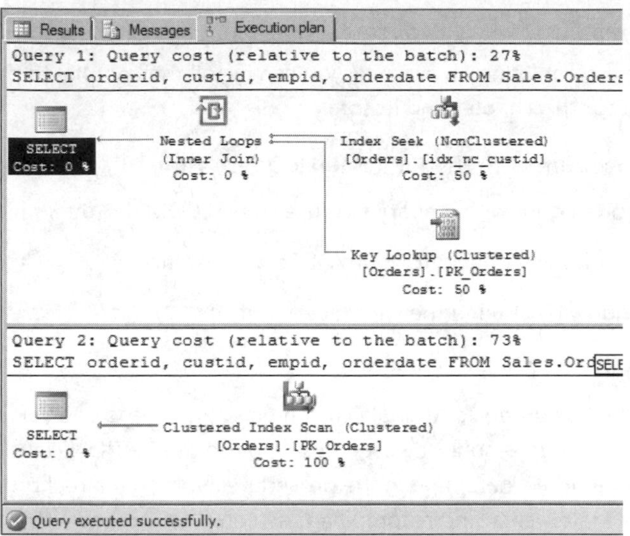

FIGURE 17-25 Two different execution plans for two calls of a stored procedure.

2. Clean up the TSQL2012 database by using the following code.

```
DROP PROCEDURE Sales.GetCustomerOrders;
```

3. Exit SSMS.

Lesson Summary

- You can force SQL Server to execute a query in a specific way by using optimizer hints.
- With plan guides, you can force a specific execution plan without modifying the query text.

Lesson Review

Answer the following questions to test your knowledge of the information in this lesson. You can find the answers to these questions and explanations of why each answer choice is correct or incorrect in the "Answers" section at the end of this chapter.

1. What kind of optimizer hints does SQL Server 2012 support? (Choose all that apply.)
   - **A.** Query
   - **B.** Join
   - **C.** Order
   - **D.** Table

2. What is not a type of plan guide?
   - **A.** JOIN
   - **B.** TEMPLATE
   - **C.** SQL
   - **D.** OBJECT
3. What does the OPTION (ORDER GROUP) query hint force?
   - **A.** Using indexes for joins
   - **B.** Hash aggregation
   - **C.** Aggregation in order—that is, a serial plan for aggregation
   - **D.** Stream aggregation

Case Scenarios

In the following case scenarios, you apply what you've learned about understanding further optimization aspects. You can find the answers to these questions in the "Answers" section at the end of this chapter.

Case Scenario 1: Query Optimization

Database administrators from a company where you are maintaining SQL Server complain that SQL Server does not use indexes for some queries from a third-party application. The queries are generated in the application directly, so you cannot modify them.

1. What actions can you take?
2. Is it possible to optimize the queries you cannot modify?

Case Scenario 2: Table Hint

There is a query in a stored procedure for which you suspect that SQL Server does not use an optimal plan. Although the very selective WHERE clause of the query is supported by a nonclustered index, SQL Server does not use it. The statistics for all indexes are up to date. You need to optimize this query.

1. Can you modify the query to use the index?
2. How would you accomplish this task?

Suggested Practices

To help you successfully master the exam objectives presented in this chapter, complete the following tasks.

Analyze Execution Plans and Force Plans

Understanding execution plans is not a simple task. Finding a better plan than using the SQL Server Query Optimizer is even more complicated. In order to better understand execution plans and plan guides, you should complete the following two practices.

- **Practice 1** In order to understand how SQL Server executes queries, use the TSQL2012 database and write additional queries that join, filter, aggregate, or sort the data. Try to predict what iterators SQL Server would use. Check how good your predictions were by executing the queries and analyzing the actual execution plans. Try to understand why SQL Server decided on the plans used.
- **Practice 2** Think of a production system you know. Does the system use stored procedures? What possibilities for optimization do you have? Are the queries embedded in an application? What options do you have to optimize them? How would you use plan guides in each case?

Answers

This section contains answers to the lesson review questions and solutions to the case scenarios in this chapter.

Lesson 1

1. **Correct Answers: B and C**
   - **A. Incorrect:** There is no merge aggregation algorithm.
   - **B. Correct:** SQL Server uses stream and hash aggregations.
   - **C. Correct:** SQL Server uses stream and hash aggregations.
   - **D. Incorrect:** There is no nested loops aggregation algorithm.
2. **Correct Answer: D**
   - **A. Incorrect:** SQL Server uses the RID Lookup operator to get data from the underlying table after a nonclustered index seek when the underlying table is organized as a heap.
   - **B. Incorrect:** There is no need for a full clustered index scan after a row is found in a nonclustered index.
   - **C. Incorrect:** The Merge Join operator is used during merge joins.
   - **D. Correct:** SQL Server uses the Key Lookup operator to get data from the underlying clustered table after a nonclustered index seek.
3. **Correct Answer: C**
   - **A. Incorrect:** When SQL Server scans the data in the physical order, this scan is called the allocation order scan.
   - **B. Incorrect:** The Clustered Index Scan is an operator that can scan data in logical or physical order.
   - **C. Correct:** When SQL Server scans the data in the logical order of an index, this scan is called the index order scan.
   - **D. Incorrect:** Seek is not used for scans.

Lesson 2

1. **Correct Answers: A, C, and D**
   - **A. Correct:** A change of a set option can be the reason that SQL Server does not reuse an existing cached plan.
   - **B. Incorrect:** SQL Server reuses cached stored procedure plans unless you force recompilation or use dynamic SQL in a procedure.
   - **C. Correct:** SQL Server does not reuse a cached plan if it cannot determine the selectivity of the parameterized predicate.
   - **D. Correct:** If a different data type is used for a parameter in the parameterized predicate, SQL Server does not reuse a cached plan.
2. **Correct Answer: C**
   - **A. Incorrect:** Batch mode processing does not lower disk I/O.
   - **B. Incorrect:** Batch mode processing has no influence on the network.
   - **C. Correct:** Lower CPU usage is the main advantage of batch mode processing.
   - **D. Incorrect:** Memory usage is not bound directly to batch processing.
3. **Correct Answer: C**
   - **A. Incorrect:** The SET STATISTICS IO command only turns on or off the statistical information about disk I/O.
   - **B. Incorrect:** When STATISTICS PROFILE is ON, each executed query returns its regular result set, followed by an additional result set that shows a profile of the query execution; it has no influence on the query plan reusage.
   - **C. Correct:** The SET CONCAT_NULL_YIELDS_NULL command has an influence on the result of a query, and therefore changing this option prevents plan reusage.
   - **D. Incorrect:** The SET STATISTICS IO command only turns on or off the statistical information about disk I/O.

Lesson 3

1. **Correct Answers: A, B, and D**
   - **A. Correct:** SQL Server supports query, table, and join hints.
   - **B. Correct:** SQL Server supports query, table, and join hints.
   - **C. Incorrect:** There is no order hint.
   - **D. Correct:** SQL Server supports query, table, and join hints.

2. **Correct Answer: A**
   - **A. Correct:** There is no JOIN plan guide type.
   - **B. Incorrect:** SQL Server supports the TEMPLATE plan guide.
   - **C. Incorrect:** SQL Server supports the SQL plan guide.
   - **D. Incorrect:** SQL Server supports the OBJECT plan guide.
3. **Correct Answer: D**
   - **A. Incorrect:** The OPTION (ORDER GROUP) query hint has no influence on joins.
   - **B. Incorrect:** The OPTION (ORDER GROUP) query hint forces stream aggregation.
   - **C. Incorrect:** The OPTION (ORDER GROUP) query hint has no influence on serial versus parallel execution plan.
   - **D. Correct:** The OPTION (ORDER GROUP) query hint forces stream aggregation.

Case Scenario 1

1. You can check whether the indexes are the most appropriate for the queries. You can also check whether the statistics for the indexes are updated. In addition, you can create plan guides for the problematic queries.
2. No, you cannot use the optimizer hints, because you cannot modify the text of the problematic queries.

Case Scenario 2

1. Yes. Because the query is inside a stored procedure and not embedded in an application, you can modify it.
2. You can use a table hint to force the index usage.

Index

Symbols

A

B

D

E

F

G

I

J

K

L

M

N

O

P

Q

R

S

T

U

V

W

X

Y

About the Authors

ITZIK BEN-GAN is a mentor and cofounder of SolidQ. A Microsoft SQL Server MVP since 1999, Itzik has delivered numerous training events around the world that are focused on T-SQL querying, query tuning, and programming. Itzik is the author of several books about T-SQL. He has written many articles for *SQL Server Pro*, in addition to articles and white papers for MSDN and *The SolidQ Journal*. Itzik's speaking engagements include Tech-Ed, SQL PASS, SQL Server Connections, presentations to various SQL Server user groups, and SolidQ events. Itzik is a subject matter expert within SolidQ for the company's T-SQL–related activities. He authored SolidQ's Advanced T-SQL and T-SQL Fundamentals courses and delivers them regularly worldwide.

DEJAN SARKA, MCT and SQL Server MVP, focuses on development of database and business intelligence applications. Besides working on projects, he spends a large part of his time training and mentoring. He is the founder of the Slovenian SQL Server and .NET Users Group. Dejan has authored or coauthored 11 books about databases and SQL Server. He also developed two courses and many seminars for Microsoft and SolidQ.

RON TALMAGE is a SolidQ database consultant who lives in Seattle. He is a mentor and cofounder of SolidQ, a SQL Server MVP, PASS Regional Mentor, and Chapter Leader of the Seattle SQL Server User Group (PNWSQL). He's been active in the SQL Server world since SQL Server 4.21a, and has authored numerous articles and white papers.